Grammatical Relations

Grammatical Relations
Theoretical Approaches to Empirical Questions

edited by
Clifford S. Burgess,
Katarzyna Dziwirek,
&
Donna Gerdts

CSLI *Publications*
CENTER FOR THE STUDY OF
LANGUAGE AND INFORMATION
STANFORD, CALIFORNIA

Copyright ©1995
Center for the Study of Language and Information
Leland Stanford Junior University
Printed in the United States
99 98 97 96 95   5 4 3 2 1

Library of Congress Cataloging-in-Publication Data

Grammatical relations : theoretical approaches to empirical questions
/ edited by Clifford S. Burgess, Katarzyna Dziwirek & Donna Gerdts.
   p. cm.
   Rev. versions of papers presented at the 6th Conference on Grammatical Relations, which was held Sept. 16-18, 1993, Simon Fraser University.
   Includes bibliographical references and index.

   ISBN 1-57586-003-1
   ISBN 1-57586-002-3 (pbk.)

   1. Grammar, Comparative and general—Congresses. I. Burgess, Clifford S. II. Dziwirek, Katarzyna. III. Gerdts, Donna B. IV. Conference on Grammatical Relations (6th : 1993 : Simon Fraser University)
P201.G679   1996
415—dc20   95-40881
                                              CIP

∞The acid-free paper used in this book meets the minimum requirements of the American National Standard for Information Sciences—Permanence of Paper for Printed Library Materials, ANSI Z39.48-1984.

Contents

Preface vii

Word-Internal Semantic Relations in Wakashan 1
EMMON BACH

Mapping Theory and Fula Verbal Extensions 15
CHRISTOPHER CULY & WILLIAM D. DAVIES

Mapping Basque Psych Verbs 33
WILLIAM D. DAVIES & ASCUNCION MARTINEZ-ARBELAIZ

Experiencers of Psych Verbs in Tagalog 45
VIDEA P. DE GUZMAN

Expletive Subjects in Lingala: A Challenge to Burzio's Generalization 63
STANLEY DUBINSKY & MAZEMBA NZWANGA

Southern Tiwa Argument Structure 75
DONALD G. FRANZ

Relational Grammar Laws, the Theory of Parameters and the Acquisition of Spanish 97
NORA GONZALES

The Structure and Surface Form of Benefactives and Other Prepositional Grammatical Relations 117
MIKA HOFFMAN

On Some Mood Alternations in Labrador Inuttut 131
ALANA JOHNS

Verb Agreement and Grammatical Relations 153
DAVID KATHMAN

Predicate-Argument Structure in Malagasy 171
EDWARD L. KEENAN

Excorporation and (Non)-1AEX 217
YOSHIHISA KITAGAWA

Mapping constructions as word templates: evidence from French 249
JEAN-PIERRE KOENIG

On grammatical reltaions in Malagasy control structures 271
PAUL LAW

Causee Prominence Constraints in French and Elsewhere 291
GÉRALDINE LEGENDRE

Lexical Case and NP Raising 309
KUMIKO G. MURASUGI

Predication Within Telugu Nominals 321
ROSANNE PELLETIER

Ergative Subjects 341
COLIN PHILLIPS

Non-terms in complex predicates: From Incorporation to Reanalysis 359
MARIA POLINSKY

A Glance at French Pseudopassives 391
PAUL M. POSTAL

Underspecifying grammatical relations in a constraint-based morphology 429
KEVIN RUSSELL

Binding and Conference in Jakaltek 449
FRANK R. TRECHSEL

Preface

This volume consists of revised versions of papers given at the 6th Biennial Conference on Grammatical Relations held at Simon Fraser University, September 16-18, 1993. The goal of this meeting was to provide a forum for discussion on grammatical relations and related concepts from the point of view of current syntactic theory.

Grammatical relations such as subject and object have always played a central role in descriptive discussions of data in the world's languages. In recent years, grammatical relations have come to play a prominent role in linguistic theory as well. Two frameworks–Relational Grammar and Arc Pair Grammar–are based on the idea that these are primitive elements. Grammatical relations/functions are derivative notions in Government/Binding, Lexical Functional Grammar, and Head-Driven Phrase Structure Grammar. Nevertheless, they are key elements in these theories as well. Thus, grammatical relations, more than any other concept, serve as a common ground for practitioners of various syntactic theories. Results of studies on grammatical relations in individual languages influence all theories. Furthermore, theoretical approaches to grammatical relations help to organize the vast amount of cross-linguistic data that has become available over the last half-century.

Several different frameworks are represented in this volume. However, what all the papers have in common is that each provides a theoretical solution to an empirically-based problem. Many of the structures dealt with are perennial favorites: passives, applicatives, causatives, psych constructions, binding, and control. Many papers also deal with morphosyntactic issues including the representation of ergativity, mood, case, agreement, and polysynthesis. A number of the authors diverge from straightforward relational accounts to ones that use linking or mapping devices or specifier positions to represent the interface of morphology and syntax. Several new morphosyntactic frameworks made their appearance at this conference.

Data from many of the world's languages and language families are discussed in this volume including: Abkhaz, Bantu (including Kinyarwanda and Lingala), Basque, Cheyenne, Dutch, Eskimo (Labrador Inuttut, Inukitut, and Qairnirmiutut dialects), French, Fula, Georgian, Italian, Halkomelem, Jakaltek, Japanese, Kwa, Malagasy, Potawatomi, Russian, Southern Tiwa, Spanish, Tagalog ,Telugu, Wakashan, and Yimas. For the most part, the data derive from original fieldwork of the authors. Thus, the volume makes an empirical, as well as a theoretical, contribution to linguistic research.

We would like to thank the many people who assisted in making the conference possible. First, funding for the conference was provided by a grant (Aid to Occasionaly Scholarly Conferences) from the Social Sciences and Humanities Research Council of Canada, and by a conference grant from Simon Fraser University. Editorial expenses were defrayed by Donna Gerdts' SSHRC Grant. We thank Katarzyna Dziwirek and Michael Rochemont for reviewing the abstracts. We also acknowledge the assistance of the Linguistics Department at SFU. Almost all of the faculty, graudate students, and staff of the SFU Linguistics Department contributed to the administration of the conference in some way. We thank Cliff Burgess for being chief administrator, Tanya Beaulieu, Georgina Carlson, Katarzyna Dziwirek, and Charles Ulrich for providing administrative support, and Mercedes Hinkson, Susan Russell, Nathalie Schapansky, Janine Toole, and Lorraine Yoshida for helping to run the conference. We especially thank Rita Gerdts, A.W. Oliver, Wayne Oliver, and Charles Ulrich for comestibles and beverages for the conference feast.

Although all of the editors participated in reviewing the papers for content and style, Cliff Burgess took on the odious task of editing the papers for form. We thank him for the careful attention he paid to each paper and trust that the volume was greatly improved by his suggestions.

Word-Internal Semantic Relations in Wakashan

EMMON BACH

University of Massachusetts (Amherst)

0. Preliminaries.

The general question in back of this paper is: Where do languages express what? I pose this question in the context of puzzlements about the relation between word structures and phrase structures in various languages and about the dimensions of differences among languages encoded in terms like "polysynthesis."

I will start with some ruminations about this general tangle of questions. The bulk of my remarks will be directed at some details of the Wakashan languages, which have been famous for building complex words. I will concentrate in this paper on complex words that show adjunctive relations between stem and affix (or other operations). I will try to show that the semantic relations that we see in most of the derived words of Wakashan languages are notably lacking in those grammatical relations that are most in focus in Relational Grammar or in the Argument Structures of some other frameworks. In particular, I will claim that no affixes directly encode argument categories for the stems to which they are attached, and hence, are not to be derived by Incorporation or Head Movement.

0.1 Words and Sentences.

Consider (1):

(1)   In (some) polysynthetic languages, words are just sentences.

This claim is often encountered in introductory linguistics books, where single words from some language like Nuu'chah'nulth (Nootka) are exhibited along with translations into English. Something like this idea is implicit in a well-known paper by Morris Swadesh (1939) called 'Nootka internal syntax.' If the idea has anything to it, then we might expect complex words in such a language to have all the characteristics that sentences have, in microcosm.

---

*I am grateful for the help of many people from Kitamaat Village, especially Gordon Robertson, Sampson Ross, Don Stewart, Amelia Grant, Irene Starr, Kay Grant, the late Jeffrey Legaik and the late Mike Shaw. I take full responsibility for all errors and misunderstandings. The research reported on here was supported in part by a Faculty Research Grant from the University of Massachusetts (Amherst).

There is something strange, however, about such a comparison between word-internal and word-external syntax: words and sentences are not concepts of the same logical order. We can see this most vividly from the semantic side. It makes sense to entertain the idea that the sentence has a special relation to a primary semantic notion, the notion of a proposition or a truth value or whatever, as in categorial systems where one of the primitive categories is t, the category of truth values. Even when we recognize that there are sentences of different types, including all sorts of minor kinds, it still is not unreasonable to take the core notions of declarative assertions as basic. The basic grammatical relations like subject, objects, 1, 2, and 3 are crucially connected to this view of the central meaning of sentences (and, to repeat, we may still say that it is not meaningful to ask about the subject of a "sentence" like "John!" or "Wow!"). In contrast, I think it would be quite crazy to ask whether there is any such core meaning for words as words.

0.2 Basic relations among linguistic elements.

Let us take a brief look at the most general relations that can hold among linguistic items in constructions. I am going to assume the general picture of linguistic elements that we find in categorial grammar, that is, as functions and arguments. That gives us a nice reconstruction of the traditional distinction between optional modifiers in endocentric constructions and function/complement (argument) relations in exocentric constructions. The transformational tradition (as in "some version of X-Bar theory") makes a further distinction in the latter type between constructions of complementation and structures of specification, depending on the relation between the input categories and the resultant category. (See Webelhuth (1992) for discussion of the basic ideas here.) In categorial systems we have the possibility of items being combined by function composition as well as by function/argument application (see Jacobson (1990)). Using a categorial notation, with no implications of ordering, we have then: Categorial perspective: functions/arguments:

(2) A/A A : endocentric, optional modification
(3) A/B B : exocentric, complementation or specification (A≠B)
(4) A/B B/C : functional composition

Besides these modes of combination, categorial systems provide for various operations on categories, which may be thought of as ways of allowing members of (sets indexed by) one category to occur as members of another systematically related one. Of these, I assume at least the possibility of "type-lifting," by which an expression is allowed to function as a higher order functor on functors defined for its original lower category:

(5) A ⟹ B/(B/A)

A familiar example is the analysis of names as generalized quantifiers, or families of sets:

(6) e ==> t/(t/e) (type: ((e,t),t), see below)

(For general discussion of type-lifting see Partee and Rooth (1983)).

The traditions of Relational Grammar and Transformational Grammar are in agreement about assigning special significance to a certain set of arguments in relation to their functions: the primary "terms" of core propositional structures, the "arguments" as complements of complement structures, especially those of verbal constructions. (I do not mean to imply that the specific instances so singled out coincide in the two frameworks, but there is a large overlap.)

From the perspective of categorial grammar, these primary relations can be reconstructed on the basis of a standard hierarchy of relations between term-phrases (NPs, DPs) and sentences, considered as truth-value bearing expressions (Dowty 1982a,b). The subject is the "last-in," (argument of a function of the form S/NP), the direct object the "next-to-last," and so on. An alternative view uses a categorial analysis of Cases to assign subject NPs (nominative, say) to a functor category as elements "looking for" predicate or VP expressions, and so on (Keenan 1987).

Most categorial theories make use of the following system (intended here as just encoding the syntactic/semantic type assignments with no implications of directionality or other purely syntactic properties):

(7) e: category of names (entities);
    t: category of sentences (truth-values);
    (a, b): category of functors (functions) from a categories (a types) to b categories (b types)

Some common functor types are these:

(8) (e,t): predicates: intransitive verbs, common nouns, predicative adjectives;
    (e,(e,t)): transitive verbs;
    (e,(e,(e,t))): ditransitive verbs;
    ((e,t),t): term phrases (noun phrases);
    ((e,t),((e,t),t)): determiners;
    ((e,t), (e,t)): attributive adjectives, intransitive verb (VP) adverbs;
    (t,t): sentence adverbs, epistemic modals;
    (((e,t),t), ((e,t),(e,t))): prepositions that make NPs into VP adverbs;
    (((e,t),t), (t,t)): prepositions that make NPs into sentence adverbs

(These examples assume a "lowest type" analysis, leaving open the possibility that some or all should be analyzed or allowed to also categorize as higher order functors, see Partee and Rooth (1983)).

You should note that these categories have their subcategorizations built into them. Thus, the category of transitive verbs is to be compared most directly with the combination in other frameworks of the category V = [+V,-N]) and something like a subcategorization frame [_NP] (or whatever combination of case government, theta-role assignment, or whatnot gets that effect).

For more particular syntactic purposes, I assume minimally the following:

(9) a. Functor categories specify the constructive operation that combines them with their arguments (as for example in the directional slashes / and \ for "right-looking" and "left-looking" functors).

b. Syntactic operations may include specification of word-internal morphological reflexes, to be triggered or checked, as in Bach (1983) according to general principles of government, agreement, and percolation (government understood here in the traditional sense).

c. The categorial system specifies a distinction between word categories and (possibly) phrasal categories. (Compare the 0-level in X-Bar systems.)

Note that in this view, every functor specifies a category of elements to which it applies (its "argument" type) and the category of elements that result when it combines with its argument (its "result" type).

The general way in which the grammar works is wholly constructive, in the sense that there are no mechanisms for filtering or "repairing." One consequence of this approach is that it is impossible to analyze bound affixes as members of lexical categories inhabited by full words, as in Williams (1981).

It would take us too far afield to try to even sketch the many competing current views of the relation between the grammar of words and the grammar of phrases. Let me just mention two points. First, many current discussions stress the role of the central set of function/argument relations just mentioned in word grammar: in compounding, in other derivational processes, and in inflectional morphology. Second, there has been a recurring tendency throughout much theoretical work in generative grammar to extend or reflect the syntax of phrases (sentences, etc.) into the internal structure of words.

In the remainder of this paper I will try to substantiate the claim that such notions play a relatively minor part in the derivation of complex words in Wakashan (concentrating on Northern Wakashan). Of far more importance are relations of optional modification. In the categorial perspective, this means that relations of type (a) above are most prominent.

[It should be noted that some writers use the term "endocentric" in a different way, more or less equivalent to the term "headed" (see e.g. Speas (1990)). For a general and helpful discussion of the notion "head," see especially, Zwicky (1985).]

1. Wakashan languages.

Here is the briefest of introductions to Wakashan. The languages themselves include, among others:

(10) a. Southern: Makah, Nuu'chah'nulth (Nootka), Kyuquot, Ditidaht

b. Northern: Kwakw'ala, Haisla, Henaksiala, Heiltsuk

The general structure of all of them is: VSO, polysynthetic, suffixing only, no compounding. A controversial claim that has been repeatedly made is that there is no lexical distinction between Nouns and Verbs (the best assessment of this claim, with extensive general discussion and a detailed examination of Makah is Jacobsen (1979)).

The general structure of words is this:

(11) (Extended)Root + DerAf* + GrAf/Clitics*

(Roots are extended by various operations of reduplication, expansion, and so on. DerAf stands for derivational affixes; GrAf/Clitics for various grammatical affixes or clitics. There are more constraints on the combinatorics of derivation than are reflected in this formula, but they have never been fully spelled out. See the Appendix for an explanation of the spellings used for examples from Haisla/Henaksiala.)

(12) x̄enaksialak'ala '*Kitlope language*'

x̄en(a)	-[k]si	-al(a)	-[k]!al	- a
few	- scattered	- continuative[?]	-language/noise	-completive

Some notion of the extent of derivational versus other resources of the languages can be given by these rough numbers for Haisla: there are about 400 roots and around five or six hundred derivational suffixes (figures based on LR, i.e. Lincoln and Rath (1986)).

Here is my general claim: word-formation in Wakashan largely expresses relations of optional modification ("adverbial" meanings). Hence there is no "incorporation." To substantiate this claim would require going exhaustively through the inventory of derivational processes, which I obviously cannot do here. But I will try to give a representative sample. (We should really speak of stem-forming affixes and operations, but I will continue to ignore this refinement and talk of word-formation.)

1.1 Some types of derivational suffixes (Haisla/Henaksiala).

One implication of the claim in (1) above (words are little sentences) might be the expectation or thesis that the categories of subword elements would be just the categories of subsentential elements; that is, just the categories of the syntax. Let us use this idea as a guide through our sampling of word- forming affixes (and other operations) in Haisla/ Henaksiala. In this section where possible I will relate categories to those familiar from the generative tradition: S, NP etc. (In the following sketch I have drawn on Boas's semantic classes of lexical affixes in Kwakw'ala (Boas 1947:236–46).

1.1.1 Argument Categories

Since in the version of categorial grammar followed here, modes of combination are encoded in functor categories, the basic categories of standard systems, e and t, could not be represented as affixes or other dependent operations. But given the option of type-lifting, there is an easy way to get affixes to fulfill the same role. Candidates for such affixes in Haisla would be the pronominal subject clitics (or grammatical affixes), such as *-(e)n/-nug^{w}a* 'I' (1sg subject form), which could be specified as higher order functions of type ((e,t),t), that is, the type of generalized quantifiers; or *-utl* 'you' (2sg object) of type ((e,(e,t)),(e,t)), that is, the type of "accusative" operators (functions from transitive verb meanings to intransitives (Keenan 1987)). Since neither of these kinds of elements function at the level of word-formation, in the sense of producing new lexical elements, I will not discuss them further here. (I will take up below other affixes that might seem to fit in here, such as the various "passive" affixes).

As far as I know there are in Haisla no affixal counterparts for the other argument—only category (t). The absence of "nominative" word-forming affixes or rules is exactly what we expect given these assumptions:

(13) a. Word-formation rules are rules for extending the membership of lexical word classes (Dowty 1978, 1979).
b. The category (t), (S, IP, CP etc.), has no lexical members.

Compare Kroeber's observation (1909[1910]:574, in Sapir, CW, V.1:544):

> If noun subject and object were both incorporated, incorporation as a process would break down of itself. All elements of the sentence, or at least of the clause, would be contained in the verb, and the syntactical word would be not only in scheme but in fact identical with the sentence.

As noted above, there has been considerable discussion as to whether there is a lexical distinction between Nouns and Verbs (and predicative

Adjectives) in Wakashan (Boas 1947; Swadesh 1939; Jacobsen 1979). From a categorial perspective, both of these classes are usually analysed semantically as predicates (that is, of type (e,t)). Without prejudice to the outcome of this dispute, I will discuss what are (notionally) two (or three) sorts of items separately, but note some implications of the discussion from and for word formation processes. As far as function/argument structures go, it is quite possible that both types act syntactically as argument categories rather than as functors. In any case, there are no affixes (or word-forming operations) that correspond directly to either type.

Observers coming to Wakashan from a background of European languages have been struck by the large number of lexical affixes that encode concepts which are expressed by separate words in their languages (see for example Boas's remarks on this point in Boas 1947:236–37). There are two general points to be made here about Wakashan. First, although there are plenty of word-forming affixes and other operations that result in forms with verbal and nominal kinds of meanings, there are none that directly encode the meanings of common nouns or intransitive verbs. Second, there is in general no synchronic relationship between affixes with particular concrete meanings and separate words that encode related meanings. Compare the following:

(14) a. =ilh   'inside, in a house'
     a'. guk^w-   'house'
     b. -qi   'on/in the head'
     b'. hi'xt'i   'head'
     c. -x̄s   'in canoe, vehicle'
     c'. gel'w'a   'canoe'

An apparent exception occurs with a pair like this:

(15) a. -x̄ina   'on/in the shoulder'
     a'. 'ux̄^{w}ina' 'shoulder'

But the free form here is derived by attaching the suffix to an "empty" root, √'u- 'place, thing.' (The example shows regular labialization of the velar after /u/).

1.1.2 Adjunctive Functors

The examples just given illustrate a very large class of adjunctive specifiers of locations, directions, areas of the body, and the like. As the glosses are intended to indicate, these affixes generally add something like an adverbial or adjectival specification to the stem to which they are attached. A few more examples:

(16) a. -bet   'in(to) hole'
     a'. gax̄ebetala   'come into a hole or opening '   [LR]

b. =zi 'on side of flat thing'
b'. qel'x̄ezi 'eggs inside body (of salmon)'; 'in or on abdomen'
c. -atus 'downriver'
c'. ḡ'atus 'get up early to go downriver' [LR]
c'. laa'tus 'go downstream' [LR]
d. =zu 'on flat thing '
d'. t'i'bezud 'step onto (something flat)'

These glosses are somewhat misleading. The last example is used as a transitive verb with an object. The suffix does not fill up an argument slot, as would be the case if it were like an incorporated object.

There are quite a few words which at first might seem to be formed by taking (for example) a body-part suffix as an argument of the stem to which it is attached:

(17) gel't'ex̄d 'long + buttocks, behind'

But (as Sapir noted for similar examples in Yana (1911:271)[CW:48] this word does not mean 'long behind' but rather has a bahuvrihi type of meaning: 'having a long behind, tall' (='long-assed').

Another kind of example is given by the word for '(playing) baseball':

(18) yayacem'a̱' (yayassm'a' [LR]) < √yes - 'hit with club or stick' +
-sem - 'round thing' + -!a (with
a-reduplication) — 'try to V'

Here -*sem* is not standing in for an object but is again modificational. In fact it is used as a regular classifier for counting round solid objects. (The form reflects a regular phonological rule s + s > c.)

The locational and directional affixes cover a wide range of meanings from quite specific ('on beach', 'in house', 'on canoe or boat', 'on surface of water') to quite general ones much like prepositional meanings in languages such as English ('into', 'onto', 'at', 'inside of', 'out of'). Very often, a certain suffix will include "extended" as well as concrete meanings:

(19) -eksala 'in all directions, randomly, wrong, mis-'

The examples given so far reflect the fact that modificational affixes can be attached to stems with a wide variety of meanings. In this respect,they resemble syntactic modifiers that are often cross-categorial (like, for example, prepositional phrases in English). But this fact would also be consistent with the idea that stems all belong to a single open class of "predicatives," as is claimed by the analyses of the language as having no lexical distinctions among Nouns, Verbs, or Adjectives.

1.1.3 Exocentric Functors

Boas's classification includes these headings: "Nominal Suffixes," "Verbs," and "Adjective and Adverbs." In view of the claim that there is no distinction among these kinds of stems (Boas 1947:280), this might seem curious, but Boas makes clear that the classification is intended just as a convenience "to give an impression of the range of ideas expressed by suffixes"(p.237). In that spirit, I will give a few Haisla examples for each of Boas's categories:

(20) NOMINAL:

a.	-as	'tree, bush'
a'.	'ui'q'as	'devil club'
b.	-bis	'particle, liquid'
b'.	cel'x̄bis	'hailstone'
c.	=ac'i	'receptacle, lair, vessel, round hollow object'
c'.	hemgila'c'i	'cooking pot'
d.	-!inix̄ʷ	'agentive, clan member'
d'.	Hel'x̄'inix̄ʷ	'Blackfish, Killer Whale'

(21) VERBAL:

a.	-utl	'to catch X'
a'.	q'i'utl	'catch a lot'
b.	-!a	'hunt for, gather X'
b'.	c'a'c'ikʷ'a	'hunt for birds' (√c'ikʷ'='bird', with a-reduplication)
c.	-!ix̄d	'want to V'
c'.	k'a'l'ix̄da	'want to sleep' [LR]
d.	-[g]ila	'to make X, go to X'
d'.	Terrace-ila	'go to Terrace'

(22) ADJECTIVAL

a.	-p'a	'tasting of, like'
a'.	'i'xp'a	'sweet'
b.	-p'ala	'smelling of'
b'.	y'a'xʷpala	'stink, skunk'
c.	-sdu	'appearing like, -colored'
c'.	'i'xsdu	'bright colored'

Many of the lexical affixes are (notionally) cross-categorial, both in the items with which they can occur and as to the resultant meanings of the derivates. For example, the last one listed, (22c), also means 'eye' and can participate in forms like those mentioned above under body parts. The suffix *-[g]ila* listed under VERBAL above, (22d), also can be used to refer to something made to look like X, an so on.

Again, none of these affixes can be related to independent words, and for some there is no independent word. Among these derivational patterns we can include operations that do not actually have any segmental existence apart from their effect, such as the (total) reduplication of stems meaning 'to eat' whatever the stem denotes.

I close this section with a brief mention of several other classes of affixes that I will not discuss here.

(23) COUNTERS—These are used primarily on number words, but some are specialized uses of affixes with other uses.

(24) MODAL, etc.—This class includes a number of affixes that relate to focus, speaker attitude, evidentiality, etc.

(25) TENSE and ASPECT—These include affixes that relate to temporal location (past, future), contour of the action (repetitive, gradual, momentaneous, etc.) but in a way that I view as derivational rather than inflectional.

(26) VALENCE AFFECTING—Here we have causative, transitivizing affixes, and so on including about five affixes that Boas calls "passive" (see Levine (1980), for persuasive arguments that these last affixes, which he calls "focus" affixes, are to be treated as word-formational—"lexical" rather than syntactic).

In general, all of the derivational affixes of Northern Wakashan languages operate at the level of stem-formation. In X-Bar terms, this would mean that their input and output categories are of level 0. It is possible that they are unspecified as to N and V features. If this is correct it would have important consequences for the general theory of syntactic categories. It is uncontroversial that in the syntax there is a clear distinction between main predicators, or verbs, and nominal constituents, but this distinction could not be directly projected from the lexicon if the items in the lexicon were unspecified.

As far as the interpenetration of word-internal and word-external syntax goes, there seems to be an interesting difference between the northern and the southern branches of the Wakashan languages. I have not seen anything in the former languages resembling the clitic-like behavior of derivational affixes that is discussed in Rose (1981) for Kyuquot. There an affix that seems to mean something like *-[g]ila* in (21d) can attach to the first element in a modified nominal constituent. (Examples and numbering are from Rose [R](1981:294 ff.):

(27) a. č'apicƚ   'He made a canoe'
        /č'apic-(č)iƚ /   'canoe-make'   R342

b. ƛuλi·ł č'apic	'He made a nice canoe'	R343
c. mu·kʷi·ł ƛuł č'apic	'He made four nice canoes'	R343
d. ʔukʷi·ł (ƛuł) č'apic	'He made a (nice) canoe'	R343
e. ʔi·hi·ł ƛuł č'apic	'He made a really nice canoe'	R352
f. ƛuλi·ł tani č'apic	'He made a really nice canoe'	R353

The last two, (22e, f) are especially telling, since the adverbial elements meaning 'really' differ syntactically in coming before and after their argument and the affix -(č)ił is attached to the first element of the phrase accordingly.

With these examples from Kyuquot we move beyond the limits of word-internal semantics.

2. Conclusions and questions.

A number of general points seem to hold for Wakashan. First, complements, internal arguments, and primary grammatical relations play a relatively minor role in word-formation. Second, affixes are functors, more or less any definable function on meanings can be the meaning of an affix. Third, the kinds of meanings that are encoded in affixes (and other word-formation operations) do not coincide with the kinds of meanings that are associated with phrase-syntactic categories. Fourth, there is a large number of stem-forming affixes and operations that in both input and output (argument and result) categories cut across typical nominal and verbal categories.

A final point: there seem to be lots of different ways of being "polysynthetic." Even within Wakashan we find striking differences among the many similarities between the two branches. Going outside the family to two neighboring families (Na-Dene and Eskimo-Aleut) would show many more differences.

APPENDIX: Note on Representations

Haisla forms are given in an orthography which is a compromise among several existing systems: ' marks glottalized segments and also indicates glottal stop; tl, tl', dl for lateral affricates; lh for voiceless l (ł); ai and au for open E and O respectively; g̅ and x̅ for back g and x; e stands for schwa (ə), including many predictable epenthetic vowels, (and em, en, el for sometimes syllabic m, n, l); Cʷ for labialized C.

Suffixes are marked according to their "end-effects" as follows (see Boas, 1947):

=	"softening" / "voicing"
-!	"hardening" (glottalizing)
-	"plain "(no special effect)
[X]	"X" present only after (roughly) vocalic or segmental segments

REFERENCES

Bach, Emmon. 1983. On the Relationship Between Word-grammar and Phrase-grammar. *Natural Language and Linguistic Theory* 1.65–89.
Bach, Emmon. 1991. Representations and Operations in Haisla Phonology. *Proceedings of the Western Conference on Linguistics* 4.29–35.
Bach, Emmon. 1992. The Semantics of Syntactic Categories. To appear in *The Logical Foundations of Cognition*, J. Macnamara and G.E. Reyes, eds. Oxford: Oxford University Press.
Bach, Emmon. 1993. On the Semantics of Polysynthesis. *BLS* 19.361–68.
Boas, Franz. 1947. Kwakiutl Grammar with a Glossary of the Suffixes. Ed. by Helene Boas Yampolsky with the Collaboration of Zellig S. Harris. *Transactions of the American Philosophical Society*. N.S. Vol. 37, Part 3, 203–377. [Reprint] New York: AMS Press.
Di Sciullo, Anna-Marie and Edwin Williams. 1987. *On the Definition of Word*. Cambridge, Massachusetts: MIT Press.
Dowty, David R. 1978. Lexically Governed Transformations as Lexical Rules in a Montague Grammar. *Linguistic Inquiry* 1.45–78.
Dowty, David R. 1979. *Word Meaning and Montague Grammar*. Dordrecht: Reidel.
Dowty, David. 1982a. Grammatical Relations and Montague Grammar. *The Nature of Syntactic Representation*, Pauline Jacobson and Geoffrey K. Pullum, eds., 79–130. Dordrecht: Reidel.
Dowty, David. 1982b. More on the Categorial Analysis of Grammatical Relations. *Subjects and Other Subjects*, ed. by Annie Zaenen, 115–53. Bloomington, Indiana: Indiana University Linguistics Club.
Jacobsen, William H. Jr. 1979. Noun and Verb in Nootkan. The Victoria Conference on Northwestern Languages, Barbara S. Efrat, ed., 83–155. Victoria: British Columbia Provincial Museum.
Jacobson, Pauline. 1990. Raising as Function Composition. *Linguistics and Philosophy* 13.423–75.
Keenan, Edward L. 1987. Semantic Case Theory. *Proceedings of the Sixth Amsterdam Colloquium [13–16 April 1987]*, ed. by Jeroen Groenendijk, Martin Stokhof, and Frank Veltman, 109–32. University of Amsterdam: ITLI.
Kroeber, A.L. 1909. Noun Incorporation in American Languages. *XVI Internationaler Amerikanisten-Kongress*, 569–76. [Repr. in Edward Sapir. 1911. Collected Works [CW] V.1.542–46.] [Citation from Sapir, in Sapir [CW] cited as Verhandlungen der [sic] XVI Amerikanisten-Kongresses, Wien, 1908, 569–76 (1910)]
Levine, Robert D. 1980. On the Lexical Origin of the Kwakwala Passive. *IJAL* 46.240–58.
Lincoln, Neville J. and John C. Rath. 1986. *Phonology, Dictionary and Listing of Roots and Lexical Derivates of the Haisla Language of Kitlope and Kitimaat*. (2 vols.) Ottawa: National Museum of Man Mercury Series. [Canadian Ethnology Service: Paper No. 103.] [LR]

Mithun, Marianne. 1986. On the Nature of Noun Incorporation. *Language* 62.32–7.
Ojeda, Almerindo. 1993. *Linguistic Individuals*. Stanford, CA: CSLI. [CSLI Lecture Notes, Number 31.]
Partee, Barbara and Mats Rooth. 1983. Generalized Conjunction and Type Ambiguity. *Meaning, Use, and Interpretation of Language*, ed. by Rainer Bäuerle, Christoph Schwarze, and Arnim von Stechow, 361–83. Berlin/New York: Walter de Gruyter.
Spencer, Andrew. 1991. *Morphological Theory: An Introduction to Word Structure in Generative Grammar*. London: Basil Blackwell.
Swadesh, Morris. 1939. Nootka Internal Syntax. *IJAL* 9.77–102.
Rose, Suzanne Maria. 1981. *Kyuquot Grammar*. Unpublished Ph.D. Dissertation: University of Victoria.
Rosen, Sara Thomas. 1989. Two Types of Noun Incorporation: A Lexical Analysis. *Language* 65.294–318.
Sadock, Jerrold M. 1980. Noun Incorporation in Greenlandic: A Case of Syntactic Word Formation. *Language* 56.300–19.
Sadock, Jerrold M. 1986. Some Notes on Noun Incorporation. *Language* 62.19-31.
Sapir, Edward. 1911. The Problem of Noun Incorporation in American Languages. *American Anthropologist (n.s.)* 13.250–82.
Speas, Margaret J. 1990. *Phrase Structure in Natural Language*. Dordrecht/Boston/London: Kluwer Academic Publishers.
Webelhuth, Gert. 1992. *Principles and Parameters of Syntactic Saturation*. New York/Oxford: Oxford University Press.
Williams, Edwin. 1981. On the Notions "Lexically Related" and "Head of a Word." *Linguistic Inquiry* 12.245–74.
Zwicky, Arnold M. 1985. Heads. *Journal of Linguistics* 21.1-29.

Mapping Theory and Fula Verbal Extensions

CHRISTOPHER CULY & WILLIAM D. DAVIES
The University of Iowa

1. Introduction

Fula has a variety of verbal extensions, including extensions that increase the valence of the verb. The arguments associated with these extensions contrast in word order, surface realization, and passivization facts. We will account for the Fula data by proposing Mapping Theory (Gerdts 1992, 1993a) mechanisms of layered structures and universal constraints on argument-to-MAP linking. These mechanisms are an important extension of Mapping Theory, and account for a wide range of data heretofore not addressed by Mapping Theory.

2. Fula Verbal Extensions: the problem

We will be looking at four constructions: monomorphemic ditransitive verbs and verbs with Dative, Causative, and Modal Extensions. The examples in (1) illustrate these constructions. All data are from Arnott (1970) unless otherwise specified.

(1) The four constructions

    a.   Monomorphemic ditransitives (p. 28)

        Bello hokkii   Mammam sheede ɗen
        Bello give-pf.act Mamman money the
        'Bello gave Mamman the money'

    b.   Dative extension (p. 354)

        ɓe kirsanii   min ngaari
        3pl slaughter-D-pf.act 1pl bull
        'They slaughtered a bull for us'

---

    [*] Acknowledgements: Thanks to Stan Dubinsky and especially Donna Gerdts for discussion of some of the issues contained here. Errors and short comings are, of course, the responsibility of the authors.

c. Causative extension (p. 347)

'o yamii puccu ndiyam
3sg drink-C-pf.act horse water
'He gave the horse water to drink'

d. Modal extension (p. 348)

'o haɓɓirii gujjo ɓoggol
3sg tie.up-M-pf.act thief rope
'He tied up the thief with rope'

The monomorphemic ditransitive in (1a) illustrates that Fula is SVO with bare NP objects; the Goal argument precedes the Theme. The Dative extension *-an-* adds a Beneficiary or Goal argument, *min* 'us' in (1b), as Object. The Causative *-n-* adds a Causer argument as Subject, *'o* 'he/she' in (1c). Finally, the Modal extension *-ir-* adds an Instrument or Manner Object argument, *ɓoggol* 'rope' in (1d). Thus, although each of the extensions increases the valence of the base verb by one, the Causative adds a Subject while the Dative and Modal extensions add Objects.

The examples illustrate other important differences as well. The new Objects of the Dative and Causative appear between the verb and the original Object (similar to the Goal/Recipient of a monomorphemic ditransitive), while the Object added by the Modal appears after the original Object. Additionally, the Modal argument can optionally occur with a preposition; no other argument of these extensions or monomorphemic ditransitives can.

One other difference among these constructions has to do with what arguments can be passivized. The Passive is one of three voices, the others being the Active (illustrated in (1)), and the Middle. Each voice is indicated by a distinct set of aspect markers. As suggested by the example in (2b), Fula has only an agentless Passive.

(2) Active and Passive of simple transitive (Appendix 13)

a. Active

'o lootii (ɗum)
she wash-pf.act it

'She washed (it)'

b. Passive

    'o   lootaama
    she wash-pf.pass
    'She was washed'

Returning to the constructions of interest, in all cases, the Object adjacent to the verb can passivize, as seen in (3).

(3) Passivization of first Object

   a. ditransitive: Object = Goal (p. 260)

      'o hollaama   puccu
      he show-pf.pass horse
      'He was shown a horse'

   b. Dative: Object = Benefactive (p. 355)

      min kirsanaama   ngaari
      1pl slaughter-D-pf.pass bull
      'We have had a bull slaughtered for us'

   c. Causative: Object = Agent (p. 260)

      'o Bornaama   ngapalewol
      he dress-C-pf.pass gown
      'He$_i$ was dressed in a gown, had a gown put on him$_i$'

   d. Modal: Object = Theme (p. 349)

      wudere nden lootiraama   saabunde
      cloth def wash-M-pf.pass soap
      'The cloth has been washed with soap'

It is in the passivization of the second Object that more differences among the constructions emerge. The second Object of the monomorphemic ditransitives, Datives, and Modals may passivize; however the second Object of the Causative may not.[1] Additionally, the first Object of the monomorphemic ditransitives and Datives is realized in immediate post-

---

[1] Arnott doesn't say this explicitly, but where both Objects can passivize, as with the Dative and Modal, he discusses it. Gnalibouly (1990) does state (p. 70) that only the first Object can passivize in Maacina Fula.

verbal position, while the first Object of Modals cannot be realized, as illustrated in (4).

(4) Passivization of second Object

  a. Ditransitive: Object = Theme (p. 230)

   'o suud'ataake   mo
   he hide from-inc.pass him
   'He won't be hidden from him'

  b. Dative: Object = Theme (p. 355)

   ŋgaari hirsanaama   min
   bull   slaughter-D-pf.pass 1pl
   'A bull has been slaughtered for us'

  c. Modal: Object = Instrument (p. 349)

   saabunde nde'e lootiraama
   soap   this wash-M-pf.pass
   'This soap has been washed with'

Note that the Goal *mo* 'him' in (4a) and the Beneficiary *min* 'us' in (4b) each occur postverbally. However, in the Modal construction in (4c) the Theme is suppressed — an overt Theme Object in post-verbal position would apparently render the clause ungrammatical. We can summarize the properties of our constructions as in Table 1.

	ditransitive	Dative	Causative	Modal
GR of added arg	OBJ	OBJ	SUBJ	OBJ
Order of new OBJ	V O X	V O X	V O X	V X O
Optional Preposition	No	No	No	Yes
Passive of 2nd OBJ	V O$_1$	V O$_1$	*	V Ø

Table 1: Properties of the constructions

3. Analysis using Mapping Theory

It is clear from the examples and Table 1 that the verbal extensions all have somewhat different properties, the Dative however having the same set of properties as the monomorphemic ditransitive. The Causative does not allow passivization of the second Object, and the first Object of the Modal must be suppressed if the second Object is passivized. Thus, any account which attempts to treat the addition of arguments by these various extensions in precisely the same manner is doomed to failure, inasmuch as it will fail to capture the crucial differences. We will propose a Mapping Theory analysis of the extensions that highlights the similarities among the extensions, but which also explains their differences.

Mapping Theory, as set forth in Gerdts (1992, 1993a), posits 4 modules: Thematic Relations, Grammatical Relations, MAPs, and Presentation. Grammatical relations in Mapping Theory correspond to initial grammatical relations in classical RG, while MAPs correspond to final grammatical relations. Presentation is the morphosyntactic correlates of a MAP. The MAP structure for a simple English transitive sentence is given in (5). As suggested by this example, each of the modules is ordered and aligned with the others. Each module is linked only to the module(s) adjacent to it.

(5) MAP structure for English "I saw you"

thematic relations	Agent	Theme
grammatical relations	1	2
MAPs	A	B
presentation (partial)	nom. case	acc. case

Given that the modules are linked, we need to have principles for governing this linking. Gerdts (1993a) proposes the Universal Principles in (6).

(6) Principles for Linking GRs and MAPs (Gerdts 1993a)

SATURATION PRINCIPLE: Every MAP must be linked to a GR or cancelled.

BIUNIQUENESS PRINCIPLE: Every MAP is linked to a single GR (except multiattachment under coreference), and every GR is linked to at most one MAP.

NO DELINKING PRINCIPLE: There are no delinkings.

In addition to these principles, there are rules for effecting the linkings. The default (or unmarked) rule is given in (7). The example in (5) illustrates the default rule.[2]

(7) Default linking rule

> Link modules in a one-to-one manner from highest (left-most) position to lowest.

We analyze Fula as a 1-MAP language. Although 1-MAP languages may be typologically rare and have not heretofore been proposed within Mapping Theory, our primary purpose here is not to argue for this position. We simply note that a 1-MAP analysis naturally captures the crucial distinction in Fula between the subject and the multiple postverbal bare NPs: the postverbal bare NPs can be relativized in either a positive or negative relative clause, while the (surface) subject can be relativized only in a negative relative clause; participial phrases perform the function that positive subject relative clauses do in other languages. This can simply be stated in terms of whether or not an element is linked to a MAP. Further, there are no properties that we know of that distinguish among the postverbal NPs which would necessitate positing additional MAPs. Finally, postverbal NP order must make reference to thematic roles rather than grammatical relations. The MAP structure for the simple transitive clause in (2a) is given in (8).

(8) MAP structure of simple transitive (=2a)

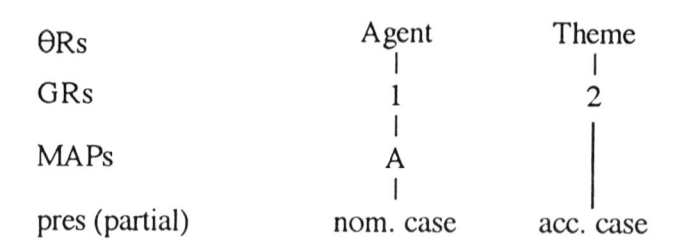

θRs	Agent	Theme
	|	|
GRs	1	2
	|	
MAPs	A	
	|	|
pres (partial)	nom. case	acc. case

The heart of Mapping Theory, though, is in the marked linking rules, some universal, some language particular. These rules are generally associated with some kind of morphology. One marked rule is the Passive, given in (9).

---

[2]This is a slight generalization of the formulation in Gerdts (1993a).

(9) Universal passive linking rule (following Gerdts (1993a), Davies (1993))

   a. Do not link the first [highest, left-most] GR
   b. Cancel one or more MAPs (language parameter)

Universal marked rules, such as the Passive, can be supplemented by language particular codicils, e.g. detailing how linking is to occur. In (10) we have the Fula Passive Codicil.

(10) Fula Passive Codicil

   a. No MAP is actually cancelled, since there is only one to begin with, and there must be at least one
   b. Any GR (other than the first) can be linked to the A MAP
   c. Thematic roles linked to a 1 GR that is not linked to a MAP have no presentation

The MAP structure for the Passive of the simple transitive clause in (2b) is given in (11). In this case, there is only one GR available to link to the A MAP.

(11) MAP structure of Passive (=2b)

'o   lootaama
she   wash-pf.pass

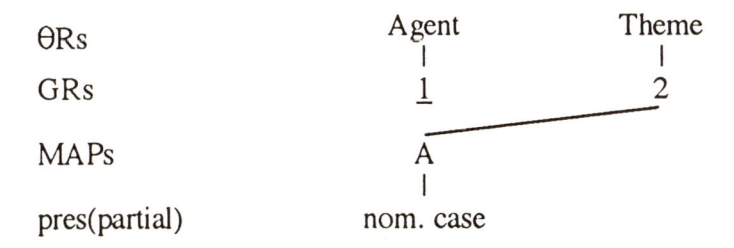

```
                     Agent         Theme
θRs                    |             |
GRs                    1_____2

MAPs                   A
                       |
pres(partial)       nom. case
```

Since Fula is a 1-MAP language, we need a principle for the realization of the additional arguments in clauses with more than a single argument. As we see in (1) and (2a), these additional arguments are usually realized as NPs. We can state this generalization as in (12). Note that the Passive Codicil prohibiting the realization of unlinked 1's takes precedence over the surplus argument principle.

(12) Fula surplus argument principle

Unless otherwise specified, unlinked arguments are realized as secondary object NPs. The object NPs higher on the thematic hierarchy precede those lower on the thematic hierarchy.

We are now ready to give the MAP structures for monomorphemic ditransitives and verbs with the Dative extension, which behave alike (see Table 1). Although Arnott gives no evidence for alternation between bare NP and PP realizations for the Goal/Recipients of the ditransitive or the Benefactive of the Dative extension, McIntosh (1984) does provide such evidence, given in (13), from Kaceccereere Fula, which is closely related to the Gombe dialect discussed by Arnott.

(13) NP/PP alternations with ditransitives and the Dative extension in Kaceccereere (McIntosh 1984: 181-183)

    a. ditransitive, NP Goal/Recipient

        Ngim   ɗume mi suuɗ- an- ta   maa mo ɗe?
        because of what 1sg hide D impf 2sg 3sg 3pl
        'Why was I going to hide them from her on your (sg.) behalf?'

    b. ditransitive, PP Goal/Recipient

        Ngim   ɗume mi suuɗ- an- ta   maa ɗe
        because of what 1sg hide D impf 2sg 3pl

        daga to maako?
        from at 3sg
        (=a)

    c. Dative extension, NP Benefactive

        Ndee min ngar- t-   id- an- ay- noo
        when 1pl come back with D   impf pst

        Muusa 'e   maakoyŋ?
        Muusa with 3pl
        'When were we going to come back with them for Muusa?'

    d. No Dative extension, PP Benefactive 273c

        Ndee min ngar- t-   id- ay- noo
        when 1pl come back with impf pst

'e   maakoyŋ ngim Muusa?
with 3pl   for   Muusa
(=c)

Notice that when the Benefactive is realized within a PP, the Dative extension is not present. There is no corresponding difference in verbal morphology with monomorphemic ditransitives. We can account for this difference by assuming that a Benefactive PP is an adjunct, and not an argument of the verb; only a Benefactive NP is an argument.

In the absence of other evidence, we assume that our analysis of Fula must reflect the NP/PP alternation for the monomorphemic ditransitives and the Datives. We thus propose that the presentation of this argument is idiosyncratically specified as being [-V]. For the structure of the active ditransitive, we suggest the MAP structure in (14)[3]

(14) MAP structure of Active of ditransitive

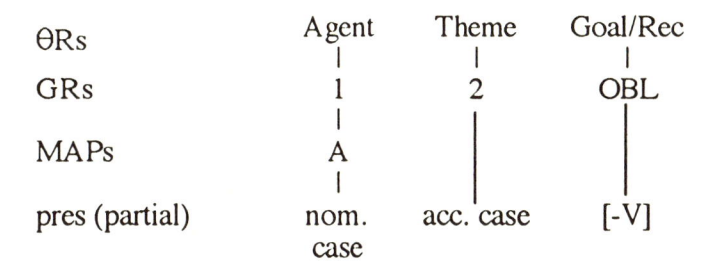

	Agent	Theme	Goal/Rec
ΘRs			
GRs	1	2	OBL
MAPs	A		
pres (partial)	nom. case	acc. case	[-V]

When the Benefactive occurs in a PP, it is an adjunct, and so is not mentioned in the MAP structure, which only concerns arguments. However, when the Benefactive occurs as an NP, it is an argument, and the Dative extension must be present. The Fula Dative rule is given in (15).

(15) Fula Dative Rule

   a. Add an object GR (i.e., 2 or 3).
   b. The Θ-Role of the Dative links to a term GR.

---

[3] While this MAP structure is less than ideal in positing that the Goal/Recipient is an Oblique, something is needed to account for examples like (13a), in which the Agent, Theme, "Goal", and Benefactive all seem to be NP arguments.

When the base verb is transitive, the resulting MAP structures will be as in (16), while when the base verb is ditransitive, the structure is as in (17).

(16) MAP structure of Active of Dative of transitive

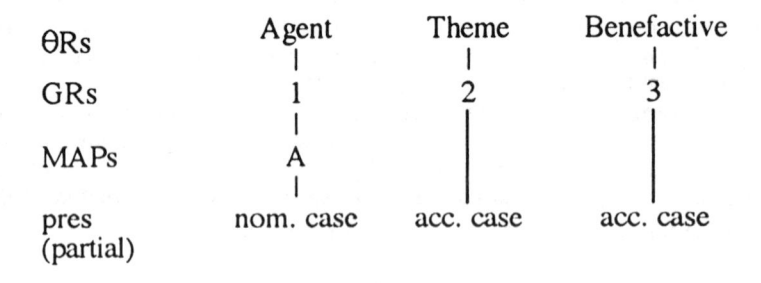

ΘRs	Agent	Theme	Benefactive
GRs	1	2	3
MAPs	A		
pres (partial)	nom. case	acc. case	acc. case

(17) MAP structure of Active of Dative of ditransitive (cf.13)

ΘRs	Agent	Theme	Goal/Rec	Benefactive
GRs	1	2	OBL	3
MAPs	A			
pres (partial)	nom. case	acc. case	[-V]	acc. case

Recall that when there are two Objects, either Object can passivize with the other still being realized (cf. (3-4, and Table 1)).[4] In (18) we give the MAP structure for the passivization of the first Object, and in (19) we give the MAP structure for the passivization of the second Object. These two structures are permitted by the Fula Passive Codicil (10), which allows either non-1 GR to link to the A MAP.

---

[4]We have no evidence about what happens in the three Object case.

(18) MAP structure of Passive of first Object of ditransitive/Dative

```
ΘRs              Agent       Theme      Goal/Ben
                   |           |           |
GRs                1           2         OBL/3
                   _____|
MAPs               A          |
                   |          |
pres (partial)  nom. case   acc. case
                   NP
```

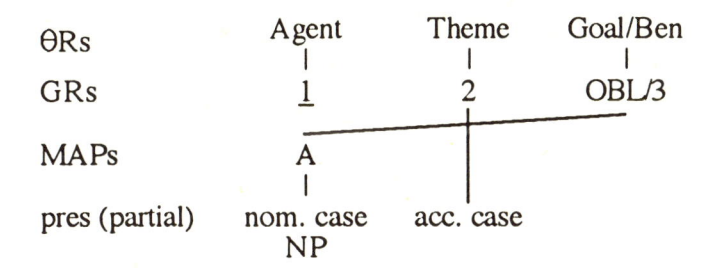

(19) MAP structure of Passive of second Object of ditransitive/Dative

```
ΘRs              Agent       Theme      Goal/Ben
                   |           |           |
GRs                1           2         OBL/3
                   _____|           |
MAPs               A                      |
                   |                      |
pres (partial)  nom. case               [-V]/
                   NP                   acc. case
```

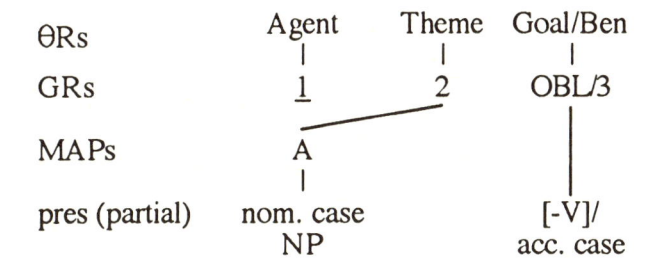

4. Layered Structures

4.1 Causative

As we have seen, verbs with the Causative extension and verbs with the Modal extension behave differently from ditransitives and verbs with the Dative extension. One way to account for these differences is to posit different structures for the Causative and Modal than we did for ditransitives and Datives.

Starting with the Causative, we suggest that when the Causative extension is added to a verb, its argument creates a new layer of GRs, as in (20).[5] The inner layer contains the GRs of the stem, and the outer layer contains the GR linked to the Causer and the inner layer. The inner layer will be ranked as a 2, after the Causer 1. Note that a layer as a whole does not link to a MAP, only its constituent GRs. We can state the Fula Causative rule explicitly as in (21).

---

[5] Our proposal for causatives differs radically from the Mapping Theory proposal of Gerdts (1993b). We offer here no comparison of the two proposals and no arguments for the superiority of our approach, noting only that our layered structure analysis allows us to capture generalizations for Fula that are unavailable under the other approach.

(20) MAP structure for active Causatives

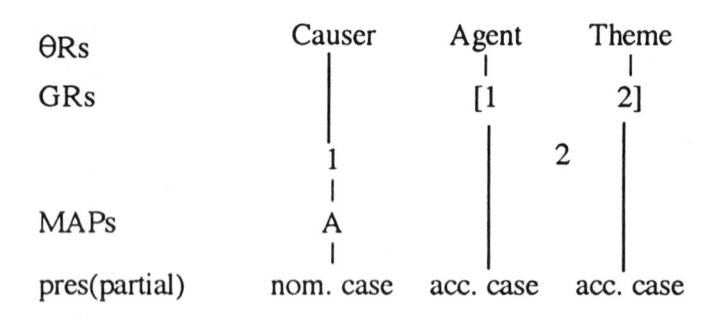

```
                    Causer      Agent      Theme
ΘRs                   |           |          |
GRs                   |          [1          2]
                      |           |          |
                      1           |  2       |
                      |           |          |
MAPs                  A           |          |
                      |           |          |
pres(partial)      nom. case  acc. case  acc. case
```

(21) Fula Causative Rule

    a. Create a layered GR structure, consisting of a 1 and the old GR structure as a 2
    b. Link the new 1 to the Causer thematic role

Since we've added layers, we need to refine the process of default linking, since there can be more than one GR of the same rank in a Mapping structure. The obvious modification is given in (22).[6]

(22) Extended default linking rule

    Starting with the outermost layer, link modules within a layer in a one to one manner from highest (left-most) position to lowest. If the position is a layer, link its positions in the same manner before linking the next position.

One motivation for positing a layered structure is that the addition of a Causer leads to a different type of action being described. Instead of the action of the stem, we now have the causation of the action of the stem. The Causative is thus in contrast with the Dative, which does not cause a change in action, merely its direction or benefit.[7] We can also note that this

---

[6] Note that some languages might have a special linking rule for certain inner layers, e.g. of the causative, instead of the default linkingrule.

[7] There may be other motivations for positing layered structures, too. It may thus be possible for languages to vary as to which constructions give rise to layered structures. For example, Alsina (1993) has proposed the analog of a layered structure for the Applicative in Chichewa (see below), which includes the functions of the Fula Dative.

layered structure is conceptually similar to causative structures proposed by Perlmutter and Postal (1974) in RG and Alsina (1992) in LFG.

Just as we had to modify the default linking rule to accomodate layers, we also need to modify the Fula passive codicil linking, given in (23).

(23) Extended Fula Passive Codicil Linking

Any GR in the Passive layer (other than the 1) can be linked to the A MAP

The account of the Passive of a Causative is now straightforward. Its Mapping structure is given in (24). The Causer is the first GR, so it is not linked, and hence not realized (by the Fula Passive Codicil). The 2 of that layer is itself the inner layer, and as a layer it cannot link to a MAP. Once we move to the inner layer, Passive linking no longer applies since the inner layer is not the Passive layer (its 1 can link). This leaves default linking to apply, linking the (inner) 1 to the A MAP. Thus, the Mapping structure in (24) is the only one possible for the Passive of a Causative in Fula.

(24) MAP structure for passive Causatives

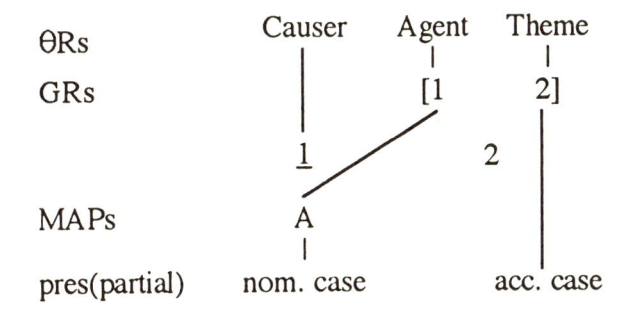

```
                    Causer    Agent   Theme
ΘRs                   |         |       |
GRs                   |        [1       2]
                      1                 2
                      |        /        |
                      |       /         |
MAPs                  A                 |
                      |                 |
pres(partial)      nom. case        acc. case
```

4.2 Modal

The final extension to discuss here is the Modal. Recall that the added argument of the Modal extension can be realized as either an NP or a PP. As with the Goal/Recipient of a ditransitive, the presentation of this argument is idiosyncratically specified as being [-V]. We can also notice that the Modal has the same semantic property as the Causative, namely that the action of the derived verb is different from the action of the stem. Hitting something with a hammer is different from hitting something with a rock. Thus, it seems that we should posit a layered structure for the Modal. The Modal Rule is given in (25). Note that this analysis is conceptually similar to Instrument Union as proposed by Gerdts and Whaley (1991) for Kinyarwanda and Alsina's 1993 analysis of applicatives in Chichewa.

(25) Fula Modal Rule

  a. Create a layered GR structure, consisting of the old GR layer as the 1 and a 2.
  b. Link the new 2 to the Instrument thematic role
  c. Specify the presentation of the new 2 as being [-V].

We can also note that the A MAP in Fula has as part of its presentation that it is an NP (26). Evidence for this comes from the lack of sentential or PP subjects.[8]

(26) Nominal presentation in Fula

The A MAP in Fula has NP as part of its presentation.

The Mapping structure for an Active Modal is given in (27). Note that it is the inner 1 which gets linked to the A MAP via Extended Default Linking (22).

(27) MAP structure for Active Modal

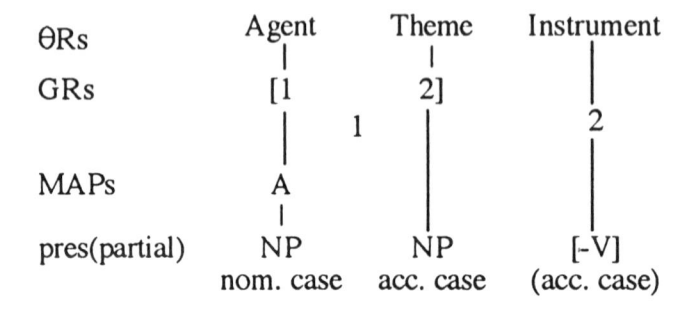

```
θRs              Agent      Theme     Instrument
                   |          |            |
GRs               [1         2]            |
                   |    1     |            2
                   |          |            |
MAPs               A          |            |
                   |          |            |
pres(partial)     NP         NP         [-V]
                nom. case  acc. case  (acc. case)
```

We are now ready to explain the Passive of the Modal. Recall from Table 1 that the original Object can passivize, with the Modal argument still realized, but if the Modal argument is passivized, the original Object cannot be realized. The key to the Passive is that a mapping structure admits two different analyses when we have an internal layer as a 1, as sketched in (28). Since Passive refers to the first GR (9a), either the 1 of the inner layer, or the 1 of the outer layer can be taken as the first GR.

---

[8]Further evidence comes from the Associative extension, whose added argument is realized only as a PP, and never passivizes.

(28) Ambiguity of Passive with layers

[[1]   2]
         [1]   2

    It is this ambiguity of the Passive which gives rise to the two passives of Modals. If we take the 1 of the inner layer as the first GR, as in (29), the 2 of the original layer (the original Object) is linked to the A MAP, and the Modal argument is realized as in the Active.

(29) MAP structure for passivization of original Object with Modal

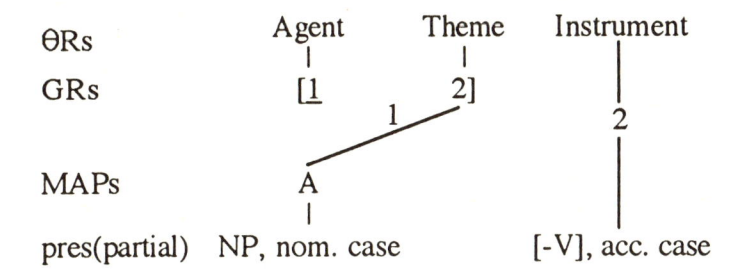

```
θRs              Agent      Theme    Instrument
                   |          |          |
GRs               [1         2]          |
                      1 ___/             2
                                         |
MAPs              A                      |
                  |                      |
pres(partial)   NP, nom. case      [-V], acc. case
```

    On the other hand, if we take the inner layer itself as the first GR, as in (30), then both the original Subject and the original Object will be unrealized, and the only GR available to link to the A MAP is the Modal argument. Since MAPs are all [+N], the modal argument must be realized as an NP subject, not a PP subject.

(30) MAP structure for passivization of Modal argument

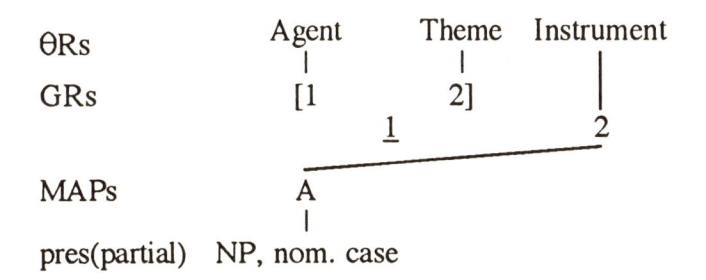

```
θRs              Agent      Theme    Instrument
                   |          |          |
GRs               [1         2]          |
                         1               2
                    _____
MAPs              A
                  |
pres(partial)   NP, nom. case
```

    While the layered structure of the Causative leads to a single passive possibility, the layered structure of the Modal leads to two passive possibilities. The difference lies in the ambiguous nature of the Modal structure as opposed to the unambiguous nature of the Causative. Furthermore, the layered structure of the Modal explains the non-realization of the original Object when the Modal argument is passivized. This is in contrast with monomorphemic ditransitives and Datives, which do not have layers and which allow the original Object to be realized when the second Object is passivized.

5. Conclusion

In this paper we have proposed one basic extension of Mapping Theory, layered structures, with attendant modification of existing Mapping Theory principles to handle these new structures. One such principle is the extended default linking rule (22), which makes precise the unmarked linking in all structures. We have also demonstrated the effectiveness of layered structures in allowing a natural treatment of a variety of facts concerning Fula verbal extensions.

The layered structure mechanism provides Mapping Theory with an analogue of the Union structure of classic RG and can be applied to causatives as well as semi-causatives, some applicatives, and many of the more recent Union proposals. For example, the Affective Union analysis of Japanese adversatives proposed by Dubinsky (1985) is handled effectively in a layered structure analysis. The sentence in (31) would have the structure in (32). In this structure, an Affectee argument is added to the basic valence of the verb, and the B MAP is cancelled, if there is one.

(31) Japanese adversative (Dubinsky 1985:180)

Tanaka ga   sensei ni   kodomo o   sikarareta
Tanaka NOM   teacher DAT child   ACC scold-pass-pf
'Tanaka was scolded [his] child by the teacher'

(32) MAP structure for Japanese adversative

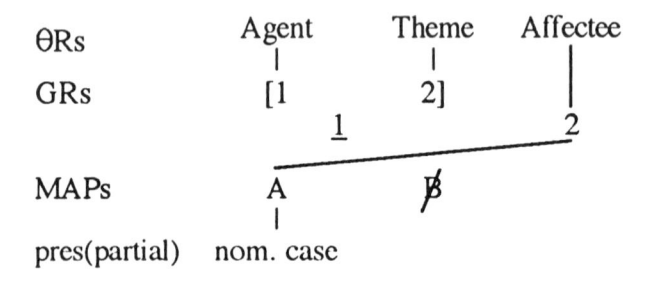

ΘRs	Agent	Theme	Affectee
GRs	[1	2]	
	1		2
MAPs	A	B̸	
pres(partial)	nom. case		

The precise domain of data open to layered structures in Mapping Theory is, of course, an empirical question, and it is unclear whether or not layered structures could account for the complete range of structures for which Union structures have been proposed. What is clear, however, is the fact that the present proposal captures facts of Fula verbal extensions in a straightforward and insightful fashion.

References

Alsina, Alex. 1992. On the Argument Structure of Causatives. *Linguistic Inquiry*. 23:4. 517-556.

Alsina, Alex. 1993. Predicate Composition: A Theory of Syntactic Function Alternations. Stanford: Ph.D. dissertation, Stanford University.

Arnott, D.W. 1970. *The Nominal and Verbal Systems of Fula*. London: Oxford University Press.

Davies, William D. 1993. Javanese Adversatives, the 1-Advancement Exclusiveness Law and Mapping Theory. *BLS* 19: 101-111.

Dubinsky, Stanley. 1985. Japanese Union Constructions: A Unified Analysis of *-sase* and *-rare*. Ithaca: Ph.D. Dissertation, Cornell University.

Gerdts, Donna B. 1992. Morphologically-Mediated Relational Profiles. *BLS* 18: 322-337.

Gerdts, Donna B. 1993a. Mapping Halkomelem Grammatical Relations. *Linguistics* 31: 591-621.

Gerdts, Donna B. 1993b. Mapping Transitive Voice in Halkomelem. *BLS* 19S: 22-33.

Gerdts, Donna B. and Lindsay Whaley. 1991. Locatives vs. Instrumentals in Kinyarwanda. *BLS* 17S: 87-97.

Gnalibouly, Bouriéma. 1990. Adressatif et Causatif en Fulfulde. *Current Approaches to African Linguistics*, ed. by John Hutchison and Victor Manfredi. vol. 7:67-72. Dordrecht: Foris.

McIntosh, Mary. 1984. *Fulfulde Syntax and Verbal Morphology*. London: Routledge and Kegan Paul.

Perlmutter, David M. and Paul M. Postal. 1974. Lectures on Relational Grammar. unpublished notes, Summer Linguistic Institute of the LSA, University of Massachusetts, Amherst.

Mapping Basque Psych Verbs

WILLIAM D. DAVIES & ASCUNCION MARTINEZ-ARBELAIZ
The University of Iowa & Cornell University

1. Introduction

Much has been written concerning the case and agreement systems of Basque; this is basically because both marking systems differ from those typically found in human languages inasmuch as they resist characterization solely in terms of final grammatical relations. One of our aims in this paper is to add to this burgeoning literature. Our rationale for doing so is that all previous accounts, whether couched in terms of initial grammatical relations (Levin 1983, Ortiz de Urbina 1989, Martinez-Arbelaiz 1992) or some combination of metastratal rules and final GRs (Mejias-Bikandi 1990, Addis 1993), prove deficient in some area. The deficiency of any particular analysis may be in needing to include a defective pattern of agreement with some auxiliary, in needing to posit metastratal rules, in some combination of the two, or simply in not considering all of the relevant data. The key to coming up with what we feel is a superior analysis is in recognizing the appropriate structure of psych verbs. In particular, we argue against an Inversion analysis of these predicates (as posited by Mejias-Bikandi and assumed by Addis). We propose instead a Mapping Theory analogue of an advancement analysis, which allows a simple account of these marking phenomena that incorporates the insights of those claiming a role for initial GRs and Addis' insight that final GRs determine agreement triggers. As a basically bistratal theory of GRs, Mapping Theory provides just the mechanisms necessary to capture the insights and is constrained in its bistratality to force just such a solution.

Before presenting arguments for the correctness of a non-inversion analysis of Basque psych verbs, we outline the analysis of case, agreement, and auxiliary selection for the unproblematic cases. However, we first present a few essentials of Mapping Theory.

2. Mapping Theory Basics

Gerdts' Mapping Theory (as outlined in Gerdts 1992, 1993) includes representations specifying three types of information about a nominal: (i) its thematic role, (ii) its grammatical relation, (iii) its MAP (morphosyntactically-licensed argument position) if it has one, and (iv) its

---

[*] Thanks to Leo Connolly, Chris Culy, Stan Dubinsky, and Donna Gerdts for discussion of issues related to this work. Errors and omissions are the sole responsibility of the authors.

presentation, language-particular statements regarding word order, case, agreement, and so on. We discuss presentation statements for Basque, but do not represent them in the structures here. In English, a 2-MAP language, a simple transitive clause such as (1) has a Mapping Theory representation such as (2).

(1) Kelly trimmed the hedges.

(2) thematic relations: agent   theme

    grammatical relations: 1   2   (initial GRs in RG)

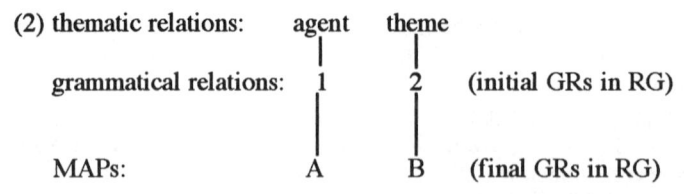

    MAPs: A   B   (final GRs in RG)

MAPs are ordered positions (represented as A, B, etc.) linked to morphological statements (e.g. active morphology licenses A, immediate postverbal position licenses B). In any given clause, the number of MAPs is based on three things: (i) the valence of the verb, (ii) MAP-reducing or -building morphology, and (iii) the MAP threshhold set for the language. Gerdts also includes a number of principles for linking GRs and MAPs, which we will not go into here; these are well-formedness conditions on linking akin to laws of RG and conditions on linking in other linking theories. (See Gerdts 1993 or Culy and Davies 1994 for statement of some of these.) A final bit of information is that unmarked associations of GRs to MAPs proceed in a vertical left-to-right fashion, as illustrated in (2). Marked associations involv non-vertical linkings or linking a nominal not present in the basic valence of the verb. These are generally accompanied by morphological conditions and marking and parallel some of the relation-changing structures of RG, e.g., passive, 3-2 advancement, and so on.

    For example, the passive clause in (3) would have the representation in (4).

(3) The hedge was trimmed by Kelly.

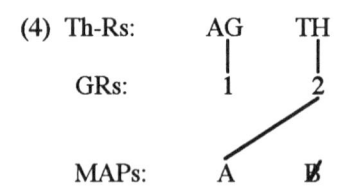

(4) Th-Rs: AG   TH

    GRs: 1   2

    MAPs: A   B̸

In passive, the highest-ranking GR goes unlinked to a MAP and a MAP is cancelled (the precise MAP being a language-particular matter). In the English passive, the theme links directly to the A MAP and the agent 1 goes unlinked, and the B MAP is cancelled (denoted here by the slash through it).

3. Mapping Basque and a Case/Agreement Proposal

Inasmuch as Basque can show agreement with up to 3 arguments, it is a 3-MAP language (Gerdts 1992), and the ditransitive clause in (5a) would have a representation as in (5b).

(5) a. Zu-k   Joseba-ri bi   dolar   eman dizkiozu.
       you-ERG J-DAT   two dollar.ABS give 3pA.ukan.3sD.2sE
       'You have given two dollars to Joseba.'

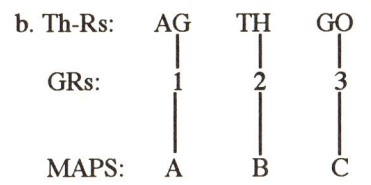

   b. Th-Rs: AG   TH   GO
          | | |
     GRs: 1   2   3
          | | |
     MAPS: A   B   C

Note here that in (5) *zu* 'you (sg)' is in the ergative case and determines ergative agreement, *bi dolar* 'two dollars' is in the absolutive case and determines absolutive agreement, and *Joseba* is in the dative case and determines dative agreement. In all instances, the verb agreement shows up on the auxiliary.

We will state our case, agreement, and auxiliary selection conditions, and then illustrate their correctness within the Mapping Theory framework for the uncontroversial constructions.[1]

---

[1]Although we use the terms 'ergative' and 'absolutive' as names of the case markers and agreement phenomena in Basque, it is fairly clear that the Basque has active/non-active case and agreement systems. That is, as the data in (10) and (11) show below, intransitive predicates split with respect to the case assigned to their subjects: unergatives take 'ergative' case and unaccusatives take 'absolutive' case. Thus Basque parallels the case marking systems noted for active/non-active languages as discussed by Sapir (1917), Klimov (1974), Mithun (1991), and many others. The non-ergativity of Basque has been noted by Anderson (1976), Levin (1983), Addis (1990, 1993), and others. Some of these works refer to the case by their traditional names *nork* (= ergative), *nor* (= absolutive), and *nori* (= dative). While we do not mean to deliberately mislead the reader or appear to claim that Basque is morphologically ergative, we use ergative and absolutive as case names here. Because of the overwhelming tendency to do so in the recent literature on Basque, we feel that using this terminology makes the analysis and the

(6) *Case Marking*
Case is marked on a nominal in accord with its GR such that
(i) ergative is marked on 1s,
(ii) absolutive is marked on 2s, and
(iii) dative is marked on 3s.

(7) *Verb Agreement*
Nominals linked to MAPs trigger agreement. The form of the agreement markers is determined by the GR of the trigger such that
(i) 1s determine ergative agreement,
(ii) 2s determine absolutive agreement, and
(iii) 3s determine dative agreement.

(8) *Auxiliary Selection*
ukan 'have' is selected as the perfect auxiliary if a 1 links to the A MAP; otherwise *izan* is selected.

The rules in (6-8) apply straightforwardly to the ditransitive clause in (5): the 1 linked to the A MAP takes ergative case and determines ergative agreement, the 2 linked to the B MAP takes absolutive case and determines absolutive agreement, the 3 linked to the C MAP takes dative case and determines dative agreement, and the auxiliary is *ukan*, since the 1 links to the A MAP.

Example (9) illustrates the passive.

(9) a. Jon-ek idatz-i-a   da   eskutitz hau.
     J-ERG write-PRF-sA 3sA.PRS.*izan* letter   this-ABS
     'This letter has been written by Jon.'

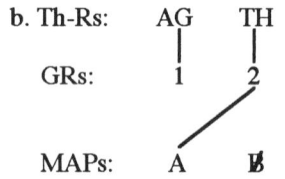

   b. Th-Rs: AG   TH
                | |
      GRs: 1   2

      MAPs: A   B

In the passive structure the 1, *Jon*, is not linked to a MAP; thus, it does not determine agreement and it takes ergative case, since it is a 1. The 2, *eskutitz hau* 'this letter', is linked to the A MAP; therefore, it triggers agreement, which is absolutive since it is a 2, and takes absolutive case.

---

points we hope to make more accessible than would be the case if we used the more obscure traditional terminology.

The perfect auxiliary is *ikan*, in accord with the rule in (8) since the 1 is not linked to the A MAP.

Unergatives and unaccusatives are illustrated in (10) and (11), respectively.

(10) a. Jon-ek kurritu du.
     J-ERG run   PRS.*ukan*.3sE
     'Jon has run.'

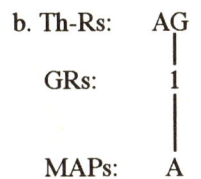

    b. Th-Rs: AG
         |
      GRs: 1
         |
      MAPs: A

(11) a. Jon   etorri da.
     J.ABS come 3sA.PRS.*izan*
     'Jon has come.'

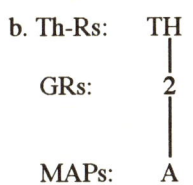

    b. Th-Rs: TH
         |
      GRs: 2
         |
      MAPs: A

The unergative in (10) has a single argument whose GR is 1, which links to the A MAP. Since it is linked to a MAP, the nominal triggers agreement; agreement and case is realized as ergative since the nominal is a 1. *Ukan* is correctly selected as the auxiliary since the 1 links to the A MAP. Conversely, the unaccusative in (11) determines absolutive agreement and takes absolutive case since it is a 2. As there is no 1 linked to the A MAP, *izan* is selected as auxiliary.

These structures are Mapping Theory analogues to structures posited in other frameworks in earlier work and should be considered relatively uncontroversial. The perfect auxiliary selection rule in (8) parallels the RG formulation proposed by Mejias-Bikandi (1990) and accepted by Addis (1993) and Martinez-Arbelaiz (1992), which states that *izan* is selected if some nominal heads both a 2-arc and a 1-arc and that otherwise *ukan* is selected.

4. Psych Predicates

Crucial to establishing the correctness of our case and agreement rules are the psych verb constructions, illustrated in (12) and (13).

(12) Miren-i lore-ak gusta-tzen zaizkio.
M-DAT flower-pABS like-HAB PRS.*izan*.3pA.3sD
'Miren likes the flowers.'

(13) Gorka-ri giltza-k ahaz-tu zaizkio.
G-DAT key-pABS forget-PRF PRS.*izan*.3pA.3sD
'Gorka forgot the keys.'

We propose the representation in (14) for psych verbs.

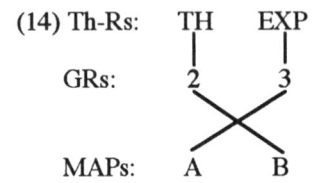

(14) Th-Rs: TH   EXP
              | |
     GRs: 2   3
               \ /
                \/
                /\
               / \
     MAPs: A   B

The representation in (14) together with the rules in (6-8) account well for the case, agreement, and auxiliary selection facts. First, the experiencer argument triggers agreement by virtue of being linked to the A MAP; the form of agreement and case is dative since its GR is 3. The theme triggers agreement since it is linked to the B MAP; agreement and case are absolutive since its GR is 2. Finally, izan is properly selected as auxiliary since there is no 1 linked to the A MAP.

Of course, the same set of case, agreement, and auxiliary facts would be accounted for if the 2 were linked to the A MAP and the 3 linked to the B MAP. It therefore remains for us to motivate the particular linking of GRs to MAPs that we propose in (14). We turn to that issue now.

4.1 A MAP Properties

There are a number of grammatical phenomena that are sensitive to which nominal is linked to the A MAP in a clause. We discuss two of these here. What we find is that the experiencer argument of psych constructions consistently displays these A MAP properties while the theme does not.

The first property to consider is binding the anaphor *bere burua* literally 'his/her head'. Nominals linked to the A MAP may bind the reference of this anaphor, while other nominals may not. The ditransitive clause in (15) illustrates.

(15) Andoni-k_i Edurne-ri_j be-re burua-rekiko_{i/*j} iritzia-k
    A-ERG E-DAT s/he-GEN head-w.r.t. opinion-pABS
    adieraz-ten dizkio.
    explain-HAB 3A.PRS.*ukan*.3sD.3sE
    'Andoni explains his opinions about himself to Edurne.'

In (15) the 1 linked to the A MAP, *Andoni*, can bind the reflexive. The 3 linked to the C MAP, *Edurne*, cannot.

As passives show, unlinked 1s cannot bind the anaphor.

(16) *Jon-ek_i idatz-i-a d a liburu hau be-re
    J-ERG write-PRF-sA 3sA.PRS.*izan* book this.ABS s/he-GEN
    burua-ren_i lagun-entzat.
    head-GEN friend-pBEN
    (This book has been written by Jon for his friends.)

In (16), *Jon* is the unlinked 1; it is unavailable to bind the anaphor. The linked theme in the passive can bind the anaphor.

(17) Gizona_i be-re burua-ren_i etsai-rik handi-ena-k
    man-ABS s/he-GEN head-GEN enemy-PART big-SUPERL-ERG
    sala-tu-a izan zen..
    betray-PRF-sA *izan* 3sA.PST.*izan*
    'The man was betrayed by his own worst enemy.'

As (17) shows, the 2 linked to the A MAP of the passives, here *gizona* 'man' can bind the anaphor. The linked argument of both unergatives (18) and (19) unaccusatives can bind the anaphor. Naturally, in both cases, the element binding the anaphor is linked to the A MAP.

(18) Jon-ek_i be-re burua-z_i hitzegiten d u maiz.
    J-ERG s/he-GEN head-INST talk *ukan*.3sE often
    'Jon talks about himself often.'

(19) Gizon-a_i be-re burua-ren_i laguntza-rekin bakar-rik
    man-ABS s/he-GEN head-GEN help-sCOM single-ADV
    e z d a ino-ra joa-ten.
    NEG 3sA.PRS.*izan* wh-ADL go-HAB
    'A man does not go anywhere only with his own help.'

As the following sentences indicate, only the experiencer and not the theme of psych verbs can bind the anaphor.[2]

(20) Joseba-ri$_i$ Miren$_j$ gusta-tzen zaio be-re burua-rekiko$_{i/*j}$
     J-DAT M.ABS like-HAB 3A.*izan*.3sD s/he-GEN head-w.r.t.
     jokaera-gatik.
     behavior-MTV
     'Joseba likes Miren because of her behavior toward him.'

(21) Sarrionandia-ri$_i$ idazle hori$_j$ interes-tzen zaio
     S-DAT writer that.ABS interested-HAB 3sA.*izan*.3sD
     be-re burua-ren$_{i/*j}$ poem-etan natura-k duen eragin-agatik.
     s/he-GEN head-GEN poem-pLOC nature-ERG *ukan*.REL influence-MTV
     'Sarrionandia likes that writer because of the influence that nature has
     in his own (S's) poetry.'

If the experiencer 3 links to the A MAP, as in our representation in (14), we can simply account for the binding of the anaphor *bere burua* with a condition restricting antecedents to arguments linked to the A MAP.

A second type of evidence for our analysis comes from what nominals can be controlled in *-teko* clauses. As illustrated in (22), a *-teko* clause is embedded as a complement of the verb *esan* 'to tell' and (can) lack the argument linked to the A MAP. The reference of this argument is supplied by the goal argument of the matrix clause.

(22) Miren-i$_i$ [Ø$_i$ Kepa-ri liburu-a ema-teko] esa-n
     M-DAT K-DAT book-ABS give-*teko* tell-PRF
     diot.
     3sA.*ukan*.3sD.1sE
     'I told Miren to give the book to Kepa.'

As Mejias-Bikandi (1990) shows, the experiencer in a psych construction can be the controllee in a *-teko* clause.

---

[2]In (20), the string *buru-zko* 'head-LOC' has nothing to do with the anaphor *bere burua* but instead is simply being used as a postposition, as in the following:
(i) Afrika-ri buru-zko liburu-a
     A-DAT head-LOC book-ABS
     'a book about Africa'

(23) Aita-k   neska-ri$_i$ [Ø$_i$ mutil-a   gusta-tzeko] esa-n
    father-ERG girl-DAT   boy-ABS like-*teko*   give-PRF
    dio.³
    3sA.*ukan*.3sD.3sE
    'The father told the girl to like the boy.'

The missing element in the embedded clause in (22) is the experiencer argument of the psych verb. As (23) shows, the theme cannot be controlled.

(24) *Aita-k   neska-ri$_i$ [Ø$_i$ mutila-ri gusta-tzeko] esa-n
    father-ERG girl-DAT   boy-DAT like-*teko* give-PRF
    dio.
    3sA.*ukan*.3sD.3sE
    (The father told the girl that the boy should like her.)

Data from passives, unaccusatives, and unergatives bear out the fact that only arguments linked to the A MAP can be controllees in -*teko* clauses.

4.2 Relativization

We now turn to an additional argument that the theme 2 is linked to a MAP (in fact, the B MAP since the experiencer 3 links to the A MAP). Relativization facts provide evidence independent of case and agreement for the linking of the 2.

In their treatment of relative clause phenomena, Keenan and Comrie (1977) establish that relativization in Basque reaches to the indirect object position on their Accessibility Hierarchy. This fact is captured within a Mapping Theory analysis by appeal to elements being linked to a MAP: the A MAP, the B MAP, or the C MAP. The fact that the agent of a passive clause cannot be relativized (hence the ungrammaticality of (25)) provides evidence that elements linked to term GRs cannot be relativized if they are not linked to a MAP.

(25) *Jon   astindua   izan zen   gizona
    J-ABS   hit.PART   *izan izan*.PAST.REL   man
    (the man who Jon was hit by)

The proposed analysis of Basque psych verbs in (14), in which the theme 2 is linked to the B MAP, predicts that it should be possible to relativize the theme, which the example in (26) shows is indeed the case.

---

³In (23) -*tzeko* is a phonologically-conditioned variant of -*teko*.

(26) Jon-i   gustatzen zaio-n   neska
     J-DAT   like.HAB   3A.*izan*.3sD-REL   girl
     'the girl that Jon likes'

The data considered above are easily accounted for given our proposed structure for psych verbs.

5. Against an Inversion Analysis

We alluded to the fact above that certain problems arise for case and agreement from assuming an inversion analysis for Basque psych verbs. The complications which arise are (i) it is necessary to invoke metastratal rules in order to account for case and agreement facts, and (ii) it is necessary to invoke the brother-in-law relation to account for agreement in inversion clauses. As we have shown above, grammatical properties which are sensitive to subject status (or in Mapping Theory terms being linked to the A MAP) invariably fall to the experiencer and not the theme in psych verbs. This forces two complications upon the inversion analysis (i) it is necessary to state all these grammatical properties in terms of the notion 'working 1', as indeed Mejias-Bikandi (1990) does, and (ii) it is actually necessary to posit an impersonal inversion structure, in which the theme is put en chomage by a silent pleonastic element which enters as a 2, as diagrammed relationally in (27). Neither Mejias-Bikandi (1990) nor Addis (1993) recognize the necessity of positing impersonal inversion rather than personal inversion.

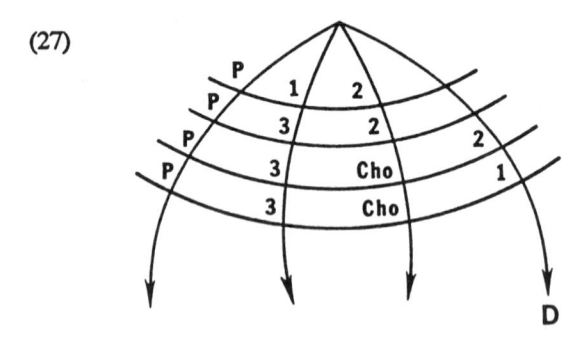

(27)

This impersonal structure is made necessary by the fact that the theme of the psych construction does not behave as a final subject, as it should if the construction were actually personal inversion. Once it is recognized that the impersonal construction must be posited, further complication ensues. Since the theme is finally a chômeur, it should not trigger agreement under Mejias-Bikandi's and Addis' analyses in which agreement tiggers are final terms. It is necessary to invoke brother-in-law agreement by which the theme determines the form of the agreement triggered by the silent pleonastic pronoun.

Our Mapping Theory proposal avoids any of these special devices. The proposal renders unnecessary any reference to working 1, brother-in-law, metastratal rules, or impersonal inversion. It neatly characterizes the case and agreement facts in terms of initial and final grammatical relations (here GRs and MAPs), and simply accounts for auxiliary selection as well. There is one more virtue missing in some previous analyses (although this is not true of Addis 1993): it is unnecessary to have agreement rules treat the two auxiliaries *ukan* and *izan* differently. Mejias-Bikandi (1990:264) is forced to state that *ukan* takes ergative agreement with its final 1 and *izan* takes absolutive agreement with its final 1; Martinez-Arbelaiz (1992) is forced to posit a defective paradigm for agreement with *izan*. Here no special disclaimers or conditions are necessary: agreement morphology is determined in terms of GRs but the property of triggering agreement is stated in terms of MAPs.

6. Conclusion

Clearly, the proposed analysis can be easily formulated in the standard RG framework. We would simply posit a 3-1 Advancement analysis, as in (28).

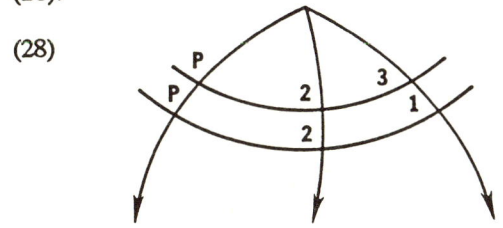

(28)

The case and agreement rules can then be reformulated in terms of initial and final GRs: agreement is triggered by final terms and the form of agreement and case marking is determined by initial terms. The auxiliary selection rule can be reformulated in terms of a nominal heading only a 1-arc (in which case *ukan* is selected). However, one potential advantage of the Mapping Theory approach taken here (which, of course, might be seen as a liability elsewhere) is that it is unnecessary to entertain the possibility of 3-2-1 advancement rather than direct 3-1 Advancement inasmuch as the theory is basically bistratal with respect to grammatical relations. Thus, the type of analysis that we propose here is for all intents and purposes dictated by the theory.

References

Anderson, Stephen. 1976. On the Notion of Subject in Ergative Languages. *Subject and Topic*, ed. by Charles N. Li, 1-24. New York: Academic Press.
Addis, Kristen. 1990. Basque as a Non-ergative Language. Cornell University ms.
Addis, Kristen. 1993. Paradigm Trimming in Basque. *Linguistics* 31:431-74.
Culy, Christopher, and William D. Davies. 1994. Mapping Theory and Fula Verbal Extensions. This volume.
Gerdts, Donna. 1992. Morphologically-mediated Relational Profiles. *BLS* 18:322-327.
Gerdts, Donna B. 1993. Mapping Halkomelem Grammatical Relations. *Linguistics* 31:591-621.
Keenan, Edward, and Bernard Comrie. 1977. Noun Phrase Accessibility and Universal Grammar. *Linguistic Inquiry* 8:63-99.
Klimov, G.A. 1974. On the Character of Languages of Active Typology. *Linguistics* 131.11-25.
Levin, Beth. 1983. Unaccusative Verbs in Basque. *Proceedings of the Thirteenth Annual Meeting of the North East Linguistic Society*.
Martinez-Arbelaiz, Asun. 1992. Dative Subjects and Case Assignment in Basque. University of Iowa ms.
Mejias-Bikandi, Errapel. 1990. Clause Union and Case Marking in Basque. *Grammatical Relations: A Cross-theoretical Perspective*, ed. by Katarzyna Dziwirek, Patrick Farrell, and Errapel Mejias-Bikandi, 263-77. Stanford, CA: CSLI.
Mithun, Marianne. 1991. Active/agentive Case Marking and Its Motivations. *Language* 67:510-46.
Ortiz de Urbina, Jon. 1989. *Parameters in the Grammar of Basque*. Dordrecht: Foris.
Sapir, Edward. 1917. Review of Uhlenbeck 1917. *International Journal of American Linguistics* 1:82-86.

Experiencers of Psych Verbs in Tagalog

VIDEA P. DE GUZMAN
The University of Calgary

1. Introduction

The Exp(eriencer) nominal of psych(ological) verbs has received a wide range of investigations in several unrelated languages. The accounts vary according to the theoretical framework adopted in a given grammatical description. One shared observation about the Exp nominal is its varying grammatical function and surface case manifestation in both accusative and ergative languages. This variation may be found even within the same language. (Belleti and Rizzi, 1986; Rosen, 1984). Usually, the Exp is marked with Nom(inative) case when functioning as subject, Acc(usative) when direct object, or Dat(ive) when indirect object. In some languages, however, the Dat-marked Exp functions as the grammatical subject (Verma and Mohanan, 1990). In such instances, the case marker of the nominal does not signal the grammatical relation with which it is associated.

In the Relational Grammar framework, two proposals have been put forth to account for the syntactic behaviour of Exps of psych verbs. They are: (i) the Inversion account, where the Exp nominal is an initial 1, and it may retreat or get demoted to a final 3 (Perlmutter, 1984; Harris, 1984); and (ii) the Advancement account in which the Exp starts out as an initial 3 (or Oblique) and it may advance to 2, and then to 1 (Gerdts and Youn, 1988). These two approaches share the feature of the Exp being assigned term 1 and term 3 at some level of structure and thus effecting Nom case marking when it is a final 1 and Dat or Obl(ique) case when it is a final 3/Obl. The Obj(ect) nominal that cooccurs with the Exp is aligned with the initial 2 in both proposals, and it ends up as a final 2 or a final 2-chomeur.

These two accounts have been well-argued in documented studies in various languages, notably Italian, Japanese, Quechua, Georgian, Udi, various South Asian languages, and Korean. However, neither one provides an adequate account of similar structures in Tagalog, a major Philippine language. This paper investigates the characteristic morphological and syntactic behaviour of Tagalog psych verbs and their complements, paticularly the Exp nominal. Approaching the description from an ergative viewpoint within the RG framework, I propose an account in which the Exp is aligned with two different initial term relations. I argue that it is an initial 1 when the verb is transitive, with an option to advance to term 2 thereby creating an antipassive structure analogous to the antipassive of action verbs.[1] The cooccurring Obj nominal, as in other transitive structures, is an initial 2. With intransitive psych verbs, the Exp is aligned with an initial 2 (Donna Gerdts, personal communication), the salient or favoured grammatical relation in ergative languages. The Exp is analogous to the Obj in an unaccusative structure rather than to the Agent or Actor in an unergative structure. Arguments for the proposed analysis will be discussed and illustrated below. Finally, some theoretical implications of the proposal will be drawn.

2. Tagalog psych verb constructions

Verbal structures in Tagalog are characterized specially by two morphosyntactic features, case-marked nominals and inflected verb forms indicating voice and aspect. A set of three case particles marks nominals; common nouns may be preceded by the Abs(olutive) ang, the Erg(ative)/Gen(itive) nang, or the Obl(ique) sa.[2] The voice affix on the verb, including its specific stem structure, is associated with the semantic role of the nominal that is chosen to be "in focus", i.e. marked by the neutral Abs case, which functions generally as the grammatical subject.

2.1 Types of psych verbs

Tagalog psych verbs are no different from action verbs in cooccurring with nominals marked by case particles and in being distinguished by their various voice forms. Four morphosemantic types of psych verbs are considered in this study, namely: (a) transitive perception, (b) transitive cognition, (c) intransitive emotion/physical state, and (d) transitive pseudo verbs, each represented by the following examples:

(1) na-kita   nang bata ang parada (sa   daan)
    St/past-see-OV Erg child Abs parade (Obl street) (St = state)
    'The child saw the parade on the street.'   (OV = Objective Voice)

(2) na-unawa-an   nang bata ang payo   nang magulang
    St/past-understand-OV Erg child Abs advice Gen parent
    'The child understood the parent's advice.'

(3) na-takot   ang bata (sa   kulog)
    St/past-fear-EV   Abs child (Obl thunder) (EV = Experiencer Voice)
    'The child was afraid of the thunder.'

---

[1]In the Ergative Analysis employed here, the hierarchy 2 > 1 > Obl is assumed. (See De Guzman, 1988).

[2]Proper nouns are correspondingly marked in the singular and plural by a different set of case particles: si/sina, ni/nina, kay/kina, respectively.

(4) kailangan   nang bata   nang/ang gamot
    Ps/pres-need   Erg child   Obl/Abs medicine   (Ps = pseudo)
                         [-spec]/[+spec]
    'The child needs medicine/the medicine.'

Based on an Ergative Analysis (De Guzman, 1988; cf. Gerdts, 1988), we will account for the different Exp voice forms of the verbs and the grammatical relations the Exp nominal is aligned with in each type, as well as the case markers it takes.

2.2 Psych verbs and their forms

A remarkable difference between action and psych verbs lies in their morphological structures. Whereas action verbs are typically marked by in/i-/-an to indicate objective voice, by -um-/m- , agentive, by -an , locative, and by i- , other voices (where each stem form may vary), psych verbs are marked by a completely different set. The typical structure of the transitive (OV) perception and cognition verbs is an unmarked form without any overt voice affix, as in ma-kita 'to see', ma-dinig 'to hear', ma-amoy 'to smell', ma-dama 'to feel', ma-puna, ma-pansin, ma-halata 'to notice', ma-tanaw 'to see from a distance', etc. It simply carries the stative marker ma- affixed to the root, and in this minimal form the verb is distinctive enough to signal the OV. The corresponding antipassive or EV form consists of the stative marker ma- plus a ka-+stem. The following antipassive constructions correspond to (1) and (2) above:

(5) na-ka+kita   ang bata nang parada sa   daan
    St/past-Adm-see-EV   Abs child Obl parade Obl street
                                    (Adm=advancement marker)
    'The child saw a parade on the street.'

(6) na-ka+unawa   ang bata nang payo   nang magulang
    St/past-Adm-understand-EV Abs child Obl advice Gen   parent
    Lit.: 'The child understood an advice of the parent.'

The structures of the transitive perception construction in (1) and its corresponding antipassive (5) may be represented by the following stratal charts (7) and (8), respectively, with the semantic roles identified:

(7)   Exp   Obj   (Loc(ation))
    P   1   2   (Obl)
    ma-kita   nang bata   ang parada   sa daan
    St-see-OV   Erg child   Abs parade   Obl street

(8)   Exp   Obj   (Loc)
     P   1   2   (Obl)
     P 2^3 2-cho   (Obl)
                                                                               (Antipassive rule)
     ma-ka+kita   ang bata   nang parada   sa   daan
     St-Adm-see-EV   Abs child   Obl   parade   Obl   street

The transitive structure is monostratal and the simple OV form of the verb corresponds to the Obj being final 2, licensing Abs case. The Exp, as an analogue of Agent (Agt), is aligned with 1 which licenses Erg case.[4] In some other perception and cognition verbs, as in (2), the form of the OV is distinguished by the occurrence of the voice affix -an attached to the stative stem with the prefix ma- . This class includes verbs such as: ma-unawa-an 'to understand', ma-limut-an 'to forget', ma-intindih-an 'to comprehend', ma-ramdam-an 'to feel/sense', ma-tanda-an 'to remember or recall', ma-tuklas-an 'to discover/find out', ma-ranas-an 'to experience', etc. The corresponding antipassive form, however, remains identical in structure to that of the preceding class, i.e. ma- + ka-stem. The stratal network representations of this class is the same as those of the first type.

In the third type of psych verb, exemplified in (3), the clause structure is intransitive with a cooccurring Exp, not an Obj, functioning as the grammatical subject. Assuming that the Exp is aligned with initial 1, as in the transitive structures, it may still be shown to function as a final 2 via the Unergative rule, where an initial 1 advances obligatorily to 2. The puzzling result, though, is that its verb consisting of ma- + root is identical in form to the OV or transitive form. (This situation is counter to what obtains in action verbs where both intransitive and antipassive forms are identical in structure.) It may be inferred from the absence of the ka- advancement marker in the verb that no advancement has taken place, in which case it is reasonable to conclude that the Exp must have been aligned with initial 2, rather than with initial 1. This would give us a monostratal representation for (3) as follows:

---

[3]It will be noted that instead of the Final 1 Law, it has been proposed and argued previously (De Guzman, 1988) that for ergative languages, it is the Final 2 Law that applies such that the hierarchy of grammatical relations likewise shifts 2 higher than 1. Despite Schachter's (1977) account of reference and role related properties of subjects, it has been shown quite convincingly by Kroeger (1991) that the 'subject properties' in Tagalog primarily converge on the Abs-marked relation, i.e. the Final 2.

[4]For economy, I will limit discussion of these two cases unless otherwise relevant. Arguments for the alignment of Exp and Obj to initial 1 and 2, respectively, will be given in the succeeding section.

(9)   Exp   (Obl)
    P   2   (Obl)
    ma-takot ang bata   (sa kulog)
    St-fear   Abs child   (Obl thunder)

From a semantic point of view, we can argue that intransitive psych verbs require only Exps to be their cooccurring nominals. With intransitive action verbs, the obligatory nominal may be either an Obj or an Actor (or Agt). The former structure is referred to as unaccusative and the latter, unergative. The question is whether the intransitive psych verb clause structure is similar to an unaccusative or an unergative structure. The Exp being the animate entity to/in whom some psychological experience occurs is better unified with the Obj or patient, rather than the Actor, in the sense that both nominals share the feature **[+affected]** (Rozwadowska, 1988). As such both Exp and Obj of intransitive structures take on the most important GR in the structure - initial 2.

There is ample evidence in other languages to show that a thematic role can be mapped onto different initial GRs (Rosen, 1984:55), hence, the suggested alignments above are not unusual. This variation can be further supported by comparing the corresponding structure in which the optional Obl nominal, which specifies the goal, cause or reason for the emotional or physical state of the Exp, advances to 2 as shown in (10) below:

(10) P   1   Obl
     P   1   2   (Obl --> 2)
     ka+takut-an   nang bata   ang kulog
     Adm-fear-RV   Erg   Abs   (RV= Referential Voice)
     k-in-a+takut-an nang bata ang kulog
     'The child was afraid of the thunder.'

In the above clause structure, the Exp can only be assigned to initial 1 when the Obl nominal is made an obligatory complement advancing to 2. The nominal that heads a final 1 necessarily heads an initial 1 and no other term. If it were an initial 2, and the cooccurring Obl advanced to 2, then the initial 2 would become a 2-chomeur. This latter analysis fails because there is no evidence that the Exp nominal is a 2-chomeur. On the contrary, it can be shown that the Exp is a final 1. (See section 3 for evidence.) For the moment, suffice it to state that the related verb form in which a non-term advances to the primary GR is construed as undergoing transitivization, in which case the occurrence of a 1 becomes inevitable. This form may be treated as a lexically derived form. (Cf. Voskuil, 1993)

The fourth type of psych verb, referred to as 'pseudo-verb' (Schachter and Otanes, 1972), consists of a small group of base forms which do not usually cooccur with an Abs case-marked nominal. Without any apparent voice affix, only the Obj, aligned with the 2, may have the option of taking the Abs case marker when it carries the specific meaning .

Otherwise, it shows up with the non-specific Obl case marker <u>nang</u>. This type of verb never allows an antipassive correspondence. Thus, the relational representation of (4) may be shown as follows:

(11)
	Exp	Obj	
P	1	2	
kailangan	nang bata	nang/ang	gamot
PsV-need	Erg child	Obl/Abs	medicine
		[-spec]/[+spec]	

3. The Exps of psych verbs

Unlike the varied grammatical manifestations of Exps observed in other languages, Tagalog Exps of psych verbs are more straightforward. They occur in only two case forms, that is, either in the Abs or in the non-Abs case, similar to the other thematic roles. It has already been shown that the Exp of intransitive verbs is properly aligned with the 2, rather than with the 1, primarily by virtue of its cooccurring verb form.

Between the Exp and the Obj complements of the transitive types in the non-Abs case, we find the Exp to be the apparent analogue of the Agt of transitive action verbs. Thus, it seems plausible to align it with initial 1. Evidence for its 1-hood comes not only from Erg case marking (particle <u>nang</u>) but also from the occurrence of the Erg/Gen forms of pronominal substitutes in this syntactic function. Further evidence comes from the morphological structure of its cooccurring verb. The form of the transitive (OV) psych verb, where the Exp is a final 1 marked Erg, is simpler than its corresponding antipassive form, where the Exp is a final 2 marked Abs. Finally, the syntactic rules that refer to initial 1, which typically realizes the semantic role Agt of action verbs, also refer to initial 1 manifesting the Exp of psych verbs. Each of these pieces of evidence that argue for mapping Exp onto initial 1, rather than initial 3/Obl, is discussed and illustrated below.

3.1. The Exp and the Agt both take Erg case

In the above transitive clauses (1) and (2), the Exp nominal appears to be the uncontroversial analogue of the Agt in action verb constructions in terms of case form. For example, the transitive action verb construction

(12) lulutu-in[5]   nang   nanay   ang   isda   sa   kusina
    will cook-OV Erg   mother   Abs   fish   Obl kitchen
    'Mother will cook the fish in the kitchen.'

---

[5]Only the future or contemplated aspect form of the objective voice with the affix <u>-in</u> shows this affix overtly, thus it is chosen for illustration. The corresponding completed and incompleted aspect forms of this verb are <u>linutu/nilutu</u> and <u>linulutu/nilulutu</u>, respectively.

has the following relational representation:

(13) | | Agt | Obj | (Loc) |
|---|---|---|---|
| P | | 1 | 2 | (Obl) |
| | lutu-in | nang nanay | ang isda | sa kusina |
| | cook-OV | Erg mother | Abs fish | Obl kitchen |

In this version of the Ergative Analysis, the basic monostratal transitive construction represented in (5.a) has the OV form of the verb marked with the voice affix -in; the Agt (aligned with initial 1) is marked with the Erg case particle nang, the Obj (term 2), with the neutral Abs case particle ang, and the optional Location (assigned to Obl non-term), with the Obl particle sa. Similarly, the transitive psych verb construction in (1) has the same stratal representation identified earlier as (7), repeated below for ease of comparison:

(14) | | Exp | Obj | (Loc) |
|---|---|---|---|
| P | | 1 | 2 | (Obl) |
| | ma-kita | nang bata | ang parada | sa daan |
| | St-see-OV | Erg child | Abs parade | Obl street |

It will be noted that despite their semantic difference both Agt and Exp, aligned with a 1, are marked Erg. Marking the Exp with the Obl case will be ungrammatical.

The Exp nominal, like the Agt, may be substituted by pronominal forms to perform the function of a 1. This form can only be the Erg (or Gen), as in:

(15) nakita ko ang parada sa daan
saw-OV 1sg/Erg Abs parade Obl street
'I saw the parade on the street.'

Using either of the two other pronominal forms, the Abs or the Obl, in this function will result in ungrammatical structures.[6]

---

[6]There are three case forms of pronouns in Tagalog. The personal ones are as follows:

		Abs	Erg/Gen	Obl
Singular:	1	ako	ko	sa akin
	2	ikaw; ka	mo	sa iyo
	3	siya	niya	sa kaniya
Plural:	1	tayo (inclusive)	natin	sa atin
		kami (exclusive)	namin	sa amin
	2	kayo	ninyo	sa inyo
	3	sila	nila	sa kanila

The same case marking can be found in the nominalized forms of these psych verbs in which the Exp (like the Agt) is also marked by the Erg case particle. For example:

(16) ang pagkakita nang bata nang parada sa daan
'the child's seeing a parade on the street'

(17) ang pagkaunawa nang bata nang/sa payo nang magulang
Lit.: 'the child's understanding of some/the advice of the parent's'

(18) ang pagkatakot nang bata sa kulog
'the child's being afraid of the thunder'

(19) ang pangangailangan nang bata nang/sa gamot
'the child's need of medicine/the medicine'

3.2 The Exp and its cooccurring verb forms

We can now compare the morphological structure of transitive psych verbs in their OV and EV forms to show that the former is simpler than the latter and parallels the pattern in action verbs. In the previous section on psych verb forms, (2.2, (7) and (8)), we noted that the typical OV form consists of ma- + root while that of the EV is made up of the more complex structure ma- + ka-stem. From example (5) above, the OV of the action verb is formed with the root + -in. This can be compared with the corresponding antipassive form below:

(20) P   1   2   (Obl)
     P   2   2-chomeur   Obl (Antipassive rule)
     m-pag-lutu   ang nanay   nang isda   sa   kusina
     AV-Adm- cook Abs mother   Obl fish   Obl kitchen
     (AV=agentive voice)
     maglulutu ang nanay nang isda sa kusina
     'Mother will cook fish in the kitchen.'

The form maglutu is analyzable as consisting of the agentive voice affix m- attached to the stem pag-lutu, pag- being claimed as the antipassive affix (Gerdts, 1988). Here, I have identified it, along with ka-, as an advancement marker (Adm). The antipassive verb forms exemplified by the infinitive forms maglutu 'to cook' and makakita 'to see' are more complex compared with their corresponding OV forms lutuin 'to cook' and makita 'to see'. (See De Guzman, 1992, for a more detailed discussion.) This supports the parallel patterning of verb forms with Exp and Agt as grammatical subjects in contrast with their corresponding OV forms.

Additionally, there is a class of verbs identified as abilitative, involuntary, or accidental (AIA), which are derived from action verbs, whose agentive forms are also prefixed by the identical form maka-. (Dell, 1983; Schachter and Otanes, 1972). For example:

(21) naka-paglutu ang nanay nang isda sa kusina
AIA-AV-cook Abs mother Obl fish Obl kitchen
'Mother was able to cook fish in the kitchen.'

The OV form for both psych and AIA verbs is marked only with ma- affixed to the root, when the corresponding OV of the source action verb takes the affix -in, as illustrated below:

(22) na-luto nang nanay ang isda sa kusina
AIA-OV-cook Erg mother Abs fish Obl kitchen
'Mother was able to cook the fish in the kitchen.'

3.3 Syntactic behaviour of the Exp[7]

The similarity between the grammatical functions of both the Agt and the Exp, treated as initial 1, is magnified when we consider the Exp's role in syntactic processes such as reflexivization, participation in control structures (equi), and inaccessibility to 'Adjunct fronting' (Kroeger, 1991: 49). It may be mentioned in passing that the Exp is also capable of fulfilling the grammatical function of subject much like that of other Abs nominals as shown in the processes of: (a) relativization, (b) quantifier floating,[8] (c) raising, (d) conjunction reduction, (e) possessor ascension, and (f) number agreement (Kroeger, 1991).[9] What I will show momentarily is the more crucial evidence involving the syntactic behaviour of the Erg Exp which is identical to that of the Erg Agt.

---

[7]The non-nominative agent/actor (referred to in Bell (1976) as a non-term being a 1-chomeur or oblique after passivization) or experiencer has been argued in Kroeger (1991: 49f.) to be a term on account of its eligibility to act as a controller or a controllee in Equi constructions. It may be noted that in the Ergative Analysis the termhood of the Agt or the Exp is assured as an Erg-marked initial/final 1. Perlmutter (1984), however, has responded to this question of Kroeger's by introducing the notion of "working 1s".

[8]The first two processes are Schachter's (1977) evidence for treating the Abs/Nom-marked nominal as the grammatical subject.

[9]The last four processes are also cited in Kroeger (1991) along with two other processes, secondary (depiction) predication and obviation, to show that the Nom/Abs nominal functions as the grammatical subject in Tagalog.

3.3.1. The Exp controls the reflexive pronoun

Like the Agt, the Exp **controls the reflexive pronoun** (and also binds other anaphors) and the PRO or gap in embedded complement clauses as in the following:

(23) na-kita   nang bata$_i$ ang sarili niya$_i$ sa salamin
     St/past-see-OV Erg child Abs self 3sg/Gen Obl mirror
     'The child saw himself/herself in the mirror.'

(24) na-ramdam-an   nang bata$_i$ -ng/na nagalit   ang nanay
     St/past-feel-OV Erg child Comp St/past-angry Abs mother
     sa   kaniya$_i$
     Obl 3sg/Obl
     'The child$_i$ felt/sensed that Mother got angry with him/her$_i$.'

(25) na-isip-(an)   nang bata$_i$ -ng/na pumunta PRO$_i$
     St/past-think of-OV Erg child Comp to go
     sa   laruan
     Obl playground
     'The child thought of going to the playground.'

(26) gusto   nang bata$_i$ -ng/na makita   PRO$_i$ ang palabas
     PsV-like Erg   child Comp to see-OV   Abs show
     'The child likes/wants to see the show.'

In the above examples, the Erg Exp of the matrix predicates is the **controller of both anaphors and PROs**.

3.3.2. The Exp can be the controllee in participial complements

As shown in Kroeger (1991: 49-57), actors (more appropriately, agents) can also be **controllees in participial complements**, regardless of whether they are in the Abs or the Erg case. The Exp, if it is a true analogue of the Agt, should likewise be able to function in the same manner. And indeed it does. Compare the action constructions in (27) and (28) (from Kroeger, 1991: 50) and the psych constructions in (29) and (30):

(27) in-abut-an   ko   siya$_i$ -ng/na [nagbabasa PRO$_i$
     past-find-OV I/Erg 3sg/Abs-Comp   AV-reading
     nang komiks sa   eskwela]
     Obl comics Obl school
     'I caught him reading a comic book in school.'

(28) in-abut-an   ko   siya̜i -ng/na [hinahalikan PROᵢ/(niya̜ᵢ)
    past-find-OV I/Erg   3sg/Abs-Comp kissing-OV   3sg/Erg
    ang katulong]
    Abs maid
    'I caught him kissing the maid.'

(29) na-halata   nang bata̜ⱼ ang nanayᵢ na   [nagagalit
    St-sensed-OV Erg child   Abs mother Comp being angry
    PROᵢ sa   kaniyaⱼ/ₓ]
          Obl   3sg/Obl
    'The childⱼ sensed mother being angry with him/her ⱼ,ₓ.'

(30) na-halata   nang bata̜ⱼ ang nanayᵢ na   [kinaiinisan
    St-sensed-OV Erg child   Abs mother Comp annoyed at-RV
    PROᵢ/(niya ᵢ) ang tatay]
    3sg/Erg   Abs father
    'The child sensed mother being annoyed with father.'

In both action and psych constructions, the Agt and the Exp controllee in the participial clause may be in either the Erg or the Abs case, as reflected in the voice form of the verb.

3.3.3. The Exp is not subject to adjunct-fronting, but to topicalization

In what Kroeger (1991: 53f.) calls 'Adjunct Fronting', i.e. moving a constituent in front of the verb within the same minimal clause, only non-terms (i.e. obliques, adjuncts or adverbials) are eligible to undergo this process. Thus, Erg Exps and Obl Objs are constrained from being fronted in this manner, as shown in the following:[10]

---

[10]This evidence constitutes Kroeger's argument for considering these two nominals - non-nominative agents and 'genitive' (or oblique) objects - as terms, contrary to the supposed chomeur status they assume as a result of an earlier advancement rule. For him, since these nominals are not subject to "adjunct-fronting', they must be terms. However, it may be mentioned that even the instrumental phrase, when introduced by the alternate particle nang instead of the phrase sa pamamagitan nang 'by means of' before the nominal, cannot be fronted either. This is also true of adverbial adjuncts that are introduced by the particle nang, and it may be countered that the constraint on adjunct-fronting is on any nang-complement or nang-adjunct or their Gen pronominal substitutes. (Compare with sa-phrases that function as terms, but which may undergo adjunct-fronting.)

(31) sa   salamin nakita   nang bata ang sarili niya
     Obl   mirror St-saw-OV Erg   child Abs self   3sg/Gen
     'In the mirror the child saw himself.'

(32) *nang bata nakita   ang sarili niya   sa   salamin
     Erg   child saw-OV   Abs self   3sg/Gen Obl   mirror

(33) *nang parada nakakita ang bata sa   daan
     Obl parade saw-EV   Abs child Obl   street

In contrast, these nominals may undergo topicalization (fronting of constituents outside the minimal clause with a pause introduced after the moved constituent) which is normally accessible to absolutive-marked nominals. For example:

(34) ang sarili niya,   nakita   nang bata sa   salamin
     Abs self   3sg/Gen # saw-OV   Erg child Obl mirror
     'Himself, the child saw in the mirror.'

(35) ang bata,   nakakita nang parada sa   daan
     Abs child # saw-EV   Obl parade Obl   street
     'The child, (he) saw a parade on the street.'

The non-absolutive Exp and non-absolutive Obj may be distinguished in topicalization (see (32) and (33) above), when the <u>nang</u> particle is replaced by <u>ang</u>, as in:

(36) ang bata,   nakita   (niya$_i$)   ang sarili (niya$_i$)   sa   salamin
     Abs child # saw-OV   (3sg/Erg)   Abs self   3sg/Gen   Obl   mirror
     'The child, (he) saw himself in the mirror.'

(37) *ang parada, nakakita ang bata sa   daan
     Abs parade # saw-EV   Abs child Obl street

While the **non-absolutive Exp may undergo this topicalization**, (a phenomenon often overlooked in previous accounts of topicalization), the non-absolutive Obj may not. As shown in (36), the Exp has the option of leaving a pronoun copy in the Erg case in its original postverbal position. With action verbs, it is also the non-absolutive Agt, and not the non-absolutive Obj, which can be topicalized in like manner, as in:

(38) ang nanay,   lulutuin   (niya)   ang isda   sa   kusina
     Abs mother # will cook-OV 3sg/Erg Abs fish Obl kitchen
     'The mother, (she) will cook the fish in the kitchen.'

(39) *ang isda,   maglulutu   ang nanay   sa   kusina
      Abs fish # will cook-AV   Abs mother Obl kitchen

This kind of topicalization of the non-absolutive Exp can be generalized to all the other types of psych constructions identified above (examples (24)-(26)).

In all these processes we see the syntactic similarities between the Agt of action verbs and the Exp of psych verbs. Thus, it is plausible to map Exp onto an initial 1 which exhibits 'subject' properties.

3.4 The Exp and the Obj case particles

The Obj nominal which cooccurs with the Exp in psych verb constructions has been taken, without argument, as being aligned with initial 2, the Abs case, as in most other basic clause structures. It is characteristic of ergative type languages for the Obj to take the primary grammatical relation, term 2, and for the cooccurring Agt, term 1. As the grammatical subject or Abs, the Obj is syntactically prominent and semantically expresses definiteness. As soon as its function is usurped by another cooccurring nominal, the Obj becomes impotent. As a 2-chomeur, it is marked by the Obl marker nang, an entity homophonous with the Erg case marker.

In this connection, the question may be raised whether this Obl nang is one and the same particle as the Erg nang.[11] I claim that a distinction exists between these two forms. As I have shown earlier, the Erg nominal is capable of undergoing topicalization, but the Obl Obj is not. Another pertinent difference can be found in the way these nominals are replaced by pronominal substitutes, where applicable. The function of the Erg nominal only allows the occurrence of the Erg/Gen form of the pronouns as illustrated in (15). When the Obl Obj nominal takes a pronominal form, it never shows up in the Erg case, but rather only in the Obl case. Thus, note the Obl pronouns in the following action and psych verb constructions:

---

[11] Other accounts (Bell, 1976, Payne 1982, Kroeger, 1991) label this particle in the two occurrences both Gen(itive) or Obl(ique) or one Gen and the other Obl.

(40) sa wakas, nakaunawa   rin   ang bata   sa kaniya /*niya
    Obl end # understood-EV also Abs child   3sg-Obl/ 3sg-Erg
    'Finally, the child also understood him/her'

(41) hihintay-in   ko   siya
    will wait for-OV 1sg/Erg 3sg/Abs
    'I will wait for her.'

(42) maghihintay   ako   sa kaniya/*niya
    will wait for-AV 1sg/Abs   3sg-Obl/ 3sg-Erg
    'I will wait for her.'

Even the semantic interpretation of the Erg-marked nominal and the Obl Obj marked by <u>nang</u> suggests a difference. The former is always interpreted as being definite, unless otherwise modified by some indefinite particle, whereas the latter consistently generates an indefinite meaning. In instances where a definite reference is possible for the Obl Obj, the Obl particle <u>sa</u> serves as an alternate form. Thus,

(43) nakakita ang bata sa   parada
    saw-EV Abs child Obl [+def] parade
    'The child saw the parade.'

(44) nakaunawa rin ang bata   sa   payo   nang magulang
    understood also Abs child Obl [+def] advice Gen parent
    'The child also understood the advice of the parent.'

The Obl Obj marked by <u>sa</u>, to mean definite, is utilized more frequently in other types of constructions, e.g. cleft, interrogative, etc. The preferred form for referring to a definite Obj is still the Abs case.

4. Mapping semantic roles onto initial GRs

From the present analysis and description, we can offer empirical support for Rosen's (1984:53) abandoning her proposed Little Alignment Hypothesis (LAH) which says: 'For any one predicate in any one language, there is a fixed mapping which aligns each semantic role with an initial GR. The alignment remains invariant for all clauses with that predicate.' It will be recalled that in (10) above the Exp of the intransitive verb <u>matakot</u> 'to be afraid' which is aligned with initial 2 has to be aligned with initial 1 with the corresponding referential voice form <u>katakutan</u> 'to be feared'. If these two forms are treated as inflected forms of the same verb, then we have a counterexample to the LAH. Carefully referring to the latter verb form earlier as being 'related' suggests implicitly that they may not necessarily be 'one and the same' verb or predicate, which the hypothesis above sets up as a condition. The notion 'one predicate' in all clauses certainly requires some thoughtful determination. It is not uncommon to observe subtle differences between using the 'same' verb form transitively and intransitively. What appears to be one and the same verb form may in fact be two different forms. One of these could have effected a change in its semantic role requirements which may have some corresponding syntactic consequences. Of course, we can account for this lexical change by means of specifying corresponding changes in morphological and/or syntactic features in the derivational process. To a certain extent, this may be what happens with respect to verb forms that focus on adjunct nominals. (Starosta, Pawley, and Reid, 1982; Voskuil, 1993). It may very well be the case that the two verb forms referred to are different and hence the hypothesis holds. If this line of thinking is correct, and there are good reasons for believing it to be so (but note that the debate between inflection and derivation of these verb forms continues), then this study has lent support to the LAH stated above.

One other contribution of this study with respect to the question of the relevance of semantic role alignment with initial GRs is the explanation it is able to provide for the morphosyntactic split between action and psych verbs in Tagalog. As previously stated, the morphological structure of intransitive action verbs, marked by -um- or m-, is identical to that of the antipassive forms. In contrast, the intransitive psych verb forms have the same pattern as the transitive or OV forms. The morphological affix ma- (and even the marked ma- -an), uniting the Obj of the transitive and the Exp of the intransitive, serves to emphasize the object-hood (or affectedness) of the Exp as a 2. Without this initial term alignment of Exp to 2 in intransitive constructions, it would have been a problem for any grammatical framework to account for this overlap.

Finally, the case system of Tagalog, as observed operating in the class of psych verbs treated here, is much simpler when compared with other languages such as English, Korean, Georgian, or Italian. Following Gerdts' (1991) distinction between cases licensed by grammatical relations (S-case) and those licensed by semantic relations (I-case), Tagalog has only one S-case, the Abs licensed by final 2. All others, including those encountered here such as Erg/Gen, Obl, and Ref are I-cases. Given this limitation, the only cases in which each nominal can be manifested is either the non-Abs (its I-case) or the Abs (its S-case). From a typological view, Tagalog may be said to belong to a one S-case type language.

5. Conclusion

The present proposal that the Exp of psych verbs aligns with initial 1 makes it resemble the Inversion account whereby its 1-hood properties are captured. Contrary to a retreat or demotion to 3 which follows from the rule, however, the initial 1 advances to 2, a higher term in the hierarchy of grammatical relations (in ergative languages). In effect therefore, the account considered to be adequate for Tagalog follows the same principle involved in the Advancement proposal. Two distinctive characteristics of the Tagalog Exp of psych verbs are: (i) its non-occurrence in Dat or Obl case, and (ii) (a) with transitive verbs, its identity with the Agt, which typically aligns with 1, and thus takes the Erg case, and (b) with intransitives, its identity with the Obj (the affected entity) which aligns with 2, the Abs case.

Drawing then from all three proposals, we conclude that the Exp of psych verbs in general aligns with a term relation and at least one of its final term manifestations must be a 1. Given this restriction on aligning this semantic relation with an initial term relation in a given language, it suggests that there is an advantage to be gained in keeping Rosen's Little Alignment Hypothesis, particularly when initial terms are inadequate to explain certain morphological devices such as verbal affixes which are linked with semantic roles.

References

Bell, Sarah J. 1976. *Cebuano Subjects in Two Frameworks*. Ph.D. Dissertation, MIT.

Belleti, Adriana and Luigi Rizzi. 1988. Psych-verbs and Th-theory. *Natural Language and Linguistic Theory* 6, 291-352.

Berinstein, Ava. 1990. On Distinguishing Surface Datives in K'ekchi. *Studies in Relational Grammar 3*, ed. by Paul M. Postal and Brian D. Joseph, 3-48. Chicago: The University of Chicago Press.

Blake, Barry J. 1990. *Relational Grammar*. New York: Routledge.

Cresti, Diana. 1990. A Unified View of Psych-verbs in Italian.*Grammatical Relations (A Cross-Theoretical Perspective)*, ed. by Katarzyna Dziwirek, Patrick Farrell & Errapel Mejias-Bikandi, 59-81. Stanford: The Center for the Study of Language and Information.

De Guzman, Videa P. 1988. Ergative Analysis for Philippine Languages: An Analysis. *Studies in Austronesian Linguistics*, ed. by Richard McGinn, 323-345. Athens, Ohio: Ohio University.

De Guzman, Videa P. 1992. Morphological Evidence for Primacy of Patient as Subject in Tagalog. *Papers in Austronesian Linguistics* No. 2, ed. by Malcolm D. Ross, 87-96. *Pacific Linguistics*, A-82.

Dell, Francois. 1981. On Certain Sentential Complements in Tagalog." *Philippine Journal of Linguistics* 12.1: 11-28.

Dell, Francois. 1983. An Aspectual Distinction in Tagalog. *Oceanic Linguistics* 22-23: 175-206.

Gerdts, Donna B. 1988. Antipassives and Causatives in Ilokano: Evidence for an Ergative Analysis. *Studies in Austronesian Linguistics*, ed. by Richard McGinn, 295-321. Athens, Ohio: Ohio University.

Gerdts, Donna B. 1991. Outline of a Relational Theory of Case. *Simon Fraser University Working Papers in Linguistics*, Vol. 1: 25-51.

Gerdts, Donna B. and Cheong Youn. 1988. Korean Psych Constructions: Advancement or Retreat? *Chicago Linguistic Society* 24: 155-175.

Grimshaw, Jane. 1990. *Argument Structure*. Cambridge, Mass.: The MIT Press.

Harris, Alice C. 1984a. Case Marking, Verb Agreement, and Inversion in Udi. *Studies in Relational Grammar 2*, ed. by David Perlmutter and Carol Rosen, 243-258. Chicago: The University of Chicago Press.

Harris, Alice C. 1984b. Inversion as a Rule of Universal Grammar: Georgian Evidence. *Studies in Relational Grammar 2*, ed. by David Perlmutter and Carol Rosen, 259-291. Chicago: The University of Chicago Press.

Kroeger, Paul R. 1991. *Phrase Structure and Grammatical Relations in Tagalog.* Ph. D. Dissertation, Stanford University.
Payne, Thomas E. 1982. Role and Reference Related Subject Properties and Ergativity in Yup'ik Eskimo and Tagalog. *Studies in Language* 6.1: 75-106.
Perlmutter, David. 1984. Working 1s and Inversion in Italian, Japanese, and Quechua. *Studies in Relational Grammar 2*, ed. by David Perlmutter and Carol Rosen, 292-330. Chicago: The University of Chicago Press.
Rosen, Carol. 1984. The Interface Between Semantic Roles and Initial Grammatical Relations. *Studies in Relational Grammar 2*, ed. by David Perlmutter and Carol Rosen, 38-77. Chicago: The University of Chicago Press.
Rozwadowska, Bozena. 1988. Thematic Restrictions on Derived Nominals. *Syntax and Semantics (Thematic Relations)* 21, ed. by Wendy Wilkins, 147-165. San Diego: Academic Press.
Schachter, Paul. 1977. Reference-related and Role-related Properties of Subjects. *Syntax and Semantics (Grammatical Relations)* 8, ed. by Peter Cole and Jerrold Sadock, 279-306. New York: Academic Press.
Schachter, Paul and Fe T. Otanes. 1972. *Tagalog Reference Grammar.* Los Angeles: University of California Press.
Starosta, Stanley, Andrew K. Pawley, and Lawrence Reid. 1982. The Evolution of Focus in Austronesian. *Papers from the Third International Conference on Austronesian Linguistics*, Vol. 2: Tracking the Travellers, ed. by Amran Halim, Lois Carrington, and Stephen A. Wurm. *Pacific Linguistics Series* C-75. Canberra: National University of Australia.
Verma, Manindra. K. and Karavannur P. Mohanan. 1990. *Experiencer Subjects in South Asian Languages.* Stanford, CA: The Center for the Study of Language and Information.
Voskuil, Jan E. 1993. Verbal Affixation in Tagalog (and Malay). (Ms., University of Leiden)

Expletive Subjects in Lingala: A Challenge to Burzio's Generalization

STANLEY DUBINSKY & MAZEMBA NZWANGA
University of South Carolina

    Lingala, a Bantu language spoken in western Zaire, has two syntactic constructions which can be used to 'background' the Agent of a transitive verb. One is a passive structure, illustrated in (2), which may be compared with its transitive analog in (1).

(1)   Mama a-beng-i   Francine
         AgrS-call-TNS
     'Mom called Francine.'

(2)   Francine a-beng-am-i   na mama
         AgrS-call-PASS-TNS by mom
     'Francine was called by Mom.'

It is fairly uncontroversial to assume a passive structure for (2), wherein the initial 2 *Francine* advances to 1, and puts the initial 1 *mama* en chômage. The initial object *Francine* is preverbal and triggers 3rd person singular subject agreement on the verb, the initial subject *mama* is the object of a preposition, and a morphological marker of passive *-am* appears on the verb. The other construction, which is largely interchangeable with (2), is illustrated in (3). This sentence type is not described in the traditional grammars (e.g. Bwantsa 1970, De Rop 1963, and Welmers 1973), although a similar construction is alluded to in Kimenyi (1980). Note that the passive translation adopted for the construction in (3) and throughout is reflective of its functional, rather than structural, properties.

(3)   Ba-beng-i   Francine na mama
     AgrS-call-TNS   by mom
     'Francine was called by mom.'
     Lit: 'They called Francine by mom.'

---

*We gratefully acknowledge the helpful suggestions and criticisms of Chris Culy, William Davies, Edward Keenan, Paul Kroeber, Joan Maling, and Ron Simango, as well as the audience of the 6th Biennial Conference on Grammatical Relations. All omissions and errors are solely attributable to the authors.

1. Analysis

Although this construction has the Agentive *by*-phrase characteristic of regular passive, it is quite distinct in other regards. It lacks passive verbal morphology. The initial direct object *Francine* is postverbal, and does not trigger subject agreement on the verb. The subject agreement prefix *ba-* is nonreferential and 3rd person plural.[1] For reasons that will be made clear shortly, we propose that (3) is an IMPERSONAL TRANSITIVE and has the relational structure given in (4).

(4)
```
              P          2          1
1             P          2          Cho
DUMMY         beng       Francine   mama
```

In (4), the initial 1 *mama* is put en chômage by a dummy nominal that is an entrant 1. The initial 2 *Francine* is a final 2. This analysis at once explains the absence of passive morphology in (3), which might be expected if the dummy were an entrant 2 that advances to 1 (i.e. an impersonal passive construction). In order to demonstrate that (4) is, in fact, the correct analysis for the impersonal transitive construction, it is necessary to show: that the initial 1 is a final chômeur, and that the initial 2 is a final 2.

Proving the initial 1 of this construction to be a final chômeur is relatively straightforward. The phrase *na mama* in the impersonal transitive, (3), has all the morphological attributes of the passive chômeur in (2), such as the oblique preposition *na* and the failure to trigger subject-verb agreement. In addition, neither it nor the regular passive chômeur can undergo topicalization or relativization. Compare the relative clauses in (5) and (6).

(5) *Mwasi [(na) oyo mama a-bengami] azali-kitoko
    woman   by   whom mom was.called is-pretty
    ('The woman by whom mom was called is pretty.')

(6) *Mwasi [(na) oyo babengi   mama] azali-kitóko
    woman   by   whom they.called mom is-pretty
    ('The woman by whom mom was called is pretty.')

---

[1]The agreement prefixes *a-* and *ba-*, glossed as AgrS (i.e. subject agreement), are respectively third person singular and third person plural. Additionally, they reflect agreement with nouns of Class 1/2, which is reserved for [+sentient] or [+human] nominals. The relevance of this last feature will be seen below.

In (5), the nominal *mwasi* 'woman' is interpreted as the initial 1 of a regular passive relative clause. In (6), the relative clause is an impersonal transitive, and *mwasi* is interpreted as its initial 1. Both sentences are ill-formed with or without the preposition *na*.

Showing that the initial 2 of the impersonal transitive is not advanced (i.e. a final 1) is also uncomplicated. As already noted above, this nominal does not trigger subject agreement on the verb (as does the initial 2 of a regular passive clause). Furthermore, the initial 2 of the impersonal transitive normally remains postverbal, and if it is moved into preverbal position, it necessarily acquires a Focus or Topic interpretation (dependent on the presence of a resumptive pronoun). Consider the sentences in (7).

(7) a. Francine ba-beng-i   na mama
         AgrS-call-TNS by mom
        'It is Francine who was called by mom.'

    b. Francine$_i$ ba-beng-i ye$_i$ na mama
         AgrS-call-TNS her by mom
        'As for Francine, she was called by mom.'

In (7a), the initial 2 *Francine* precedes the verb, but is interpreted as a Focus nominal and does not trigger subject agreement on the verb. In (7b), a resumptive pronoun *ye* occupies the postverbal direct object position, and the nominal *Francine* has a Topic reading.

Further supporting the claim that *Francine* does not advance in (3) is the fact that this nominal can be replaced by an object clitic in the Makanza dialect of Lingala. Compare (1) and (3) with (8a) and (8b), in which the nominal *Francine* has been replaced by the third person singular object clitic *mu-* (n.b., the plural object clitic *ba-* is homophonous with the subject agreement marker of the same type).

(8) a. Mama a-mu-beng-i
         AgrS-AgrO-call-TNS
        'Mom called her.'

    b. Ba-mu-beng-i   na mama
         AgrS-AgrO-call-TNS by mom
        'She was called by mom.'

Demonstrating the initial 2 is also a final 2 in the impersonal transitive is a little more difficult, since 2s and 2-Chos are not distinguished by any special marking. We can observe the similarity of 2s and 2-Chos in the Benefactive-applicative construction. Example (9) illustrates the advancement of Benefactives.

(9) a. Paul a-lamb-i   loso mpo-na mama
          AgrS-cook-TNS rice for   mom
        'Paul cooked rice for mom.'

   b.   Paul a-lamb-el-i   mama loso
          AgrS-cook-APP-TNS mom   rice
        'Paul cooked mom rice.'

Example (9a) shows a simple transitive clause, containing a prepositional Benefactive (i.e. preceded by the preposition *mpo-na*). In (9b), this Benefactive nominal *mama* is advanced, triggering the applicative morpheme *-el* on the verb, and the movement of the Benefactive to immediate postverbal position (preceding the initial 2 *loso*).

Through the interaction of passive with Benefactive-applicative, we can determine that the Benefactive in (9b) advances to 2, putting the initial 2 en chômage. In (10), we see that the initial 2 cannot passivize in the Benefactive-applicative.

(10) a. Loso e-lamb-am-i   mpo-na mama na Paul
          rice AgrS-cook-PASS-TNS for   mom   by
        'The rice was cooked for mom by Paul.'

   b.   *Loso e-lamb-el-am-i   mama na Paul
          rice AgrS-cook-APP-PASS-TNS mom   by
        ('Rice was cooked mom by Paul.')

The object of *lamb* 'cook' is passivized in (10a), which contains a prepositional Benefactive. In (10b), the Benefactive is advanced, triggering the applicative morpheme, and passivization of the initial 2 is impossible. This is readily explained if we assume that Ben advances to 2, putting the initial 2 *loso* en chômage.

At the same time, we find that the Benefactive nominal can passivize, but only in the presence of the applicative morpheme. This fact, illustrated in (11), would suggest that Ben-2 and 2-1 advancement are both involved in the passivization of a Benefactive nominal.[2]

---

[2]As might be expected, the Benefactive can also surface as the final 2 in an impersonal transitive construction. This is illustrated in (i).

(i)   Ba-lamb-el-i   Paul loso na mama
       AgrS-cook-APP-TNS   rice by mom
      'Paul has been cooked rice by mom.'

(11) a. *Paul a-lamb-am-i   loso na mama
        AgrS-cook-PASS-TNS rice by mom
        ('Paul was cooked rice for by mom.')

   b. Paul a-lamb-el-am-i   loso na mama
       AgrS-cook-APP-PASS-TNS rice by mom
       'Paul was cooked rice by mom.'

Together, (10) and (11) show that the Benefactive is advanced to 2 in an applicative construction, and that both 2s and 2-Chos are morphologically unmarked in this language. This second inference makes it difficult to determine whether the initial 2 of example (3) is actually a final 2. Although it is clear from (11b) that final 2s precede final 2-Chos, we can also see that both 2s and 2-Chos precede 1-Chos, and the impersonal transitive construction only contains a single postverbal prepositionless nominal. Passivization tests of the sort just utilized are unhelpful, since the nominal *Francine* in example (3) would not be able to undergo passive even if it were a final 2, this being precluded by the Nuclear Dummy Law which rules out Dummy chômeurs.[3] Fortunately, the behavior of object clitics provides the needed evidence. Example (12) shows that an initial 2 cannot cliticize in the Benefactive-applicative construction.

(12) a. Mama a-mu-bet-i   mpo-na Paul/ye
        AgrS-AgrO-beat-TNS for   him
        'Mama beat her for Paul/him.'

   b. Mama a-mu-bet-el-i   Paul/ye
       AgrS-AgrO-beat-APP-TNS   him
       'Mama beat Paul/him for her.'
       (NOT: 'Mama beat her for Paul/him.')

In (12a), in which the Benefactive is preceded by the preposition *mpo-na*, the initial 2 is represented by the object clitic *mu-*. Example (12b) is an applicative construction in which the Benefactive nominal has advanced to 2. Under these conditions, only the Benefactive nominal can be replaced by an object clitic, and the nominal *Paul* is necessarily interpreted as the Theme. If the 2-Cho could cliticize, then (12b) ought to be ambiguous.

---

[3]The Nuclear Dummy Law (Perlmutter and Postal 1983) is stated as follows: If A is an arc whose head is a dummy nominal, A is a nuclear term arc (i.e., a 1-arc or 2-arc).

The evidence still does not tell us that access to object cliticization is determined on the basis of **absolute** final GRs, since the failure of the 2-Cho to cliticize in (12b) might be due to the presence of an available final 2 which outranks it, or because the final 2 (and not the 2-Cho) is adjacent to the verb. The data in (13) through (16) provides the needed information.

(13) Francine a-bet-i   Paul mpo-na mama
             AgrS-beat-TNS   for
     'Francine beat Paul for mama.'

(14) Francine a-bet-el-i   mama Paul
             AgrS-beat-APP-TNS
     'Francine beat Paul for mama.'

(15) Mama a-bet-el-am-i   Paul na Francine
          AgrS-beat-APP-PASS-TNS   by
     'Mama was beaten Paul for by Francine.'

(16) *Mama a-mu-bet-el-am-i   na Francine
           AgrS-AgrO-beat-APP-PASS-TNS by
     ('Mama was beaten him for by Francine.')

In (14), the Benefactive *mama* is advanced to 2, triggering the applicative morpheme *-el* and putting the initial 2 *Paul* en chômage. In (15), the Ben-2 advancee passivized, leaving the 2-Cho *Paul* adjacent to the verb. Example (16) shows that a 2-Cho cannot cliticize, even when the Benefactive nominal is passivized, leaving the 2-Cho as the only bare nominal following the verb (see Zaenen 1984 for similar observations concerning Kikuyu). This should dispel any suspicions that access to object cliticization might be mediated by a relational hierarchy or string adjacency rather than absolute final relations. Returning now to the expletive construction, recall from example (8b) that the initial 2 can indeed be replaced by an object clitic, as would be predicted by the hypothesis that it is a final 2. It can be concluded then that the analysis given in (4) is in fact the correct one, and that impersonal transitive is an apt label for the construction.[4]

---

[4]The stratum immediately preceding the entrance of the dummy 1 must be transitive, as can be seen from the fact that this construction cannot be formed with intransitive predicates, either unergative or unaccusative (although see Kimenyi (1980) for impersonal unaccusatives in Kinyarwanda). This is illustrated in (i) and (ii).

2. Relation between the expletive subject and the initial 1

We now turn to a brief discussion of the relation between the expletive subject of the Lingala impersonal transitive and the initial 1 of the construction, which will play a role in the conclusions that we draw in section 3. In English, when certain purportedly 'Case'-less NPs show up where they shouldn't, the subject position of the clause is filled by the expletive *there*. The examples given in (17) are easy to come by.

(17) a. There were seen two men near the bank.
     b. There appears to be a frog in the pool.

Verbal agreement in (17b) with the nominal *a frog* is presumed to arise as result of some relation between it and the expletive *there*. This relation is characterized in Perlmutter (1983) as the Brother-in-Law relation, and formalized in Aissen (1990) in her work on agreement controllers.[5] In the Government and Binding literature, Chomsky (1986) proposes an EXPLETIVE CHAIN relation formed by the coindexation of the two relevant nominals.

In the Lingala impersonal transitive construction, there is no justification for positing a relation of this sort between the expletive and the initial 2 of the clause. This is because the initial 2 retains its grammatical relation into the final stratum, and fails to trigger subject-verb agreement. If there is a dependency between the expletive and any nominal of the clause, it is between the expletive and the initial 1 rather than the initial 2. This is despite the fact that the person/number features of the expletive are

---

(i) *Ba-kim-i   na Francine
      AgrS-run-TNS by
      ('It was walked by Francine.')

(ii) *Ba-kuf-i   na Francine
      AgrS-die-TNS by
      ('It was died by Francine.')

We have no explanation for why this is so, other than the aforementioned suggestion that the impersonal transitive and regular passive have the same function, namely, that of causing a 2 to outrank the initial 1 in the final stratum. Since intransitive clauses have only one initial term, there is no motivation for the rule to apply.

[5]In Aissen (1990), it is proposed that a nominal may pass its case and agreement features to another nominal if the second OVERRUNS the first (i.e. puts the first en chômage).

consistent and independent of the initial 1, as shown in (18).

(18) Ba-beng-i   Francine na yo/ye/biso/bino/bango
      AgrS-call-TNS   by you/him/us/you/them
      'Francine was called by you/him/us/you/them.'[6]

In (18), the expletive subject of the impersonal transitive construction triggers 3rd person plural agreement on the verb (i.e. *ba-*) regardless of the number or person of the initial 1. Nonetheless, there is evidence of a dependency between the expletive subject of the impersonal transitive and the initial subject of the clause. The subject agreement marker *ba-* is a prefix associated with Class 1/2 (i.e. [+human] or [+sentient]) nouns, and it turns out that the initial 1 of an impersonal transitive clause must also belong to Class 1/2.[7] This can be seen through a comparison of impersonal transitives and regular passives, in (19) and (20), where the relevant class features have been made explicit in the interlinear gloss.

(19) a. Ba-bet-i   Paul na mwasi
         CL1/2-beat-TNS CL1/2 by CL1/2.woman
         'Paul was beaten by a woman.'

     b. *Ba-bet-i   Paul na nzete
         CL1/2-beat-TNS CL1/2 by CL9/10.stick
         ('Paul was beaten by a stick.')

(20) a. Paul a-bet-am-i   na mwasi
         CL1/2 CL1/2-beat-PASS-TNS by CL1/2.woman
         'Paul was beaten by a woman.'

     b. Paul a-bet-am-i   na nzete
         CL1/2 CL1/2-beat-PASS-TNS by CL9/10.stick
         'Paul was beaten by a stick.'

In (19a), the initial subject of the clause is a class 1/2 noun *mwasi* 'woman'.

---

[6]Compared to the other pronominals, an impersonal transitive having a first person singular initial 1 is somewhat marginal. This anomaly may have to do with pragmatic constraints on the construction, and is an issue that we leave for future research.

[7]Strictly speaking *a-* is Class 1 and *ba-* is Class 2, where Class 1 is [+human] singular and Class 2 is [+human] plural. We have collapsed the singular/plural distinction in this discussion, as the determining feature encompasses both classes.

If this nominal is replaced with the class 9/10 noun *nzete* 'stick', as in (19b), the sentence is ungrammatical. Example (20) shows that regular passive is immune to such effects. A [-human] 1-Cho is perfectly acceptable in a passive clause, as shown in (20b). No such similar relation is observed to hold between the expletive subject and the initial 2 of an impersonal transitive. Compare (19a) with (21).

(21) Ba-bet-i   tapi   na mwasi
      CL1/2-beat-TNS   CL9/10.rug   by CL1/2.woman
      'The rug was beaten by a woman.'

In (21), the class 1/2 object of (19a) has been replaced with the class 9/10 nominal *tapi* 'rug', and the grammaticality of the sentence is unaffected.

Further confirmation of this dependency is obtained from an examination of nouns which can fluctuate between two noun classes. Terms for some animals, such as *mbwa* 'dog', can trigger either class 1/2 or class 9/10 agreement, dependent on whether the speaker anthropomorphizes the creature. This is illustrated in (22), where the agreement prefix varies according to this parameter.

(22) a. Mbwa   a-ling-i Francine
          CL1/2.dog   CL1/2-like-TNS
          'The dog[+human] likes Francine.'

      b. Mbwa   e-ling-i Francine
          CL9/10.dog   CL9/10-like-TNS
          'The dog[-human] likes Francine.'

This alternation proves significant to our analysis when regular passive and impersonal transitive analogues of (22) are constructed, as in (23).

(23) a. Francine a-ling-am-i   na mbwa
                   CL1/2-like-PASS-TNS by dog
          'Francine is liked by the dog.'

      b. Ba-ling-i   Francine na mbwa
          CL1/2-like-TNS   by CL1/2.dog
          'Francine is liked by the dog[+human].'

While the regular passive in (23a) can express the meaning of either (22a) or (22b), the impersonal transitive construction in (23b) can only express the meaning of (22a). Taken together, these facts suggest that Lingala has a single subject expletive which has inherent noun class, person and number features. The relevant restriction on the distribution of this expletive is that it can only put en chômage a nominal belonging to the same noun class.

3. Conclusion

The impersonal transitive construction of Lingala, together with the regular passive, presents a formidable challenge to a theory which motivates NP-movement on the basis of Case assignment, and further links Case assignment capacity to particular θ-role properties of a predicate. The approach commonly identified as Burzio's (1986) generalization claims that a verb cannot assign structural Case unless it assigns an external θ-role. Apparent violations of this generalization, exemplified in (17), above, have been approached in one of two ways.

Belletti (1988) claims that definiteness plays a key role, wherein an object NP in a Caseless position (such as the object *two men* in (17a)) can get inherent partitive Case as long as it is indefinite. This ability of indefinite NPs to be rescued from the Case Filter in positions where they fail to get structural Case is what is argued to distinguish (17a) from (24).

(24) *There was seen Francine near the bank.

Comparing (17a) and (24) with the impersonal transitive clauses of Lingala, it is clear that inherent partitive Case cannot be a crucial factor here. The object in (23b), for example, is [+definite], and should be licensed by structural Case under Belletti's account. Since the predicate of this clause fails to assign an external θ-role, it stands as a counterexample to Burzio's generalization in the model proposed by Belletti.

Chomsky (1991) appeals to chain formation at LF to guarantee that the argument NP *two men* in (17a) gets the Case (nominative) associated with the expletive *there*. Therein, it is claimed that expletive *there* is an LF affix, lacking inherent person and number features. In order to satisfy agreement, which is assumed to be checked at LF, the NP adjoins to the expletive producing the LF derivation for (17a) shown in (25).

(25) [$_{NP}$There [$_{NP}$two men]$_i$] were seen t$_i$ near the bank.

In (25), the adjunction structure [$_{NP}$ there [$_{NP}$ two men]] occupies a Case-position, and the trace of [$_{NP}$ two men] occupies a θ-position, in accordance with the Chain Condition of Chomsky (1986). However, clear evidence for a dependency between the expletive subject and initial subject of (23b) precludes any sort of chain formation involving the expletive and the initial object. One would have to assume, in Chomsky's terms, that the nominal *Francine* is a one-membered chain occupying a Case and θ-position. Thus, under Chomsky's (1991) account as well, the impersonal transitive construction violates Burzio's generalization.

An analysis of passive proposed in Baker, Johnson, and Roberts (1989) seeks to derive Burzio's generalization from more general principles, suggesting that the passive morpheme is itself an argument and that it is responsible both for the absorption of accusative Case assigned by the transitive verb as well as for the absorption of the verb's external θ-role. Goodall (1993) cites evidence from Ukrainian (Sobin 1985) and other languages which suggests that passive morphology does not always absorb Case. Equally problematic for the Baker, Johnson, and Roberts account are the constructions examined here. From a comparison of regular passive and impersonal transitive clauses in Lingala, we find that the absorption of external θ-roles passive morpheme is not dependent on the presence of the passive morpheme -*am*. A more reasonable explanation for the distribution of this affix is that it is triggered by a passive subnetwork (i.e. a 2-1 advancement out of a transitive stratum) in a clause.

References

Aissen, Judith. 1990. Towards a Theory of Agreement Controllers. *Studies in Relational Grammar 3*, ed. by Paul Postal and Brian Joseph, 279-320. Chicago: University Press.

Baker, Mark, Kyle Johnson, and Ian Roberts. 1989. Passive Arguments Raised. *Linguistic Inquiry* 20: 219-51.

Belletti, Adriana. 1988. The Case of Unaccusatives. *Linguistic Inquiry* 19: 1-43.

Burzio, Luigi. 1986. *Italian Syntax: A Government-Binding Approach*. Dordrecht: Reidel.

Bwantsa, Kafungu. 1970. *Esquisse de grammaire de Lingala*. Kinshasa: Université Lovanium.

Chomsky, Noam. 1986. *Knowledge of Language*. New York: Praeger Publishers.

Chomsky, Noam. 1991. Some Notes on Economy of Derivation and Representation. *Principles and Parameters in Comparative Grammar*, ed. by Robert Freidin, 415-54. Cambridge, MA: MIT Press.

De Rop, A. 1963. *Introduction a la linguistique Bantoue Congolaise*. Bruxelles: Mimosa.

Goodall, Grant. 1993. On Case and the Passive Morpheme. *Natural Language and Linguistic Theory* 11: 31-44.

Kimenyi, Alexandre. 1980. *A Relational Grammar of Kinyarwanda*. Berkeley: University of California Press.

Perlmutter, David. 1983. Personal vs. Impersonal Constructions. *Natural Language and Linguistic Theory* 1: 141-200.

Perlmutter, David, and Paul Postal. 1983. Some Proposed Laws of Basic Clause Structure. *Studies in Relational Grammar 1*, ed. by David Perlmutter, 81-128. Chicago: Chicago University Press.

Sobin, Nicholas. 1985. Case Assignment in Ukrainian Morphological Passive Constructions. *Linguistic Inquiry* 16: 649-62.

Welmers, W.E. 1973. *African Language Structures*. Berkeley: University of California Press.

Zaenen, Annie 1984. Double Objects in Kikuyu? *Cornell Working Papers in Linguistics 5*: 199-206.

Southern Tiwa Argument Structure

DONALD G. FRANZ
University of Lethbridge

1. Introduction

Rosen (1990) has shown that the salient facts about Southern Tiwa (ST) which were presented in a series of papers by Allen and others (see in particular Allen, Gardiner, and Frantz (1984) and Allen et al. (1990)) can be described elegantly without a rule of Indirect to Direct Object advancement. Inspired by Rosen's paper and by the work of Gerdts (1992, 1993a,b,c), this paper explores an essentially bistratal treatment of the same facts as well as some not previously discussed in the literature.

In applying Gerdts' Mapping Theory, one must refer repeatedly to individual lexical items and their features, and occasionally to their referential status. Therefore I have made provision for such information in the framework by expanding it to include referential and lexical tiers. My Encoding tier (see below) includes some information which Gerdts includes in her Presentation tier along with that from the MAP tier.

2. Dimensions of Argument Structure

I assume at least the following five DIMENSIONS of information are relevant to argument structure:

Referential (ref): Not only referential status (and indexing) of referents, but the semantic content associated with the lexical material on the Lexical dimension (see below). For present purposes, representation of semantic content will be limited to an English gloss.

Semantic Role (role): The semantic role (if any; see discussion of "empty arguments" in section 5) of arguments, not necessarily limited to the thematic roles seen in the work of Gruber (1965) and Jackendoff

---

* I gratefully acknowledge support for this research from the Social Sciences and Humanities Research Council of Canada. And of course my debt to Barbara Allen and Donna Gardiner for supplying data and analysis through the years remains immense.

(1976,1990).[1] In the examples below, the role labels used are Ag(ent), Exp(eriencer), Th(eme), Pat(ient), Recip(ient), Poss(essor-of-absolutive), Dest(ination), and Stim(ulus).

Grammatical Relational (gr): Following Gerdts, this is generally equivalent to the "initial" level of grammatical relations in Relational Grammar. In addition to term relations 1, 2, and 3, there are oblique relations.

Encoding (cod): The morphosyntactic argument status, whether one of the direct syntactic arguments of the verb (Gerdts' MAPs), or some other; when representing information on this dimension, MAP labels will be in bold print to distinguish them from non-MAP arguments such as Ben, Instr, and Gl. MAPs of ST are here labeled **ERG**, **ABS**, **DAT**,[2] and **REFL**. These are the arguments whose features are reflected in the verb prefixes. (Nominals as MAPs are not themselves case-marked in ST.)

Lexical (lex): The lexical realization of the argument. For present purposes I am merely listing the stem of the Head of the argument; or in the case of a "null pronoun" Head, I list pro. Items listed on this dimension carry a subscript indicating person and number features or morphological category; in the case of MAPs these features or categories will be reflected in the verb prefix. Of course the individual lexical items will carry features (not shown

---

[1] I agree with Marantz (1984.32) that even though semantic roles of arguments of different verbs can be grouped usefully into sets that can be characterized by labels such as those I have listed, this does not mean that all individual semantic roles must belong to this relatively small number of labeled sets. There probably are many verbs which take arguments the semantic roles of which are not readily classifiable.

[2] These arguments could as well be labeled A, B, and C following Gerdts' conventions. I have two reasons for not using those labels. First, as indicated in footnote 5, the letters A, B, and C are already well established in Tanoan studies as labels for the three morphological categories relevant primarily to verb agreement. Second, the portmanteau verb prefixes do not enable a principled assignment of arguments to such a scheme in all cases. That is, in some cases it is not clear whether an argument should be considered first, second, or third. However, with the case-like labels, there is at least a correlation in the unmarked cases to values on the gr dimension. (I am aware, however, that this prevents what might have been an interesting claim about ST: that not all clauses have a first MAP. Perhaps it is just this situation which defines the class of languages which have Ergative-Absolutive surface case systems.) See the final paragraph of section 11.

here) relevant to the grammar such as noun class.

Any of the above dimension values may be empty for a given argument (i.e. in any given row). The term dimension is chosen because each of these parameters of information can be viewed as linking to all of the others. So even though I list the dimensions as columns in a particular order, my intent is to view them as associated tiers (represented vertically rather than horizontally), or better, as parameters of a multidimensional matrix.

2.1 Verb specifications

Each verb of the ST lexicon will be specified for any associations or array value restrictions which are not predictable by universal or language-specific rule. This of course will include the number and semantic roles of arguments, their grammatical relations if not predictable by redundancy rule (e.g. the unmarked association of an Agent is with a 1 on the **gr** dimension)[3], and any other facts idiosyncratic to individual verbs. See section 6 below for examples of verbs which are particularly idiosyncratic.

3. Association Rules

Here I present some rules governing associations between values on the different dimensions. Most of these cover facts already discussed in the literature, so are only briefly illustrated.

In the quasi-formal notation used here, the following conventions and abbreviations apply:

^ indicates association of the two items it links; ABSOLUTIVE, ERGATIVE, NUCLEAR TERM, and OBJECT are secondarily defined as usual in relational grammar in terms of 1, 2, 3 on the **gr** dimension;[4] $\underline{i}$ and $\underline{u}$ are referential indices for first and second person, respectively.

3.1 Unmarked associations [see examples (1)-(3) below]:[5]

---

[3] The unmarkedness of this association is unidirectional, and can be distinguished from other associations to be listed below which are bidirectional (and indicated by the symbol ^).

[4] A 1 is an ergative in the presence of a 2, else it is an absolutive. A 2 is an absolutive. 1 and 2 are nuclear terms; 2 and 3 are objects.

[5] The following abbreviations and conventions are used in the morpheme-by-morpheme glosses of the examples: 1 = first person, 2 = second person, 3 = third person, s/sg = singular, p/pl = plural, d = dual, pass = passive, fut = future, pres = present, refl = reflexive. The letters A, B, and C represent the three third person morphological categories relevant to verb agreement, in which the six possible

1, 2, and 3 are associated with MAPs as follows (unless individual verb specifications or other constraints overrule):

    ergative^ERG   absolutive^ABS   3^DAT

(1) **ref**   **role**   **gr**   **cod**   **lex**
     dog$_w$ Ag   1   ABS   khwian$_A$

Kwien-ide Ø-teurawe-we.
dog-sg A-run-pres
"The dog is running."

(2) **ref**   **role**   **gr**   **cod**   **lex**
     dog$_w$ Ag   1   ERG   khwian$_A$
     cats$_x$ Th   2   ABS   musa$_B$

Kwien-ide i-musa-hum-we.
dog-sg A:B-cat-chase-pres
"The dog is chasing the cats."

(3) **ref**   **role**   **gr**   **cod**   **lex**
     i   Ag   1   ERG   pro$_{1s}$
     cats$_x$ Th   2   ABS   musa$_B$
     woman$_y$ Recip   3   DAT   hliawra$_A$

Tam-musa-wia-ban hliawra-de.
1s:A\B-cat-give-past woman-sg
"I gave the cats to the woman."

3.2 Some Constraints on Associations:

The first constraint accounts for cases of necessary passive involving a

---

combinations of two numbers (singular and plural) with the three genders (i, ii, and iii) are reduced to three as follows: A = isg or iisg; C = iipl or iiipl; B = ipl or iiisg. In verb prefix glosses I have retained the notation used in earlier papers, including use of a backslash to separate features of a **DAT** argument from the category of the **ABS**. So if a prefix gloss contains no backslash, then there is no **DAT**. A colon is placed after features of an **ERG**. For example, 1s:A reflects first person singular **ERG** with A as **ABS**; A\B reflects A as **DAT** and B as **ABS**; 2s:A\C reflects second person singular **ERG** with A as **DAT** and C as ABS. See Allen, Gardiner, and Frantz (1984) or Allen et al. (1990) regarding the orthography. In this paper, a macron over a vowel (e.g. â) indicates nasalization.

third person ergative. Rosen described this situation by saying that passive in ST exists to replace just these particular combinations among those which are ruled out by her "hierarchy".[6]

> I. A third person ergative (i.e. one which is not associated with i̱ or u̱ on the **ref** dimension) does not *link* to a MAP if either of the following is true:
>
> **a.** absolutive^{i/u} (i.e. absolutive is first or second person) [see ex. 4]
> **b.** there is a **DAT**; [see ex. 5]
> otherwise, it optionally links to a MAP.

The phrase "does not link to a MAP" in the above constraint means that the associated value on the **cod** dimension must be other than **ERG, ABS, DAT**, or **REFL**. A non-null ergative which does not link to a MAP is an Instr on the **cod** dimension, as seen in (4) and (5). The non-linking of an ergative argument to a MAP is one of the two circumstances (described below) which call for passive morphology. (Compare (5) to (6) in which the ergative can link to a MAP because there is no **DAT** argument due to an alternate association of the 3 with an oblique rather than with **DAT**.)[7]

(4)	**ref**	**role**	**gr**	**cod**	**lex**
	man$_v$	Ag	1	Instr	seuan$_A$
	u	Th	2	**ABS**	pro$_{2s}$

A-hube-ban   seuan-ide-ba.
2s-chase:pass-past man-sg-instr
"The man chased you."

---

[6]Constraint I.a is equivalent to the Person Constraint in Allen et al.(1990); constraint I.b is equivalent to their Non-initial 2 Constraint.

[7]I have kept the 3 value for the Recipient in (6), assuming that, given a Mapping Theory version of Baker's (1988, p.46) Uniformity of Theta Assignment Hypothesis, the Recipient of this verb must always associate with the same **gr** value.

(5) | **ref** | **role** | **gr** | **cod** | **lex** |
|---|---|---|---|---|
| man_w | Ag | 1 | Instr | seuan_A |
| cats_x | Th | 2 | **ABS** | musa_B |
| woman_y | Recip | 3 | **DAT** | hliawra_A |

Hliawra-de   am-musa-wia-che-ban   seuan-ide-ba.
woman-sg   B\A-cat-give-pass-past   man-sg-instr
"The man gave the cats to the woman."

(6) | **ref** | **role** | **gr** | **cod** | **lex** |
|---|---|---|---|---|
| man_w | Ag | 1 | ERG | seuan_A |
| cats_x | Th | 2 | ABS | musa_B |
| woman_y | Recip | 3 | Gl | hliawra_A |

Seuan-ide   i-musa-wia-ban   hliawra-de-'ay.
man-sg   A:B-cat-give-past   woman-sg-to
"The man gave the cats to the woman."

The next constraint is also one which can be read off Rosen's hierarchy. It accounts for the fact that there is never a **DAT** argument if the absolutive argument is first or second person (unless coreferent with the ergative, in which case the **ABS** will link to be on the **lex** dimension as required by **V** below):[8]

II. A **DAT** is not possible in a given clause if absolutive^pro_{i/u}.

The third constraint accounts for data only briefly mentioned in footnote 28 in Allen, Gardiner, and Frantz (1984); the generalization stated here was first suggested to me by David Perlmutter (p.c.) in 1989:

III. *Cancel* a 3 coreferent with an ergative (where "cancel" means here that the 3 is associated with empty cells on the **cod** and **lex** dimensions).

Example 7 illustrates the effect of this cancellation where the 3 is a Possessor.[9] It also comes into play for Recipients as 3. Note that it results

---

[8]Constraint II rules out sentences which are blocked in Allen et al. (1990) by the Participant Chômeur Ban.

[9]This cancellation never comes into play with reflexive verbs, apparently due to a constraint that a 1, 2 and 3 may not all be coreferential. This explains why sentence (ii) is not ambiguous, i.e. cannot mean "He is listening to

in ambiguity.[10]

(7)

ref	role	gr	cod	lex
i	Ag	1	ERG	pro$_i$
	Poss	3		
dog$_x$	Th	2	ABS	khwian$_A$

Ti-khwian-thâ-ban.
1s:A-dog-find-past
"I found my dog." (= "I found the dog.")

The fourth constraint comes into play with what Allen and Frantz (1983) called "impersonal passives" and are briefly discussed below under the section titled **Passive Morphology**. It requires that if **ref** has the value ON (unspecified but presupposed to be capable of exerting will), then the associated value on the **lex** dimension must be pro$_A$, as in (12).

---

himself.", even though this verb can take a 3 as seen in (i):

(i) Ka-be-t'awiani-we.
    1:2s\A-refl-listen-pres
    "I'm listening to you."

(ii) Ø-Be-t'awiani-we.
    A-refl-listen-pres
    "He's listening."

During discussion of this paper, a question from Frank Trechsel brought out the fact that in a context where a third person possessor might or might not be coreferent with the subject, lack of cancellation of the 3 makes it clear that the possessor is not coreferential with the subject. So in the following example (iii) it is clear that the subject 'man' is not also possessor of 'dog', else the possessor 3 would be cancelled, as in (iv), and constraint I.b (requiring passive in (iii)) would not come into play:

(iii) Seuan-ide-ba a-khwian-thâ-che-ban.
     man-sg-instr A\A-dog-find-pass-past
     "The man$_j$ found his$_k$ dog."

(iv) Seuan-ide Ø-khwian-thâ-ban.
     man-sg   A:A-dog-find-past
     "The man$_j$ found a/his$_j$ dog."

[10]Though it does not result in ambiguity if the cancelled 3 is possessor of an obligatorily possessed stem such as a kin term, as in the following:

(i) Ti-p'echu-hwea-ban.   "I took my sister."
    1s:A-sister-take-past

IV. ON^pro_A

The following constraint accounts for reflexive inflection:

V. If 1&2^k then if there is a **DAT** then **ABS^be_A**   [see (10)]
    else 1&2^REFL   [see (8) and (9)]

That is, following Rosen's analysis, the presence of a **DAT** argument in a clause with a 2 and 1 which are coreferential requires be as **ABS**[11], otherwise coreference of the 1 and 2 calls for the regular reflexive prefixes. Note that these rules hold not only for logically transitive verbs with coreferent subject and object like that in (8), but also for exceptionally reflexive verbs, which I here treat as requiring an empty[12] second argument "coreferent" with the first argument; see (9) and (10).

(8) | **ref** | **role** | **gr** | **cod** | **lex** |
|---|---|---|---|---|
| dogs_x | Ag / Pat | 1 / 2 | REFL | khwian_3d |

Khwian-nin in-khoy-ban.
dog-pl   3d:refl-bite-past
"The dogs (2) bit themselves."

(9) | **ref** | **role** | **gr** | **cod** | **lex** |
|---|---|---|---|---|
| dogs_x | Ag | 1 / 2 | REFL | khwian_3d |

Khwian-nin in-t'awiani-ban.
dog-pl   3d:refl-listen-past
"The dogs (2) listened."

---

[11]Discussion of reflexive unaccusatives (Frantz to appear,b) will show that there may be reason to add that either the presence of a **DAT** or Ø^1 requires **ABS^be_A**.

[12]See discussion of empty arguments below.

(10)
ref	role	gr	cod	lex
i	Ag	1	ERG	pro_{1s}
		2	ABS	be_A
dog_x	Stim	3	DAT	$khwian_A$

Ta-be-t'awiani-ban   khwian-ide.
1s:A\A-refl-listen-past dog-sg
"I listened to the dog."

4. Passive Morphology

A verb is passivized if either of the following is true:

1. an ergative does not link to a MAP

2. {UN/ON}^ergative

Condition 1 here is the result of constraints I.a and I.b above. Condition 2. covers cases of unspecified ergatives, as seen in (11), and the construction called an "impersonal passive" in Allen and Frantz (1983), as illustrated in (12) and (13) (where the argument structure of only the embedded clauses are shown). In (12), the fact that khwian 'dog' is incorporated is accounted for by the fact that ON is third person (pro_A) as **ERG**, a situation which calls for the incorporation of a noun as Head of **ABS** (see section 9).[13] In (13), however, ON does not link to a MAP, according to constraint **I.a** above.[14]

---

[13]This treatment of sentences such as (12) does require one more ad hoc statement than the analysis offered in Allen and Frantz, which, given "brother-in-law" agreement, correctly predicted that the verb prefix will reflect dual number of the initial 2 as seen in (i) because the dummy as final subject is brother-in-law of the initial 2. (Third person dual number is otherwise reflected in verb prefixes only if the third person is (final) subject.) To account for the same fact under the current analysis, we must state that a third person dual **ABS** will be reflected as dual in the verb prefix iff there is no **ERG**, unless that **ERG** is ON. It is the "unless..." clause which would be unnecessary in the dummy advancement analysis.

(i) Nat'aratawe-'ay   [in-khwian-thâ-che-hi-'i].
    difficult-past   (A:)du-dog-find-pass-fut-sub
    "It was difficult to find the two dogs."

[14]According to this analysis, the verb of (13) has two reasons for being passive: it has a third person ergative (pro_A) with i as absolutive, and it has ON as ergative.

(11) | **ref** | **role** | **gr** | **cod** | **lex** |
|---|---|---|---|---|
| UN | Ag | 1 | | |
| dog$_x$ | Th | 2 | ABS | khwian$_A$ |

Khwian-ide Ø-thâ-che-ban.
dog-sg A-find-pass-past
"The dog was found."

(12) | **ref** | **role** | **gr** | **cod** | **lex** |
|---|---|---|---|---|
| ON | Ag | 1 | ERG | pro$_A$ |
| dogs$_x$ | Th | 2 | ABS | khwian$_B$ |

Nat'aratawe-'ay [i-khwian-thâ-che-hi-'i].
difficult-past A:B-dog-find-pass-fut-sub
"It was difficult to find the dogs."

(13) | **ref** | **role** | **gr** | **cod** | **lex** |
|---|---|---|---|---|
| ON | Ag | 1 | | pro$_A$ |
| i | Th | 2 | ABS | pro$_i$ |

Nat'aratawe-'ay [te-thâ-che-hi-'i].
difficult-past 1s-find-pass-fut-sub
"It was difficult to find me."

5. Empty Arguments

As will be detailed in Frantz (to appear,a), a large number of ST verbs behave as if they have syntactic arguments which are semantically empty and phonologically null. [See (14), (15), and (16) for examples.] Such arguments must have values on the **cod** dimension to account for the fact that they are represented in the verb prefix. The null pro on the **lex** dimension carries the inflectional category they trigger on the verb. The value associated with these arguments on the **gr** dimension is always an absolutive. I have assigned these arguments no semantic role[15], and except for exceptionally reflexive verbs such as that seen in (9) and (10), no value is assigned on the **ref** dimension.

---

[15]One might assign these a "quasi-argument" theta role as Chomsky (1981.324ff) suggests for meteorological verbs in English.

(14) | **ref** | **role** | **gr** | **cod** | **lex** |
|---|---|---|---|---|
| u | Th | 1 | ERG | pro_{2s} |
| | | 2 | ABS | pro_C |

Ku-weuri-ban.
2s:C-exit-past
"You went out."

(15) | **ref** | **role** | **gr** | **cod** | **lex** |
|---|---|---|---|---|
| | | 1 | ABS | pro_C |
| u | Exp | 3 | DAT | pro_{2s} |

Kow-far-ban.   "You finished."
2s\C-finish-past

(16) | **ref** | **role** | **gr** | **cod** | **lex** |
|---|---|---|---|---|
| u | Ag | 1 | ERG | pro_{2s} |
| | | 2 | ABS | pro_C |
| $lady_k$ | Exp | 3 | DAT | $hliawra_A$ |

Ow-t'am-ban hliawra-de.
2s:A\C-help-past lady-sg
"You helped the lady."

6. Adjuncts[16]

Frantz (to appear,b) discusses the status of ST nominals which are not MAPs, yet have Heads which are incorporated in the idiosyncratic verbs of which they are arguments. Examples are presented in (17) – (20). Note that the incorporated nouns of these idiosyncratic verbs are not the Heads of MAPs, since they do not determine verb prefixes. Like other incorporated nouns of the language, they may be modified by a demonstrative,[17] as seen in (18) - (20). The Head of an Adjunct may be external to the verb if it

---

[16] I am tentatively using the label "Adj(unct)" for want of a better term, even though I realize the term "adjunct" is used in quite a different way by others.

I have done extensive revision of this section of the delivered version of this paper, largely under the influence of an impressive description of "deponent" verbs in a related language, Towa, by Bob Sprott (1992, pp.180-188).

[17] If we follow Baker (to appear) in saying that verb prefixes license null pronouns, we may also say that incorporated nouns license null pronouns in the cases I am calling Adjuncts.

references a human, as seen in the second variant in (18).[18]

(17)
ref	role	gr	cod	lex
i	Exp	1	ABS	pro_{1s}
shirt(s)$_k$	Stim	2	Adj	shut

Te-shut-beaw-a.
1s-shirt-want-pres
"I want shirts/ a shirt."

(18)
ref	role	gr	cod	lex
u	Ag	1	ABS	pro_{2s}
baby$_k$	Th	2	Adj	'u'u

A-'u'u-hliami-ban yede? / Yede 'u'u-de a-hliami-ban?
2s-baby-steal-past that   that baby-sg 2s-steal-past
"Did you steal that baby?

(19)
ref	role	gr	cod	lex
i	Exp	1	ABS	pro_{1s}
man$_k$	Stim	2	Adj	seuan$_A$

Yede te-seuan-kheuap-a.
that 1s-man-like-pres
"I like that man."

The expected associations of semantic roles with **grs** leads to those shown in (17) – (19). The fact that the 2 does not link to a MAP in these sentences is the equivalent in this framework of antipassive in a standard RG treatment. So the idiosyncracy here can be captured by a specification that for these verbs a 2 associates with an Adjunct. However, things are not quite so simple. So long as the Stimulus is third person, the verb illustrated in (19), heuap 'like', may have the argument structure shown there, or it may have an alternate argument structure in which the experiencer is associated with a **DAT** value, the Stimulus is again an Adjunct, and there is an empty Absolutive argument belonging to category C, as shown in (20). Note that I have kept the initial **gr** values the same in (20) as in (19), as one would be

---

[18] It may be that the nominal in such a case bears some "overlay" relation such as Focus. This would be consistent with the sentence-initial position of most unincorporated Heads of Adjuncts.

required to do, given a mapping theory version of Baker's (1988, p.46) Uniformity of Theta Assignment Hypothesis. Given the correctness of the **gr** values shown, (20) looks like the mapping theory equivalent of RG's inversion, with the added wrinkle that there is a marked association of an empty argument with **ABS**.[19]

(20)	**ref**	**role**	**gr**	**cod**	**lex**
i	Exp	1	DAT	pro$_{1s}$
man$_k$	Stim	2	Adj	seuan$_A$
			ABS	pro$_C$

(Na) yede iw-seuan-kheuap-a.
1 that 1s\C-man-like-pres
"I like that man."

However, if the Stimulus is first or second person, it is associated with a **DAT** and the experiencer is marked as an Instrumental (i.e. like a passive chômeur, though the verb is not marked as passive); there is then no Adjunct; see (21).

(21)	**ref**	**role**	**gr**	**cod**	**lex**
man$_k$	Exp	1	Instr	seuan$_A$
i	Stim	2	DAT	pro$_{1s}$
			ABS	pro$_C$

Yede seuan-ide-ba iw-kheuap-a.
that man-sg-instr 1s\C-like-pres
"That man likes me."

Notice that the non-association of a third person ergative with a MAP here is already accounted for by constraint **I.a.**, which rules out such an association if the 2 is first or second person. The linking of the 2 with a **DAT** is the Mapping Theory version of 2-3 retreat in RG, and must be specified for this class of verbs just in case the 1 does not link to a MAP.

There are two problems which remain for this type of verb, however, both apparently connected with the fact that the 2 is associated with a **DAT**. The first problem is that our rule for passive morphology incorrectly requires passive morphology on the verb. This can be rectified by adding to the first condition on the passive morphology rule that the 2 link to an **ABS**. The

---

[19] I have no idea what **gr** value, if any, to assign this empty argument.

rule for passive morphology will then read as follows:

Passive Morphology (revised)

A verb is passivized if either of the following is true:

1. an ergative does not link to a MAP and a 2^**ABS**
2. { UN/ON}^ergative

The second problem is in Association constraint **II** which rules out cooccurence of a **DAT** in a clause in which the absolutive is first or second person. In this case the mitigating factor is obviously that these two, the absolutive and the **DAT,** are one and the same argument. This problem can be rectified either by rewording **II** so that it clearly refers to distinct arguments, or by changing reference in the rule to the **cod** dimension only, i.e. make it rule out a first or second person **ABS** in a clause with a **DAT**. I will not attempt to choose between these solutions here.

7. Causatives

Morphological causative verbs have the causee as a Patient argument and the causer as Agent, as illustrated in (22) – (24).[20] (I have followed Gerdts (1993a) in showing the two sectors of argument structure involved in causative verbs, though I am using a different notation. I show two values for nominals which are arguments of both the outer verb (the Head) and the inner verb; arguments of the inner verb are in parentheses.)

As stated in Allen, Gardiner, and Frantz (1984), a lexical Head of the Theme of the verb stem to which the causative suffix is added is incorporated, as shown in (22) where p'akhu 'bread' is the Theme of kar 'eat'. However, data collected more recently indicate that if this nominal references a human, it is not necessarily incorporated, as seen in (24). Thus the Theme seems to have the same status as what I have called Adjuncts above. (Note that were it not for the demonstrative in (24), the number of the Theme would be indeterminate.)

---

[20]This is as expected if these two are arguments of the Causative, and the latter is Head of the complex stem (see section 9 regarding the status of arguments of the lexical portions of complex stems). See Alsina (1992) regarding the claim that such a derivational causative morpheme has more than an Agent and complement as arguments.

As described in Frantz (to appear,b) ST also has a less productive causative suffix -wi ~ -i which takes Agent, Theme, and Patient arguments. The Theme is realized as a 2^**ABS** and the Patient as either a 3^**DAT** or a 3^Gl.

(22)

ref	role	gr	cod	lex
i	Ag	1	ERG	pro_1
u	Pat(Ag)	2(1)	ABS	pro_{2p}
bread$_k$	(Th)	(2)	Adj	$p'akhu_C$

Ma-p'akhu-kar-'am-ban.
1:2p-bread-eat-cause-past
"I made you eat the bread."

(23)

ref	role	gr	cod	lex
man$_k$	Ag	1	Instr	$seuan_A$
i	Pat(Ag)	2(1)	ABS	pro_{1s}
u	(Th)	(2)	Adj	$'i_2$

Seuan-ide-ba te-hwiat-'abe-ban 'î.
man-sg-instr 1s-hit-cause:pass-past 2
"The man made me hit you."

(24)

ref	role	gr	cod	lex
u	Ag	1	ERG	pro_2
i	Pat(Ag)	2(1)	ABS	pro_{1s}
baby	(Th)	(2)	Adj	$'u'u_A$

Yede bey-'u'u-khoa-'am-ban. / Yede 'u'u-de bey-khoa-'am-ban.
that 2:1s-baby-carry-cause-past   that baby-sg 2:1s-carry-cause-past
"You made me carry that baby."

8. Other Complex Stems

Arguments of only the Head of a complex verb may be MAPs in this language. Therefore arguments of the verb to which the Head is attached in complex stems which are not also arguments of the Head will be Adjuncts, as is the second argument of pû 'see' in (25):[21]

---

[21]Rosen (1990:706) cites the following sentence from Leap (1970), but it is not acceptable to any speakers with whom we have checked it. This unacceptability is to be expected, for as stated above, in Southern Tiwa the last verb root of a stem (i.e. its Head) determines the morphological transitivity of the stem, and the root mi 'go' is intransitive:

(i) *Pî-ide   ti-sheu-mi-we.
    deer-sg 1s:A-hunt-go-pres

(25)	**ref**	**role**	**gr**	**cod**	**lex**
men$_k$	Ag	1(1)	**ABS**	seuan$_B$
lady$_m$	Stim	(2)	Adj	hliawra$_{A/B}$

Yedi(n) seuan-nin i-hliara-**pû-mi**-ban.
those man-pl B-lady-see-go-past
"Those men went to see the lady/ladies."

9. Noun Incorporation

For the examples covered in this paper, all incorporated noun stems are lexical Heads of either 2^**ABS** or Adjuncts. Incorporation of the former is necessary or not possible under conditions summarized nicely by Rosen (1990:679–689). Adjunct incorporation, as mentioned above, is necessary unless human (and in focus? See note 15.). Allowing incorporation of 2^**ABS** will also account for incorporation of inanimate arguments of intransitive verbs if these are unaccusative 2s on the **gr** dimension, as exemplified in (26) (fushi is of class ii and so is an A when singular). In such cases the incorporation is necessary due to a constraint that inanimate Heads of nominals must be incorporated if they meet conditions which allow incorporation.

(26)	**ref**	**role**	**gr**	**cod**	**lex**
balloon$_k$	Th	2	**ABS**	fushi$_A$

Ø-fushi-teuap-pan .
A-balloon-burst-past
"The balloon burst."

Unaccusative animate nouns such as that in (27) will not be incorporated due to the constraint against incorporation of a "sole animate argument" (Rosen 1990:681).

("I'm going to hunt deer.")

The acceptable form to express the intended meaning is as follows (Frantz, to appear,b):

(ii) Te-pî-sheu-mi-we.
1s-deer-hunt-go-pres
"I'm going to hunt deer."

(27) | **ref** | **role** | **gr** | **cod** | **lex** |
|---|---|---|---|---|
| man$_k$ | Ag | 2 | ABS | seuan$_A$ |

Seuan-ide Ø-k'euwe-m.
man-sg A-old-pres
"The man is old."

There seems to be no way of escaping the conclusion that there are incorporated Heads of **ABS** which have the value 1 on the **gr** dimension (i.e. unergatives) just in case there is a 3 which is understood as possessor of that 1:

(28) | **ref** | **role** | **gr** | **cod** | **lex** |
|---|---|---|---|---|
| man$_k$ | Poss | 3 | DAT | seuan$_A$ |
| sister$_m$ | Ag | 1 | ABS | tutu$_A$ |

Seuan-ide a-tutu-feuri-we.
man-sg A\A-sis-dance-pres
"The man's sister is dancing."

Finally, we take up what Allen, Gardiner, and Frantz (1984) called incorporation of passive chômeurs, as seen in (29); compare the same sentence without incorporation in (30).

(29) Seuan-ide Ø-pîru-khoake-ban.
man-sg A-snake-bite:pass-past
"The man was bitten by the snake."

(30) Seuan-ide Ø-khoake-ban pîru-de-ba.
man-sg A-bite:pass-past snake-sg-instr
"The man was bitten by the snake."

In the framework of this paper, this is incorporation of a 1^Instrument; (31) would represent the argument structure of both (29) and (30):

(31) | **ref** | **role** | **gr** | **cod** | **lex** |
|---|---|---|---|---|
| man$_k$ | Th | 2 | ABS | seuan$_A$ |
| snake$_m$ | Ag | 1 | Instr | pîru$_A$ |

In summary, then, an incorporated noun will be the lexical Head of an Adjunct, an **ABS**, or a 1^Instr. Heads of Adjuncts are necessarily incorporated unless they reference a human (and are in focus?). The Head of a

1^Instr is optionally incorporated.[22] The Head of an **ABS** is necessarily incorporated if it is inanimate and/or in the presence of a **DAT**, and may not be incorporated if it is the sole animate MAP of the clause. Otherwise, the optionality vs. necessity of incorporation of the Head of an **ABS** varies, depending upon a combination of factors such as focus or emphasis, the presence of modifiers, person of an accompanying **ERG**, and even number of the **ABS** itself.[23]

---

[22] At least one speaker rejects the presence of a demonstrative as modifier of the incorporated noun. That is, the following sentence, which was included in Allen, Gardiner, and Frantz (1984), is not acceptable to one of our current consultants, though it is to others:

(i) % Yede-ba te-pîru-khoake-ban.
    that-instr 1s-snake-bite:pass-past
    "That snake bit me."

This suggests a difference in the status of such incorporated nouns.

Also, preliminary investigation indicates that an ergative^Instr may not be incorporated if there is a **DAT** in the clause. Sentences with the Head of the ergative incorporated are not acceptable in that case:

(ii) In-seuan-khwian-wia-che-ban.
     1s\A-man-dog-give-pass-past
     *"The man gave me the dog."

This can be given an interpretation only if <u>seuan-khwian</u> is a understood as a compound noun meaning 'male dog'. And it is not the double incorporation which prevents the intended reading; substituting a null pronoun or proper noun as **ABS**, either of which would leave 'man' as the only incorporated noun, still does not allow the intended reading.

[23] Allen, Frantz, and Gardiner (1984, p.303) state an additional factor which seems to require incorporation of a 2^**ABS**: the presence of what is a 3^Gl in the present framework; see (6) for an example. More recent work confirms this to be true, but only if there is no modifier. This might be construed as bearing on the correctness of the **gr** value assigned in sentences such as (6); however, the presence of a Benefactee oblique such as that in (i) also requires incorporation of the 2^**ABS** unless the latter is modified. So (i) is bad without the demonstrative <u>yede</u>, whereas (ii) is good with or without the demonstrative:

(i) *(Yede) musa-de ti-tuwi-ban 'î-'um'ay.
    that cat-sg 1s:A-buy-past 2-Ben
    "I bought (that) cat for you."

(ii) (Yede) ti-musa-tuwi-ban 'î-'um'ay.
     that 1s:A-cat-buy-past 2-Ben

10. Conclusion

It seems clear that associations between the **gr** and **cod** dimensions of ST can be captured without recourse to intermediate representations, so long as the association rules have access to information on the other dimensions. Constraints **I**, **II**, and **IV** cover virtually all the data in the literature. The first of these constraints actually goes beyond Rosen's hierarchy in that it requires Instrument status on the **cod** dimension for ergatives in a specific subset of cases that the hierarchy rules out.

There is an added advantage to the treatment here for two-MAP clauses, one MAP of which is a **DAT**. For example, in a passive clause such as that seen in (32), it is not clear, under a standard relational grammar analysis, which argument is the final Subject. Is 'dog' or 'speaker' the final Subject? According to Allen et al., 'speaker' is final Subject, but for Rosen (p.688) 'dog' is final Subject. Similarly, in a sentence such as (33)[24], in which a Destination is associated with a **DAT,** it is unclear which argument has final Subject status. I have been unable to find any syntactic facts which decide among these alternatives. Yet under the framework utilized in this paper, the choice need not be made, since in the association of the values on the **gr** dimension with those on the **cod** dimension we claim for (32) only that the ergative **gr** does not link to a MAP; the remaining arguments have their unmarked associations, **ABS** and **DAT**. And in (33) I propose that an Obl has a marked association with a MAP (the Mapping Theory equivalent of Goal advancement) and the 2 has its unmarked association. There is no reason to claim Subject status for either nominal; in fact, Subject is not even a possible value on the **cod** dimension.

(32)

ref	**role**	**gr**	**cod**	**lex**
child$_j$	Ag	1	Instr	'u$_A$
i	Recip	3	**DAT**	pro$_{1s}$
dog$_k$	Th	2	**ABS**	khwian$_A$

'U-ide-ba yede in-khwian-wia-che-ban.
child-sg-instr that 1s\A-dog-give-pass-past
"The child gave me that dog."

"I bought (that) cat for you."

It is not clear to me how to capture, in the present framework, what the Gl and Ben have in common, in contrast to other obliques which do not have any bearing on incorporation.

[24]This sentence has another reading in which the **DAT** is associated with Poss on the **role** dimension.

(33)

ref	role	gr	cod	lex
child$_j$	Ag	2	ABS	'u$_A$
i	Dest	Obl	DAT	pro$_{1s}$

In-'u-wan-ban.
1s/A-child-come-past
"The child came to me."

REFERENCES

Allen, Barbara J. and Donald G. Frantz. 1983. An Impersonal Passive in Southern Tiwa. *Work Papers*, Vol. 25. Summer Institute of Linguistics and University of North Dakota.

Allen, Barbara J., Donna B. Gardiner, and Donald G. Frantz. 1984. Noun Incorporation in Southern Tiwa. *IJAL* 50.292–311.

Allen, Barbara J., Donald G. Frantz, Donna B. Gardiner, and David M. Perlmutter. 1990. Verb Agreement, Possessor Ascension, and Multistratal Representation in Southern Tiwa. In Postal and Joseph 1990.321-383.

Alsina, Alex. 1992. On the Argument Structure of Causatives. *Linguistic Inquiry* 23:4.517–555.

Baker, Mark C. 1988. *Incorporation; A Theory of Grammatical Function Changing*. Chicago & London: University of Chicago Press.

Baker, Mark C. To appear. The Polysynthesis Parameter. Ms.

Chomsky, Noam. 1981. *Lectures on Government and Binding*. Dordrecht; Foris.

Frantz, Donald G. 1991. Null Heads and Noun Incorporation in Southern Tiwa. *Papers from the Special Session on American Indian Linguistics*. Berkeley Linguistics Society. Pp. 32–50.

Frantz, Donald G. To appear,a. Empty Arguments in Southern Tiwa. Ms.

Frantz, Donald G. To appear,b. Southern Tiwa Grammar. In preparation.

Gerdts, Donna B. 1992. Morphologically-mediated Relational Profiles. *BLS* 18.322–337.

Gerdts, Donna B. 1993a. Mapping Halkomelem Grammatical Relations. *Linguistics* 31.591–621.

Gerdts, Donna B. 1993b. Mapping Korean Grammatical Relations. *Proceedings of the Fifth (1993) International Symposium on Korean Linguistics, 299–318*. S. Kuno et al. Seoul: Hanshin Publishing Company.

Gerdts, Donna B. 1993c. Mapping Transitive Voice in Halkomelem. *Proceedings of the Nineteenth Annual Meeting of the Berkeley*

Linguistics Society, Special Session on Syntactic Issues in Native American Linguistics, 22–23.

Gruber, Jeffrey. 1976. *Lexical Structures in Lexical Semantics.* Lingustic Series No. 25. North Holland. Amsterdam.

Jackendoff, Ray. 1976. Toward an Explanatory Semantic Representation. *Linguistic Inquiry* 7.89–150.

Jackendoff, Ray. 1990. *Semantic Structures*. MIT Press. Cambridge, MA.

Leap, William Lester. 1970. The language of Isleta, New Mexico. Dallas, TX: Southern Methodist University dissertation.

Marantz, Alec P. 1984. *On the Nature of Grammatical Relations*. Linguistic Inquiry Monograph Ten. MIT Press. Cambridge, MA.

Postal, Paul M. and Brian D. Joseph., editors. 1990. *Studies in Relational Grammar 3*. Chicago & London: University of Chicago Press.

Rosen, Carol G. Rethinking Southern Tiwa: the Geometry of a Triple Agreement Language. *Language* 66.669-713.

Sprott, Robert W. 1992. Jemez Syntax. Ph.D. dissertation. University of Chicago.

Relational Grammar Laws, the Theory of Parameters and the Acquisition of Spanish

NORA GONZALES
University of Iowa

1. Introduction.

Chomsky's (1981) Principles and Parameters proposal for language acquisition theory assumes that the child is genetically equipped with principles of Universal Grammar (UG). These principles interact with environmental data to determine a particular language.[1] The innate principles of grammar contribute to solving the problem of learnability in that they guide the construction of the child's grammar (Borer and Wexler 1987).

Current studies on language acquisition address a fundamental question derived from the principles and parameters proposal, which is, to distinguish which aspects of linguistic structure belong to the a priori knowledge-endowment (UG principles) and which have to be learned with the experience of exposure to a particular language. To my knowledge most such studies shed light on problems within the Goverment-Binding theory (e.g. Hyams 1986). The present study is innovative in that it assumes the parametric theory of language acquisition, but is developed within the Relational Grammar (RG) framework to account for empirical data from 7- to 14-year-old Spanish speakers. The set of UG principles assumed here are the RG universal laws.

Among the UG principles postulated in RG, we find the Relational Succession Law (RSL) (Perlmutter and Postal 1983), which restricts the possibilities of raising in human languages. The nominal that raises must

---

[*] This study has been made possible in part by the Center for International and Comparative Studies, The University of Iowa, and by a travel-research grant from MUCIA Travel-Research Grant. The author thanks Bill Robboy for valuable comments, Philip Klein for proofreading a draft of this paper, Andra Crull for entering the data in the computer and for running some statistical tests, and Claudia Martinez for drafting the graphs. Finally, I thank the director, teachers and students of the Cerro Navia School in Santiago, Chile for their enthusiastic collaboration with this study.

[1] See also Lenneberg (1967).

inherit the grammatical relation of the host nominal in the matrix clause as illustrated in (1).

(1)   a. Vimos [que ella salía]
        b. La vimos salir.
           'We saw her leave.'

In (1a) [que ella salía] is the 2 of the matrix clause; therefore, the final 1 of **salir** raises to 2 of **ver** in accord with the RSL (**la** is the relevant accusative clitic).

Most of the studies that utilize the parametric theory of acquisition assume that the formal principles of UG available to the child are constant and fixed through the course of development (Pinker 1984). On the other hand, Borer and Wexler (1987:124) challenge this assumption and propose a maturational theory, which assumes that UG principles mature with the development of linguistic competence. The principles are not learned and therefore are not dependent on the child's obtaining evidence for their development.

The two hypotheses outlined above make two different predictions. The "continuity" hypothesis (Pinker 1984) predicts that children's intermediate-grammars should have access to the fixed principles and, therefore, should reject sentences that violate the principles. On the other hand, the maturational hypothesis predicts that children's intermediate-grammars should be sensitive to the UG principles of language in a progressive manner with increasing age. The prediction of the maturational hypothesis is shown to hold true in the present study with data from 299 subjects who were asked to perform grammaticality judgements on sentences that obey principles of UG, such as the RSL illustrated in (1b), and (2a) below, versus sentences that violate such principles as shown in section 2.1.

The results of this study provide a tangible method to distinguish between the UG principles (the a priori knowledge endowment) and the aspects of linguistic structure that need to be learned with experience. The results indicate that the children have access to the UG principles in a natural developmental manner, showing very stable grammars progressing with increasing age. In addition, the results show that the children are actively reformulating hypotheses to fix the appropiate parameters to learn different linguistic structures, showing drastic declines and advances in the development of their grammars, especially so to set the Raising-restriction parameter, a newly identified parameter. Finally, the results provide empirical support for the UG principles of RG and for the theory of parameters.

2.0. The Syntax of Spanish Raising Constructions

One of the UG principles assumed in the present study is the RSL, with parametric variations with respect to the type of raising constructions that particular languages choose within the limited repertoire: Subject to subject raising (SSR), Subject to object raising (SOR) and Object to subject raising (OSR); Spanish being among the languages that chooses all three types of raising constructions.

The effects of the three types of raising are illustrated in (2b) to (4b). The predicate that triggers the raising is underlined. The structures assumed here for each raising construction (which are argued for in Gonzalez 1988) are simplified in (2c) to (4c).

SSR:
(2)   a.   Parece que Juan trabaja bien.
                'It seems that Juan works well.'
     b.   Juan parece trabajar bien.
                'Juan seems to work well.'
     c.

parecer	2		
	1		U. Adv.
	chô	1	SSR
trabajar		1	
	sub. clause	Juan	

In (2c) the final 1 of *trabajar*, *Juan*, raises to 1 of *parecer* in accord with the RSL and the subordinate clause is an initial 2 of *parecer*, which undergoes unaccusative advancement to 1 before being put en chômage by the raised 1. An alternative analysis would involve raising to 2 followed by unaccusative advancement of the raisee. The latter analysis has been argued against for Spanish in Gonzalez (1988).

SOR:
(3)   a.   Vimos que los niños jugaban en el patio.
                'We saw that the children were playing in the yard.'
     b.   Vimos a los niños jugar en el patio.
                'We saw the children play in the yard.'

c.

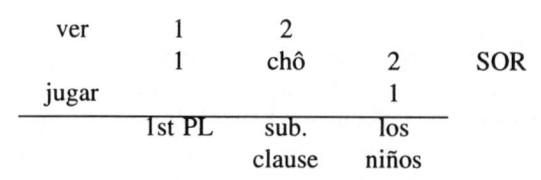

	ver	1	2		
		1	chô	2	SOR
	jugar			1	
		1st PL	sub. clause	los niños	

In (3c) the final 1 of *jugar*, **los** *niños* raises to 2 of *ver* putting the subordinate clausal 2 of *ver* en chômage.

OSR:
(4) a. Es fácil que convenzamos a Juan.
    'It is easy for us to convince Juan.'
  b. Juan <u>es fácil</u> de convencer.
    'Juan is easy to convince.'
  c.

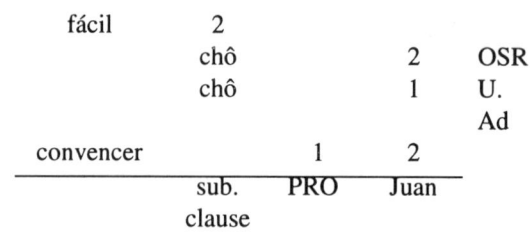

	fácil	2			
		chô		2	OSR
		chô		1	U.
					Ad
	convencer		1	2	
		sub. clause	PRO	Juan	

In (4c) the final 2 of *convencer* raises to 2 of *fácil* putting the subordinate clausal 2 of *fácil* en chômage and then advancing to 1 by unaccusative advancement. Structures (2c), (3c) and (4c) are in accord with the RSL.

2.1. UG Principles within RG

From the set of UG principles proposed within RG, the present study focuses on four principles: the Stratal Uniqueness Law (SUL), the Chômeur Law (CL), the 1 Advancement Exclusiveness Law (1AEXL), and the RSL. It was shown above that the RSL limits the possibilities of raising in human languages, allowing sentences like (2b) to (4b), while prohibiting sentences like (5a) to (8a) below. See their corresponding analyses in (5b) to (8b).

Perlmutter and Postal (1983:49-51) demonstrate with examples from English that violation of the RSL may turn an initially intransitive raising-governing predicate into a transitive one. Consequently, if such a transitive structure is involved in a 2-1 passive advancement the result is ungrammatical. Perlmutter and Postal claim that these facts are universal. Observe that this prediction holds true for Spanish in (5a) and (6a).[2]

(5) a. *Trabajar bien es parecido por Juan
(To work well is seemed by Juan)
b.
parecer	2		
	2	1	*RSL
	1	chô	
trabajar		1	
sub. clause	Juan		

(6) a. *(De) convencer es fácil por Juan
(To convince is easy by Juan.)
b.
fácil	2			
	2		1	*RSL
	1		chô	
convencer		1	2	
sub. clause	PRO	Juan		

In (5b), *Juan* raises to 1 of *parecer* transitivizing that stratum. The subordinate clause advances to 1 by passive putting *Juan* en chômage. A similar structure is involved in (6b). Both structures (5b) and (6b) violate the RSL.

Passivization in a structure with a transitive raising predicate like **ver** 'see' is also ruled out because such a structure involves violation of both the SUL and the Chômeur Law. The SUL claims that no stratum can contain more than one term-arc (1, 2, or 3). The Chômeur Law rules out a structure that would violate the SUL if a nominal were not put en chômage (Perlmutter and Postal 1983:92-96). Consider (7a) with its analysis (7b).

(7) a. *Jugar en el patio fue visto a los niños
(To play in the yard was seen the children)

---

[2] A structure similar to (5b), but without the third stratum of *parecer* would produce an opaque result: *Juan parece trabajar bien*. We need to passivize in the third stratum in order to determine whether the RSL has been violated or not.

b.

		ver	1	2		
			1	2	2	*SUL
						+CL
			chô	1	2	
	jugar				1	
		PRO	sub. clause	los niños		

The structure in (7b) violates both the SUL and the CL. Note that the raised nominal, *los niños*, raises to 2 in accord with the RSL but it fails to put the host en chômage. The embedded clause then advances to 1 by passive yielding the ungrammatical (7a).[3] One further ungrammatical sentence type explored in this study involves violation of the RSL and the 1AEX Law. The 1AEX Law claims that there cannot be more than one advancement to 1 per clause (Perlmutter and Postal 1984:84-87). Consider the sentence in (8a) (which violates both the RSL and the 1AEXL) and its analysis in (8b).[4]

(8) a. *Juan fue parecido trabajar bien
         (Juan was seemed to work well.)
     b.

	parecer	2		
		1		
		1	2	*RSL
		Chô	1	*1AEXL
	trabajar		1	
		sub. clause	Juan	

---

[3] An alternative analysis for (7a) would involve no violation of the two laws, such that the raised 2 would put the host en chômage. The ungrammaticality of (7a) would be accounted for by the illegal advancement to 1 from a 2-chô, which is against the Chômeur Advancement Ban (Perlmutter and Postal 1983:117).

[4] An alternative analysis would assume that *parecer* is an initially unergative predicate, thus the initial grammatical relation of the host would be a 1. The resulting structure would still be violating the RSL. Arguments have been given against the initial unergativity of *parecer* 'seem' (Gonzalez 1988). The present study assumes the structure (8b) for the ungrammatical sentence (8a).

In (8b) the subordinate clausal 2 of *parecer* advances to 1 by unaccusative advancement and a second advancement to 1 is undergone by the raisee nominal, *Juan*, violating the 1AEX Law. Also, the RSL is violated in the third stratum of *parecer*.

To claim that raising-predicates are not lexicalized for passive does not suffice. See sentence [B-13] in the Appendix, which involves the SSR predicate *empezar* in a Clause Reduction (CR) and passive structure, as well as the simple passive clause with the SOR predicate *ver* in (9) below.

(9) El accidente fue visto por Juan.
     'The accident was seen by John.'

2.2. Parametric variation in interaction of Raising Constructions

Gonzalez (1988) argues for a raising constraint (henceforth Spanish raising constraint (SRC)), which prohibits iterative interactions of raising to/from object as illustrated in (10b) and (11b).

OSR+SOR:
(10) a. Vimos que los árboles eran fáciles de cortar.
        We saw that the trees were easy to cut.
     b. *Vimos los árboles ser fáciles de cortar.
        (We saw the trees be easy to cut.)

SOR+Passive+SOR:
(11) a. Vimos que los aviones eran escuchados aterrizar.
        'We saw that the planes were heard to land.'
     b. *Vimos los aviones ser escuchados aterrizar
        'We saw the planes be heard to land.'

García-Mayo (1989, 1990) argues that the same restriction holds for French and Portuguese. However, English appears to have a softer restriction since it allows sentences with interaction of SOR+ Passive+SOR (Postal 1974:198). Given that within RG there is no principle that prohibits sentences like (10b) and (11b), a theoretical question suggests itself: Does this raising restriction obey a universal law or is it construction-specific? A study with 292 Chilean children (Gonzalez 1992) addressed this question showing that the children had great difficulty acquiring the raising restriction. Those results suggested that the raising restriction is not a UG principle. The present study assumes that the SRC is one value of a newly identified universal parameter, the "Raising-restriction" parameter. This parameter has to be set by all children regardless of the language they learn.

I assume further, that the default setting value is "0", no restriction at all; so that the children accept all sentences as grammatical. In the course of development the children will entertain three hypotheses, until they fix the adequate value for the Raising-restriction parameter: 1) The "0" value hypothesis, (shown to be prefered by the younger children in this study), 2) the softer-restriction value instantiated by English, and 3) the stronger-restriction value (SRC), which is found in the adult grammar of Spanish, French and Portuguese. The present study shows that the SRC value is set very late in the acquisition of Spanish.

2.3. Working hypothesis

The working hypothesis for the present study is two-fold. If the ungrammaticality of sentences like (5a) to (8a) is due to violations of UG principles, then, (under the maturational hypothesis), (a) The children's intermediate grammars should show a progressive indication of the availability of the UG principles with increasing age. That is, they should progressively reject the ungrammatical sentences, even without negative evidence. (b) The children will have more difficulty rejecting the ungrammatical sentences that violate the SRC than rejecting the sentences that violate the UG principles. This is because the children need to fix the Raising-restriction parameter to the SRC value, while the UG principles will be available through the language development requiring no effort on the part of the children.

3.0. Subjects and Data Collection

One questionnaire was given to 299 students in a public school in Cerro Navia, Santiago, Chile. The students were attending the last month of classes in first through eighth grades with ages ranging between 6;9 to 15;1. The socioeconomic level of the subjects' families is lower working class. All the sentences were read aloud followed by a pause for the students to render grammaticality judgements. The distribution of the students by age group is shown in Table 1.

3.1. Methodology

In studies of adult grammars, data based on grammaticality judgements are often used. This seems to be an effective method to elucidate linguistic knowledge while avoiding problems of attention and memory limitation. This method also allows for access to knowledge of grammatical sentences which occur rarely in speech, as well as knowledge of UG principles which prohibit ungrammatical sentences of the type crucial for the present study. De Villiers and de Villiers (1978) propose that children acquire metalinguistic abilities around five years of age. The data used in this paper was constructed with grammaticality judgements by children older than five.

AGE	f	%	Cum %
6;09-6;11	18	6.0	6.0
7;00-7;11	39	13.1	19.1
8;00-8;11	39	13.1	32.2
9;00-9;11	27	9.1	41.3
10;00-10;11	46	15.4	56.7
11;00-11;11	41	13.7	70.5
12;00-12;11	37	12.4	82.9
13;00-13;11	29	9.7	92.6
14;00-14;11	20	6.7	99.3
15;00-15;01	2	0.7	100.0
Missing	1	0.3	
TOTAL	299	100.0	

TABLE 1
Frequencies and Percents of Population by Age[5]

The experimental sentences selected for statistical analyses represent different syntactic structures. (See the Appendix). In group (a) the selection includes simple Passive (B-11, B-26) and the three types of Raising structures: SSR (B-5, B-19, B-8, B-14), SOR (B-1, B-15) and OSR (B-3, B-17). Also included in group (a) are interactions of two constructions, represented by sentences which involve two consecutive SSR (iv-18, iv-24), two consecutive Equi (iv-29, iv-30), interaction of SSR and Equi (iv-16, iv-17), and Clause Reduction (CR)/Passive (B-13, B-27).[6] Group (b) (in the Appendix) illustrates sentences that violate the RSL in OSR (B-4, B-18) and in SSR structures (B-6, B-20, B-7, B-21, B-9, B-23) as well as sentences that violate the SUL and the CL in a SOR structure (B-2, B-16). Finally,

---

[5] For purpose of statistical analyses the group of 6-year-olds was merged with the group of 7-year-olds and the two 15-year-olds were included in the 14-year-old group.

[6] See Aissen and Perlmutter (1983) for a discussion on this type of construction.

examples that violate the Spanish Raising Constraint are also included in group (b) (iv-3, iv-5, iv-11, iv-12). The construction-governing predicate is underlined in each sentence.

4.0. Statistical Analyses and Results

A fundamental issue in this study is to determine whether the subjects were able to discriminate between 'correct' and 'incorrect' sentences. To answer this question, the z-test (standard version) was used with all responses by all subjects. The results of the z-test indicate that the responses were not randomly made. The majority of the children's responses were statistically significant (equal to or greater than 1.96) in their discrimination between correct and incorrect responses. The percentages of correctly marked grammatical versus ungrammatical sentences by the entire population are summarized in table 2 below.[7]

The results of Table 2 (a) suggest that Passive (group 1), SOR (group 2) and SSR (group 3) are the easiest constructions obtaining the highest percentages of correct responses (97%, 96% and 94% respectively); whereas the interaction of two constructions seems to be more difficult. Table 2 (b) shows that the lowest percentages of correct responses for the ungrammatical sentences were obtained by the sentences in group 13, which involve violation of the Spanish Raising Constraint (57%-67%). On the other hand, the sentences that violate the UG principles (groups 10 to 12) obtained higher percentages (67%-80%).

---

[7] The complete table is in Gonzalez (in preparation).

(a) Grammatical Sentences	1 %	2 %	3 %	4 %	5 %	6 %	7 %	8 %	9 %
	91	96	94	90	90	64	89	72	74
	97	89	93	88	86	81	85	88	75

(b) Ungrammatical Sentences	10 %	11 %	12 %	13 %
	78	77 74 70	80	62 67
	74	73 67 67	67	61 57

1=passive, 2=SOR, 3=SSR-*parecer*, 4=SSR-*empezar*, 5=SSR/SSR, 6=Equi/Equi, 7=OSR, 8=SSR/Equi, 9=CR/passive, 10=SUL+CL, 11=RSL, 12=RSL+1AEXL, 13=SRC.

TABLE 2
Percentages Summary of Correct Responses

4.1. Order of Difficulty for Grammatical and Ungrammatical Sentences

All selected sentences were grouped by construction type. A degree of difficulty was obtained by assigning the value of '1' to the right responses and '0' to the wrong responses and then obtaining the means and standard deviations (SD) for each group of sentences.[8] This information is graphically represented in Figure 1 for the grammatical sentences and Figure 2 for the ungrammatical sentences.

Figure 1 displays the mean scores by age groups for eight different trunks or clusters of sentences: Trunk 1 (Passive), Trunk 2 (SSR), Trunk 3 (SOR), Trunk 4 (OSR), Trunk 5 (SSR/SSR), Trunk 6 (SSR/Equi), Trunk 7 (CR/Passive) and Trunk 8 (Equi/Equi). We can observe three distinct groups: (i) The older children, 11- to 14-year-olds, scored above .80 for all constructions except the CR/Passive (Trunk 7). They also show some

---

[8] The means and SD of each group of sentences for all subjects are exhibited in Gonzalez (in preparation).

difficulty with the two consecutive Equi construction (Trunk 8). (ii) The 9- and 10-year-olds scored between the older and the younger children. Their scores are .80 or above except for CR/Passive (Trunk 7) and OSR (Trunk 4). For the Equi/Equi construction (Trunk 8), the 10-year-olds scored very close to the 11- and 12-year-olds. In contrast, the 9-year-olds scored close to the 7- and 8-year-olds for Equi/Equi (Trunk 8) and SSR/Equi (Trunk 6). (iii) The 7- and 8-year-olds scored .80 or below. They had greater difficulty with OSR (Trunk 4), SSR/Equi (Trunk 6) and CR/Passive (Trunk 7).

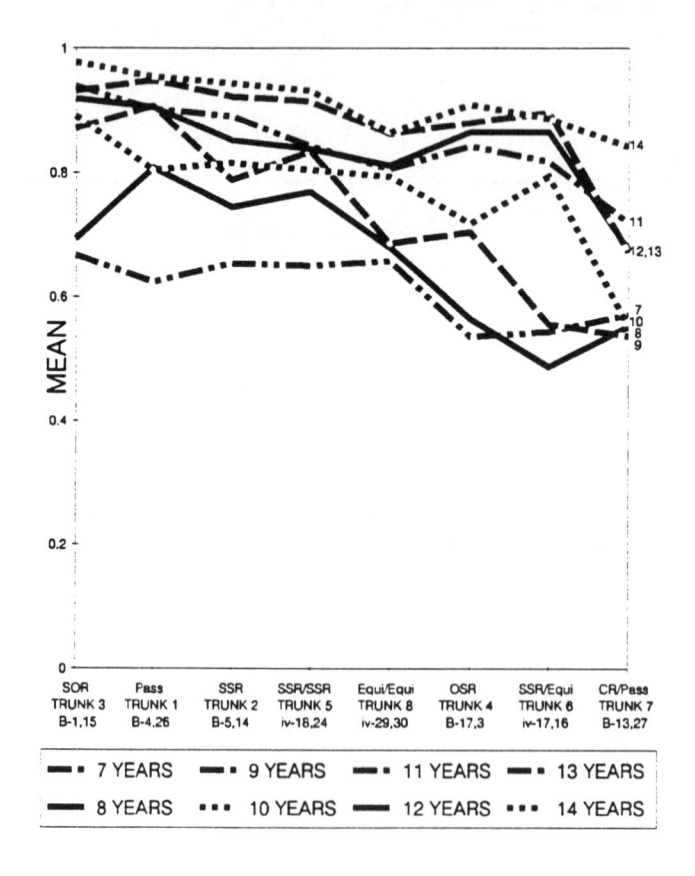

FIGURE 1
Mean Trunk Scores by Age for the Grammatical Sentences

The results in Figure 1 reflect the fact that the children's intermediate grammars are being reevaluated, showing drastic declines and advances, especially by the younger children ages 7 to 10. The declines and advances are evidence that the children are actively reformulating hypotheses in order to achieve complete linguistic development.[9] The older children, 11- to 14-year-olds, seem to have more stable grammars and their scores are higher, suggesting that they are closer to the adult's grammar.

4.1.1. Order of Difficulty for Grammatical Sentences

Results of the means of the entire population without age distinctions suggest the following acquisition order:

(12) I. SOR (.84) and simple passive (.83) followed by SSR (.81) and SSR/SSR (.80).
  II. Equi/Equi (.75), OSR (.73) and SSR/Equi (.71).
  III. CR/Passive (.63) (acquired by age 14).

4.1.2. Development of UG Principles

Figure 2 illustrates the development of the UG principles (Trunk 1-5) and the acquisition of the SRC (Trunk 6-7), based on the mean-trunk scores by age group for the ungrammatical sentences.

Figure 2 displays three distinct groups: (i) The oldest children, 13- and 14-year-olds, successfully scored above .80, except for the SRC in Trunk 6 which was lower (.72 and .75). (ii) The 10 to 12-year-olds were relatively successful in rejecting the sentences that violate the UG principles in Trunk 1-5 and they had some troubles with the sentences that violate the SRC in Trunk 6-7. (iii) The 8- and 9-year-olds scored between .41 and .65 for the sentence-trunks that violate the UG principles and they scored .33 to .48 for the sentence trunks that violate the SRC (Trunk 6-7). Finally, the youngest group, 7-year-olds scored only between .18 and .27. The results of Figure 2 seem to confirm our initial hypotheses: (a) Overall, the children tend to reject the sentences that violate the UG principles in a progressive developmental fashion with increasing age. (b) There is a clear distinction between the intermediate grammars for the UG principles (Trunk 1-5) and the SRC (Trunk 6-7). The intermediate grammars for the SRC show sudden declines and advances similar to what was observed in Figure 1 for the grammatical sentences. This is evidence that the children are reformulating their hypotheses to fix the parameters as they learn the SRC. On the other

---

[9] This kind of fluctuation is observed in child language development in English and is taken to be a natural transitional phase as the child reformulates its hypotheses, cf. Brown (1973).

hand, the intermediate grammars for Trunk 1-5 (UG principles) seem to be more stable; with the exception of Trunk 2 for the 8-year-olds, who show a sudden advance, and Trunk 4 for the 10-year-olds, who show a decline. The rest of the lines look very smooth, suggesting that the children do not need to hypothesize to reject the ungrammatical sentences. They just seem to have access to the appropiate principles in a progressive developmental fashion.

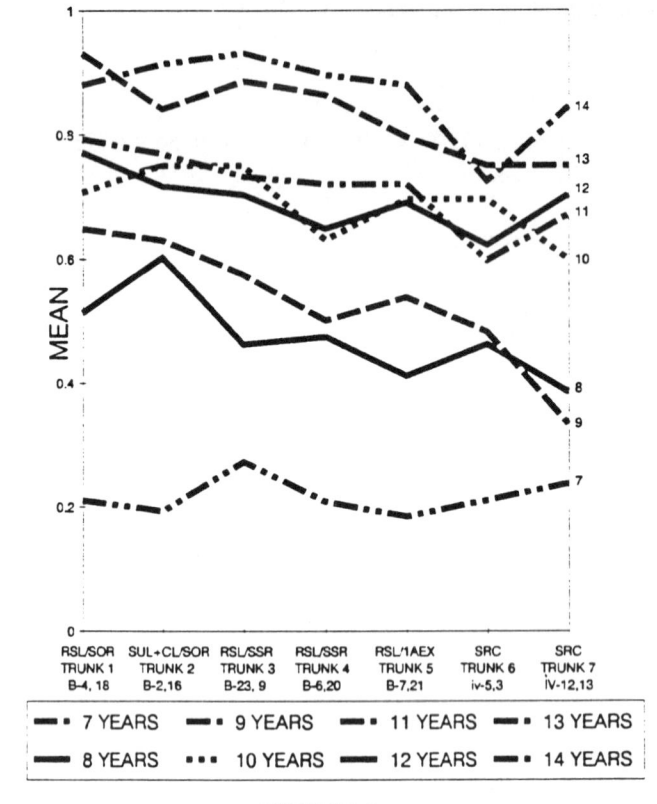

FIGURE 2
Mean Trunk Scores by Age for the Ungrammatical Sentences

It could be claimed that the low scores for the 7-year-olds is due to non-linguistic factors; however, my claim is that in the grammars of the youngest, the principles have not yet matured and they are not easily available. This claim is based on the results of the z-test (section 4.0). The children accepted the ungrammatical sentences as "correct" not by chance. Furthermore, the 7-year-olds' performance for the grammatical sentences in the most difficult construction (CR/Passive) was better than the 8-, 9- and 10-year-olds (see Figure 1). This shows that even the youngest children were doing their best with their metalinguistic task. What is apparently surprising is the results for the 12- and 14-year-olds; they should have scored higher in this developmental tendency. However, statistical tests determined that their scores are not significantly different from the 11- and 13-year-olds respectively.[10]

4.1.3. Stages in the Development of UG Principles and the Acquisition of the SRC

The stages of development for the UG principles and the acquisition of the SRC are graphically illustrated in Figure 3 below. This order was obtained by calculating the mean scores of the entire population without age distinctions for the ungrammatical sentences. The results in Figure 3 suggests a developmental order with the constructions with *fácil* and *ver* at the top (.63), followed by *empezar* (.62); the two clusters with *parecer* in the middle (.57), and at the bottom, the constructions that violate the SRC (.53).[11] These results provide additional evidence in favour of hypothesis (b). There is a difference between the rejection of the sentences that violate the UG principles and those that violate a language particular constraint.[12]

---

[10] The 13-year-olds scored .9000 out of a possible score of 1.0, while the 14-year-olds scored .8636 for the five clusters of sentences that violate the UG principles. A paired t-test was run and the difference mean between the two groups was .364. The 2-tail probability was .509 suggesting that there is no difference between the 13- and 14-year olds. The same is true for the 11- and 12-year olds, their means are .7463 and .8636 respectively and the 2-tail probability is .483.

[11] The different scores between the constructions with *parecer* and *empezar* may be due to the different syntactic behavior of these predicates: unlike *parecer*, *empezar* is a CR governor. See the discussion of CR in 5.0.

[12] The five groups of sentences that violate the UG principles (Trunk 1-5) scored .6084 out of a possible score of 1.0, while the two groups of sentences that violate the SRC (Trunk 6-7) scored .5368. A paired t-test was run and the difference mean between the two groups was .0716. The p-value showed that the difference between these two groups is significant at p= .000.

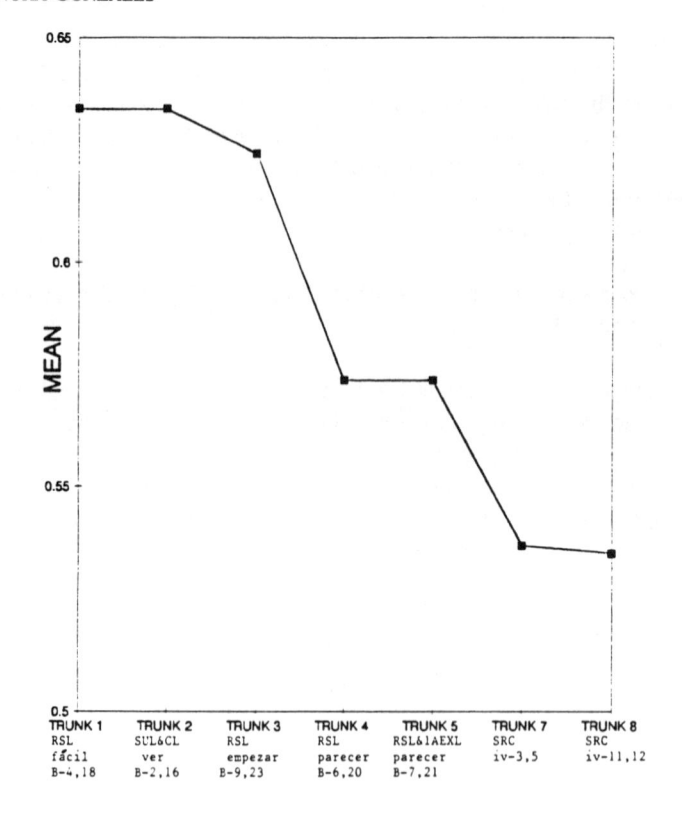

FIGURE 3
Developmental Stages of UG Principles and Acquisition of the SRC.

5.0. Discussion and Theoretical Implications

The most revealing aspect of this study was the confirmation of our working hypotheses: (a) The UG principles postulated in RG are latent in the children's grammars. The children do not have to learn the restrictions subsumed in the UG principles; but rather, they have access to the UG principles in a natural developmental manner in accord with the maturational hypothesis (Borer and Wexler 1987). Certain principles mature, guided by the biological program; when they are ready, they are activated and become available to the child. If the principles were constant during the course of linguistic development, then the children acquiring a language should know the restrictions subsumed in the UG principles and therefore they should be able to reject sentences that violate UG principles, even without negative evidence. (b) There is a distinction between the children's ability to reject sentences that violate the SRC and sentences violating the UG principles. The children are actively reevaluating their grammars to set the Raising-restriction parameter to the the SRC value; while their grammars are more stable for the innate UG principles.

It seems to be clear from the results of the grammatical sentences that the child is constantly reformulating hypotheses through the different stages of acquisition: Some drastic declines and advances in the different constructions were shown. On the other hand, for the ungrammatical sentences that violate the UG principles, there is a much smoother progressive development in the activation of the Laws. The child is not testing hypotheses, but is progressively using the laws inasmuch as he is acquiring the structures necessary to observe the application of the laws.

The difficulty of the CR/Passive construction (Trunk 7 in Figure 1) tends to confirm the parametric theory of acquisition argued for in this study. The CR/Passive sentences involve a structure with Union and passive of the subordinate dependent in the matrix clause. The problem faced by the child is with the linguistic input. There are individual differences among speakers as to which SSR predicates are also CR (Union) governors. In other words, the linguistic input is varied -sometimes with CR, sometimes without CR. It seems that the younger children's (7-10) strategy is to assume a hypothesis without CR, and then later (12-14) they entertain both hypotheses, with and without CR, until they fix the CR parameter.

Future work needs to compare results of the laws with minor violations of language-particular rules.[13] The present theory predicts that the intermediate grammars for the latter constructions should show drastic declines and advances in their acquisition.

References

Aissen, Judith & David Perlmutter. 1983. Clause Reduction in Spanish. *Studies in Relational Grammar 1,* ed. by David M. Perlmutter, 360-403. Chicago: U. Chicago Press.
Borer, Hagit & Kenneth Wexler. 1987. The Maturation of Syntax. *Parameter Setting,* ed. by Thomas Roeper & Edwin Williams, 123-172. Dordrecht: D. Reidel.

---

[13] Also needed is a study that focuses on explaining the order of acquisition of the constructions in (12). My conjecture is that the hierarchy of GRs (1>2>3) may provide such an explanation.

Brown, Roger. 1973. *A First Language: The Early Stages*. Cambridge, MA: Harvard University Press.
Chomsky, Noam. 1981. *Lectures on Goverment and Binding*. Dordrecht: Foris.
De Villiers, Jill & Peter de Villiers. 1978. *Language Acquisition*. Cambridge, Mass.: Harvard U. Press.
García-Mayo, Pilar. 1989. Constraints on Raising in English. ms. U. of Iowa.
García-Mayo, Pilar. 1990. Constraints in Raising. ms. U. of Iowa.
Gonzalez, Nora. 1988. *Object and Raising in Spanish*, ed. by Jorge Hankamer. New York: Garland Publishing Co.
Gonzalez, Nora. 1992. Desarrollo de la sintaxis del español en niños de 7 a 14 años: Elevaciones y la teoría paramétrica. Delivered at the Spanish in America Conference, December 1992, Santiago, Chile.
Gonzalez, Nora. *Raisings, Parameters and Spanish Acquisition*. (in preparation). U. of Iowa.
Hyams, Nina. 1986. *Language Acquisition and the Theory of Parameters*. Dordrecht: D. Reidel.
Lenneberg, Eric. 1967. *The Biological Foundations of Language*. New York: John Wiley & Sons.
Perlmutter, David & Paul Postal. 1983. The Relational Succession Law. *Studies in Relational Grammar 1*, ed. by David M. Perlmutter, 30-80. Chicago: U.of Chicago Press.
Perlmutter, David & Paul Postal. 1983. Some Proposed Laws of Basic Clause Structure. *Studies in Relational Grammar 1*. ed. by David M. Perlmutter, 81-128. Chicago: U.of Chicago Press.
Perlmutter, David & Paul Postal. 1984. The 1 Advancement Exclusiveness Law. *Studies in Relational Grammar 2*, ed. by David M. Perlmutter & Carol G. Rosen, 81-125. Chicago: U.of Chicago Press.
Pinker, Steven. 1984. *Language Learnability and Language Learning*. Cambridge: Harvard U. Press.
Postal, Paul. 1974. *On Raising*. Cambridge: MIT Press.

Appendix

Sentences Selected for Analysis
  (a) Grammatical Sentences
    Passive:
      [B-11]   El problema fue <u>comprendido</u> por los estudiantes.
                'The problem was understood by the students.'
      [B-26]   Jesucristo fue <u>amado</u> por sus discípulos.
                'Jesus was loved by his disciples.'

SSR:
[B-5]   Juan <u>parece</u> trabajar bien.
         'Juan seems to work well.'
[B-19]   La orquesta <u>parece</u> tocar bien.
         'The orchestra seems to play well.'
[B-8]   Los pájaros <u>empiezan</u> a hacer sus vidas.
         'The birds start to make their lives.'
[B-14]   Los vecinos <u>empezaron</u> a pintar las paredes.
         'The neighbors started to paint the walls.'

SOR:
[B-1]   <u>Vimos</u> a los niños jugar en el patio.
         'We saw the children play in the yard.'
[B-15]   <u>Vimos</u> a los perros jugar en el jardín.
         'We saw the dogs play in the garden.'

OSR:
[B-3]   Juan es <u>fácil</u> de convencer.
         'Juan is easy to convince.'
[B-17]   Una tortuga no es muy <u>fácil</u> de cuidar.
         'A turtle is not easy to take care of.'

SSR/SSR:
[iv-18] <u>Debemos</u> <u>terminar</u> de hacer la tarea.
         'We must finish doing the homework.'
[iv-24] <u>Podemos</u> <u>empezar</u> a contar.
         'We can start to count.'

Equi/Equi:
[iv-29] <u>Quiero</u> <u>tratar</u> de sacar buenas notas.
         'I want to try to get good grades.'
[iv-30] <u>Quiero</u> <u>insistir</u> en visitar esa ciudad.
         'I want to insist in visiting that city.'

SSR/Equi:
[iv-16] No me <u>permitieron</u> <u>volver</u> a comprar.
         'They did not allow me to rebuy again.'
[iv-17] <u>Decidieron</u> <u>empezar</u> a construir la casa.
         'They decided to start constructing the house.'

CR/Passive:
[B-13]   Las paredes fueron <u>empezadas</u> a pintar en la tarde.
         'The walls were started to be painted in the afternoon
[B-27]   Los edificios fueron <u>empezados</u> a limpiar en la tarde.
         'The buildings were started to be cleaned in the
                   afternoon.'

(b) Ungrammatical Sentences
   RSL (OSR):
   [B-4]   (De) <u>convencer</u> es fácil por Juan.
           (To convince is easy by Juan.)
   [B-18] (De) cuidar no es muy <u>fácil</u> por una tortuga.
           (To take care of is not easy by a turtle.)
   RSL (SSR):
   [B-6]   Trabajar bien es <u>parecido</u> por Juan.
           (To work well is seemed by Juan.)
   [B-20] Tocar bien es <u>parecido</u> por la orquesta.
           (To play well is seemed by the orchestra.)
   [B-7]   Juan fue <u>parecido</u> trabajar bien.
           (Juan was seemed to work well.)
   [B-21] La orquesta fue <u>parecida</u> tocar bien.
           (The orchestra was seemed to play well.)
   [B-9]   (A) hacer sus vidas es <u>empezado</u> por los pájaros.
           (To make their lives is started by the birds.)
   [B-23] (A) volar es <u>empezado</u> por las mariposas.
           (To fly is started by the butterflies.)
   SUL/CL (SOR):
   [B-2]   Jugar en el patio fue <u>visto</u> a los niños.
           (To play in the yard was seen the children.)
   [B-16] Jugar en el jardín fue <u>visto</u> a los perros.
           (To play in the garden was seen the dogs.)
   SRC (OSR+SOR):
   [iv-3] <u>Oímos</u> la música ser <u>fácil</u> de interpretar.
           (We heard the music be easy to interpret.)
   [iv-5] <u>Vimos</u> los árboles ser <u>fáciles</u> de cortar.
           (We saw the trees be easy to cut down.)
   SRC (SOR+PASSIVE+SOR):
   [iv-11] <u>Vimos</u> los aviones ser <u>escuchados</u> aterrizar.
           (We saw the planes be heard to land.)
   [iv-12] <u>Notamos</u> el concierto ser <u>escuchado</u> interpretar.
           (We noticed the concert be heard to interpret.)

The Structure and Surface Form of Benefactives and Other Prepositional Grammatical Relations

Mika Hoffman
ETS & Swarthmore College

      The dative and benefactive constructions are the only constructions in English which allow double objects (neither object of the verb is marked by a preposition). For this reason, they are often put together in a class of "double object verbs". I will show, however, that in fact the dative and benefactive have two different structures; the dative looks much like constructions in which a verb takes a direct object and a prepositional object, while the benefactive has its own distinctive structure. In addition, I want to show that in languages that allow a broader range of double object constructions than English does, the benefactive is consistently different from other semantic relations represented by these constructions.

      The examples in (1)-(3) show three types of constructions in English in which a verb appears to take two objects.[1] All of them alternate; that is, the objects can occur in either order, with some modification of the preposition used. (1) and (2) are dative and benefactive constructions, while the examples in (3) are of locative alternation verbs, which do not have variants without a preposition.

(1) a   I gave a book to Chris.
    b.   I gave Chris a book.
    c.   A book was given *(to) Chris.
    d.   Chris was given a book (*to).

(2) a   I baked a cake for Robin.
    b.   I baked Robin a cake.
    c.   A cake was baked *(for) Robin.
    d.   Robin was baked a cake (*for).

(3) a   I stuffed the feathers into the pillow.
    b.   I stuffed the pillow with feathers.
    c.   The feathers were stuffed into the pillow (*with).
    d.   The pillow was stuffed with feathers (*into).

      Consider first (1) and (3). I have given examples of locative alternation verbs because I claim that their structure is essentially identical to that of datives. Rather than accounting for 'dative shift' by deriving the

---

[*] This paper grew out of research I did for my dissertation at MIT; I would like to thank Ken Hale, Jay Keyser, and Alec Marantz for helping me with that research. I would also like to thank Peter Ihionu for providing me with some of the data and for extensive discussions of some of the points made here. All misinterpretations or errors are, of course, nobody's fault but my own.

[1] I use the term 'object' here loosely; the object of *for* in the sentences in (2), for example, is not an argument of the verb. In (1) and (3), however, both postverbal NPs are selected by and constitute arguments of the verb.

double-object form of the dative from the prepositional form (Larson 1988) or the prepositional form from the double-object form (Aoun & Li 1989), I claim, following the spirit of Kayne (1984), Pesetsky (1990), and Hale & Keyser (1992), that in the double object dative the second object (the theme) is in fact syntactically the object of a preposition; the preposition just happens to be phonologically null. What this means is that the basic structure for both the sentences in (1) and the sentences in (3) is as shown in (4). The structure in (4a) is the l-syntactic structure (Hale 1989, Hale & Keyser 1992): this is the structure of the lexical entry for the verb *give* or *stuff* that indicates how the verb relates to its arguments. When this structure is projected from the lexicon into the syntax at D-structure, it looks like (4b), with NP1 as the sister of V and the PP adjoined to V'.[2]

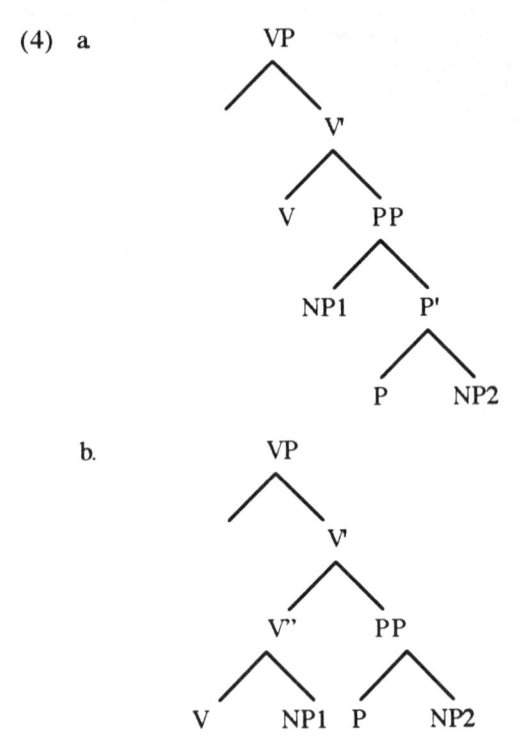

(4) a.

```
            VP
           /  \
              V'
             /  \
            V    PP
                /  \
             NP1    P'
                   /  \
                  P    NP2
```

b.

```
            VP
           /  \
              V'
             /  \
           V"    PP
          / \   /  \
         V  NP1 P   NP2
```

What is interesting about the dative is not that it has a double object variant, but that it shares with the locative alternation verbs the feature that its two objects may show up in either order, depending on the preposition used. Thus, in the dative, the theme is in the NP1 position if the

---

[2] The reason why the PP must adjoin to V' is not immediately clear; since NP1 and V behave like a constituent in the syntax, I am assuming that something like (4b) must be the structure. One speculation could be that in the surface syntax PPs are not allowed to take arguments in their specifiers. For my purposes here, it suffices to have the structure in (4a) available in the lexicon; what happens on the surface in English is beside the main point of this paper.

preposition is *to*, and the recipient is in the NP1 position if the preposition is the phonologically null 'double object' preposition. In other work I have developed a theory of how this works (Hoffman 1991a, b), so I will not go into it in detail here. The gist of the analysis is that a preposition, in expressing a relation between two things, can express that relation equivalently in either direction, just as the family relationship between two people can be expressed either as 'X is Y's niece' or as 'Y is X's uncle'. Verbs such as datives and locative alternation verbs that select for a prepositional complement in the lexicon can in principle select either direction of the preposition they select for; for example, the preposition in the dative might be classified as a change of possession preposition, with two different phonological forms (*to* and null) depending on which way the relation is to be expressed. The preposition selected by *stuff* might be expressed as a directional preposition, with two different phonological forms (*into* and *with*) depending on whether the object of the preposition is in motion or the endpoint of the motion.

In (5) and (6) I have sketched out how these differences look in the lexicon, filling in the arguments with words in parentheses for concreteness. In the lexicon, of course, there would be no NPs or specific Ps in the lexical entry, simply the verb and the semantic features selected by the V for the P. In these cases, the feature of the P that determines 'directionality' (Hale (1989) calls this feature [central]) is underspecified; the (a) and (b) sentences are how the lexical entry would look for the two different values for this feature;[3] the lexical prepositions in parentheses are merely shorthand for these bundles of features.

---

[3] See Hoffman (1991a) for a fuller discussion of prepositional features.

(5) a.

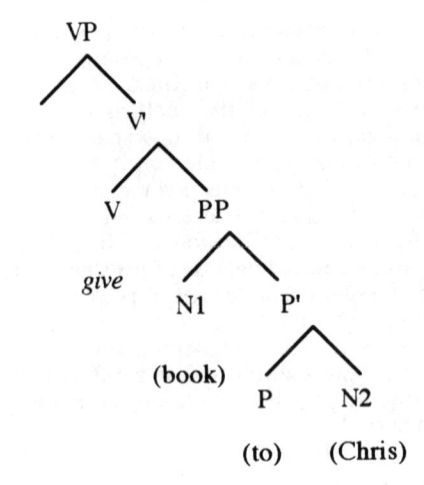

```
        VP
        |
        V'
       / \
      V   PP
    give  / \
         N1  P'
       (book)/ \
            P   N2
          (to) (Chris)
```

b.

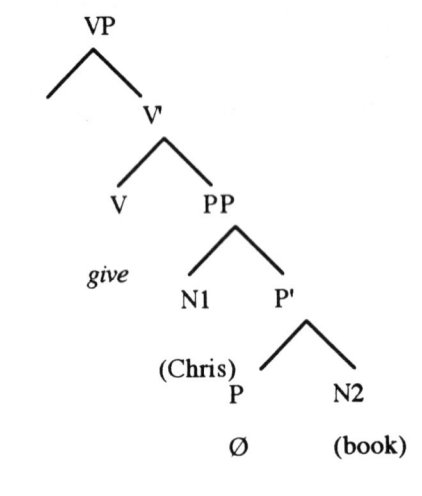

```
        VP
        |
        V'
       / \
      V   PP
    give  / \
         N1  P'
      (Chris)/ \
            P   N2
            ∅  (book)
```

(6) a.

```
        VP
        |
        V'
       / \
      V   PP
    stuff / \
         N1  P'
              / \
      (pillow) P  N2
            (with) (feathers)
```

b.

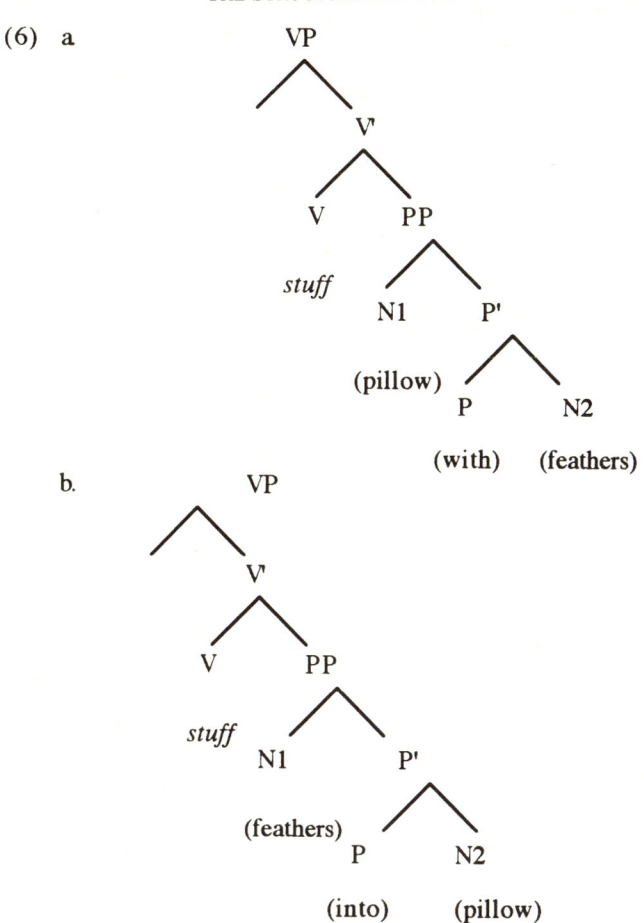

```
        VP
        |
        V'
       / \
      V   PP
    stuff / \
         N1  P'
              / \
      (feathers) P  N2
              (into) (pillow)
```

So far, then, I have claimed that prepositions can express their relations in two directions, which accounts for alternating verbs; note that not all verbs alternate (*pour*, for example, is unidirectional, as is *fill*, and in fact these two verbs form a pair, expressing essentially the same action and semantic relations, but in reverse directions from each other). This is easily explained by appealing to the fact that it is in the lexicon that these choices are taking place, and some verbs select for a preposition with unspecified direction, while others select for a preposition with one specific direction only. This, I claim, is due to the fact that the object closest to the verb is always the 'affected object' (Tenny 1987), and some verbs' lexical entries specify which object can be the affected one.

Now consider benefactives. Are the sentences in (2) just like the sentences in (1), with the structure in (5)? No; and the big difference is that datives select for two objects as part of their lexical entry, whereas the benefactive adds an optional argument to the already complete argument structure of a verb. Consider the sentences in (7)-(10). In (7), we have datives with the goal argument missing; context is required to make the meaning clear, and there is a definite sense of something being missing. In (8), we have verbs that can appear in benefactive constructions without the benefactive, and there is no hint of the benefactive relation or of something being missing.

(7) a. ?Chris sent a book yesterday. (anomalous without context)
    b. At the Red Cross blood drive, I gave my 30th pint. (to the Red Cross)

(8) a. I baked a cake yesterday.
    b. At the Red Cross blood drive, I found $100. (no implication of for the Red Cross')

(9) a. I baked a cake for Robin.
    b. I baked Robin a cake.
    c. I baked for Robin.
    d. I baked Robin. (* on benefactive reading)

(10) a. I sang a song for Pat.
     b. I sang Pat a song.
     c. I sang for Pat.
     d. *I sang Pat.

The examples in (9) and (10) illustrate another difference between datives and benefactives: whereas datives can be seen roughly as bringing about a relation between two entities, benefactives are not always interpretable in that way. In the (a) and (c) sentences, there is a relation between the action described by the verb and the beneficiary which is independent of the object (if any) of the verb. That is, (9a) may mean that my baking the cake benefited Robin by being Robin's birthday present or by being a job Robin was supposed to do; Robin need not even be aware of being benefited, as (9a) is perfectly good describing my baking of a cake in Robin's memory on the anniversary of Robin's death. In the (c) sentences, the relation is even clearer: it is the action of baking or singing that benefits Robin or Pat, not necessarily the products of the action.

In the (b) sentences, however, there must be a relation between the two objects of the verb: (10b) cannot mean, for example, that Pat was supposed to sing, but got laryngitis, so I sang instead. The song and Pat, or the cake and Robin, must be related: Robin must come to possess or benefit from the cake (not necessarily its baking), and Pat must hear or otherwise respond to the song. The (d) sentences, where there is no object to which the beneficiary may be related, are just plain impossible with a benefactive reading.[4]

The generalization is this: when the phonologically overt preposition is present, the relation expressed by the preposition is not between the two objects, but between the action and the benefactive object; when the

---

[4]This is probably just because there is no way to tell the difference between a theme and a beneficiary without some sort of clue, such as the presence of two bare postverbal NPs or a benefactive preposition.

preposition is phonologically unrealized, the relation seems to be at least in part between the two objects. The first part of this is not hard to see: in English, verbs can freely take a number of prepositions as adjuncts, that is, not as part of their lexically defined argument structures, as in 'Chris read the book in a chair by the fire on a cold, stormy night'. Prepositions cannot be inserted as verbal arguments in the surface syntax; they can only do that in the l-syntax. Since verbs that take benefactives do not select for them in the lexicon, the prepositional benefactive simply falls into this category: the verb takes a PP adjunct that expresses a relation between the phrase headed by the verb (that is, VP, the verb plus its object) and the beneficiary of the action described by that phrase. The structure for a prepositional benefactive is given in (11a) below.

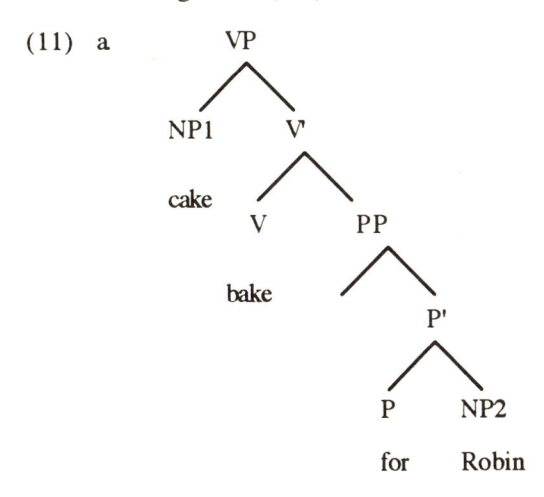

(11) a.

```
           VP
          /  \
        NP1   V'
        cake /  \
            V    PP
           bake  / \
                   P'
                  / \
                 P   NP2
                for  Robin
```

What about the double object benefactive? To capture the close relation between the two objects, I claim that this variant, unlike the *for*-benefactive, is realized in the lexicon. Within the theory of prepositions I have oulined, the obvious thing to say would be that the benefactive preposition alternates just like other prepositions, but it differs in that it expresses a relation between an entity and an event rather than between an entity and another entity. Thus, instead of a PP being the complement of a V in the lexicon, the VP in a sense appears as an argument of the P; where an entity-entity P takes an NP complement, an event-entity P takes a VP complement. The l-syntactic structure is given in (11b).

(11) b.
```
         PP
        /  \
      NP1   P'
      |    /  \
     Robin P   VP
           |   / \
           ø  V'
              / \
             V   NP2
             |    |
            bake cake
```

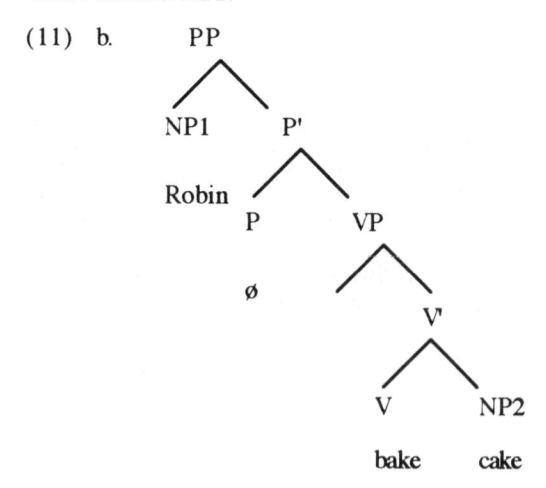

In this structure, the P is strictly speaking the head of the construction, an unusual case for English, to say the least. In English, Ps cannot head verbal projections because they are incapable of taking on verbal morphology by moving through INFL. What needs to happen in order for the word order to work out right is that the V moves up into the P node and then raises to INFL. Since this kind of incorporation of one lexical category into another is generally frowned upon in English, if we adopt the sort of system of lexical syntax proposed by Hale & Keyser, we can do the incorporation in the lexicon, where it is allowed for things like *en-* causative prefixes and so forth. After this is done, the structure is put into the syntax with the structure shown in (12).

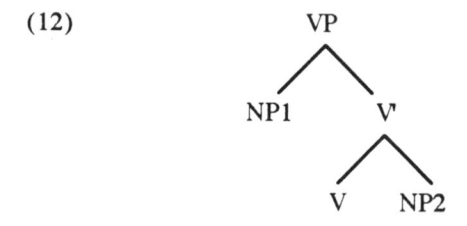

(12)
```
       VP
      /  \
    NP1   V'
          / \
         V   NP2
```

I would now like to look at some languages other than English to show how the analysis I've sketched works. The problems with the structure in (11b) exist because English does not allow incorporation in the syntax and because in English prepositions and verbs are different categories. In the Bantu languages, which have a rich system of incorporation, the structure in (11b) shows up in the syntax as the benefactive applicative. In at least the Kwa languages I've looked at briefly, one could argue that structures such as the ones above are the basis for 'serial verb constructions', if we take a liberal view of what a verb is. Essentially, the claim is that Bantu and Kwa languages, unlike English, allow at least certain prepositional morphemes to take on verbal morphology, thus allowing structures like (11b) to exist without running into problems with INFL. In other words, I claim that the structure in (11b) is a more or less universal structure for benefactives, and that general morphological constraints of particular languages will determine how (11b) is realized on the surface.

I should point out that in fact it is the structure in (11a) that seems odd for benefactives: as far as I have been able to determine, it is unusual for Bantu or Kwa languages to have a benefactive alternation: in general, it seems the structure in (11b) is the only option available. My guess is that English, since it has a fairly rich system of prepositions used both as optional adjuncts and as selected arguments of verbs, has allowed benefactives to fall into this pattern, especially since the structure in (11b) is unusual in the language, while the Bantu and Kwa languages, which do not have rich preposition systems and which have no problem dealing with structures like (11b), prefer to keep the basic benefactive structure as is.

Let me elaborate on Bantu for a moment. Chichewa has applicative constructions for benefactives, instrumentals, and locatives. While instrumentals and locatives allow either order of objects after the verb, the benefactive applicative typically allows only one word order.

(13) Chichewa (data from Alsina & Mchombo 1990)
    a   Chitsîru chi-na-gúl-ír-a atsíkána mphâtso.
        fool subj-pst-buy-appl-fv girls gift
        'The fool bought a gift for the girls.'

    b   *Chitsîru chi-na-gúl-ír-a mphátsó atsíkāna.
        fool subj-pst-buy-appl-fv gift girls
        'The fool bought a gift for the girls.'

    c   Anyăni a-ku-phwány-ír-a mwăla dēngu.
        baboons subj-pres-break-appl-fv stone basket
        'The baboons are breaking the basket with a stone.'

    d   Anyăni a-ku-phwány-ír-a dēngu mwăla.
        baboons subj-pres-break-appl-fv basket stone
        'The baboons are breaking the basket with a stone.'

While applicative constructions vary across Bantu languages with respect to object symmetry and word order, as far as I know all Bantu languages are like Chichewa in allowing only one order for the postverbal objects in benefactive applicatives, and that word order is the one in (13a). According to the account of prepositions in general and benefactives in particular that I have sketched above, the Chichewa facts can be explained by claiming that the instrumental applicative is a preposition that can express its relation in either direction, while the benefactive preposition is unidirectional. The structures for the sentences in (13c-d) are given in (14); the surface form of the applicative is arrived at by the head-to-head movement of the lower head into the upper.

(14) a.

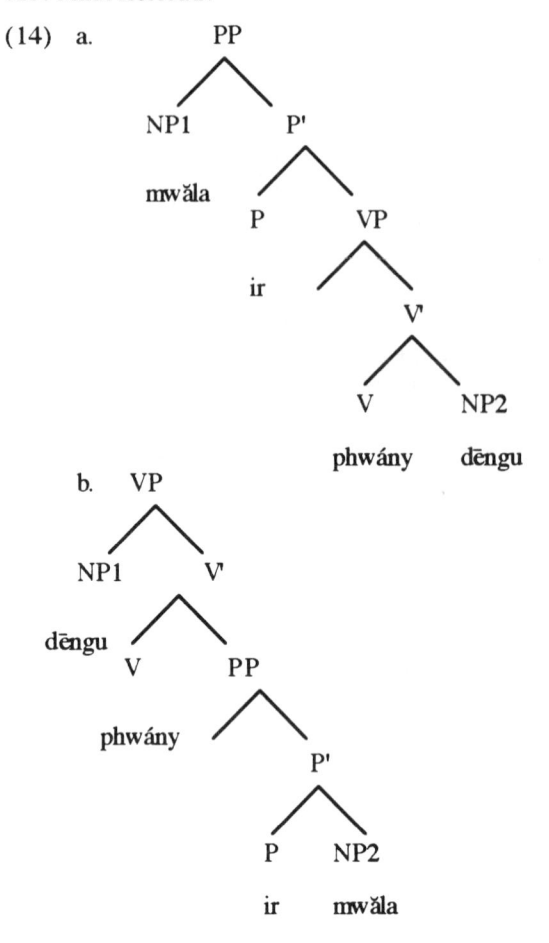

```
        PP
       /  \
     NP1   P'
      |   / \
    mwăla P  VP
          |   \
          ir   V'
              / \
             V   NP2
           phwány dēngu
```

b.
```
        VP
       /  \
     NP1   V'
      |   / \
    dēngu V  PP
          |   \
        phwány P'
               / \
              P   NP2
              ir  mwăla
```

Note that these are surface-syntax structures; Bantu, unlike English, allows incorporation in the surface syntax, and allows Ps to bear verbal morphology. Both structures in (14) involve an event-entity P, but the structure in (14b) deserves some attention: in this variant, the event (VP) should by rights be in the specifier of the PP, since that is one of the two positions for entities being related by a P. However, since VPs generally cannot occupy specifier positions (and certainly not if there were to be head-to-head movement of P into V), the relation between P and V can be satisfied by having a projection of V (V in this case, rather than VP if VP were in the specifier of PP) be a sister to a projection of P (PP in this case, rather than P'). I justify this position elsewhere (Hoffman 1991b); for my purposes here it is sufficient to illustrate the mechanism.

The structure for (13a) is the same as that for (13c), that is, (14a). The structure for (13b) would be (14b) if it were grammatical, but the benefactive preposition, unlike the instrumental preposition, does not alternate. Note that the same phonological form is used for all variants of all applicative prepositions in Chichewa; while it may seem odd to have all these different prepositions looking so much the same phonologically, recall that Bantu languages generally do not have much phonological variety in their prepositions. This particular set is peculiar in being bound morphemes, and it may be that in Chichewa there is a single phonological form for any bound preposition.

The next question is why the benefactive fails to alternate. I have no conclusive answer, but it may somehow be tied in to the availability of free prepositions. Chichewa has a free instrumental preposition *ndi*, 'with'; this preposition would fit into the structure in (14b), just as the corresponding English preposition would. There is no preposition corresponding to 'for', however. I suggest that (14a) is the usual form for applicatives, that is, that in general the applicative morpheme heads the applicative construction. The instrumental allows structures such as (14b) because there is a free preposition that could fit into that structure.

The situation in Bantu, then, is that verbs and prepositions can incorporate into each other in the surface syntax, and the head which appears uppermost can vary. Unlike English, applied verbs do not involve adjunction to VP, although Bantu does have free-standing prepositions that do adjoin to VP.

I would like to add a brief observation about Kwa languages. Like English, Kwa does not allow syntactic incorporation, but unlike English, Kwa does not generally allow phonologically null prepositions. (15) illustrates this point: *de* is a dummy predicate that has no specific semantic content, but is merely a placeholder that allows a predicate to take two objects.

(15) Kwawu Akan (data from Campbell 1990)
    a   yaw de bOOl má kòfí.
          Yaw DE ball gives Kofi
          'Yaw gives a ball to Kofi.'

    b.   yaw tó bOOl má kòfí.
          Yaw throws ball gives Kofi
          'Yaw throws a ball to Kofi.'

Like Bantu, Kwa does not make a clear distinction between prepositions and verbs with respect to verbal morphology: in serial verb constructions it is often unclear whether a predicate should be interpreted as a verb or as a preposition. The examples in (16) illustrate this. Again, notice that there are no phonologically null predicates; the dative alternates in just the same way locative alternation verbs do in English, with two different overt prepositions. (17) illustrates a benefactive: to my knowledge, there is no variant with the objects in reverse order, although my search of the data has not been extensive. If this holds, then Kwa is the opposite of Bantu in that its only benefactive has the beneficiary below the theme.

(16)   Yoruba (data from Manfredi 1988)
a   ó mú owó fún mi.
3ps took-hold-of money give me
'He/she gave money to me.'

b.   ó fún mi ní owó.
3ps gave me prep. money
'He/she gave me some money.'

(17)   Bàbá mi ra èwù bùn mi.
father my buy garment present me
'My father bought me a garment.'

The brief look at Kwa was simply intended to illustrate the variety of ways in which prepositional relations can be expressed. (18) summarizes the parametric differences among English, Bantu, and Kwa that account for the variation in surface form of these relations.

(18)   English
--many predicates leave [central] unspecified, including benefactive
--all prepositions are free morphemes
--verbs and prepositions are always morphologically distinct

Bantu
--few predicates leave [central] unspecified (only locative and instrumental applicatives)
--some prepositions are free morphemes, some are bound to verbs
--verbs and prepositions are generally morphologically distinct

Kwa
--few predicates leave [central] unspecified
--all prepositions are free morphemes
--verbs and prepositions are not always morphologically distinct

Underlying the differences outlined in (18) is a fundamental similarity in the structure of predicates that take prepositional relations as arguments. Many verbs can take PP complements, at least in the lexicon, and a PP can take a VP as one member of the relation it describes. Benefactives differ from datives in that datives are verbs that express the bringing about of a relation between two NPs and thus take an entity-entity PP in the lexicon, while benefactives always involve an event-entity PP. This difference is at least partly responsible for the difference in surface realization options for benefactives and datives, together with language-particular constraints on incorporation in the syntax.

References

Alsina, Alex, and Sam Mchombo. 1990. The Syntax of Applicatives in Chicheŵa: Problems for a Theta Theoretic Asymmetry. *Natural Language and Linguistic Theory* 8.493-506.

Aoun, Joseph, and Yen-hui Audrey Li. 1989. Scope and Constituency. *Linguistic Inquiry* 20.141-172.

Baker, Mark. 1988. *Incorporation: a Theory of Grammatical Function Changing.* Chicago: University of Chicago Press.

Baker, Mark. 1989. Object Sharing and Projection in Serial Verb Constructions. *Linguistic Inquiry* 20.513-553.

Campbell, Richard. 1990. Argument- Sharing Serial Verbs in Akan. Ms., University of Pennsylvania.

De Guzman, Videa. 1987. Indirect Objects in SiSwati. *Studies in African Linguistics* 18.309-325.

Hale, Ken. 1989. The Syntax of Lexical Word Formation. Ms., MIT.

Hale, Ken, and S. J. Keyser. 1992. The Syntactic Character of Thematic Structure. MIT Working Papers in Linguistics Occasional Papers.

Hoffman, Mika. 1991a. Movement, Traces, and Incorporation in the Lexicon. *Proceedings of the Second Annual Leiden Conference for Junior Linguists*, ed. by John van Lit, René Mulder, and Rint Sybesma, 109-120. Leiden: Rijksuniversiteit Leiden.

Hoffman, Mika. 1991b. The Syntax of Argument-Structure-Changing Morphology. Doctoral dissertation, MIT.

Kayne, Richard. 1984. *Connectedness and Binary Branching.* Dordrecht: Foris.

Larson, Richard. 1988. On the Double Object Construction. *Linguistic Inquiry* 19.335-391.

Levin, Beth, and Malka Rappaport. 1986. The Formation of Adjectival Passives. *Linguistic Inquiry* 17.623-661.

Manfredi, Victor. 1988. Draft of doctoral dissertation, Harvard.

Marantz, Alec. 1990. Implications of Asymmetries in Double Object Constructions. Ms., University of North Carolina at Chapel Hill.

Pesetsky, David. 1990. Experiencer Predicates and Universal Alignment Principles. Ms., MIT.

Tenny, Carol. 1987. Grammaticalizing Aspect and Affectedness. Doctoral dissertation, MIT.

On Some Mood Alternations in Labrador Inuttut

ALANA JOHNS

Memorial University of Newfoundland

0. Introduction

In this paper I will examine a number of instances in Labrador Inuttut where the inflectional paradigms differ from those of Qairnirmiutut,[1] a related dialect of Inuktitut. I will show that paradigms from the two dialects involve the same clause structure, but that Labrador Inuttut has a certain lexical restriction, which Qairnirmiutut does not. Using a) the Inuktitut clause structure of Johns (1992), b) lexical restrictions which

---

*This research has been funded in part by the Social Sciences and Humanities Research Council of Canada (grant number 410-88-0432). Thanks to Sybella Tuglavina, Harriet Lyall for help with the data, and Phil Branigan for discussion. All errors are mine.

[1] I will use the term Qairnirmiutut for the language and Qairnirmiut as the adjective.

determine whether or not a particular head may combine with another local head, and c) a notion of economy based on the minimalist program of Chomsky (1992), it will be shown that a large number of seemingly idiosyncratic alternations in mood in Labrador Inuttut are in fact the product of two lexical restrictions. One of the these restrictions holds throughout the entire language, while the other is dialect specific. The latter restriction, since it is the source of numerous dialect specific properties, resembles a parameter.

1. Mood Alternations

As discussed in Johns (1993), among the moods of the Qairnirmiut dialect of Inuktitut, are the participial and the indicative moods. In declarative sentences, the participial mood is regularly found,[2] and, in the same context, the indicative mood conveys a meaning of surprise or immediacy which I refer to here as SPECIAL.[3] Each of these moods may be fully inflected for person and number. A partial intransitive paradigm is shown in (1).[4]

(1) **Qairnirmiutut**

Intransitive *niri-* 'to eat'

		Participial	Indicative (special)
a.	1s	nirijunga	nirivunga
b.	2s	nirijutit	nirivutit
c.	3s	nirijuq	nirivuq
		etc.	

---

[2]The participial is also found in nominal constructions, such as relative clauses, etc. (see Johns 1992).

[3]The meaning and function of the indicative mood varies slightly across dialects. While in the western dialects, it has a narrative function (see Fortescue 1983), in West Greenlandic, it is the normal declarative mood. In all dialects, it is associated with question forms. In Labrador Inuttut, evidence suggests that the indicative has an aspectual character as well.

[4]Abbreviations used in this article are the following: s for singular; intr. for intransitive; tr. for transitive; rel. for relative (ergative) case; abs.for absolutive case; part. for participial mood; indic. for indicative mood; neg. for negative; irr. for irrealis mood, and 1, 2, 3 for first, second and third person.

A partial transitive[5] paradigm is shown in (2). To the left of the examples is indicated the person and number of the agent followed by a slash, and then the person and number of the patient. For example, this notation means that 1s/3s is 'I to him, her, or it.'

(2)   Qairnirmiutut

                          Transitive *taku-* 'to see'

		Participial	Indicative (special)
a.	1s/3s	takujara	takuvara
b.	2s/3s	takujait	takuvait
c.	3s/3s	takujaa	takuvaa
d.	3s/1s	takujaanga	takuvaanga
e.	3s/2s	takujaatit	takuvaatit

                                  etc.

As is obvious in (1) and (2), the participial mood in Qairnirmiutut is indicated by /j/, while the indicative mood is indicated by /v/.[6]

In Labrador Inuttut, however, we see that while the indicative mood is again completely inflected for person and number, the participial mood is only partially so, as shown in (3) and (4).[7]

---

[5]It should be noted that the terms intransitive and transitive in Inuktitut do not mean minus or plus object. Instead the term intransitive indicates single agreement on the verb (possible either i. where there is no logical object at all in the sentence, or ii. where there is a logical object in oblique case). The term transitive indicates double agreement on the verb (possible only where there is a grammatical object, as well as subject).

[6]In Qairnirmiutut, these consonants vary according to the phonological properties of the stems to which they attach, /j/ becoming [t] and /v/ becoming [p] after consonants. In Labrador Inuttut verb roots behave for the most part as if they all end in vowels.

[7]The Labrador Inuit Standardized Spelling system differs from that used in the N.W.T. and northern Quebec in that K is used for q, â for aa, e for ii, and o for uu.

(3) **Labrador**

Intransitive *nigi-* 'to eat'

		Participial	Indicative
a.	1s	*nigi**j**unga	nigi**v**unga
b.	2s	*nigi**j**utit	nigi**v**utit
c.	3s	nigi**j**uk	nigi**v**uk (special)

etc.

(4) **Labrador**

Transitive *takunna-* 'to look at'

		Participial	Indicative
a.	1s/3s	takunna**j**aga	takunna**v**aga (special)
b.	2s/3s	takunna**j**ait	takunna**v**at (special)
c.	3s/3s	takunna**j**anga	takunna**v**auk (special)
d.	3s/1s	*takunna**j**ânga	takunna**v**ânga
e.	3s/2s	*takunna**j**âtit	takunna**v**âtit

etc.

If we compare the data from Qairnirmiutut in (1) and (2) with that from Labrador Inuttut in (3) and (4), we see that the differences between the two dialects revolve around the person features of intransitive subject (theme) and transitive object (patient). More specifically, if the theme or patient is first or second person in Labrador Inuttut, the indicative is the regular mood form, and the participial mood is ungrammatical, as in (3a-b) and (4d-e). This contrasts with Qairnirmiutut, where, as we saw above, the regular declarative mood is always participial (and the indicative mood is always special). In Labrador Inuttut, when the theme or patient is third person, the participial is the regular mood, and the indicative mood is special,[8] exactly as is the case across all persons in Qairnirmiutut. These facts are summarized in (5).

---

[8] The facts are somewhat more complicated than given here, since indicative is also associated with aspect in third person (see footnote 3).

(5)   Qairnirmiutut   Labrador

                        Indic.   Part.   Indic.   Part.

1/2 theme   special regular   regular   *
1/2 patient   special regular   regular   *

3 theme   special regular   special   regular
3 patient   special regular   special   regular

The person of the agent of the transitive verb is not a factor in differences between the two dialects, since all three persons can appear as agents in the participial and the indicative moods in both Qairnirmiutut and Labrador Inuttut (whereas theme/patient in the participial mood is restricted to third person in Labrador Inuttut).

2. Syntactic Scaffolding and the Labrador Parameter

In Johns (1993) it is shown that the clause structure first argued for in Johns (1987) and (1992) can be viewed as a type of syntactic scaffolding for dialect comparison. What this means is that while the general analysis holds across dialects, variation can be expected in details concerning the existence and properties of functional projections. An example of this variation is the dialect differences we observed between Qairnirmiutut and Labrador above. Consider the structure for the Qairnirmiut example in (6a) given in (6b).

(6) a. angutiup   arnaq   taku-jaa
        man-rel.   woman(abs)   see-tr.part.3s/3s
        'The man sees/saw the woman'

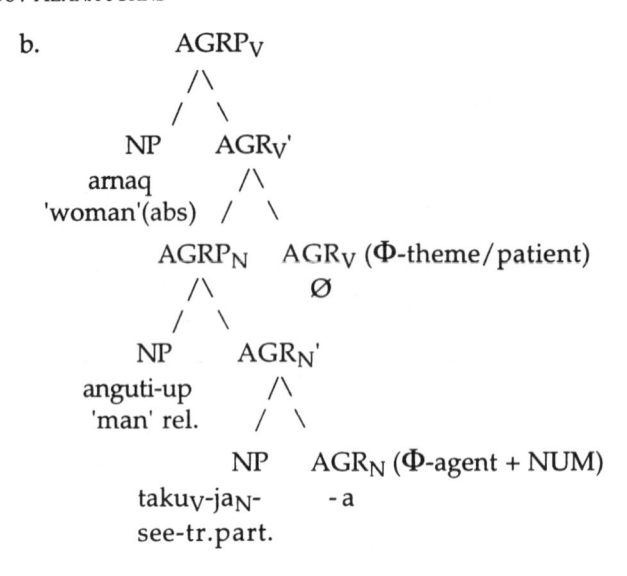

b. AGRP$_V$
   /\
  / \
 NP   AGR$_V$'
 arnaq   /\
 'woman'(abs) / \
        AGRP$_N$ AGR$_V$ (Φ-theme/patient)
         /\   ∅
        / \
       NP   AGR$_N$'
      anguti-up /\
      'man' rel. / \
              NP   AGR$_N$ (Φ-agent + NUM)
           taku$_V$-ja$_N$-   -a
           see-tr.part.

In (6b) we see that the structure contains two inflectional projections (following Pollock 1989, Chomsky 1991 [9]). The lower inflectional head AGR$_N$ takes the participial (NP) as a complement. AGR$_N$ conveys the Φ-features of the agent, i.e. its person and number, plus whatever number the participial has.[10] The higher inflectional projection AGRP$_V$ conveys the Φ-features of the theme/patient, i.e. its person and number. In Qairnirmiutut, a verb affixed with the participial mood is able to move to AGR$_N$ and subsequently to AGR$_V$ producing the form *taku-ja-a* or 'She/he/it sees him/her/it'. An important outcome of this analysis is that it correctly predicts that patient agreement is external to agent

---

[9]Pollock (1989) proposes an agreement projection for subject, while Chomsky (1991) proposes agreement projections for both subject and object. The structure in (6b) also has two agreement projections, except that the"subject" projection is internal to the "object" projection. In Johns (1992) this property is attributed to the presence of a passive participle morpheme. This morpheme is glossed as the transitive participle in this article.

[10]The number of the participial probably has a projection of its own. In fact, the number features of the agent and patient should also be investigated for this property. A discussion of number as a projection can be found in Ritter (to appear). Such an analysis is beyond the scope of this work, and does not bear upon the discussion.

agreement, as shown by the form *taku-ja-a-nga* see-tr.part.-3s.-1s. 'He sees me' from (2d). Note that the participial mood only moves up to AGR$_V$, when it functions as a verb. When it functions as a nominal, it maximally has the structure of an AGRP$_N$, thus explaining similarities and differences between the two constructions (see Johns 1992 for details). The indicative mood morpheme must always end up in AGR$_V$.[11] As a result, while the participial forms are sometimes ambiguous as to category, the indicative forms are always verbal.

For intransitive verbs, the structure is similar, except that the lower agreement head and its projection are missing, i.e. there is no AGRP$_N$.[12]

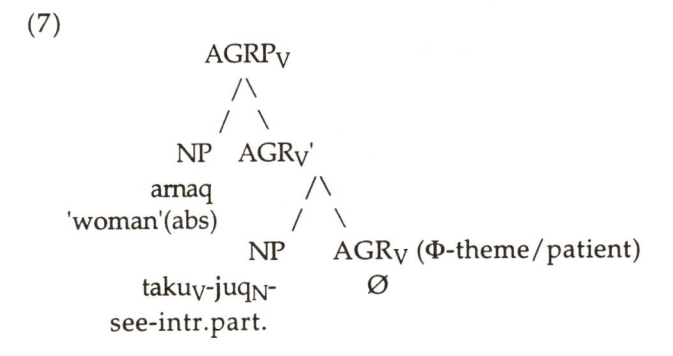

(7)
```
                AGRP_V
                /\
               /  \
             NP   AGR_V'
            arnaq   /\
         'woman'(abs) / \
                    NP   AGR_V (Φ-theme/patient)
               taku_V-juq_N-    Ø
               see-intr.part.
```

Once again, in Qairnirmiutut, the participial form may optionally move to AGR$_V$. Again, the indicative must always move to AGR$_V$.

I assume exactly the same structures for Labrador Inuttut as those shown in (6b) and (7). In addition, I will also assume that the Labrador dialect is specified for the following.

(8) **Labrador Parameter:**
The participial mood may not move to AGR$_V$.

Recall from (6b) and (7) that AGR$_V$ is the head of the level at which theme/patients receive Φ–features. Given that in Labrador

---

[11]The reasons behind this remain an object for future research.

[12]In Johns (1987) it is argued that AGR$_N$ can only appear when both complement and specifier are referential, thus explaining the overlap between transitive clauses and possessives. An intransitive predicate is not referential, and therefore cannot be a complement of AGR$_N$.

the participial mood cannot move to AGR$_V$, the analysis correctly predicts that the participial mood will never appear with the Φ–features associated with the AGR$_V$ level. This accounts for the ungrammaticality of the first and second person participial forms in the Labrador examples in (3a, b) and (4d,e). There we saw that only forms with indicative mood (which can and must move to AGR$_V$) are grammatical.

Note, however, that in Labrador Inuttut the participial mood is permitted in examples with third person theme/patient, such as (3c)and (4a-c). How is it that the participial can be marked for third person? One possibility is that the parameter in (8) is incorrect, and the participial mood in Labrador Inuttut can move to AGR$_V$ only when it needs third person features. Another possibility is that (8) is correct and the participial forms in (3c) and (4a-c) have not moved to AGR$_V$. In Johns (1993) it is argued that the latter is the correct conclusion. Following Silverstein (1985), Ritter (to appear) and references cited by these authors, it is assumed that third person is not a person in the same sense as first or second person (see also Rice and Saxon to appear). Third person derives from the nominal properties of the participial. As a result, forms with third person theme/patient simply do not need Φ-features, and therefore do not need to move to AGR$_V$. Under this view the participial forms in (3c) and (4a-c) are functionally nominals, since they have not been "verbified" by movement to AGR$_V$. How then do we explain Labrador Inuttut examples such as (9)?

(9)   angutik   takunna-jaga
      man(abs)   look at-tr.part1s/s
      'I look at the man'

The example in (9) shows a transitive participial form with a third person patient. The participial form appears to be the main verb. Yet I have just stated that participial forms can only be nominals in Labrador. As a result, the participial form in (9) cannot be a verb. If this is so, then there is no verb at all in example (9). How can there be a sentence without a verb? The solution to this paradox lies in the fact that Inuktitut allows nominals to be predicates without requiring the presence of a verbal auxiliary. Consider examples of nominal clauses from Labrador Inuttut, given in (10).[13]

(10) a. annak   ilinniatitsijik
         woman(abs) teacher(abs)
         'The woman is a teacher'

       b. annak   ilinniatitsiji-ga
          woman(abs) teacher-1s.
          'The woman is my teacher'

These examples illustrate that nominals in Inuktitut can function as predicates without the presence of a copula verb. In (10) both *ilinniatitsijik* 'teacher' and *ilinniatitsijiga* 'my teacher' appear as nominal predicates.[14] With this in mind, the example in (9) can be explained as a nominal clause consisting of a subject *angutik* 'the man' and a nominal predicate *takunnajaga*. There is no main verb in this sentence.

As we have seen, the parameter in (8) predicts that forms requiring first or second person theme/patient may never occur in the participial mood in Labrador Inuttut. This was seen to be correct, as shown by the ungrammaticality of the participial examples in (3a-b) and (4d-e). In these examples, the presence of the indicative mood morphemes is required in order for the verb to reach the Φ-features in AGR$_V$. At the same time, forms that do not need Φ-features from AGR$_V$ (third person theme/patient) are predicted to be possible in the participial mood. This is borne out by the grammaticality of the examples in participial mood in (3c) and (4a-c). These forms are not main verbs, but nominals, and can appear as nominal predicates.

What remains to be explained is why, in (3c) and (4a-c), the

---

[13]For an example of another language where the copula may be absent in nominal clauses, see the discussion of Modern Hebrew in Rapoport (1987).

[14]As discussed in Woodbury (1985), most dialects require that nominal predicates be "complex", i.e. have some additional morphology (possessive inflection, etc.). This rules out NPs without extra morphology from appearing as nominal predicates. Labrador Inuttut is distinct in that it allows simple NPs, such as ilinniatitsijik 'teacher' in (10a), as nominal predicates. Thus while an example similar to (10b) is grammatical in Qairnirmiutut, an example similar to (10a) would be ungrammatical, except in certain discourse contexts.

forms with the indicative mood morphemes carry the special meaning which characterises the entire indicative mood in Qairnirmiutut, while in (3a-b) and (4d-e), the indicative forms do not carry the special meaning. The generalization seems to be that the special meaning is absent whenever an alternate participial form is also absent, and that it is present whenever an alternate participial form exists.

That the special meaning of the indicative mood is correlated with the presence of a participial alternate can be explained as a form of economy, similar to that discussed in Chomsky (1992). In cases where the indicative mood morpheme is required in order for the verb to attain Φ-features, there is no other significance to the presence of indicative mood on the verb. On the other hand, where movement to AGR_V is not necessary for Φ-features, and a participial form suffices, economy will prevent the verb from appearing with the indicative mood. The reason that economy will always prefer the participial over the indicative is that the indicative involves an extra projection (AGR_V), and an extra movement of the head to this higher position. Where the participial mood suffices (i.e. third person theme/patient), an indicative mood morpheme can only be justified by an independent requirement for an AGR_V node. Special meaning, which we saw in Qairnirmiutut is always conveyed by the indicative mood, must require AGR_V.

In Qairnirmiutut, which does not have the parameter in (8), both the participial and the indicative mood may move to AGR_V. Since the participial mood may move there whenever Φ-features for theme/patient are needed from AGR_V, the sole function of the indicative mood in declarative clauses is to convey special meaning. In Labrador Inuttut, on the other hand, the indicative mood is utilized both to convey special meaning and as a means of reaching AGR_V (prohibited to the participial). The indicative mood, while forming a semantic contrast in Qairnirmiut declaratives, to some extent forms a grammatical contrast in Labrador Inuttut (AGR_V vs. AGR_N). As we shall see in the next section on negatives, however, moods other than the indicative can appear in AGR_V position.

3. Negation and the Indicative

In this section we will explore another set of paradigm differences between Qairnirmiutut and Labrador Inuttut. First consider the examples from Qairnirmiutut shown in (11).

(11) a. tiki-nngi-tunga   *tiki-nngit-punga
       arrive-neg.-intr.**part**.1s.   arrive-neg.-intr.**indic**.1s.
       'I didn't arrive'

     b. tiki-nngi-tutit   *tiki-nngit-putit
       arrive-neg.-intr.**part**.2s.   arrive-neg.-intr.**indic**.2s.
       'You(s.) didn't arrive'

     c. tiki-nngit-tuq   *tiki-nngit-puq
       arrive-neg.-intr.**part**.3s.   arrive-neg.-intr.**indic**.3s.
       'He/She didn't arrive'

     d. taku-nngi-taanga   *taku-nngit-paanga
       see-neg.-tr.**part**.3s/1s   see-neg.-tr.**indic**.3s/1s
       'She/her didn't see me'

     e. taku-nngi-tara   *taku-nngit-para
       see-neg.-tr.**part**.1s/3s.   see-neg.-tr.**indic**.1s/3s
       'I didn't see him/her/it'

As we can see, in Qairnirmiutut, the participial mood follows the negative morpheme -*nngit*- in declarative verbs. The indicative mood is ungrammatical in this context.[15] Now consider similar examples from the Labrador dialect, shown in (12).

(12) a. tiki-nngi-langa   *tiki-nngi-tunga   *tiki-nngi-vunga
       arrive-neg.-irr.1s   **part**.   **indic**.
       'I didn't arrive'

     b. tiki-nngi-latit   *tiki-nngi-tutit   *tiki-nngi-vutit
       arrive-neg.-irr.2s.   **part**.   **indic**.
       'You(s.) didn't arrive'

---

[15]In the righthand column of examples in (11), the indicative, were it grammatical, would appear as [p] following the final /t/ at the end of the negative (see footnote 6.). That there is no restriction against the sequence [tp] is shown by Qairnirmiutut *tikitpunga* 'I arrive (special)', where the verb stem *tikit*- 'arrive' ends in /t/.

c. tiki-nngi-tuk   tiki-nngi-lak   *tiki-nngi-vuk
    arrive-neg.intr.part.3s.   irr.   indic.
    'He/She didn't arrive'   (special)

d. taku-nngi-lânga   *taku-nngi-tânga   *taku-nngi-vânga
    see-neg.-irr.3s/1s   part.   indic.
    'He/she didn't see me'

e. taku-nngi-taga   taku-nngi-laga   *taku-nngi-vaga
    see-neg.-tr.part.1s/3s   irr.   indic.
    'I saw him/her/it'   (special)

Once again, the verb forms of the Labrador dialect vary in places from those in Qairnirmiutut. Whereas in Qairnirmiutut the participial mood appears after the negative affix, as in (11), in Labrador, the negative affix is often followed by a morpheme -la- in (12), which I will provisionally gloss as an irrealis mood (possibly the same morpheme as that found in the optative mood). In particular, first person and second person theme/patients, as in (12a, b and d), always appear with -la-. In contrast, third person theme/patients, such as (12c and e), can be either in the participial mood or appear with -la-. In these instances, the forms with -la- convey special meaning.[16] A final observation is that Labrador Inuttut, like Qairnirmiutut, does not allow the indicative mood to follow the negative affix.

It seems that there is a general restriction in Inuktitut against the negative morpheme combining with the indicative.[17] The explanation for this probably has to do with the semantics of

---

[16]One might expect that forms consisting of the negative followed by -la- will be present in Qairnirmiutut with special meaning. The data is unavailable to me at present.

[17]I have not been able to elicit an example with the negative followed by the indicative mood in either Qairnirmiutut or in Labrador Inuttut, although Smith (1977, 39) attests to these constructions in his discussion of Labrador intransitive verbs. Labrador speakers tell me that young people make such constructions as errors in what they term "babytalk." Dorais (1993, 59) reports that young speakers in Igloolik were using the negative plus indicative in 1975.

the two morphemes, as discussed in Lowe (1988).[18] This restriction can be stated as in (13).

(13) Negation Generalization:
The negative affix is incompatible with the indicative mood.

I will assume then that this constraint is a pan-dialectal property of Inuktitut. This restriction accounts for the ungrammaticality of all the negative plus indicative examples in Qairnirmiutut (11) and Labrador (12).

What about the cases where the verb requires Φ-features for theme/patient? In Qairnirmiutut, the negative morpheme plus participial mood (-*nngi(t)-tu-*) moves to AGR$_V$, just as the participial mood does in affirmative declaratives. Compare (1a), (2d) with (11a,d).[19]

In the Labrador dialect, the interaction of the Negative Generalization in (13) with the Labrador Parameter in (8) induces a dilemma. On the one hand, the [negative + participial mood] can't move to AGR$_V$ for first/second person features for theme/patient because of the prohibition against the participial mood moving to the higher position (Labrador Parameter). On the other hand, the negative can't combine with the indicative mood to get to AGR$_V$ (Negative Generalization).

As a result of these competing restrictions,[20] we might expect that forms with negative + first/second person theme/patient might be missing from Labrador paradigms, i.e. that it would be impossible to say 'I don't walk' or 'He doesn't see me'. More plausibly, we might expect that some element other than the indicative mood must exist which enables the verb to reach the AGR$_V$ position. This is the mood morpheme -*la*-. We observe that -*la*- appears in exactly those instances where the verb must reach the AGR$_V$ in order to obtain Φ-features, e.g. (12a,b,d) which all

---

[18]Lowe suggest that the participial indicates possible events, while the indicative indicates real events. He also offers one example (source not mentioned), illustrating what a negative plus indicative might mean.
[19]I leave open the question of whether in Qairnirmiut the participial mood moves up to AGR$_V$ when it does not need these features.
[20]See Grimshaw 1993 for a model dealing the issue of competition between syntactic restrictions.

involve first or second person theme/patient. For third person, which, as we saw above, does not need Φ-features, the presence of *-la-* is optional, and it conveys the special meaning, as in (12c,e). Both the indicative mood and the morpheme *-la-* allow the predicate to move to AGRV, and the appearance of either on third person forms, which do not have to go to AGR$_V$, always marks the presence of an independent requirement (special meaning). This accounts for the slight semantic differences between the third person forms in the participial and the ones with *-la-*, as in (12c,e). That the regular form in these cases is the one in the participial mood, rather than the one with *-la-*, indicates that some principle of economy is in force, since the form with *-la-* is syntactically more complex.

To summarize, the combination of the syntactic scaffolding of Johns (1992), the Labrador Parameter in (8), and the Negative Generalization in (13) predicts exactly the set of facts that hold of the paradigms of the two different dialects. These are:

(14) **Qairnirmiutut** **Labrador**

a. participial regular participial regular only in third person theme/patient.

b. indicative special i) indicative special only in third person theme/patient

ii) indicative regular in first or second person theme/patient.

c. negative followed by participial negative followed by participial only in third person theme/patient.

d. negative followed by *-la-* special?[21] i) negative followed by *-la-* special only in third person theme/patient

ii) negative followed by *-la-* regular in first or second person theme/patient.

---

[21]See footnote 16.

These facts, as stated in prose in (14), give the impression of somewhat irregular or idiosyncratic systems. The same facts, however, follow in the present account, where the necessity of obtaining first or second person features from AGR_V interacts with the means available to move to this position within each dialect.

Variation then results from a) whether or not it is necessary for a predicate to move to AGR_V, and b) restrictions on the morphemes that can move there. In the case of Qairnirmiutut, the participial mood is the normal means of moving to AGR_V, resulting in little variation. In the case of Labrador Inuttut, a restriction on the participial mood[22] necessitates the substitution of other mood morphemes (which may have their own restrictions, as was seen with the indicative). The outcome is more numerous alternations.

4. The Indicative Mood and Existential Predicates

We have seen in section 3. that in Inuktitut, mood alternations between the participial, the indicative and forms with -*la*- are governed by the structure of the clause and various general or dialectal restrictions. In this section we will see further evidence from a set of verbs that must appear in AGR_V which supports the claim that mood alternations are linked with syntactic structure.

In Inuktitut, the affix meaning 'have' also serves as an existential predicate (similar to Chinese; see Huang 1987). Consider the following typical example from the Labrador dialect.

(15)   Labradorimi   tuttu-**Ka**-vuk
       Labrador-locative   caribou-have-intr.indic.3s.
       'There are caribou in Labrador'

In (15) there is no overt subject and the verb is obligatorily marked with third person intransitive singular agreement. That this is an expletive subject is suggested by the facts that a) there is no overt NP with which the third person agrees, and b) there can be no variation in number. What is interesting is that the mood marker is indicative rather than participial. Recall that we saw above that third person intransitive verbs in Labrador Inuttut frequently appear with the participial mood, and alternate with the

---

[22]We might view this restriction as a variation in the verbal potential of the participial mood. In Qairnirmiutut, the verbal potential of the participial mood exceeds that in Labrador.

indicative mood. In constructions such as (15), there is no special meaning involved in the use of the indicative. More interesting is the fact that the participial mood is ungrammatical in these cases, as shown in (16).

(16) tuttu-Ka-juk
 caribou-have-intr.part.3s.
 * 'There are caribou'
 BUT 'He/she has a caribou'

The example in (16) is ungrammatical with the participial mood morpheme where the intended meaning of -Ka- is that of an existential predicate; however the participial mood is possible if a subject is present, or implied, as shown by the second translation in (16), in which a particular person has one or more caribou. In these cases the -Ka- necessarily means 'to own or possess'.

I assume then that existential predicates, because of their semantics, are not capable of taking an individuated subject. I assume also that there is a licensing requirement that a predicate must itself be licensed (for a discussion of predication, see Rothstein 1983). Predicate licensing requires that there be some property that links the predicate with a real or imaginary world. This linking can take place either through the subject,[23] or through reference to time. I also assume that AGR_V is a level of utterance time for verbs. Under this reasoning, the only way in which existential predicates (which lack subjects) can be licensed is for them to appear in AGR_V. This explains why -Ka- as an existential predicate must appear in the indicative mood, which allows it to reach AGR_V. It can appear in the participial mood only when it means 'to have or possess', and therefore has a subject to license the predicate.

Similarly, weather predicates, which also do not have

---

[23]This would explain why nominal clauses, which I argue in Johns (1987) do not appear in AGR_V, are ungrammatical without an overt (and presumably definite) subject. In Labrador Inuttut one can say s[*angut ilinniatitsijik*] man(abs) teacher(abs) 'The man is a teacher', but not *s[ilinniatitsijik] for 'He/she is a teacher', even though null subjects are fine with verbs. In order to express the latter, one would have to add a verbal affix -*u*- meaning 'to be', giving s[*ilinniatitsiji-u-juk*] teacher-be-intr.part.3s. 'He/she is a teacher'. This issue also relates to third person participials, which also seem to require overt subjects in Labrador Inuttut.

subjects, require the indicative mood in Labrador, as shown in (17).

(17) a. silalu-vuk *silalu-juk
 rain-intr.**indic**.3s. **part**.
 'It's raining'

 b. anugi-vuk *anugi-juk
 wind-intr.**indic**.3s. **part**.
 'It's windy'

Unlike the affix -*Ka*- 'to have', which can take a subject when it means to have or possess, weather verbs have no alternative meaning, and therefore are ungrammatical in the participial.[24] Thus weather verbs behave like existential predicates.[25]

Now consider the implication of this analysis with respect to the negative morpheme. Recall that the negative can never appear along with the indicative mood in Inuktitut, and yet existential predicates must appear in AGR$_V$ in order to be licensed. If an existential predicate is negated, it must reach AGR$_V$ by some means other than the indicative mood (which can't appear following the negative) or participial mood (which can't move to AGR$_V$). Once again, the only means left is the mood morpheme -*la*-. The examples below follow from the account presented here.

(18) a. tuttu-Ka-nngi-**lak**
 caribou-have-neg.-**irr**.3s.
 'There aren't any caribou'

---

[24]Labrador Inuttut speakers inform me that the participial mood is possible for these verbs when the weather is taking place in a location away from the speaker, e.g. another town. Further research on this construction is necessary to determine if and how this fact can be reconciled with the account given here.

[25]The analysis presented in this section predicts that in Qairnirmiutut, where the participial is permitted to move to AGR$_V$, existential predicates should be able to appear with the participial. While I do not have the data for Qairnirmiutut, evidence from another dialect where the participial predominates - Kangiryuarmiutun - supports this analysis. Lowe (1983) gives *nipaluk-tuq* rain-intr.part.3s. for 'It's raining' and *kikturia-qaq-tuq* mosquito-have-intr.part.3s. for 'There are mosquitoes'.

b. tuttu-Ka-nngi-tuk
   caribou-have-neg.-**intr.part.**3s
   *'There aren't any caribou'
   BUT 'He/she doesn't have a caribou'

c. silalu-nngi-**lak**   *silalu-nngi-**tuk**
   rain-neg.-**irr.**3s.   rain-neg.-**intr.part.**3s
   'It's not raining'

As can be seen from (18a) and (18b), the morpheme -*la*- following the negative morpheme is required when the preceding -*Ka*- 'have' is to be interpreted as an existential predicate. If it is a predicate of possession, the participial mood suffices (since the possessive will have a subject). Following the same reasoning, the morpheme -*la*- is required in the negation of weather verbs, as shown in (18c); however, since there is no alternative interpretation for these predicates involving subjects, the participial mood will be ungrammatical.[26]

5. Conclusion

In grammars of Inuktitut, individual moods are normally introduced with the agreement morphemes attached, e.g. Smith (1977), Dorais (1988), similar to the presentation of the examples in (1), (2), etc. We have seen, however, that the mood markers are independent of the agreement elements, although they interact with them in complex and interesting ways. The nature of this interaction is revealed through a common clause structure, shown in (6b), on which certain local restrictions associated with individual morphemes operates.

One of the restrictions we have seen is the Labrador Parameter, given in (8), which prevents the participial mood from moving to the head AGR_V.[27] The result of this parameter is to

---

[26]But see footnote 24.

[27]The nature of AGR_V and the indicative mood morpheme deserves further research. AGR_V may be similar to T(ense), or even C(omplementizer), in other languages. The indicative mood morpheme is found frequently, but not always, in question forms, even in those dialects in which declaratives are formed predominantly with the participial mood. In some Labrador dialects, the indicative mood morpheme also appears to be related to perfective aspect, being more likely to occur with punctual verbs like *tiki*- 'arrive' than activity

render all Labrador participials non-ambiguously nominal (in contrast to other dialects where they may move into verbal positions, i.e. AGR$_V$). Another restriction is the Negative Generalization in (13). Although this restrictions is uniform across all dialects, its effects are different, depending on what other restrictions are present in each dialect. A final but crucial feature of the analysis is the notion of economy (based on Chomsky 1992), whereby the minimal grammatical structure is preferred (see also Grimshaw 1993).

Related dialects of a language have similar phrase structures, resulting from sharing the same sets of functional categories,[28] e.g. AGR$_N$ and AGR$_V$. While the inflectional paradigms found in these functional categories may vary quite a bit between dialects, these variations are systematic and are linked to phrase structure. Without the syntactic scaffolding of the clause, the generalization of the Labrador Parameter would have been cumbersome to state.[29] We therefore expect that the properties of other inflectional paradigms, both in Inuktitut and other languages, will mirror clause structure.

References

Chomsky, Noam. 1991. Some Notes on Economy of Derivation and Representation. *Principles and Parameters in Comparative Grammar*, ed. by R. Freidin, 417-454. Cambridge: MIT Press.
Chomsky, Noam. 1992. A Minimalist Program for Linguistic Theory. *MIT Occasional Papers in Linguistics* 1. Cambridge: MIT, Dept. of Linguistics.
Dorais, Louis-Jacques. 1988. *Tukilik: An Inuktitut Grammar for All*. Association Inuksiutiit Katimajiit Inc. Québec: Université Laval.

---

verbs like *nigi-* 'eat'.

[28]As to differences between languages, either languages do not all have the same clause structure, as suggested in Johns (1992), or they differ in morphological properties that utilize the elements of a universal clause structure.

[29]For example, without the clause structure, we would have to say that in Labrador Inuttut the participial mood is only found in third person intransitive subjects and third person objects, i.e. is an ergative restriction. As well, such a morphological "rule" would have to include existential predicates as an unexplained exception.

Dorais, Louis-Jacques. 1993. *From Magic Words to Word Processing. A History of the Inuit Language*. Association Inuksiutiit Katimajiit Inc. Québec: Université Laval.

Fortescue, Michael. 1983. *A Comparative Manual of Affixes for the Inuit Dialects of Greenland, Canada, and Alaska (Man & Society 4)*. Copenhagen: Meddelelser om Grønland.

Grimshaw, Jane. 1993. *Minimal Projection Heads and Optimality, Technical Report #4*. Rutgers University Center for Cognitive Science.

Huang, C.-T. James. 1987 Existential Sentences in Chinese and (In)definiteness. *The Representation of Indefiniteness*, ed. by E. Reuland and A. ter Meulen, 226-253. Cambridge: MIT Press.

Johns, Alana. 1987. Transitivity and Grammatical Relations in Inuktitut. Doctoral dissertation, University of Ottawa.

Johns, Alana. 1992. Deriving Ergativity. *Linguistic Inquiry* 23:1, 57-87.

Johns, Alana. 1993. Symmetry in Labrador Inuttut. MIT Working Papers in Linguistics 18, 43-58. Cambridge: MIT, Dept. of Linguistics.

Lowe, Ronald. 1983. *Kangiryuarmiut uqauhingita numiktittitdjutingit: Basic Kangiryuarmiut Eskimo Dictionary*. Committee for Original Peoples Entitlement, Inuvik, N.W.T. [Distributed by the Association Inuksiutiit Katimajiit Inc., Université Laval, Quebec.]

Lowe, Ronald. 1988. La forme déclarative et l'alternance des suffixes -vu- et -ju- dans les dialectes inuit de l'arctique canadien de l'est. *Revue québécoise de linguistique* 17:1, 137-165.

Pollock, Jean-Yves. 1989. Verb Movement, Universal Grammar, and the Structure of IP. *Linguistic Inquiry* 20, 365-424.

Rapoport, Tova. 1987. Copular, Nominal and Small Clauses: A Study of Israeli Hebrew. Doctoral Dissertation, MIT.

Rice, Keren and Leslie Saxon. To appear. The Two Subject Positions in Athapaskan Languages. MIT Working Papers in Linguistics. Cambridge: MIT, Dept. of Linguistics.

Ritter, Elizabeth. To appear. On the Syntactic Category of Pronouns and Agreement. *Natural Language and Linguistic Theory*.

Rothstein, Susan. 1983. The Syntactic Form of Predication. Doctoral Dissertation, MIT.

Silverstein, M. 1985. Hierarchy of Features and Ergativity. *Features and Projections*, ed. by P. Muysken and H. van Riemsdijk, 163-232. Dordrecht: Fortis.

Smith, Lawrence. 1977. *Some Grammatical Aspects of Labrador Inuttut (Mercury Series No. 37)*. National Museum of Man [Canadian Museum of Civilization].

Woodbury, A. 1985. Noun Phrase, Nominal Sentence and Clause in Central Alaskan Yupik Eskimo. *Grammar Inside and Outside the Clause*, eds. J. Nichols and A. Woodbury, 61-88. London: Cambridge University Press.

Verb Agreement and Grammatical Relations

DAVID KATHMAN
University of Chicago

I. Introduction

Most theories of agreement assume a more or less direct correlation between verb agreement, morphology, and grammatical relations — that is, one set of agreement markers indicates features of the subject, another set (in those languages with object agreement) indicates features of the direct object, and so on. However, such a correlation does not always hold; in some languages, a single set of morphological agreement markers can correspond to different grammatical relations under different circumstances. For example, the South Caucasian language Georgian has a construction called 'Inversion', in which agreement markers which otherwise indicate features of the indirect object instead indicate features of the subject, and markers which otherwise indicate features of the subject instead indicate features of the direct object. Some such cases are dealt with in the Relational Grammar (RG) literature, where they are generally taken as evidence for multiple levels of grammatical relations. (Harris (1981) for Georgian and Davies (1986) for Choctaw are two of the most detailed RG analyses of this kind.) Stephen Anderson, in a series of papers and books (Anderson 1977, 1982, 1984, 1992) has argued for an alternative to the RG approach, in which such mismatches are handled by manipulating the features in an independent 'Morphosyntactic Representation'. However, I would like to suggest that neither of these approaches is the best way of looking at things, and that there is a third option which is simpler and more versatile. In this paper I examine two instances of mismatches between grammatical relations and verb agreement morphology — Georgian 'Inversion' and ergative verb agreement in Abkhaz — and show how they can be given a unified treatment in a theory which postulates separate but parallel morphological and syntactic subcategorization frames.

---

[*] I would like to thank all the people whose comments and criticisms have helped improve this paper, including V.A. Chirikba, Amy Dahlstrom, Donald Frantz, Donna Gerdts, Rich Janda, Edward Keenan, Joan Maling, and Jerrold Sadock. The usual disclaimers apply.

II. Georgian

Georgian has several distinct sets of verb agreement markers; table (1) below shows three of these, which, following Anderson (1984, 1992), I will refer to as 'v-series', 'm-series', and 'u-series'.[1] With a verb in the present or future tense, these are used to mark features of the subject, direct object, and indirect object respectively, as the examples in (2) demonstrate. These examples also illustrate the use of morphological case with third person nominals in Georgian: here, the subject is marked with nominative case, and the direct and indirect objects are both marked with dative case.[2]

(1)

	v-series	m-series	u-series
1sg.	v-	m-	mi-
2sg.	∅	g-	gi-
3sg.	-s	∅	u-
1pl.	v- -t	gv-	gvi-
2pl.	-t	g- -t	gi- -t
3pl.	-en, -an, -es, -on, -nen	∅	u-

(2) a. rezo   m-   xedav-   s
       rezo.NOM   1.SG.M–see.PRES–3.SG.V
       'Rezo sees me'

   b. me   da- v-   u-   xat'av   deda-   s   surat-   s
       I   PVB–1.SG.V–3.U–paint   mother–DAT   picture–DAT
       'I will paint mother a picture'

There is another pattern of agreement and case marking in Georgian, found in what is commonly called the 'Inversion' construction. This construction is illustrated by the sentences in (3), which are parallel to those in (2) except they are in the Perfect tense[3] instead of the Present. In

---

[1] There are other sets of agreement markers (from one to three, depending on what one counts as a separate series), all of which are parallel to the u-series in that they represent features of the indirect object, except in the Inversion construction to be described below. I use the u-series here to represent all of these series, since they all behave alike in the relevant respects; details of their use can be found in Aronson (1990) and Kathman (1994, Chapter 4).

[2] I use the term 'dative' here in accordance with the usual practice of English-speaking linguists studying Georgian, but some other term, such as 'objective', might be more appropriate. The term 'dative' is used because the indirect object takes this case in a wider variety of circumstances than the direct object does; see Aronson (1990) for details.

[3] What is here called the 'Perfect' can have a meaning similar to the English perfect, but it also, in simple declarative sentences like those in (3), implies that

this construction, the subject is in the dative case and is marked on the verb with the u-series markers; the direct object is in the nominative case and is marked on the verb with the v-series markers; and the indirect object is expressed in a postpositional phrase and thus not marked on the verb at all.

(3) a. rezo-s   v-   u- naxav-   xar
    rezo-DAT   1.SG.V-3.U-see.PF-   1.SG.V.be
    'Rezo has (apparently) seen me'

   b. me   da- mi-   xat'av- s   dedis-tvis   surat- i
    I   PVB-1.SG.U-paint.PF-3.SG.V   mother-for   picture-NOM
    'I have (apparently) painted mother a picture'

These two case/agreement patterns are summarized in (4), with the 'regular' pattern in (4a) and the Inversion pattern in (4b):[4]

		Subject	Direct Object	Indirect Object
(4)	a. Agr.	v-series	m-series	u-series
	Case	NOM	DAT	DAT
	b. Agr.	u-series	v-series	(none)
	Case	DAT	NOM	(tvis-phrase)

The distribution of Inversion is based on two factors: which conjugation the verb belongs to, and which screeve it is in. Georgian verbs can be divided into four conjugations (conventionally referred to as simply the First through Fourth Conjugation), based on a combination of morphological and semantic factors; Georgian verb tenses (or screeves, as Aronson 1990 calls them) can also be divided into four groups, conventionally called series (Present, Future, Aorist, and Perfect Series), with this latter grouping also based on a combination of morphological and semantic factors. The Inversion case/agreement pattern occurs in Fourth Conjugation verbs of any screeve, and in First or Third conjugation verbs in Perfect Series screeves. The verbs in (2) are both First Conjugation verbs and are in Present and Future Series screeves, so these sentences do not exhibit the Inversion pattern; in (4), these same First Conjugation verbs are in a Perfect Series screeve, so they do exhibit the Inversion pattern.

Despite the agreement and case marking facts, a number of (primarily syntactic) tests converge to pick out a class of arguments which are heterogeneous in terms of agreement, but which correspond to the

---

the speaker does not have firsthand knowledge of the events being described. Aronson (1990) contains discussion of the use of the various Georgian tenses.

[4] There is a third pattern which is identical to (4a) in terms of agreement, but which has a case pattern which is somewhat misleadingly called 'ergative'. I will not deal with this pattern here for reasons of space, but accounts of it can be found in, among others, Harris (1981), Anderson (1992), and Kathman (1994).

"notional subject". For instance, the reflexive word *tavi* (literally 'head') must have as its antecedent the subject; when the verb is in a Present Series screeve, as in (5), this will be the NP which triggers v-series agreement and appears in the nominative case:

(5)　　mxat'var-i　　da- xat'av- s　　　　vano-s　　tavis-tvis
　　　　painter-NOM　PVB-paint.FUT-3.SG.V　vano-DA　self-for
　　　　'The painter$_i$ will paint Vano$_j$ for himself$_{i/*j}$'

When the same verb appears in a Perfect Series screeve, the restriction on the reflexive remains constant, even though the same NP is now in the dative case and is represented on the verb by u-series agreement:

(6)　　mxat'var-s　　da- u- xat'av- s　　　　vano　　tavis-tvis
　　　　painter-DAT　PVB-3.U-paint.PERF-3.SG.V　vano　self-for
　　　　'The painter$_i$ has (apparently) painted Vano$_j$ for himself$_{i/*j}$'

If we assume that reflexive binding makes reference to syntactic factors (be they c-command, atomic grammatical relations, or whatever), then we have evidence that 'the painter' is the subject of both the above sentences, despite the differences in morphology.

Further evidence comes from word order. Though Georgian has relatively free word order in theory, some generalizations can be made; one of these states that the neutral word order has the subject in sentence-initial position, followed by the verb and direct object in either order (that is, either SVO or SOV is an unmarked word order in Georgian).[5] Thus, the sentences in (7) (one with Inversion, one without) are stylistically neutral, while those in (8) would be used only if the speaker wanted to focus 'his children':

(7) a.　mama　　　　xedav- s　　　　　tavis　švil- eb- s
　　　　father.NOM　see.PRES-3.SG.V　his　　child-PL-DAT
　　　　'Father sees his children'

　　b.　mama-s　　　u- naxav- s　　　　　　tavisi　švil-eb-i
　　　　father-DAT　3.U-see.PERF-3.SG.V　his　　　child-PL-NOM
　　　　'Father has (apparently) seen his children'

(8) a.　tavis　švil-eb-s　　　　xedav- s　　　　　mama
　　　　his　　child-PL-DAT　see.PRES-3.SG.V　father.NOM
　　　　'Father sees his children' (≈ 'His children, Father sees')

---

[5] This generalization was noted by Vogt (1971) on the basis of a study of texts, and the judgements in (6) were confirmed for me by Gia Gec'adze, a native speaker of Georgian.

(8) b. tavisi   švil-eb-i   u- naxav- s   mama-s
       his   child-PL-NOM   3.U-see.PERF-3.SG.V father-DAT
       'Father has (apparently) seen his children'
       (≈ 'His children, Father has apparently seen')

What is significant here is that for the purposes of this generalization, the same NP comes first whether it is marked on the verb with v-series or u-series agreement. This suggests that this NP bears the same syntactic relation in both sentences, since word order is a prototypically syntactic property.

Another way in which notional subjects pattern alike in Inversion and non-Inversion sentences has to do with number marking in the third person. Recall that the v-series agreement markers, most often used for subjects, distinguish number in the third person (cf. 9), while the other series, most often used for objects, do not (cf. 10):

(9) a. es   k'ac- i   m-   icnob- s
       this   man-NOM   1.SG.M-know-3.SG.V
       'This man knows me'

   b. es   k'ac-eb- i   m-   icnob- en
      this   man-PL-NOM   1.SG.M-know-3.PL.V
      'These men know me'

(10) a. am   k'ac-s   v-   icnob
        this   man-DAT   (3.M)-1.SG.V-know
        'I know this man'

    b. am   k'ac-eb- s   v-   icnob
       this   man-PL-DAT   (3.M)-1.SG.M-know
       'I know these men'

However, there is one circumstance where a third person NP can trigger number agreement in a series other than the v-series: in Inversion structures, the dative NP (the notional subject) triggers number agreement, while the nominative NP does not:

(11) a. st'udent'-eb-s   gamo-u- gzavni- a-   t   gela
        student- PL-DAT   PVB-3.U- send.PERF-3.SG.V-PL   gela.NOM
        '(Apparently) the students have sent Gela'

    b. gela-s   gamo-u- gzavni-   a   st'udent'-eb-i
       gela-DAT   PVB-3.U- send.PERF-3.SG.V   student-PL-NOM
       '(Apparently) Gela has sent the students'

Here, as with reflexive binding, it is the dative NP rather than the nominative NP which patterns with the nominative NP in non-inverted sentences. This fact is easily accounted for if the dative NPs in (11) are syntactic subjects despite their morphology. Furthermore, the fact that all three of the above tests (reflexive binding, word order, and plural agreement) converge to pick out the same class of NPs suggests that we are dealing with a real phenomenon.

These facts have led to a variety of analyses, some of which, upon close examination, are more successful than others. For example, Van Valin (1990), in the context of a Role and Reference Grammar analysis of Georgian split intransitivity, proposes a basically semantic analysis of Georgian Inversion. He argues that Inversion verbs differ from other Georgian verbs in that they are semantically transitive (i.e. they assign two thematic roles) but are lexically specified as only having a single 'macrorole' (roughly, core quasi-syntactic argument). This macrorole is assigned to the logical direct object by general principles of the theory, and language-specific principles then determine the agreement and case-marking facts; essentially, the logical direct object gets v-series agreement and nominative case because of its macrorole status, and the logical subject gets u-series agreement and dative case by default. However, this analysis has empirical problems; among other things, it is unable to account for Inversion in semantically intransitive activity verbs (e.g. *mušaobs* '(he) works'). A fuller critique of Van Valin's proposal for Georgian can be found in Kathman (1994, Chapter 4).

A more common position is that the discrepancies between agreement/case morphology and other tests is the result of arguments bearing different grammatical relations at different levels of analysis. This approach is typified by Relational Grammar (RG), and Harris' (1981) analysis of Georgian exemplifies the RG approach very well. Harris argues that Inversion is a syntactic process: the initial 1 (essentially the subject) demotes to 3 (i.e. indirect object), and the initial 2 (essentially the direct object) raises to become the final 1. Agreement and case marking are based on final relations, and reflexivization and (presumably) word order are based on initial relations. Harris' analysis correctly accounts for all the relevant facts, and she argues that its two components, 1-to-3 demotion and 2-to-1 advancement, are each found in many other languages and thus form part of universal grammar.

Anderson (1984, 1992), however, points out that all of Harris' evidence for final relations in Inversion is morphological (agreement and case) and that her evidence for initial relations is syntactic. He thus suggests that the syntax of these verbs remains the same as that of non-Inversion verbs, and that Inversion involves the movement of features within an independent Morphosyntactic Representation, with realization rules then determining the surface form of inflected words. One problem with this analysis is that manipulation of morphosyntactic features is an extremely powerful device which Anderson makes no attempt to constrain;

additionally, the account, while empirically adequate, is extremely complicated and requires numerous ad-hoc assumptions.

I suggest that a simpler solution can be provided in a framework in which syntactic and morphological subcategorization are kept separate, with syntactic subcategorization in terms of grammatical relations (as in Relational Grammar and Lexical-Functional Grammar) and morphological subcategorization in terms of sets of morphological agreement markers.[6] As an illustration, consider the following diagrams, which represent the First Conjugation, present screeve verb *davc'er* '(I) write (it)'. The syntactic frame, essentially an LFG functional (f-)structure, is on the left; the morphological frame, which is similar except that it contains agreement markers instead of grammatical relations, is on the right. Here, AGR1 represents the v-series agreement markers, AGR2 the m-series, and AGR3 the u-series; the specific morphological realization of such slots will, of course, be language-specific.

(12) a.
(syntax)

PRED 'write'	
TENSE future	
SUBJ$_i$	PERS 1
	NUM SG
OBJ$_j$	PERS 3
	NUM SG

b.
(morphology)

ROOT 'write'	
TENSE future	
AGR1$_i$	PERS 1
	NUM SG
AGR2$_j$	PERS 3
	NUM SG

All the slots in (12) contain person-number features, though these serve different functions in the two frames: in the syntactic frame, they restrict the types of NPs which can unify with the verb to form a sentence (e.g., only a first person singular NP can be the SUBJ of a sentence containing the verb in (12)), while in the morphological frame they restrict the form of the affixes which appear on the verb (e.g., the features in AGR1 above mean that this verb will contain a first person singular v-series affix, namely *v*-). The slots in each frame are arranged according to the hierarchies in (13), where the leftmost slot in each hierarchy is the highest ranked:

(13) a. Syntax: SUBJ > OBJ > OBJ2
   b. Morphology: AGR1 > AGR2 > AGR3

Each slot is linked to a corresponding slot in the other frame, with these linking relationships indicated here both by subscripts and by lines connecting the two frames; slots which are linked to each other must

---

[6] In Kathman (1993), I argue that such a separation of syntactic and morphological subcategorization is independently needed to account for languages such as Abkhaz, in which morphological 'agreement' markers can occur without any corresponding syntactic argument.

contain the same person/number features. For the most part the relationship between the frames of a verb are governed by the following principles:

(14) a. Optimality: The highest-ranking slot present in a verb's syntactic frame will link with the highest morphological slot present; the second-highest syntactic slot will link with the second-highest morphological slot; and so on.

b. Reciprocity: A verb which contains a syntactic SUBJ slot will also contain a morphological AGR1 slot and vice versa; similarly for OBJ and AGR2, and OBJ2 and AGR3.

These principles will account for the linking seen in (12): SUBJ, which is the highest syntactic slot, is linked to AGR1, which is the highest morphological slot, and OBJ, the second-highest syntactic slot, is linked to AGR2, the second-highest morphological slot. Another way of stating Optimality is to say that no line-crossing is allowed if linking is represented by lines connecting slots, as in (12).

There are, however, instances where each of the above principles can be overridden by language-specific linking principles, and I suggest that Georgian Inversion is just such a case. The following frames represent what an Inversion verb looks like in our framework: the syntactic subject (SUBJ) is linked to the AGR3 slot (representing the u-series markers), and the syntactic direct object is linked to the AGR1 slot, representing the v-series markers:

(15) a. (syntax)

PRED 'write'
TENSE perfect
SUBJ$_i$ | PERS 1
        | NUM SG
OBJ$_j$ | PERS 3
        | NUM SG

b. (morphology)

ROOT 'write'
TENSE perfect
AGR1$_j$ | PERS 3
        | NUM SG
AGR3$_i$ | PERS 1
        | NUM SG

This linking clearly violates Optimality, as the crossing lines in (16) attest: the highest syntactic slot is linked to the lowest, rather than the highest, morphological slot present. What allows such a violation to occur? I suggest that Georgian has the following marked linking rule, which overrides Optimality under the appropriate circumstances:

(16)   Link AGR3 to SUBJ if there is no corresponding OBJ2 slot.

This rule provides for the linking of SUBJ to AGR3 in (16), since there is in fact no OBJ2 (i.e. indirect object) slot in (16a); the direct object (OBJ) must then link to AGR1 (the v-series markers) by default, since the slot it should link to according to Optimality (AGR3) is already linked.

The frames in (15) also violate Reciprocity, since there is an AGR3 present instead of the AGR2 we would expect. Such violations, I suggest, can be accounted for in terms of lexical rules, similar to those used in (early) LFG (e.g. Bresnan 1982) except that they apply in the morphological frame instead of the syntactic f-structure. In the case of Georgian Inversion, the following rule would apply:

(17)   (AGR2) ---> (AGR3)   in Perfect Series screeves

Like the lexical rules of standard LFG, this rule is intended as a static condition on representations rather than a process. It does not 'change' an AGR2 into an AGR3; rather, it states that under the appropriate conditions (a Perfect Series screeve), a verb's morphological frame will contain an AGR3 where we would expect an AGR2 by Reciprocity.[7]

The analysis of Inversion outlined above also allows us to account for the case-marking facts in a straightforward manner. In LFG, case is generally treated as a feature of NPs, found in f-structures alongside agreement features such as person and number (see, for example, the analysis of Warlpiri in Simpson and Bresnan (1984)). In terms of our framework, this means that the lexical frames of a Georgian transitive verb such as the one in (12) would contain case features as shown below:

(syntax)   (morphology)

(18) a. | PRED 'write'   b. | ROOT 'write'
         | TENSE future | TENSE future
         | SUBJ$_i$ | PERS 1 |─AGR1$_i$ | PERS 1 |
         | | NUM SG | | NUM SG |
         | | CASE NOM | | | CASE NOM |
         | OBJ$_j$ | PERS 3 |─AGR2$_j$ | PERS 3 |
         | | NUM SG | | NUM SG |
         | | CASE DAT | | | CASE DAT |

The case features in the syntactic frame ensure that only NPs which contain the correct features can unify with this verb; thus the NP filling the SUBJ

---

[7] This rule also allows an explanation of why certain intransitive verbs (those in the Third Conjugation) exhibit Inversion in Perfect screeves, while other intransitives (those in the Second Conjugation) do not. Kathman (1994, Chapter 4) argues that Third Conjugation verbs are morphologically transitive (containing a dummy AGR2 slot) but syntactically intransitive; rule (17) would thus apply to Perfect screeves of these verbs, but not of Second Conjugation verbs. For details see Kathman (1994) or the similar analysis, using a slightly different framework, in Anderson (1984, 1992).

role must have the CASE feature NOM, and the NP filling the OBJ role must have the CASE feature DAT. Since the linking relationship involves the sharing of all the features in two slots, the CASE features are also present in the morphological frame despite the fact that they are not directly relevant to the morphological form of the verb; however, their presence there does have at least one advantage. Consider the distribution of the feature CASE in the frames of an Inversion verb:

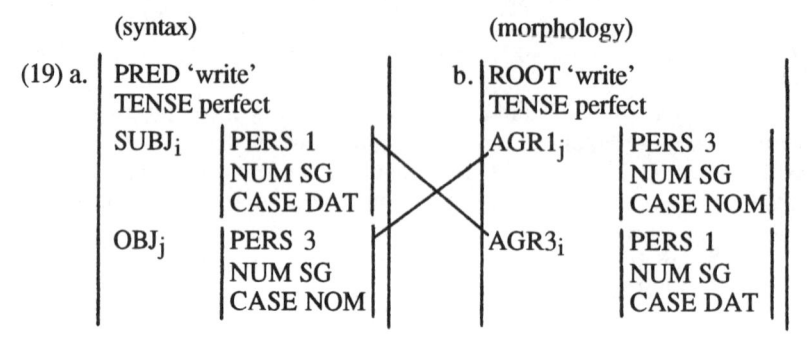

(19) a.
```
         (syntax)                              (morphology)
      PRED 'write'                         b.  ROOT 'write'
      TENSE perfect                            TENSE perfect
      SUBJ_i  | PERS 1                         AGR1_j  | PERS 3
              | NUM SG                                 | NUM SG
              | CASE DAT                               | CASE NOM
      OBJ_j   | PERS 3                         AGR3_i  | PERS 1
              | NUM SG                                 | NUM SG
              | CASE NOM                               | CASE DAT
```

The distribution of the CASE feature in the syntactic frame here is the opposite of that in (18): the subject is DAT and the object is NOM. However, in the morphological frame the distribution is identical: the AGR1 slot has the CASE:NOM feature, and the AGR2 slot has the CASE:DAT feature. This suggests that we can state the distribution of the feature CASE in terms of morphological slots, as in the following rule:

(20)   Default Case Marking: the highest available morphological slot is assigned NOM case; all lower slots are assigned DAT.

This rule is very similar to the Default Case Marking rule given by Zaenen, Maling, and Thráinsson (1985: 466) as part of an LFG analysis of case marking in Icelandic; the major difference between the two rules is that ZMT's rule applies in f-structure (i.e. in the syntax), while rule (20) applies in the morphology; if it applied in the syntax, we would not get the correct results. The fact that this case distribution rule is easily stated in terms of the morphological but not the syntactic frame lends some independent support to the notion of a separate morphological subcategorization frame.[8]

---

[8] The so-called 'ergative' case marking pattern of Georgian (found in the Aorist series of screeves) can be handled with the addition of another case assignment rule which assigns ERG case to the AGR1 slot under the appropriate conditions, as detailed in Chapter 4 of Kathman (1994).

III. Abkhaz

Abkhaz, like Georgian, has three distinct sets of verb agreement markers. However, unlike Georgian, Abkhaz verb agreement is ergative; the same set of markers is used for subjects of intransitive verbs and direct objects of transitives, as the examples in (21b-c) illustrate.

(21) a.

	Absolutive	Dative	Ergative
1sg.	s-	s-	s-/z-
2sg. masc.	w-	w-	w-
2sg. fem.	b-	b-	b-
3sg. masc.	d-	y-	y-
3sg. fem.	d-	l-	l-
3sg. nonhum.	y-/∅	a-/∅	a-/na-
1pl.	h-	h-	h-/aa-
2pl.	šʷ-	šʷ-	šʷ-/žʷ-
3pl.	y-/∅	r-	r-
relative	y-	z-	z-

b. sará sə- yʷná-le- yt'
   I   1.SG.ABS–in–come–AOR.ACT
   'I came in'

c. Zaíra sará sə- l- bé- yt'
   zaira me 1.SG.ABS–3.SG.F.ERG–see–AOR.ACT
   'Zaira saw me'

Despite this morphological ergativity, however, Abkhaz syntax is completely nominative-accusative according to various standard syntactic tests. For instance, in Abkhaz, as in Georgian, only subjects can antecede reflexives, whether they are marked on the verb by ergative (22a-b, d) or absolutive (22c) agreement.

(22 a. Zaíra l- xə ∅- l- dər- weyt'
      zaira 3.SG.F.DAT–self 3.SG.ABS–3.SG.F.ERG–know–PRES.A
      'Zaira knows herself' (antecedent=ergative; reflexive=absolutive)

b. sará a- sarkʸ'a-čə
   I   DEF–mirror–IN

   s- xə ∅- z- be- yt'
   1.SG.DAT–self 3.SG.ABS–1.SG.ERG–see–AOR.ACT
   'I saw myself in the mirror' (antecedent=erg; reflexive=abs)

(22) c. Zaíra   l-   xә
         zaira   3.SG.F.DAT–self

        d-   á-   s- weyt'
        3.SG.H.ABS–3.SG.DAT–hit–PRES.ACT
        'Zaira hits herself' (antecedent=abs; reflexive=dat)

    d. sará   s-   xә   a- hámta
        I   1.SG.DAT–self   DEF–present

        Ø-   á-   s-   te- yt'
        3.SG.ABS–3.SG.DAT–1.SG.ERG–give–AOR.ACT
        'I gave myself a present' (antecedent=erg; reflexive=dat)

As the examples below show, non-subjects cannot antecede reflexives, though they, too, can be marked on the verb with either absolutive (23a) or ergative (23b) agreement:

(23) a. *Axra   l-   xә   Zaíra
        axra   3.SG.F.DAT–self   zaira

        d-   a-   cʷә- y-   xʸčʸe- yt'
        3.SG.H.ABS–3.SG.DAT–from–3.SG.M.ERG–protect–AOR.ACT
        'Axra$_i$ protected Zaira$_j$ from herself$_j$' (antecedent=abs; reflexive=dat)

    b. *Axra Zaí'ra   lә-   x   a-   zә   a-hámta
        axra   zaira   3.SG.F.DAT–SELF   3.SG.DAT–for   DEF–present

        Ø-   á-   d-   te- yt'
        3.SG.ABS–3.SG.DAT–3.SG.M.ERG–give–AOR.ACT
        'Axra$_i$ gave Zaira$_j$ a present for herself$_j$' (antecedent=erg; reflexive= oblique)

Thus, the kind of verb agreement an argument corresponds to is irrelevant to whether it can antecede a reflexive. There must be some other factor involved; it seems reasonable to conclude that this factor is syntactic, since the possible antecedents in the above examples correspond to the notional subjects of the sentences, while the impossible antecedents correspond to notional objects.

    Equi/Control structures provide some parallel evidence. In each of the following sentences, the subject of the embedded clause cannot be overtly present and must be coreferent with the matrix subject (in GB terms, it must be a PRO coindexed with the matrix subject), even though this argument is referenced by absolutive agreement in (24a) and ergative in (24b).

(24) a. s-   cá- rc   Ø-   s-   taxə́- wp'
         1.SG.ABS–go–PTNTL   3.SG.ABS–1.SG.ERG–want–STAT.PRES
         'I want to go'

   b. áxra   də-   s-   šə́- rc   Ø-   s-
       axra   3.SG.ABS–1.SG.ERG–kill–PTNTL 3.SG.ABS–1.SG.ERG–

       taxə́- wp'
       want–STAT.PRES
       'I want to kill Axra'

Here, again, NPs referenced by different sets of agreement markers pattern together by a syntactic criterion, thus providing further evidence that the correlation between agreement markers and grammatical relations is not always direct.

Similarly with Conjunction Reduction, which has been a standard test in discussions of ergativity since Dixon's (1972) analysis of Dyirbal. When two English sentences are conjoined, the subject of the second sentence may be omitted if it is coreferential with the subject of the first; thus, in the sentence 'The man saw the woman and (then) left', the missing subject of 'left' must be interpreted as being 'the man', since this is the subject of the first verb ('saw'). The same is true in most other languages, but Dixon points out that in the analogous sentence in Dyirbal, the opposite holds true: the notional subject of 'left' must be interpreted as being 'the woman', the notional *direct object* of the first verb, and Dixon uses this fact in arguing that Dyirbal has ergative syntax to go along with its ergative case marking. When we consider parallel sentences in Abkhaz, we see that the pattern is the same as in English; as Hewitt (1989) notes, the example in (25) can only be interpreted as meaning that the man, not the woman, went out:

(25)   a- xác'a a- ph^{w}ə́s   də-   y-   bá- n
       DEF–man DEF–woman   3.SG.H.ABS–3.SG.M.ERG–see–PAST

                                   də-   d^{w}ə́l- c'ə́- yt'
                                   3.SG.H.ABS–out–go–AOR.ACT
       'The man saw the woman and (he/*she) went out'

Thus Abkhaz, despite its ergative verb morphology, patterns with nominative-accusative languages such as English in this respect, rather than with the 'deep ergative' language Dyirbal.

Finally, there is word order; like Georgian, Abkhaz has relatively free word order, but the unmarked order[9] is for the subject to come sentence initially, whether it is marked with absolutive (26a) or ergative (26b) agreement:

(26) a. Zairá   Ø-   y^{w}ná-le- yt'
        zaira   3.ABS– in–come–AOR.ACT
        'Zaira came in'

     b. Zairá   sará   sə-   l-   bé- yt'
        zaira   me   1.SG.ABS–3.SG.F.ERG–see–AOR.ACT
        'Zaira saw me'

As with the other tests we have seen, this fact is easily explained if *Zaira* is the syntactic subject in both (26a) and (26b), despite the fact that it is referenced on the verb by different sets of agreement markers.

Given the framework described above, we can account for such a pattern very simply: Abkhaz has the language-specific linking rule (27) in addition to the universal principles of Optimality and Reciprocity that we saw in (14) and (15):

(27)   Link OBJ to AGR1.

This rule will have no effect on the linking in intransitives, since such verbs do not subcategorize for an OBJ function (cf. 28). In transitives, however, this rule will take precedence over Optimality, resulting in the linking shown in (29); once OBJ has been linked to AGR1 by (27), the only slot left for SUBJ to link to is AGR2.

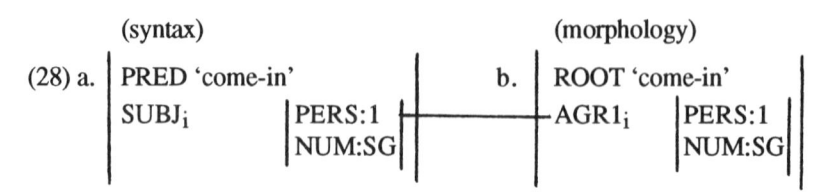

              (syntax)   (morphology)

(28) a. | PRED 'come-in' | b. | ROOT 'come-in'
          | SUBJ$_i$ | PERS:1 | AGR1$_i$ | PERS:1 |
                        | NUM:SG | | NUM:SG |

---

[9] The unmarked Abkhaz word order in simple sentences is S-IO-O-V; Hewitt (1989) contains the most extensive discussion in English of word order patterns in the language.

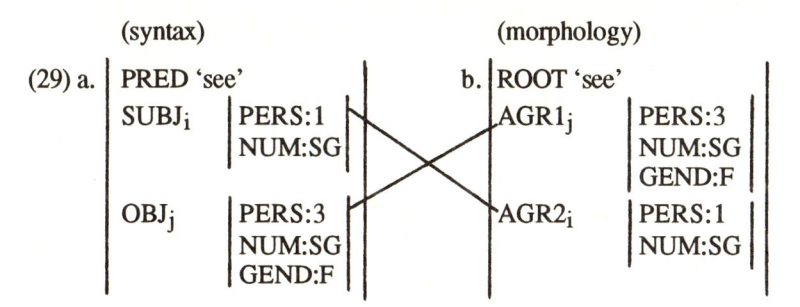

(29) a. (syntax)
PRED 'see'
SUBJ$_i$ [PERS:1, NUM:SG]
OBJ$_j$ [PERS:3, NUM:SG, GEND:F]

b. (morphology)
ROOT 'see'
AGR1$_j$ [PERS:3, NUM:SG, GEND:F]
AGR2$_i$ [PERS:1, NUM:SG]

Thus AGR1 in Abkhaz represents the absolutive markers, and AGR2 represents the ergative markers; AGR3 (not shown here) represents the dative markers and is always linked to the indirect object, regardless of transitivity.

Thus, Georgian Inversion and Abkhaz ergative verb agreement can each be handled by a language-specific linking rule which overrides the universal principle of Optimality given earlier in (14a). For purposes of comparison, these rules are repeated in (30)-(33), along with the respective linkings they license:

(30) Georgian: Link AGR3 to SUBJ if there is no corresponding OBJ2 slot.

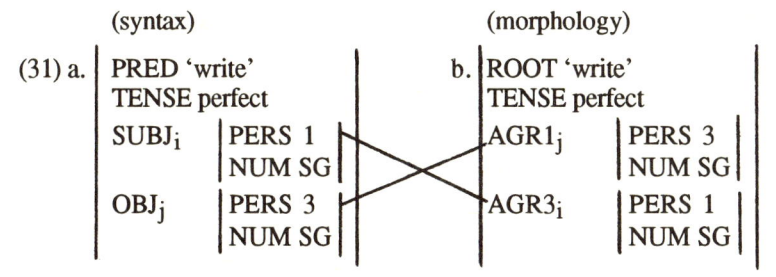

(31) a. (syntax)
PRED 'write'
TENSE perfect
SUBJ$_i$ [PERS 1, NUM SG]
OBJ$_j$ [PERS 3, NUM SG]

b. (morphology)
ROOT 'write'
TENSE perfect
AGR1$_j$ [PERS 3, NUM SG]
AGR3$_i$ [PERS 1, NUM SG]

(32) Abkhaz: Link OBJ to AGR1.

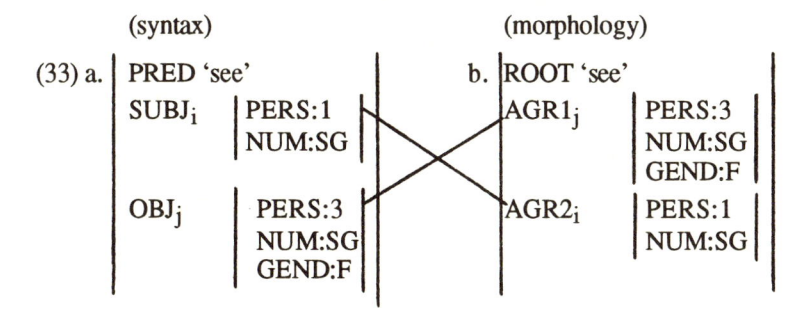

(33) a. (syntax)
PRED 'see'
SUBJ$_i$ [PERS:1, NUM:SG]
OBJ$_j$ [PERS:3, NUM:SG, GEND:F]

b. (morphology)
ROOT 'see'
AGR1$_j$ [PERS:3, NUM:SG, GEND:F]
AGR2$_i$ [PERS:1, NUM:SG]

A look at these rules, and the associated linkings, suggests that there is a generalization to be made, which can be stated informally as in (34):

(34) A language-specific linking rule may allow a given slot to link one slot higher in the opposite frame than it would under Optimality.

This metarule is only a first approximation, based as it is on only two languages, but it provides a reasonable starting point for restricting the type of language-specific linking rules which can exist. Whether it will apply to all instances of marked linking between grammatical relations and agreement markers is a matter for further research.[10]

IV. Summary and Conclusions

The theory proposed here does not exist in a vacuum, of course; it bears similarities to those of, among others, Anderson (1992) and Gerdts (1993a,b). Anderson (1992) posits a Morphosyntactic Representation independent of syntax, similar in principle to the morphological subcategorization frame proposed here except that it uses layering of features rather than labels such as AGR1 to distinguish subject from object agreement features. Anderson proposes to account for such phenomena as Georgian Inversion by moving features around within this representation, but unfortunately he makes no attempt to constrain this extremely powerful device. Furthermore, the nature of Anderson's theory often causes analyses to become more complicated than necessary; space will not allow a detailed demonstration of this, but the interested reader may compare, for instance, the analysis of Georgian case marking in Anderson (1992) with that in Section II above. Nevertheless, Anderson's work has been extremely important and influential in demonstrating the usefulness of separating the morphological and syntactic aspects of verb agreement.

The Mapping Theory of Gerdts (1993a,b) is even more similar, and indeed the analysis given here could be translated fairly easily into Gerdts' notation. In Gerdts' model a clause contains four parallel levels of representation: a level of thematic roles, corresponding to similar levels in many other theories (such as the Theta Grid of GB and the a-structure of LFG); a level of Grammatical Relations, corresponding roughly to initial GRs in traditional Relational Grammar; a level of Morphosyntactically-licensed Argument Positions (MAPs), corresponding roughly to final GRs

---

[10] Kathman (1994) proposes another metarule, parallel to (34) but applying over lexical rules such as we saw in (17) for Georgian. This second metarule states that a lexical rule may allow a verb's morphological frame to contain a slot which is lower on the morphological hierarchy than we would expect under Reciprocity; thus it allows lexical rules of the form (AGR2) ---> (AGR3) (as in (17)), but not (AGR3) ---> (AGR2). There is thus a symmetry between the metarules which license violations of the two principles of Optimality and Reciprocity.

in traditional Relational Grammar; and a level which specifies how the MAPs are realized (generally in terms of case, agreement, word order, etc.). Gerdts' level of GRs corresponds closely to the level of syntactic f-structure in the present theory, and her level of MAPs corresponds closely to morphological subcategorization frames; furthermore, unmarked associations between GRs and MAPs in Gerdts' theory 'proceed in a vertical, non-crossing, left-to-right fashion' (Gerdts (1993a, b)), a principle which is quite similar to Optimality. There are, of course, differences between the two models; probably the most significant of these is that, as the above quote shows, Gerdts explicitly forbids line crossing in her linkings, though I hope to have shown in this paper that such crossing is sometimes necessary. Nevertheless, the similarity of the two models (developed simultaneously but independently) is striking, and suggests that the notion of linking as a means of accounting for morphosyntactic mismatches is a promising area for future study.

I hope to have shown in this paper that the seemingly unrelated phenomena of Georgian Inversion and Abkhaz ergative agreement can both be seen as instances of mismatches between grammatical relations and agreement morphology, and that both can be stated very simply in terms of marked linking rules between independent syntactic and morphological subcategorization frames. The above discussion does not by any means exhaust the uses of this framework, (Kathman (1994) contains analyses of many other related phenomena in a variety of languages), but it does demonstrate that the relation between grammatical relations and verb agreement is not always as straightforward as many models of language implicitly assume.

References

Anderson, Stephen. 1976. On the Notion of Subject in Ergative Languages. *Subject and Topic*, ed. by Charles N. Li, 1–23. New York: Academic Press.

Anderson, Stephen. 1977. On the Formal Description of Inflection. *CLS* 13.15–44.

Anderson, Stephen. 1982. Where's Morphology? *Linguistic Inquiry* 13.571–612.

Anderson, Stephen. 1984. On Representations in Morphology: Case, Agreement, and Inversion in Georgian. *Natural Language and Linguistic Theory* 2.157–218.

Anderson, Stephen. 1992. *A-morphous Morphology.* Cambridge: Cambridge University Press.

Aronson, Howard. 1990. *Georgian: A Reading Grammar* (Second Edition). Columbus, Ohio: Slavica.

Bresnan, Joan, ed. 1982. *The Mental Representation of Grammatical Relations.* Cambridge, MA: MIT Press.

Davies, William. 1986. *Choctaw Verb Agreement and Universal Grammar*. Dordrecht: Kluwer.

Dixon, R. M. W. 1972. *The Dyirbal Language of North Queensland*. Cambridge Studies in Linguistics 9. Cambridge: Cambridge University Press.

Gerdts, Donna. B. 1993a. Mapping Transitive Voice in Halkomelem. *BLS* 19S.22–33.

Gerdts, Donna. B. 1993b. Mapping Halkomelem Grammatical Relations. *Linguistics* 31.591–621.

Harris, Alice. *Georgian Syntax*. Cambridge: Cambridge University Press.

Hewitt, B. G. 1989. *Abkhaz*. New York: Routledge.

Kathman, David. 1993. Expletive Verb Marking in Abkhaz. Paper presented at the 19th Annual Meeting of the Berkeley Linguistics Society.

Kathman, David. 1994. The Morphosyntax of Verb Agreement. Ph.D dissertation, University of Chicago.

Simpson, Jane, and Joan Bresnan. 1983. Control and Obviation in Warlpiri. *Natural Language and Linguistic Theory* 1.49–64.

Spruit, Arie. 1986. Abkhaz Studies. Doctoral dissertation, Rijksuniversiteit of Leiden.

Van Valin, Robert D., Jr. 1990. Semantic Parameters of Split Intransitivity. *Language* 66.221–260.

Vogt, Hans. 1971. *Grammaire de la langue georgienne*. Oslo: Universitetsforleget.

Predicate-Argument Structure in Malagasy

EDWARD L. KEENAN
University of California at Los Angeles

1. Introduction

In **2** we show that Malagasy, although highly configurational, compares with Philippine languages like Tagalog and Cebuano with regard to the richness of its voice system and the split of "subject properties" between active and non-active Agent Phrases. These results are consistent with the point of view in Manaster-Ramer (1992), Guilfoyle, Hung and Travis (1992) and Voskuil (1993) but modify somewhat those in Keenan (1976).

In **3** we study non-active Ss in Malagasy, defending a predicate level analysis (Mulder and Schwartz 1981, Bach 1980, Keenan 1980, Keenan & Timberlake 1985a,b and Dukes 1993) over a clause level advancement analysis (Bell 1983, Payne 1982, Gerdts 1988 and De Guzman 1988 for Philippine languages).

2. Western Austronesian Clause Structure

We define a language L to be a WESTERN AUSTRONESIAN TYPE (= WA Type) language if there is a structural way of identifying an NP in each basic clause of L which satisfies (1a,b) below, where we write **NP(S)** for the NP identified[1] in S:

---

[*]I am particularly indebted to Dr. Cecile Manorohanta for consultation on many of the claims.

[1]To say that there is a structural way of identifying an NP (occurrence) in each basic clause is to say that there is a *structure dependent* function, here noted **NP**, which maps each basic clause to an NP occurring in it. A function F is *structure dependent* iff whenever S and S' are isomorphic (= have the same structure, whatever it is) then the value of F at S must be the isomorphic image of its value at S'. For example, suppose that a complex expression ABC is isomorphic to A'B'C' by a function which maps A to A', B to B' and C to C'. Then if a structure dependent F maps ABC to B then F must map A'B'C' to B'. See Keenan & Stabler (1991). In some languages a syntactic isomorphism (technically *automorphism*) must

(1) a. the verbal morphology covaries with the semantic role of NP(S) and
  b. many syntactic and interpretative processes, such as relativization, apply only to NP(S).

WA Type languages include Malagasy (Madagascar), the Philippine languages (Tagalog, Cebuano, etc.), Toba Batak (Sumatra; Schachter 1984) and Kimaragang Dusun (Sabah (= N.Borneo); Kroeger 1988). (2) from Cebuano (Bell 1983) is illustrative. NP(S) is marked *ang-* (*si-* if a proper noun, *ako, ka, siya...* if a pronoun).

(2) a. Mag+luto' ang   babaye ug bugas sa kulon
       act+cook nom   woman obl rice obl ricepot

  '*The woman will cook rice in the ricepot.*'

  b. Luto'+on sa   babaye ang   bugas sa kulon
      cook +obj gen woman nom   rice   obl ricepot

  '*The rice will be cooked in the ricepot by the woman.*'

  c. Luto'+an sa   babaye ang   kulon   ug bugas
      cook +loc gen woman nom   ricepot obl rice

  '*The ricepot will be cooked rice in by the woman.*'

The markings *ang-*, *sa-*, *ug-* on a given NP in (2) vary but its semantic role (Agent, Location, etc.) is invariant. The verb root *luto'* 'cook' is also constant, but its voice morphology (*mag-,-on,* ...) varies with the choice of *ang* marked NP. Cebuano has four verbal "voice" forms: the *i*-form, not illustrated, is a catch-all voice, used when the *ang-* NP bears e.g. an instrumental, temporal, or (sometimes) benefactive relation to the verb. The *ang-* NP in these Ss is interpreted as definite. NP(S) in WA Type Ls is typically required to satisfy some sort of definiteness requirement. See Bell (1978).

---

preserve certain morphemes, that is, map them to themselves, just as they must preserve hierarchical structure. Case marking on NPs is typical. So identifying an NP in terms of its case markings or lexical identity may be just as "structural" as identifying an expression in terms of its hierarchical position in a derivation tree.

Regarding (1b), only the *ang-* NP may be relativized (Bell 1983:156). Relative clauses (RCs) in Cebuano have the form '...N *nga* S*, where S* is an S with its *ang-* NP missing. The head N is interpreted as bearing to the verb of S* whatever semantic role its *ang-* NP would have. Thus it is the verbal morphology (and not the invariable "linker" *nga*) which determines the role of the head N in the RC. So the S* for "the rice that the woman cooked", must be built from (2b). If it was built from (2a), that is, (2a) less its *ang* NP, it could only mean "the rice that cooked rice in a ricepot", violating the selection restrictions of the verb *magluto*.

Similarly limited to *ang* NPs is hosting Possessor Ascension (Bell 1983:193), Raising from Complement Clauses (Shibatani 1983:122) and, largely, launching floating quantifiers (Bell 1983:154). These same phenomena are among those limited to **NP(S)** in Tagalog (Schachter 1976, 1977, Kroeger 1993).

But properties like anteceding reflexives and controlling missing arguments of complement verbs, are not vested in **NP(S)** in Cebuano (or Tagalog). An antecedent of a reflexive in Cebuano (Bell 1983:161) is the NP which bears the same semantic role to the verb as does the *ang* NP when the verb is in the *mag-* (= "active" Bell p.205) form.[2] We adapt Schachter's term ACTORS for NPs identified in this partially semantic way.[3] Extensionally it is the *ang* NPs of active Vs and the *ni/sa* (= genitive) NPs of non-actives which antecede reflexives. Similarly it is the Actor NPs of "promise" verbs which control the missing argument of their verbal complement. In Tagalog (Schachter, Kroeger op cit) additional properties like expressing the addressee of imperatives are associated with Actors as opposed to **NP(S)**.

---

[2] I am being a bit pedantic here to stress that the terms "active", etc. are just cover terms for the morphologies given; they do not presuppose any similarity with clauses in, e.g., English, which are also called "active".

[3] So contrary to Schachter's usage, the *Actor* NP in a clause is simply whatever NP bears the same semantic role to the verb as the *ang* NP does to the active (= *mag-*) verb. Our usage does not imply that there is some common semantic or pragmatic factor that all verbs assign to their **NP(S)**. So our claims remain true even if Cebuano presents some verbs which select arguments with "weird" or heretofore unheard of semantic roles.

2.1 An Advancement/Demotion Analysis

Within a Relational Grammar (RG) framework, Bell provides an analysis of Cebuano which accounts for the array of facts above in terms of ADVANCEMENT RULES, thought of as conditions which allow representations of a certain sort. See Bell (1983:148–52) and Perlmutter and Postal (1983) for clear statements of the theoretical background assumed.

In sketch form, the structure of a basic clause in RG terms can be given by a finite matrix, the rows of which are called *strata*, while the columns represent relations that expressions bear to the clause. So the (i,j)th entry gives the relation that expression j bears to the clause in stratum i. The relations we are concerned with here are Predicate, the *Term* relations: Subject (1), Direct Object (2), Indirect Object (3); various non-terms relations like Benefactive, Instrument, Locative, and so forth. For each term relation n the Cho(n) relation discussed below.

In building a RN (relational network) for a basic clause it appears (Perlmutter and Postal 1984) that, despite a little latitude (Rosen 1984), the assignment of relations borne by expressions at the initial stratum is determined semantically — the Universal Alignment Hypothesis (UA). For non-term relations like Ben, Loc, Inst, etc. the assignment is perhaps transparent (though just how many locative relations we should distinguish is not obvious). For term relations the assignment is less obvious, but following "tradition", highly Agentive NPs will be 1s, Recipients with verbs of transmission will be 3s, etc.

RG constrains the allowable transitions from one stratum to the next. Advancement transitions sanction the reassignment of an expression at position n on the hierarchy 1 > 2 > 3 > non-term at a stratum i to a higher position n' stratum i+1. An n at stratum i is then demoted (=assigned the Cho(n) relation) at stratum i+1. Cho(n)s are not present in initial strata. The advancements Bell posits for Cebuano are:
2 → 1, 3 → 1, Loc → 1, Ben → 3, and x → 1, all non-terms x ≠ Cho(n), any n. Representing *Joe cooked rice in the pot* by (3) and *Rice was cooked in the pot by Joe* by (4) and ordering strata top down, (4) says that *rice* bears the 2 relation to the clause at stratum 1 and the 1 relation at stratum 2.

(3) P   1   2   Loc
     cook Joe rice in the pot

(4) P   1   2   Loc
     P   î   1   Loc
     cook Joe rice in the pot

The RNs for (2b) and (2c) in Cebuano extend that for (2a) in the same way that (4) extends (3): the initial stratum of (4) is the same as the only stratum of (3). So in (2c) the locative changes relation, becoming a 1 in the final stratum, demoting 'Joe' to Cho(1) as in (4). In these terms the 'split subject' facts can be stated as follows:

(5)   a.   Only final 1's relativize, launch quantifiers, raise from their clause, and host Possessor Ascension.
       b.   Antecedence of reflexives and control of missing arguments is determined at the initial stratum and preserved by advancement operations.

Note that the RNs in (3) and (4) do not express the voice (*mag-*,...) marking on the verb or the case marking on the NPs. Bell (1983:184–5) explicitly gives the additional, feature assigning, rules. (And of course to properly generate clauses, rules spelling out the actual morphology would be needed). Informally:

(6)   Mark the verb +*active* if no transition to 1 was used, mark it +*objective* if a 2 → 1 was used, +*locative* if 3 → 1 or Loc → 1 was used, and +*inst* if any other advancement rule was used. Thus,

       a.   The voice morphology on the verb is determined as a function of the Advancements that have taken place.
       b.   The case marking on NPs is determined as a function of the final grammatical relations they bear.

2.2 Malagasy Clause Structure

Malagasy is a WA Type language with a split in subject properties comparable to (but not identical with) that seen in the Philippine case. Compare (7) and (8) with Cebuano (2). Glosses on the verbal morphology and the constituent bracketing anticipate usage defined later.

(7) a. [N+an+tolotra (Nanolotra) vary (hoan)' ny
past+act+present rice (to)' the

vahiny t+amin'ny lovia vaovao] aho[4,5]
guest past+on'the dishes new 1sg(nom)

'I presented rice to the guests on the new dishes.'

b. [N+a+tolotra+ko (Natolotro) (hoan)' nyvahiny
past+pass$_1$+present-1sg(gen) (to)' theguests

t+amin'ny lovia vaovao] nyvary
past+with'the dishes new therice

'The rice was presented by me to the guests on the new dishes.'

c. [No+tolotra+ana+ko (Notolorako) vary t+amin'ny
past+offer+pass$_2$-1sg(gen) rice past+with'the

lovia vaovao] ny vahiny
dishes new the guests

'The guests were presented rice on the new dishes by me.'

---

[4]I use standard orthography (except for the use of +). The orthography–phonology correspondence is direct: o = /u/, j = /dz/, and word final -y = word internal -i = /i/. Stress is phonemic and with some exceptions penultimate except in words ending in "weak" syllables -*ka*, -*na*, -*tra* where it is antepenultimate.

[5]Most of my textual examples do not use the preposition. Malzac (1926) asserts its optionality for several other ditransitive verbs, and the double accusative paradigm is well established in Malagasy, both for *manome* 'give' and causatives of transitives. Either can be **NP(S)** with the passive -*ina* morphology.

d. [N+an+tolotra+(C)ana+ko (Nanolorako) vary (hoan)'
    past+act+present+circ-1sg(gen)   rice (to)'

    ny   vahiny] ny   lovia   vaovao
    the   guests the   dishes new

'The new dishes were presented rice on to the guests by me.'

As in (2) the semantic role of each NP (PP) in (7a) is the same in (7b-d). **NP(S)**, the NP whose semantic role covaries with the verbal morphology, is the last NP. (Sometimes PPs and S-level adverbials follow this NP, but other argument NPs do not). The correlation is given by: AGENT – *an-* in (7a), THEME – *a-* in (7b), RECIPIENT – *-ana* in (7c) and INSTRUMENT – *an-* ...-(C)*ana* in (7d). Rajemisa-Raolison (1971) cites 12 oblique semantic roles compatible with the morphology in (7d): BENEFACTIVE, CAUSE, REASON, PRICE, LOCATION, TEMPORAL, etc. In (8) it is *i-* which correlates with AGENT, *-ina* with THEME and *i-...-ina* with OBLIQUE, in this case BENEFACTIVE or CAUSE are natural.

(8) a. [N+i+vidy   ity   lobaka ity
        past+act+buy   this   shirt   this

        hoan-dRasoa]   Rabe
        for-Rasoa   Rabe

   'Rabe bought this shirt for Rasoa.'

   b. [No+vidi+ina+Rabe (=novidin-dRabe)   hoan-dRasoa]
       past+buy+pass+Rabe   for-Rasoa

       ity   lobaka ity
       this   shirt   this

   'This shirt was bought for Rasoa by Rabe.'

c. [N+i+vidi+ana+dRabe (= nividianan-dRabe) ity
    past+buy+circ+Rabe   this

    lobaka   ity]   Rasoa
    shirt   this   Rasoa

'Rasoa was bought this shirt by Rabe.'

2.2.1 Constituency

There is massive evidence that the bracketed strings in (7) and (8) form a constituent, one we shall theory neutrally call PREDPH (=PREDICATE PHRASE). Thus, in addition to position (and pronoun form) NP(S) in Malagasy can be identified as the NP sister to the PredPh. Despite theoretical differences, all those who have considered the issue of phrasal constituency (Keenan 1972, 1976, 1993; Randriamasimanana 1986; Guilfoyle, Hung and Travis 1989; Voskuil 1993); Dukes 1993; Law, this volume) agree that in (7) and (8) the bracketed strings are a constituent (though they may disagree as to its category). We note just some of the evidence which bears on our later claims.

2.2.2 Evidence from Quantifier and Particle Placement

The placement of the universal quantifiers *avokoa* and *daholo*, the yes-no question particle and negative polarity items all involve identifying the right PredPh boundary.

(9) M+i+jery   ny   mpianatra   daholo ny
     pres+act+watch the   student   all   the

     mpampianatra   (rehetra)
     teacher   all

'All the teachers watched the student(s).'
(*The teacher(s) watched all the students.)

Daholo and *avokoa* (which may replace *daholo* in (9)), occur only at the right edge of the PredPh and do not form a constituent with the following NP. They cooccur with the N level quantifier *rehetra* but may not replace it. Nor may they precede *ny mpianatra* 'the student(s)' in (9). Thus placing these quantifiers requires identifying the Pred-Ph boundary but does not motivate a rule of Quantifier Float. But interpretatively they only pertain to the relation between the PredPh and NP(S), as with the "floated" quantifiers in Cebuano and Tagalog.

The yes-no question particle *ve* (*va*) separates the Pred-Ph and NP(S):

(10) a.   M+i+vidy   mofo   eto   ve   izy   ireo?
         Pres+act+buy   bread   here   ?   they   (nom)

'Do they buy bread here?'

     b.   *Mividy ve mofo eto izy ireo?
         *Mividy mofo ve eto izy ireo?

     c.   No+sasa+ana+Rasoa (= nosasan-dRasoa)   ve   ireto
         past+wash+pass$_2$+Rasoa   ?   those

         akanjo   ireto?
         clothes   those

'Have those clothes been washed by Rasoa?'

     d.   An+sasa+ana+Rasoa (= anasan-dRasoa)   lamba   ve
         act+wash+circ+Rasoa   clothes   ?

         ity   savony   ity?
         this   soap   this

'Is this soap used by Rasoa to wash clothes?'

Negative expressions such as *not...even*, *no...longer*, *not...at all* frame the Pred-Ph:

(11)   Tsy   h(o)+amp+i+asa+ina+nay (hampiasainay)   intsony
       not   fut+cause+act+work+pass+us(excl)   longer

       ireto   fanaka   ireto
       these   furniture   these

'These pieces of furniture will no longer be used by us.'

2.2.3 Evidence From Relative Clauses, Embedded Questions, Raising Contexts and Nominalizations

PredPhs (regardless of verbal morphology) constitute a semantic unit: They are interpreted as properties which (possibly abstract) objects may have (or fail to have): the property expressed by the PredPh in (7a) holds of an object x iff x offered rice to the guests on the new dishes; that in (7b) holds of an object y iff y was presented by Rabe to the guests on the new dishes, etc. And PredPhs recur with this property denoting meaning in a very wide range of syntactic contexts besides that which defines them as PredPhs.

2.2.3.1 Relative Clauses

Relative clauses (RCs) are of the form **Det + N + (izay) + PredPh + (Det)**. *Izay* is the optional morphologically constant complementizer (≈ Cebuano *nga*). Deriving RCs from full Ss after *izay* we see that only NP(S) in Malagasy is relativizable. The parallel with the Philippine case is exact. Thus,

(12) a. ny   olona   (izay) n+i+vidy   ny   mofo
         the   person   that   past+act+buy   the   bread

   hoan'ny zaza
   for'the child

   'The person that bought the bread for the child.'

   b.   ny   mofo   (izay) no+vidi+n-dRabe
         the   bread   that   past+buy+pass-Rabe

   hoan'ny zaza
   for'the child

   'The bread that was bought by Rabe for the child.'

c. ny   zaza   (izay) n+ividi+anan-dRabe
    the   child that   past+buy+circ-Rabe

    ny   mofo
    the   bread

    'The child that was bought the bread for by Rabe.'

d. *ny   zaza   (izay) no+vidi+n-dRabe
    the   child that   past+buy+pass-Rabe

    ny   mofo
    the   bread

Replacing the verb in any of the relatives with those of any of the others forces a reinterpretation and usually ungrammaticality. (12d) results from (12c) by replacing the +circ verb with the one of (12b), uninterpretable since *ny mofo* 'the bread' lacks a semantic role, the child being understood to be what is bought.

2.2.3.2 Embedded Questions

Embedded questions are of the form [*izay* + (N) + **PredPh**]. Relevant examples are in (13).

(13) a. Tsy   fantatro   izay   [PredPh nividy   mofo
         not   known+1sg   comp   bought   bread

         hoan'ny   zaza]
         for'the   child

         'Who bought bread for the child isn't known by me.'

     b. Tsy   fantatro   izay   [novidin-dRabe
         not   known+1sg   comp   pst+buy+pass-Rabe

         hoan'ny   zaza]
         for'the   child

         'What was bought by Rabe for the child isn't known by me.'

c.   Tsy fantatro izay zaza [nividianan-dRabe mofo]
not known+1sg comp child pst+buy+circ-Rabe bread

'For/because of which child Rabe bought bread isn't known by me.'

2.2.3.3 Raising to Object Contexts

Samples of these constructions, [V + **NP**$_{acc}$ + **ho** + **PredPh** + **NP**$_{nom}$], are shown in (14).

(14) a.   Mihevitra an-dRasoa ho [$_{PredPh}$ n+i+vidy
thinks acc-Rasoa as past+act+buy

akanjo hoan'ny zaza] Rabe
clothes for'the child Rabe

'Rabe thinks Rasoa to have bought clothes for the child.'

b.   Mihevitra ny akanjo ho [no+vidi+n-dRasoa
thinks the clothes as past+buy+pass-Rasoa

hoan'ny zaza] Rabe
for'the child Rabe

'Rabe thinks the clothes as having been bought for the child by Rasoa.'

c.   Mihevitra ny zaza ho [n+ividi+anan-dRasoa
thinks the child as past+buy+circ-Rasoa

akanjo] Rabe
clothes Rabe

'Rabe thinks the children as having been bought clothes for by Rasoa.'

d.   *Mihevitra ny akanjo ho [n+i+vidy hoan'ny
    thinks the clothes as past+act+buyfor'the

    zaza Rasoa] Rabe
    child Rasoa Rabe

Deriving (14a-d) by NP raising from an "S" following *ho* we see that just NP(S) raises; (14d) is uninterpretable.

2.2.3.4 Tensed Nominalizations

[**Det** + **PredPh** + **(Det)**] constructions are displayed in (15).

(15) a.   Zava-dratsy sy maha+menatra ny
       thing-bad and cause+shame the

       m+an+galatra omby
       pres+act+steal cow

      'Stealing cows is shameful and a bad thing.'

b.   Tsy tia+n-dRakoto ny n+a+tao+nao azy
     not like+pass-Rakoto the past+pass+do+2sg(gen)3acc

      'Rakoto didn't like what you did to him.'

c.   izy no nitantara ny nitondran' ny
     she foc relate the past+carry+circ' the

     jirika sy ny namonjen-dRainilaimanga azy
     brigand and the past+save+circ-Rainilaimanga her

     'It was she who recounted the carrying-off by the brigand and the saving by Rainilaimanga of her.' [**IKM.47**]

d. Faly   amin'   izao   h+ananan'i   Soa
    happy   about'   this   fut+have(circ)'art Soa

    tokantrano   izao   izahay   mivady
    household   this   we(excl)   spouses

'We (husband and wife) are happy about Soa's future founding a household (=getting married).' **[PM]**

A **regularity** is observed: Determiners and **NP(S)**s are in complementary distribution. A PredPh combines with a Det to make an NP or with an **NP(S)** to make an S.

Note that non-verbal PredPhs like predicate nominals enter these same paradigms:

(16) a. Mp+i+solo   ahy   izy
         er+act+replace   1sg(acc)   3(nom)

'He is my replacement.'

b. ny   vehivavy   izay   mpampianatra
    the   woman   that   teacher

    t+any   Betafo
    past+there   Betafo

'The woman who was a teacher in Betafo.'

c. Nihevitra   azy   ho   mpamboly   ve   ianao?
    thought   him   as   planter   ?   you(nom)?

'Did you think he was a planter?'

d. ny   mpianatra   any
    the   students   there

2.2.4 Summary

(9) − (16) establish the constituency of the PredPh and show that **NP(S)** in Malagasy shares crucial properties with **NP(S)** in Cebuano/Tagalog. Relativization and Raising are limited to **NP(S)** and predicate level quantifiers are interpreted only as quantifying over **NP(S)**.

(**NP(S)**) also hosts Possessor Ascension in Malagasy, but recent observations suggest other NPs also do, though not Actors different from **NP(S)**s).

2.3 Case

Like its Philippine cousins, Malagasy pronouns distinguish three cases:

(17) Singular: 1　　2　　3

nom	aho	(h)ianao	izy
acc	ahy	anao	azy
gen	-ko	-nao	-ny

Plural:	1 excl	1 incl	2	3
nom	izahay	isika	(h)ianareo	izy
acc	anay	antsika	anareo	azy
gen	-nay	-tsika	-nareo	-ny

A plural interpretation in 3rd person may be forced by augmenting them with an overtly plural demonstrative like *ireo* or a kin term like *mivady* in *izy mivady* 'they husband & wife'. There are other, familiar, 2nd person forms like *ialahy* and *ise*. Pronouns in the **gen** series, like their full NP counterparts, are always bound to a host. Except for the monosyllabic *-ko* and *-ny* they may carry stress (phonemic in Malagasy) and so are not in general clitics. Case marking on full NPs in Malagasy is less explicit than in Cebuano/Tagalog. But pronouns occur where the corresponding full NPs do, whence pronominal replacement is a test for the case of an NP.

2.3.1 Nominative

This is the case of **NP(S)**. It has no distinctive markings other than the pronoun forms. Equally, Predicate nominals, (16a), adjectives and PPs combine solely with nominative NPs to form Ss. **nom** is never selected by Vs in forming PredPhs or by Ns or As in forming NPs and APs. In general it is structurally assigned rather than *selected* by heads (though two Preps select **nom** NPs: *noho* 'than, because of', and *afa-tsy* 'except', lit: 'free-not').

2.3.2 Accusative

Accusative case is distinguished by its pronoun series (**acc**). In addition proper nouns, some kin terms and, optionally, demonstratives are overtly marked accusative with *an-*. **acc** is selected by many Vs, (7a) and (8a), some Ns (below), a few Ps (*tahaka azy* 'like him') and a few as (*feno azy* 'full (of) it'). The definite article *ny* plus NP$_{acc}$ translates predicate possessives (*ny ahy* 'the me' = 'mine', as in *Mine is black, yours is white*).

2.3.3 Genitive

Genitive is the master case in Malagasy. It is the dominant case selected by Ns, As, and Ps. Vs divide on the issue. Vs which cannot take an argument in the genitive, as in (7a) and (8a), will be called **active** and those which can **non-active**, e.g. (7b,c,d) and (8b,c). Formally, genitive NPs are morphologically bound to their hosts by a complex process I call *n-bonding*, which we exemplify without defining (for lack of space).

2.3.3.1 n-bonding

This process combines a host H and an NP$_{gen}$ α to form an expression **nbond**(H,α) whose category depends on that of H. For example, if H is a Prep then the category of **nbond**(H,α) is PP. The precise form of **nbond**(H,α) depends on whether H is "weak" (= ends in *-na, -ka, -tra*, stressed on the antepenult) or not. Weak endings are dropped or modified according to whether NP$_{gen}$ is a pronoun, an augmented pronoun, a coordinate NP, or a full NP beginning with a vowel, the proper noun articles *Ra-* or *i-*, or the definite article *ny*. If H is not weak, a segment *-n-* is inserted between it and a non-pronominal NP$_{gen}$. NP$_{gen}$'s occur as Possessors of Ns, (18a), complements of transitive N's, (19), objects of most prepositions, (20), complements of most adjectives, (21), and Actor NPs with non-active predicates: (18b), (15b), (10c), (8b,c); (7b,c,d). (*nr* ⇒ *ndr* is phonologically regular in Malagasy).

(18) a. trano ity   trano+ n+Rabe (=tranon-dRabe) ity
         house this   house+ gen+Rabe   this

   'this house of Rabe's'

   b. a+roso+n+Rabe (aroson-dRabe)
       pass+serve+gen+Rabe

   'served by Rabe'

Note that Possessor's do not compete for position with Dets. They do compete somewhat with Adjectives modifying the head, and their joint presence is often felt as awkward even when acceptable. Adjectives may always follow and sometimes (e.g. inherent property Adjectives; Jan Voskuil p.c.) precede NP$_{gen}$:

(19) a. ny   trano+n-dRabe fotsy
         the   house+gen-R   white

   b. ny   trano   fotsi+n-dRabe
       the   house   white+gen-R

   c. ny   mpiasa+n-dRabetezitra
       the   worker+gen-R angry

   d. *ny   mpiasa tezi-dRabe
       the   worker angry+gen-R

In (20) we see both lexical Ns (*tahotra* 'fear' and *alahelo* 'sadness') and the derived N *fitiavana* 'love' (with *f-* replacing the tense marker) selecting two complements, **gen** and **acc** ones.

(20) a. ny   taho-dRabe
         the   fear+gen+Rabe

   'the fear Rabe has'

   b. ny   tahotra an-dRabe
       the   fear   acc-Rabe

   'the fear of unspec.for Rabe'

c. ny   taho-dRabe   azy
    the   fear+gen+Rabe+3sg(acc)

   'Rabe's fear of him.'

d. ny   alahelo+n-dRazay   an-drai+ny
    the   sadness+gen-R.   acc-father+her

   'Razay's sadness for her father'

e. ny   f+i+tia+van'ny   zaza   azy
    the   nom+act+love+circ+gen'the   child   him

   'the child's love of him'

Most prepositions (Rajemisa-Raolison (1971) lists 30+) select a genitive NP complement.

(21) a. amina
         'with'

   b. ami+ko
       'with me'

   c. amin-dRabe
       'with Rabe'

   d. amin'ny zaza
       'with the child'

   e. imason'ny vahoaka
       'in view of the populace'

   f. hatry ny ela
       'since the long time'

Also directional and measure expressions take **gen** complements: *roa kilometra atsimo+n'ny tanantsika* 'two kilometers to the South of our village'; *ny haben'ny trano* 'the size of the house'. And adjectives productively take **gen** complements usually with an Agent or Cause interpretation, but sometimes with an Experiencer one:

(22) a. *maty* 'dead'
matin'ny jirika 'killed by the brigands';

b. *jamba* 'blind'
jamban'ny vola 'blinded by money';

c. *marary* 'sick'
mararin'ny tazo 'sick from the fever;

d. *sasatra* 'tired'
sasatry ny dia 'tired from the trip';

e. *mamy* 'sweet'
mamiko 'sweet to me'.

2.3.4 Summary

Statistical counts of the distribution of NPs in the various cases support the grammaticality facts above.[6] In a text count based on two newspaper articles and three random selections from novels/short stories, there were a total of 1,237 NPs. Their case distribution is given in the table below and compared with a sample from English (also two newspaper articles and page selections from 3 novels) are given for comparison:

	number of NPs	nom	acc	gen
Malagasy	1,237	33.6%	23.0%	43.4%
English	1,345	38.9%	47.1%	14.1%

Table 1

Genitive is the most widely occurring in Malagasy, compared with accusative in English, nominative falling in second place in the two

---

[6]Tensed S complements, predicate nominals and appositives were not counted. Pronoun replacement was the major criterion for deciding the case of an NP. *of the town* was counted as genitive in *the mayor of the town*. The OPrep in strongly locative or temporal PPs, as in *John was ready in five minutes*, was not counted accusative. A conjunction of two NPs was counted twice (not three times). In Malagasy if the second was animate it was counted nominative since that is the "default" case it would have on pronoun replacement.

languages. Clearly the dominant expression of the Predicate + Argument relation in English is the Verb + Object one, whereas it is the Head + Possessor one in Malagasy.

2.4 Voice

We defined NON-ACTIVE (ACTIVE) Vs as ones which may (may not) take a genitive argument. By extension, affixes which form (non-)active Vs will also be called (non-)active. Other morphology distinguishes active from non-active Vs: Only active Vs mark present tense with *m*-; non-actives use ∅-. And only actives form agent nominalizations with *mp*- replacing the tense marker. In Malagasy, grammars active affixes are accompanied with the present tense *m*-, as Vs in Malagasy never occur untensed (as with English infinitives, gerunds or participles).

Active affixes are all prefixes: PRIMARY ones such as *i*- and *an*- (and a few others) build active Vs from roots. SECONDARY ones like *amp*- 'cause', *if*- 'reciprocal' and *aha*- 'abilitative/cause' prefix to other active prefixes. Tense marking prefixes to secondary affixes if present, otherwise to primary ones. There are two TERTIARY active prefixes, *iha*- 'become' and *iaraka* 'do/be together'. They combine with tensed active Vs forming tensed active Vs and carry their own tense markers. So such Vs are marked twice for tense.

Non-active morphology consists of CIRCUMSTANTIAL and OTHER. To form a circumstantial V add the suffix -*(C)ana* to an active verb, sometimes with reduplication of the syllable -*na*, shifting stress one syllable to the right (for Vs not stressed on their final syllable). The choice C of consonant is determined by the root, many roots not taking any. All other non-active morphology will be called PASSIVE, although the class is not morphologically or relationally uniform. The passive prefixes are *a*-, *voa*- and *tafa*-; suffixes are -*ina* and -*ana*. All these morphologies are similar to the active in that they combine directly with roots to form verbs. Thus in distinction to the circumstantial morphology they do not in general cooccur with active morphology.[7]

We observe finally that the semantic role assigned to the **NP(S)** of an active V is the same as that assigned to the genitive NP of any non-active

---

[7]There are two exceptions to this claim. First a very few suffix passives, clearly recognized as exceptional in descriptive grammars, are built on the active form: (*m*)*angataka* 'ask', *angatahina* 'be asked'. By contrast, causatives are productively passivized, as in (11) built from the active $h+amp+i+asa$ = *hampiasa* 'will use'.

form of that V. This role is Agent if the V takes one (but of course many do not).

2.5 Split Subjects in Malagasy

We first note a definiteness requirement (23) on **NP(S)** in Malagasy which differentiates it from Cebuano and Tagalog. Then we see that like those languages, control of missing arguments and antecedence of anaphors are vested in Actors rather than **NP(S)**.

Bare Ns in Malagasy do not occur as **NP(S)**, even with a cardinality quantifier.

(23) a. *Nijery   azy   olona   maro
         watched   him   people   many

   'Many people were watching him.'

   b. Nojeren'   olona   maro   izy
       watched+pass'   people   many   he

   'He was being watched by many people.'

   c. Nijery   azy   ny   olona maro
       watched   him   the   people many

   'Many people were watching him.'

   d. Nisy   olona   maro   nijery azy
       Existed   people   many   watch   him

   'There were many people watching him.'

So a semantically indefinite **NP(S)** must be overtly marked definite (23c) in distinction to Cebuano and Tagalog.

2.6 Reflexive & Reciprocal Antecedence in Malagasy

Reciprocals, expressed as verbal affixes, and bare N reflexives are locally anteceded by Actors: noms of active Vs, gens of non-active Vs.

(24) a. N+if+an+soratra (= Nifanoratra)   taratasy
         past+rec+act+write   letters

   Rabe   sy   Rasoa
   Rabe   and   Rasoa

   'Rabe and Rasoa wrote letters to each other.'

   b. N+if+an+soratra+ana+Rabe   sy
       past+rec+act+write+circ Rabe   and

   Rasoa (=nifanoratan-dRabe sy Rasoa)   ireto
   Rasoa   these

   taratasy   ireto
   letters   these

   'These letters were written to each other by Rabe and Rasoa.'

   c. ireto   taratasy   (izay)   nifanoratan-dRabe
       those   letters   (that)   wrote+to+each+other+by+Rabe

   sy   Rasoa   ireto
   and   Rasoa   those

   'Those letters that were written to each other by Rabe and Rasoa.'

In (24a) **NP(S)** *Rabe sy Rasoa* antecedes the reciprocal affixes on the verb, but in (24b) it is the genitive Agent Phrase which is the semantic antecedent. The **NP(S)** in (24b) is 'those letters'. It is replaceable by a nominative pronoun, takes question particles in front of it, and relativizes as in (24c).

(25) a. M+an+vono (=mamono) tena$_i$ hoan'ny zanaka
         pres+act+kill   self   for'the children

         ny   ray aman-dreny   rehetra$_i$
         the   parents   all

   'All parents kill themselves for the children.'

   b. Amonoan'ny ray aman-dreny rehetra$_i$ tena$_i$
       kill+circ'the parents   all   self

       ny   zanaka$_j$ (j ≠ i)
       the   children

   Same meaning as (24a).

In the active (25a) **NP(S)** 'all parents' antecedes the reflexive *tena* 'self'. But in (25b), (Manaster-Ramer (1992)), the antecedent is the genitive Agent. **NP(S)** is *ny zanaka* 'the children' which bears a benefactive relation to the circumstantial predicate and cannot be interpreted as antecedent. The Patient here just happens to be reflexive. It could be replaced by any (animate) accusative NP. Here are a few other examples which show non-nominative Actor antecedence in somewhat different contexts.

(26) ny   antony izay tsy
      the   reason that not

      Ø+an+haja+ana+Rabe (=anajan-dRabe$_i$)   self
      pres+act+respect+circ+Rabe   tena$_i$

   'The reason that Rabe does not respect himself.'

(27) a. M+an+doka   tena$_i$ ny   mpianatra tsirairay
         pres+act+flatter self   the   student   each

   'Each student flatters himself.'

b. | Fatatra | loatra | ny | f+an+doka+n'ny |
    | extreme | too | the | nom+act+flatter+circ'the |

   | mpianatra | tsirairay_i | tena_i |
   | student | each | self |

'Each student's flattering himself was too extreme.'

These examples are comparable to the Philippine anaphora pattern. But (23) blocks the simplest cases:[8]

---

[8]But more must be said to account for the pattern below:

i. a. | ?Novonoin-dRabe | ny | tena+ny |
       | kill+pass-Rabe | the | self+his |

    b. | ??Novonoin'ny | miaramila | rehetra | ny | tena+ny |
       | kill+pass' the | soldiers | all | the | self+their |

NP(S) *ny tena+ny* 'the self+his' is definite. (i.a) is less natural than the active (24a) but not ungrammatical. See Randriamasimanana (1986). (i.b) with a quantified antecedent is less good than (i.a). But in contrastive contexts like (ii) the definite reflexive seems good (but more extensive consultant work is needed here):

ii. | Derain'ny | olona | rehetra_i | ny | ray |
    | praise+pass'the | person | all | the | father |

   | aman-dreni+ny_i | sy | ny | tena+ny_i |
   | and-mother+his | and | the | self+his |

'His_i parents and himself_i are praised by each person_i.'

The judgmental problems here concern the binding relation, not absolute grammaticality. NPs of the form *ny tena +NP[gen]* 'the self of NP' are used emphatically and need not be bound:

(28) a. Namono   tena   Rabe
         killed(act) self   Rabe

   'Rabe killed himself.'

   b.   *Novonoin-dRabe   tena
        killed(pass)-Rabe self

2.7 Control

Control in Malagasy is studied in Law (this volume). Here we just illustrate that, like anteceding anaphors, control is vested in NP_{nom}s of active Vs and NP_{gen}s of non-active ones.

(29) a. N+i+tsahatra   n+an+doko (nitsaha-nandoko)
         past+act+stop   past+act+paint

         ny   trano   Rabe
         the   house   Rabe

   'Rabe stopped painting the house.'

---

iii. Ekena   fa   ho   soa   tokoa   raha   tonga   mamangy
      agreed   that   fut   good   very   if   arrive   visit

      any   Sahavato ny   tenan'ny   Profesora   Zafy   Albert
      there   Sahavato the   self'the   Prof.   Zafy   Albert

   'To be sure it would be very good if Prof. Zafy Albert himself comes visit Sahavato.' [**LK** 20/10/92]

iv. A^{toa}Bill   Clinton   no   nofidiny
      Mr. Bill   Clinton   foc   chosen+by+them

   'It was Bill Clinton who was chosen by them.'

      Miarahaba   azy   ny   tenako
      Congratulate   him   the   self+my

   'My humble self (Ross Perot) congratulates him.' [**LK** 12/13/92]

b. N+a+tsaha-dRabe   no+loko+ina   ny   trano
    past+pass+stop-Rabe past+paint+pass the   house

'The house was stopped being painted by Rabe.'

In both Ss *Rabe* controls the missing argument of 'paint'. *ny trano* 'the house' is clearly **NP(S)** in (29b). For example it takes questions particles, (30a) and relativizes (30b):

(30) a. Natsaha-dRabe   nolokoina   ve   nytrano?

'Was the house stopped being painted by Rabe?'

b. ny   trano   izay   natsaha-dRabe   nolokoina

'the house that was stopped being painted by Rabe.'

A related paradigm is given in (31) where 'paint the house' is nominalized, taking the definite article *ny*, and behaving grammatically as an argument of 'stop'. In particular it occurs as **NP(S)** in the passive, (31b), from which *ny* cannot be omitted preserving grammaticality:

(31) a. N+i+tsahatra   ny   n+an+doko
         past+act+stop   the   past+act+paint

         ny   trano   Rabe
         the   house   Rabe

'Rabe stopped painting the house.' = (29a)

b. N+a+tsaha-dRabe   ny   n+an+doko
    past+pass+stop-Rabe the   past+act+paint

    ny   trano
    the   house

Same meaning as (31a).

Rabe is the painter in both (31a,b). **NP(S)** in (31b) is *ny nandoko ny trano* – it takes question particles and clefts:

(32) a. Natsaha-dRabe ve ny nandoko ny trano?

'Has Rabe stopped painting the house?'

b. Ny   n+an+doko   ny   trano
the   past+act+paint   the   house

no   natsaha-dRabe
foc   was+stopped+by+Rabe

'It was painting the house which was stopped (being done) by Rabe.'

Observe that genitive NPs of predicate nominals also control into such NP(S)s:

(33) a. Adidy+n+ny (=Adidin'ny) tsirairay   ny
duty+gen+the   each   the

m+an+aja   ireny fananam-pokonolona   ireny
pres+act+respect   those goods of the collectivity those

'Respecting the possessions of the group is everyone's duty.'
[T3]

b. Anjara+n'ny hafa   ny   m+an+angana
role+gen'the others   the   pres+act+pick

amim-   pitiavana   ny   potiky   ny
up with-   love   the   pieces+gen   the

maha-olona ao   amin'ny zazavavi+
personality there   from'the young women+

n'izao   tontolo   izao [E]
gen'this   world   this

'It is the role of others to pick up with love the pieces of the personality chez the "young women of this world".'

3. Predicate Building vs. Advancement

Here I pursue a Predicate Building (PB) approach, one that addresses what I consider to be some conceptual and empirical shortcomings of the RG one.

Conceptually, non-active Ss (RMs) in RG extend active ones by changing the relations that NPs bear to the Clause. So we may expect non-actives to differ from their actives in NP-level markings and clause level markings. But only the former is instantiated, e.g., no language forms passives by putting a particle at the beginning or end of an active S, or by modifying the intonation contour of the active, though Yes-No Question Formation, a properly clause level operation, routinely uses these options (Keenan 1985).

But most importantly, RG does not lead us to expect differences in the morphology of active and non-active verbs since the relation the verb bears to the clause is unchanged under advancements. We can, as Bell (1978,1983) does for Cebuano, observe correlations between verbal inflection and advancements, but the degree to which Cebuano satisfies the empirically non-trivial laws of RG would not change if verbs did not inflect at all for voice.

Furthermore, RG builds in a syntactic asymmetry between actives and non-actives (the latter extending the former) which seems to me not present in WA Type languages. We might expect that the more complex (non-active) forms would have a more restricted distribution. But by a variety of criteria the Malagasy (and I believe the Philippine) data do not conform to this expectation. I cite three instances of this disconformity.

3.1 Active/Passive Symmetries in Malagasy

First, as with Tagalog (Schachter, Kroeger) the major voice categories in Malagasy — actives, prefix passives, suffix passives, circumstantials — have their own imperative forms.

For example, the verbs in (7) [in order] have the following imperatives: *manolora* (act), *atolory, tolory, anolory*. So Imperative Formation treats all four types of verbs alike, rather than restricting its application to active verbs, which is largely the case in English. (But NB: *voa-* and *tafa-* passives lack imperative forms).

Second, genitive Actors present a frequency spectrum characteristic of core arguments, not classical chomeurs.

In German only 17.6% of passives present Agent Phrases (Stein 1979). The figures for English run from 13% to 20% (Svartvik 1966, Duskova 1971, Givon 1979). By contrast K&M (Keenan and Manorohanta, in prep) show that 60% of non-actives in Malagasy present overt Agent Phrases (a percentage comparable to that found by Shibatani (1988) for Cebuano). And this percentage is inaccurately low since many overtly agentless passives have their missing Agent controlled. Contexts like (29b) are common. Another case is the first conjunct in (34a,b), counted by K&M as agentless but whose Agent is clearly understood to be that of the second conjunct.

(34) a. A+tao+ko   fa   voa+jery sy
         pass+do+1sg(gen)   that pass+see and

         voa+dinika+nao (=voadinikao) tsara ireo
         pass+examine+2sg(gen)   good   those

         sary   teo
         pictures there

   'I think that those pictures there have been seen (by you) and examined well by you.' **[VR]**

b. araka   izao ahitana   sy   a hafantaranareo
    according that see+circ   and know+circ+2pl

    ahy izao
    me   that

   'according to that which is seen and understood by you of me.' **[VR.43]**

Third, empirically, voice morphology in Malagasy is not definable as a function of the advancement (or even revaluation) history of the clause. I touch here on two problems; the first has two parts.

3.1.1 Anomalies in Malagasy Active/Passive Morphology

(i) Active morphology which varies in the absence of revaluations (and so advancements in particular), cannot, therefore, be given as a function of revaluation history.

(ii) In basic cases, active and passive morphology are in complementary distribution, so neither is built from the other. But circumstantial morphology is added to active morphology.

With respect to (i), we have already seen active Vs built from *i-* and *an-* (there are two other primary active morphologies and a very few active roots). In basically all cases the Ss they build present no argument changing operations. Note that many *i-* verbs are transitive (and thus not unaccusastive): *mikapoka* 'beats', *mifidy* 'chooses', *miorina* 'builds'. And many *an-* verbs are intransitive — *mandainga* 'tell lies', *mandihy* 'dance', *mandeha* 'go', *mangovitra* 'shudder', *mandrivotra* 'be windy' — so *an-* cannot be identified as a causative operator.

The more positive point here is that the argument structure (number, case marking, and semantic role of the arguments) of an active V is predictable from the voice morphology plus root and so must be handled independently of revaluation history. And doing this explicitly is just the Predicate Building approach.

As far as (ii) goes, many examples show that affixal active and passive verbs are each built by directly affixing the root. Neither is derived by affixing the other, even though the most widespread passive affixes *-ina* and *-ana*, being suffixes, do not compete for position with the active prefixes. So active and passive Vs are morphologically independent. But in RG active and (anti-)passives clauses are not: the RN for the latter includes that for the former. So active and (anti-) passive Vs have the same quantity of voice morphology but differ in number of advancements (0 vs.1). Again voice morphology is not correlated with revaluation history.

Passive versus circumstantial Vs present the opposite problem. The Ss they build exhibit one advancement each in RG. But the circumstantial V retains the active morphology and thus has two voice affixes, while the passive only has one. Again the presence of voice morphology fails to correlate with advancement history.[9] Note that circumstantial Vs are not blindly derived from actives, they must see their internal structure. First, whether to reduplicate *na* and which initial consonant (if any) to use depends on the root, not the active prefix:

---

[9] Morphology - advancement mismatches also occur in Cebuano. For each aspect (durative, volitional, potential) in the Realis Mode, the locative morphology suffixes *-an* to the objective form of the verb (Bell 1983:205).

(35)	root	active (pres)	circ (pres)
tao 'do'	manao	anaovana
ome 'give'	manome	anomezana
lefa 'send'	mandefa	andefasana
didy 'cut'	mandidy	andidiana
leha 'go'	mandeha	andehanana

And second, active Vs built from tertiary affixes — ones that go outside the tense marker — do not have circumstantial forms. Contrast second order (m)aha 'cause/abilitative' with third order (m)iha 'inchoative':

(36) a. tsara   mahatsara(act)   ahatsarana (circ)
         good   make good   circ. of making good

   b.   mihatsara (act)   *ihatsarana (circ)
        become good   circ. of becoming good

Similarly from *vizana* 'tired' we have *ahavizanana* 'circumstance of tiring' but *ihavizanana* 'circ. of becoming tired'. Thus circumstantial verb formation must also be able to see the active prefix as well as the root.

3.1.2 Advancement Morphology

The second problem concerns advancements. The advancements n → 1, n = 2, 3, Inst, have no consistent morphological correlate, and the common morphologies correlate with two or more advancements. We have seen cases of passive 2 → 1 correlated with *a-*, *-ina* and even *-ana* (9c), and *voa-* (34). And there are at least two cases where passive 2 → 1 correlates with circumstantial morphology.

First, 2 to 1 advancement with reciprocal verbs triggers circumstantial morphology, as in (24c). Second, there are several roots which do not take passive affixes but use a circumstantial form instead:

(37) a.   M+i+anatra   teny   vahiny   Rabe
          pres+act+study   languages foreign   Rabe

'Rabe studies foreign languages.'

b. ny   teny   vahiny   izay   i+anar+an-dRabe
    the   languages foreign that   act+study+circ-Rabe

'*The foreign languages that are studied by Rabe.*'

Second, many passive Vs in Malagasy are simply roots, as *haino* 'be listened to' in (38). The active V in (38b) is built by prefixing *i-* to the passive, so the morphological inclusion relation is the opposite of the syntactic one on an RG analysis.

(38) a. Haino+ko   izy
          listen-to+1sg(gen)   he(nom)

   '*He is being listened to by me.*'

      b. M+i+haino   azy   aho
          pres+act+listen   him(acc)   1sg(nom)

   '*I am listening to him.*'

Keenan & Manorohanta (in prep.) found that 30% of the 1,829 occurrences of passives in their sample were root passives, with meanings like 'understood', 'captured', 'seen', 'heard', 'listened to', 'sent', 'damaged', 'cured', 'sought', 'caught', 'broken', 'perceived from afar', 'defeated', 'is able to'. (But affixal passives outnumber root passives by about 10 to 1 when number of distinct verbs as opposed to occurrences of verbs is considered).

Equally, most verbs in Malagasy are built from roots plus affixes and the semantic interpretation of such verbs is expected to be some function of those of the root and the affixes used (compositionality being the only means we have of accounting for how we understand novel utterances. We understand what their parts mean and how things built in that way take their interpretation as a function of their parts). And this says that we should interpret the verb in (38b) as a function of its root, *haino*, which is a passive form. One might consider taking (38a) as basic and deriving (38b) by an Antipassive rule. But then by UA the genitive NP should be the 1 and the nominative the 2, vitiating the Malagasy particular generalizations that only final 1's relativize, final 1's are drawn from the **nom** pronominal series, etc.

Thus many morphologies, including none at all, correlate with passive 2 → 1. Moreover many roots accept 3 or even 4 of these morphologies. So choosing among them involves more than simply knowing which advancements have taken place. Here is one rather widespread paradigm.

(39) a.   m+i+kapoka   ny   alika   amin'ity
        pres+act+beat   the   dog   with'this

        langilangy   ity   Rabe
        stick   this   Rabe

       'Rabe beats the dog with this stick.'

   b.   No+kapoh+in-dRabe   ny   alika
        past+beat+pass-Rabe   the   dog

       'The dog was beaten by Rabe.'

   c.   ny   langilangy   (izay)   n+a+kapoka   ny   alika
        the   stick   (that)   past+pass+beat   the   dog

       'The stick that the dog was beaten with.'

In (39b) *-ina* correlates with 2 → 1 as in (8b). But that *a-* marks Inst → 1 in (39c) is surprising. In many other cases, (7d) and (40), Inst → 1 triggers circumstantial morphology:

(40) a.   manasa   lamba   amin'ity   savony   ity   aho
        wash(act)   clothes   with'this   soap   this   I

       'I wash clothes with this soap.'

   b.   an+sasa+ana+ko (=anasako)   lamba   ity   savony   ity
        act+wash+circ+1sg(gen)   clothes   this   soap   this

       'This soap is washed clothes with by me.'

But in fact the example in (39c) is typical. Dez (1980) even calls the *a-* voice "Instrumental". My own judgment is that it is best to think of **NP(S)** in an *a-* clause as a kind of "intermediary" in an action. That will be the Theme with a verb of transmission but in many other cases an Instrument. Roots like *sasa* in (39) which don't take *a-* use the circumstantial form when the instrument is **NP(S)**.

Finally, there are other cases where a given morphology correlates with more than one type of advancement: In (7c) passive *-ana* licensed 3 → 1, but in (9c) and several other cases it correlates with 2 → 1. Also circumstantial morphology sometimes licenses 3 → 1:

(41) a.   N+i+laza   izany   t+amin-dRabe   aho
            past+act+say   that   past+to-Rabe   1sg(nom)

'I told that to Rabe.'

b.   N+i+laza+ana+ko (=nilazako)   izany   Rabe
     past+act+say+circ+1sg(gen)   that   Rabe

'Rabe was told that by me.'

These and other data show that overall we have little predictability of the verbal morphology merely given the advancement history of a clause. So to generate verbal clauses we need independent access to the verb root and morphology. But given that alone we have excellent predictability (see fn. 5) of the argument structure of the clause; viz. given the verbal morphology and root we can generate the range of nuclear clauses intended to be accounted for by active clauses + advancements in RG, so it seems to me that the independent apparatus of advancement rules is unnecessary. This, at least, is the Predicate Building approach taken here.

3.2   A Predicate Building [PB] Analysis of Voice in Malagasy

PB does not posit any direct syntactic relation among e.g. the Ss in (7). They are similar in that all are formed by combining a PredPh with an NP_{nom}. Their differences all lie within the PredPh. PB treats the voice morphology as functions which build PredPhs, beginning with roots. So we give the form and interpretation of a PredPh as a function of that of the root it is derived from. In general (Keenan 1980) the only semantic relations which obtain between active and non-active Ss are those determined by their PredPhs. Here we show that antecedence of reflexives by NP(S) in actives and NP_{gen} in non-actives falls out of the semantics we give for PredPhs without reference to the notion of subject (at any level).

Syntactically, we treat active transitive verbs like *mividy* 'buys' (ignoring tense, always) as expressions which combine first with an accusative NP, NP_{acc} to form a PredPh, which in turn combines with an NP_{nom} to form an S. Extending standard subcategorization notation to include subjects and writing it on a single line we note this category as

S[NP$_{nom}$,NP$_{acc}$]. So the thing it combines with first to form a constituent is written on the right, and the constituent structure of *nividy azy izy* 'He bought it' is given by [[*nividy azy*] *izy*]. 'PredPh' itself now just abbreviates S[NP$_{nom}$], the category of expressions which combine with nominative NPs to yield Ss. Passive *vidina* 'is bought' has category S[NP$_{nom}$,NP$_{gen}$] as it combines first with a genitive NP to form a PredPh. And circumstantial *ividianana* in (8c) has category S[NP$_{nom}$,NP$_{acc}$,NP$_{gen}$]. As a cover term we write P$_n$, *n-place predicate*, for expressions which combine with n NPs in appropriate cases to form an S.

The P$_3$ category of circumstantial *ividianana* 'is bought for by' already makes a somewhat surprising prediction: combining it with an NP$_{gen}$ yields an expression of category S[NP$_{nom}$,NP$_{acc}$], ordinary transitive verbs. We expect then to be able to coordinate active transitive Vs and agented circumstantial forms of transitive Vs, and we can. ((42c) is adapted from a first grade reader!)

(42) a. Nividianako   ilay   boky ianao
         bought(circ)+1sg(gen)   that   book you

   'You were bought that book by me.'

   b. Namaky   ilay   boky ianao
       read(act)   that   book you

   'You read that book.'

   c. Nividianako   sy   namaky
       bought(circ)1sg(gen)   and   read(act)

       ilay   boky   ianao
       that   book   you

   'You [[were bought+for by me and read] that book.]'

(43) a. Nanondroako   ilay   toerana ianao
         past+point+out(circ)+1sg(gen)   that   place   you

   'You were indicated that place by me.'

b. Nanondroako   sy   nijery
    past+point+out(circ)+1sg(gen) and   saw(act)

    ilay   toerana ianao
    that   place   you

'You [[were indicated by me and saw] that place.]'

Semantically we interpret P_ns as n-ary relations, R_ns. R_1s, one place relations, are functions mapping objects (possibly quite abstract ones) from the domain D of discourse into {**True,False**}. R_2s are functions mapping objects to R_1s and R_3s are functions mapping objects to R_2s. So we represent "a bought b" compositionally in Malagasy as **nividy**(b)(a). (Bracketing is always to the left: F(y)(x) means (F(y))(x) – F is a one place function whose value at y is a function taking x as argument. We interpret common nouns as sets of objects.

NPs are interpreted as generalized quantifiers (GQs), enriched shortly to account for semantic roles like AGENT. GQs are functions mapping n+1 ary relations to n-ary ones. In fact here we can restrict NP_{nom}s to just take P_1s as arguments, mapping them into {**T,F**}. For example (**every boy**) maps **laugh** to **T** iff **laugh**(b) = **T**, all b $\in$ **boy**. (We write denotations over a given domain D in boldface. (**exactly two boys**)(**laugh**) = **T** iff {b $\in$ **boy** | **laugh**(b) = **T**} has exactly two members.

We classically think of a proper noun like *Mary* as directly denoting an object, say m, in the domain D, and an S like *Mary laughed* would have the truth value **laugh**(m). But to interpret NPs like *neither Mary nor Sue*, *Mary and some student*, *everyone but Mary*, etc. we treat proper nouns as GQs, ones called *individuals*. Given an object m $\in$ D, the *individual* I_m *generated by* m is that GQ mapping each P_1 function **p** to whatever truth value **p** maps m to. A function F from P_1 denotations into {**T,F**} is an *individual* iff F = I_m for some m $\in$ D. We interpret proper nouns as individuals, obtaining the same truth values as the classical approach in simple cases but yielding correct interpretations for complex NPs built from proper nouns as well.

NP_{acc}s and NP_{gen}s can be restricted to map R_2s to R_1s and R_3s to R_2s. E.g. accusative **an-dRabe** maps an R_2 like **see** to that R_1 true of an object d iff 'd sees Rabe', i.e. iff **see**(r)(d) = **T**. (**every boy**)$_{acc}$(**see**)(d) = **T** iff for each b $\in$ **boy**, **see**(b)(d) = **T**, that is iff 'd sees every boy'.

Generally we are not concerned here with which functions a given NP denotes, the one exception being the reflexive pronoun *tena*. It combines with P_2s to form P_1s and denotes that function **self** mapping each binary relation F to that unary relation **self(F)** which maps each object d ∈ D to the truth value F(d)(d). Thus the compositional representation for 'Rabe praises himself' is as in (44). It is true iff (**praise Rabe**) is true of Rabe.

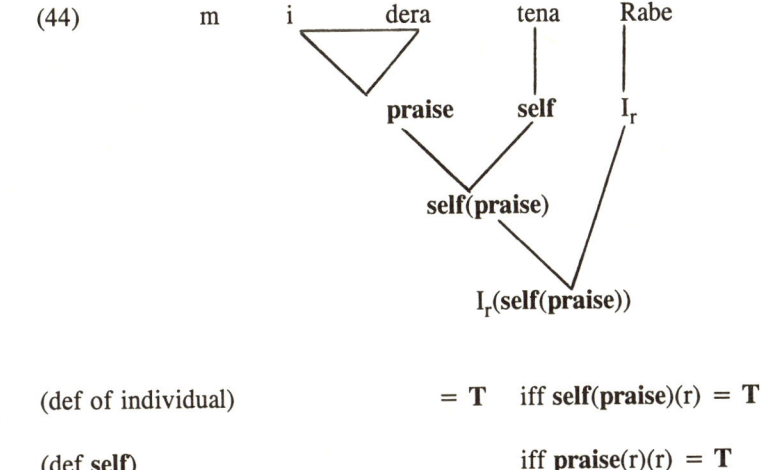

(44)

```
        m    i    dera      tena      Rabe
                    ▽         |         |
                  praise     self       I_r
                     ▽_____/        /
                  self(praise)        /
                        ▽_____/
                     I_r(self(praise))
```

(def of individual)   = T   iff self(praise)(r) = T

(def **self**)   iff praise(r)(r) = T

3.2.1 Roots and Affixes

We illustrate the analysis for one active, one passive, and one circumstantial case. See Rajaona (1972) and Rabenilaina (1993) and Abinal et Malzac (1976) for empirically extensive studies. Consider the active S *nividy ny boky Rabe* 'Rabe bought the book'. *nividy ny boky* 'bought the book' is a P_1 of category $S[NP_{nom}]$. Semantically it is true or false of objects like Rabe. The P_2 *nividy* 'buy' has category $S[NP_{nom}, NP_{acc}]$. The active morphology *i-* combines with the root *vidy* to form a P_2, so semantically it can denote a function **I** which maps root denotations to R_2s, possible P_2 denotations. We represent the denotation of the root *vidy* as a set **VIDY** of ordered pairs. **I** maps this set to a P_2 function which places semantic role conditions on its arguments. Specifically, for R any set of pairs (such as **VIDY**), and x and y elements of D,

(45) I(R)(y)(x) = **True** iff THEME(y,R) & AGENT(x,R) & R(x,y)

So THEME, AGENT, etc. are relations between objects and relations denoted by roots. THEME(y,R) says that y bears the THEME relation to R. *i-* only combines with roots so the domain of **I** may be given by listing. It may contain relations with semantic roles different from {AG,TH}. For each distinct sort of argument, conditions analogous to those in (45) must be given. A compositional representation for 'Rabe bought the book' is:

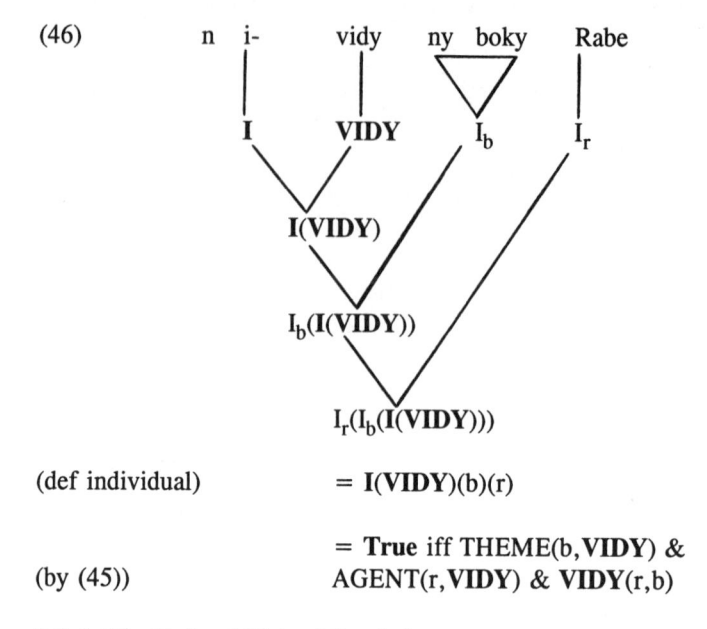

(46)

```
    n    i-      vidy     ny boky    Rabe
         |        |          ∨         |
         I       VIDY        I_b       I_r
          \____ ____/       /         /
              ∨            /         /
           I(VIDY)        /         /
              _____ /         /
                    ∨             /
                I_b(I(VIDY))     /
                    _____ /
                         ∨
                   I_r(I_b(I(VIDY)))
```

(def individual)   = I(VIDY)(b)(r)

                        = **True** iff THEME(b,VIDY) &
(by (45))   AGENT(r,VIDY) & VIDY(r,b)

3.2.2 The Role of Voice Morphology

Like *i*-, the role of voice morphology is to build argument structure:

(47) **Syntactically**, voice morphology builds predicates, determining the number and case of the NPs they combine with. **Semantically**, voice morphology assigns semantic roles to the arguments of the relation which interpret the predicates it builds.

Note that it is the compositional interpretation which associates NP denotations with the arguments of the verb, the verbal morphology just tells us what semantic roles those arguments have.

Now consider the passive morphology *-ina*. It combines with the root *vidy* to form *vidina* of category S[NP$_{nom}$,NP$_{gen}$]. The argument of **INA** is, as with **I**, the root denotation **VIDY**. So both active and passive morphology are functions on the same roots rather than the passive being a function of the active. The value of **INA** is given generally for arguments of this type in (48) and compositional interpretation illustrated in (49):

(48)   **INA**(R)(a)(b) = **True** iff AGENT(a,R) & THEME(b,R) & R(a,b)

(49)   no- vidy -in- drabe ny boky

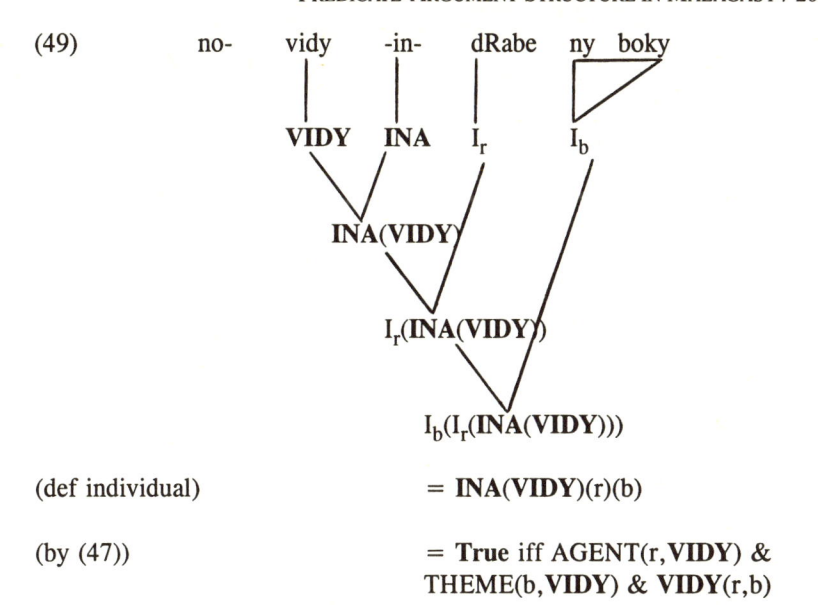

```
        VIDY   INA   Iᵣ    Iᵦ
           \   /    /    /
           INA(VIDY)    /
              \       /
              Iᵣ(INA(VIDY))
                   \
                   Iᵦ(Iᵣ(INA(VIDY)))
```

(def individual)   = INA(VIDY)(r)(b)

(by (47))   = **True** iff AGENT(r,VIDY) &
                            THEME(b,VIDY) & VIDY(r,b)

The last lines in (46) and (49) are logically equivalent, differing only by order of conjuncts. The equivalence falls out of the independently assigned interpretations to roots, affixes, and the NPs rather than any syntactic relation between the Ss themselves. Keenan (1980) notes that actives and agented passives typically fail to be paraphrases when the arguments are not of the individual sort. *No editor read every poem* is not logically equivalent to *Every poem was read by no editor*.

The reflexive pronoun *tena* has category NP_{acc} and so combines with P_2s (= $S[NP_{nom}, NP_{acc}]$) to form P_1s (= $S[NP_{nom}]$) but will not combine with P_1s (It is not an NP_{nom}). Keenan (to appear) provides a syntax and semantics for the Batak reflexive which, like those of Cebuano and Tagalog, does combine with P_1s.

3.2.3 Circumstantial Verbs

We treat predicate level PPs as Predicate Modifiers (PredMods). They denote restricting functions mapping R_1s, P_1 denotations, to R_1s. So *sing in the park* denotes **(IN THE PARK)(SING)**. (F is *restricting* iff for each P_1 denotation **P** and each object b, F(P)(b) = **T** implies P(b) = **T**). PredMods in English are in general restricting: If Joe sang in the park, he sang; if he bought a shirt for Sue, he bought a shirt. Preps themselves denote functions mapping NP denotations to PredMod denotations. Call this set of functions Den(Prep). Observe the compositional interpretation of (50) 'Rabe bought the hat for Rasoa':

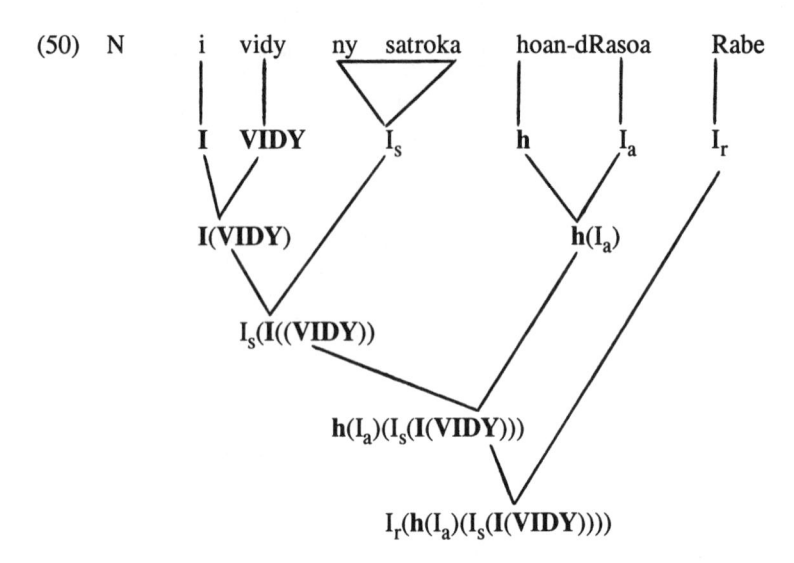

(50)

```
N      i    vidy    ny  satroka    hoan-dRasoa    Rabe
       I    VIDY      I_s             h    I_a     I_r
           I(VIDY)                    h(I_a)
            I_s(I((VIDY)))
                   h(I_a)(I_s(I(VIDY)))
                          I_r(h(I_a)(I_s(I(VIDY))))
```

Consider the circumstantial form *ividianana* 'is bought for by'. Syntactically circumstantial *-ana* maps the pair (*i-*, *vidy*) to *ividanana* of category S[NP$_{nom}$,NP$_{acc}$,NP$_{gen}$]. So *-ana* sees both the prefix and the root, (35). The denotation **ANA** of *-ana* is given in (51). F,G, and H range over GQs and ACT is any active prefix denotation:

(51) ANA(ACT,R)(F)(G)(H) = True iff $\exists p \in$ Den(Prep), F(p(H)(G(ACT(R)))) = T

(52) gives the compositional interpretation of the circumstantial 'Rasoa was bought the shirt for by Rabe'. It differs from (50) only in quantifying over the Prep denotation where (50) has **h**. So (50) entails (52) but not conversely. In (52) we just know that Rasoa stands in some Prep type relation to the buying of the hat, but we don't know which relation. And this is empirically correct, Rasoa could have been the cause or even the instrument of the buying in (52) but not in (50). So contra Bell (1983) and Guilfoyle, Hung and Travis (1992), (52) is not ambiguous but merely unspecified as to which relation Rasoa bears to the action of Rabe's buying.

(52)

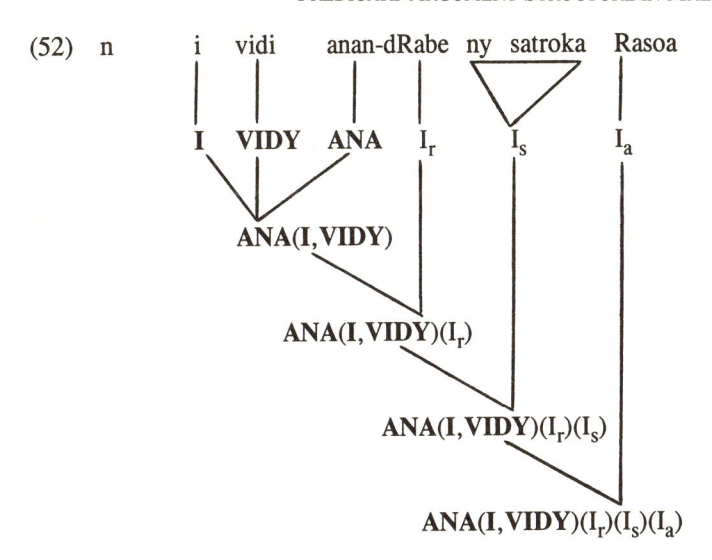

```
n    i    vidi    anan-dRabe   ny satroka   Rasoa
|    |     |         |              △          |
I   VIDY  ANA       I_r            I_s         I_a
 \   |   /
  ANA(I,VIDY)
        \
         ANA(I,VIDY)(I_r)
              \
               ANA(I,VIDY)(I_r)(I_s)
                    \
                     ANA(I,VIDY)(I_r)(I_s)(I_a)
```

= T iff ∃p ∈ Den(Prep), $I_r(p(I_a)(I_s(\text{ANA}(I(\text{VIDY})))) = T$

So the syntax and semantics of the circumstantial suffix has been given with enough adequacy to capture the basic semantic relation between Ss like (50) and their circumstantial correspondents (52). And coupled with the independently given semantics for *tena* it predicts **nom** NP antecedence for reflexives in actives (53) and **gen** NP antecedence in circumstantials, (54). Here the child is I_z and Rabe is I_r:

(53) a. M+an+vono (mamono) tena   hoan'ny zanaka Rabe
          pres+act=kill   self   for'the child   Rabe

'Rabe kills himself for the child.'

b. $I_r(h(I_z)(\text{self}(\text{AN}(\text{VONO}))))$

(def individual)   = $(h(I_z)(\text{self}(\text{AN}(\text{VONO}))))(r)$

($h(I_z)$ is restricting)   ⇒ $\text{self}(\text{AN}(\text{VONO}))(r)$ *'Rabe kills himself.'*

(54) a. an+vono+ana+Rabe (= amonoan-dRabe) tena
         act+kill+circ+Rabe   self

   ny   zanaka
   the   child

   Same meaning as (53a)

   b. ANA(AN,VONO)(I$_r$)(self)(I$_z$)

   = T iff ∃p ∈ Den(Prep), I$_r$(p(I$_z$)(self(AN(VONO))))= T

(def individual)   iff ∃p ∈ Den(Prep), (p(I$_z$)(self(AN(VONO))))(r)= T

(p(I$_a$) is restricting) ⇒ self(AN(VONO))(r) *'Rabe kills himself.'*

For reasons of space this will have to suffice to show what a Predicate Building approach looks like. We conclude by resuming some of the advantages of a PB approach.

3.3 Summary

First, verbal morphology has a non-trivial role: it determines the argument structure of predicates (47).

Second, PB accounts for the syntactic and interpretative independence of actives and passives. But circumstantials are partially dependent on the actives. The interpretation of a circumstantial verb refers to the value of the active affix applied to the root, that is, to the interpretation of the active verb.

Third, with respect to lexical exceptions on a PB approach we must give the domains and values (= define) of the twenty odd voice functions *i-*, *an-*, *a-*, etc. The fact that the roots of transitive Vs like *mianatra* 'study' and *miorina* 'build' do not lie in the domains of any of the passive functions is unremarkable – many roots do not lie there. But on an RG (or other standard) approach these facts are "exceptions" to supposedly structure dependent rules. Similarly the existence of suppletive passive forms is unremarkable on a PB approach. For example, one might expect the passive of *mitondra* 'carry' to be *tondraina* or *atondra*, or *tondrana*, but in fact it is *entina*, an *-ina* form built from a different root. In RG the rules spelling out rules *mitondra*[+passive] will have to have an exception (as will several other verbs). On a PB approach *entina* is listed as a root passive in the lexicon, its relation to *mitondra* being merely semantic, as in *buy* and *sell* in English. More could be said here, but the general point is clear.

References

Abinal, Frédéric G.P. & V. Malzac. 1987 [1888]. *Dictionnaire Malgache-Francais*. Ambozontany: Fianarantsoa.
Bach, Emmon. 1980. In Defense of Passive. *Linguistics and Philosophy 3*.297-341.
Bell, Sarah J. 1978. Two Differences in Definiteness in Cebuano and Tagalog. *Oceanic Linguistics 17*.1-9.
Bell, Sarah J. 1983. Advancements and Ascensions in Cebuano. *Studies in Relational Grammar 1*, ed. by David M. Perlmutter, 143-218. Chicago & London: University of Chicago Press.
De Guzman, Videa P. 1988. Ergative Analysis for Philippine Languages: An Analysis. *Studies in Austonesian Linguistics*, ed. by Richard McGinn, 323-345. Athens, OH: Ohio University Center for International Studies [Center for Southeast Asia Studies].
Dez, J. 1980. *Structures de la Langue Malgache*. Paris: P.O.F.2 rue de Lille.
Dukes, M. 1993. Variation in Western Austronesian Clause Structure. To appear in the Proceedings of SEALS III.
Duskova, L. 1972. On Some Functional and Stylistic Aspects of the Passive Voice in Present-Day English. *Philologica Pragensia 15*.117-143.
Gerdts, Donna B. 1988. Antipassives and Causatives in Ilokano: Evidence for an Ergative Analysis. *Studies in Austronesian Linguistics*, ed. by Richard McGinn,295-321. Athens, OH: Ohio University Center for International Studies [Center for Southeast Asia Studies]
Givón, Talmy. 1979. *On Understanding Grammar*. New York: Academic Press.
Guilfoyle, Eithne; Henrietta Hung & Lisa Travis. 1992. Spec of IP and Spec of VP: Two Subjects in Austronesian Languages. *NLLT 10*.375-414.
Keenan, Edward L. 1976. Remarkable Subjects in Malagasy. *Subject and Topic*, ed. by Charles N. Li, 247-301. New York: Academic Press.
Keenan, Edward L. 1980. Passive is Phrasal (not Sentential or Lexical). *Lexical Grammar*, ed. by Teun Hoekstra, Harry van der Hulst & Michael Moortgat, 181-213. Dordrecht: Foris.
Keenan, Edward L. 1985. Passive in the World's Languages. *Language Typology and Syntactic Description*; Volume I, Clause Structure, ed.

by Timothy Shopen, 243–281. Cambridge: Cambridge University Press.
Keenan, Edward L. 1993. Identifying Anaphors. to appear in *BLS 19*.
Keenan, Edward L. & Cecile Manorohanta. in preparation. A Quantitative Study of Voice in Malagasy. ms. UCLA.
Keenan, Edward L. & Edward P. Stabler. 1991. Language Invariants. *Proceedings of the Eighth Amsterdam Colloquium*, ed. by Paul Dekker & Martin Stokhof, 309–328. Amsterdam: University of Amsterdam Institute for Logic, Language and Computation.
Keenan, Edward L. & Alan Timberlake. 1985a. Predicate Formation Rules in Universal Grammar. *WCCFL 4*.
Keenan, Edward L. & Alan Timberlake. 1985b. Valency Affecting Rules in Extended Categorial Grammar. *Language Research 21*.415–434.
Kroeger, Paul. 1993. *Phrase Structure and Grammatical Relations in Tagalog*. Stanford, CA: CSL1.
Kroeger, Paul. 1988. Verbal Focus in Kimaragang. *Papers in Western Austronesian Linguistics 3*. Pacific Linguistics, A-78.
Law, Paul. 1994. On Grammatical Relations in Malagasy Control Structures. This volume.
Malzac, Victorin. 1926. *Grammaire Malgache*. Paris: Societe d'editions Geographiques, maritimes et Coloniales.
Manaster-Ramer, Alexis. 1992. Malagasy and the Topic/Subject Issue. *Oceanic Linguistics 31*.267–279.
Mulder, Jean & Arthur Schwartz. 1981. On the Subject of Advancements in the Philippine Languages. *Studies in Language 5*.227–268.
Payne, Thomas E. 1982. Role and Reference Related Subject Properties and Ergativity in Yup'ik Eskimo and Tagalog. *Studies in Language 6*.75–106.
Perlmutter, David M. (ed.) 1983. *Studies in Relational Grammar 1*. Chicago & London: University of Chicago Press.
Perlmutter, David M. & Paul M. Postal. 1983. Some Proposed Laws of Basic Clause Structure. *Studies in Relational Grammar 1*, ed. by David M. Perlmutter, 81–128. Chicago & London: University of Chicago Press.

Perlmutter, David M. & Paul Postal. 1984. The 1-Advancement Exclusiveness Law. *Studies in Relational Grammar 2*, ed. by David M. Perlmutter & Carol G. Rosen, 81–125. Chicago & London: University of Chicago Press.
Perlmutter, David M. & Carol G. Rosen (eds.) 1984. *Studies in Relational Grammar 2*. Chicago & London: University of Chicago Press.
Rabenilaina, R.B. 1993. *Le Verbe Malgache: Constructions transitives et intransitives*. Antananarivo: Centre d'Etudes et de Recherches sur le Malgache, Universite d'Antananarivo. (Revised version of *Lexique-grammaire du malgache. Constructions transitives et intransitives*. 1985. these de doctorat d'Etat, Universite Paris 7:D.R.L. et L.A.D.L.)
Rajaona, S. 1972. *Structure du malgache — Etude des formes predicatives*. Ambozontany: Fianarantsoa, Madagascar.
Rajemisa-Raolison, R. 1971. *Grammaire Malgache*. Enseignement Secondaire $6^{eme} - 3^{eme}$. 7eme edition. Ambozontany: Fianarantsoa, Madagascar.
Randriamasimanana, Charles. 1986. *The Causatives of Malagasy*. Honolulu: University of Hawaii Press.
Rosen, Carol G. 1984. The Interface Between Semantic Roles and Initial Grammatical Relations. *Studies in Relational Grammar 2*, ed. by David M. Perlmutter and Carol G. Rosen, 38–77. Chicago & London: University of Chicago Press.
Schachter, Paul. 1976. The Subject in Philippine Languages: Topic, Actor, Actor-Topic, or None of the Above. *Subject and Topic*, ed. by Charles Li, 491–518. New York: Academic Press.
Schachter, Paul. 1977. Reference-Related and Role-Related Properties of Subjects. *Grammatical Relations*, ed. by Peter Cole & Jerrold M. Sadock, 279–306. New York: Academic Press. [*Syntax and Semantics 8*].
Schachter, Paul. 1984. Semantic-Role-Based Syntax in Toba Batak. *Studies in the Structure of Toba Batak*, ed. by Paul Schachter, 122–150. UCLA Occasional Papers in Linguistics No. 5. Los Angeles: UCLA Department of Linguistics.
Shibatani, Masayoshi. 1988. Voice in Philippine Languages. *Passive and Voice*, ed. by Masayoshi Shibatani, 85–142. Amsterdam and Philadelphia: John Benjamins.
Stein, Gabriele. 1979. *Studies in the Function of the Passive*. Tübingen: Gunter Narr Verlag.
Svartvik, Jan. 1966. *On Voice in the English Verb*. Berlin: Mouton.
Voskuil, Jan F. 1993. Abstract Case and Malagasy. ms. McGill University.

Source materials

[E] *Etsy ho ahy ny Tananao*. 1988. Novel by Lucien Razanadrakoto. A.C.E.: Antananarivo, Madagascar.

[IKM] *Ilay Kintana Mamirapiratra*. 1963. Novel by Philippe Rajohanesa. Imprimerie Lutherienne: Tananarive, Madagascar.

[LK] *Lakroa*. Contemporary Malagasy newspaper.

[PM] *Parler Malgache*. 1966. Short instruction manual widely used in Madagascar. By Prosper Rajaobelina. Imprimerie Lutherienne: Tananarive, Madagascar.

[T3] *Fiarahamonina*. 1985-6. Third grade reader by Andre Rakotondranaivo.

[VR] *Volavola Ranomaso*. 1957. Novel by Onja A. Benjamina Ranaivo. Imprimerie Lutherienne: Tananarive, Madagascar.

Excorporation and (Non)-1AEX

YOSHIHISA KITAGAWA
Indiana University

In this paper, I will explore a syntactic approach to morphologically complex predicates, adhering to the spirit, though not the technical details, of the minimalist approach proposed by Chomsky (1992). After summarizing the major theoretical assumptions adopted, I will outline the content and motivations of what I will refer to as the Excorporation Approach to complex predicates in Japanese, which was originally proposed in Kitagawa (1986). I then proceed to extend this approach to the analysis of passivization in English, which will permit us to minimize artificial assumptions and mechanisms in accounting for the mysterious properties of this construction. Finally, I will attempt to capture under the Excorporation Approach certain typological distinctions among different languages regarding the compatibility of passive and other morphosyntactic constructions with different verb classes. In the process of this attempt, I will also reach the conclusion that the 1-Advancement Exclusiveness Law (Perlmutter and Postal (1984)) captures only a special case of a much larger generalization, and hence cannot be regarded as a universal principle of grammar.

---

[*]Portions of this paper were presented at UCSD (March 1992), La Jolla Japanese Syntax Workshop (November 1991), and Rochester Workshop on Japanese Linguistics, Universal Grammar, and Their Implications to Language Pedagogy and Human Cognition (May 1991). I would like to express my gratitude to Greg Carlson, Marco Haverkort, Yuki Kuroda, Peter Lasersohn, Shigeru Miyagawa, and David Pesetsky for their comments at various stages of this paper. I would also like to thank the following participants of the Sixth Biennial Conference on Grammatical Relations at Simon Fraser University for their comments — Phil Branigan, David Perlmutter and Paul Postal. Finally I would like to express my gratitude to Donna Gerdts for providing me with this wonderful opportunity to interact with the grammatical relational community.

1. Theoretical Background

1.1 The Minimalist Hypothesis

Chomsky (1992) advocates the minimalist hypothesis, whose main features and consequences can be summarized as in (1):

(1) a. Interface levels (PF and LF) are the only levels of representation.
 b. Interface conditions are the only conditions on representations and derivations.
 c. Interface conditions must be satisfied in the 'optimal' way, where 'optimality' is determined by such economy conditions as the Principle of Full Interpretation (FI), and the Last Resort Principle.

With the assumption (1a), D-structure and S-structure are eliminated as independent levels of representation, and the Projection Principle is discarded. UTAH (Baker (1988)), if ever maintained, must also be assumed to hold at LF rather than at D-structure. Because of the assumption (1b), the Binding Theory, θ-Criterion, etc. (as subcases of FI) now are satisfied only in the LF component. In accordance with the assumption (1c), FI as in (2) below, for instance, requires all symbols in the linguistic representation to acquire legitimacy at LF by way of one or more of the licensing procedures listed in (3):

(2) **The Principle of Full Interpretation (FI):**
 A representation at interface must consist entirely of legitimate objects.

(3) a. θ-saturation
 b. θ/Case-discharge
 c. Categorial selection
 d. Operator-variable binding
 e. Modification

Especially noteworthy here is the requirement that all selectional properties of predicates must be satisfied not at D-structure or S-structure but in the LF component. Throughout this paper, I will adopt these leading ideas, though not the technical details, of the minimalist hypothesis.[1]

1.2 The Internal Subject Hypothesis

I will also adopt one particular version of the so-called Internal Subject Hypothesis (ISH), which may be distinguished from other versions in two respects. First, this version of ISH is regarded crucially as a hypothesis concerning the syntactic representations at LF rather than at D-structure. The

---

[1] The essence of the minimalist hypothesis has significant overlap with the Gricean approach to the theory of conversation.

external argument of a predicate is θ-saturated within the maximal projection of the predicate at LF, as illustrated in (4): (The linear order is irrelevant.)

(4) LF: [$_{VP}$ **External argument** [$_{V'}$ Internal argument V^0]]
where External argument may be a trace.
(Kitagawa 1986, Koopman and Sportiche 1986, Kuroda 1988, et al.)

Second, as illustrated in (5) below, it is combined with the head-directionality parameter and analyzes English as having VOS rather than SVO LF-order within a VP (Kitagawa (Ibid.)):

(5) LF: We$_1$ [$_{VP}$ [$_{V'}$ love Vancouver] t$_1$]

Kitagawa (1989) extends Belletti's (1988) 'Case for unaccusative' to unergative verbs, and argues for this hypothesis, pointing out that the post-verbal subject in English may surface overtly in the extraposition and presentational there constructions as in (6) below, because the subject does not require Case in the former and it can receive Case VP-internally in the latter:

(6) a. It [$_{VP}$ proves his innocence **that he has come back**].
b. There [$_{VP}$ walks **a man** into the room].

2. Excorporation in Japanese

2.1 Binding Puzzle

Kitagawa (1986) pointed out that Japanese sentences involving morphologically complex predicates exhibit quite peculiar facts concerning various LF-related matters. For instance, binding of anaphors and pronominals in causative constructions show up in quite a puzzling way. First, when the anaphor mizukara 'self' and a zero pronoun appear in a regular complementation structure as in (7) below, they exhibit the expected complementarity with respect to the locality restrictions on their binding:[2]

(7) John$_1$-ga [$_{CP}$ Bill$_2$-ga   { **mizukara**$_{2/*1}$ self   }-o
        nom   nom   **pro**$_{1/*2}$ acc
    hihansuru   to]-wa omowanakatta (koto)
    criticize-pres comp-top didn't think (fact)
                                           himself
    'John didn't think that Bill would criticize {   }.'
                                           him

---

[2] See Zubizarreta (1985) for a similar observation concerning binding in Romance causatives.

When these items appear in a causative construction as in (8) below, on the other hand, the expected complementarity breaks down in a very puzzling way. First, the zero pronoun may be bound by the causer NP John but not by the causee NP Bill. These facts will follow if the causative construction is **syntactically complex**, and the causee NP is analyzed as the subordinate subject. Quite surprisingly, however, the anaphor mizukara can be bound not only by the causee NP Bill but also by the causer NP John. Note that the successful long-distance binding of the anaphor by the causer NP suggests that the entire sentence be analyzed as **syntactically simplex**:

(8) John$_1$-ga [Bill$_2$-ni   aete   { mizukara$_{2/1}$ / self / pro$_{1/*2}$ }-o   acc
     nom   dat   intentionally
     hihans]-ase-ta   (koto)
     criticize-CAUSE-past   (fact)

'John intentionally had Bill criticize { himself / him }.'

Essentially the same range of facts can be observed in the indirect passive construction like (9) as well: [3] (cf. Kitagawa and Kuroda 1992)

(9) John$_1$-ga [Bill$_2$-ni   koosyuu-no-menzen-de   { mizukara$_{1/?2}$ / self / pro$_{1/*2}$ }
     nom   dat   publicly
     -o hihans]-are-ta   (koto)
     acc criticize-PASS-past   (fact)

'John had { himself / him } criticized by Bill in public.'

In short, given the minimalist assumption that the Binding Theory must be satisfied solely in the LF component, the binding facts in the complex predicate constructions in Japanese will lead us to the conclusion that **both simplex and complex representations must be available** for these constructions in the LF

---

[3] It is somewhat difficult to let the anaphor mizukara to refer to the causee Bill in (9) presumably due to the difficulty of imagining a situation in which John is affected by Bill's criticizing himself in public. This slight awkwardness due to pragmatics, however, contrasts with the grammatical restriction on pronominal binding involving pro in (9).

component.[4] Note, especially, that the facts in question will remain unaccounted for if we adopt an analysis in which a complex predicate is derived in overt syntax. This is so whether a monoclause is derived in overt syntax from a biclause as in Kuroda (1965), Shibatani (1973) and Aissen (1974), or whether a biclausal structure is maintained after verb raising in overt syntax and a specially-tailored government convention is stipulated for head movement as in Baker (1988).

2.2 LF-Excorporation and the Revised Lexical Integrity

When we juxtapose our minimalist assumption and our observation concerning complex predicate constructions in Japanese as in (10 a-c), we naturally arrive at the conclusion as in (10d):

(10) a. All conditions belong to the interface level (PF and LF components).
  b. The LF representations are the only syntactic representations relevant to semantic interpretation.
  c. **Both simplex and complex** LF representations must be available for the correct interpretation of the complex predicate constructions in Japanese.
  d. Derivation of or from the complex predicates in Japanese take place in the LF component, making available both their input and output to (the syntactic encoding of) semantic interpretation.

As an analysis to provide such LF-derivation, I will adopt the Excorporation approach to complex predicates summarized in (11):

(11) a. Complex Predicates in Japanese, including inflectional endings, are morphologically derived in the Lexicon:[5]
  eg) [s Causer Causee ... [v **V-sase-ru**]]
                                     CAUSE-PRES
  b. Affixes excorporate (= undergo Move α) in the LF component in order to satisfy their selectional properties. — See (12), (13a).
  c. In accordance with the minimality hypothesis, movement leaves behind traces iff principles of grammar require their presence. (cf. Pesetsky 1982, Lasnik and Saito 1984) — See (13b).

---

[4]We will reach the same conclusion by examining other LF phenomena such as scope interpretation and adverbial interpretation. It can be also shown that the observation in question is caused neither by tenselessness of the complement involved in complex predicate constructions nor by the matrix predicate's government into the complement. The reader is referred to Kitagawa (1986) as well as Kitagawa (In preparation) for further details.

[5]Kitagawa (Ibid.) provides various arguments for such lexical derivation of complex predicates, examining accentuation, downdrift, voicing spread, and inflection.

d. Due to the application of Excorporation, complex syntactic representation is derived in the LF component from a simplex syntactic representation. — See (13b) and (13a).
e. The derived complementation is a predicate phrase containing the internal subject. — See (13b).
f. No principles and rules are extrinsically ordered within a single component. — See (14).

The sample selectional properties of excorporating affixes referred to in (11b) are provided in (12):

(12) a. ru (PRES): Morphological: +[V⁰ __]
     Syntactic: +[EVENTUALITY __]
  b. sase (CAUS): Morphological: +[V⁰ __]
     Syntactic: +[AGENT [EVENTUALITY __]]
  c. rare (PASS): Morphological: +[V⁰ __]
     Syntactic: +[AFFECTEE [EVENTUALITY __]]

The LF application of Excorporation is illustrated in (13):

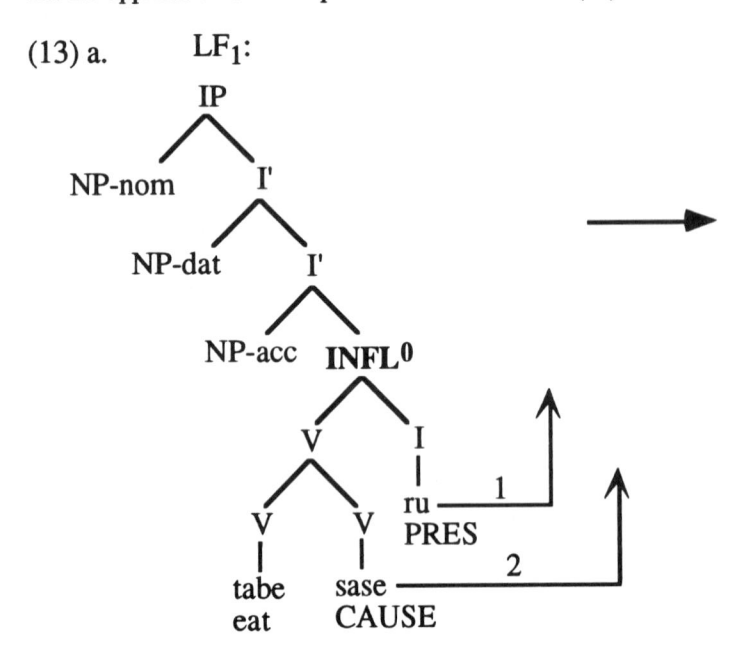

(13) a.   LF₁:

```
              IP
             /  \
         NP-nom  I'
               /  \
           NP-dat  I'
                  /  \
              NP-acc  INFL⁰
                     /    \
                    V      I
                   / \     |
                  V   V    ru ──1──▶
                  |   |    PRES
                 tabe sase ─────2──▶
                 eat  CAUSE
```

b. LF$_n$:

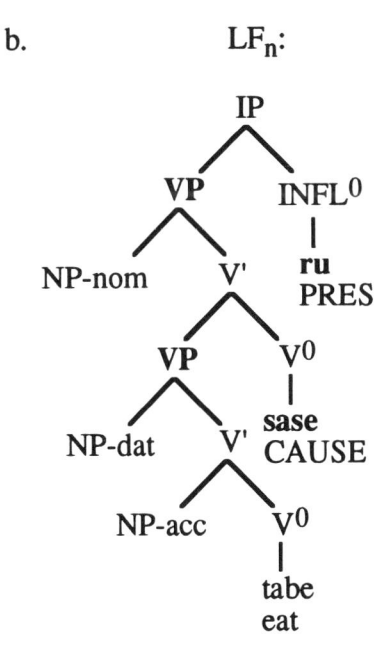

```
              IP
             /  \
            VP   INFL⁰
           /  \   |
      NP-nom  V'  ru
             /  \ PRES
            VP   V⁰
           /  \   |
       NP-dat  V' sase
              /  \ CAUSE
          NP-acc  V⁰
                  |
                  tabe
                  eat
```

Note that under the minimalist assumption (12c), Excorporation does not leave any trace behind, and superfluous nodes and edges of the syntactic tree are deleted in (13b). Note also that under the assumption (12f), any syntactic licensing (or syntactic encoding of semantic interpretation) may be done **either before** ((13a)) **or after** ((13b)) **Excorporation takes place.** Such a mode of LF-licensing is schematically illustrated in (14):

(14)   LF Component

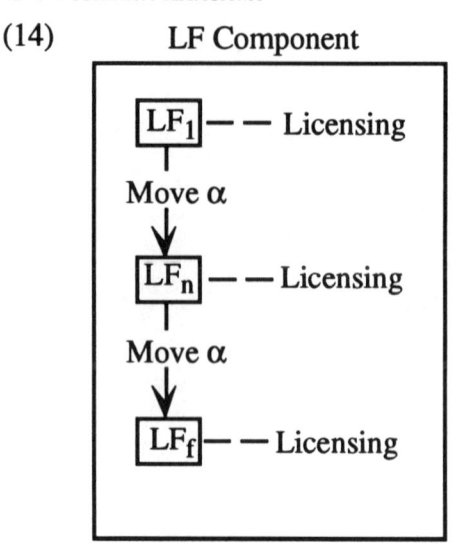

```
┌─────────────────────────┐
│  [LF₁] — — Licensing    │
│    │                    │
│  Move α                 │
│    ↓                    │
│  [LFₙ] — — Licensing    │
│    │                    │
│  Move α                 │
│    ↓                    │
│  [LF_f] — — Licensing   │
└─────────────────────────┘
```

This permits us to capture, for instance, the otherwise puzzling binding facts in the complex predicate constructions as observed in (8) above. Note that the anaphor *mizukara* can be licensed either before or after Excorporation applies and be bound either by the causer or causee. The zero pronoun, on the other hand, has a chance to be successfully bound only by the causer NP after Excorporation applies.[6]

---

[6]One may attempt to account for these binding facts by making an appeal to 'reanalysis' or 'coanalysis' (Zubizarreta 1985, Di Sciullo and Williams 1987). Kitagawa (Ibid.), however, also observes that a morphologically complex predicate as in (i a) sometimes can be ambiguously interpreted, forcing us to postulate for this construction an LF-representation as in (i b) in addition to (i a):
 (i) a. [causer causee nagur-sase-aw]
      punch-CAUSE-RECIPROCAL
   b. [causer [causee nagur-____-aw] **sase**]
         |_____↑

The ambiguity here can be accounted for if we assume that not only hierachical but also linear reordering of morphemes can be performed in the LF component as our Excorporation Approach claims. The same ambiguity cannot be handled, on the other hand, by a mere 'rebracketing' as in (ii a) or by 'coanalysis' as in (ii b):

An important theoretical device underlying this Excorporation approach is feature percolation as described in (15): (cf. Lieber 1981, Williams 1981, Selkirk 1982)

(15) a. Features percolate up from the head morpheme to the top-most node within a word.
  b. After (i) is completed, features percolate up from the non-head morphemes as well.

I will also assume that feature percolation is blocked by 'percolation barriers' as defined in (16):

(16) a. **Universal:**
  All features create barriers to percolation of the sametype of feature.
  b. **Parameterized:**
  Lexical categorial features ($[\pm N],[\pm V]$) create absolute barriers to percolation of any feature.

Due to (16a), the categorial features of the head morpheme, for example, will block the percolation of the categorial features of a non-head morpheme. The same will be true with two external θ-features, internal θ-features, external Case features, internal Case features, and so on.[7] As a case of the parametric variation stated in (16b), I will tentatively assume that lexical categorial features create percolation barriers in English but not in Japanese.[8]

Finally, I will adopt a version of the Lexical Integrity Hypothesis as stated in (17), following the spirit of Williams' (1981) Atom Condition:

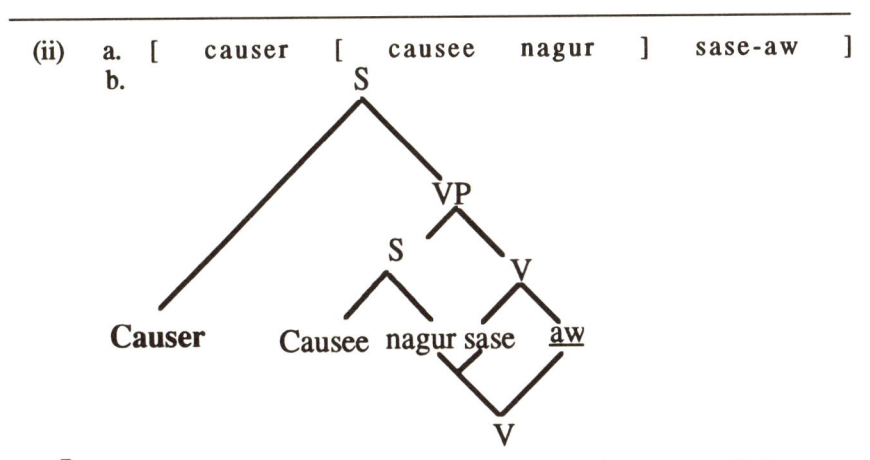

(ii) a. [causer [causee nagur] sase-aw]
  b.

```
         S
        / \
       /   VP
      /   / \
     /   S   V
    /   / \ / \
Causer Causee nagur sase  aw
                    \___/
                      V
```

[7]The constraints here imposed by (15) and (16) on feature percolation may, in fact, be regarded as a special case of Relativized Minimality (Rizzi 1990).

[8]Kitagawa (1986) discusses a possible dialectal/idiolectal variation on this parametric choice among Japanese speakers.

(17) **Revised Lexical Integrity Hypothesis:**
Morphemes are subject to syntactic principles (eg, θ-Criterion (= FI)) and operations (eg, Move α) only when they become visible in syntax due to their feature percolation up to word level.

Roughly, unlike its predecessor, this constraint permits syntax to affect elements of words only if they are visible due to feature percolation. The corollary of the definition of percolation barriers in (16) and the Revised Lexical Integrity Hypothesis, then, will be as in (18):

(18) a. Head morphemes are always visible to syntax.
   b. Non-head morphemes are visible only when their feature percolation is not blocked by barriers.

A variety of morpho-syntactic interactions become naturally explicated when we make an appeal to this corollary. For instance, in English, the θ and Case features of the non-head morpheme need not be discharged in a nominal compound as in (19a) below, while they still must be discharged in an inflected verb as in (19b). This distinction naturally follows from the distinct category of the head morpheme — in English, the lexical feature N creates a barrier for percolation of any feature but the categorial feature INFL does not.

(19) **Visibility to Syntactic Principles:**

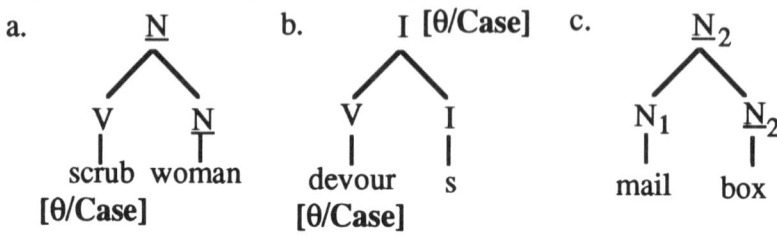

a. N   b. I [θ/Case]   c. N_2
   /\   /\   /\
  V   N   V   I N_1 N_2
  | | | | | |
scrub woman   devour s   mail box
[θ/Case]   [θ/Case]

That a nominal morpheme does not require Case in a non-head position as in (19c) can be also ascribed to its invisibility to the syntactic principle requirig Case for overt nominals. Note that the nominal status of the head morpheme blocks the percolation of any feature from this non-head morpheme. Hence, it is invisible to syntax. The corollaries in (18) also explain why, on the one hand, Excorporation tends to apply string-vacuously. The reason, of course, is that words are generally head-final. It also predicts, on the other hand, that the non-string-vacuous application of Excorporation can be observed when non-head morphemes percolate up their features, as in the case of the morphology-syntax mismatches mentioned in footnote 6. Recall that the lexical features are assumed not to create absolute percolation barriers in Japanese. Therefore, when the head morpheme lacks thematic features, as in the case of the reciprocal affix <u>aw</u> in (20) below, the non-head morpheme becomes visible to syntax due to the percolation of its thematic features, and undergoes Excorporation in order to satisfy its selectional properties:

(20) **Visibility to Syntactic Operation**:

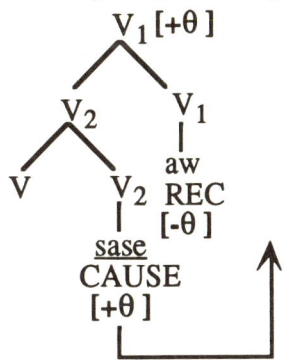

$$\begin{array}{c} V_1[+\theta] \\ \diagup\,\diagdown \\ V_2 \quad\; V_1 \\ \mid \quad\;\; \mid \\ \quad\;\; \text{aw} \\ V \quad V_2 \;\; \text{REC} \\ \mid \quad\;\; [-\theta] \\ \text{sase} \\ \text{CAUSE} \\ [+\theta] \end{array}$$

3. Excorporation in English

The Excorporation Approach can be further motivated when we extend it to the analysis of passives in English. In (21) below are listed those properties of passive which are often assumed to distinguish this construction from others:

(21) a. Absorb OBJ Case (but not OBJ θ)
b. Absorb SBJ θ (but not OBJ θ)
c. Implicit Argument in short passive
d. There is a cooccurrence restriction between passive and certain auxiliary verbs like (be/get)
e. Incompatible with unaccusative and raising verbs

In the Principles and Parameters approach exemplified in (22) below, the absorption of internal Case ((21a)) is generally assumed to trigger Move α, and the absorbed SBJ (or external) θ-role ((21b)) is optionally realized as an adjunct by-NP:

(22) **JFK**$_1$ might have been killed t$_1$ (by the **CIA**).

When the absorbed SBJ θ-role is not realized as an adjunct, on the other hand, it is often assumed to be **lexically** realized as an implicit argument ((21c)), which is known to be capable of licensing agent-oriented adverbs as in (23):

(23) The ship was sunk **deliberately**.

The cooccurrence restriction in (21d) is well-known, and can be demonstrated, for example, by the obligatoriness of was in (23). Finally, the phenomenon in

(21e) is exemplified by (24 a-b) below, which is often described as a violation of the 1-Advancement Exclusiveness Law (1AEX: Perlmutter and Postal (1984)):[9]

(24) a. Unaccusative: *Time was elapsed.
b. Raising: *John$_1$ was seemed t$_1$ to be unhappy.

We can extend our Excorporation Approach and analyze passive in English as summarized in (25):

(25) a. V-EN is derived in the Lexicon.
b. The abstract passive morpheme -EN has its own selectional properties. — See (26).
c. -EN undergoes Excorporation in the LF component to satisfy its selectional reqirements. — See (27).

The selectional properties of -EN are stated in (26), and the application of Excorporation to this suffix is illustrated in (27):

(26) **Morphological:** **Syntactic:**
-EN: +[V^0 __] +[__ EVENTUALITY][10]

(27) **Excorporation in Passive:**

---

[9]We will examinine the 1AEX in detail in Section 4 below:

[10]We will modify the syntactic selectional property of -EN in Section 4 below.

a. $\underline{\text{D/S/PF/LF}_1}$:

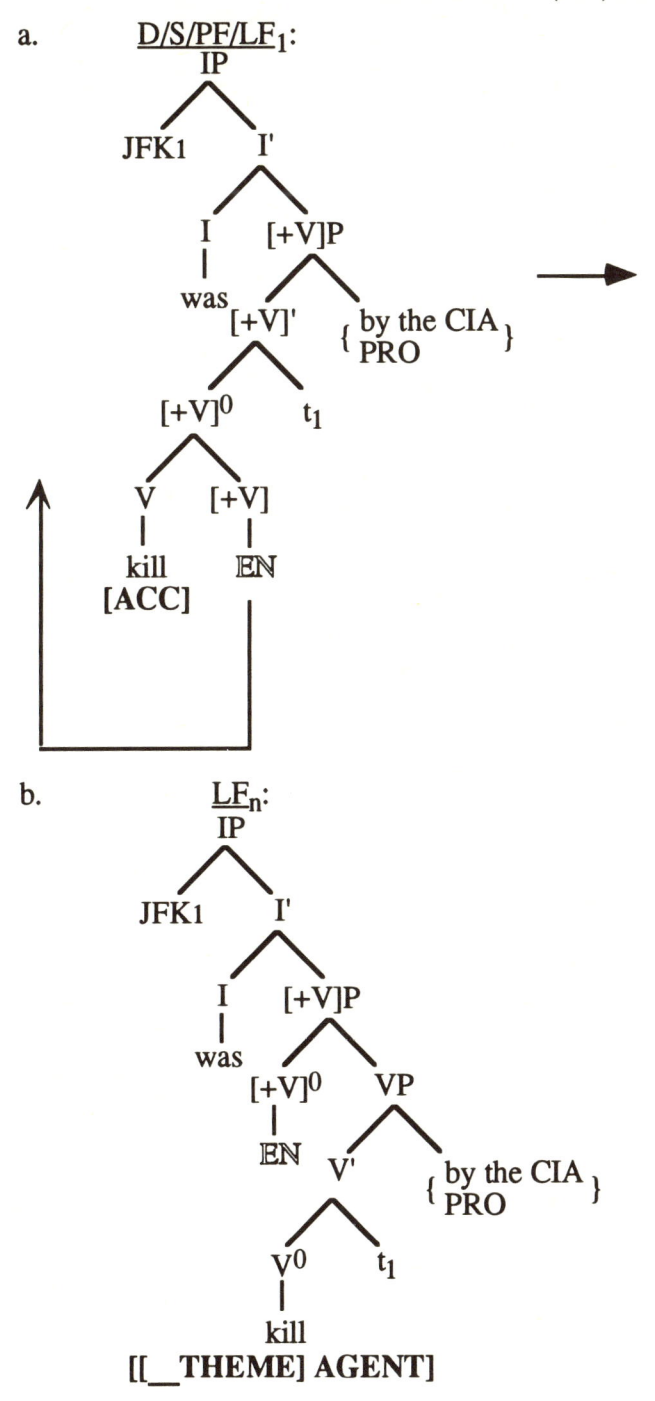

```
              IP
            /    \
         JFK₁     I'
                /    \
               I     [+V]P
               |    /      \
              was [+V]'   { by the CIA }
                  /  \    { PRO        }
              [+V]⁰   t₁
              /   \
             V    [+V]
             |     |
            kill   EN
           [ACC]
```

b. $\underline{\text{LF}_n}$:

```
              IP
            /    \
         JFK₁     I'
                /    \
               I     [+V]P
               |    /      \
              was [+V]⁰    VP
                   |      /    \
                  EN     V'    { by the CIA }
                        /  \   { PRO        }
                       V⁰   t₁
                       |
                      kill
              [[_THEME] AGENT]
```

We can summarize the highlights of this analysis as follows. First, $[+V]^0$ in (27a) is a percolation barrier before Excorporation takes place. This blocks the percolation of the Case feature from the non-head verb, and yields an Absorb Case effect.

Second, as illustrated in (27b), the verb kill θ-marks both internal and external arguments after Excorporation applies. Both arguments of the verb kill, in other words, are syntactically realized as arguments.

Third, by is a Case marker for the post-verbal subject in (27a) licensed by -EN. This yields a seeming dethematization effect (cf. Murasugi 1990). The role of by is comparable to that of of, which is regarded as the Case marker for internal arguments licensed under N' (Chomsky 1981, Stowell 1981). Recall also that we regard English as a VOS language (see Section 1.2.).[11]

Fourth, the post-verbal subject may be realized as PRO in (27a). This yields the seeming implicit argument effect.[12]

---

[11]Phil Branigan (p.c.) pointed out to me that the NP-movement of the internal argument involved in (27) would incorrectly yield a violation of Relativized Minimality under the proposed analysis since the post-verbal internal subject should be regarded as the closest relevant potential antecedent for the NP-trace left behind. Two possible ways come to mind to explain why such violation is not caused. First, we may consider that the post-verbal internal subject position, being a thematic position, does not count as A-specifier in Rizzi's (1990) sense. The internal subject, therefore, does not count as the closest potential A-binder. An alternative will be to reinterpret the notion Relativized Minimality in terms of 'actual' rather than 'potential' antecedent at least for A-binding.

[12]The implicit argument is straightforwardly identified as syntactically realized PRO, sometimes with an arbitrary interpretation. The syntactic tests involving short passive in (i) support this analysis, marking a sharp contrast with those involving 'lexically saturated understood objects' in English in (ii), while being comparable to those involving syntactically realized object pro in Italian in (iii) (Rizzi 1986):
  (i) a. **As a controller:**
        A ship was sunk [**PRO** in order to collect insurance].
     b. **As the local antecedet of an anaphor:**
        In this computer system, no message can be sent back to **oneself/ourselves.**
     c. **As the subject of an adjunct small clause:**
        In this theater, no dance can be performed **nude.**
  (ii) a. **As a controller:**
        *This leads ___ [PRO to conclude what follows].
     b. **As the local antecedet of an anaphor:**
        *Good music reconciles ___ with **oneself.**

Fifth, as a result of Excorporation, -EN comes to be in a position from which it can locally select a specific type of verb phrase in (27b). I will crucially make an appeal to this result of Excorporation in order to capture the 1AEX effects ((21e)). I will, however, defer the discussion until Section 4. In (27b), -EN also comes to be in a position where it can be locally selected by the auxiliary verb be. One possibility, in fact, is that -EN even adjoins to be and makes up a constituent in the LF component. In either case, the Excorporation analysis permits us to capture the cooccurrence restrictions between passive and certain auxiliary verbs ((21d)) in a natural way.

One big advantage of this approach is that it allows us to minimize artificial assumptions and extra mechanisms by ascribing most of the peculiar behaviors of passive to the general theory of percolation supplemented by the notion of barriers and the Revised Lexical Integrity Hypothesis. For instance, neither Case nor θ needs to be actually absorbed by or assigned to the passive morpheme. (See Chomsky (1981) and Jaeggli (1986) for the former analysis, and Baker, Johnson, and Roberts (1989) for the latter.) Instead, Case absorption and Dethematization are regarded as epiphenomena arising from the interaction of morphology and syntax. It also is unnecessary to introduce any extra mechanism to ensure the transmission of the external θ-role from the passive morpheme to the by-phrase, which is necessitated in all of the proposed approaches mentioned just above.[13]

---

      c. **As the subject of an adjunct small clause:**
         [A serious doctor]$_1$ visits ___$_2$ **nude**$_{1/*2}$.

(iii) a. **As a controller:**
         Questo conduce ___ a [PRO concludere quanto segue]
         'This leads ___ [PRO to conclude what follows].'
    b. **As the local antecedet of an anaphor:**
         La buona musica riconcilla ___ con **se stessi**.
         'Good music reconciles ___ with **oneself**.'
    c. **As the subject of an adjunct small clause:**
         Un dottore serio vista ___$_1$ **nudi**$_1$.
         '[A serious doctor] visits ___$_1$ **nude**$_1$.'

[13]Kitagawa (In preparation) further argues that the Excorporation Approach can and should be extended to the analyses of process derived nominals in English (Lebeaux 1986), pointing out a quite striking parallelism between nominalization and passivization, summarized in (i):

(i) a. **Absorb Object Case (but not θ):**
      kids' devouring *(of) the pasta
    b. **Absorb Subject (but not Object) θ:**
      the devouring of pasta (**by kids**)
    c. **Implicit Argument:**
      the devouring of pasta [**PRO** to challenge **one's** limit of appetite]
    d. **1AEX Effects:**
      Unaccusative: *time **elapsing**
      Raising: *John$_1$'s **seeming** [t$_1$ to believe in God]

4. Possible Extension to Universal Grammar

The Excorporation Approach may also shed new light on certain parametric variation concerning complex predicate constructions in different languages of the world.[14]

4.1 1AEX Effects

Let me start with an examination of the 1AEX effects, which we briefly mentioned in our investigation of English passives and nominals. 1AEX, the 1-Advancement Exclusiveness Law in (28) below proposed by Perlmutter and Postal (1984) has proven itself to be a quite interesting and useful generalization, which provides the researchers of various thoughts with a clue to investigate into the natures of different grammatical constructions:

(28) The 1-Advancement Exclusiveness Law (informal):
      No clause can have more than one advancement to 1 (= subject).
      (Perlmutter and Postal 1984:87, Perlmutter and Rosen 1984:xi)

The contrast observed in (29) below between the possibility of unergative impersonal passive and unaccusative impersonal passive in Dutch was originally provided by Perlmutter (1978) as motivation to postulate the 1AEX as a universal principle:

(29) a. Er   wordt hier   veel   **geskied**.
         it   is   here   lot   skied
         'It is skied here a lot.'
     b. *Er   werd   door de   kinderen in   Amsterdam **gebleven**.
         it   was   by the children in   remained
         'It was remained in Amsterdam by the children.'

Although a similar example involving a transitive verb as in (30a) below has been presented to suggest the rather complicated nature of Dutch passives, Marco Haverkort (p.c.) has pointed out to me that the source of the ill-formedness in (30a) might in fact be the definiteness of the involved argument, as the well-formedness of (30b) with an indefinite argument indicates:

(30) a. *Er   werd **het** boek **gelezen** door Karel
         there was   the   book read   by
     b. Er   werd **een** boek **gelezen** door Karel
         there was   a   book read   by

---

[14]We will focus here on those languages which exhibit the Nominative-Accusative Case system, leaving the pursuit of the topic of Ergative languages for another occasion.

hus, tentatively regarding the ungrammaticality of (30a) as a type of
lefiniteness effect' arising when an unaccusative verb assigns Case to its
iternal argument along the line of Belletti's (1989) analysis, I will consider that
ie impersonal passives in Dutch constitute a paradigm that compeletely falls
nder the explanation offerd by the 1AEX.[15]

2 Anti-1AEX Effects

Despite such descriptive success in the analysis of Dutch, the 1AEX is known to
ave counterexamples. As illustrated by the examples in (31), for instance, Keenan
nd Timberlake (1985:127-128) point out that there are languages such as Lithuanian
nd Turkish, in which unaccusative verbs (in addition to transitive and unergative
erbs) permit an impersonal passive construction:

31) a. Ko   c̨ia   **degta?**
what here burn (nt.sg.PASS)
'By what was (it) burned here?'
b. Jo   **pasorodyta**   esant didvyrio
gen.m.sg.3 seem (nt.sg.nom.PASS) being hero
'By him (it) was seemed to be a hero.'

3 Quasi-1AEX Effects

Furthermore, when we attempt to extend the 1AEX to Japanese, we
ncounter another set of obviously related but unexpected facts. First, when we
bserve the contrast between the possibility of transitive passive and unergative
assive in (32) below and the impossibility of unaccusative passive in (33), we
et the impression that we have a straightforward case of the 1AEX Effect:

32) a. Taroo ga   Sensei ni   (musuko o)   **home-are**-ta
nom   teacher dat (son   acc) praise-PASS-past
'Taro was affected by the teacher's praising his son.'
b. Hanako ga   kodomo ni   **hasir-are**-ta
nom   child   dat run-PASS-past
'Hanako was affected by the child's running.'

33) a. *Taroo ga   oyu   ni   **wak-are**-ta
nom hot-water dat boil-PASS-past
'Taro was affected by the water's boiling.'

---

[15]Perlmutter and Zaenen (1984), on the other hand, analyze a sentence like
30b) as an 'indefinite extraposition construction'. Whichever analysis may turn
ut to be correct, however, the approach to be proposed in 4.7. below will be
apable of handling the case.

b. *Hanako ga   taoru ni   **kawak-are**-ta
   nom   towel dat dry-PASS-past
   'Hanako was affected by the towel's getting dry.'

What we find puzzling, then, is a similar contrast we can observe between the transitive and unergative causative in (35) and the unaccusative causative in (36) (Miyagawa 1989):[16]

(35) a. Hanako ga   kodomo-tati ni   gohan o   **tabe-sase**-ta
        nom   children   dat   meal acc eat-CAUSE-past
        'Hanako had the children have a meal.'

---

[16]Counterexamples to this generalization as in (i) have been also reported in the literature, which Kuroda (1993:42-44) characterizes with the notion 'Noninterventive causation'. (See also Dubinsky (to appear)): (The judgments indicated on Kuroda's examples in (i a-b) are mine.)
(i) a. [statement concerning the ever more leaning Tower of Pisa]
       ?katamuku mama ni   **katamuk-ase**-te   oku   yori
       lean   as   lean-CAUSE   leave other than
       sikata ga nai
       means   not exist
       'There is nothing to do but leave it to lean.'
   b. [statement concerning boiling water in the kettle suspended above a camp fire when no tool is available to take the kettle off the fire]
       ?*ano oyu wa/o   wak-u   mama ni   **wak-ase**-te   oku
       that hot water   boil   as   boil-CAUSE   leave
       yori   sikata ga nai
       than   means   not exist
       'There is nothing to do but to let that water boil as it is.'
Note that similar counterexamples can be found with respect to passivization as well:
(ii) a. ?ima kokode kono kabe ni   **kuzure-rare**-tara
        now   this wall dat   collapse-PASS-if
        hitotamarimo nai
        fatal
        'We will be in big trouble if that wall collapses.'
    b. ?ima kono kuruma ni   **koware-rare**-tewa   komaru
       now this car   dat   break-PASS-if   troubled
       'We will be in trouble if this car breaks down.'
I will assume that such 'Noninterventive causation/passivization' can be regarded as involving a marked strategy of lexicalization, which is made possible only when the subordinate subject can be regarded as having 'potency'. Such semantic restriction, as well as the marginality of the resulting sentences, and the fact that such a construction is only idiosyncratically permitted for a limited number of verbs all suggest the plausibility of this assumption.

b. kooti ga   sensyu-tati o   **hasir-ase**-ta
   coach nom players   acc run-PASS-past
   'The coach made the players run.'
c. Hanako ga koi o ike de **oyog-ase**-ta
   nom   carp acc pond in swim-PASS-past
   'Hanako let the carp swim in the pond.'

(36) a. *Taroo ga oyu   o   **wak-ase**-ta
        nom   hot-water acc boil-CAUSE-past
        'Taro made the water boil.'
     b. *Hanako ga taoru o   **kawak-ase**-ta
        nom   towel acc dry-CAUSE-past
        'Hanako made the towel dry.'

Note that, if the 1AEX is indeed a principle prohibiting more than one instance of advancement to 1, it should not rule out the causativization of unaccusative verbs in (36 a-b), since it will involve only a single instance of such GF-change. One possibility, of course, is that the phenomena in (35) and (36) are independent, and that we can still maintain the 1AEX, which accounts only for the facts concerning passive. It is more desirable, however, if we can provide a single account to these totally parallel phenomena.

4.4 Super-1AEX Effects

Still another obviously related but unexplained fact is that Dutch personal passive is possible with transitive verbs, but is prohibited not only with unaccusative but also with unergative verbs, as illustrated in (37):

(37) a. Het boek werd **gelezen** door Karel
         the book was   read   by
     b. *De   rots werd **gevallen**
         the rock was   fallen
     c. *De   kinderen werden **gelachen**
         the children were   laughed

As illustrated in (38), the situation is similar in English as well:

(38) a. JFK might have been **killed** by the CIA.
     b. *Time was **elapsed**.
     c. *John was **swum**.

In fact, we can find another such case in English if we closely analyze action nominal compounds as in (39 a-e):

(39) a. **Transitive-Nominal (SBJ):**   *chíld devouring
                                        (child as AGENT)
     b. **Transitive-Nominal (OBJ):**   pásta devouring

		1 2 3
c.	**Transitive-Nominal (SBJ-OBJ):**	?child pasta devouring
d.	**Unergative-Nominal:**	*girl **swimming/**
		(girl as AGENT)
		(Selkirk 1982, Pesetsky 1985)
e.	**Unaccusative-Nominal:**	*time-**elapsing**
		(as a process nominal)

As illustrated by (39 d-e), such compounding is not possible with either unergative or unaccusative verbs.[17] The situation is the same, as illustrated in (39a), when the compound incorporates a subject nominal of a transitive verb. What is puzzling, then, is that the same compounding is possible when an object nominal is incorporated as in (39b) and when both subject and object nominals are incorporated as in (39c). Thus, though it admittedly is not the most felicitous expression, many speakers agree that pasta devouring and child pasta devouring with their correct compound stress patterns as indicated in (39 b-c) are basically grammatical, and make a sharp contrast with a totally ungrammatical example like (39a) with the agentive reading of the incorporated nominal.

When we examine the examples in (39 a-b) further, it will turn out that the restriction on compounding observed here is identical to the restriction on passivization observed in (38). First, as is well-known, English does not permit any empty pronominal as an object argument, whether it is PRO or pro, while at least PRO is known to be permitted as a subject argument. Thus, we can analyze the example in (39b) above as legitimately involving a PRO subject, as in (40b) below, and the example in (39a) as illegitimately involving an object empty pronominal as in (40a):[18]

---

[17] Paul Postal (p.c.) provided me with an example like computer malfunctioning as a case in which the nominalization in question is possible with an unaccusative verb. The example, however, is possible only as a result nominal rather than a process nominal, as can be seen from its incompatibility with an aspectual modifier like for three hours in (i):

(i) ?*The computer malfunctioning for three hours today
    slowed down our project.

Compare (i) with a process nominal in (ii):

(ii) **The bombardment of the city by A-1 Fighters** for three consecutive days appalled everyone.

[18] An example similar to (39b), in fact, passes all the tests for the presence of a syntactic empty argument as illustrated in (i a-c) (See footnote 10):

(i) a. **As a controller:**
       Pasta cooking [**PRO** to prove **one's** familiarity with
       Italian cuisine] is foolish.
   b. **As the local antecedet of an anaphor:**
       [Pasta cooking just for **oneself/yourself**] is not much fun.
   c. **As the subject of an adjunct small clause:**

(40) a. [child { *PRO / *pro } devour]-ing → *(39a)
   b. [PRO pasta devour]-ing → ok(39b)

Then, when we assume that the compounding in question is compatible with a transitive verb with its two argument nominals incorporated, all the facts in (39 a-c) will follow straightforwardly. Thus, we conclude that the compounding in question is possible in English with transitive verbs but not with unaccusative verbs or unergative verbs, which is a situation identical to that in passivization both in English and Dutch.

Again, the two cases could in principle be totally unrelated, or the incompatibility of unergative verbs with these morphosyntactic processes in Dutch and English in principle could be independent of that of unaccusative verbs. It will be nice, however, if we can bring in both cases under one same umbrella.

4.5 Contra-1AEX Effects

Finally, we can also observe a case in which a certain morphological process is incompatible with a selected group of verbs, but this time in a completely opposite way to 1AEX Effects. The case in question is the formation of action/process nominal compounds in Japanese as in (41): (cf. Kageyama 1982, Sugioka 1984, Miyagawa 1989)

(41) **Action-Nominal Compounds (Neologism) in Japanese:**
   a. ***Transitive Subject:**
      *yakuza-naguri   *kodomo-yomi   *inu-kami
      'gang-punching'   'kid-reading'   'dog-biting'
   b. ***Unergative Subject:**
      *inu-boe   *kodomo-hasiri   *roozin-aruki
      'dog-barking'   'child-running'   'elderly-walking'
   c. **Unaccusative Subject:**
      dote-kuzure   kabe-kuzure   hei-kuzure
      'bank-collapsing'   'wall-collapsing' 'fence-collapsing'
   d. **Transitive Object:**
      kuruma-migaki   tukue-migaki   kabe-migaki
      'car-polishing'   'desk-polishing' 'wall-polishing'

First, as illustrated in (41 a-b), the compounding in question for **neologisms**, which seems to permit only action (or process) readings, is prohibited when it incorporates the subject nominal of a transitive verb or an unergative verb. On

---

Pasta cooking **completely nude** sounds to me to be a sign of insanity.

the other hand, as illustrated in (41c), the subject nominal of an unaccusative verb can be rather freely incorporated. Thus, when we pay attention to the compatibility of this compounding with the subject of three types of verbs, we notice exactly the opposite effect of the 1AEX. Finally, for the sake of completeness of observation, let us add that, as illustrated in (41d), the object nominal of a transitive verb is also incorporable.[19]

4.6 Summary: 1AEX and Non-1AEX Effects

All these empirical phenomena revolving around the 1AEX can be summarized as in (42) when we pay attention to passivization:

(42) **Passivization:**

	English	Dutch (personal)	Dutch (impersonal)	Japanese	Lithuanian
Trans:	ok	ok	ok	ok	ok
Unerg:	*	*	ok	ok	ok
Unacc:	*	*	*	*	ok

Note that, in English, unergative and unaccusative verbs make up a natural class while in Japanese, transitive and unergative verbs do. In Lithuanian (and Turkish), on the other hand, no subgroup of verbs make up such natural classes with respect to passivization. Dutch is somewhat peculiar in that its personal passive calls for the same natural class as English, while its impersonal passive calls for the natural class observed in Japanese.

Furthermore, the same set of empirical phenomena can be summarized also in a language-by-language fashion, as in (43)-(45):

(43) **English:**

	Passive	Nominal Compound
Transitive:	ok	ok
Unergative:	*	*
Unaccusative:	*	*

(44) **Japanese:**

	Passive	Causative	SBJ-V Nominal
Transitive	ok	ok	*
Unergative	ok	ok	*
Unaccusative	*	*	ok

(45) **Dutch:**

	Personal Passive	Impersonal Passive
Transitive:	ok	ok
Unergative:	*	ok
Unaccusative:	*	*

---

[19] Further investigation of this fact will raise an interesting problem, which will lead us to another possible motivation for the Excorporation Approach. I will not, however, pursue this topic in this paper.

These charts rather clearly indicate that, except for Dutch, the natural class of verbs we have observed with respect to passivization in (42) does carry over to other morphosyntactic processes in each language. I believe that these observations suggest to us that the 1AEX now should be regarded as a special case of a much larger generalization, which in turn suggests that it cannot be regarded as a universal principle of grammar. The task that is assigned to us, then, is to come up with the analyses of various morphologically complex predicates that are general enough to let us capture not only (i) but also (ii) below: (i) the universality (if we can ever identify it) and the cross-linguistic variation observed with respect to passivization in (42), and (ii) the compatibility/incompatibility of the same specific group of verb classes to different morpho-syntactic processes within each single language in (43)-(45). In the rest of this article, I would like to point out that our Excorporation Approach can offer a quite simple and unified account for both of (i) and (ii), when it is coupled with the view of syntactic projection spelled out directly below and the requirement under the minimalist hypothesis such that each predicate must satisfy its selectional properties in the LF component.

4.7 Categorial Projection and Thematic Projection

The first step we will take is to assume that the traditional syntactic projection in fact conflates two distinct types of projection. One type of projection is created by the percolation of categorial features, which I will refer to as '**categorial projection**'. In categorial projection, as illustrated in (46a) below, the topmost projection of a category X is labelled as X^{max}, the terminal projection as X^{min}, and any other projection in between as X^{med}:

(46) **Categorial Projection:**
    a. Transitive: b. Unergative/Unaccusative:

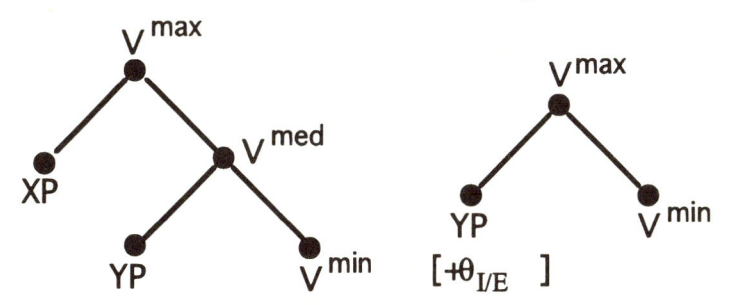

```
         V^max                                V^max
        /    \                               /    \
      XP     V^med                         YP     V^min
            /    \                        [+θ_{I/E}]
           YP    V^min
```

Note that, as illustrated in (46b), the categorial projection of a one-place predicate, whether it is unergative or unaccusative, contains only a maximal projection and a minimal projection.[20]

In addition to categorial projection, the thematic features of a predicate and their saturation are also encoded on a syntactic tree, making up its **'thematic projection'**. Crucially, then, we will assume that UG provides two distinct ways of realizing thematic projection as possible options, and that each language or language group may be parametrized with respect to the choice of such options. In particular, as illustrated in (47a) below, a language may choose to project thematic information by counting the **number of θ-roles** to be saturated within the maximal projection of a predicate. We will refer to this mode of thematic projection as 'Quantity (QNT)-sensitive' thematic projection. In (47a), V^2 represents a thematic projection in which two θ-roles are discharged, and V^1 represents a thematic projection in which only one θ-role is discharged:

(47) **Thematic Projection:**
    a. **Transitive:**   b. **Transitive**
        (QNT-sensitive Projection)   (QLT-sensitive Projection):

---

[20]The definitions of maximality, minimality and mediality in categorial projection can be provided in simple graph-theoretic terms like 'indegree' and 'outdegree' with the assumption that the rooted trees utilized in linguistic representations are 'acyclic unipathic digraphs' combined with categorial features as 'non-numerical weight' of vertices.

Given, such categorial projections, we can now redefine UTAH as an LF-principle as in (i):

(i) **Revised UTAH (RUTAH):**
    a. There exist two distinct sets of θ-roles:
        External θ-roles and Internal θ-roles
    b. Each set of θ-roles are discharged in their designated LF-positions as follows:
        1) External θ-roles: $[X^{max}$ __ $]$
                                  (Immdediately dominated by X^{max})
        2) Internal θ-roles: $[$ __ $X^{min}]$
                                  (Being a sister to X^{min})

One possibility is that the definition of each set of θ-roles in (i a) is parameterized so that what count as external θ-roles and internal θ-roles differ among (groups of) languages. See Keenan (1994: this volume) for Malagasy as one possible case to illustrate such parametric variation.

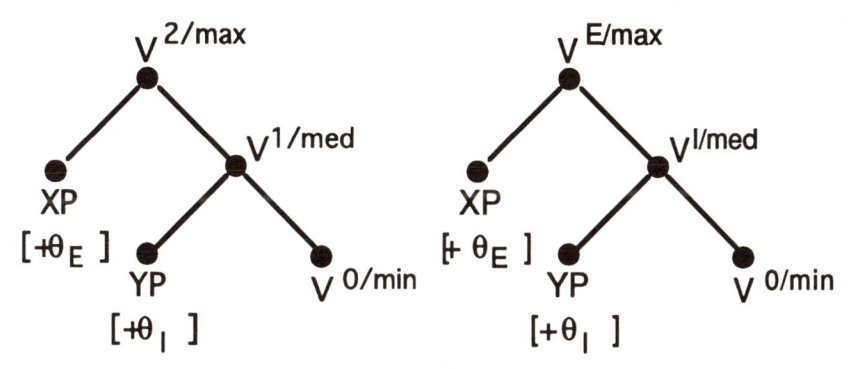

```
    V 2/max              V E/max
     •                    •
    / \                  / \
   /   \ V 1/med        /   \ V I/med
  /    •               /    •
 /    / \             /    / \
XP   /   \           XP   /   \
[+θ_E] • •           [+θ_E] • •
      YP  V 0/min         YP  V 0/min
     [+θ_I]              [+θ_I]
```

A different language, on the other hand, may also choose to project thematic information of a predicate by paying attention to the **types of θ-roles** to be saturated, as in (47b). We will refer to this mode of thematic projection as 'Quality (**QLT**)-sensitive' thematic projection. In (47b), V^E represents a thematic projection in which an external θ-role is discharged and V^I represents a thematic projection in which an internal θ-role is discharged.

Now, when we are dealing with the thematic projection of transitive verbs as in (47) above and that of unaccusative verbs as in (48) below, the distinction between the two types of thematic projection does not surface since the QNT-sensitive thematic projection V^1 always corresponds to the QLT-sensitive thematic projection V^I, and likewise, V^2 corresponds to V^E:

(48) **Unaccusative:**
    a. **QNT-sensitive Projection:**   b.   **QLT-sensitive Projection:**

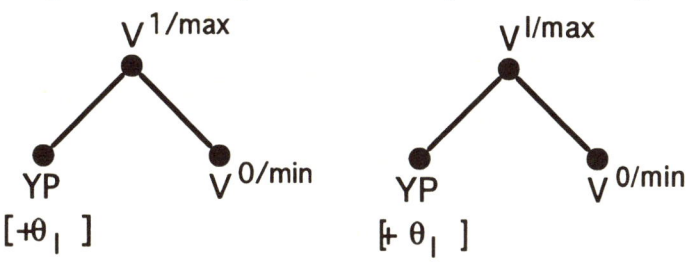

```
    V 1/max                  V I/max
     •                        •
    / \                      / \
   /   \                    /   \
  •     • V 0/min          •     • V 0/min
  YP                       YP
 [+θ_I]                   [+θ_I]
```

When we have to deal with unergative verbs, on the hand, the situation becomes different, since, as illustrated in (49 a-b), the QNT-sensitive projection V^1 now has V^E instead of V^I as its counterpart of the QLT-sensitive thematic projection:

(49) **Unergative:**
    a. **QNT-sensitive Projection:**   b.   **QLT-sensitive Projection:**

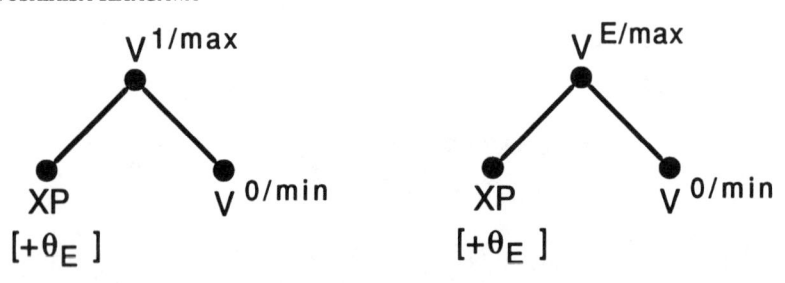

```
    V¹/max                    VE/max
    ●                         ●
   / \                       / \
  ●   ●                     ●   ●
  XP  V⁰/min                XP  V⁰/min
 [+θE]                     [+θE]
```

Finally, we also assume that UG permits certain languages to adopt both QNT- and QLT-sensitive thematic projections, as illustrated in (50), possibly as a marked option:

(50) **Transitive (QNT- & QLT-sensitive Projection):**

```
         V²/E/max
         ●
        / \
       ●   ● V¹/I/med
       XP  / \
      [+θE]●  ● V⁰/min
           YP
          [+θI]
```

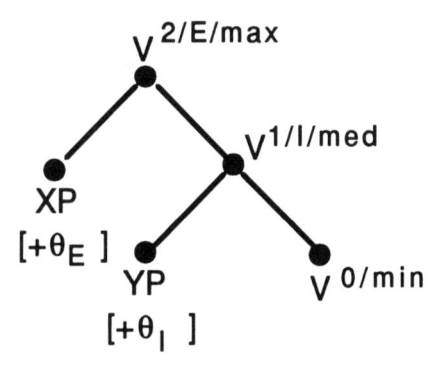

Note that the moment we adopt a percolation-based X-bar Theory as well as the notion of θ-features, postulation of thematic projection, in fact, might become not only a natural move but also a necessary one.

The chart in (51) below summarizes the thematic status of each verbal maximal projection under distinct parametric choices of thematic projection:

(51) **Parametric Variations of Thematic Projections:**

	Transitive	Unergative	Unaccusative
QNT-sensitive	V²	V¹	V¹
QLT-sensitive	VE	VE	VI
QNT/QLT-sensitive	V²/E	V¹/E	V¹/I

Note that, in a language with QNT-sensitive projection, unergative and unaccusative verbs make up a natural class, and in a language with QLT-sensitive projection, transitive and unergative verbs make up a natural class. Finally, in a language with both choices, either subgroup may make up a natural class.

I then propose to make an appeal to Excorporation and the concomitant thematic selection by the excorporated affixes in the LF component in order to account for the generalization we came up with concerning all different types of 1AEX-related effects. In particular, in a language with QNT-sensitive projection like English, the passive morpheme -EN and the nominal morpheme like -ing are analyzed as thematically selecting V^2, and hence only the maximal projection of a transitive verb, as stated in (52):

(52) Thematic Selection in English = Q N T-sensitive:
    a. Passive (-EN): [_ _ V^2]
    b. Nominal (-ing): [_ _ V^2]

This explains why unergative and unaccusative verbs make up a natural class and reject both passivization and nominalization in English. (See (43) above.)

In a language with QLT-sensitive projection like Japanese, on the other hand the passive morpheme -rare and the causative morpheme -sase can be analyzed as thematically selecting V^E, and the null nominal morpheme to select V^I, as stated in (53):

(53) Thematic Selection in Japanese = **QLT**-sensitive:
    a. Passive (-rare): + [V^E __]
    b. Causative (-sase): + [V^E __]
    c. Nominal (-∅): + [V^I __]

This allows us to capture why transitive and unergative verbs make up a natural class and permit passivization and causativization, while they reject SBJ-Verb nominalization in Japanese. (See (44) above.)[21]

---

[21]Kageyama (1982, 222), Sugioka (1984, 83) and Miyagawa (1989, 95-97), all examine **actual** examples and regard 'weather verbs' on a par with unaccusative verbs with respect to their susceptibility to the nominal compounding in question. Miyagawa, for example, provides the following three examples (the last of which is not in the vocabulary of any of my informants):
    (i) a. ame-huri   'rain-falling (= rainy weather)'
          b. hi-deri   'sun-shining (= drought)'
          c. kaze-huki 'wind-blowing'
None of them, however, seem to provide action/process readings. Moreover, when we examine the **neologism** of weather verbs, none of the examples seem to be acceptable (as action/process nominal):
    (ii) a. *yuki-huri   'snow-falling'
           b. *arare-huri 'hail-falling'
           c. *tuki-deri   'moon-shining'

d. *hosi-deri   'star-shining'
e. *kaze-huki   'wind-blowing'

We may consider, therefore, that 'weather verbs' are classified as unergative rather than unaccusative verbs, although I refrain from making any definitive statement. The possibility of both passivization and causativization with <u>hur</u> 'fall' and <u>huk</u> 'blow' as in (iii)-(iv) is compatible with such classification:

(iii) a. ame ni **hur-are**-te oozyoosita
    rain dat fall-PASS-and troubled
    'We were troubled by the rain.'
  b. kita kara   haridasita   kookiatu   ga
    from north overhanging high pressure system nom
    ame o   **hur-ase**-ta
    rain acc fall-CAUSE-past
    'The high pressure system overhanging from the north made it rain.'

(iv) a. konoha ga   kaze ni   **huk-are**-te   yureteita
    leaf   nom wind dat blow-PASS-and   swinging
    'The leaf was swinging, being blown by the wind.'
  b. Siberia-tairiku   no   kookiatu   ga
    Siberia-continent gen   high pressure system nom
    Kantootihoo ni   karakkaze o   **huk-ase**-ru
    Kanto-region at   dry wind   acc fall-CAUSE-pres
    'The high pressure system from Siberia makes the dry wind blow.'

The verb <u>ter</u> 'shine' at least marginally permits passivization but seems to reject causativization:

(v) a. ?itinitizyuu   manatu no taiyoo   ni   **ter-are**-te
    all day long   mid-summer sun   dat shine-PASS-and
    makkuro ni hiyakeshitesimatta
    much tanned
    'Being exposed to the mid-summer sun all day, I got a good tan.'
  b. *taiyoo ga   tuki   o   **ter-ase**-teiru
    sun   nom   moon   acc shine-CAUSE-being
    'The sun makes the moon shine.'

I do not have any account of this breakdown of the generalization except for noting the possibility of blocking effects due to the existence of expressions as in (vi):

(vi) a. ?X o **kagayak-ase**-ru
        acc shine-CAUSE-pres
        'have X shine'
  b. ?X o **hikar-ase**-ru
        acc shine-CAUSE-pres
        'have X shine'

See Rosen (1984) for a warning against identifying unaccusativity of verbs solely in terms of sematics.

In Dutch, which permits both QNT- and QLT-sensitive projections, two different choices may arise for thematic selection. As stated in (54), the personal passive morpheme is analyzed as selecting V^2, while the impersonal passive morpheme as selecting V^E. Alternatively, we may assume that one and only passive morpheme in Dutch selects V^E, and when it has an additional restriction of having to select V^2, it functions as personal passive:

(54) Thematic Selection in Dutch = **QNT-** & **QLT**-sensitive:
    a. Dutch Personal passive: + [$V^{2(/E)}$ __]
    b. Dutch Impersonal passive: + [V^E __]

We, thus, can capture the fact that unergative and unaccusative verbs make up a natural class and reject personal passivization, while transitive and unergative verbs make up a natural class and permit impersonal passivization in Dutch. (See (45) above.)

I do not have enough basis to determine the parametric choices of thematic projection in Lithuanian and Turkish, but we can at least characterize the impersonal passive morphemes in these languages as selecting the categorial maximal projections rather than thematic projections in the LF component, as stated in (55):

(55) Thematic Selection in Lithuanian/Turkish = ?:
    Passive: + [V^{max} __]   (= Categorial projection)

Then, we can offer a generalization that **a passive morpheme universally selects a 'maximal projection'**, though whether this maximal projection is categorial or thematic, and if it is thematic, whether it is QNT-sensitive projection or QLT-sensitive projection, (i.e. V^{max}, V^2 or V^E) depends on the parametric choice of each individual language.

Thus, the Excorporation Approach coupled with the notion 'thematic projection' and its parameterization will systematically capture: (i) the universality (which otherwise may go unnoticed!) and the cross-linguistic variation observed with respect to passivization ((42)), and (ii) the fact that a specific group of verb classes makes up a natural class and is either compatible or incompatible with different morphosyntactic processes within each single language ((43)-(45)). The underlying hypothesis playing a crucial role here is the requirement imposed by the minimalist hypothesis that each predicate must satisfy its selectional properties in the LF component to satisfy the Principle of Full Interpretation.

References

Aissen, Judith. 1974. *The Syntax of Causative Constructions*. Doctoral dissertation, Harvard University.
Baker, Mark. 1988. *Incorporation*. Chicago: The University of Chicago Press.

Baker, Mark, Kyle Johnson, and Ian Roberts. 1989. Passive Arguments Raised. *Linguistic Inquiry* 20..2. 219-251.
Belletti, Adriana. 1988. The Case of Unaccusatives. *Linguistic Inquiry* 19.1. 1-34.
Chomsky, Noam. 1981. *Lectures on Government and Binding*. Dordrecht: Foris.
Chomsky, Noam. 1992. A Minimalist Program for Linguistic Theory. *MIT Occasional Papers in Linguistics 1*.
Di Sciullo, Anna Maria and Edwin Williams. 1987. *On the Definition of Word*. Cambridge, MA: MIT Press.
Dubinsky. Stanley. to appear. *Journal of Linguistics*.
Jaeggli, Osvaldo. 1986. Passive. *Linguistics Inquiry* 17,. 587-622.
Kageyama, Taro. 1982. Word Formation in Japanese. *Lingua* 57. 215-258.
Keenan, Edward. 1994. Predicate-Argument Structure in Malagasy. This volume.
Keenan, Edward L. and Alan Timberlake. 1985. Predicate Formation Rules in Universal Grammar. *WCCFL* 4. 123-138.
Kitagawa, Yoshihisa. 1986 = 1994. *Subjects in Japanese and English*. New York: Garland.
Kitagawa, Yoshihisa. 1989. Internal Subjects. unpublished manuscript: University of Rochester.
Kitagawa, Yoshihisa. in preparation. Excorporation: A Minimalist Approach to Morphology-Syntax Interaction. Kluwer.
Kitagawa, Yoshihisa and S. -Y. Kuroda. 1992. Passive in Japanese. unpublished manuscript. University of Rochester and University of California at San Diego.
Koopman, Hilda. and Dominique Sportiche. 1986. A Note on Long Extraction in Vata and the ECP. *Natural Language and Linguistic Theory* 4.3. 357-376.
Kuroda, S. -Y. 1965. Causative Forms in Japanese. *Foundations of Language* 1. 31-50.
Kuroda, S. -Y. 1988. Whether We Agree or Not: A Comparative Syntax of English and Japanese. *Linguisticae Investigationes* 12.1. 1-47.
Kuroda, S. -Y. 1993. Lexical and Productive Causative in Japanese: An Examination of the Theory of the Paradigmatic Structure. *Journal of Japanese Linguistics* 15. 1-81.
Lasnik, Howard and Mamoru Saito. 1984. On the Nature of Proper Government. *Linguistic Inquiry* 15.2. 235-289.
Lebeaux, David. 1986. The Interaction of Derived Nominals. *CLS* 22: 231-247.
Lieber 1981. *On the Organization of the Lexicon*, Indiana University Linguistics Club.
Miyagawa, Shigeru. 1989. *Structure and Case Marking in Japanese, Syntax and Semantics* 22, New York: Academic Press.
Murasugi, Kumiko. 1990. The Derivation of Derived Nominals. unpublished manuscript, MIT.
Perlmutter, David. M. 1978. Impersonal Passives and the Unaccusative Hypothesis in *Proceedings of the Fourth Annual Meeting of the Berkeley Linguistics Society* 157-189.

Perlmutter, David M. and Paul Postal. 1984. The 1-Advancement Exclusiveness Law in Perlmutter, David M.. and Carol. Rosen eds., *Studies in Relational Grammar* 2, 81-125, Chicago: University of Chicago Press.

Perlmutter, David. M. and Annie Zaenen. 1984. The Indefinite Extraposition Construction in Dutch and German. in Perlmutter, David M.. and Carol. Rosen eds., *Studies in Relational Grammar* 2., 171-216, Chicago: University of Chicago Press.

Pesetsky, David. 1982. *Paths and Categories*. Doctoral dissertation, MIT.

Pesetsky, David. 1985. Morphology and Logical Form. *Linguistic Inquiry* 16.2. 193-246.

Rizzi, Luigi. 1986. Null Objects in Italian and the Theory of pro. *Linguistic Inquiry* 17.3. 501-557.

Rizzi, Luigi. 1990. *Relativized Minimality*. Cambridge, MA: MIT Press.

Rosen, Carol. 1944. The Interface between Semantic Roles and Initial Grammatical Relations. in Perlmutter, David M.. and Carol. Rosen eds., *Studies in Relational Grammar* 2, 38-80, Chicago: University of Chicago Press.

Selkirk, Elisabeth O. 1982. *The Syntax of Words*. Cambridge, MA: MIT Press.

Shibatani, Masayoshi. 1973. Semantics of Japanese Causativization. *Foundations of Language* 9. 327-373.

Stowell, Timothy. 1981. *Origins of Phrase Structure*. Doctoral dissertation, MIT.

Sugioka, Yoko. 1984. *Interaction of Derivational Morphology and Syntax in Japanese and English*. Doctoral dissertation, University of Chicago.

Williams, Edwin. 1981. On the Notions 'Lexically Related' and 'Head of a Word'. *Linguistic Inquiry* 12.2. 245-274.

Zubizarreta, Maria Luisa. 1985. The Relation between Morphology and Morphosyntax: The Case of Romance Causatives. *Linguistic Inquiry* 16.2. 247-289.

Mapping constructions as word templates: evidence from French

JEAN-PIERRE KOENIG
University of California at Berkeley

In this paper, I will outline a monotonic approach to what Jackendoff (1990) calls the correspondence problem, i.e. the mapping of semantic structure to surface syntax. My approach is based on three simple ideas. The first is that mapping principles are word templates, i.e. abstractions over fully specified lexical entries (or certain subparts of lexical entries): they constitute generalizations over the way classes of words associate their semantic arguments to their syntactic complements. The second is that mapping principles can include complex information, and, crucially, that the kind of complex information found in mapping principles spans the range of information found in lexical entries. The third idea is that the set of mapping principles (or word classes in the present approach) found in a grammar do not constitute an amorphous list of principles. They form a hierarchy of more or less general mapping types and this hierarchy of mapping types allows us to capture generalizations while accounting for the full range of phenomena.

It is beyond the purview of this paper to completely justify the hypothesis that mapping principles are word templates. Part of the motivation stems from general considerations in favor of declarative, monotonic approaches to grammatical knowledge which I cannot review here (see Bresnan and Kaplan (1982), Sag (1991) for some arguments from both a learning and processing point of view). I concentrate here instead on presenting a few French mapping principles which support the three ideas I mentioned above. The paper is organized as follows. First, I present a French linking construction that is language-specific and informationally rich and show that the range of information this mapping principle makes use of is similar to the range of information we find in fully specified lexical entries. Second, I present a brief overview of an actual linking theory which embodies the three leading ideas mentioned at the outset. I particularly stress how this theory can model idiosyncratic, informationally rich mapping principles as well as the most general ones. Third, I study some of the consequences of the third leading idea, namely the hypothesis that mapping principles are organized in a hierarchy of word types. I show that assuming the set of mapping principles a grammar contains is so organized, we are able to model some well-known dependencies between

---

* I thank Adele Goldberg for discussing some of the material included in this paper, and Paul Kay for comments on an earlier version. All remaining errors are mine, of course.

mapping principles with the simple notion of inheritance of information.[1]

1. A language-specific linking pattern

The idiosyncratic pattern which I use to illustrate the claim that mapping principles can be informationally rich is exemplified in (1a), which is truth-conditionally equivalent to (1b). The pattern, which I call the Dative Predication pattern or DP, was first discussed at length in Ruwet (1982). It is specific to French; it does not exist in closely related Romance languages like Italian. There are four facts concerning the DP construction which are relevant here.[2]

First, the pattern applies productively to a set of about sixty verbs which are semantically defined, basically verbs of saying and of mental representation. Some of the verb classes are mentioned below. What is interesting here is that all verbs which alternate between a Dative Predication and a sentential complementation structure like *croire* in (1a) vs. (1b) can also occur in so-called non-verbal subject-to-object-raising structures illustrated in (2). Even more striking is the fact that of the small class of French verbs which can occur in verbal raising-to-object structures, but not in non-verbal raising-to-object structures, none can enter in a Dative Predication structure (see (3)). Given the well-known idiosyncrasies of verb class selection by lexical rules or linking constructions (see Green (1974), Pinker (1989), Goldberg (1992)), I take these two facts as strong evidence that the Dative Predication pattern is an instance of non-verbal raising-to-object (or its equivalent in other frameworks).

(1) a. Je veux bien croire des circonstances atténuantes à certains criminels...
I want well believe some circumstances mitigating to some criminals...
b. Je veux bien croire que certains criminels ont des circonstances atténuantes...
I want well believe that certain criminals have ART circumstances mitigating
'I am willing to grant mitigating circumstances to certain criminals'

---

[1] In this paper, I talk about linking patterns proper, i.e. principles governing the assignment of grammatical functions to semantic arguments, as well as mapping principles in general, i.e. the various principles regulating the mapping between semantic structure and syntactic structure (surface syntax within the monostratal framework of this paper). I use the term linking to refer to linking proper, and use mapping to refer to the more general notion.

[2] My discussion in this section is for the most part a summary of the findings of Koenig (1993) to which I refer the reader for a more complete discussion of each point.

(2) Je croyais Marc heureux.
I believe.IMPF Marc happy
'I thought Marc happy'

Some verb classes which participate in the alternation

Assertives: *affirmer* 'affirm', *assurer* 'insure', *proclamer* 'proclaim'...
Verbs of saying: *dire* 'say', *murmurer* 'whisper'...
Commissives as assertives: *promettre* 'promise', *parier* 'bet', *jurer* 'swear'...
Verbs of guessing: *imaginer* 'imagine', *deviner* 'guess', *soupçonner* 'suspect'...

Verb classes which cannot participate in the alternation

verbs of learning and understanding: *apprendre* 'learn'; *comprendre* 'understand'
verbs of explanation or signaling: *montrer* 'show', *expliquer* 'explain', *signaler* 'signal', *indiquer* 'indicate'.

(3) a. La personne qu'il a montré/indiqué être responsable de l'attentat était innocente
'The person he showed to be responsible for the bombing was innocent'
b. *La personne qu'il a montré/indiqué responsable de l'attentat était innocente
'The person he showed responsible for the bombing was innocent'
c. *Je lui ai montré des ennuis
'I showed that he had troubles' (intended meaning)

Second, the two non-external complements of the verb do not form a constituent, specifically not a small clause, contra Guéron (1985). As the ungrammaticality of (4b) and (4c) shows, the direct and indirect objects of (4a) do not behave as a single constituent for purposes of clefting and pseudo-clefting. The constituent-structure of (1a) is therefore as shown in (5), where the direct and indirect object do not form a single subconstituent of *croire* 'to believe'. Now, given that the direct and indirect objects in (5) express together the second semantic argument of *croire*, the two objects cannot both be semantic arguments of *croire*. One at least must be an argument of the belief argument of *croire* rather than an argument of *croire* itself. The constituency of sentences like (1a) thus also suggests that we are dealing with a case of raising, since at least one of the non-subject complements of *croire* satisfies a semantic argument of one of its arguments rather than one of its own semantic arguments.

(4) a. Je trouve beaucoup de charme à cette musique.
I find.PR a.lot of charm to this music
'I find that this music has a lot of charm'
b. *C'est beaucoup de charme à cette musique que je trouve.
It be.PR a.lot of charm to this music that I find.PR
c. *Ce que je trouve, c'est beaucoup de charme à cette musique.
That which I find.PR it be.PR a.lot of charm to this music.

(5) Je veux bien [$_{VP}$ [$_V$croire] [$_{NP}$des circonstances atténuantes] [$_{PP}$à certains criminels]]

Third, the Dative Pattern constrains the semantic relation internal to the second semantic argument of the verb *croire* in sentences like (1a). More specifically, the relation which constitutes the main predicate of the believed proposition of (1a) must be one of extended-possession, where extended-possession is defined as literal possession or any output of a metaphorical mapping taking possession as its source domain (see sentences (6)-(10) for examples of the various semantic relations that can hold between the DO and IOBJ of (1a). See Lakoff et al. (1991) for more details on the mappings).

OWNERSHIP
(6) Tiens, il a une Toyota. Je lui croyais une Renault 18.
     Hold, he have.PR a Toyota. I to.3SG believe.IMPF a Renault 18.
     'Hmm! He has a Toyota. I thought he had a Renault 18'

ABSTRACT PROPERTY
(7) Je lui aimerais davantage d'enthousiasme
     I to.3SG like.COND more of enthusiasm
     'I would like him to have more enthusiasm'

INALIENABLE POSSESSION
(8) Je lui crois le bras gauche plus fort que le bras droit.
     I to.3SG believe.PR the arm left more strong than the arm right
     'I believe that he has a stronger left arm (than the right one)'

SOCIAL RELATIONSHIPS (INCLUDING KINSHIP)
(9) Nous lui savons plusieurs contacts au pentagone.
     We to.3SG know.PR several contacts at.the Pentagon
     'We know that he has several contacts in the Pentagon'

EXPERIENCES (EVENTS THAT HAPPEN TO AN INDIVIDUAL)
(10) Je lui prédis de nombreux accidents avec ce tas de feraille.
     I to.3SG predict.PR some numerous accidents with this heap of scrap
     'I predict that he will have a lot of accidents with this pile of junk'

Fourth, the linking subpart of this construction, i.e. the assignment of an IOBJ function to *à certains criminels* in (1a) is idiosyncratic to this pattern. Whether we choose to say that this *à*-PP denotes an extended-possessor or the extended-possession relation itself, there is no other linking rule with quite the same semantics (i.e. the notion of extended-possession I just defined) in the rest of the grammar of French.[3]

To account for all the facts just mentioned, we must introduce in the grammar of French a Linking rule/construction along the lines of the informal statement in (α):

Dative Predication Linking rule:
(α) If a non-verbal raising-to-object verb V has a propositional argument A whose predicate is the relation of extended possession (of the *belong* variety), realize A as an IOBJ.

What does the existence of language-specific patterns like the DP tell us about the nature of linking patterns in general? To answer this question, let's consider the kind of information necessary to state the DP construction: (i) the syntactic category of lexical entries whose subcategorization requirements the DP specifies (i.e. that the DP applies to verbs here); (ii) some specific semantic condition on the subcategorization requirement the DP specifies the grammatical function of (i.e. that it denotes a relation of extended possession); (iii) the relationship between the DP and another mapping pattern (i.e. that the the DP is a subtype of non-verbal raising-to-object).

Although the French DP is relatively exceptional cross-linguistically, many other linking patterns are constrained by the same kind of information. First, Pinker (1989) and Goldberg (1992), among others, show that many valence alternations are sensitive to the detailed semantics of verbs. As we have seen, the same is true indirectly of the DP, which by virtue of being a subcase of non-verbal raising is constrained to apply only to verbs that denote certain kinds of relations. Furthermore, linking rules are also known to be sensitive to the

---

[3] In particular, even in cases where the dative or indirect object function is assigned to a complement coding something like a possession or a possessor, including metaphorical possession, not exactly the same range of metaphorical possessors or possession relations can be coded by the indirect object. Witness the following examples to be compared with (7)-(8) and (10) above (thanks to Adele Goldberg for suggesting the relevance of the examples):

(i) Cela lui a donné de l'enthousiasme.
'This gave him some enthusiasm'
(ii) *Deux heures d'exercice par jour lui a donné le bras droit plus fort que le bras gauche.
'Two hours of exercise per day gave him a right arm that is stronger than the left one'
(iii) *Sa conduite rapide lui a donné de nombreux accidents.
'His fast driving gave him a lot of accidents' (literal gloss).

So, despite similarities between the notion of extended-possession involved in the DP and other notions of possession involved in other French mapping principles, the specific semantics associated with the IOBJ is particular to this pattern.

semantic type of the arguments whose grammatical function they specify. For example, locational and directional argument requirements must be satisfied by expressions which denote locational and directional predications. To be sure, the exact semantic relation relevant to the IOBJ assignment in the DP is more specific than that involved in many other linking rules. But there is no difference in kind as to the nature of the information relevant to the linking rule: in both cases, it is the semantic relation denoted by the dependent to which a grammatical function is assigned. The general kind of information the DP rule makes reference to is therefore not limited to this language-specific pattern. Other, more common patterns make reference to a combination of the syntactic category and semantics of the targeted lexical item and the syntactic category and semantics of the targeted subcategorization requirement.[4]

We may now ask ourselves the question: what groups together these various types of information? Why can mapping rules be sensitive to these four specific types of information? The answer, I suggest, lies in the nature of linking rules: mapping rules are word classes, the kind of information they can make reference to is therefore the kind of information found in lexical entries, the syntactic category and semantics of the entry and the syntactic category and semantics of its subcategorization requirements.[5] In other words, if linking rules are word classes, we directly account for the identity of the informational domain relevant to mapping principles and lexical entries. Linking rules are classifications of words. Hence, they can make reference to any of the major classes of information which lexical entries can contain.

The first characteristic of the DP pattern I mentioned above — that it is a subcase of non-verbal raising-to-object — also indirectly supports the hypothesis that linking patterns are word classes. Classes are easily related to each other via set inclusion (or any formally more complex notion of set inclusion, like subsumption in attribute-value grammars). In this section, I have argued that the general characteristics of patterns like the DP lends support to the claim that mapping principles are word classes. In the next section, I present in some detail a specific linking theory based on this hypothesis. I then show how this approach can not only model the usual linking patterns as easily as other approaches, but that it can also account for more complex linking constructions like the DP.

---

[4] Although the DP does not specify the syntactic category of the argument to which it assigns the IOBJ function, other linking constructions do. Consider the conative alternation in *Marc shot at Joe* which specifies not only that the patient argument must bear an oblique function, but that it must be realized by a PP headed by *at*.

[5] See Pollard and Sag (1994) and Fillmore and Kay (1993) for evidence that the subcategorization requirements of lexical entries contain both syntactic and semantic information.

2. A formalism for capturing generalizations

The formalism I use is a minimal variant of Typed Feature Structures, as defined in Carpenter (1992) and Pollard and Sag (1994) after the initial studies of Flickinger (1988) and Pollard and Sag (1987) on the hierarchial lexicon.[6] Basically, typed feature structures are like ordinary feature structures used in most brands of attribute-value grammars, except that feature structures are grouped into categories to form a hierarchy of more or less general types. One important aspect of this classification of feature structures into types is that feature structures can be classified by several cross-cutting dimensions, as if one were to classify animals not only by genetic similarities, but also by food habits, habitats, and so forth. Each dimension in this multi-dimensional hierarchy represents a linguistically relevant classification of grammatical objects or feature structures. In the somewhat simplified diagrams you will see, I use traditional attribute-value matrices to represent feature structures and write their types in italics at the bottom left of each attribute-value matrix or AVM. I represent the relation of subtype to type by drawing a line between the subtype below and its supertype above it, where *a* is a subtype of *b* iff it contains all the information contained in *b* and maybe more.

In the specific framework being developed here, called Construction Grammar (see Fillmore and Kay (1993) for more details), lexical entries are stored radically underspecified, i.e. stripped of all predictable information, notably any information regarding the grammatical function and other syntactic aspects of their subcategorization requirements. Fully specified lexical entries, i.e. lexical entries used in the processing of actual sentences, are the result of combining the information of underspecified stored entries with that of various possible alternatives or choices in a hierarchy of linking and mapping patterns.

---

[6] The two major differences between the typed feature structures system adopted here and the one presented in Carpenter (1992) are (i) that type definitions are not necessarily local, i.e. restricted to the immediate attributes of the type being defined; (ii) the type hierarchy is constructed on-line, and is not necessarily compiled in advance.

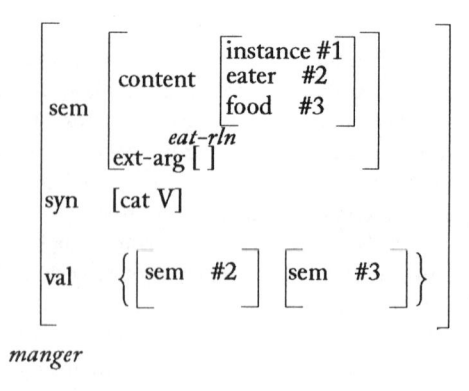

$$\begin{bmatrix} \text{sem} & \begin{bmatrix} \text{content} & \begin{bmatrix} \text{instance } \#1 \\ \text{eater } \#2 \\ \text{food } \#3 \end{bmatrix} \\ \text{ext-arg} & \overset{eat\text{-}r/n}{[\ ]} \end{bmatrix} \\ \text{syn} & [\text{cat V}] \\ \text{val} & \left\{ \begin{bmatrix} \text{sem } \#2 \end{bmatrix} \begin{bmatrix} \text{sem } \#3 \end{bmatrix} \right\} \end{bmatrix}$$

manger

Figure 1: The minimal entry for *manger*

2.1 General linking constructions

A simple example will make this clearer. Take a sentence like (11):

(11) Marc a mangé du poulet.
  'Marc ate some chicken'

The minimal, stored entry for French *manger* 'eat' only mentions the semantics of the entry, its syntactic category, as well as its having two subcategorization or valence requirements which must be satisfied (see Figure 1[7]). The fully specified entry for *manger* which licenses sentences like (11), on the other hand, specifies the syntactic functions of the subcategorization requirements corresponding to the eater and food arguments and which semantic argument functions as the external argument (leaving aside the syntactic category of the subcategorization requirements, which is irrelevant here). It is represented in Figure 2. The entry in Figure 2, which is the fully specified entry for (11), results from the combination of the stored entry represented in Figure 1 with two types of mapping constructions.

---

[7] Pound signs followed by identical numbers in the diagrams represent identity of structure. The diagrams are somewhat simplified, as well as stripped of all irrelevant information for the purposes of this paper; I also use three dots whenever the path leading to a given attribute is irrelevant. The attributes I use should be self-explanatory, but for the INSTANCE attribute, which stands for the referential index associated with each semantic object.

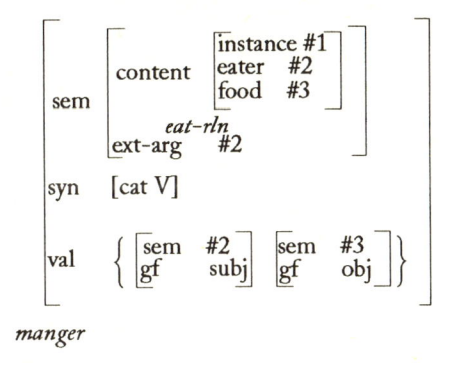

$$\begin{bmatrix} \text{sem} & \begin{bmatrix} \text{content} & \begin{bmatrix} \text{instance} & \#1 \\ \text{eater} & \#2 \\ \text{food} & \#3 \end{bmatrix} \\ \begin{bmatrix} eat\text{-}rln \\ \text{ext-arg} & \#2 \end{bmatrix} \end{bmatrix} \\ \text{syn} & [\text{cat V}] \\ \text{val} & \left\{ \begin{bmatrix} \text{sem} & \#2 \\ \text{gf} & \text{subj} \end{bmatrix} \begin{bmatrix} \text{sem} & \#3 \\ \text{gf} & \text{obj} \end{bmatrix} \right\} \end{bmatrix}$$

manger

Figure 2: The fully specified entry for *manger*

First, *manger* combines with an external argument assignment construction. The specific construction relevant to *manger* is represented in the top row of Figure 3. This construction says that semantic predicates one of whose participants is of type actor have this actor as their distinguished or external argument, where distiguished or external argument is a semantic notion here which does not necessarily entail that the corresponding syntactic dependent is realized structurally as a subject (i.e. external to the VP) at any level of representation. Another typical construction is diagrammed in the bottom row of Figure 3. This construction says that the external argument of predicators which denote a relation of semantic type REPRESENT (corresponding to the notion of having a representation, like *know, believe...*), is the participant role which can be analyzed as being of type experiencer. Obviously, these constructions are similar to the various AGENT and EXPERIENCER rules which have been assumed since Fillmore (1968) and Williams (1981), among others. There are several differences between the mapping constructions proposed here and such rules. First, ACTOR or EXPERIENCER in these constructions are simply meant as supertypes or abstractions over actual participant roles, like EATER or BELIEVER, very much in the spirit of Dowty (1991) and Knowledge Representation systems (see Wilensky (1986) for an overview). In other words, what is primary in lexical entries is participant roles. So-called theta-roles are merely a classification of participant roles invoked by certain mapping and linking constructions.[8]

Second, as can be seen from a comparison of the two constructions in Figure 3, the rules determining the external argument of a predicator are specific to the types of situations denoted by various predicators.[9] Each construction checks the semantic type of the relation denoted by the lexical entry and, if the denoted situation is of the right type, identifies the external argument of the verb with a participant role of a given type. Each construction does not consider any other argument of the relation denoted by the verb but the one which is assigned external argumenthood. Nor does it consider theta-roles of other entries in assigning external argumenthood. There is thus no theta-hierarchy, i.e. postulation of an abstract hierarchy of theta-roles, which is independent of the actual set of semantic arguments carried by a given predicator and which orders its entire set of arguments. External argument selection constructions merely distinguish one argument from all the others.

The difference between the two approaches is not merely conceptual. The theory presented here makes different predictions as to the class of possible linking rules from those made by theories which rely on a theta-hierarchy. To take but one example, within the theory presented here, either a linking rule

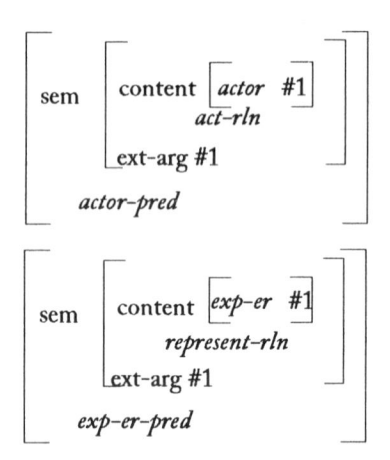

$$\begin{bmatrix} \text{sem} & \begin{bmatrix} \text{content} & \begin{bmatrix} \textit{actor} & \#1 \\ \textit{act-rln} & \end{bmatrix} \\ \text{ext-arg } \#1 \end{bmatrix} \\ \textit{actor-pred} \end{bmatrix}$$

$$\begin{bmatrix} \text{sem} & \begin{bmatrix} \text{content} & \begin{bmatrix} \textit{exp-er} & \#1 \\ \textit{represent-rln} & \end{bmatrix} \\ \text{ext-arg } \#1 \end{bmatrix} \\ \textit{exp-er-pred} \end{bmatrix}$$

Figure 3: Two external argument constructions

---

[8] The specific formalism I use to implement semantic typing is adapted from Pollard and Sag (1994) and Tony Davis, p.c., who has been independently developing a linking theory within hpsg which shares many similarities with the one presented here.

[9] In that respect, the theory of external argument assignment assumed here is closer in spirit to Fillmore (1977) who claims that meanings are relativized to scenes.

targets the external argument (or the (complement) set of non-external arguments), or a linking rule targets a thematically specified argument. Linking rules cannot be constrained semantically in any other way. In all other cases, linking rules must therefore be free to apply to arguments of any semantic type. To put it differently, there can be no linking rule that mentions the second or third highest argument of a verb along the theta-hierarchy. To my knowledge, this prediction is borne out in English, French, and many other languages.

Third, there is no implication that there is a small set of predefined universal types of participant roles which are necessarily relevant for the determination of the external argument of a verb. In particular, it is not assumed that all predicators have their external argument specified by one of these constructions. Some predicators idiosyncratically specify their external argument, as in the case of *undergo*, or *receive*.

This last point illustrates one important general characteristic of the approach to linking advocated here. It is best explained by drawing a parallel with feature underspecification in non-linear phonology. Regular lexical entries, as mentioned before, are stored radically underspecified. The function of mapping constructions is to specify this underspecified information, so as to end up with a fully specified entry. Lexical entries which are irregular with respect to a given type of mapping construction— external argument assignment constructions in the case of *undergo* and *receive*— PRELINK or lexically PRE-SPECIFY the value of the relevant set of attributes; here, which argument is the external argument of the entry. Such prelinking prevents more general patterns from applying (see section 3 for more examples).

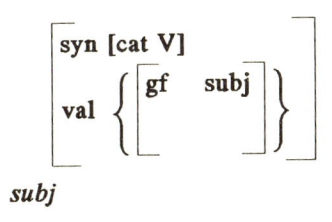

$$\begin{bmatrix} \text{syn [cat V]} \\ \text{val} \ \left\{ \begin{bmatrix} \text{gf} & \text{subj} \end{bmatrix} \right\} \end{bmatrix}$$

subj

Figure 4: The *subject* linking construction

The second set of constructions necessary to account for sentences like (11) include linking patterns proper. Two are represented in Figures 4 and 5. The first construction says that a transitive verb (i.e. a verb of type TRANSITIVE) subcategorizes for a dependent bearing the OBJ grammatical function provided this dependent does not correspond to the external argument of the semantic representation of the verb. The second construction is the subject construction represented in Figure 5 which simply says that a verb can have one dependent bearing the subject function whatever its semantic type. We see with patterns such as the transitive and subject constructions that linking templates can be as

$$\begin{bmatrix} \text{sem} & [\text{ext-arg } \#2] \\ \text{syn} & [\text{cat V}] \\ \text{val} & \left\{ \begin{bmatrix} \text{sem} & \#1 \\ \text{gf} & \text{obj} \\ \#1 \neq \#2 \end{bmatrix} \right\} \end{bmatrix}$$

trans

Figure 5: The *transitive* linking construction

general as necessary, as in other approaches to linking. In fact, the three constructions just mentioned, the actor external argument mapping construction and the transitive and subject linking constructions are not incommensurable with various current proposals within both LFG and GB. They are as general as more well-known descriptions of these patterns and use a comparable amount of information. Well-known linking patterns are thus as easily represented in a theory that views linking patterns as abstract word templates as they are in other theories.[10]

What distinguishes more particularly the word class approach to linking, though, is its ability to model less ordinary linking patterns using the same notion of word templates and the same formal mechanism of typed feature structures. More language-specific or idiosyncratic templates are simply less general, less abstract templates than the ones I just discussed. They do not require added formal stipulations. Let's see, for example, how we can describe the Dative Predication pattern within the approach to linking just outlined.

---

[10] Even so, there are significant conceptual and empirical differences between the approach taken here and more traditional approaches, some of which I mentioned when discussing the status of theta-roles and the theta-hierarchy.

MAPPING CONSTRUCTIONS AS WORD TEMPLATES / 261

$$\begin{bmatrix} \text{sem [cont } saying \lor represent]] \\ \text{syn [cat V]} \\ \text{val} \left\{ \begin{bmatrix} \text{syn} & \begin{bmatrix} \text{cat } \neg V \\ \text{pred +} \end{bmatrix} & \#1 \begin{bmatrix} \quad \end{bmatrix} \\ \text{val} & \{ \#1[\ ] \} \end{bmatrix} \right\} \end{bmatrix}$$

non-verbal-raising

$$\begin{bmatrix} \text{val} \left\{ \begin{bmatrix} \text{syn [pred +]} \\ \text{gf iobj} \\ \text{sem} \quad \text{cont} \begin{bmatrix} \text{ext-poss-or} \\ \text{ext-poss-ed } \#1 \\ \textit{ext-possession-rln} \end{bmatrix} \\ \text{ext-arg } \#1 \end{bmatrix} \right\} \end{bmatrix}$$

dative-predication

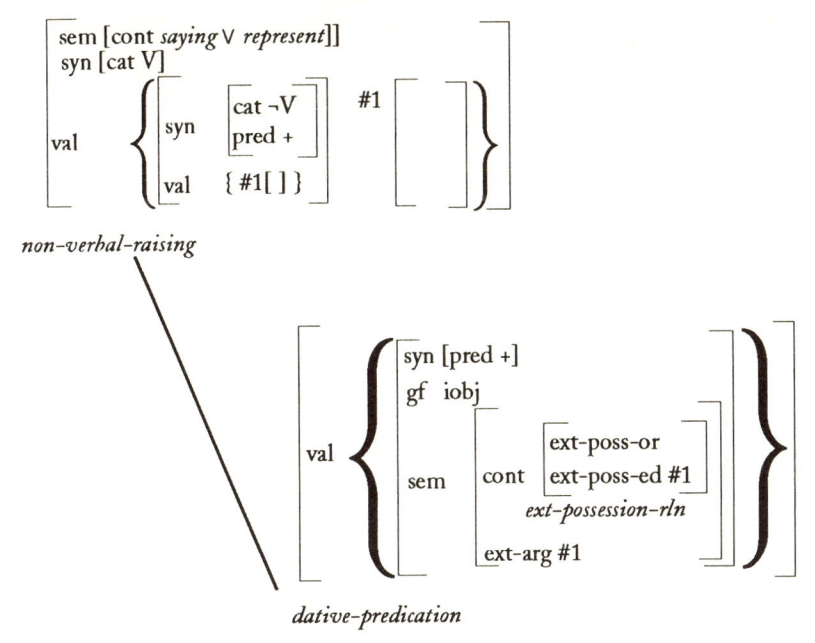

Figure 6: The *dative-predication* construction

First, we need to describe non-verbal raising, exemplified in (2). The construction is represented in Figure 6. Aside from its restricting raising to non-verbal predicates, like *heureux* in (2), this pattern simply identifies the subject sucategorization requirement of the non-verbal predicate with a subcategorization requirement of the predicator the non-verbal predicate depends on, i.e. *croire* in (2), as is standard in both HPSG, LFG, and CG, and is indicated in the diagram by *#1*. Now, as I mentioned before, the Dative Predication construction only applies when non-verbal raising applies. This means that any fully specified lexical entry which instantiates the Dative Predication pattern also instantiates the non-verbal raising pattern. Formally, the Dative Predication construction is declared to be a subtype of the non-verbal raising construction, as indicated in Figure 6 by the line joining the two types in the diagram.[11]

---

[11] The points at each end of the line are the AVM representations of the type declaration for each construction. The line joining the two types is meant to be iconic for the relevant subpart of the type hierarchy, where being lower entails being a subtype of. Note that I have included the general definition of raising structure in the

Given such a declaration, we need not repeat in the statement of the Dative Predication construction all the information contained in the non-verbal raising construction. The presence of this information in any verb to which the DP applies is entailed by the fact that the Dative Predication is a subtype of non-verbal raising. We only need to specify what is added by the Dative Predication pattern. As shown in the bottom AVM of Figure 6, we therefore only need to say that the semantic relation denoted by the non-verbal predicate dependent of this special kind of non-verbal raising-to-object is a relation of extended-possession, its grammatical function, IOBJ, and that the (extended)-possessed object of this non-verbal predicate is the external argument of this PP (and will thus turn out to be the target of raising).[12]

When applied to *croire* as used in (1a), the construction described in the bottom AVM of Figure 6, insures that the IOBJ *à certains criminels* receives the right semantic interpretation and that its external argument, *des circonstances atténuantes* is raised. Our ordinary TRANSITIVE and SUBJECT constructions then apply, as they would in any ordinary sentence, like our (11) above. Note that I did not use any new mechanism to account for the idiosyncratic, language-specific DP pattern. I simply used the notion of type hierarchy and abstraction over fully specified phrases or words which is used in all areas of grammatical structure to capture generalizations within CG and HPSG: morphology, constituent structure, including the description of our most general linking patterns. Although there is a difference of degree in the amount of information linking templates like the DP and the transitive constructions require any verb they apply to to contain, the two patterns are the same kind of object, i.e. a word type (i.e. a subtype of the WORD type). Assuming linking patterns to be word classes thus leads to a theoretically parsimonious description of language-specific linking rules, by allowing us to vary levels of abstraction within the statement of

---

type definition for the French non-verbal raising-to-object construction. To distinguish between a universal raising construction and language-specific conditions on particular raising constructions, we need to distinguish between universal type declarations and language-specific type declarations, a matter I cannot pursue here.

[12] Literally, the type declaration diagrammed in Figure 6 says that if a verb is an instance of the DP construction, then it is an instance of non-verbal raising. In the first section, I made the stronger claim that the classes of verbs that can enter the two patterns are identical. But the weaker statement made here *de facto* entails the identity of the two verb classes. Verbs are stored underspecified between a raising and non-raising alternation (for those verbs that alternate). Morever, there are no additional restrictions on the target verb imposed by the DP pattern. Consequently, if a given verb belongs to the set of verbs to which non-verbal raising-to-object can apply, it also belongs to the set of verbs to which the DP can apply. I thank Christopher Culy (p.c.) for clarifying my thoughts on the issues discussed in the last two footnotes.

each linking pattern and to relate more complex patterns to simpler patterns they informationally contain. In the next section, I illustrate further with some other examples of French linking constructions the latter use of the word class hypothesis.

3. Other examples

3.1 Positive absolute exceptions

The approach to linking outlined above easily handles cases where a rule/construction which is optional otherwise must apply in the case of a specific lexical item (what Lakoff (1970) called "positive absolute exceptions"). Take the verb *prêter* in French, as illustrated in example (12a):

(12) a. On lui prête l'intention de démissionner.
    3.INDEF 3SG.DAT lend.PRES the intention of resign.INF
    'People say he will resign'
 b. *On prête qu'il a l'intention de démissionner
    3.INDEF lend.PRES that he have.PR the intention of resign.INF

Prêter has a special meaning in this pattern, something like *say* with the added nuance that the speaker makes explicit its non-commitment to the truth of the statement. It only occurs in the Dative Predication with this meaning (see (12b)). To capture the fact that this lexical entry is an instance of a well-established French linking pattern and is not completely arbitrary in its surface syntax, we only need declare one entry for *prêter* to be an instance of the Dative Predication construction. Its irreducible stored information can thus be reduced to the minimum, as shown in Figure 7, where the minimal entry for *prêter* at the bottom left of this partial type hierarchy does not contain more information than what was in the minimal entry for *manger* except for the specification that *prêter* necessarily inherits the Dative Predication pattern. The familiar distinction between productive and unproductive patterns is here simply a distinction between a word class being defined by a specification of common properties of its members, or by their mere listing. Moreover, a single pattern can use both ways of specifying the word classes it applies to, as the DP construction illustrates. By inheritance, the general DP construction specifies the classes of verbs to which it applies productively, i.e. any verb whose denotation is of type SAYING v REPRESENT. Within these classes, the DP is productive. But there are also idiosyncratic subcases of the DP construction. Each of these subclassses is specified by listing its members, like *prêter*.

3.2 Localizing Global Rules

The well-known French clause-union structures and particularly the rule/pattern responsible for the assignment of the IOBJ function to the external argument of the complement verb in sentences (16)-(19), illustrate a second additional advantage of the word class *cum* inheritance view of linking.

(13) Marc a fait tomber Paul.
      'Marc made Paul fall'
(14) Dieu fait pleuvoir tous les vendredis
      'God makes it rain every Friday'
(15) Napoléon a fait peindre le tableau par David
      'Napoleon had the painting done by David'
(16) Marc a fait manger des épinards à Paul
      'Marc made Paul eat spinach'
(17) a. Nous leur avons fait essuyé une de ces défaites
          'We made them endure such a defeat!'
      b. Un vent violent a fait perdre de la vitesse à l'avion
          'A strong wind made the plane loose speed'
(18) a. Nous n'avons pas pu faire parler de son voyage à Marc
          'We couldn't make Marc speak of his trip'
      b. *Cela leur fait appartenir à leur maître.
          'This made them belong to their master'
(19) Cela lui a fait patienter (Authier and Reed (1991), (3))
      'This made him wait'

I will make the assumption here that the process of clause-union consists in merging the subcategorization requirements of the causative *faire* and its complement, i.e. that it is a subtype of raising as defined above. But nothing crucial depends on this assumption here. The same point can be made if clause-union is analyzed differently. The crucial facts for my point are the following.

(i) The process of clause-union does not *per se* specify the GF/case of the external argument of the complement verb, *contra* Legendre (1989) for French. Note first that FAIRE-À does not need to apply to the external argument of the complement verb. This external argument can be a DO, as in sentence (13), or be expressed by an adjunct phrase (see (15)). The complement verb might even have no external argument to be expressed, as in (14). There is thus no common GF assigned to this external argument by clause-union.

Second, the assignment of DO to the external argument of the complement verb in (13) is predicted by the general transitive linking construction mentioned in Figure 3. Letting clause-union itself specify this GF would miss a generalization.

(ii) There are more than one type of FAIRE-À linking rule, as shown by Postal (1984), Morin (1980), and Authier and Reed (1991). Aside from the usual FAIRE-À illustrated in (16), which applies to syntactically transitive, semantically dyadic complement verbs, many dialects of French allow the application of FAIRE-À to a class of dyadic intransitive verbs provided the entity denoted by the IOBJ *à Marc* is in control of the event denoted by the complement verb (see (18a) *vs.* (18b)). Note that this semantic constraint does not bear on cases where FAIRE-À applies to syntactically transitive dyadic complement verbs, as shown in (17). The two patterns are therefore distinct. Moreover, some dialects (not mine, though) apparently allow even the external argument of monadic complement verbs to be realized as an IOBJ under the same semantic conditions, with the added syntactic constraint that the IOBJ be always realized as a clitic (*lui* in (19)). Given the differences in semantic and syntactic constraints bearing on these patterns, we must recognize at least two and even three FAIRE-À linking rules for those speakers which accept sentences like (19). Moreover, these three FAIRE-À patterns are specific to clause-union structures and cannot be predicted from other French linking patterns, a point already made for transitive FAIRE-À by Baker (1988).[13]

As in the case of the DP construction, we therefore need to make the application of FAIRE-À dependent on the application of clause-union. We can easily accomplish this by (i) positing an abstract clause-union construction which does not specify the GF of the external argument of the complement verb, but merely merges two subcategorization sets; (ii) having this abstract construction be inherited by or be a supertype of the general FAIRE-À construction, which assigns an IOBJ function to the raised external argument of the complement verb, (ii) having each specific FAIRE-À construction inherit from the general FAIRE-À construction, as succintly illustrated in Figure 7.

Notice that inheritance of word classes, as used here, allows us to capture in a constrained fashion and via a mechanism amply motivated elsewhere in the description of natural languages, what would have been basically global rules in old TG, as seen in the condition (β) on the application of the dyadic, intransitive version of FAIRE-À and where 'only applies if' replaces the information-theoretic notion 'is subsumed by':

(β) The dyadic, intransitive FAIRE-À construction only applies if the controlled event FAIRE-À construction applies. This pattern, in turn, only applies if the general FAIRE-À applies, which is itself dependent on the application of the general clause-union construction.

The two uses of typed feature structures I mentioned in the last two subsections are very similar. In both cases, we specify a class of words to be a subclass of another subclass. The first case is simply the degenerate case where a subclass contains only one member. In the next section, I present a somewhat different example. I show that treating linking patterns as word classes allows us to capture the common structure among patterns which are not necessarily all

---

[13] Some scholars have tried to derive the assignment of IOBJ in the general FAIRE-À construction from more general facts about Romance. I cannot review the evidence against such a proposal here. Note, though, that, if true, this fact would not detract from my main point in this section, since the controlled event FAIRE-À linking constructions are uncontroversially restricted to clause-union contexts.

linking patterns, but are all word class constructions.

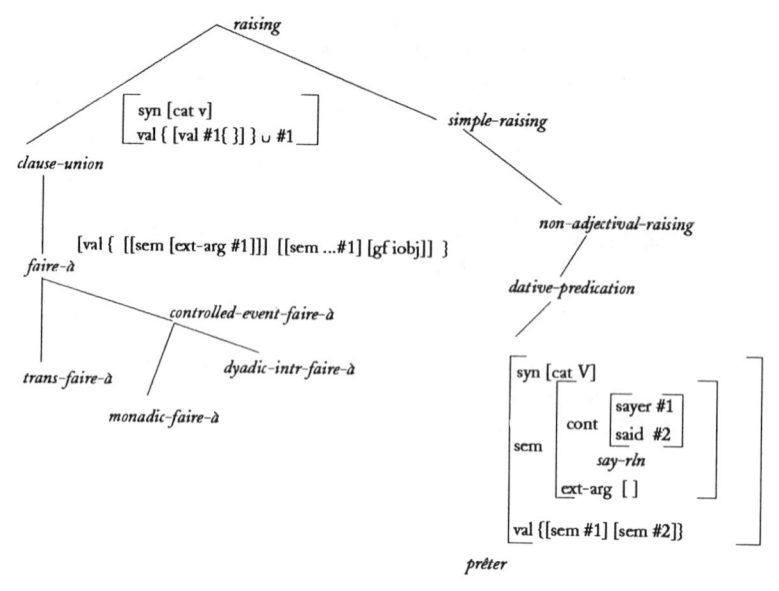

Figure 7: The French *raising* type hierarchy

3.3 Abstraction over different types of rules/constructions

As is well-known, French reflexive verbs are used for many different purposes: for ordinary co-reference or reciprocal interpretation (20a), for deriving inchoative verbs from lexical causatives (20b), i.e. for a process which belongs to derivational morphology, for a linking pattern very similar to passive (20c), and idiosyncratically with verbs like *s'en aller* 'to leave' (20d) or *se ficher* 'to make fun'.[14]

(20) a. Ils se sont regardés.
Marc REFL be.PR look.PPT
'They looked at themselves/each other'
b. Le vase s'est brisé.

---

[14] Many other scholars have considered what is common among all reflexive uses in Romance, (see Zribi-Hertz (1980) and Wehrli (1986) among others). I cannot review these various proposals here. My point is simply that word typing offers an elegant way of explicitly capturing the common morphosyntactic manifestation of reflexivity in Romance.

The vase REFL be.PR break.PPT
'The vase broke'
c. Le Gazpacho se mange froid.
The Gazpacho REFL eat.PR cold
'Gazpacho is eaten cold'
d. Jean s'est en allé.
Jean REFL be.PR of.it go.PPT
'Jean went away'

The syntactic consequences of being a reflexive verb are always the same, though. (i) The verb requires (or subcategorizes for) a reflexive clitic which can attach directly to the verb, or can be passed onto an auxiliary as in (20c) vs. (20a). (ii) This clitic must agree in person and number with the subject. (iii) The auxiliary marking preterite past tense is être and not avoir, when its complement is a reflexive verb.

We can capture this entire set of morphosyntactic properties which are shared among all constructions marked by a reflexive marker by positing an abstract reflexive type, represented at the top of the type hierarchy in Figure 8 that all the more specific patterns mentioned in the diagram inherit. Witness the case of the passive reflexive or se-moyen, which simply says that the external argument need not be realized syntactically (marked in the diagram by the GF ⊘). What is specially interesting in this last example is (i) that the abstract reflexive construction which is shared is an abstract morphosyntactic construction, not a linking pattern per se and (ii) that the types which share the abstract reflexive construction belong to what are usually considered very different areas of grammars: linking principles proper, as in the case of the passive reflexive or se-moyen, derivational morphology, as in the case of the inchoative reflexive, and binding constructions. Finally, as with other instances of word classes, the abstract reflexive construction also applies idiosyncratically to a few inherently reflexive verbs like s'en aller 'to leave' or se ficher 'to make fun'. Under a view that linking patterns, derivational morphology, and morphosyntactic patterns are all word templates, i.e. classification of actual entries, although along different dimensions, such an interaction between these

$$\begin{bmatrix} \text{syn} & [\text{aux } \hat{e}tre] \\ \text{clitic} & \left\{\begin{bmatrix} ..\text{agr } \#1 \\ \text{case refl} \end{bmatrix}\right\} \\ \text{val} & \left\{\begin{bmatrix} \text{gf subj} \\ ..\text{agr } \#1 \end{bmatrix}\right\} \end{bmatrix}$$

reflexive-verb

co-referential

inchoative

idiomatic-refl *passive-refl*

reflexive *reciprocal*

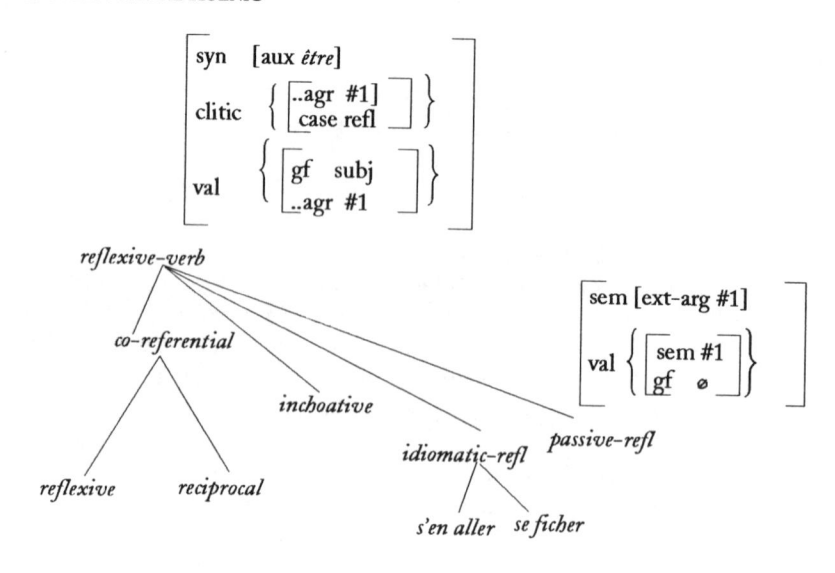

s'en aller *se ficher*

$$\begin{bmatrix} \text{sem } [\text{ext-arg } \#1] \\ \text{val} \left\{ \begin{bmatrix} \text{sem } \#1 \\ \text{gf } \emptyset \end{bmatrix} \right\} \end{bmatrix}$$

Figure 8: The French *reflexive-verb* type hierarchy

various patterns is expected and easily modelled.

Conclusion

Part of the motivation for having different levels or representation in generative linguistics has come from the desire to represent what is common among various surface patterns. In a flat grammar, i.e. in a grammar where rules and principles can bear no relationship to each other, this might be the easiest way to go. What I hope to have shown is that if we allow for a hierarchical organization of grammars, i.e. grammars where linguistic objects can be related to each other in a multi-dimensional abstraction hierarchy, this motivation for multi-stratalism might well disappear. In particular, the same high-level generalizations and regularities that proponents of multi-stratal approaches have pointed out in favor of their organization of grammars are easily captured and accounted for. Of course, as I suggested in this paper, taking a hierarchical view of grammars in general, and linking patterns in particular, has independent advantages. Less general patterns do not force us to alter our principles and our theory of the nature of linking. Observable dependencies between patterns can be accounted for without resorting to *ad hoc* mechanisms, like context-sensitive rules or global rules. But there is one more reason to prefer *ceteris paribus* an approach to linking as word classes: it allows for a truly declarative, bottom-up approach to the problem, with all the usual benefits from a learning and processing perspective of approaches where hypothesized abstract structures not directly reflected in surface patterns are reduced to a minimum.

References

Authier, J.-Marc, and Lisa Reed. 1991. Ergative Predicates and Dative Cliticization in French Causatives. *Linguistic Inquiry* 22(1).197-205.
Bresnan, Joan, and Ronald Kaplan. 1982. Introduction: Grammars as Mental Representations of Language. *The Mental Representation of Grammatical Relations*, xvii-lii. Cambridge, Mass.: MIT Press.
Carpenter, Bob. 1992. *The Logic of Typed Feature Structures*. Cambridge: Cambridge University Press.
Dowty, David. 1991. Thematic Proto-roles and Argument Selection. *Language* 67(3).547-619.
Fillmore, Charles. 1968. The Case for Case. *Universals in Linguistic Theory*, ed. by Emmon Bach and Robert Harms, 1-87. New York: Holt, Rinehart and Winston.
Fillmore, Charles. 1977. The Case for Case Reopened. *Grammatical Relations*, ed. by Peter Cole and Jerold Sadock, 59-81. New York: Academic Press.
Fillmore, Charles, and Paul Kay. 1993. *On Construction Grammar*. University of California at Berkeley: Ms.
Flickinger, Daniel. 1988. *Lexical Rules in the Hierarchical Lexicon*. Ph. D. Dissertation, Stanford University.
Goldberg, Adele. 1992. The Inherent Semantics of Argument Structure: The Case of The English Ditansitive Construction. *Cognitive Linguistics* 3(1).37-74.
Green, Georgia. 1974. *Semantics and Syntactic Regularity*. Bloomington: Indiana University Press.
Guéron, Jacqueline. 1985. Inalienable Possession, PRO-Inclusion and Lexical Chains. *Grammatical Representation*, ed. by Jacqueline Guéron et al., 42-86. Dordrecht: Foris.
Jackendoff, Ray. 1990. *Semantic Structures*. Cambridge: MIT Press.
Koenig, Jean-Pierre. 1993. Linking Constructions vs. Linknr Rules: Evidence from French. *Proceedings of BLS 19*, ed. by Guenter et al., 217-231. Berkeley: Berkeley Linguistics Society.
Lakoff, George. 1970. *Irregularity in Syntax*. New York: Holt, Rinehart and Winston.
Lakoff, George, Jane Espenson, and Alan Schwartz. 1991. *Master Metaphor List*, 2nd Edition. Berkeley: Berkeley Linguistics Dept.
Legendre, Géraldine. 1989. Unaccusativity in French. *Lingua* 79.95-164.

Morin, Yves-Charles. 1980. Les Bases Syntaxiques des Règles de Projection Sémantique: l'Interprétation des Constructions en *faire*. *Linguisticae Investigationes*. 1, 203-212.
Pinker, Steven. 1989. *Learnability and Cognition: the Acquisition of Argument Structure*. Cambridge, Mass.: MIT Press.
Pollard, Carl, and Ivan Sag. 1994. *Head-Driven Phrase-Structure Grammar*. Chicago: Chicago University Press.
Pollard, Carl, and Ivan Sag. 1987. *Information-based Syntax and Semantics*, vol.1. Stanford: CSLI.
Postal, Paul. 1984. French Indirect Object Cliticization and SSC/BT. *Linguistic Analysis* 14(2-3).111-172.
Ruwet, Nicolas. 1982. *Grammaire des Insultes et Autres Etudes*. Paris: Seuil.
Sag, Ivan. 1991. Linguistic Theory and Natural Language Processing. *Natural Language and Speech*, ed. by Ewan Klein and F. Veltman, 69-83. Berlin: Springer-Verlag.
Wehrli, Eric. 1986. On some properties of French clitic *se*. *Syntax and Semantics. Vol. 19*, The Syntax of Pronominal Clitics, ed. by Hagit Borer, 263-283. Orlando: Academic Press.
Wilensky, Robert. 1986. Some Problems and Proposals for Knowledge Representation. Berkeley Cognitive Science Report 40. Berkeley: Institute of Cognitive Studies.
Williams, Edwin. 1981. Argument Structure and Morphology. *The Linguistic Review* 1(1).81-114.
Zribi-Hertz, Anne. 1982. La Construction *se-moyen* du Français et son Statut dans le Triangle: Moyen, Passif, Réfléchi. *Linguisticae Investigationes* 6.345-401.

On grammatical relations in Malagasy control structures

PAUL LAW
Université du Québec à Montréal

0. Introduction

In Malagasy, there is a class of sentences like those in (1) (Keenan 1976) that recall the Equi-NP Deletion or control construction in languages like English:[1]

(1) a. mikasa hanasa ny zaza Rasoa.
    intend.ACT FUT.wash.ACT the child Rasoa
    'Rasoa intends to wash the child.'
  b. mikasa ho-sasan-dRasoa ny zaza.
    intend.ACT FUT-wash.PASS-by-Rasoa the child
    'The child intends to be washed by Rasoa.'
  c. kasain-dRasoa ho-sasana ny zaza.
    intend.PASS-by-Rasoa FUT-wash.PASS the child
    'It is intended by Rasoa that the child be washed by her.'

(2) a. John tried to leave.
  b. John persuaded Bill to leave
  c. John promised Bill to leave.

A characteristic of these examples is that not all arguments of the verbs appear in the surface form. As indicated in the interpretations in (1), there should be three arguments: one for the matrix verb, and two for the embedded verb. But the surface forms have only two arguments. In the same manner, we should expect two arguments for the example in (2a), and three for those in (2b)-(2c), but the surface forms in these cases have one argument fewer than expected.

Despite their superficial similarities, I show in this paper that the examples in (1) do not have the particular property of the English examples in (2) in having a null pronominal subject that appears only in non-finite clauses. Although one can show that the examples in (1), and others that are similar to them, might be accounted for by a theory of control that makes crucial use of grammatical functions (GFs) like SUBJ(ECT), OBJ(ECT) and OBL(IQUE) as theoretical primitives (e.g., Bresnan's (1982) Lexical Functional Grammar (LFG), Perlmutter and Postal's (1974) Relational Grammar (RG)), I argue that syntactic representations of these examples are no more than a reflection of an independent property of argument-binding in Malagasy.

The paper is organized as follows. Section 1 considers some control analyses of these examples in terms of structural configuration, thematic roles, and GFs. Section 2 shows that there exists a general property of argument-binding in Malagasy, which also holds in complex structures, as discussed in section 3. Section 4 presents further evidence for the argument-binding property of the language, which is problematic for the control analyses considered in section 2. Section 5 concludes the paper with some remarks on the typological difference between languages like English and those like Malagasy with respect to the existence of the control structure.

1. Some control analyses

In this section, I discuss some control analyses that appeal to syntactic configuration, thematic roles or GFs, and argue that they should be rejected on empirical and conceptual grounds.

1.1. A structural account

Whether one assumes the complement of the matrix verb in the control structure as a VP (Bresnan 1978) or a clause (S', Koster and May 1982, i.e., CP, cf. Chomsky 1986), the matrix subject clearly c-commands the arguments of the embedded verb. Thus, a structural account might attribute the grammaticality of the examples in (1a) and (1b) to the fact that the matrix subject c-commands, and hence can control, the missing argument of the embedded verb (cf. Larson 1991).

However, such a structural account would fail to account for the grammatical contrast between the example in (1c) and those in (3). In these examples, the Agent phrase *Rasoa* of the matrix verb *mikasa* 'to intend' is apparently in the same position, but the control relationship holds only in (1c) but not in (3):

(3) a. *kasain-dRasoa   hanasa   ny zaza.
       intend.PASS-by-Rasoa FUT.wash.ACT   the child
       'It was intended by Rasoa that she will wash the child.'
    b. *kasain-dRasoa   hanasa   Rabe.
       intend.PASS-by-Rasoa FUT.wash.ACT   Rabe
       'It was intended by Rasoa that Rabe will wash her.'

That is, whatever the position of the Agent phrase turns out to be in the syntactic representation, it either c-commands (Reinhart 1976) or does not c-command the missing argument of the embedded verb; therefore, it either can or cannot control the missing argument in all three examples. Yet, while the example in (1c) is grammatical, those in (3) are not.

1.2. A thematic account

Noticing that the thematic roles borne by the controlling and the controlled arguments are identical in (1a), one might suppose that there is a like-constraint on control to the effect that the controlling and the controlled arguments must bear the same thematic role (cf. Jackendoff 1972). This thematic account would explain why the example in (1c) is possible, but that in (3b) is not. In (1c), the argument *Rasoa* of the matrix verb *mikasa* 'to intend' bears the Agent role, the same thematic role that is borne by the missing argument of the embedded verb. In (3b), the argument *Rasoa* of the matrix verb *mikasa* 'to intend' bears the Agent role, but the missing argument of the embedded verb bears the Theme role.

Nevertheless, the thematic account makes incorrect predictions for the example in (1b) and (3a). It predicts that (1b) should be ungrammatical, since the controlling argument bears the Agent role, but the controlled argument of the embedded verb bears the Theme role. Under this view, the example in (3a) should be grammatical, contrary to fact. The controlling argument in this example bears the same thematic role as that of the controlled argument, namely, Agent. Moreover, the ungrammaticality of the example in (4) is unexpected, since the controlling argument bears the Agent role, the same thematic role that is borne by the controlled argument of the embedded verb:

(4) *mikasa   ho-sasana   ny zaza   Rasoa.
     intend.ACT FUT-wash.PASS   the child Rasoa
     'Rasoa intends that the child will be washed by her.'

We can conclude from the examples in (1), (3)-(4) that the thematic role of the controlling argument need not be the same as that of the controlled argument.

1.3. A grammatical relation account

The examples that we have been discussing so far can be accommodated in an analysis in terms of GFs like SUBJ, OBJ, and OBL (cf. Bresnan 1978, 1982) as theoretical primitives. Suppose there is a like-constraint on control along the lines of (5):

(5) The like-constraint on control
    The controlling and the controlled arguments must bear the same grammatical relation.

then the reason why the examples in (1a)-(1c) are possible, but those in (3)-(4) are not is because the controlling and the controlled arguments bear the same GF in (1a)-(1c), but those in (3)-(4) do not. The controlling and the controlled arguments are both SUBJs in (1a)-(1b), and are both OBLs in (1c). In (3), while the controller is an OBL, the controlled argument is a SUBJ in (3a) and an OBJ in (3b), violating the like-constraint on control in (5). The ungrammaticality of the example in (4) is due to the fact that the controller is a SUBJ and the controlled argument is an OBL.

The like-constraint can be formulated in RG terms with the final stratum being the relevant level of representation. The controlling argument and the controlled arguments are final 1-arcs (also initial 1-arcs) in (1a), and in (1b) where the initial 2-arc borne by the Theme of the embedded verb is promoted to a 1-arc in the final stratum by 2-to-1-Advancement, whereas those in (1c) are final 1-chômeurs. The same constraint explains why the examples in (3) are impossible. In (3a) the controlling argument is a final 1-chômeur, and the controlled argument is a final 1-arc, whereas in (3b) the controlling argument is a final 1-chômeur and the controlled argument is a final 2-arc.

To the extent that an account in terms of structural relations, thematic roles or primitive GFs works (cf. some problematic data in section 4), we need an independent theory of control as embodied in the constraint in (5). There are three reasons why we should not adopt such an approach. First, the embedded verb in structures known as control in languages like English has a distinctive morphology, which we might call non-finite.[2] Syntactically, the non-finite form of the verb does not appear in the matrix clause without an auxiliary. If we make a connection between finite morphology and the presence of a lexical subject (cf. Rouveret 1980), it then follows directly that the subject of a non-finite verb cannot be lexical, although it might be represented syntactically as a null pronominal subject PRO (cf. Chomsky and Lasnik 1977):

(6) a. John persuaded Mary that she/*PRO should be leaving.
    b. John persuaded Mary [PRO/*she to leave]

However, such a finite/non-finite morphological distinction does not exist in Malagasy. The same form of the embedded verb in the examples discussed above can appear as the sole verb in the matrix clause:

(7) a. hanasa   ny zaza Rasoa
    FUT.wash.ACT the child Rasoa
    'Rasoa is washing the child.'
    b. ho-sasan-dRasoa   ny zaza.
    FUT-wash.PASS-by-Rasoa the child
    'The child will be washed by Rasoa.'

The lack of verbal morphology encoding the finite/non-finite distinction thus appears to be a good reason to suppose that the embedded clauses in (1), (3)-(4) do not have a null pronominal subject PRO. In other words, these examples are not control structures.

Second, a control structure generally does not allow a variant in which all arguments of the embedded verb are lexical. As shown in (8), all arguments of the embedded verb can be overtly realized in syntax (cf. (1c)):

(8) kasain-dRasoa   ho-sasa-ko   ny zaza.
intend.PASS-by Rasoa FUT-wash.PASS-by me the child
'It is intended by Rasoa that the child will be washed by me.'

Further examples of sort are given in (9) (Edward Keenan, personal communication):

(9) a. neken-dRabe   ho   lokoin'i Bema   ny trano.
agree.PASS-by Rabe   FUT   paint.PASS-by Bema   the house.
'It was agreed by Rabe that the house will be painted by Bema.'
b. niren-dRabe   ho   lokoin'i Bema   ny trano.
desire.PASS-by Rabe   FUT   paint.PASS-by Bema   the house.
'It was desired by Rabe that the house will be painted by Bema.'
c. notetehin-dRabe   ho   lokoin'i Bema   ny trano.
plan.PASS-by Rabe   FUT   paint.PASS-by Bema   the house.
'It was planned by Rabe that the house will be painted by Bema.'
d. nantenain-dRabe   ho   lokoin'i Bema   ny trano.
hope.PASS-by Rabe   FUT   paint.PASS-by Bema   the house.
'It was hoped by Rabe that the house will be painted by Bema.'
e. nokasain-dRabe   ho   lokoin'i Bema   ny trano.
intend.PASS-by Rabe   FUT   paint.PASS-by Bema   the house.
'It was intended by Rabe that the house will be painted by Bema.'
f. tian-dRabe   ho   lokoin'i Bema   ny trano.
want.PASS-by Rabe   FUT   paint.PASS-by Bema   the house.
'It was wanted by Rabe that the house will be painted by Bema.'

The facts in (8)-(9) clearly lie beyond the purview of control theory, since there is simply no null arguments to be controlled. Therefore, to the extent that a unified analysis of these examples and that in (1c) can be given, there is no justification for a separate theory of control to account for (1c) alone.

Third, appealing to an independent theory of control in order to account for the grammaticality of the examples in (1), (3) and (4) would seem to miss the connection between the property underlying these examples and the more general property of argument-binding in Malagasy. In fact, I claim that these examples are not control structures of the sort that involve a null pronominal subject PRO, but rather are a reflection of a general property of argument-binding of the language, and that there is no need for an independent theory of control to accommodate these cases. I discuss in the next section what argument-binding means in considering simple sentences involving only one verb.

2. VP-external binding of arguments in Malagasy

The surface word-order of a transitive sentence in Malagasy is V NP2 NP1. The rightmost argument, the NP1, has specific properties like having nominative Case (which is morphologically distinguishable from non-nominative Cases in the pronominal system), being definite, taking the yes/no question particle *ve* and and the negative particle *intsony* 'longer', a kind of negative polarity item, when the predicate is negated with *tsy* 'not' (the ordering of the particles with respect to NP1 is *intsony ve* NP1), as well as being able to be clefted, questioned and relativized (Keenan 1976).

Clefting, questioning and relativizing would of course give rise to the surface word-order NP1 V NP2.

Directly relevant to our discussion here are the following two properties of NP1 (Keenan 1976, 1994): (a) specific morphology on the verb correlates with the specific theta-role of the NP1, and (b) NP1 occurs outside the constituent formed by V and NP2.

The verb in Malagasy may in general have one of three voice morphologies: active, passive, and circumstantial. The active voice correlates with NP1 bearing the Agent role and the passive voice with it being the Theme. NP1 bears a variety of Oblique roles like Instrumental, Benefactee, Location, Temporal, etc, when the verb is in the circumstantial voice. (The final vowel of the verb drops when the Agent phrase is present. Cf. Keenan 1976, 1994 and more discussion of the Agent phrase and the Oblique phrase below):

(10) a. hanasa   lamba   amin'   ity   savony   ity   Rasoa
        wash.ACT clothes with   this soap   this Rasoa
        'Rasoa will wash clothes with this soap.'
    b. sasana-(dRasoa)   amin' ity   savony ity ny   lamba.
       wash.PASS-by-Rasoa   with   this soap   this the clothes
       'The clothes are washed with this soap (by Rasoa).'
    c. anasana-(dRasoa)   lamba   ity   savony ity.
       wash.CIRC-by-Rasoa   clothes this soap   this
       'This soap is being washed clothes with (by Rasoa).'

Crucially, when the argument appears in the NP1 position, but cannot be naturally interpreted as bearing the specific thematic role that the verbal morphology requires, the examples would sound pragmatically odd, if they are grammatical at all:

(11) a. *hanasa   Rasoa lamba   amin' ity   savony ity.
        wash.ACT   Rasoa clothes with   this soap   this
    b. *sasana   amin' ity   savony ity ny   lamba   Rasoa.
       wash.PASS with   this soap   this the clothes Rasoa
    c. #anasan-(dRasoa)   ity   savony ity ny   lamba.
       wash.CIRC-by-Rasoa   this soap   this the clothes

The example in (11a) is ungrammatical, since the argument *Rasoa*, presumably the Agent of the verb, does not appear in the NP1 position with the verb in the active voice (cf. (10b)). The ungrammaticality of the example in (11b) is due to the argument *ny lamba* 'the clothes', presumably the Theme of the verb, not being in the NP1 position. In (11c), *ny lamba* 'the clothes' would be understood as the Instrument or Benefactee of the washing and the soap is being washed, a pragmatically odd interpretation. More significant is the fact that these examples cannot have the pragmatically natural interpretations in (10).

The Agent phrase must be present when the verb is in the active voice; the Theme phrase must also appear when the verb is in the passive voice. However, the Oblique phrase may be absent with the verb in the circumstantial voice when the discourse context makes it sufficiently salient. Thus, the example in (12b) without an Instrumental phrase is quite possible, if it is preceded by a question like that in (12a) (Charles Randriamasimanana, personal communication):[3]

(12) a. n-ataon-dRasoa inona ny savony?
PAST-do.CIRC-by Rasoa what the soap?
'What did Rasoa do with the soap?'
b. n-anasana-(dRasoa) ny lamba. (cf. (10c))
PAST-wash.CIRC-by-Rasoa the clothes
'It was used for washing the clothes (by Rasoa).'

In all three voices, the rightmost NP is marked with the nominative Case, which shows up in the pronouns.

Cross-linguistically, NPs in dislocated positions are generally definite (cf. Rizzi 1986, Cinque 1990). In Malagasy, the argument appearing in the NP1 position is required to be definite (cf. the example (10c) where the Theme *lamba* 'clothes' need not have the definite article *ny* 'the', in contrast to that in (10b) where it must), showing that it is in a dislocated position.

Evidence that NP1 is not part of the constituent formed by the verb and the rest of the clause (for concreteness, let us call this constituent a VP) comes from facts about nominalization, and the distribution of discontinuous expressions like *tsy intsony* 'not any longer' or *na (dia) aza* 'even ... though'. A VP may be nominalized to the exclusion of NP1, by putting the definite determiner *ny* 'the' to the left of the VP (Keenan 1976):

(13) a. sarotra ny mitondra taxi.
difficult the drive.ACT taxi
'Driving taxis is difficult.'
b. mahamenatra ny tsy fitiavan-dRakoto an-dRasoa.
shameful the not love.CIRC.by-Rakoto ACC-Rasoa
'Rokoto's not loving Rasoa is shameful.'

Furthermore, the VP can also be framed by discontinuous expressions like *tsy intsony* 'not any longer' or *na (dia) aza* 'even ... though', with the last element of the expressions at the right-edge of the VP, effectively excluding NP1 (cf. Keenan 1976, 1994 for more evidence of a constituent that excludes the subject):

(14) a. tsy manasa lamba intsony Rasoa.
not wash.ACT clothes longer Rasoa
'Rasoa is no longer washing clothes.'

b. mbola marary Rabe na efa mikarakara azy aza Rasoa.
    still sick Rabe even now care-for.ACT him though Rasoa.
    'Rabe is till sick even though Rasoa is now taking care of him.'

The facts discussed in (10)-(11) and (13)-(14) thus show that there exists a general constraint regulating the relationship between voice morphology on the verb and the right most NP. We may think of this as argument-binding property:

(15) *Argument-binding in Malagasy*
  a. [[$_{VP}$ V.ACT t_i Theme (Oblique)] Agent$_i$]
  b. [[$_{VP}$ V.PASS (Agent) t_i (Oblique)] Theme$_i$]
  c. [[$_{VP}$ V.CIRC (Agent) Theme t_i] Oblique$_i$]

We might view the position indicated as t_i in (15) as the base position of an argument from which it is externalized to the rightmost position (Travis and Williams 1983).[4] For our purposes here, however, we can simply take it to be the argument-place that is bound by the VP-external NP bearing the same index. (Indices are being used here for expository convenience, and have no theoretical import). The structures in (15) show clearly that the VP-external NP c-commands the VP containing the bound argument-place. We can thus take this to be the structural condition for binding.

Some remarks concerning the Agent phrase and the Oblique phrase in (15b)-(15c) are in order. First, there seems to be some reason to assume that the Agent phrase is syntactically optional. Charles Randriamasimanana (personal communication) points out to me that the Agent phrase is syntactically optional only if the verb has perfective morphologies as marked by the prefixes *voa* or *tafa*; otherwise, it is obligatory. However, according to Keenan (1994), 60% of non-active sentences in texts that he examined have overt Agent phrases. We can thus infer that the rest of them do not. It thus seems that the difference can be accounted for only if the Agent phrase is syntactically optional, and cases where an Agent phrase is present is due to some other factors. Second, the Oblique phrase binding an argument-place of the verb in the circumstantial voice is usually in the rightmost position when it bears the Instrumental role as in (10c) or the Benefactee role as in (16a):

(16) a. n-anasana-dRasoa lamba Rabe.
         PAST.wash.CIRC-by Rasoa clothes Rabe
         'Clothes were washed by Rasoa for Rabe.'
     b. io trano io no n-anasana-dRasoa lamba.
         this house this cleft PAST.wash.CIRC-by Rasoa clothes
         'It's (in) this house that clothes were washed by Rasoa.'
     c. omaly no n-anasana-dRasoa lamba.
         yesterday cleft PAST.wash.CIRC-by Rasoa clothes
         'It's yesterday that clothes were washed by Rasoa.'

Oblique phrases with the Location or Temporal role usually cannot appear in the rightmost position, but occur in the leftmost position in the cleft construction with the particle *no*, as shown in (16b)-(16c). Therefore, to the extent that an Oblique phrase binding an argument-place of the verb in (15c) is possible, it should be taken to be restricted to those that bear the Instrumental or Benefactee role (cf. (12b)). I will not attempt here to give a precise formulation of the constraint in (15c) that also covers cases of the Oblique phrase bearing the Location or Temporal role.

Lastly, I assume along the lines of Bresnan's (1978) analysis of control verbs in English that verbs like *mahazo* 'can', *mikasa* 'to intend', and *tia* 'to want' in Malagasy select VP-complements.

Having established the general property of binding of arguments in Malagasy, we can now see how the grammaticality of the examples in (1), (3) and (4) can be accounted for. For ease of reference, let us call the structures in these examples complex structures.

3. Binding of arguments in complex structures

The examples in (1a)-(1b) are straightforward, as their structures in (17) show:

(17) a. [[$_{VP}$ mikasa t_i [$_{VP}$ hanasa t_i ny   zaza]] Rasoa$_i$]
        intend.ACT   wash.ACT   the   child   Rasoa
    'Rasoa intends to wash the child.'
  b. [[$_{VP}$ mikasa t_i [$_{VP}$ ho-sasan-dRasoa t_i]] ny   zaza$_i$]
        intend.ACT   wash.PASS-by-Rasoa   the   child
    'The child intends to be washed by Rasoa.'

The Agent phrase, the rightmost NP, (simultaneously) binds an argument-place of the matrix and the embedded verb, satisfying the constraint on argument-binding in (15).[5]

The example in (17a) would become ungrammatical if the Agent phrase of the embedded verb were syntactically overt, or if the Agent of the matrix verb were inside the matrix VP and the Theme of the embedded verb is in the VP-external position in the matrix clause:

(18) a. *[[$_{VP}$ mikasa t_i [$_{VP}$ hanasa   Rabe ny   zaza]] Rasoa$_i$]
         intend.ACT   FUT.wash.ACT   the   child   Rasoa
    'Rasoa intends that Rabe will wash the child.'
  b. *[[$_{VP}$ mikasa   Rasoa [$_{VP}$ ho-sasan-dRabe t_i]] ny   zaza$_i$]
         intend.ACT   FUT-wash.PASS-by Rabe   the   child
    'Rasoa intends that the child will be washed by Rabe.'

The ungrammaticality of these examples is just what we would expect, given the constraints on argument-binding in (15). The embedded VP in

(18a) and the matrix VP in (18b) do not have an argument-place bound by an argument external to the respective VP.

The example in (1c) is a bit more complicated. It is not immediately clear if the matrix verb in the passive voice has an argument-place bound externally to the VP. The matrix verb obviously has two arguments, the Agent and the VP-complement. Recall that the argument in the VP-external position must be definite as marked by the definite article *ny* 'the'. It is therefore not unexpected that a VP without the definite article *ny* 'the' may not appear in this position. In fact, when a VP-complement of the verb *mikasa* 'to intend' is nominalized with the prefixing of the definite article *ny* 'the', it may occurs either inside the matrix VP if the verb is in the active voice, or outside the matrix VP, if it is in the passive voice (Ed Keenan, personal communication):

(19) a. mikasa   ny hamangy   an-dRabe   Rasoa.
       intend.ACT   the FUT.visit.ACT   ACC-Rabe   Rasoa
       'Rasoa intends to visit Rabe.'
   b. kasain-dRasoa   ny hamangy   an-dRabe.
       intend.PASS   the FUT.visit.ACT   ACC-Rabe
       'It was intended by Rasoa that he will visit Rabe.'

The claim that the nominalized VP in (19b) appears in a VP-external position is supported by the fact that it has all the properties like undergoing clefting, relativization, taking the yes-no question particle *ve* and the exclamative particle *anie* (cf. Keenan 1976).

If this is correct, then the VP-complement stays in its base-position when the verb taking it as a complement is in the passive voice. The structure of the example (1c) would be as in (20) (on the indicated interpretation), where the argument *ny zaza* 'the child' must be taken as the binder of the Theme argument-place of the embedded verb in the passive voice, sastifying the constraint on argument-binding in (15b):[6]

(20)   [[$_{VP}$ kasain-dRasoa   [$_{VP}$ sasana t_j]]   ny   zaza$_i$]
        intend.PASS-by-Rasoa   wash.PASS   the child
        'It was intended by Rasoa that the child be washed by her.'

The Agent phrase of the embedded verb is not realized in syntax, but this is fine since it need not be present syntactically when the verb has non-active morphology (cf. the discussion after (15)). Only the embedded verb needs to have a Theme argument-place bound VP-externally, which it does in this representation. I attribute to pragmatic factors the most natural interpretation of (20) according to which the embedded Agent and the matrix Agent are the same, since the matrix Agent, the only other argument that is syntactically present, is salient for interpretation.

If Keenan (1994) is correct in that the Agent phrase forms a constituent with the verb in the passive voice, then the ungrammaticality of the example in (3a), whose structure is given in (21), would be due to the fact that the Agent phrase does not c-command the VP containing the Agent argument-place, and hence cannot bind it from outside the embedded VP, violating the constraint on argument-binding in (15a):

(21) *[[VP [kasain-dRasoa]   [VP hanasa   ny   zaza]]]
         intend.PASS-by-Rasoa   wash.ACT the child
    'It was intended by Rasoa that she will wash the child.'

Note that the embedded Theme in (21) cannot possibly appear outside the embedded VP. First, nominalizing the embedded VP necessarily includes the embedded Theme, as shown in (22a):[7]

(22) a. ny hanasa   *(ny zaza).
          the FUT.wash.ACT   the child
         'The washing of the child.'
      b. *[[VP [kasain-dRasoa]   [VP hanasa t_i]] ny zaza$_i$]
            intend.PASS-by-Rasoa   wash.ACT   the child
         'It was intended by Rasoa that she will wash the child.'

Second, if the embedded Theme appeared external to the embedded VP as in (22b), it would violate the constraint on argument-binding in (15a) with the embedded verb in the active voice.

The contrast between (20) and (21) is telling. In particular, it shows that we should not treat the Agent argument-place of the embedded verb in the two examples in the same way. In these representations, the Agent phrase of the matrix verb is in the same structural position (cf. section 1.1), if the Agent argument of the embedded verb may be bound VP-externally (or controlled in a control analysis), then there is no reason why there should be a grammatical contrast. If the Agent argument-place of an active verb must be bound VP-externally, in contrast to that of a non-active verb, then the grammatical contrast between (20) and (21) follows.

The example in (3b) is ruled out in a simple fashion. As its structure in (23) shows, the Agent of the embedded verb is VP-external, but its Theme argument is missing (indicated as ∅), violating the subcategorization property of the transitive verb *sasa* 'to wash' in the active voice:

(23) *[[VP kasain-dRasoa   [VP hanasa t_i ∅]] Rabe$_i$]
         intend.PASS-by-Rasoa   wash.ACT   Rabe
    'It was intended by Rasoa that Rabe will wash her.'

As shown in (24), when the embedded verb is in the active voice, and the Theme is present inside the embedded VP, the examples are grammatical (Edward Keenan, personal communication):

(24) a. neken-dRabe   handoko   ny trano   i Bema.
        agree.PASS-by Rabe   paint.ACT the house Bema
        'It was agreed by Rabe that Bema will paint the house.'
    b. nirin-dRabe   handoko   ny trano   i Bema.
        desire.PASS-by Rabe   paint.ACT the house Bema
        'It was desired by Rabe that Bema will paint the house.'
    c. notetehin-dRabe   handoko   ny trano   i Bema.
        plan.PASS-by Rabe   paint.ACT the house Bema
        'It was planned by Rabe that Bema will paint the house.'
    d. nantenain-dRabe   handoko   ny trano   i Bema.
        hope.PASS-by Rabe   paint.ACT the house Bema
        'It was hoped by Rabe that Bema will paint the house.'
    e. nokasain-dRabe   handoko   ny trano   i Bema.
        intended.PASS-by Rabe paint.ACT the house Bema
        'It was intended by Rabe that Bema will paint the house.'
    f. tian-dRabe   handoko   ny trano   i Bema.
        want.PASS-by Rabe   paint.ACT the house Bema
        'It was wanted by Rabe that Bema will paint the house.'

The example in (4) is impossible on the indicated interpretation according to which *ny zaza* 'the child' is understood as the Theme of the embedded verb. As the structure in (25) shows, the Agent of the matrix verb is in the VP-external position, but the Theme of the embedded verb in the passive voice stays inside the embedded VP, violating the constraint on argument-binding in (15b):

(25) *[[$_{VP}$ mikasa t_i [$_{VP}$ ho-sasana   ny   zaza]]   Rasoa$_i$]
        intend.ACT   FUT-wash.PASS   the child   Rasoa
    'Rasoa intends that the child be washed by her.'

The example in (25) would be grammatical with *ny zaza* 'the child' as the Agent, inducing the dropping of the final vowel of the verb, and *Rasoa* as the Theme of the embedded verb (cf. the example in (17b)):

(26) [[$_{VP}$ mikasa t_i [$_{VP}$ ho-sasan'   ny   zaza t_i]]   Rasoa$_i$]
        intend.ACT   FUT-wash.PASS   the child   Rasoa
    'Rasoa intends to be washed by the child.'

In the representation in (26), the two verbs have an argument-place bound by the argument *Rasoa*, which is external to the two VPs.

We thus have considerable evidence that complex structures like the ones discussed here are not control structures. The apparent absence of an argument of the embedded verb is in fact regulated by the general property of argument-binding of the language.

4. Further evidence for argument-binding

In this section, we will look at some more complex structures in which the constraint on argument-binding is also at work. As shown in (27), the argument-place of the matrix verb and that of the embedded verb may be bound by two different arguments:

(27) a. [[$_{VP}$ niangavy t_i an-dRabe$_j$ [$_{VP}$ handoko t_j io trano io]] Rasoa$_i$]
   ask.ACT   ACC-Rabe   paint.ACT   this house this   Rasoa
   'Rasoa asked Rabe to paint this house.'
b. [[$_{VP}$ manampy t_i an-dRabe$_j$ [$_{VP}$ mametraka t_j ny kodiarana]] Rasoa$_i$]
   help.ACT   ACC-Rabe   put-on.ACT   the tire   Rasoa
   'Rasoa is helping Rabe put on the tire.'

The argument *Rasoa* binds the Agent argument-place of the matrix verb. The accusative-marked argument *Rabe* is clearly external to the embedded VP, since a verb does not mark its Agent phrase with the accusative Case. It thus binds the Agent argument-place of the embedded verb. Given the different positions of the accusative binder in (27) and the nominative binder in previous cases, we have to suppose that for the constraints on argument-binding in (15), the binder may appear either to the left or to the right of the VP containing the bound argument-place, as long as it is external to that VP. However, we must have an independent way to ensure that the VP-external nominative NP appear to the right of the VP. I will not pursue this question here.

There is a question of whether the accusative NP in (27) is a syntactic argument of the embedded verb, raising from the embedded VP to be marked the accusative Case by the matrix verb, or it is actually a syntactic argument of the matrix verb, binding an argument-place of the embedded verb. Keenan (1976) suggests that the example in (28c) is derived by first raising the Agent of the embedded verb to the matrix VP where it is marked with the accusative Case as in (28b),[8] and then passivizing the matrix verb. The result of this is that the Agent of the embedded verb would end up in the subject position of the whole clause:

(28) a. nanantena [fa   sasan-dRasoa   ny zaza] Rabe.
       hope.ACT that wash.PASS.by-Rasoa   the child   Rabe
       'Rabe hoped that the child is being washed by Rasoa.'
   b. nanantena ny zaza [ho-sasan-dRasoa   ] Rabe.
       hope.ACT the child FUT-wash.PASS.by-Rasoa   Rabe
       'Rabe hoped the child to be washed by Rasoa.'
   c. nantenain-dRabe   [ho-sasan-dRasoa   ] ny zaza.
       hope.PASS-by-Rabe   FUT-wash.PASS.by-Rasoa   the child
       'It was hoped by Rabe that the child will be washed by Rasoa.'

Along these lines, then, the examples in (27) are but the intermediate steps of the derivations of the examples in (29):

(29) a. [[$_{VP}$ niangavian-dRasoa t_j [$_{VP}$ handoko t_j io trano io]] Rabe$_j$]
ask.PASS-by-Rasoa   paint.ACT   this house this Rabe
'Rabe was asked by Rasoa to paint this house.'
b. [[$_{VP}$ ampian-dRasoa t_j [$_{VP}$ mametraka t_j ny kodiarana]] Rabe$_j$]
help.PASS-by-Rasoa   put-on.ACT the tire   Rabe
'Rabe is helped by Rasoa to put on the tire.'

However, evidence from selectional restrictions seems to indicate that this is perhaps not the correct way to view these examples. Not just any argument of the embedded verb can be raised and marked with the accusative Case:

(30) a. #[[$_{VP}$ niangavy t_i io   trano io$_j$ [$_{VP}$ ho-lokoin-dRabe t_j] Rasoa$_i$]
ask.ACT   this house this   paint.PASS.by-Rabe Rasoa
'Rasoa asked this house that it be painted by Rabe.'
b. #[[$_{VP}$ nanampy t_i ny   kodiarana$_i$ [$_{VP}$ apetra-dRabe t_j]] Rasoa$_i$]
help.ACT   the tire   put-on.PASS.by-Rabe Rasoa
'Rasoa helped the tire be put on by Rabe.'

The pragmatically odd interpretations of these examples thus appear to suggest that there is a selectional restriction imposed by the matrix verb. In other words, the accusative NP in (27) seems to be an argument of the matrix verb.

What is perhaps surprising is the fact that the embedded Theme may occur in the VP-external position in the matrix clause when the matrix verb is in the passive voice, even though the presumed intermediate steps of the derivation in (30) are impossible:

(31) a. [[$_{VP}$ niangavian-dRasoa [$_{VP}$ ho-lokoin-dRabe t_i]] io trano io$_i$]
ask.PASS-by-Rasoa   FUT.paint.PASS-by-Rabe this house this
'It was asked by Rasoa that this house be painted by Rabe.'
b. [[$_{VP}$ ampian-dRasoa   [$_{VP}$ apetra-dRabe t_j]]   ny kodiarana$_j$]
help.PASS-by-Rasoa   put-on.PASS-by-Rabe the tire
'It is helped by Rasoa that the tire is put on by Rabe.'

It it even more surprising that in (31) the argument *Rabe* can appear within the embedded VP as the Agent of the embedded verb. This should be impossible if the argument *Rabe* is truly an argument of the matrix verb.

One possibility of accounting for these problematic examples would be to treat the accusative NP in (27) as an optional argument of the matrix verb. Selectional restrictions on this optional argument are just as we should expect since it is in an argument position of the matrix verb. Not only do the pragmatically odd interpretations of the examples in (30) follow directly, the fact that the argument would be marked with the accusative Case would also require no additional assumption since the verb assigns accusative Case to this position.

The impossible representations in (30) have no bearing on the examples in (31), however. The examples in (31) need not be derived from the representations in (30). Indeed, the representations in (31), as well as those in (27), (28b-c) and (29) all conform to the constraint on argument-binding in (15).[9] The fact that the Agent phrase *Rabe* occurs in the embedded VP in (31) is due to its being an argument of the verb in the passive voice, just as it does in general. In (28b) and (29), the accusative argument of the matrix verb is absent, sanctioned by its being an optional argument.

Particlularly relevant to the analysis of complex structures in Malagasy is the fact that the accusative NP in examples like (27) may be related to an argument of the embedded verb. This is unexpected under the control analysis in terms of GFs. The accusative NP is clearly an OBJ or a 2-arc, but the missing argument of the embedded verb is a SUBJ or a final 1-arc. The examples in (27) should thus violate the like-constraint on control relationship in (5).

5. Conclusion

It is therefore rather clear from the discussion in the foregoing sections that there is no need for an independent theory of control in order to account for the grammatical patterning of complex structures in Malagasy. To a significant degree, the data can be brought under the purview of the general property of argument-binding of the language (cf. footnote 9, however). We should note also that the conclusion reached here does not argue against the existence of GFs as theoretical primitives, since they may turn out to be necessary for other parts of the grammar.

From a typological perspective, one might ask what property that distinguishes Malagasy from languages like English bears on the question of why the language lacks the control structure. As pointed out in section 1.3, Malagasy differs significantly from languages like English in that it does not have the finite/non-finite morphological distinction. Thus, if a null subject PRO appears only when the verb which it is the subject of is non-finite (cf. footnote 2), then the fact that Malagasy does not allow PRO follows from the lack of the non-finite form of the verb. In other words, since the verb always requires a lexical subject in non-complex structures, there is no reason to assume that in complex structures the same form of the verb does not require a lexical subject, but instead allows a null subject PRO. The striking difference between languages like Malagasy and those like English with respect to the existence of the control structure is reduced to an independent difference with respect to the morphology encoding the finite/non-finite distinction.

Notes

[*]I am particularly grateful to Ed Keenan for many hours of discussion about the grammar of Malagasy, and for giving me access to his extensive notes that

are pertinent to the issues discussed here. I also would like to thank Ileana Paul and Lisa Travis for lending notes, offering helpful comments and suggestions, and especially for making their informant resources available to me. I am aslo indebted to Cécile Manorohanta, Roger-Bruno Rabenilaina, Charles Randriamasimanana for their patience with my solicitation of judgments. Inadequacies are my responsibility.

[1] Abbreviations: V.ACT, V.PASS, and V.CIRC mean that the verb V has active, passive, and circumstantial voice morphology, respectively. FUT and ACC are respectively abbreviations of future and accusative.

[2] One way of characterizing the finite/non-finite distinction is in the Tense and agreement morphology on the verb. In English, apart from modals like *must* and *will*, finite verbs show number agreement:

(i) a. John believed Mary to be intelligent.
    b. John believed Mary and Sue to be intelligent.
    c. John believed that Mary is/*are intelligent.
    d. John believe that Mary and Sue are/*is intelligent.

[3] In cases like (ia) where the verb is in the circumstantial voice and the Oblique phrase is absent, the rightmost NP has a partitive interpretation, in contrast to cases like (ib) where the verb is in the passive voice and the rightmost NP does not have such interpretation (Edward Keenan, personal communication):

(i) a. namonoana   ny   akoho.
       PAST.kill.CIRC   the   chicken
       'Some chickens were killed.'
    b. novonoina   ny   akoho.
       PAST.kill.PASS   the   chicken
       'The chickens were killed.'

I will not pursue here an analysis for this particular case, however.

[4] The representations in (15) raise some issues with regard to clause structure of Malagasy. Guilfoyle, Hung and Travis (1992) suggest that the unlabelled brackets in (15) are IPs, and an argument inside the VP moves to its Spec position for Case reasons, depending on the voice morphology of the verb. They propose that a verb with active morphology does not assign Case to the Agent (and similarly, passive and circumstantial morphologies do not, respectively, assign Case to the Theme and Oblique arguments). The argument that thus lacks Case must move to SpecIP. One problem for this view is that cross-linguistically there seems to be no definiteness requirement for movement to a Case position.

If one assumes that all arguments of the verb are within the VP-projection at D-structure (Fukui and Speas 1985, Koopman and Sportiche 1985), then the word-order facts in (10c) indicate that the Agent precedes the Theme at D-structure. In addition, if the Agent phrase always appears higher than the Theme at D-structure (e.g., SpecVP), then the fact that the verb appears to the left of the Agent phrase implies that the verb has moved out of its base-position (to INFL, according to Guilfoyle, Hung and Travis 1992). Consequently, it must be the case that an argument appearing to the left of a verb is external to the VP-projection of that verb.

The issue of clause structure of Malagasy is rather complex (cf. Keenan (1994) on the problems of coordination and of the morphological relationship between a non-active verb and the genitive Agent phrase, which bear on the issue of clause structure of the language). For our purposes here, it suffices that there be one argument-place bound by an VP-external argument whose thematic role is determined by the verbal morphology.

[5] One might think of this as a case of across-the-board (ATB) extraction (Williams 1978), but we will see in section 3 that it does not generalize to some other cases.

[6] Given that the argument *ny zaza* 'the child' in (18) binds only one argument-place (of the embedded verb), there thus seems to be reason to suppose that these complex structures should not be considered as a case of ATB movement (cf. footnote 5).

[7] The representation in (22b) would correspond to a grammatical surface form if the embedded verb is *misasa* 'to wash (oneself)', the intransitive verb derived from the root *sasa* 'to wash'. In this case, the argument *ny zaza* 'the child' would bind the sole argument-place of the verb, conforming to the constraint in (15a).

[8] The *fa*-complements cannot appear to the left of the matrix subject, i.e. they cannot stay in their base-positions, and must occur to the right of the matrix subject (Keenan 1976):

(i) a. *mino   [fa hanasa   ny zaza Rasoa] Rabe.
       believe.ACT wash.ACT the child Rasoa   Rabe
       'Rabe believes that Rasoa will wash the child.'
    b. mino Rabe [fa hanasa ny zaza Rasoa]

Thus, (26a) is impossible as the surface form.

[9] In the oral presentation of this paper, I brought up the examples in (i) as problematic cases for VP-external binding of arguments:

(i) a. mikasa   ho-vangian-dRasoa   Rabe.
       intend.ACT FUT-visit.PASS-by-Rasoa Rabe
       'Rasoa intends to visit Rabe.'
    b. Te-ho-vangian-dRasoa   Rabe
       want-FUT-visit.PASS-by-Rasoa Rabe
       'Rasoa wants to visit Rabe.'

On these particular interpretations, the argument-place of the Agent phrase of the matrix verb is bound by the Agent of the embedded verb, which appears in the VP-projection inside the matrix VP. That is, the argument *Rasoa* is not external to the matrix VP, but binds its Agent argument.

It turns out that these unexpected judgments (of one speaker) obtain only with a few verbs. In addtion to those in (i), the following example also has an unexpected interpretation (Edward Keenan, personal communication):

(ii) nangatahin-dRasoa   ho   lokoin-dRabe   io   trano io.
     ask.PASS-by Rasoa   FUT   paint.PASS-by Rabe   this house this
     'Rabe was being asked by Rasoa to paint this house.'

One of my informants does not have these unexpected interpretations at all. Both of them, though, do get the expected interpretations where the argument *Rabe* is the Agent of the matrix verb in (i) and the unspecified person being asked in (ii) is someone else. There might very well be some dialectal variations here. A thorough investigation of these cases is necessary before a firm conclusion can be reached.

I also brought up the example in (iii), which requires a further assumption on the distribution of VPs:

(iii) [[$_{VP}$ niangavy t_i] Rasoa$_i$] [[$_{VP}$ ho-lokoina t_j] io   trano io$_j$]
      ask.ACT   Rasoa   FUT-paint.PASS   this house this
      'Rasoa asked that this house be painted.'

In comparison with (ib), (iii) differs in having the VP complement to the right of the matrix subject. I suggested that on the assumption that VPs cannot appear in an adjunct position, the embedded VP actually has another category on top of the VP (whose brackets are unlabelled here, probably an IP), and the whole is extraposed to the right of the embedded subject.

It turns out that the example in (iii) may have a complementizer *fa* as in (iv), with the same interpretation:

(iv) [[[$_{VP}$ niangavy t_i] Rasoa$_i$] [[$_{VP}$ fa ho-lokoina t_j] io   trano io$_j$]]
      ask.ACT   Rasoa   FUT-paint.PASS   this house this
      'Rasoa asked that this house be painted.'

Given that a *fa* complement must be extraposed (cf. footnote 8), it is not unreasonable to assume that the complement in (iii) is a *fa* complement, which is extraposed to the right of the matrix subject, and the complementizer *fa* is subsequently deleted.

Nevertheless, the informant that gave the judgments in (iii) rejected the example in (v), which differs from (iv) in having the embedded verb in active voice:

(v) *[[[_VP_ niangavy t_i] Rasoa$_i$] [[_VP_ fa handoko t_j io   trano io   Rabe$_j$]]
      ask.ACT   Rasoa   paint.ACT   this house this Rabe
  'Rasoa asked that Rabe paint this house.'

As with the examples in (i), it is not clear whether the judgments are rock solid or represent a dialectal variation. They need to be rechecked before drawing a conclusion. The intriguing question that arises is why voice morphology makes a difference with respect to the position of the complement.

References

Bresnan, Joan 1978. A Realistic Transformational Grammar. *Linguistic Theory and Psychological Reality*, ed. by Morris Halle, Joan Bresnan, and Geroge A. Miller, 1-59, Cambridge, MA: MIT Press.
Bresnan, Joan 1982. *The Mental Representation of Grammatical Relations.* Cambridge, MA: MIT Press.
Chomsky, Noam. 1986. *Barriers.* Cambridge, MA: MIT Press.
Chomsky, Noam and Howard Lasnik. 1977. Filter and Control. *Linguistic Inquiry* 8: 425- 504.
Cinque, Guiglemo. 1990. *Types of A'-dependencies.* Cambridge, MA: MIT Press.
Fukui, Naoki and Margaret Speas. 1986. Specifiers and Projection. *MIT Working Papers in Linguistics*, volume 8: 128-172.
Guilfoyle, Eithne, Henrietta Hung, and Lisa Travis. 1992. Spec of IP and Spec of VP: Two Subjects in Austronesian Languages. *Natural Language and Linguistic Theory* 10: 375-414.
Jackendoff, Ray 1972. *Semantic Interpretation in Generative Grammar.* Cambridge, MA: MIT Press.
Keenan, Edward. 1976. Remarkable Subjects in Malagasy. *Subject and Topic*, ed. by Charles Li, 247-301, New York: Academic Press.
Keenan, Edward. 1994. Predicate-Argument Structure in Malagasy. this volume.
Koopman, Hilda and Dominique Sportiche. 1985. θ-theory and Extraction. Abstract in *GLOW Newsletter,* number 14, Department of Language and Literature, Tilburg University, Tilburg.
Koster, Jan and Robert May. 1982. The Constituents of Infinitives. *Language* 58: 117-143.
Larson, Richard. 1991. *Promise* and the Theory of Control. *Linguistic Inquiry* 22: 103-139.
Perlmutter, David and Paul Postal. 1974. Unpublished lectures on Relational Grammar at the Summer Institute of the Linguistic Society of America, Amherst, Massachusetts.
Reinhart, Tanya. 1976. *The Syntactic Domain of Anaphora*, doctoral dissertation, MIT.
Rizzi, Luigi. 1986. On the Status of Subject Clitics in Romance. *Studies in Romance Linguistics*, ed. by Osvaldo Jaeggli and Carmen Silva-Corvalán, 391-419. Dordrecht: Foris.
Rouveret, Alain. 1980. Sur la Notion de Proposition Finie: Governement et Inversion. *Langages* 60: 75-107.
Travis, Lisa and Edwin Williams. 1983. Externalization of Arguments in Malayo-Polynesian Languages. *The Linguistic Review* 2: 57-78.
Williams, Edwin 1978. ATB Rule Application. *Linguistic Inquiry* 9: 31-43.
Williams, Edwin 1990. The ATB Theory of Parasitic Gaps. *The Linguistic Review* 6: 265-279.

Causee Prominence Constraints in French and Elsewhere

GÉRALDINE LEGENDRE
University of Colorado at Boulder

1. Introduction

At least since Aissen (1974), it's been known that the complement of a causative union construction can be severely constrained, though the extent of variation and an explanation for the patterns observed cross-linguistically have remained elusive. The purpose of this paper is three-fold: 1) to document the patterns found cross-linguistically, 2) to formulate four Causee Prominence Constraints which arguably have the effect of constraining the mapping between thematic roles and final GRs, and 3) to make a preliminary proposal concerning the parameterization of these constraints in individual languages.

2. The French pattern

The French pattern appears to be very complex because in causative union complements some revaluations are allowed, others are required, while yet others are forbidden. French allows one type of revaluation in the complement of causative union: unaccusative advancement (or 2-1 advancement from an intransitive stratum). This can be shown by considering unaccusative verbs which in simple sentences require the reflexive morpheme *se*. As extensively discussed in Legendre (1986), "inherent" *se* is optional in union complements.[1]

(1) a.   J'ai fait taire/se taire les enfants.   (Legendre 1986)
         'I made the children keep quiet.'

---

* Thanks to Paul Smolensky for extensive discussion of the constraints and editorial assistance, and to the participants at the 6th Biennial Conference on Grammatical Relations for helpful comments and criticisms. This research has been supported in part by NSF (grant # SBR-9209265).

[1] Not to distract from the issues addressed here, union diagrams in this paper represent only the complement of union predicates. The union clause is never represented.

b.　　P　　2　　　　　c.　P　　2
　　　P　　1　　　　　　　P　　2:1
　　　　　　　　　　　　　　P　　1
　　taire　les enfants　　　se taire　les enfants

When *se* corresponds to an argument of the verb (i.e., is semantically reflexive), *se* must appear. Assuming the analysis argued for in Legendre (1986), this means that the multiattachment must be resolved. Following Rosen (1981), Legendre (1986) argues that this is accomplished by cancellation of the lowest GR. *Se* then marks the cancellation of the 2, as represented in diagrams (1c) and (2b).

(2) a.　J'ai fait se laver les enfants.
　　　'I made the children wash themselves.'

　　b.　　P　　1:2
　　　　　P　　1
　　　　se laver　les enfants

Legendre (1993) argues that psych verbs of the *préoccuper* "preoccupy" class occur in three distinct antipassive constructions. Two are exemplified in (3) and (4). (3) exemplifies retroherent antipassive while (4) exemplifies "pseudo-passive" antipassive (see Legendre 1993 for details).

(3) a.　Pierre se préoccupe de ses enfants.
　　　'Peter worries about his children.'

　　b.　　P　　Obl　　1
　　　　　P　　Obl　　1:2
　　　　　P　　Obl　　1
　　　se préoccupe　de ses enfants　Pierre

(4) a.　Pierre est préoccupé par/de ses enfants.
　　　'Peter is preocuped by his children.'

　　b.　　P　　Obl　　1
　　　　　P　　Obl　　2
　　　　　P　　Obl　　1
　　　préoccupé　par ses enfants　Pierre

Both may appear under a causative predicate[2]; when retroherent antipassive is embedded under *faire*, *se* is obligatory.

(5) Ça ferait se préoccuper Pierre de ses enfants.
     'This would make Peter worry about his children.'

On the other hand, French forbids revaluation in a number of syntactic contexts. *Faire par* involves a union complement frequently assumed to involve passive. Legendre (1990) however reviews all the evidence proposed in the literature and concludes that *faire par* does not involve passive, but rather chômage of the embedded 1 induced by the causer in the union clause. Legendre (1990) argues that the structure of the union complement in (6a) is (6b).

(6) a. J'ai fait réparer la voiture par le mécanicien.
         'I had the car repaired by the mechanic.'

     b. P   1   2
         réparer   le mécanicien   la voiture

The no-passive analysis is confirmed by instances of 3-2-1 advancement in French. Postal (1982) argues that a few French verbs including *(dés)obéir* which exceptionally allow their oblique arguments to passivize (as noted in Kayne 1975) are instances of 3-2 advancement followed by passive; (7b) is represented in (7c).

(7) a. Les soldats ont désobéi au capitaine.
         'The soldiers disobeyed (to) the captain.'

     b. Le capitaine a été désobéi par les soldats.
         'The captain has been disobeyed by the soldiers.'

     c. P   1   3
         P   1   2
         P   cho   1
         désobéi   les soldats   le capitaine

(Dés)obéir allows 3-2 advancement only when combined with subsequent

---

[2]The antipassive structure in (4) may only appear under *rendre* "render" which is the causative union predicate for adjectives in French.

passive; (7b) cannot be embedded under *faire* however, showing that *faire par* is ungrammatical when passive is required.

(8) a. Ca fera désobéir les soldats au capitaine.
'This will make the soldiers disobey (to) the captain.'

    b. * Ca fera désobéir le capitaine par les soldats.   (Kayne 1975)
'This will make the captain be disobeyed by the soldiers.'

French allows locative subjects as shown in (10)—which is synonymous with (9). Under standard RG assumptions, (10) appears to be a good candidate for Loc-1 advancement inducing chômage of the initial 1.

(9) La vermine grouille dans le jardin.
'The vermin swarms in the garden.'

(10) Le jardin grouille de vermine.
'The garden is swarming with vermin.'

Legendre (1993) however argues that (10) does not involve a Loc-1 revaluation; rather it is monostratal.[3] Note that both (9) and (10) can be embedded under causative *faire*, as shown in (11) and (12):

(11) a. Ça fera grouiller la vermine dans le jardin.
'This will make the vermin swarm in the garden.'

    b.   P   1   Loc
       grouiller la vermine   dans le jardin

(12) a. Ça fera grouiller le jardin de vermine.
'This will make the garden swarm with vermin.'

    b.   P   1   Obl
       grouiller le jardin   de vermine

The third antipassive construction in which *préoccuper*-type psych verbs appear (Legendre 1993) is exemplified in (13):

---

[3]Farrell (1991) argues against a similar biclausal analysis of locative subjects in Italian.

(13) a. Ses enfants préoccupent Pierre.
'His children preoccupy Peter.'

    b.

P	Obl	1
P	Obl	2
P	1	2
préoccupent	ses enfants	Pierre

Legendre (1993) argues that in (13), the experiencer, *Pierre*, heads an initial 1-arc and a final 2-arc while the stimulus, *ses enfants*, heads an initial oblique-arc and a final 1-arc. What distinguishes this type of antipassive from the other two presented in (3) and (4) is the fact that both arguments in (13) revaluate—in (3) and (4), the stimulus does not revaluate—and that the final 1 is distinct from the initial 1. As it turns out, (13) cannot be embedded under *faire*. Note that (14) is constructed on the model of well-formed French causative constructions whose complement is finally transitive (*faire à/faire par*).

(14) * Ça fera préoccuper Pierre à/par ses enfants.
'This will make his children preoccupy Peter.'

Finally, French inversion constructions present some interesting complexities. Legendre (1989) argues that a separate class of French psych verbs—the *plaire* class exemplified in (15)—involve a combination of two revaluations: the initial 1 (experiencer) revaluates to 3 (inversion), and the initial 2 (stimulus) revaluates to 1 (unaccusative advancement).

(15) a. Marie plaira à Pierre.
'M. will be pleasing to P. (= P. will be attracted to M.).'

    b.

P	1	2
P	3	2
P	3	1
plaira	à Pierre	Marie

Embedding (15) under *faire* yields the unacceptable sentence (16):

(16) * Ça fera plaire Marie à Pierre.
'This will make Mary attractive to Peter.'

Observe that in the complement of (16), represented in (15b), the final 1—the stimulus—is distinct from the initial 1—the experiencer. This confirms the striking generalization, based on a comparison of all the allowed or required vs. forbidden patterns above, that French does not allow in causative complements combinations of revaluations which result in a final 1 being distinct from an initial 1; on the other hand, French allows an argument to revaluate to 1 when no distinct argument heads an initial 1 (as shown in (1)-(5)). This generalization is obscured by the fact that one verb governing inversion—*ressembler* "resemble"—can appear under *faire*:

(17) Ça fera ressembler Marie à Pierre.
      'This will make Marie resemble Peter.'

Though *ressembler* and *plaire* have the same syntax (Legendre 1989, 1994), they obviously have different semantic properties. The arguments of *plaire* are not equal thematically while those of *ressembler* are (regardless of the actual label, perhaps theme). I propose to account for the generalization on combinations of revaluations on the one hand and the *ressembler* case on the other in terms of two prominence constraints stated informally in (18). One is syntactic (referencing GRs) and the other is thematic (referencing thematic roles).[4]

(18) Causee Prominence Constraints in French union complements:
     #1) Syntactic: the causee bears the highest embedded final GR.
     #2) Thematic: the causee is the highest thematic argument.

Impossible revaluations in French violate constraint #2: Passive, Inversion with *plaire*, and plain antipassive all involve misalignments between thematic roles and final GRs: the causee or embedded final 1 is the lowest thematic argument. Inversion with *ressembler* however satisfies constraint #2, given that the two arguments are thematically equal (therefore highest), and also constraint #1 (the causee is the final 1). Possible revaluations do not violate any constraint; in each case the causee bears the highest final GR as well as the highest thematic role, as the reader may verify.

Postal (1989) argues that the union complement of superficially transitive verbs like *connaître* involves inversion which is "masked". His

---

[4] The constraints stated in (18) subsume the bi-conditional Causee Prominence Constraint (CPC) of Legendre (1993). The present formulation is intended to capture the French pattern from a cross-linguistic perspective which is the focus of this paper.

analysis is primarily intended to account for a mysterious contrast between standard transitive verbs like *choisir* and non-standard *connaître* with respect to the distribution of clitics in union structures. Postal, however, does not settle the issue of what type of masked inversion is involved in the union complement of *connaître*. In the absence of "evidence which could distinguish the distinct proposals" (p. 46), he suggests two alternative analyses of masked inversion consistent with all his claims, represented below in their RG version. They are dubbed absolute inversion (I) and personal inversion with redemotion of the advancee 1 to 2 (II).

(19)   I: P 1 2   II: P 1 2
            P 3 2   P 3 2
                               P 3 1
                               P 3 2

Note that the prominence constraints settle the issue: I must be the correct analysis because this is the only one which is consistent with both constraints stated in (18)—II violates constraint #2. The constraints stated in (18) assume GR and thematic hierarchies, the existence of which is uncontroversial; while many versions of the thematic hierarchy have been proposed in the literature, I assume only a partial one covering only Agent, Experiencer, and Theme or Stimulus; their relative ranking on the hierarchy is, to the best of my knowledge, accepted by all:

(20)   GR hierarchy: 1 > 2 > 3 > Obl (including chô)
       Thematic hierarchy: Agent > Experiencer > Theme/Stimulus

This is turn requires that thematic roles gain official status in RG representations, a move independently motivated in Farrell (1991).The prominence constraints refer to the causee which is defined as the embedded argument which is displaced by the causer; universally the causee revaluates to 2, 3, or chômeur depending on the particular language (Gibson and Raposo 1986; Legendre 1994).[5]

---

[5] All three revaluation strategies exist in French, thus requiring an extension of Gibson and Raposo's 1986 parametric proposal. They propose that the causee may only revaluate to 2 or 3; Legendre (1994) argues that *faire par* involves "revaluation to chômeur", sometimes called the no-revaluation strategy; see Rosen (1983) for Italian and Gerdts (1990) for Korean.

The prominence constraints on the union complement stated in (18) reference a particular argument, the causee; they cannot be general constraints that affect all embedded arguments because revaluations and subsequent misalignments of arguments other than the causee are possible in French.[6] For example, certain French verbs govern 3-2 advancement which, unlike the 3-2 advancement posited by Postal (1982) for *(dés)obéir*, causes the initial 2 to go en chômage (Legendre 1986). This is shown in (21a) and (21c). (21a) can be embedded under *faire*, as shown in (21b):

(21) a. L'hôtesse a averti les passagers d'un danger imminent.
'The flight attendant warned the passengers of an imminent danger.'

b. Le pilote a fait avertir les passagers d'un danger imminent (par L'hôtesse).
'The pilot had the passengers warned about an imminent danger.'

c.   P   1   2   3
    P   1   cho   2
    avertir   l'hôtesse   d'un danger im.   les passagers

Constraints #1 and #2 amount to restricting the mapping between thematic roles and **final** GRs. This is quite different from Baker's (1988) Uniformity of Theta Assignment Hypothesis (UTAH) or Postal's (1986) Universal Alignment Hypothesis which are principles contraining the mapping between thematic roles and **initial** GRs.[7] When we turn to cross-linguistic evidence on union complements, we cannot fail to notice two other major patterns, one represented by Inuktitut—which does not constrain the form of union complements—and the other represented by Italian—which severely constrains it. Two more patterns with added complexities—those of Labrador Inuttut and Halkomelem—merit

---

[6] This appears to be true of Turkish—which otherwise patterns like Italian— based on Özkaragöz (1986).

[7] I am assuming here that the initial stratum is only constrained by language-particular rules which offer direct evidence for an initial syntactic level distinct from a level of thematic roles (see Farrell 1991 for discussion).

consideration.[8]

3. The Inuktitut pattern

The Inuktitut (Eskimo) data available to me (Jensen and Johns 1989) is not as complete as that of French but what is available points to a distinctly different pattern. The Inuktitut morphological causative formed by the bound morpheme *-tit-* involves clause union, according to Woodbury (1977). Interestingly enough, Inuktitut—an ergative language—allows passive and antipassive in the complement of clause union. It is unclear whether Inuktitut antipassive involves just one revaluation—e.g., 1-2 demotion as in French or spontaneous 2-chômage as in Halkomelem, according to Gerdts (1984)—or two revaluations inducing a misalignment—as in Choctaw antipassive (Davies 1984). However, the possibility of passive (a clear case of misalignment in Inuktitut, according to Jensen and Johns (1989)) allows us to propose that Inuktitut union complements allow both revaluations and misalignments, while French allows only revaluations. (22) and (23) exemplify intransitive and transitive union complements, respectively. (24) exemplifies a union complement with antipassive while (25) exemplifies a union complement with passive.

(22) Nutara-up   arnaq   ani-ti-taa.
     child-erg   woman-abs   go out-CAUS-3sg/3sg
     'The child made the woman go out.'

(23) Nutara-up   arna-mut   angut   aktuq-ti-taa.
     child-erg   woman-all   man-abs   touch-CAUS-3sg/3sg
     'The child made a woman touch the man.'

(24) Nutara-up   arnaq   anguti-mik aktuq-si-ti-taa.
     child-erg   woman-abs   man-comit   touch-ANTIPASS-CAUS-sg/3sg
     'The child made the woman touch the man.'

(25) Nutara-up   angut   arna-mit   aktuq-tau-ti-taa.
     child-erg   man-abs   woman-abl   touch-PASS-CAUS-3sg/3sg
     'The child made the man be touched by the woman.'

The fact that Inuktitut allows misalignments (as in passive) shows that

---

[8]The existence of these distinct patterns was brought to my attention by Alana Johns and Donna Gerdts, respectively.

thematic constraint #2 posited for French does not operate in Inuktitut. Only syntactic constraint #1 applies.

(26) Causee Prominence constraints in Inuktitut union complements:
   #1: Syntactic: the causee bears the highest embedded final GR.

Verbal agreement on the complex verb actually shows the effects of constraint #1. In transitive clauses, the verb agrees with its two arguments, the ergative agent and the absolutive theme (Jensen and Johns 1989).

(27) Arna-up   angut   kunik-paa.
     woman-erg   man-abs   kiss-3sg/3sg
     'The woman kissed the man.'

In passive sentences, however, the verb only agrees with the absolutive theme (the agent is an oblique):

(28) Angut   arna-mit   kunik-tau-vuq.
     man-abs   woman-abl   kiss-PASS-3sg
     'The man was kissed by the woman.'

In antipassive sentences, the verb agrees only with the absolutive agent (the theme here is an oblique):

(29) Arnaq   angum-mik   kunik-si-vuq.
     woman-abs   man-comit   kiss-ANTIPASS-3sg
     'The woman kissed a man.'

The pattern appears to be that the verb agrees with the surface ergative and absolutive arguments regardless of their thematic role. This might be couched in RG in terms of agreeing with final nuclear term GRs only. Interestingly, the same pattern of agreement is found in causative union constructions. In (22)-(25), the complex causative verb agrees with the relationally highest two arguments—surfacing in the ergative case (causer) and the absolutive case (embedded argument), regardless of the thematic role borne by the absolutive argument: it is an agent in (22) and (24) and a theme in (23) and (25). The generalization about agreement obviously cannot be stated in terms of highest thematic arguments.

4. The Italian pattern

The Italian pattern is well known and has been extensively discussed in the RG literature, based on Carol Rosen's work (Rosen initially proposed her account for all of Romance). Unlike "free" Inuktitut and "semi-free" French, Italian severely restricts the form of its union complements. All revaluations appear to be banned (Rosen 1983). For example, passive, as registered by *essere*, is impossible in the Italian *fare da* construction.

(30) * Faremo essere accompagnato il grupo da un interprete. (Rosen 1983)
    'We'll make the group be accompanied by an interpreter.'

Rosen (1983) provides additional evidence that the complement of *fare da* does not involve passive. Unaccusative advancement registered by *si* is also impossible:

(31) Carlo ha fatto arrabbiare/*arrabbiarsi il vigile.   (Rosen 1983)
    'Carlo made the cop get angry.'

Psych verbs which involve a misalignment between their thematic arguments and their final GRs, such as *preoccupare* "preoccupy" and *piacere* "please" cannot appear under *fare* according to Belletti and Rizzi (1988):

(32) * Questo lo ha fatto preoccupare ancora di più a Mario
    'This made Mario worry him even more.'

Thus Italian has a "downstairs freeze", to use Rosen's initial characterization; in our terms, neither revaluations nor misalignments are allowed in Italian. Italian then requires (at least) one more constraint. The question is: how should it be formulated? One alternative would be to say that the causee cannot head more than one distinct GR. In combination with the other two constraints, this would rule out revaluations (for revaluations mean among other things that a single nominal bears more than one GR, albeit in different strata); it would also rule out multiattachment (MA) structures, i.e. structures in which a single nominal bears more than one GR in a single stratum. There is evidence (shown in (33)), brought forward by Farrell (1991), that certain MAs are fine under *fare* as long as *si* does not appear (*si* would signal the resolution of the MA, i.e., an additional stratum). Crucial, of course, is the fact that sentence (33) has a semantically reflexive interpretation, according to Farrell (1991).

(33) Maria ha fatto tagliare Gianni (*tagliarsi).
'Mary made Gianni cut himself.'

Farrell (1991) further reports that in union complements, MA structures which lack resolution (without *si*) but which involve more than one stratum are nonetheless unacceptable. Sentence (34) involves a 3-2 revaluation combined with a MA according to La Fauci (1986). (35) shows that it cannot be embedded under *fare*.

(34) I professori si sono concessi/a una pausa.
'The teachers allowed themselves/each other a break.'

(35) *Questo ha fatto concedere i professori una pausa.
'This made the teachers allow themselves a break.'

These additional facts suggest that the constraint in Italian is not simply a matter of heading more than one GR, but of heading more than one GR in **different** strata. In other words, the causee cannot revaluate. I thus propose that a third constraint operating in Italian is a revaluation ban. I consider this revaluation ban to be a prominence constraint because revaluations map relative changes in syntactic prominence.

(36) Causee Prominence Constraints in Italian union complements:
#1: Syntactic: the causee bears the highest embedded final GR.
#2: Thematic: the causee is the highest thematic argument.
#3: Syntactic: the causee must not revaluate.

5. Other patterns: Halkomelem and Labrador Inuttut

Halkomelem is an ergative Salish language which allows antipassive and passive in simple sentences. The union pattern is discussed in Gerdts (1984): union is possible only if the complement clause involves antipassive. Antipassive is registered by the presence of the intransitive suffix -∂m preceding the causative suffix -$st\partial x^w$ on the main verb.

(37) a.   ni cən q'^{w}əl-əm-stəx^w θə słéni?   ʔə   k^{w}θə səplíl.
       aux 1sub bake-intr-caus det woman   obl det bread
      I had the woman bake the bread.

     b.   P   1   2   (Gerdts, 1984)
            P   1   chô
        q'^{w}əl   słeni?   səplíl

Transitive (38a) as well as passive complements (38b) are impossible (passive is registered by the presence of both transitive -ət and intransitive -əm suffixes):

(38) a. * ni cən q'ʷəl-ət-stəxʷ kʷθə səplíl ʔə łə słéniʔ.
    aux 1sub bake-tr-caus det bread obl det woman
    'I had the woman bake the bread.'

  b. * ni q'ʷəl-ət-əm-stəxʷ-əs kʷθə səplíl ʔə łə słéniʔ.
    aux bake-tr-intr-caus-3erg det bread obl det woman
    'He had the bread baked by the woman.'

Gerdts (1984, 1991) further argues that Halkomelem distinguishes two classes of intransitives: unergatives, which can occur in union complements, and unaccusatives, which cannot.[9]

(39) a. ni cən ʔəłtən-əstəxʷ kʷθə sqwəméyʔ.
    aux 1sub eat-caus det dog
    'I let the dog eat.'

  b. * ni cən kʷəł-stəxʷ kʷθə tí.
    aux 1sub spill-caus det tea
    'I made the tea spill.'

Gerdts (1984) concludes that Halkomelem, much like Italian, has a downstairs freeze preventing passive and unaccusative revaluations. In our terms, this means that constraint #3 operates in Halkomelem, just like in Italian. But Halkomelem is different from Italian since the former (but not the latter) does not allow transitive union complements. In Halkomelem, transitive union complements must undergo antipassive, which detransitivizes the complement, as shown in diagram (37b), adapted from Gerdts (1984). This suggests that a fourth constraint is at work in Halkomelem and that constraint #4 requires the causee to be the only

---

[9] Gerdts (1991) mentions that she knows of no evidence in favor or against unaccusative advancement per se in Halkomelem union complements. The analysis proposed here provides evidence that (39b) is ungrammatical as a result of a violation of constraint #3 presumably caused by unaccusative advancement.

prominent (= nuclear term) final argument on the GR hierarchy.[10] Constraint #4 guarantees that the final stratum of a union complement is intransitive (= contains only one nuclear term, 1 or 2). Constraint #4 also guarantees that constraint #1 (the causee bears the highest embedded final GR) will be satisfied. Finally, constraint #2 (the causee is the highest thematic argument) is satisfied in Halkomelem antipassive union complements. Halkomelem, then, is even stricter than Italian in the sense that all four constraints operate.

(40) Causee Prominence Constraints in Halkomelem union complements:
   #1: Syntactic: the causee bears the highest embedded final GR.
   #2: Thematic: the causee is the highest thematic argument.
   #3: Syntactic: the causee must not revaluate.
   #4: Syntactic: the causee is the only prominent final argument on the GR hierarchy.

Halkomelem is not unusual in requiring an additional constraint (#4) which guarantees a finally intransitive complement. Jensen and Johns (1989) mention that according to Lawrence Smith, as reported in Grimshaw and Mester (1985), the equivalent of Inuktitut (23) with a transitive complement is impossible for some speakers of Labrador Inuttut (a related dialect), while (24) and (25) with antipassive and passive, respectively, are fine. Smith (1982) argues that, generally speaking, in LI the transitive complement of what he appears to consider unions must be detransitivized by passive or antipassive. Passive—a clear case of revaluation—violates constraint #3, which operates in Italian and in Halkomelem. In addition, LI violates constraint #2, since the passive causee is not the highest thematic argument. LI satisfies constraint #4 since it requires that there be only one nuclear term argument. Note that satisfying #4 automatically satisfies constraint #1: the causee is the highest embedded final GR, a consequence of removing one of the nuclear term GRs.

(41) Causee Prominence Constraints in LI union complements:
   #1: Syntactic: the causee bears the highest embedded final GR.
   #4: Syntactic: the causee is the only prominent final argument on the GR hierarchy.

---

[10]This raises the question of whether "nuclear term" or "term" is the correct characterization. In RG, term R-signs include 3s (Indirect Objects) while nuclear term R-signs exclude 3s. I do not have any data from Halkomelem or Labrador Inuttut bearing on this question.

6. Summary of cross-linguistic patterns

A preliminary survey yields the patterns of Table (42).

(42) Cross-linguistic patterns:

Revaluation #3	Misalignment #2	Transitive #4	Language
OK	*	OK	French
OK	*	*	?[11]
OK	OK	OK	Inuktitut, Korean[12]
OK	OK	*	Labrador Inuttut
*	*	OK	Italian, Turkish[13]
*	*	*	Halkomelem
*	OK	OK	logically impossible
*	OK	*	logically impossible

This survey indicates that various languages fall under the same patterns, regardless of differences between periphrastic vs. morphological causative and case marking systems (accusative or ergative). Note that only three constraints are included because constraint #1 is satisfied by all languages. Note further that the seventh and eighth combinations are impossible because misalignment subsumes revaluation, making it logically impossible to have possible misalignment and impossible revaluation in a single language. The prominence constraints giving rise to the patterns in (42) are claimed to operate in union complements only. What is it about union structures that makes these constraints operate on the causee? I can only conjecture at this point that union structures have two relevant properties:

---

[11] Algonquian languages have been mentioned as allowing only unions of intransitives, both of unergatives and unaccusatives. If true, this may indicate that (unaccusative) revaluation is fine. I have not been able yet to check whether Algonquian might fit the missing pattern.

[12] This pattern holds of periphrastic *ha-ta* causatives in Korean, based on Gerdts (1990): Korean allows passive and unaccusative advancement in the complement of *ha-ta* unions.

[13] The classification of Turkish is based on Özkaragöz's (1986) study: Turkish does not allow reflexive, passive, or unaccusative advancement in union complements.

the causative verb initializes its own 1 (the causer) and all embedded arguments raise to the matrix or union clause to presumably satisfy the valence of the complex predicate while remaining subservient (the causee cannot put the causer en chômage). Constraints on the union complement insure that the raising of embedded arguments will not create havoc in the main clause.

7. Conclusion: parameterization issues

To summarize, I have proposed that the complexity of causative union complements cross-linguistically derives from a small set of syntactic and thematic prominence constraints. The set of four constraints determines a set of six possible patterns, five of which are exemplified in the paper. Further research may confirm the existence of the sixth one. The four constraints proposed here are universal in the sense that they belong to the universally available set. Two parameterization alternatives can be entertained. One, individual languages select from this set—e.g., Inuktitut selects #1, French selects #1 and 2, Italian selects #1, 2, and 3, and Halkomelem selects them all. Another possibility is that all the constraints are available in all the languages but they are ranked differently in terms of their violability. The highest ranked constrained are inviolable while the lower ranked ones can be violated. What I am suggesting here is a system of constraint interaction made available by Optimality Theory (Prince and Smolensky to appear; Legendre, Raymond, and Smolensky 1993; Grimshaw 1993). This formal approach posits that linguistic constraints are highly general, they are ranked with respect to one another differently in different languages, and they are soft in the sense that they are frequently violated. Violation of constraints is itself constrained: a lower ranked constraint can be violated **only if** violating it allows another higher ranked constraint to be satisfied. Two things are clear from the discussion above: One, constraint #1 operates in all languages examined in this paper, and two, not all remaining constraints operate in all the languages. This suggests that an optimality approach may be the next thing to pursue.

REFERENCES

Aissen, Judith. 1974. Verb Raising. *LI* 5.3:325-366.
Baker, Mark. 1988. *Incorporation: A Theory of Grammatical Function Changing.* University of Chicago Press.
Belletti, Adriana and Luigi Rizzi. 1988. Psych-verbs and Theta-Theory. *NLLT* 6:291-352.
Davies, William D. 1984. Antipassive: Choctaw Evidence for a Universal Characterization. In *Studies in Relational Grammar 2*, D.M. Perlmutter and C. Rosen (eds.), 331-76. University of Chicago Press.
Farrell, Patrick. 1991. *Thematic Relations, Relational Networks, and Multistratal Representations.* UCSD Ph.D. dissertation.
Gerdts, Donna. 1984. A Relational Analysis of Halkomelem Causals. In *Semantics and Syntax 16: The Syntax of Native American Languages*, E.D. Cook and D. Gerdts, (eds.), 169-204. Academic Press Inc.
Gerdts, Donna. 1990. Revaluation and Inheritance in Korean Causative Union. In *Studies in Relational Grammar 3*, P.M. Postal and B.D. Joseph (eds.), 203-246. University of Chicago Press.
Gerdts, Donna. 1991. Unaccusative Mismatches in Halkomelem Salish. *IJAL* 57.2: 230-250.
Gibson, Jeanne and Eduardo Raposo. 1986. Clause Union, the Stratal Uniqueness Law, and the Chômeur relation. *NLLT* 4:295-331.
Grimshaw, Jane. 1993. Minimal Projection, Heads, and Optimality. Rutgers U. manuscript.
Grimshaw, Jane and Ralf-Armin Mester. Complex Verb Formation in Eskimo. *NLLT* 3: 1-19.
Harris, Alice. 1981. *Georgian Syntax: A Study in Relational Grammar.* Cambridge University Press.
Jensen, John T. and Alana. Johns. 1989. The Morphosyntax of Eskimo Causatives. In *Theoretical Perspectives on Native American Languages*, D.B. Gerdts and K. Michelson (eds.), 209-229. State University of New York Press.
Kayne, Richard. 1975. *French Syntax: The Transformational Cycle.* MIT Press.
La Fauci, Nunzio. 1986. Sulla natura assoluta del controllore dell'accordo del participio passato in italiano. *La Memoria. Annali della Facoltà di Lettere e Filosofia dell'Università di Palermo.*
Legendre, Géraldine. 1986. Object Raising in French: A Unified Account. *NLLT* 4: 137-183.
Legendre, Géraldine. 1989. Inversion with Certain French Experiencer Verbs. *Language* 65.4:752-782.

Legendre, Géraldine. 1990. French Causatives: Another Look at *faire par*. In *Grammatical Relations: A Cross-Theoretical Perspective*, K. Dziwirek, P. Farrell, and E. Mejias-Bikandi (eds.), 247-262. Stanford: CSLI Publications.

Legendre, Géraldine. 1993. Antipassive with French Psych-Verbs. To appear in *WCCFL Proceedings*.

Legendre, Géraldine. 1994. *Topics in French Syntax*. Garland Publishing, Inc., New York.

Legendre, Géraldine, William Raymond, and Paul Smolensky. 1993. An Optimality-Theoretic Typology of Case and Grammatical Voice Systems. *BLS Proceedings* 464-478.

Özkaragöz, Inci. 1985. *The Relational Structure of Turkish Syntax*. UCSD Ph.D. dissertation.

Prince, Alan and Paul Smolensky. to appear. *Optimality Theory: Constraint Interaction in Generative Grammar*. MIT Press.

Postal, Paul M. 1982. Arc Pair Grammar Descriptions. In *The Nature of Syntactic Representation*, P. Jacobson and G. Pullum (eds.), 341-425. Reidel, Dordrecht.

Postal, Paul M. 1989. *Masked Inversion in French*. University of Chicago Press.

Rosen, Carol. 1983. Universals of Causative Union: A Co-Proposal to the Gibson-Raposo Typology. *CLS 19*.

Smith, Lawrence R. 1982. An Analysis of Affixal Verbal Derivation and Complementation in Labrador Inuttut. *Linguistic Analysis* 10.2: 161-189.

Woodbury, Anthony. 1977. Greenlandic Eskimo, Ergativity, and Relational Grammar. In *Syntax and Semantics 8: Grammatical Relations*, P. Cole and J. Sadock, eds., 307-336. Academic Press.

Lexical Case and NP Raising

KUMIKO G. MURASUGI
McGill University

1. Two Types of Movement

The concept of ECONOMY as a universal principle has recently emerged as an important development with the principles-and-parameters approach to language (see Chomsky 1991, 1992). For example, the derivation of grammatical structures seems to involve operations that require the LEAST EFFORT, either in terms of the distance moved or the number of steps involved. Similarly, at each level of representation, such structures should not contain any unlicensed or superfluous symbols. In this paper, I investigate a specific derivational principle of economy: SHORTEST MOVEMENT. I define 'shortest movement' as movement involving the shortest distance between two points in a structure.

Following Chomsky (1991), I assume that arguments are generated within the VP, and raise to the specifiers of functional projections to receive Case. When there is a choice of potential NPS for movement, the principle of Shortest Movement will create NESTED PATHS, shown in (1). The subject, NP1, raises to the Spec of the lower functional projection, Tr(ansitivity)P, and the object raises to the Spec of the higher one, IP. Evidence for Nested Paths, found in ergative languages (see Murasugi 1992), is provided in section 3.

---

[*]I would like to thank the ausience at the 6th Biennial Grammatical Relations Conference for their helpful questions and comments, and the participants of the 1993 Conference of the Canadian Linguistic Association, where an earlier version of this paper was presented. This work was supported by a Social Sciences and Humanities Research Council of Canada Postdoctoral Fellowship (#756-92-0529).

(1) Nested Paths (Ergative Languages)

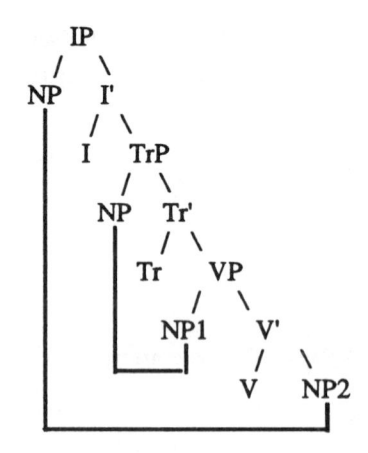

```
          IP
         /  \
        NP   I'
            /  \
           I    TrP
               /  \
              NP   Tr'
                  /  \
                 Tr   VP
                     /  \
                   NP1   V'
                        /  \
                       V    NP2
```

In accusative languages we find CROSSING PATHS, shown in (2). The subject raises to the higher projection, and the object to the lower.

(2) Crossing Paths (Accusative Languages)

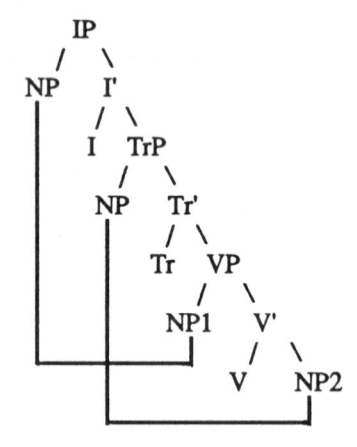

```
          IP
         /  \
        NP   I'
            /  \
           I    TrP
               /  \
              NP   Tr'
                  /  \
                 Tr   VP
                     /  \
                   NP1   V'
                        /  \
                       V    NP2
```

In section 4, I demonstrate how Crossing Paths are possible in accusative languages given my proposal that the Principle of Shortest Movement generates Nested Paths. I claim that the difference in the two types of languages results from the assignment of lexical Case to the complement of the verb in accusative, but not in ergative, languages. The assignment of lexical Case restricts the choice of NPs that are available for raising to Spec positions.

The discussion of ergativity in section 3, in particular the existence of Nested Paths, is presented more fully in Murasugi (1992). The analysis of accusative languages presented in section 4 is different from the analysis discussed in previous work.

2. Principle of Shortest Movement

The Principle of Shortest Movement is stated formally in (3).

(3) *Principle of Shortest Movement*
At each level of a derivation, a target must select the closest available NP.

This principle states that a target (i.e. the Spec of a Case assigning functional head) must select the closest available NP to move into that Spec position. Suppose that functional heads must assign their Case if they have one (see, for example, the Saturation Principle of Fukui and Speas 1986). Since Case is assigned in a Spec-head configuration, it is necessary that NPs move into the Spec positions to receive the Case of the heads. Given a choice of available NPs, the one that is selected is the one that moves the shortest distance to reach the target.

Some additional diefinitions are provided in (4), (5) and (6).

(4) An NP is **available** for movement if it has not been assigned structural Case.

(5) The **closest** NP is the one that crosses the least number of A-positions to reach its target.

(6) An **A-position** is a position in which an argument is base-generated (i.e. specifiers and complements of V), or moves into in order to receive Case (i.e. specifiers of Case-assigning functional heads).

3. Ergative Languages

3.1 Ergativity

Consider again the Nested Paths structure in (1) above. I will assume some kind of cyclicity condition, where targets are filled 'bottom-up', i.e. lower ones are filled before higher ones. Thus in (1), Spec TrP is filled first. There are two NPs that are available to move there, the subject and the object, since neither one has structural Case. The closer one is NP1, the subject, as there are no A-positions between it and Spec TrP. It is therefore the NP that movers to the Spec position.

Next, consider Spec IP. There is only one NP remaining, the object NP2, that is available for movement to this position. The subject in Spec

TrP is actually 'closer' in terms of actual distance, as it will not cross any A-positions, whereas the object must cross two, Spec VP and Spec TrP. However, the subject is no longer available for movement as it receives structural case in Spec TrP.

Nested Paths is not the type of movement that is commonly assumed in the literature. In fact, Chomsky (1992) claims that Crossing Paths are universal, and argues against the existence of Nested Paths. Recently, however, studies of ergative languages have proposed an 'object raising' analysis where the object appears in a position higher than the subject (e.g. Johns 1987, 1992; Bittner 1988, 1994; Bittner & Hale 1993; Campana 1992; and Murasugi 1992).[1]

An ergative language is distinguished from an accusative language in its Case-marking pattern. The two patterns of Case are shown in (7), where A = transitive subject, S = intransitive subject, and O = object.

(7) a.   *Accusative*   b.   *Ergative*

$$\left.\begin{array}{c}A\\S\end{array}\right\} \text{Nom}$$

$$O - \text{Acc}$$

$$A - \text{Erg}$$

$$\left.\begin{array}{c}S\\O\end{array}\right\} \text{Nom}$$

In (7a), A and S have the same Case, nominative, while the object has accusative Case. In (7b), S and O have nominative Case,[2] while the transitive subject has ergative Case. Examples from actual languages are shown in (8) and (9).[3]

(8) Japanese (Accusative)

    a. Jon-ga   hon-o   yon-da
       John-Nom bool-Acc read-Past
       'John read the book'
    b Jon-ga   warat-ta
       John-Nom laugh-Past
       'John laughed'

---

[1] In Johns (1987, 1992) the object does not actually raise to a higher position, but is generated above the subject.

[2] This Case is also known as 'absolutive.'

[3] The following abbreviations are used in the glosses: 1/2/3 = first/second/third person, s/p = singular/plural, Acc = Accusative, AP = Antipassive, Erg = Ergative, Fin = Finite, Incomp = Incompletive, Ind = Indicative, Intr = Intransitive, Nom = Nominative, Part = Participal, Suff= Suffix,Tr = Transitive

(9) Inuktitut (Ergative)

a. Jaani-up   tuktu-ø   taku-vaa
   John-Erg   caribou-Nom   see-Ind.3s.3s
   'John saw the caribou'
b. Jaani-ø   sinik-puq
   John-Nom   sleep-Ind.3s
   'John slept'

In both ergative and sbsolutive languages, nominative Case is assigned by I to the NP in Spec IP. Tr assigns accusative or ergative Case to the NP in its Spec.[4] In an accusative language, the NPs that raise to Spec IP are the two subjects (A and S). The object receives accusative Case in Spec TrP. For transitive clauses, this gives the familiar Crossing Paths movement shown in (2) above. In an ergative language, the two arguments that raise to Spec IP are S and O. The A argument raises to Spec TrP, where it receives ergative Case. In a transitive clause, then, with O raising to Spec IP and A to Spec TrP, we get Nested Paths.

3.2 Evidence for Nested Paths

I will provide two pieces of evidence for Nested Paths in ergative languages: (i) relativization, discussed in section 3.2.1, and (ii) the order of verbal agreement morphemes (see section 3.2.2).[5]

3.2.1 Relativization

In ergative languages such as Inuit and Dyirbal, relativization is restricted to S and O. An argument cannot be relativized unless the clause becomes intransitive by antipassivization. In (10a), the relativized noun is S, and in (10b), it is O. The ungrammatical (10c) involves the relativization of A. When the clause becomes an antipassive, as in (10d), the A argument becomes an S, and relativization of the argument is possible

(10) Inuit (Ergative)

a. angut   [sinik-tuq]   (S)
   man(Nom)   sleep-Part.Intr.3s
   'the man who e is sleeping'

---

[4]The Case assigned by Tr is given a different name in accusative and ergative languages.

[5]For additional evidence, see Campana (1992) and Murasugi (1992).

b. angut   [arna-up   kunik-taa]   (O)
   man(Nom) woman-Erg   kiss-Part.Tr.3s.3s
   'the man who the woman kissed e'
c. *anguti-up [amaq   kunik-taa]   (A)
   man-Erg   woman(Nom)   kiss-Part.Tr.3s.3s
   'the man who e kissed the woman'
d. angut   [arna-mik   kunik-si-juq]   (A > S)
   man(Nom) woman-Inst   kiss-AP-Part.Intr.3s
   'the man who e kissed the woman'

Various analyses have been proposed to account for this restriction on relative clauses in ergative languages (e.g. Johns 1987, 1992; Bittner 1988, 1994; Campana 1992; Murasugi 1992). Although the analyses are based upon differing theoretical assumptions, the general idea is that relativization is restricted to the Spec IP position (or the equivalent in the particular theory). Since it is S and O that raise to this position, these are the arguments that may be relativized. A similar restriction is found for wh-movement, topicalization and focus clefting in other ergative languages.

3.2.2 Order of Verbal Agreement Morphemes

In the unmarked order of verbal agreement morphemes in ergative languages, subject agreement is closer to the verb than object agreement.

(11) a. Tzutujil (Mayan)

   n-e7-a-kamsa-aj
   Incomp-3p-2s-kill-Suff
   'you kill them'   (Dayley 1985:83)

b. Abkhaz (Caucasian)

   harà š°arà š°-aa-bò-yt'
   we   you.p 2p-1p-see-Fin
   'we see you'   (Hewitt 1979:104)

We can account for the ordering if we assume that the order of agreement morphemes relative to the verb correlates with the hierarchical structure of arguments in the tree (see, for example, Baker's (1988) Mirror Principle). The NP lowest in the tree will show agreement closest to the verb, and a higher NP will show agreement further away from the verb. The fact that subject agreement appears closer to the verb in ergative languages shows that the subject is lower in the tree than the object.

In this section, I have provided evidence for Nested Paths in ergative languages, claiming that this type of movement is determined by the Principle of Shortest Movement. In the next section, I tuen to accusative languages.

4. Accusative Languages

4.1 Conditions on Case Assignment

My claim is that the difference between ergative and accusative languages results from the Case-assigning properties of the transitive verb. The traditional assumption is that transitive verbs assign Case to their objects (e.g. Chomsky 1981). There are two types of Case that a verb may assign: structural and lexical. Structural Case is dependent solely on a structural relation between the Case assigner and the NP receiving Case. In the theory presented here, this relation involves a functional head and an NP in its Spec.

The second type of Case is lexical Case. It has been assumed that this type of Case is assigned by the verb to the argument to which it assigns a theta role. I propose, however, that the assignment of lexical Case is also dependent on a structural relation, and not necessarily on theta roles. I define lexical Case as in (12):

(12) Lexical Case is the Case assigned by the verb to its complement, or to the specifier of its complement.

The second part of (12) applies when the complement is VP or IP. In these cases, the verb assigns Case to the NP in Spec VP or Spec IP. This is what we find in biclausal structures involving ECM and causative verbs, for example, which I assume do assign lexical Case (see Murasugi 1993). A verb usually assigns lexical Case to its Theme, since the Theme is most commonly the complement of the verb.

The two types of Case (lexical and structural) that are assigned by a verb are unified with the following condition:

(13) *Condition on Lexical and Structural Case Assignment*

If a verb assigns lexical Case to an NP, it must also participate in structural Case assignment to that NP.

An NP receives lexical Case by being in a complement relation with the verb. It receives structural Case in a Spec-head configuration with the verb following head-to-head movement of the verb to a functional head.

For a verb to participate in structural Case assignment, it must satisfy the conditions in (14). These conditions apply to all instances of structural Case assignment, i.e., to functional heads as well as verbs.

(14) Conditions on Structural Case Assignment
To be a structural Case assigner, an X^0 must be in a Spec-head relation with an NP in:
a. Spec XP, or
b. Spec YP, where X is adjoined to Y

The two cases are illustrated in (15).

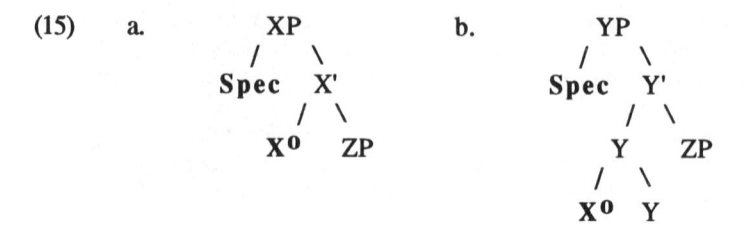

(15)   a.
```
        XP
       /  \
     Spec  X'
          /  \
         X⁰   ZP
```
b.
```
        YP
       /  \
     Spec  Y'
          /  \
          Y   ZP
         / \
        X⁰  Y
```

(15a) is the case where a functional head assigns Case to its Spec. In (15b), an X^0, say a verb, assigns structural Case to Spec YP when it adjoins to the head, Y. The verb, however, does not actually assign this second Case. Rather it is the functional head that it adjoins to that assigns the structural Case, but by condition (13), the verb has to participate in structural Case assignment. This is accomplished by the verb adjoining to a Case-assigning functional head, which places it in the proper configuration for structural Case assignment.

A crucial consequence of (14b) is that the verb, which assigns lexical Case to its object, can participate in structural Case assignment to this object only when it is in Spec TrP. When the verb raises to Tr, the resulting structure is (15b), with Y being Tr. The verb is in the proper Spec-head configuration required for Case assignment/participation to the NP in Spec TrP.

When the V+Tr complex raises further to I, however, the verb itself is too deeply embedded in the adjoined structure to participate in Case assignment to the NP in Spec TrP (see(16)).

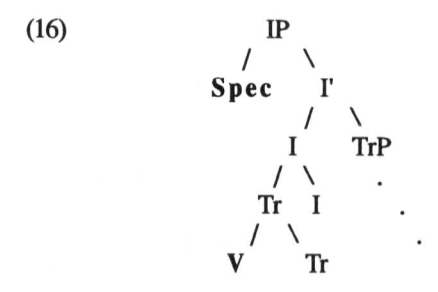

(16)
```
            IP
           /  \
         Spec  I'
              / \
             I   TrP
            / \    .
           Tr  I   .
          / \      .
         V   Tr
```

For condition (13) to be satisfied, then, the object must raise to Spec TrP, and not Spec IP. It is this raising of the object to Spec TrP that gives Crossing Paths. In accusative languages, Crossing Paths result from the Case-assigning properties of the transitive verb along with condition (13).

It has been proposed in the literature that verbs in ergative languages do not assign Case to their objects, forcing the object to raise (see, for example, Bok-Bennema 1991, Campana 1992, and Bittner 1994). In (17), I make this claim more specific.

(17)   Verbs in ergative languages do not assign **lexical** Case.

There appears to be no evidence of lexical Case in ergative languages, such as the quirky Case or Case-preserving passives found in German and Icelandic. Since verbs do not assign lexical Case, it is not necessary that they participate in structural Case assignment to the object. Therefore, the object is not required to move to Spec TrP. The subject and object are equally available for movement to the functional Specs. The Principle of Shortest Movement determines that the subject raises to Spec TrP. The remaining object moves to Spec IP, resulting in Nested Paths.

The fact that Crossing Paths are found in accusative languages demonstrates that economy principles, at least the one presented here, are operative only in cases where there is a choice available. Given two potential NPs for movement, as in ergative languages, the one that is selected is the one that is more economical. In accusative languages the object **must** raise to Spec TrP in order not to violate condition (13), leaving only the subject to raise to the other Spec. In such cases where a choice is not available, the Principle of Shortest Movement does not apply.

4.2 Raising and Shortest Movement

In this final section, I will demonstrate how Shortest Movement applies to raising constructions in English. Examples with intransitive embedded verbs will be used to avoid the issue of Crossing or Nested Paths. It is necessary to make one modification to the theory presented so far with respect to the Extended Projection Principle. I have been assuming that Specs must be filled in order for the functional heads to assign their Case. However, in raising constructions we find movement to Spec IP when I is [-tense], and therefore has no Case to assign. I will have to assume some sort of EPP, where it is required that Spec IP be filled in English.

Consider the sentence in (18) with the structure in (19).

(18)   [$_{IP1}$ John$_j$ seems [$_{IP2}$ t$_j$ to [$_{VP}$ t$_j$ be intelligent]]]

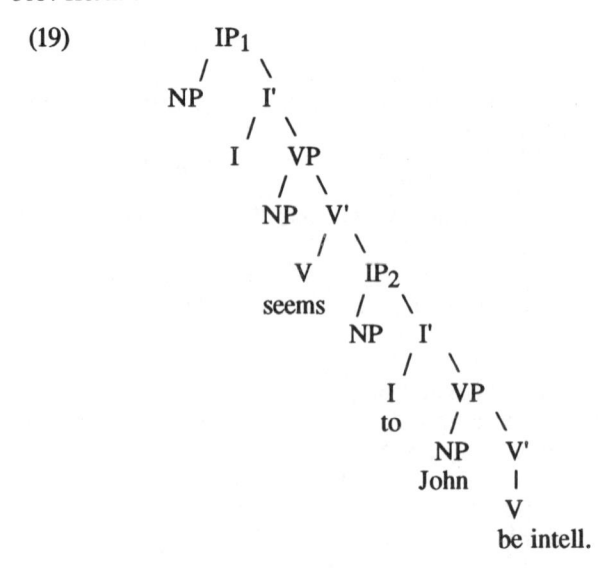

(19)
```
                IP₁
               /  \
             NP    I'
                  / \
                 I   VP
                    /  \
                  NP    V'
                       / \
                      V   IP₂
                    seems / \
                         NP  I'
                            / \
                           I   VP
                          to  /  \
                             NP   V'
                            John   |
                                   V
                                be intell.
```

Both the lower and higher IPs have Specs that need to be filled. The lower Spec, IP₂, is filled first, with the only (and hence closest) available NP, *John*. Since *John* does not receive Case here, it is still available to move to Spec IP₁.

Consider next the case where the lower clause is tensed.

(20) [IP₁ it seems that [IP₂ John is intelligent]]

When *John* raises to Spec IP₂, it receives Case there and is therefore no longer available for movement. IP₁ is satisfied with the insertion of *it*, which I claim is a language-specific last-resort strategy like *do*-support. *it*-insertion is required in English to satisfy the EPP. Since this is a last-resort strategy, it applies only after all other possible movements have occurred.

Now consider the examples in (21).

(21) a. [IP₁ it seems [IP₂ it is likely [IP₃ John is intelligent]]]
   b. [IP₁ it seems [IP₂ John is likely [IP₃ to be intelligent]]]

In (21a), *John* raises only to IP₃, where it receives Case. The other Is are satisfied with the insertion of *it*. In (21b), John raises from Spec IP₃, where it does not receive Case, to Spec IP₂, where it does receive Case. *it* is inserted in Spec IP₁.

Finally, consider the ungrammatical sentence in (22).

(22) *[IP₁ John seems [IP₂ it is likely [IP₃ to be intelligent]]]

In (22), Spec IP$_3$ is filled first, with the only available NP, *John*. *John*, however, does not receive Case in this position, and is therefore still available for movement. Next, Spec IP$_2$ must be filled. Instead of selecting *John*, *it* is inserted. This is not a legitimate strategy, since *John* is still available in Spec IP$_3$ to move into that position.

An alternative way to derive (22) is for *John* to raise all the way to Spec IP$_1$ directly from Spec IP$_3$, and insert it in IP$_2$ afterwards. Such a move, however, is not permitted, since Spec IP$_2$ must be filled before Spec IP$_1$.

5. Conclusion

In this paper, I presented an economy principle of Shortest Movement based on available NPs raising the shortest distance to target positions. It was demonstrated that when the subject and object are both available for movement, as in ergative languages, the resulting movement is Nested Paths. In accusative languages, where transitive verbs assign lexical Case to their objects, the object is required to raise to Spec TrP, creating Crossing Paths. With the recent assumption that arguments are generated within the VP, and raise from VP to Specs of functional categories, we expect there to be two types of movement paths, which I claim, in this paper, do in fact exist.

References

Baker, Mark C. 1988. *Incorporation: A Theory of Grammatical Function Changing*. Chicago: University of Chicago Press.
Bittner, Maria. 1988. *Canonical and Noncanonical Argument Expressions* Doctoral Dissertation, Universtiy of Texas at Austin.
Bittner, Maria. 1994. *Case, Scope, and Binding*. Dordrecht: Kluwer.
Bittner, Maria and Kenneth Hale. 1993. *Ergativity: Towards a Theory of Heterogeneous Class*. Ms., Rutgers University and MIT.
Bok-Bennema, Reineke. 1991. *Case and Agreement in Inuit*. Doctoral Dissertation, Katholieke Iniversiteit Brabant.
Campana, Mark. 1992. *A Movement Theory of Ergativity*. Doctoral Dissertation, McGill University.
Chomsky, Noam. 1981. *Lectures on Government and Binding*. Dordrecht: Foris.
Chomsky, Noam. 1991. Some Notes on Economy of Derivation and Representation. *Principles and Parameters in Comparative Grammar*, ed. by Robert Frieden, 417–54. Cambridge, MA: MIT Press.
Chomsky, Noam. 1992, *A Minimalist Program for Linguistic Theory*. MIT Occasional Papers in Linguistics, Number 1. Distributed by MIT Working Papers in Linguistics, Cambridge, MA.

Dayley, Jon P. 1985. *Tzutujil Grammar*. Berkeley/Los Angeles: University of California Press.
Fukui, Naoki and Margaret Speas. 1986. Specifiers and Projections. *MIT Working Papers in Linguistics* 8.128–72.
Hewitt, B.G. (with Z.K. Khiba). 1979. *Abkhaz*. Linguistic Descriptive Series, vol. 2. Amsterdam: North-Holland.
Johns, Alana. 1987. *Transitivity and Grammatical Relations in Inuktitut*. Doctoral Dissertation, University of Ottawa.
Johns, Alana. 1992. *Deriving Ergativity*. Linguistic Inquiry 23.57–87.
Murasugi, Kumiko G. 1992. *Crossing and Nested Paths: NP Movement in Accusative and Ergative Languages*. Doctoral Dissertation: MIT.
Murasugi, Kumiko G. 1993. *Shortest Movement is Shortest Distance*. Ms., McGill University.

Predication Within Telugu Nominals

ROSANNE PELLETIER

Yale University

1. Introduction

This paper provides an analysis of noun phrases in the Dravidian language Telugu, and shows that they parallel clauses in an important respect: Noun phrases, like clauses, are headed by predicates. As discussed in Rosen (1987), positing this clause-like internal syntax for nominals reflects the semantically predicative nature of the common nouns which head them. Moreover, given this subclausal predication structure, an account of otherwise anomalous facts concerning word order, agreement, and case marking follows.

The parallels between clausal and nominal-internal predication are captured straightforwardly in Relational Grammar, since this framework makes direct reference to grammatical relations such as 'predicate' without regard to the categorial status of the element bearing this relation.

2. Nominal Predication Within Clauses

Before demonstrating predication within Telugu nominals, I will first illustrate nominal predication in general, in Telugu main clauses. Cross-linguistically, clausal nominal predicates are far from unusual. In Telugu, however, predicative nouns are clearly marked as such, thus making it possible to track the evidence for nominal-internal predication in this language.

2.1 General Properties

First, compare the examples in (1) and (2):

---

[*]I would like to express my appreciation to the following linguists for their help in writing this paper: Miles Beckwith, Elizabeth Owen Bratt, Stanley Dubinsky, David Greenspon, Heidi Harley, Caroline Heycock, Keith Langston, and Carol Rosen. I would also like to thank those Telugu speakers whose judgments have helped in the writing of this paper, especially Ramesh Chitturi, Usha Kanithi, and K. P. Krishna. Of course, none of the people named here are responsible for the use I have made of their help.

(1) a. neenu   uttaram   raas-aa-nu
       I   letter   write-PST-1S
       'I wrote a letter.'
    b. meemu   uttaram   raas-aa-mu
       we   letter   write-PST-1PL
       'We wrote a letter.'

(2) a. neenu   maaSTaru-nu
       I   teacher-1S
       'I am a teacher.'
    b. meemu   maaSTaru-la-m
       we   teacher-PL-1PL
       'We are teachers.'

In (1a) and (1b), the predicates raasaanu 'I wrote' and raasaamu 'we wrote' occur in rightmost position and bear agreement morphology. The predicates in (2) consist of the nouns maaSTaru 'teacher' and maaSTaru-lu 'teachers'.[1] These nominal predicates resemble the predicates in (1) in that they too occur clause-finally and bear agreement morphology, two characteristics unique to predicates.

In (3), I give further examples of nominal predicates:

(3) a. meemu   sneehitu-la-m
       we   friend-PL-1PL
       'We are friends.'

    b. meemu   aaDawaaL-La-m
       we   woman-PL-1PL
       'We are women.'

    c. meemu   vaidyu-la-m
       we   doctor-PL-1PL
       'We are doctors.'

Another set of examples consists of numerals: Telugu numerals are nominal, and behave like other nominals when used predicatively, in that they occur in clause-final position and bear agreement morphology, as seen below:

(4) a. meemu   naalugu-ra-m
       we   four-HUM-1PL
       'We are four people.'

b. meemu antaa oka-ra-m
   we   all   one-HUM-1PL
   'We are all one.'

Notice in (4b) that the inherently singular predicate oka-ru 'one-HUM' bears plural agreement morphology, indicating that its number features match those of its subject, regardless of this predicate's own lexical specifications.

A similar example is (5), where the lexically third person noun manciwaaLLu 'good people' bears first person plural agreement morphology:

(5)   meemu manci-waaL-La-m
       we   good-person-PL-1PL
       'We are good people.'

manci 'good, goodness' belongs to a subclass of Telugu nominals traditionally called 'abstract nouns'. While these nouns are distributionally similar to typical nouns, and also bear case suffixes, they differ from other nouns in that when they occur as clausal predicates, they must bear a suffix which specifies number and gender features. Thus, in (5), manci bears the third person plural substantivizing suffix -waaLLu. In spite of the third person suffix borne by this predicate, the suffix -m is nevertheless first person, in agreement with its first person subject.

(6) illustrates a further similarity between verbal and nominal predicates: Just as the two classes of predicates are similar with respect to word order and agreement, they also resemble each other in that both allow non-overt subject arguments, as seen below:

(6) a. _ raas-aa-mu
       write-PST-1PL
       'We wrote.'
    b. _ manci-waaL-La-m
       good-person-PL-1PL
       'We are good people.'

The facts presented in (1)–(6) corroborate the data in Perlmutter (1979), where it is shown that the similar behavior of nominal and other Ps evidences a grammatical relation 'P', whose instantiation is independent of category membership.

2.2 Relational Structure

While the point of Section 2.1 was to show that both nominal and verbal elements bear the grammatical relation predicate in Telugu clauses, the two types of predicates differ in that the nominal predicates are uniformly UNACCUSATIVE. That is, while the subject of a verbal predicate such as raas- 'write' in (1) is initialized as a 1, the subject of a nominal predicate such as maaSTaru 'teacher' in (2) is initialized as a 2. This unaccusative VALENCE of noun predicates is mentioned in Perlmutter (1979) and discussed more fully in Rosen (1987, 1990) and Mirto & Rosen (1993). The contrast in relational structure is borne out in (7) and (8) below.

The chart in (7), consisting of a single stratum, represents a clause containing a typical verbal predicate
such as that in (1):

(7)   1   2   P
    meemu   uttaram   raas-aa-mu
    we   letter   write-PST-1PL
    'We wrote a letter.'

On the other hand, I claim that the structure of a clause headed by a nominal predicate contains an initial unaccusative stratum, as shown in (8):

(8)   2   P
        1   P
    meemu   aaDawaaL-La-m
    we   woman-PL-1PL
    'We are women.'

My proposal of (8) is based on semantic grounds—the semantic role which a noun assigns to its argument is simply membership in the set denoted by that noun—and also the evidence discussed in Rosen (1987, 1990) and Mirto & Rosen (1993).

One further point regarding nominal Ps is demonstrated in (9a) and (9b):

(9) a. neenu   vaidyu-nu   kaa-nu
        I   doctor-1S   NEG-1S
        'I am not a doctor.'
    b. meemu   vaidyu-la-m   kaa-mu
        we   doctor-PL-1PL NEG-1PL
        'We are not doctors.'

These examples illustrate the behavior of nominal Ps which have been put en chômage. The relational structure of (9a), in which the negative auxiliary kaa- places the nominal predicate vaidyu-nu 'doctor-1S' en chômage, is given in (10):

(10) 2   P
      1   P
      ----
      1   CHO   P
      neenu vaidyu-nu kaa-nu
      I   doctor-1S NEG-1S

This formalization follows the analysis of unions advanced in Davies & Rosen (1988): A union contains a single clause, but multiple successive predicates within this clause. The negative auxiliary kaa- is represented as a non-initial, non-valent P, and like all auxiliaries, it inherits the 1 of the predicate which it places EN CHOMAGE. (See Rosen 1993.)

The point of (9a) and (9b) is that nominal P-chômeurs precede final Ps, and behave like final nominal Ps in that they bear agreement morphology. I will return to the issue of nominal P-chômeurs in Sections 3.2.2 and 3.3.2 below.

3. Predication Within Nominals

In the preceding section, I showed that Telugu nominals bear the grammatical relation 'predicate' within clauses, and then provided the relational structure of clauses headed by these nominal Ps. Here, I will present the respects in which Telugu nominals resemble clauses headed by noun Ps. These parallel features call for a parallel relational structure, including a nominal-internal element which bears the grammatical relational P.

First, look at (11) and (12):

(11) a. [neenu manci-waaN-Ni]   vaidyu-nu
         [I   good-man-1S   ]   doctor-1S
     'I, a good man, am a doctor.'

   b. [meemu manci-waaL-La-m   ]   vaidyu-la-m
       [we   good-person-PL-1PL]   doctor-PL-1PL
     'We good people are doctors.'

(12) a. [neenu manci-waaN-Ni]   raas-aa-nu
         [I   good-man-1S   ]   write-PST-1S
     'I, a good man, wrote.'

   b. [meemu manci-waaL-La-m   ]   raas-aa-mu
       [we   good-person-PL-1PL]   write-PST-1PL
     'We good people wrote.'

While the clausal predicate in (11) is vaidyuDu 'doctor' and the clausal predicate in (12) is raas- 'write', I will show that the subject nominals in (11) and (12) contain their own predicates, namely the appositives manci-waaN-Ni 'good-man-1S'/manci-waaL-La-m 'good-person-PL-1PL'. It has been argued on syntactic and semantic grounds that appositives are predicates. (See, for example, Doron 1992, Napoli 1989, and Rothstein 1985.) In the following section I will present four additional arguments from the Telugu data that appositives are indeed predicates.[2]

3.1 Appositives: Similarities with Clausal Predicates

There are several indicators of the predicative status of the appositives manciwaaNNi/manciwaaLLam in (11) and (12). The first is word order: Just as the predicate manciwaaLLam 'good-people-1PL' in the main clause example in (5) is in the rightmost position in this clause, manciwaaNNi/manciwaaLLam in (11) and (12) is in the rightmost position within the subject nominal. Since Telugu is a head-final, predicate-final language, manciwaaNNi/manciwaaLLam occupies the normal predicate position within the nominals in (11) and (12).

Furthermore, those same elements which bear the predicate relation in clauses can also bear the predicate relation within nominals. For example, the subject nominals of the following clauses contain appositive Ps consisting of a numeral:

(13) a. [meemu naalugu-ra-m] vaidyu-la-m
        we   four-HUM-1PL   doctor-PL-1PL
    'We four are doctors.'

   b. [meemu naalugu-ra-m] raas-aa-mu
        we   four-HUM-1PL   write-PST-1PL
    'We four wrote.'

By comparing (13a) and (13b) with (4a), we see that a numeral such as naaluguru 'four-HUM' functions both as a clausal P (in (4a)) as well as a nominal-internal P (in (13a) and (13b)). This comparison again demonstrates identical word order facts with clausal and nominal-internal Ps.

Another important parallel between the rightmost elements in the nominals in (11) and (12), and the rightmost elements in the clauses in (2)–(5) is the presence of agreement morphology. Just as the form of the clausal predicate in (2) varies according to the person and number features of its subject, so the forms of the rightmost nouns in the subject nominals in (11) and (12) vary according to the features of their pronominal arguments within these nominals.

Finally, the nominal-internal predicates parallel main clause nominal predicates in that expletive subjects are possible nominal-internally as well as in clauses. Just as the clause in (6b) is grammatical without an overt subject, variants of (11) and (12) whose appositional nominals lack overt first person plural arguments are grammatical as well:

(14) a. [_ manci-waaN-<u>Ni</u>]   vaidyu-<u>nu</u>
       [good-man-<u>1S</u>]   doctor-<u>1S</u>
    'I, a good man, am a doctor.'

   b. [_ manci-waaL-La-<u>m</u>   ]   vaidyu-la-<u>m</u>
      [good-person-PL-<u>1PL</u>]   doctor-PL-<u>1PL</u>
    'We good people are doctors.'

(15) a. [_ manci-waaN-<u>Ni</u>]   raas-aa-<u>nu</u>
       [good-man-<u>1S</u>]   write-PST-<u>1S</u>
    'I, a good man, wrote.'

   b. [_ manci-waaL-La-<u>m</u>   ]   raas-aa-<u>mu</u>
      [good-person-PL-<u>1PL</u>]   write-PST-<u>1PL</u>
    'We good people wrote.'

Thus, the nominal-internal predicates resemble clausal predicates with respect to four characteristics: 1) constituent-final position; 2) subtypes of nominals which can bear the predicate relation, for example, numerals; 3) agreement morphology; and 4) the option of non-overt arguments.

3.2 Relational Structure of Nominals

3.2.1 The Structure of Appositions

To capture the facts just discussed, I propose the following as the internal structure of the appositions in (13a) and (13b):

(16)   1
                    |

    | 2   P |
    | CHO   2,P |
    | meemu   naalugu-ra-<u>m</u> |
    | we   four-HUM-<u>1PL</u> |

The '1' label on this nominal node indicates that this particular nominal bears the 1 relation within the clause. As for the internal structure of (16), notice that the appositive <u>naalugu-ra-m</u> 'four-HUM-1PL' is the head of this nominal. (Recall that Telugu is head-final across all constructions.) The appositive bears the predicate relation, and, by virtue of its nominal category, initializes its single argument meemu 'we' as a 2. The initial stratum of (16) is thus identical to the initial stratum of (8), in which the clausal predicate is nominal and therefore initializes a 2. naaluguram agrees with the argument it initializes in humanness, as well as in person and number, and thus bears the human suffix and also first person plural agreement morphology.

In the second stratum, the head naaluguram acquires the 2 relation, putting meemu en chômage. Notice that naaluguram continues to bear the P relation in this stratum, and thus heads a P-2 MULTIATTACHMENT.[3] Multiattachment exists when a single element bears two distinct relations in the same stratum (Perlmutter & Postal 1984). Such a P-2 multiattachment has been proposed in Rosen (1987) for common nouns in nominals used referentially, on the basis of data from Tzotzil. The dual relational status of the multiattached nominal head reflects the dual semantic status of common nouns such as friends, women, four.people, and so forth. In (16), for example, the P-2 multiattachment of the nominal head naalugu-ra-m reflects the fact that the same element which predicates being a group of four is also the head of a phrase which refers to this group.

3.2.2 Comparison With Modified Noun Structure

I will now present and discuss the related structure which accounts for the facts concerning modificational nominals. The head of a modified noun complex, like that of an apposition, also heads a P-2 multiattachment. However, the P-2 multiattachment of the modified noun complex is derived from a different initial structure than that of the apposition in (16). (17) illustrates the structure which Rosen (1987) posits for modified nouns:

```
(17)        P             2
       -----------------------------------
           CHO           2,P
        naalugu-ru    aaDawaaL-Lu
        four-HUM      woman-PL
              'four women'
```

In (17), as in (16), the numeral naaluguru heads a P arc in the initial stratum. Unlike (16), however, the initial 2 of (17) acquires the predicate relation, putting the initial predicate naaluguru en chômage.[4]

There is thus a significant difference between (16) and (17): In (16), the rightmost element is an initial P which takes on the 2 relation in accordance with the referential nature of the nominal it heads. The rightmost element of (17), by contrast, is an initial 2 which takes on the P relation in accordance with its predicative nature. Therefore, (17) contains two distinct elements which head P-arcs in different strata.

The structure in (17) correctly captures the facts concerning modified nouns in Telugu. With respect to word order, (17) correctly predicts that adnominal elements such as naaluguru will precede the nouns they modify, since, as seen in the clauses in (9), Telugu P-chômeurs precede Ps.

In addition to the linearization of Ps and P-chômeurs, another parallel between the clausal predicates and the adnominal modifier Ps should be mentioned: As was the case with appositional nominals, similar types of nominal elements bear the P relation in clauses and modified nominals. In fact, Telugu distinguishes as parts of speech only nouns and verbs (Steever 1988:5); thus, no basic category 'adjective' is distinguished for adnominal modificational uses of nouns.

Evidence from person and number agreement is not available in the case of modificational nominals as it was in the appositional nominals. The reason is that morphology for person and number agreement on nominal Ps in Telugu is present only with first and second person arguments, the very arguments which can never head modification structures. I will first demonstrate the fact that nominal Ps inflect for agreement only with first and second person arguments, and then discuss the impossibility of first and second person heads—namely pronouns—in modificational nominals.

That nominal predicates with third person subjects do not bear agreement morphology within Telugu clauses is shown in (18c) and (18d):

(18) a. neenu   maaSTaru-nu   (kaa-nu)
        I   teacher-1S   (NEG-1S)
        'I am (not) a teacher.'
     b. nuwwu   maaSTaru-wu   (kaa-wu)
        you.S   teacher-2S   (NEG-2S)
        'You are (not) a teacher.'
     c. waaDu   maaSTaru(*-Du)   (kaa-Du)
        he   teacher(*-3SM)   (NEG-3SM)
        'He is (not) a teacher.'
     d. waaru   maaSTaru-lu(*-ru)   (kaa-ru)
        they   teacher-PL(*-3PL.HUM) (NEG-3PL.HUM)
        'They are (not) teachers.'

The ungrammaticality of the person and number inflection in (18c) and (18d) is apparently due to the fact that since Ps consisting of nouns are inherently third person, nominal predicates with third person arguments require no inflection for additional third person agreement morphology. Since nominal predicates never bear third person agreement morphology, the predicate naaluguru in (17) does not inflect for person and number agreement when it modifies a third person common noun such as aaDawaaL-Lu 'women'.

While third person arguments do not trigger person and number agreement, no first or second person argument—that is, no pronoun—can head a modification structure, since in order to do so, this pronominal head would have to bear a P relation as well as a 2 relation in the final stratum. As Rosen (1990) notes, however, pronouns differ from common nouns in that the former do not predicate, but only refer. Therefore, since pronouns cannot be predicates, such a modified-pronoun structure is ungrammatical:

(19) *   P   2

                 CHO   2,P
              naalugu-ra-m   meemu
              four-HUM-1PL   we

Note that (19) would also be ungrammatical without revaluation, that is, if the initial stratum of (19) were also the final stratum, with naaluguram bearing a final P relation: The phrase with such a structure, * naaluguram meemu, would be ungrammatical because final Ps must be constituent-final.

If modified-pronoun structures such as that in (19) were licit, the modifier would be predicted to bear first person plural agreement morphology, given the analysis
under which modifiers are predicates. Since (19) is not a possible nominal configuration, however, it is therefore only in appositions, where first and second person arguments are possible that evidence for nominal-internal predication is available from person and number agreement.

While person and number agreement are not available as evidence in modificational nominals, there is a single type of agreement in these constructions, namely agreement with respect to the feature 'HUMAN'. The distinction HUMAN/NON-HUMAN is made in the following nominals, where the modifier in (20a) bears the human suffix -ru, while the modifier in (20b) does not:

(20) a. naalugu-ru   aaDawaaL-Lu
        four-HUM   woman-PL
        'four women'
     b. naalugu   pustakaa-lu
        four   book-PL
        'four books'

This distinction is in fact the only one made in clausal predicate agreement in the third person plural, as seen in (21a) and (21b):

(21) a. waaru   naDic-aa-ru
        they   walk-PST-3PL.HUM
        'They (human) walked.'

b. avi   naDic-aa-yi
they   walk-PST-3PL.NON-HUM
'They (non-human) walked.'

Thus, nominal-internal predicates in Telugu agree in all grammatical features for which agreement is possible in clauses.

Additionally, several other facts presented in this section indicate that the predication structure in (17) is the correct one for modified nouns: One fact is that the modifier is always a type of nominal which functions as a P within clauses. More importantly, given that Telugu P-chômeurs precede Ps, the linearization of the modifier to the left of its head is exactly the linearization to be expected under this analysis, in which a modifier is an initial P which is put en chômage by the P-2 multiattachment of the nominal head.

3.3 Case Marking

I will now present evidence from nominal-internal case marking which supports the structures in (16) and (17). I will show that these structures, which feature nominal-internal predication, correctly predict the case facts in the two types of complex nominals.

3.3.1 Case in Appositions

I begin by introducing the following example in which all elements of the complex nominal maaku naaluguriki bear non-nominative case:

(22)   waaru   [maaku   naalugu-ri-ki]   pustakaa-lu
       they   [we.DAT   four-HUM-DAT]   book-PL

       icc-aa-ru
       give-PST-3PL.HUM
       'They gave books to us four.'

In this example, both the appositive predicate naaluguriki and also the argument which it initializes bear dative case.

The structure of (22) is given in (23):

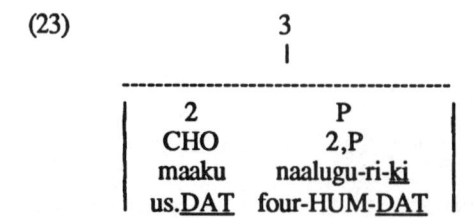

(23)
```
                3
                |
    ----------------------------------
    |   2           P                |
    |   CHO         2,P              |
    |   maaku       naalugu-ri-ki    |
    |   us.DAT      four-HUM-DAT     |
```

The internal structure of (23) is identical to that of (16), the representation of the nominative apposition; (23) differs relationally only in that the clausal dependent to which it is subordinated bears the 3 relation, as opposed to the 1 relation. As in the nominative apposition in (16), we see that here too the rightmost element heads a P-2 multiattachment in the final stratum, indicating that this element is not solely predicative, but is also referential.

Since the nominal maaku naaluguriki bears the 3 relation, the nominal head naaluguriki licenses dative case. Such a situation constitutes an instance of PRIMARY CASE licensing, by which a nominal's grammatical or semantic relation determines its case (Gerdts 1991).

Opposed to this primary case licensing is SECONDARY CASE licensing, the mechanism by which a nominal which does not license primary case acquires case indirectly, via association with a primary case licenser (Gerdts 1991). The dative case of maaku is secondary case; specifically, it is acquired by CASE AGREEMENT with naalugu-ri-ki 'four-HUM-DAT'. Case agreement operates within constituents such as nominals, as opposed to CASE SPREAD, which involves two non-constituents.

Note that the structures (16) and (23) predict that the leftmost element in an apposition will necessarily lack primary case: Since this element is not a P, it cannot license nominative case. (Recall from (18c) and (18d) that nominal Ps and P-chômeurs which are uninflected for agreement are nominative.) At the same time that the leftmost noun is not predicative, it is also not a phrasal head and is therefore not eligible for primary case licensing, since it does not bear a clausal grammatical relation.

However, the leftmost element of an apposition must acquire case by some means, in order for it to obey the principle of RELATIONAL VISIBILITY:

(24)   RELATIONAL VISIBILITY:
        Every nominal must be relationally identified
        by some morphosyntactic means. (Gerdts 1990)

This principle requires each nominal to be relationally distinguishable from other nominals. In (23), maaku signals its relationship of membership in the same nominal as its head naaluguriki by agreeing in case.

Another variant of (22) exists, however, in which the leftmost element does not agree in case with its nominal head:

(25) waaru ⎡maa naalugu-ri-<u>ki</u> ⎤ pustakaa-lu
     they ⎣we.<u>GEN</u> four-HUM-<u>DAT</u>⎦ book-PL

   icc-aa-ru
   give-PST-3PL.HUM
   'They gave books to <u>us four</u>.'

(25) shows that when a nominal does not acquire case via either primary or secondary case licensing, the nominal bears the default case, genitive.

In terms of Relational Visibility, what genitive case in Telugu signals is actual exemption from clause-level relational status. For example, in (25), no sentential grammatical relation, only a nominal-internal grammatical relation, is borne by <u>maa</u>. While under certain circumstances, an adnominal genitive element is possessive, under other circumstances, as in the appositions, it is not. In all instances, however, Telugu genitive case is non-clausal; no clausal dependents license genitive case.

Finally, one obvious difference between (16) and (23) is that unlike the head of the nominative apposition in (16), the head of the dative apposition in (23) does not bear morphology for person and number agreement. Case and person-number agreement morphology compete for a single slot on the noun, and thus, if the nominal head bears any overt case morphology, no agreement morpheme can attach, regardless of the syntactic context. The following two nominals, headed by nouns bearing both case and agreement morphology, are ungrammatical:

(26) a. * maaku/maa   naalugu-ri-<u>ki</u>-<u>m</u>
          we.DAT/we.GEN   four-HUM-<u>DAT</u>-<u>1PL</u>
          'to us four'
     b.* maaku/maa   naalugu-ra-<u>mu</u>-<u>ki</u>
          we.DAT/we.GEN   four-HUM-<u>1PL</u>-<u>DAT</u>
          'to us four'

The ungrammaticality of (26a) and (26b) cannot be due to a requirement that in order for a nominal-internal P to bear agreement morphology, its argument (the agreement 'trigger') must be nominative. That nominative case is not required on the argument of a nominal-internal P is shown in (27), where, just as in (25), there exists a variant of <u>meemu naaluguram</u> 'we four-HUM-1PL' in which the argument initialized by the nominal-internal predicate <u>naaluguram</u> is genitive:

(27) $\begin{bmatrix} \text{maa} & \text{naalugu-ra-}\underline{m} \\ \text{we.GEN} & \text{four-HUM-}\underline{\text{1PL}} \end{bmatrix}$ raas-aa-mu
       write-PST-1PL
'We four wrote.'

In fact, the requirement is not that the agreement 'trigger' be nominative, but rather that the agreement 'target', the predicate itself, be nominative.

One further point illustrated by (27) is that nominative case in Telugu, although morphologically null, is not a default case, the absence of case, but rather a primary case. If nominative were a default case, meemu naaluguram would be the only possible version of this subject nominal, since meemu would be the realization of both the case-agreement and the default form of the appositive's argument. Instead, since the subjects in both (13b) (meemu naaluguram) and (27) are possible, we see that meemu in (13b) is nominative by virtue of its relationship with naaluguram, which, as the head of the clausal subject, licenses nominative case. Thus, (27) indicates that nominative is always an instance of primary case in Telugu, licensed by specific grammatical relations, namely clausal 1s and both clausal and nominal-internal Ps and P-chômeurs. Further evidence that nominative is a primary case in Telugu is presented in the following section.

As for the rightmost element of the apposition, due to the fact that this appositive bears the P relation within the nominal, it licenses nominative case, which is morphologically null. Any case morphology licensed by the sentential grammatical relation of the nominal then attaches to the head, preempting agreement morphology which the head would bear by virtue of its nominal-internal P relation. Therefore, while all appositives bear the nominal-internal grammatical relation P, it is only in appositions which are nominative that this P relation will be registered via predicate agreement morphology.

To summarize the facts regarding case in appositional nominals: The leftmost element, the argument of the nominal P, always bears either secondary case via agreement with its head, or default (non-clausal) case. These facts are expected, given the structures in (16) and (23). According to (16) and (23), the leftmost element is non-predicative and therefore cannot license the case of nominal predicates in Telugu which are not inflected for agreement, namely nominative case. While its referentiality prevents this nominal from being nominative, the fact that it is subordinated with respect to the clause prevents this nominal from licensing primary case.

3.3.2 Case in Modificational Nominals

What about the case of adnominal modifiers, such as naalugu-ru 'four-HUM' in (17)? For the sake of comparison, I will illustrate the case facts in a version of the modified nominal in (17) which bears the 3 relation:

(28) waaru   ⌈naalugu-ru   aaDawaaL-Li-ki⌉   pustakaa-lu
      they   ⌊four-HUM   woman-PL-DAT ⌋   book-PL

   icc-aa-ru
   give-PST-3PL.HUM
   'They gave books to <u>four women</u>.'

This example shows that when <u>naaluguru</u> functions as an adnominal modifier, it is always in the zero-marked nominative case, regardless of the case of the noun which it modifies. The case marking in this construction is invariant; versions of the nominal in (28) with case agreement ((29a)) or default case ((29b)) are both ungrammatical:

(29) a.*   naalugu-ri-ki   aaDawaaL-Li-ki
           four-HUM-DAT   woman-PL-DAT

     b.*   naalugu-r-i   aaDawaaL-Li-ki
           four-HUM-GEN   woman-PL-DAT

Given the structure for modified nouns in (17), along with the requirement that nominal Ps and P-chômeurs which are uninflected for agreement be nominative, the ungrammaticality of (29a) and (29b) is predicted. Recall (18c) and (18d), repeated as (30a) and (30b) below:

(30) a. <u>waaDu</u>   maaSTaru(<u>*-Du</u>)   (kaa-<u>Du</u>)
         he   teacher(<u>*-3SM</u>)   (NEG-<u>3SM</u>)
         'He is (not) a teacher.'
     b. <u>waaru</u>   maaSTaru-lu(<u>*-ru</u>) (kaa-<u>ru</u>)
         they   teacher-PL(<u>*-3PL.HUM</u>) (NEG-<u>3PL.HUM</u>)
         'They are (not) teachers.'

In (30a) and (30b), the nominal Ps, like all solely predicative, non-referential nominals which lack inflection for agreement, are nominative.

The same case facts hold of solely predicative nominals which are nominal-internal. Therefore, since the adnominal modifying predicate in (28) must be nominative, it will not receive secondary case, namely dative, from its head, as shown in (29a); nor will it have the default genitive case, as shown in (29b). The fact that this nominative noun always precludes both case agreement as well as default case indicates that nominative is not itself a default case in Telugu; rather, nominative is the case licensed by nominals bearing specific grammatical relations, namely the 1 relation and the P relation, both clausal and nominal-internal. Note that the nominative case of adnominal modifiers constitutes yet another respect in which nominal-internal Ps parallel clausal Ps.

It should be pointed out that Telugu has a single construction in which a modificational noun is genitive rather than nominative: A modifier will be genitive only if it is in turn modified by another noun. An example of such a modified modifier is wandala 'hundreds' in the following:

(31)   muuDu   wanda-l-a   ruupaayi-lu
       three   hundred-PL-GEN   rupee-PL
       'three hundred rupees'

In (31), wandala is the modifier of ruupaayilu 'rupees'; yet wandala is itself modified by muuDu 'three'.

While the genitive case in such a construction is classified by Krishnamurti & Gwynn (1985:107) as the result of an extremely specific case-marking rule, the genitive case of nouns such as wandala, which are modified modifiers, is in fact predicted by the structures proposed for adnominal modification constructions. The structure of muuDu wandala is the following:

(32)   P   2
        CHO   2,P
        muuDu   wanda-l-
        three   hundred-PL-
        'three hundred(s)'

(32) shows that the nominal wandala, as the argument of the modifying predicate muuDu, heads a P-2 multiattachment, and thus is not eligible for the nominative case of solely predicative nominals such as muuDu, which (32) correctly predicts to be nominative.

While wandala cannot be nominative, it also cannot license primary clausal case, since it does not head the nominal. (33) represents the structure of the entire nominal in (31):

(33)   P   2

             CHO   2,P
             CHO   P   2

             CHO   CHO   2,P
             muuDu   wanda-l-a   ruupaayi-lu
             three   hundred-PL-GEN rupee-PL
             'three hundred rupees'

(33) contains two nominal-internal serializations; twice a noun predicate is placed en chômage by another noun predicate. As mentioned in Section 3.2.2, such treatment of adnominal modifiers as Ps captures the word order facts within nominals, since in Telugu, P-chômeurs precede the Ps which place them en chômage.

wandala bears the P relation in the stratum subsequent to that in which it is multiattached, in accordance with the assumption that multiattachments must be resolved by CANCELLATION of the lower relation (Rosen 1988). For discussion of the ranking of the 2 relation below the P relation, see Postal (1985) and Dubinsky (1990).

Similar to (31), examples such as the following are also listed separately by Krishnamurti & Gwynn (1985:382-3):

(34) padi lakSa-l-a Tannu-l-a biyyam
ten lakh-PL-GEN ton-PL-GEN rice
'ten lakhs (unit of measure of 100,000)
of tons of rice'

In (34), both lakSala and Tannula are modified modifiers; both are genitive.

Given the rules concerning case marking in Telugu, the nominal-internal predication analysis predicts that a modified modifier such as wandala 'hundreds' in (31), or lakSala 'lakhs' and Tannula 'tons' in (34), must be genitive: The status of these elements as arguments of their modifying predicates prevents them from being nominative, the case of purely predicative nouns; their status as the modifying Ps to other nouns prevents them from licensing primary case; therefore, modified modifiers in Telugu will always be genitive.

To summarize the facts concerning the case of the modifier in examples such as (17): This modifier is always nominative; it never acquires secondary case or default case. These facts support the structure in (17), in which the adnominal modifier naalugu-ru 'four-HUM' bears the final relation P-chômeur. Since nominal Ps and P-chômeurs in Telugu are invariably nominative, neither secondary case nor default case will ever appear on the adnominal modifier; by virtue of its nominal-internal P-chômeur relation, the modifier is obligatorily nominative.

3.3.3 Summary

The facts concerning case in the appositional and modificational nominals provide important evidence for the structures in (16) and (17), respectively, in which Telugu nominals of both types contain predicates. Given these structures, the contrast between the case of the leftmost elements in the two types of nominals is exactly that which we expect: The leftmost element in the modification structure (17), as a P-chômeur, must be nominative, like all Telugu Ps and P-chômeurs. On the other hand, the leftmost element in the apposition (16), as a referential noun which is a final 2-chômeur, must either acquire secondary case via case agreement with its head, or else bear default case indicating its status as a referential nominal which is subordinated to the nominal node and is therefore unable to license primary case.

4. Conclusion

I have demonstrated that in Telugu, the nominal as well as the clause constitutes a domain of predication. I first illustrated features of clausal nominal predicates in Telugu, most notably their agreement morphology and constituent-final position. I then showed that these same features of nominal predication exist internal to Telugu nominals as well. The case-marking facts summarized above also support the predication structures proposed for the two types of nominals: In the apposition, the secondary or default case on the non-head indicates its initial status as an argument of the head; by contrast, in the modificational nominal, the invariant nominative case on the non-head points to its initial status as a predicate. Thus, a network of facts concerning word order, agreement, and case marking is accounted for straightforwardly, given the proposal that the nominal, like the clause, is headed by an element bearing the grammatical relation 'predicate'.

Notes

[1] Note that the form of this plural noun varies: In (2b), maaSTaru-la- is the plural stem, to which affixes are attached. On the other hand, maaSTaru-lu is the nominative plural form. Telugu stem formation is too complicated to discuss in this paper. (See Krishnamurti & Gwynn 1985.) In addition to differences inherent to the stems themselves, the form of nominal stems also varies according to vowel harmony processes. Again, I will not discuss the details of these processes here.

[2] Since Telugu has no true adjectives, but only nouns used adjectivally, all complex nominals are technically appositions. In this paper, I will describe constructions such as the subject nominals in (11) and (12) as appositions, and contrast these constructions with the nominals introduced in Section 3.2.2. I describe the latter constructions, whose corresponding English constructions contain an adjective, as 'modificational nominals' (e.g. naaluguru aaDawaaLLu 'four women'), as opposed to 'appositional nominals' (e.g. meemu naaluguram 'we four').

[3] In this paper the word 'head' is used in two distinct ways: One use is very common: When used in expressions such as 'the head of a nominal', reference is simply to the central element of this nominal. On the other hand, when used in expressions such as 'to head a P-2 multiattachment' or 'to head a P arc', I refer to the fact that an element bears a grammatical relation, e.g. P, to the constituent of which it is a dependent.

[4] In addition to Rosen (1987), another recent work proposes phrase-internal revaluations: Dziwirek (1990) proposes a MODIFIER-to-HEAD promotion within Polish numeral phrases to account for agreement facts with subjects consisting of these numeral phrases.

References

Davies, William D. and Carol Rosen. 1988. Unions as Multi-Predicate Clauses. Language 64: 52-88.
Doron, Edit. 1992. Appositive Predicates. Predication (Belgian Journal of Linguistics 7.) 23-33.
Dubinsky, Stanley. 1990. Light Verbs and Predicate Demotion in Japanese. Grammatical Relations: A Cross-Theoretical Perspective, ed. by Katarzyna Dziwirek et al, 127-145. Stanford University: CSLI.
Dziwirek, Katarzyna. 1990. Default Agreement in Polish. Grammatical Relations: A Cross-Theoretical Perspective, ed. by Katarzyna Dziwirek et al, 147-161. Stanford University: CSLI.
Gerdts, Donna B. 1990. Relational Visibility. Grammatical Relations: A Cross-Theoretical Perspective, ed. by Katarzyna Dziwirek et al, 199-214. Stanford University: CSLI.
Gerdts, Donna B. 1991. An Outline of a Relational Theory of Case. Working Papers in Linguistics 1: 25-53. Simon Fraser University.
Krishnamurti, Bhadriraju and J.P.L. Gwynn. 1985. A Grammar of Modern Telugu. Delhi: Oxford University Press.
Mirto, Ignazio M. and Carol Rosen. 1993. Meronyms as Predicates: An Apparent 'Inalienable Possession' Construction. ms., Cornell University.
Napoli, Donna Jo. 1989. Predication Theory. Cambridge: Cambridge University Press.
Perlmutter, David M. 1979. Predicate: A Grammatical Relation. Linguistic Notes from La Jolla 6: 127-149. University of California, San Diego.
Perlmutter, David M. and Paul M. Postal. 1984. Impersonal Passives and Some Relational Laws. Studies in Relational Grammar 2, ed. by David M. Perlmutter and Carol Rosen, 126-170. Chicago: University of Chicago Press.
Postal, Paul M. 1985. La Dégradation de Prédicat et un Genre Négligé de Montée. (Subpredicates and a New Type of Raising). Recherches Linguistiques 13: 33-68.
Ramanarasimham, P. 1985. An Intensive Course in Telugu. Mysore: Central Institute of Indian Languages.
Rosen, Carol. 1987. Possessors and the Internal Structure of Nominals. Paper presented at the Third Biennial Conference on Relational Grammar, Iowa City, Iowa.
Rosen, Carol. 1988. The Relational Structure of Reflexive Clauses: Evidence from Italian. [Harvard University dissertation, 1981.] New York: Garland.
Rosen, Carol. 1990. Rethinking Southern Tiwa: The Geometry of a Triple-Agreement Language. Language 66: 669-713.

Rosen, Carol. 1993. Auxiliation and Serialization: On Discerning the Difference. to appear in Proceedings of the Workshop on Complex Predicates, May 1993, ed. by Alex Alsina. Stanford: CSLI.

Rothstein, Susan. 1983. The Syntactic Forms of Predication. Doctoral dissertation, MIT [distributed by IULC in 1985].

Steever, Sanford B. 1988. The Serial Verb Formation in the Dravidian Languages. Delhi: Motilal Banarsidass.

Ergative Subjects

COLIN PHILLIPS
Massachusetts Institute of Technology

The most striking feature of ergative systems is the fact that subjects of transitive and intransitive verbs behave differently for purposes of case and agreement. Why should this be so? One possible answer is that the transitivity of the verb directly affects how its subject behaves syntactically. That is, transitive and intransitive subjects have differing D-structure positions (Marantz 1984, B. Levin 1983), or conditions on case assignment force intransitive subjects to bear a particular case (Bobaljik 1993, Campana 1992, Chomsky 1993, Laka 1993, J. Levin & Massam 1985).[1] Alternatively, the differential behaviour of subjects is not directly determined by the transitivity of the verb: an independent syntactic requirement, such as the Extended Projection Principle (EPP, Chomsky 1982), causes subjects to behave differently in ergative systems. This paper argues for the second of these two possibilities.

If the transitivity of the verb is directly responsible for the fact that transitive and intransitive subjects behave differently, then we expect the two kinds of subjects to *always* behave differently for case and agreement. On the other hand, if the EPP is responsible for the contrast between transitive and intransitive subjects, then we allow for intransitive subjects to behave just like transitive subjects — provided that the EPP can be taken care of by another element, such as a non-argument. In other words, we allow for the possibility of *variability* in the behaviour of intransitive subjects. In section 1 I show that the Papuan language Yimas (Foley 1991) provides an example of an ergative system with precisely this kind of variability: when the EPP is satisfied by a non-argument, *all* subjects are marked by ergative agreement.

Section 2 shows how the variable marking of intransitive subjects, and an ergative pattern in which absolutive is assigned higher than ergative, follows from a theory of economy of derivation. Section 3 gives evidence from the distribution of anti-agreement effects in subject extraction in Yimas, which support the idea that arguments may A-bar move for Case as a last resort.

---

* I would like to thank Mark Baker, Jonathan Bobaljik, Andrew Carnie, Ken Hale, Heidi Harley, Alec Marantz, Kumiko Murasugi, David Pesetsky and Andrea Zukowski for valuable discussion of the material in this paper. All of the Yimas examples and translations are taken from Foley (1991), to which I am greatly indebted. The *glosses* are my own interpretation of the data, and differ from Foley's in a number of places. All errors are entirely my own.

[1] Bobaljik, Chomsky and Laka assume that in an intransitive clause a setting of the *Obligatory Case Parameter* dictates the case of the subject. Campana assumes a similar requirement, which is not parameterized.

In section 4 I discuss the consequences of intransitive ergative subjects in Yimas for the analysis of subject-oriented phenomena in ergative languages. Phenomena which treat subjects as a natural class are widely attested in ergative languages; most of the examples in the literature involve binding-related phenomena. It has been claimed that subjects are picked out as a natural class only by virtue of sharing the same VP-internal position. The subject property from Yimas that I am highlighting is a Case-related phenomenon, which implicates a position outside VP. This suggests a different account of which positions are targeted by subject-oriented phenomena.

1. Ergativity and the Extended Projection Principle

The aim of this section is to show that the appearance of an ergative agreement system in Yimas is due to the effects of the Extended Projection Principle. Intransitive subjects are normally marked absolutive, satisfying the demands of the EPP. However, when the EPP can be independently satisfied, intransitive subjects are not absolutive but ergative — identical to transitive subjects.

Case distinctions are marked by inflectional affixes on the verb in Yimas. Independent nominals are caseless, and they are both liberally ordered and freely omitted (Foley 1991, p.194). As a result, almost all of the sentences that follow consist of just an inflected verb. Case differences are encoded by different sets of agreement inflections.

Agreement marking for 3rd person arguments follows a classic ergative-absolutive pattern (Foley, p.196). Objects of transitive verbs and subjects of intransitive verbs are marked identically, by *absolutive* markers (1a-b). There is a separate *ergative* inflectional paradigm for subjects of transitive verbs (1c).

(1) a. **pu-**   n-   tay
       3pl-Abs   3sg-Erg   see
       'He saw them.'
    b. **pu-**   wa -t
       3pl-Abs   go   Perf
       'They went.'
    c. na-   **mpu-**   tay
       3sg-Abs   3pl-Erg   see
       'They saw him.'

1.1 Agreement Alternations

For our purposes here the most interesting property of Yimas is the fact that a given argument can be marked by different agreement affixes, depending on what other arguments and functional elements are in the clause. For example, a 2nd person subject is marked either nominative or absolutive. The factors governing the choice are given in (2). They appear complicated at first, but they reduce to a simple generalization.

(2) 2nd person subjects are marked:

Nominative — when there is a 3rd person object, marked absolutive.
Absolutive — when the 2nd person subject is the sole argument.
Absolutive — when there is a 1st person object, marked accusative.

(3) a. na-   n-   tay
       3sg-Abs 2sg-Nom see
       'You saw him.'
    b. paŋkra- wa -t
       2pc-Abs go Perf
       'You few (paucal[2]) went.'
    c. ma-   ŋa-   tay
       2sg-Abs 1sg-Acc see
       'You saw me.'

This alternation is explained by the general requirement that any finite verb form in Yimas be marked by absolutive inflection. This requirement overrides other principles of agreement marking. When another argument is marked absolutive, as in (3a), 2nd person subjects are marked by nominative agreement; but in the absence of another absolutive marked argument, 2nd person subjects satisfy the requirement for an absolutive.[3]

(4a-b) shows an alternation due to the same requirement, this time between between ergative and absolutive. (4a) repeats (1a), and shows that a 3rd person subject is marked ergative when there is a 3rd person object marked absolutive. In (4b), however, the object is 2nd person, and therefore marked accusative. In this case the 3rd person subject becomes absolutive, in order to make the verb well-formed.

---

[2]Yimas distinguishes 4 different numbers: singular, dual, plural, and paucal, which generally refers to groups of 3-7.

[3]See Phillips (1993, to appear) for discussion of the person-based ergative split in Yimas. Roughly, 1st and 2nd person arguments may be Case-licensed through incorporating into the verb.

(4) a. pu-   n-   tay
       3pl-Abs 3sg-Erg see
       'He saw them.'
    b. **na-**   nan-   tay
       3sg-Abs 2sg-Acc see
       'He saw you.'

I take the requirement for an absolutive agreement marker to be the reflex in Yimas of a version of the Extended Projection Principle, which requires that the head Agr1⁰ be governed at S-structure. I assume that Agr1P is the XP immediately below CP, and that Agr1 is associated with absolutive case. Therefore, movement of a *pro* argument to the specifier of Agr1P both satisfies the EPP and triggers the realization of absolutive agreement.

Crucially for the argument being developed, the presence of an absolutive agreement marker is only one of the ways of satisfying the EPP in Yimas. The EPP is also satisfied when the verb is prefixed by one of a small class of prefixes, which I assume to be of category C⁰. I assume that these become attached to the verb root and its inflectional material by head movement of V⁰ to C⁰ via Agr2⁰ and Agr1⁰.

(5)   Complementizer prefixes:
       m-   relativizing complementizer
       ta-   negation
       ant- modal — 'potential'
       ka-   modal — 'likely'

(6a-b) shows that these prefixes have the same effect on subject marking as the presence of a 3rd person object: the 2nd person intransitive subject is marked nominative in (6a), contrasting with absolutive in (3b); the 3rd person transitive subject is marked ergative in (6b), contrasting with the absolutive in (4b).

(6) a. ta-   **nan-**   wa -r   -um
       Neg **2pl-Nom** go Perf PL
       'You all didn't go.'
    b. ka-   mpu-   ŋa-   tput-n
       LIKE **3pl-Erg** 1sg-Acc hit   Pres
       'They are going to hit me.'

Although the Complementizer prefixes do away with the need for an absolutive marker, they are *not* in competition with absolutive agreement. (7) shows that a Complementizer prefix and an absolutive agreement marker may cooccur. This also shows that what I have been calling absolutive case is not just a word-initial allomorph of the normal agreement markers.

(7) ta- **pu-** n- tpul-c -um
Neg 3Abs[4] 3sg-Erg hit Perf PL
'He didn't hit them.'

1.2 Uniformly Ergative Subjects

With these preliminaries in mind, we can now ask the main question of this section: what happens to the ergative agreement system in Yimas when the effects of the EPP are controlled for? In other words, does the ergative system arise *because of* the EPP?

We have already seen what happens to 3rd person *transitive* subjects and objects when the EPP is independently satisfied. (6b) and (7) show that transitive subjects are ergative, and objects are absolutive. All that is missing from the paradigm are the intransitive subjects.

To test how intransitive 3rd person subjects are marked when the EPP is independently satisfied, we need to look at examples of intransitive verbs with complementizer prefixes. Unfortunately, this test is not easy to apply, due to the following confound: most of the complementizer prefixes are part of a complex C^0 containing an agreement suffix, such as the suffix *-um* in (7), which is in 'competition' with Absolutive and Ergative prefixes. This agreement suffix agrees in number with the leftmost agreement prefix, which in turn leads to the deletion of that prefix, if it is Absolutive or Ergative.[5] Nevertheless, we can show for each complementizer prefix that it causes intransitive subjects to be treated as ergative rather than as absolutive.[6] This confirms the claim that the ergative agreement system is an artifact of the EPP.

---

[4]*pu-* is glossed as a number neutral form here, although it is normally the 3rd person absolutive plural marker. This is because *pu-* can be used for all numbers in negated verbs. In these cases it can be seen that the number suffix (eg. *-um* in (7)) disambiguates the number of the object.

[5]Apart from combinations with *ka-*, which never involve deletion of agreement prefixes, absolutive or ergative prefixes always disappear. The only exceptions involve combinations of the negative marker *ta-* with 3rd person agreement markers: the agreement prefixes are not deleted, rather they are replaced by the number neutral form *pu-*. See Phillips (1993, to appear) for discussion of why complementizer agreement competes with absolutive and ergative agreement.

[6]Here my analysis disagrees with Foley's — he assumes that C-prefixes have no effect on agreement marking apart from the deletions already mentioned. However, the examples in Foley (1991, especially pp.255-258) seem more consistent with the assumption that C-prefixes take away the need for an absolutive marker.

1.2.1 ka-

ka-, 'likely modality', is the one complementizer prefix which does not cause the deletion of ergative or absolutive prefixes: this is because is does not introduce an agreeing suffix. Hence it provides the clearest test of how the EPP affects intransitive subjects. (8) shows an intransitive subject marked ergative following *ka-*.

(8) balus-ɲan ka- ŋkl- ya -ka -arm -n
airplane-Obl[7] LIKE 3pl-Erg come Seq board Pres
'Those few will board the plane now.'

1.2.2 ta-/ant-

With the complementizer prefixes *ta-* 'negation' and *ant-* 'potential modality' it is impossible to see directly whether an intransitive subject is marked ergative or absolutive, due to competition with the complementizer agreement suffixes which these prefixes introduce. However, the form of the complementizer agreement suffixes used with instransitive subjects indicates that they are being treated as ergatives.

For most numbers, the complementizer agreement suffixes do not encode case differences, i.e. the form of agreement for absolutive dual is identical to the form for ergative dual, as in (9).[8]

(9) a. ta- mpu- tpul -c -**rm**
Neg 3pl-Erg hit Perf **DL**
'They didn't hit those two.'
b. ta- pu- nan- tpul-c -**rm**
Neg 3Erg 2pl-Acc see Perf **DL**
'Those two didn't hit you.'

Case differences *are* encoded for singulars, however: singular transitive objects (absolutive) are marked *-ak*, whereas singular transitive subjects (ergative) are marked by zero agreement (10a-b; Foley, p.252-256). In this respect, the intransitive subject in (10c) patterns just like the transitive subject in (10b).

---

[7] The oblique marker *-ɲan* is the only case-marker found on independent nominals in Yimas. Nominals marked with *-ɲan* are never associated with agreement inflections on the verb.

[8] I assume that the prefix *pu-*, used as a number-neutral 3rd person prefix in negated verbs is also *case-neutral*.

(10) a. ta-   Ø-   mpu-   tay -c   -ak   *transitive object*
        NEG Ø$_{3sg\text{-}Abs}$ 3pl-Erg see perf SING
        'They didn't see him.'

   b.   ta-   Ø-   kra-   tpul -Ø   *transitive subject*
        NEG Ø$_{3sg\text{-}Erg}$ 1pl-Acc hit SING
        'He didn't hit us.'

   c.   anan- Ø- mal -Ø   *intransitive subject*
        POSS   3 die SING
        'He almost died.'

This shows that, although not overtly marked, intransitive subjects behave as ergatives when *ta-* or *ant-* satisfies the EPP.[9]

1.2.3 *m-*

The relative complementizer *m-* also introduces an agreeing suffix, which leads to deletion of absolutive or ergative markers in the same way as *ta-* and *ant-* do. So again we cannot directly see the form of intransitive subject agreement. But there is independent evidence that all 3rd person subjects are treated alike when *m-* takes care of the EPP. In this case, the evidence comes from wh-question formation. A 'clefting' strategy is used for extraction of transitive or intransitive subjects (11a-b), but is not required for object extraction (11c)(Foley, p.430). I assume that the clefting strategy, which supplies the C-prefix *m-*, is used as a last resort when there is no potential absolutive marker. Again the parallel between transitive and intransitive subject extraction indicates that 3rd person intransitive subjects are being treated as ergatives.[10]

---

[9]It might be objected that the suffixes are encoding a thematic contrast rather than a case contrast in (10). This hypothesis is reinforced by the observation that singular 1st person subjects (i.e. nominatives) are also marked by a zero agreement suffix. However, if the suffixes reflect thematic distinctions, then we might expect agreement with a 2nd person object to be identical to that with a 3rd person object. (i) shows that singular 2nd person objects are also marked by a zero agreement suffix. Therefore, the suffix -*ak* is restricted to absolutives.

i.   ipa   ta-   mpan-   tpul -Ø
        1pl   Neg   1ag/2sg-Acc   hit   SG
        'We didn't hit you.'

[The prefix *(ka)mpan* is a portmanteau used for combinations of a 1st person agent (any number) with a 2nd person singular patient. The free pronoun in (i) shows that the agent is plural, and therefore that zero agreement is with the object. Agreement with the plural subject would be -*um*.]

[10]Again, we need to exclude the possibility that Yimas simply chooses a different question form for subject and object questions, in which case the facts in (11) would not be telling us anything about Case distinctions. However, subject questions do not always require clefting: transitive subject questions in which the object is a 3rd person — providing an absolutive to satisfy the EPP — are not clefts. Therefore, the clefting strategy is not simply a property of subject questions.

(11) a. nawm   m-   Ø-   kul-   cpul -um?   *transitive subject*
        who-pl   Comp Ø$_{3pl-Erg}$ 2pl-Acc   hit   PL   *question*
        'Who hit you all?'
   b.   nawn   m-   Ø- na- ya   -n   -Ø?   *intransitive subject*
        who-sg   Comp 3 DEF   come Pres SING   *question*
        'Who is coming?'
   c.   nawn   impa-   Ø-   tpul?   *transitive object question*
        who-sg   3sg-Abs Ø$_{3sg-Erg}$ hit
        'Who did he hit?'

Reiterating the main point of this section: 3rd person agreement in Yimas follows an ergative-absolutive system, in which transitive and intransitive subjects are normally marked differently. We asked whether the contrast between transitive and intransitive subjects is a direct consequence of the transitivity of the verb, or whether it is the result of an independent phenomenon. We saw that case alternations in Yimas are explained by the demands of the EPP, and most importantly, that once the EPP is controlled for, transitive and intransitive subjects behave identically. Therefore, in Yimas at least, ergative case patterns are not directly determined by verb transitivity.

Bobaljik (1993) claims that: "given two structural ... Cases, languages must determine which will be realised on the sole argument of an intransitive clause. ...this is the result of a very simple parameter, the *Obligatory Case Parameter"* On the contrary, we have seen that there is no 'obligatory Case' in Yimas. This opens up the possibility that grammars in general do not need to include conditions which force a special treatment of intransitive subjects for Case purposes.

However, we have only partly explained the behaviour of subjects in Yimas so far. We still need to know why in transitive clauses it is objects that satisfy the EPP, rather than subjects, in contrast with English? And why are intransitive subjects marked ergative when the EPP is independently satisfied. Put in slightly more leading terms: why do subjects appear to 'prefer' ergative to absolutive? The next section addresses these questions.

---

i.   nawn   pu-   n-   tpul
        who-sg   3pl-Abs   3sg-Erg   hit
        'Who hit them?'

[The lack of anti-agreement in this wh-question is an independent effect, discussed in section 3 below.]

2. Deriving Agreement Alternations

I assume a version of the Case theory developed by Shlonsky (1987) and Baker (1991) known as *Generalized Visibility*. The key claim of this approach is that Case licensing is a precondition for interpretation, where 'interpretation' means phonetic interpretation at PF, and semantic interpretation at LF.

(12) *Generalized Visibility*
If X is a potential Case-bearing element, X can be interpreted at level α only if X is Case-marked at level α.

This implies that an expletive element, like *there*, which is overtly realized, but is presumably not interpreted, requires Case licensing only at PF. *pro*, on the other hand, which is interpreted, but not overtly realized, requires Case licensing only at LF.

I also assume that agreement heads are potential Case bearing elements, and following reasoning from Baker (1991), that overt case-bearing heads force nominal arguments to be phonologically null, for the following reasons.[11]

If we assume that Spec-head agreement can Case-license one element at a time, then a conflict arises in the situation where both the specifier and the head require Case-licensing. *Generalized Visibility* offers a solution to this conflict, provided that the argument in the specifier position is *pro*.[12] In such a situation, the agreement head but not *pro* requires Case-licensing at SS/PF, since only the agreement head is phonologically realized; and *pro*, but not the agreement head, requires Case-licensing at LF, since only *pro* enters into thematic interpretation.

Since all of the actual arguments of the clause are *pro*, any overt nominal expressions that we see must be coindexed adjuncts. This explains the free ordering and omission of overt nominal expressions in a rich agreement language like Yimas.

Generalized Visibility predicts which elements require Case-licensing, and at which levels, but does not predict *where* arguments will move for Case. I assume that syntactic movement conforms to a relativized notion of economy of derivation, in which the candidate set of operations, from which the shortest is chosen at any point in a derivation, consists of all operations which immediately satisfy the same requirement. This economy condition does not care whether the element which moves satisfies a requirement of its own, or a requirement on the site which it moves to. For example, if an

---

[11] This prevents overt nominals from appearing in A-positions; it does not prevent them from being realized altogether. Both adjunct and A-bar positions are available for overt nominals.

[12] In fact, the specifier could fail to be *pro*, provided that it is some other phonologically null element, eg. wh-trace.

NP requires Case itself, it moves to the closest position which can satisfy its Case requirement. On the other hand, if an agreement head needs a specifier to agree with, the closest available NP to that head is moved to its specifier.[13] This view of economy differs from more familiar versions, in that it assumes no component of greediness (cf. Chomsky 1993).

In (13a-b) I combine this version of economy with the assumption that lower elements in tree get the first opportunity to satisfy their requirements, and illustrate the derivations predicted for transitive clauses in a language with overt NP arguments (13a, eg. Icelandic), and a language with *pro* arguments and overt agreement heads (13b, Yimas). Depending on whether movement is driven by XPs or by heads, 'nested' or 'crossing' paths of Case movement result (cf. Murasugi 1992, this volume).

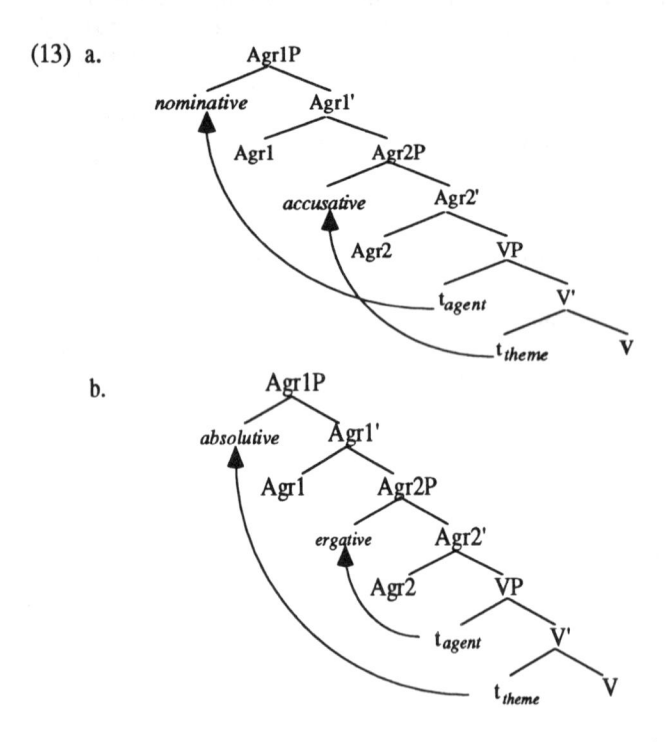

(13) a.

b.

(13b) shows that in a transitive clause in Yimas, the EPP is automatically satisfied by movement of the object to [Spec,Agr2]. This is not the case in an intransitive clause. Economy dictates that the subject move to [Spec,Agr2], and be marked ergative, just as the transitive subject does in (13b); this is only possible, however, when the EPP is independently taken

---

[13]This version of economy owes a lot to ideas in Murasugi (1992).

care of (cf. 8, 10c, 11b above). When the EPP is not independently satisfied, as in an intransitive clause, the subject is forced to move to [Spec,Agr1], and is marked by absolutive agreement.

3. Anti-Anti-Agreement

The previous sections set out one argument for the transitive clause structure in (13b), which was based on the assumption that the EPP is a requirement on the head Agr1. In this section I present another argument for the structure in (13b), based on observations of where agreement is and is not permitted in wh-questions. In addition, this provides a reason to assume that XPs move for Case by S-structure in Yimas, contrary to recent proposals of Campana (1992) and Murasugi (1992) for ergative systems; finally, Case-motivated movement turns out not to be uniformly A-movement.

One of the most striking features of the wh-questions in (11) is that extracted arguments are not marked by agreement prefixes (Foley, p.431), as we have come to expect. This phenomenon is known as *anti-agreement*, and is found in subject extraction contexts in many languages with rich subject agreement (cf. Ouhalla 1993). In Yimas, anti-agreement is found with both subject and object extraction, as can be seen in (11a) and (11c), repeated below.

(11) a. nawm   m-   Ø-   kul-   cpul -um?   *subject extraction*
         who-pl   Comp   Ø$_{3pl-Erg}$ 2pl-Acc   hit   PL
         'Who hit you all?'
    c.   nawn   impa-   Ø-   tpul?   *object extraction*
         who-sg   3sg-Abs Ø$_{3sg-Erg}$ hit
         'Who did he hit?'

There is, however, one environment where extraction does not trigger anti-agreement. (14) is a question in which the extracted argument is marked by a normal agreement prefix. The only difference between (11a) and (14) is that the *non*-extracted argument, the object, is 2nd person in (11a), and 3rd person in (14).

(14)   nawn   pu-   n-   tpul
         who-sg   3pl-Abs 3sg-Erg hit
         'Who hit them?'

We might term the unexpected agreement in (14) *anti-anti-agreement*. I assume here that this effect is essentially the same as the effect of negation on subject extraction found in some anti-agreement languages, discussed by Ouhalla (1993). Ouhalla observes that in languages in which negation intervenes between subject position and [Spec,CP], it blocks the anti-agreement normally found with subject extraction in the language: Welsh, Breton and Berber show this interaction. On the assumption that negation occupies an A-bar position between IP and CP, anti-anti-agreement is triggered when subject extraction violates *Relativized Minimality*. The pair of examples in (15) come from Breton: (15a) shows anti-agreement with subject extraction; (15b) shows the reappearance of subject agreement in a negated relative.

(15) a. Ar vugale   a   lenne (*lennent) al levrioù
         the children COMP   read   read-3pl the books
         'The children who read the books.'
    b.   Ar vugale   ne (*lenne) lennent ket al levrioù
         the children NEG read   read-3pl NEG the books
         'The children who did not read the books.'   (Hendrick 1988)

Ouhalla's explanation of anti-agreement focusses on the *A-bar Disjointness Requirement* (ABDR) of Aoun & Li (1990, 1993), which requires roughly that a pronoun must not be bound by the most local A-bar binder. On the assumption that (i) rich agreement licenses *pro*, and (ii) that *pro* may be the legitimate tail of an A-bar chain, *pro* cannot be the tail of an A-bar chain that satisfies Minimality: for if *pro* is the tail of such a chain, the ABDR will be violated. Impoverishing agreement is a way of preventing the licensing of *pro* in such contexts, and of thereby ensuring that the ABDR is satisfied. Rich subject agreement becomes possible in negated sentences like (15b), according to Ouhalla, because negation is the closest A-bar binder of *pro*.

I suspect that the effects are incorrectly attributed to the ABDR. First, Aoun & Li (1990, 1993) argue that the ABDR must hold only at LF, since in Chinese an illicit sequence *$quantifier_i...pronoun_i$ is improved by the insertion of a wh-operator which does not 'shield' the pronoun until LF: $quantifier_i ... pronoun_i ... wh\text{-}phrase_j$. Meanwhile, related facts force Ouhalla to assume that the ABDR holds at S-structure: wh-in-situ appears not to trigger anti-agreement effects. This makes it difficult to account for anti-agreement effects and Chinese pronoun binding effects using the same principle.

Second, Ouhalla claims that anti-agreement involves *impoverishing* subject agreement in order to avoid licensing *pro*. This seems to be descriptively incorrect. Yimas, Palauan (Georgopoulos 1991) and the languages cited by Ouhalla *delete* agreement with extracted subjects where at all possible. Default 3rd person singular agreement (i.e. impoverished agreement) appears only where tense and agreement are spelled out as a portmanteau, i.e. only in cases where it is impossible to delete agreement without also deleting tense. If the function of anti-agreement is merely to avoid the licensing of *pro*, as Ouhalla claims, then we should not expect

ERGATIVE SUBJECTS / 353

anti-agreement to impose so strong a requirement as complete deletion on agreement morphemes.

As an alternative, I suggest that anti-agreement effects reflect different ways in which A-bar traces can be licensed. Where possible, familiar antecedent government relations hold (16a); but antecedent government fails when an A-bar specifier intervenes (16b). Where antecedent government fails, a head chain may mediate the relation between [Spec,CP] and the extraction site. Each specifier is governed by its head, and the two heads are related by Baker's (1988) *Government Transparency Corollary*, or an analogue. The two ways of licensing A-bar traces are shown in (16a-b): I assume that licensing *via* a head chain is exploited only where normal antecedent government fails (16b: *pro* in Agr1 occupies an A-bar position), due to the extra chain-links involved, which are dispreferred for reasons of representational economy.

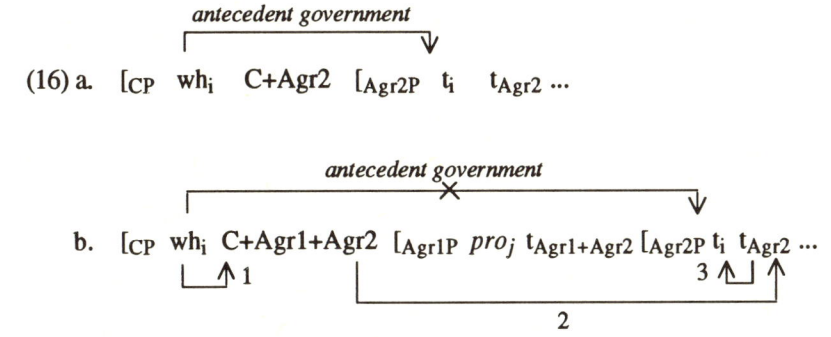

(16) a. [$_{CP}$ wh$_i$ C+Agr2 [$_{Agr2P}$ t$_i$ t$_{Agr2}$ ...

      antecedent government (with arrow from wh$_i$ to t$_i$)

b. [$_{CP}$ wh$_i$ C+Agr1+Agr2 [$_{Agr1P}$ *pro$_j$* t$_{Agr1+Agr2}$ [$_{Agr2P}$ t$_i$ t$_{Agr2}$ ...

      antecedent government (blocked, marked X)

      head-mediated government (links labeled 1, 2, 3)

In both (11a) and (14), the site of wh-extraction is presumably [Spec,Agr2], but only in (14) does any material intervene between Agr2P and CP — there is an object *pro* in [Spec,Agr1] in (14). For (11a) I assume that the 2nd person object is Case-licensed without needing to exit VP (see Phillips, to appear). If the object in [Spec,Agr1] occupies an A-bar position, then we predict the same anti-anti-agreement effect found in negated questions in Breton, Welsh or Berber.

Two questions arise at this point: first, why should the object in [Spec,Agr1] be in an A-bar position, given that the same position is generally taken to be an A position in familiar accusative languages? Second, why do we not find anti-anti-agreement in the object question (11c), which also seems to involve extraction across a filled [Spec,Agr1]?

For a possible reason why objects can only reach [Spec,Agr1] by A-bar movement, we can look to criticisms of the derivation in (13b): Bobaljik (1993) and Chomsky (1993) argue that the 'nested paths' derivation of a transitive clause in (13b) is impossible, since no pattern of A-movements will yield it, given the conditions on movement which they assume.[14] We might in fact assume that Bobaljik and Chomsky are correct in their claim that objects cannot A-move to [Spec,Agr1] across a subject, but incorrect in their assumption that impossible A-movement entails impossible movement for Case. A-bar movement for Case is also possible, but only as a last resort, as argued in Miyagawa (1993).[15]

Also, assuming something akin to Chomsky's (1993) conditions on A-movement offers an answer to the second question: why does extraction across a subject allow anti-agreement (11c)), whereas extraction across an object does not (14)? Objects can only reach [Spec,Agr1] by A-bar movement, which is why they induce Relativized Minimality effects for extraction, including anti-anti-agreement. Subjects can reach [Spec,Agr1] by A-movement, which is why they do not interfere with A-bar movement across them, and hence why they do not interfere with anti-agreement. In effect, what I am claiming here is that [Spec,Agr1P] in Yimas has mixed status, in just the same way as Diesing has claimed for Yiddish (Diesing 1990).

A further consequence of the intervention effect diagnosed in (14) is that the Case-movements shown in (13b) must take place by S-structure, and cannot be delayed until LF. This conclusion is based on an observation of Ouhalla, who notices that anti-agreement effects are not found in languages which lack overt wh-movement in subject questions. Therefore, he argues, anti-agreement effects must reflect S-structure configurations. If anti-agreement effects reflected LF configurations, we would not expect variation in when wh-movement takes place to predict variation in the presence of anti-agreement effects.[16]

---

[14]They assume that no A-movement may cross two intervening A-specifiers.

[15]Miyagawa (1993) shows that although there is a scope interaction in Japanese between a head noun and the NP which it exceptionally Case marks genitive, the interaction disappears when a third nominal intervenes and is in an A-position. Miyagawa attributes the loss of scope interaction to the fact that the genitive NP is forced to A-bar move for case in the case with an intervening A-position.

[16]The conclusion that objects move to [Spec,Agr1] at S-structure in ergative systems conflicts with claims of Campana (1992) and Murasugi (1992), who both assume that at least Case-movement of objects must be delayed until LF.

4. Subject Properties

In the remainder of the paper I discuss possible cross-linguistic implications of the following findings about Yimas from sections 1 and 2:

    i. Transitive and intransitive subjects may occupy the same case position (Spec,Agr2) in an apparently 'ergative' system.
    ii. In transitive clauses, objects are higher than subjects at S-structure.
    iii. [Spec,Agr1] is a 'mixed' position.

In an important 1976 paper, Anderson points out that despite the differences in case and agreement inflection between ergative and accusative languages, there are striking parallels across the two language types in binding phenomena: in transitive clauses subjects can bind object anaphors, but objects cannot bind subjects.[17]

Anderson's response to the contrasting natural classes of arguments picked out by case and binding was to assume that the binding phenomena reflect true syntactic configurations, and that the case phenomena are merely morphological in nature.

Faced with various kinds of evidence that the distribution of Case-marking does reflect syntactic properties, and armed with a wider range of syntactic positions, recent authors such as Campana (1992) and Murasugi (1992) have claimed that Anderson's contrasts arise because different syntactic phenomena are sensitive to different classes of syntactic positions. Case sensitive phenomena involve Case positions like [Spec,Agr1] and [Spec,Agr2] in (13b) above. Subject oriented phenomena, on the other hand, such as binding, involve primarily thematic positions inside VP.

Neither Campana nor Murasugi stipulate directly that different phenomena look at different syntactic positions. Instead, they achieve the contrast by assuming that different classes of phenomena are sensitive to different syntactic levels. Binding conditions crucially apply at S-structure, at which point objects are still inside VP, and hence asymmetrically c-commanded by subjects.[18] This derives Anderson's observations about binding in ergative languages. Case-sensitive phenomena refer to LF structures, in which objects now asymmetrically c-command subjects.

The findings about Yimas listed in (i-iii) above challenge Campana and Murasugi's assumptions in two respects. First, we found evidence in section 3 that objects move to [Spec,Agr1] by S-structure. Second, evidence from sections 1 and 3 shows that transitive and intransitive

---

[17]Examples are Basque (Control: Anderson 1976); West Greenlandic Inuit (Bittner 1994: Control, Reflexive & Pronominal Binding, Switch Reference); Abkhaz (Murasugi 1992: Reflexive Binding).

[18]This is not strictly correct for Murasugi's theory: she assumes that subjects do raise to [Spec,Agr2] at S-structure, and only objects remain in situ. However this difference is not important to the points that follow.

subjects have more in common than just originating in [Spec,VP]: section 1 showed that both transitive and intransitive subjects may occupy [Spec,Agr2]; a consequence of section 3 is that even when objects move across subjects for Case, the highest *A-position* in a clause will always be filled by a subject. We may then assume that subject-oriented phenomena target the highest A-position in a clause.

Taken together, these findings remove the need for an approach to Anderson's Problem in which case movement of objects must be delayed until LF in order to derive appropriate subject-object asymmetries in binding phenomena. The binding facts noticed by Anderson follow straightforwardly from the standard assumption from accusative languages, that binding conditions apply to all and only A-positions.

5. Conclusions

This paper has discussed the implications of a *subject property* rather different from most examples of subject properties in the ergativity literature.

First, in Yimas it is possible to control for the effects of the Extended Projection Principle on agreement marking patterns, and it can be shown that it is the EPP that is responsible for the ergative agreement system. When the EPP is independently satisfied, all 3rd person subjects are marked ergative. This has the consequence that grammars do not need to include conditions which apply specifically to intransitive verbs, or requirements that a given case be obligatorily assigned — this conclusion diverges from a good deal of the recent literature on ergativity.

Second, alternations in agreement marking for subjects due to the EPP motivate an approach to Case movement in ergative and accusative systems based on a greed-free notion of economy of movement.

Third, alternations in agreement marking for extracted subjects, due to the person of the object, lend support to the assumption that in ergative systems objects are case-marked (a) higher than subjects (Campana 1992; Murasugi 1992, 1994; Bittner & Hale 1993; Bittner 1994), and (b) in an A-bar position (Campana 1992).

References

Anderson, Stephen. 1976. On the Notion of Subject in Ergative Languages. In C.N. Li (ed) *Subject and Topic*. New York: Academic Press.

Aoun, Joseph & Yen-hui Audrey Li. 1990. Minimal Disjointness. *Linguistics* 28, 189-204.

Aoun, Joseph & Yen-hui Audrey Li. 1993. *Syntax of Scope*. Cambridge, MA: MIT Press.

Baker, Mark. 1988. *Incorporation: A Theory of Grammatical Function Changing.* Chicago: University of Chicago Press.
Baker, Mark. 1991. On some Subject/Object Non-Asymmetries in Mohawk. *Natural Language and Linguistic Theory* 9, 537-76.
Bittner, Maria. 1994. *Case, Scope and Binding.* Dordrecht: Kluwer.
Bittner, Maria, & Kenneth Hale. 1993. *Ergativity: Towards a Theory of Heterogeneous Class.* ms. Rutgers U. & MIT.
Bobaljik, Jonathan. 1993. Ergativity and Ergative Unergatives. In C. Phillips (ed) *Papers on Case & Agreement II,* MITWPL 19, 45-88.
Campana, Mark. 1992. *A Movement Theory of Ergativity.* Doctoral dissertation, McGill University.
Chomsky, Noam. 1982. *Some Concepts and Consequences of the Theory of Government and Binding.* Cambridge, MA: MIT Press.
Chomsky, Noam. 1993. A Minimalist Program for Linguistic Theory. In K. Hale & S.J. Keyser (eds) *The View from Building 20.* Cambridge, MA: MIT Press.
Diesing, Molly. 1990. Verb Movement and the Subject Position in Yiddish. *Natural Language and Linguistic Theory* 8, 41-79.
Foley, William. 1991. *The Yimas Language of New Guinea.* Stanford: Stanford University Press.
Georgopoulos, Carol. 1991. *Syntactic Variables: A-bar Chains and Resumptive Pronouns in Palauan.* Dordrecht: Kluwer.
Hendrick, Randall. 1988. *Anaphora in Celtic and Universal Grammar.* Dordrecht, Kluwer.
Laka, Itziar. 1993. Unergatives that Assign Ergative, Unaccusatives that Assign Accusative. In J. Bobaljik & C. Phillips (eds) *Papers on Case & Agreement I,* MITWPL 18, 149-172.
Levin, Beth. 1983. *On the Nature of Ergativity.* Doctoral dissertation, MIT: MITWPL.
Levin, Juliette & Diane Massam. 1985. Surface Ergativity: Case/Theta Relations Reexamined. In S. Berman (ed) *Proceedings of NELS XV.* Amherst, MA: GLSA.
Marantz, Alec. 1984. *On the Nature of Grammatical Relations.* Cambridge, MA: MIT Press.
Miyagawa, Shigeru. 1993. Case Checking and Minimal Link Condition. In C. Phillips (ed) *Papers on Case & Agreement II,* MITWPL 19, 213-254.
Murasugi, Kumiko. 1992. *Crossing and Nested Paths: NP Movement in Accusative and Ergative Languages.* Doctoral dissertation, MIT: MITWPL.
Murasugi, Kumiko. 1994. This volume. Lexical Case and NP-Raising.
Ouhalla, Jamal. 1993. Subject Extraction, Negation and the Anti-Agreement Effect. *Natural Language and Linguistic Theory* 11, 477-518.

Non-terms in complex predicates: From Incorporation to Reanalysis

MARIA POLINSKY

University of Southern California

This paper analyzes grammatical relations in a particular type of the existential construction, known as Locative Inversion (Bresnan and Kanerva 1989) or existential presentative (Hetzron 1971; 1975; Kirsner 1979). Locative Inversion is characterized by the switching of the positions of the argument NP and the prepositional phrase (hence inversion) and by the presence of an obligatory prepositional phrase, often locative or directional (hence locative). For example, in English (from Levin and Hovav 1994: 199):

(1) a. Out of the house came a tiny old lady

Sometimes, however, the locative is omitted, as in (1b) or may remain in situ, which makes the term Locative Inversion questionable.[1]

(1) b. Enter Hamlet

Such constructions may be superficially described as ones undergoing an inversion of the subject. Since inversion of the subject also characterizes constructions such as (1a), below, the term Subject Inversion (SI) will be used in reference to such constructions.

In this paper, I will examine the SI construction in Kinyarwanda and then compare it to the so-called distributive construction in Russian. Both constructions serve a particular function in discourse: they introduce a

---

*I am grateful to Daphrose Mukadisi, Gaspard Bagumanshaka, and Jeanine Ntihirageza for their help with the Kinyarwanda data. The Russian data were discussed with John Bailyn, Catherine Chvany, Steven Franks, and Valentina Zaitseva. I am indebted to Beth Levin and Jakov Testelec for their comments on the earlier draft of this paper. All errors are my sole responsibility.

The following abbreviations are used: ABS - Absolutive; ACC - accusative; AGR - agreement marker; AOR - Aorist; ASSOC - Associative; APP - Applicative; CAUS - Causative; CL# - grammatical class; DISTR- Distributive; DO - Direct Object; FEM - Feminine; FUT - Future; GEN - Genitive; IMPF - Imperfective; INDIC - Indicative; INF - Infinitive; INSTR - Instrumental; IO - Indirect Object; LOC - Locative; MASC - Masculine; NEG - Negation; NOM - Nominative; PASS - Passive; PF - Perfective; PL - Plural; PRES - Present; PROGR - Progressive; REFL - Reflexive; REL - Relative; SI - Subject Inversion; SUBJ - Subjunctive.

[1]Another criticism of the term is related to the architecture of the inversion analysis: the analysis may be rejected as not structure-preserving (Levin and Hovav 1994: 194-5).

referent that is new, or is viewed as new, on the scene (the predicate verb in such a case denotes the activity or state as characterizing the existence of this referent). This function, known as presentative, has been widely discussed in the literature (see Levin and Hovav 1994: Ch. 6 for an extensive review). In this paper, I will take this function of the constructions as a given and will concentrate on their grammatical properties.

The main question addressed in this paper concerns the grammatical relation borne by the inverted nominal in Kinyarwanda and the distributive genitive in Russian. I will show that, despite the differences in internal grammars, the two constructions are characterized by the same syntactic phenomenon: the verb and the inverted/genitive nominal form a single constituent in the clause structure. The inverted/genitive nominal has no term properties and cannot be identified, as has been suggested elsewhere, for Bantu, as an object (Bresnan and Kanerva 1989); as a head NP of a small clause (Hoekstra and Mulder 1990), or as a VP-internal subject (Diesing 1992; Freeze 1992).

Under the syntactic approach adopted here, the clause is viewed as a linguistic sign having three distinct levels of representation, namely: the meaning of the clause, represented by thematic roles and verbal semantics, and the form of the clause represented by grammatical relations, on the one hand, and by communicative functions, on the other. Thematic roles remain unchanged in the analysis; these roles can be mapped differently onto grammatical relations, resulting in different syntactic structures, for example:

(2) Mapping thematic roles onto grammatical relations
    a.   REGULAR ACTIVE TRANSITIVE CONSTRUCTION:

Thematic roles:	Agent	Theme
Grammatical relations:	subject	direct object
Communicative functions:	topic	focus

    b.   PERSONAL PASSIVE CONSTRUCTION:

Thematic roles:	Agent	Theme
Grammatical relations:	non-term	subject
Communicative functions:	focus	topic

A crucial feature of the syntactic approach adopted here is that it permits direct reference to grammatical relations. Each grammatical relation is characterized by a set of grammatical properties. These properties are of two types:
    (i) the form and/or position assumed by the respective nominal in the clause;

(ii) the form and/or position of other clausal and/or sentential constituents determined by the respective nominal (agreement; null copy, pronominalization, reflexivization, etc.).[2]

Nominals that have properties of both types are syntactically active, that is, they determine the form and/or position of some other constituent(s). Nominals that only have type (i) properties are syntactically inactive. This opposition underlies the distinction between terms (which include subject, direct object, indirect object, and oblique object) and non-terms or adjuncts. The following hierarchy of grammatical relations is assumed:

(3)   subject > direct object > indirect object > non-term corresponding to term[3] > default non-term

Non-terms that correspond to terms in other structures and default non-terms differ in that the former can retain some syntactic properties of type (ii) above; the difference between the two types of non-terms is discussed in (Gerdts 1992; Gerdts and Whaley 1991; 1992a; 1992b; Polinsky 1993a, b).

The nominal whose syntactic status is central to the discussion in this paper will be shown to be different from any element in (3). In section 1, I will examine such nominals in Kinyarwanda; in section 2, I will present evidence for a similar type of nominal in Russian. In section 3, I will argue for a unified Incorporation analysis for such nominals and will demonstrate their difference from the category of the VP-internal subject.

1. Subject Inversion in Kinyarwanda

In Kinyarwanda, non-inverted clauses such as (4a) are related, through Subject Inversion, to clauses such as (4b) (note that the word order in Kinyarwanda is strictly SVO.):

(4)   a.   aba-shyitsi   ba-ra-ririimb-a   mu gisagâra
           CL2-guest   CL2-PROGR-sing-IMPF   in village
           'The guests are singing in the village.'

---

[2]The set is established as a generalization of properties obtained for a comparable grammatical relation, e.g. subject, across different constructions (intransitive, transitive, middle, passive, etc.). Of course, a relevant question here is: do all the properties in a set have to be present for the identification of a specific nominal with a certain grammatical relation, or is there a necessary and sufficient subset of properties that would allow us to identify a specific nominal as a certain grammatical relation? If the former solution is accepted, each individual syntactic construction will have its own grammatical relations. If the latter solution is chosen, a problem arises with regard to what properties can be treated as necessary and sufficient. I am leaving this question open here.

[3]The closest correspondence to this relation is a chômeur in Relational Grammar.

b. mu gisagára   ha-ra-riríimb-a   aba-shyítsi
in village.CL7   CL16-PROGR-sing-IMPF CL2-guest
'In the village, guests are singing.'

In (4b), the locative nominal is fronted; the presumable subject follows the verb and no longer determines verbal agreement by class.
In addition to (4b), Kinyarwanda has a construction with the locative phrase *in situ*, as illustrated by (4c):

(4)   c.   ha-ra-riríimb-a   aba-shyítsi mu gisagâra
CL16-PROGR-sing-IMPF CL2-guest   in   village
'Guests are singing in the village.'

In the discussion below, I will refer to clauses such as (4b, c) as SI clauses and to nominals such as 'guests' as inverted nominals. Note that the *in situ* locative cannot precede the inverted nominal, as shown by (4d):

(4)   d.   *ha-ra-riríimb-a   mu gisagára aba-shyítsi
CL16-PROGR-sing-IMPF in   village   CL2-guest
'Guests are singing in the village.'

1.1. Arguments that the inverted nominal is not a subject

In what follows, I will examine the grammatical relation borne by the inverted nominal in (4b) and (4c). This analysis is based on several prior analyses of the grammatical relations in Kinyarwanda (Kimenyi 1980; Dryer 1983; Gerdts and Whaley 1991; 1992a; 1992b; Polinsky and Kozinsky 1992; Polinsky 1993a; 1993b; 1993c).[4] The results of these analyses are summarized in (5).[5]

As the summary in (5) shows, the subject in Kinyarwanda is characterized by a number of syntactic effects: it determines verbal agreement, occurs with a special subject delimiter *-nyiné* (also agreeing with it in class), has a number of control properties, and is accessible to extractions and topicalization.

---

[4]For arguments that Kinyarwanda has a distinct oblique object relation, different from other objects but also different from non-terms, see Gerdts and Whaley 1992; Polinsky 1993b.

[5]In the summary in (5), I am leaving out word order distinctions (Dryer 1983; Gerdts and Whaley 1992a), which vary depending on animacy (Polinsky and Kozinsky 1992). Also, in several cases, my consultants differed from the consultants of other authors in consistently rejecting certain multiple applicatives. In such cases, the analysis of grammatical relations reflects the grammar of my consultants.

(5)   Properties of grammatical relations in Kinyarwanda

PROPERTY	SUBJECT	DO	IO	OO	NON-TERM
verbal agreement	yes	no	no	no	no
selection of delimiter 'only'	-nyiné	gusa	gusa	gusa	gusa
control of the purpose clause	yes*	no	no	no	no
control of reflexivization	yes	no	no	no	no
control of the null copy across clause	yes	yes	no	no	no
control of the incorporated pronoun in the verb	yes	yes	yes	no	no
accessibility to Plain Topicalization	yes	yes	yes	no	no
accessibility to passivization	N/A	yes	yes	no	no
accessibility to relativization	yes	yes	yes	yes	no
accessibility to clefting	yes	yes	yes	yes	no

*For some speakers only; see (7) below

Unlike the preposed subject, which determines class verbal agreement (for example, in (4a)), the inverted nominal does not determine verbal agreement at all. The SI predicate is invariably marked for the so-called locative class (class 16).

Next, the inverted nominal cannot occur with the subject-selected delimiter *-nyine*, as shown by (6a).

(6) a. *muri iyi inzu ha-ra-síinzíir-a aba-shyítsi
      in this house CL16-PROGR-sleep-IMPF CL2-guest
      bóo-nyîne
      CL2-only
      'In this house are sleeping only guests.'

    b. muri iyi inzu ha-ra-síinzíir-a aba-shyítsi gusa
      in this house CL16-PROGR-sleep-IMPF CL2-guest only
      'The only thing happening in this house is guests sleeping.'[6]

While the subject in Kinyarwanda controls the purpose clause (7a),[7] the inverted nominal does not have this property, as shown by (7b):

(7) a. %aba-shyítsi$_i$ ba-ra-síinzíir-a muri iyi ínzu
      CL2-guest CL2-PROGR-sleep-IMPF in this house
      [[Ø$_i$ ku-ruhuuka mbere yo gu-kora]]
      Ø INF-rest before of INF-work
      'The guests are sleeping in this house to get some rest before work.'

    b. *muri iyi inzu ha-ra-síinzíir-a aba-shyítsi$_i$
      in this house CL16-PROGR-sleep-IMPF CL2-guest
      [[Ø$_i$ kuruhuuka mbere yo gukora]]
      Ø rest.INF before of work.INF
      'In this house, guests are sleeping to get some rest before work.'

Unlike the preposed subject in (8a), the inverted nominal does not determine the reflexive marker on the predicate; this is shown by the ungrammatical sentence in (8b):

(8) a. aba-shyítsi ba-r-íi-ríriimb-ir-a muri iyi inzu
      CL2-guest CL2-PROGR-REFL-sing-APP-IMPF in this house
      'The guests are singing to/for themselves in this house.'

---

[6]As the translations show, (6a) and (6b) have different interpretations; this semantic difference will be discussed in section 3.2 below.

[7]Some speakers do not allow subject-controlled purpose clauses at all; this is indicated by the % symbol.

b. *ha-r-íi-ríriimb-ir-a aba-shyítsi
CL16-PROGR-REFL-sing-APP-IMPF CL2-guest
muri iyi inzu
in this house
'Guests are singing to/for themselves in this house.'

Unlike the subject, the inverted nominal does not control the null copy across clause and does not determine an incorporated pronoun on a verb (Polinsky 1993c). All this proves that this inverted nominal is not a subject.

1.2. Arguments that the inverted nominal is not an object
The next question is if the inverted nominal can be identified with an object. As mentioned above, Kinyarwanda has three types of object terms: direct, indirect, and oblique object. A clause involving all three types of objects is shown in (9):

(9) umwaána y-a-há+an-ye inká ibíryo umunéezeero
     child CL1-PAST-give+ASSOC-PF cow food joy
     SUBJECT   IO   DO   OO
     'The child gave food to the cow with joy.'

As the summary in (5) shows, there are two minimal properties that distinguish an oblique object from a non-term: accessibility to relativization and clefting. Thus, the nominal 'joy' in (9) can relativize and is accessible to clefting. The inverted nominal, however, is inaccessible to either process; the impossibility of its relativization is illustrated by the following examples, which correspond to (4b) and (4c):

(10) a. *aba-shyitsi mu gisagára haa-ra-ríríimb-a
         CL2-guest in village CL16.REL-PRES-sing-IMPF
         'the guests that in the village are singing' (cf. (4b))
     b. *aba-shyitsi haa-ra-riríimb-a mu gisagára
         CL2-guest CL16.REL-PRES-sing-IMPF in village
         'the guests that are singing in the village' (cf. (4c))

Thus, the inverted nominal is not an object. Since it is syntactically inactive, it should be identified with non-terms. However, there are significant differences between the inverted nominal and Kinyarwanda non-terms.

1.3. Difference between the inverted nominal and other non-terms
In this section, I will compare the inverted nominal to such non-terms as the passive agent, prepositional instrumental phrase, prepositional manner phrase, and locative phrase. These nominals are syntactically inactive, which qualifies them as non-terms. Of these non-terms, the passive

agent always corresponds to a term (subject of the active clause) under a different mapping strategy.

The instrumental prepositional phrase and the manner prepositional phrase are obligatorily mapped to an oblique object in a clause with a prototypical ditransitive verb.[8] An example of a sentence where the instrumental NP is an oblique object, hence a term, was given above, in (9).

In all other types of double object clauses, where the second object has the thematic role benefactive, causee, possessor, or instrument, this second nominal can be mapped either to an indirect object or to a non-term. In such clauses, the instrument or manner nominal can be encoded only by a prepositional phrase. Thus, in (11a), the causee is the indirect object and the manner nominal is a prepositional phrase; as (11b) shows, the term manner NP, co-indexed with the manner advancement marker -*an*- in the verb and appearing without a preposition, is ungrammatical:[9]

(11) a. umugóre y-a-súbiz-físh-ije umuhuúngu ikibázo
woman CL1-PAST-answer-CAUS-PF boy question
n' umujínya
with anger
'The woman angrily made the boy answer the question.'
b. *umugóre y-a-súbiz-físh-an-ye umuhuúngu
woman CL1-PAST-answer-CAUS-ASSOC- PF boy
ikibázo umujínya
question anger
'The woman angrily made the boy answer the question.'

Finally, locative phrases, such as the locatives in the above examples (4), (6)-(8), are default non-terms: they never correspond to terms in any other construction.[10]

1) PHRASAL PHONOLOGY. The first difference between the inverted nominal and the non-terms just mentioned is that the inverted nominal has to form a single tonal phrase with the verb it follows, as shown by (12)

---

[8]A prototypical ditransitive verb is one that selects theme and recipient (but not benefactive, causee, possessor) as obligatory thematic roles. Clauses with a prototypical ditransitive verb as the predicate differ from other double object clauses in that a recipient can be only mapped to indirect object and cannot be mapped to a non-term. See also (Dryer 1983: 132; Polinsky and Kozinsky 1992: 431; Polinsky 1993b).

[9]For a detailed analysis of these clauses, see (Polinsky 1995; Polinsky and Kozinsky 1992: 434-439).

[10]For the reasons of space, I won't be discussing the problem of Locative Advancement in Kinyarwanda (Polinsky and Kozinsky 1992: 428). In any event, this problem is extraneous to the locative phrases discussed here.

(single tonal phrases are parenthesized).[11]

(12) a. (harariríimba abashyítsi)
     b. *(hararirríimba) (abashyitsi)
        'Guests are singing.'

Default non-terms in Kinyarwanda cannot form a single tonal phrase with the verb; in a clause that includes one or several objects, these non-terms don't form a single tonal phrase with an object either. As for the passive agent, it can only marginally form a single tonal phrase with the verb (13a), and this is a less preferred variant than the one with separate tonal phrases, illustrated by (13b):

(13) a. ?(imy-eénda) (i-ø-meshe-ejw-e   n'umukoôbwa)
        CL4-clothes CL4-PAST-wash-PASS-PF by girl
     b. (imy-eénda) (i-ø-meshe-ejw-e) (n'umukoôbwa)
        CL4-clothes CL4-PAST-wash-PASS-PF by girl
        'The clothes were washed by the girl.'

2) FUSION WITH THE VERB. The second difference between the inverted nominal and other non-terms is that the inverted nominal cannot be separated from the verb by any intervening lexical material. Kinyarwanda linearization rules are generally quite strict; however, manner adverbials and sentential particles (emphatic and question particles) float in the sentence. These lexical items can separate the verb and the direct or indirect object, compare (9) and (14a, b), where *nivyo* 'indeed' can intervene between the verb and all its objects (14a) or between two objects (14b):

(14) a. umwaána y-a-há+an-ye   nivyo ínka ibíryo
        child   CL1-PAST-give+ASSOC-PF indeed cow food
        umunéezeero
        joy
     b. umwaána y-a-há+an-ye   inká nivyo ibíryo
        child   CL1-PAST-give+ASSOC-PF cow indeed food
        umunéezeero
        joy
        'True, the child gave the food to the cow with joy.'

The intervening lexical material can separate a verb from a passive agent, compare (13) and (15):

---

[11]See Kimenyi (1979) for a detailed discussion of tonal rules in Kinyarwanda; also see Bresnan and Kanerva (1989: 5-9) for a discussion of similar rules in Chichewa.

(15) imy-eénda   i-ø-mesh-éjw-e   cyaane n'umukoôbwa
     CL4-clothes CL4-PAST-wash-PASS-PF hard   by girl
     'The clothes were washed well by the girl.'

Meanwhile, the inverted nominal and the verb cannot be separated by a particle or an adverbial; thus, (16a, b) is ungrammatical:

(16) a. *ha-ri   koko   ibi-tí   bi-ba   mu múgi?
        CL16-PRES-be indeed CL8-tree CL8-be in city
        'Are there indeed trees in the city?'
     b. *mu máazi h-ø-oog-a   cyaane aba-húungu
        in water CL16-PRES-swim-IMPF hard   CL2-boy
        'In the water, there swim boys a lot.'

3) LICENSING OF THE NULL WORD. The third difference between the inverted nominal and other non-terms is in the ability to license the NON-SPECIFIC NULL WORD $\emptyset_{\exists x}$, i.e. the null word with the existential interpretation ('for some existing X that...').[12] For passive, compare (13), where the passive agent is overtly expressed, and (17), where the agent is expressed by the null word:

(17) imy-eénda   i-ø-meshe-ejw-e $\emptyset_{\exists x}$
     CL4-clothes CL4-PAST-wash-PASS-PF
     'The clothes were washed (by someone).'

Similarly, all the other non-terms mentioned above (instrumentals, locatives) license the non-specific null word. The inverted nominal, however, is an exception: thus, (18), where 'guests' is replaced by the non-specific null word, is ungrammatical:

(18) *mu gisagára ha-ra-riríimb-a $\emptyset_{\exists x}$
     in village CL16-PROGR-sing-IMPF
     'In the village, there occurs singing (by someone).'

In general, expression by the non-specific null word is evidence of the optional or adjunct status of a nominal. The obligatory non-null expression of the inverted nominal then indicates that it is a complement, rather than an adjunct. However, it is a complement that is syntactically inactive.

---

[12]This null word is contrasted with the referential null word, whose interpretation is determined by the referential properties of the antecedent (see Polinsky 1993c for details). The distinction between the non-specific and the referential null word is similar to that between PRO and *pro* in GB.

4) RESTRICTIVE RELATIVE CLAUSE. Finally, all the non-terms discussed here except the inverted nominal can be modified by either the restrictive or the descriptive relative clause. For example, the passive agent can be modified by a restrictive relative clause, as in (19a), and by a descriptive clause, as in (19b):

(19) a. imy-eénda ya-ø-mesh-w-e   n'umu-koôbwa
       CL4-cloth CL4-PAST-was-PASS-PERF by CL1-girl
       waa-je   hano ejo
       CL1.REL-come here yesterday
       'The clothes were washed by the girl who came here yesterday.'
    b. imy-eénda ya-ø-goomb-ye   ku-mesh-w-a
       CL4-cloth CL4-PRES-should-PERF INF-wash-PASS-IMPF
       n'aba-koôbwa baa-kóra   néeza
       by CL2-girl   CL2.REL-work well
       'Clothes should be washed by such girls who are hard-working.'

Meanwhile, the inverted nominal can only be modified by a descriptive relative clause:

(20) a. *ha-ø-ri   i-nyoni   za-boon-w-e   ejo
       CL16-PRES-be CL10-bird CL10.REL-see-PASS-PF yesterday
       'There are the birds that were seen yesterday.'
    b. ha-ø-ri   i-nyoni   zi-tá-gurûk-a
       CL16-PRES-be CL10-bird CL10.REL-NEG-fly-IMPF
       'There are such birds that don't fly.'

This last dissimilarity between the inverted nominal and other non-terms cannot be explained only with reference to syntax.[13] Here, this ban on restrictive relative clauses is interpreted as a semantic correlate of the three formal distinctions between the inverted nominal and other non-terms: phrasal tonal rules, (in)separability from the verb, and licensing of the non-specific null word.

These distinctions indicate that the inverted nominal, though syntactically inactive as other non-terms, is also different from the two possible types of non-terms and, therefore, requires special analysis. I will return to this analysis in section 3, after examining the Russian distributive construction.

---

[13]Given the presentative discourse function of the construction, use of the restrictive relative clause would create a conflict between the introduction of the respective referent as new and the presupposition of its existence, necessary for restrictive relativization.

2. Russian intransitive distributive clause with the bare genitive

Following Dressler (1968), distributive is defined as a process/event that occurs at a single reference point and that has the same effect when it involves at least one whole participant as when it involves parts of that participant or multiple participants. This definition includes two major points: first, that one of the participants in the situation has to be viewed as multiple (consisting of parts), and second, that the reference time remains the same for all the parts involved. Since one of the participants is interpreted as a multiple entity, the distributive verb selects, as one of its arguments, a noun in the plural, or a mass noun, or a collective noun. To illustrate by lexical distributives in English:

(21) a. the parliament dissolved - *the MP dissolved
 b. spill the beans - *spill the bean

A number of languages, Russian included, have regular morphology for the derivation of distributive verbs. In Russian, distributive verbs are formed from non-distributive verbs with the help of prefixes *iz-, na-; o(b)-, pere-, po-, raz-, s-*; some of the prefixes can also combine, yielding composite prefixes (for details, see Knjazev 1989).[14] Of the prefixes listed above, *na-* and *po-* form perfective verbs that can take an argument either in the nominative/accusative (depending on whether it is subject or object) or genitive. Compare (22), where the argument of the distributive verb corresponds to the logical subject, and (23), where it corresponds to object. Note that in both clauses, the genitive nominal appears without a modifier, i.e. bare; it is invariably interpreted as consisting of multiple parts (for a detailed discussion of the quantification parameter, see Franks to appear).

(22) a. na jabloki na-lete-l-i ptic-y
 on apples DISTR-fly-PAST-PL bird-NOM.PL
 b. na jabloki na-lete-l-o ptic-ø
 on apples DISTR-fly-PAST-NEUTER bird-GEN.PL
 'Many birds flew over to the apples.'
(23) a. povar na-gotovi-l-ø ed-u
 cook DISTR-cook-PAST-MASC food-ACC
 b. povar na-gotovi-l-ø ed-y
 cook DISTR-cook-PAST-MASC food-GEN
 'The cook has prepared a lot of food.'

In general, Russian word order is notoriously free. However, the contextually neutral order has the subject precede the verb (and the object follow it), as in (23). In the distributive construction with the subjective

---

[14]Russian distributive verbs are most commonly perfective; if imperfectivized, they still retain their telic semantics.

distributive argument, either in the nominative or in the genitive (22a, b), the contextually neutral order is the one where the argument follows the verb. Note that (22) also includes the fronted locative, which is a recurrent feature of the construction with the subjective genitive: the spatio-temporal argument is either overtly expressed, or is easily recoverable from the context. This argument is typically fronted, as in (22). This presence of the spatio-temporal argument, often topicalized, points to a similarity between the subjective distributive and Subject Inversion.

The fronting of the spatio-temporal argument, however, does not prevent the fronting of the distributive argument. An example of a fronted distributive argument is given in (24), which corresponds to (22b):

(24) ptic-ø   na jabloki   na-lete-l-o!
     bird-GEN.PL on apples   DISTR-fly-PAST-NEUTER
     'It's amazing how many birds flew to the apples.'

The fronted distributive genitive should be differentiated from the genitive of topicalization, shown in (25a, b):

(25) a   gost-ej   na obed   sbežа-l-o-s'
         guest-GEN.PL on dinner gather running-PAST-NEUTER-REFL
         'Lots of guests came to dinner.'
     b. kniž-ek   ona pokupaet
         book-GEN.PL   she buys
         'Boy, does she buy many books.'

Unlike the genitive in the distributive, the genitive of topicalization does not correspond to a non-fronted genitive. Compare (25a, b) with (26a, b), which show that the genitive *in situ* is ungrammatical:[15]

(26) a. *na obed sbežalos' gostej
     b. *ona pokupaet knižek

In what follows, I will concentrate on the distributive clause with the so-called subjective genitive, as in (22b); this type of genitive will be referred to as the distributive genitive. Similarly, a nominative such as the one in (22a) will be referred to as a distributive nominative.

The main question addressed here is: what is the grammatical relation borne by the genitive in the distributive construction? It is argued that the genitive nominal differs from terms (subject, direct object, indirect object) and from non-terms as well.

---

[15]A more detailed analysis of the construction with the genitive of topicalization and an analysis of the semantics of the distributive construction are beyond the scope of this paper.

2.1. Arguments against the subjecthood of the distributive genitive

There have been several studies of Modern Russian, examining the syntactic properties of subjects (Chvany 1975; Babby 1980a,b; Pesetsky 1982; Kozinsky 1983; Rappaport 1984; Neidle 1988). Some of the elicited properties are complicated because they can spill over to topics, particularly *u*-phrases and datives (Timberlake 1980); hence the mention of subjectoids and pseudo-subjects in several studies of Russian syntax (Rappaport 1984; Neidle 1988).

The main reservation about the properties elicited by several authors so far is that little or no distinction is made between subjects and topics and, even within subjects, no distinction between the subject of a transitive verb, the subject of an unergative, and the main argument of an unaccusative.[16] On the other hand, this lack of distinction results in a wider range of subject properties or 'effects', which will be applied to the distributive genitive below.

An important, though not obligatory, property of Russian subjects is their ability to determine verbal agreement, see (23a, b), where the past tense verb agrees with the subject *povar* in gender and number.[17] The distributive genitive clearly does not determine verbal agreement: the verb in the distributive construction is invariably 3 person singular, neuter.

Next, Russian subjects obligatorily control the gerund, as illustrated by (27a) for a non-distributive subject and by (27b) for the distributive nominative:

(27) a. pomoščnik-i$_i$ rinulis' k nemu, Ø$_i$ uznav   ob oplate
        helper-NOM.PL rushed to him   Ø having learnt about pay
        'Having heard of the pay, helpers rushed to him.'
    b. pomoščnik-i$_i$ na-leteli   k nemu, Ø$_i$ uznav   ob oplate
        helper-NOM.PL DISTR-flew to him Ø having learnt about pay
        'Having heard of the pay, many helpers rushed to him.'

---

[16]Kozinsky (1983) is an exception to this because he distinguishes between transitive and intransitive subjects as well as subjects and topics but does not differentiate between the arguments selected by unergatives and by unaccusatives. Meanwhile, the unergative/unaccusative distinction is relevant for Russian syntax, see section 3.1 below.

[17]A notable exception is the subject of the infinitival predicate which has other relevant properties, e.g., it controls coreference across clause, but not agreement; thus:

(i) a carica$_i$ xoxotat' i   Ø$_i$ upa-l-a   pod krovat'
    and queen laugh.INF and Ø fall-PAST-FEM under bed
    'So the queen started to laugh and fell under the bed.'

The distributive genitive does not control the gerund, as shown by (27c):

(27) c. *pomoščnik-ov$_j$ na-lete-l-o   k nemu,
       helper-GEN.PL DISTR-fly-PAST-NEUTER to him
       Ø$_i$ uznav   ob   oplate
       Ø having learnt about pay

In some cases, control of the gerund is facilitated if the gerund clause is fronted (Rappaport 1984). But such fronting does not improve the results for the distributive genitive, compare (27c) to (27d), which is also ungrammatical:

(27) d. *Ø$_i$ uznav   ob   oplate, pomoščnik-ov$_j$
       Ø having learnt about pay   helper-GEN.PL
       na-lete-l-o   k nemu
       DISTR-fly-PAST-NEUTER to him

Another property of Russian subjects is control of the purpose clause, illustrated by (28a) for a non-distributive subject and (28b) for a distributive nominative:

(28) a. gost-i$_i$ priexali Ø$_i$ posmotret'   novyj dom
       guest-NOM.PL arrived Ø take a look.INF new house
       'Guests arrived to see the new house.'
    b. gost-i$_i$ po+na-exa-l-i   Ø$_i$ posmotret'
       guest-NOM.PL DISTR-go-PAST-PL Ø   take a look.INF
       novyj dom
       new house
       'Many guests arrived to see the new house.'

The distributive genitive does not control the purpose clause, thus:

(28) c. *gost-ej$_i$ po+na-exa-l-o   Ø$_i$ posmotret'
       guest-GEN.PL DISTR-go-PAST-NEUTER Ø take a look.INF
       novyj dom
       new house

The subject can be the antecedent of the argument reflexive *sebja* and possessive reflexive *svoj*, thus:

(29) on$_i$ kormit sebja$_i$ i   svoix$_i$ roditelej
     he feeds   self.ACC and self's.ACC.PL parents.ACC.PL
     'He supports himself and his parents.'

Passive agents (example (30)), possessor genitives, and topics (31) can also be the antecedents of the reflexive (Padučeva 1985: 180-208; Kozinsky 1983: 15; Perlmutter 1990).

(30) ètot dvorec byl postroen sultan-om$_i$ dlja sebja$_i$ i svoej$_i$
 this palace was built sultan-INSTR for self and self's
 naložnicy
 concubine
 'This palace was built by the sultan for himself and his concubine.'

(31) ?u nego$_i$ net vzaimoponimanija so svoimi$_i$ roditeljami
 by him there is no mutual understanding with self's parents
 'There is no understanding between him and his parents.'

The distributive genitive, even if topicalized, cannot antecede the reflexive:

(32) *gost-ej$_i$ po+na-exa-l-o na svoix$_i$ mašinax
 guest-GEN.PL DISTR-arrived-PAST-NEUTER on self's cars
 'There arrived many guests in their cars.'

Another syntactic property that characterizes subjects and direct objects is control of the adjectival co-predicate in the instrumental (Kozinsky 1983: 10-12). Importantly, the predicative adjective can be controlled by both subject and direct object, which explains the ambiguity of (33c) below. The relevant adjectives include *pervyj* 'first', *poslednij* 'last', *sledujuscij* 'next', *molodoj* 'young', *staryj* 'old'. Thus:

(33) a. my$_i$ zametili ego$_j$ perv-ym-i$_i$
 we noticed him first-INSTR-PL
 'We were the first to notice him.'
 b. my$_i$ zametili ego$_j$ perv-ym$_j$
 we noticed him first-INSTR.MASC
 'We noticed him first.' (= He was the first person we noticed)
 c. oni$_i$ zametili ix$_j$ perv-ym-i$_{i/j}$ (ambiguous)
 they noticed them first-INSTR-PL
 'They$_i$ noticed them$_j$ first$_{i/j}$.'

Non-terms, including the commonly topicalized *u*-phrase, do not have this property. This is illustrated in (34a) for the *u*-phrase and in (34b) for the passive agent.

(34) a. *u nego voznikla èta mysl' perv-ym
 by him appeared this thought first-INSTR.MASC
 'This idea occurred to him first.'

b. *Kreml' byl podožžen tatar-ami perv-ym-i
Kremlin was set on fire Tatars-INSTR.PL first-INSTR.PL
'The Tatars were the first to set the Kremlin on fire.'

The distributive genitive does not have this property either; compare (35a), where the distributive nominative controls *pervyj*, and the ill-formed (35b), with the distributive genitive:

(35) a. det-i na-bilis' v zal perv-ym-i
children-NOM DISTR-packed.PL.REFL in hall first-INSTR-PL
'Children were the first to fill up the hall.'
b. *det-ej na-bilos' v zal
children-GEN DISTR-packed.NEUTER.REFL in hall
perv-ym-i
first-INSTR-PL
'Children were the first to fill up the hall.'

Thus, the distributive genitive has no subject properties.[18]

2.2. Arguments that the distributive genitive is a non-term

Direct objects in Russian can become subjects of the passive, control the adjectival co-predicate in the instrumental (33b, c), can control the infinitival purpose clause, and can marginally antecede the reflexive (Timberlake 1979). Next, Russian has a varied group of arguments, coded by the dative, which can control the purpose clause (only in the absence of a direct object) and can marginally antecede the reflexive (Timberlake 1979; Perlmutter 1990; Polinsky 1993b; Polinsky to appear). These properties overlap with the subject properties discussed in the preceding section. As was shown above, the distributive genitive has none of these properties. Thus, it cannot be characterized as an object.

Since it is syntactically inactive, the distributive genitive qualifies as a non-term. However, it also differs from other non-terms.

2.3. Differences between the distributive genitive and other non-terms

1) CONTROL OF REFLEXIVES. Unlike other non-terms, the distributive genitive cannot control reflexivization. This inability to serve as the

---

[18]Another characteristic of Russian subjects is that only subjects can be controlled in infinitival complement constructions (Perlmutter 1990: 25). However, this property cannot be checked for the distributive genitive because it would be indistinguishable from a nominative nominal occurring with a distributive infinitive:

(i) *gostjam ne xvatit naglosti Ø po+na-exat' sjuda
guests.DAT.PL NEG will suffice impudence.GEN Ø DISTR-arrive.INF here
'Guests won't dare arrive here in large numbers.'

antecedent of a reflexive distinguishes the distributive genitive from the passive agent (see (30) above), the possessor genitive, and some other presumable non-terms, which can all be antecedents of a reflexive (Polinsky to appear).

2) LICENSING OF THE NULL WORD. The distributive genitive differs from other non-terms in that it does not license the non-specific null word (see section 1.3 above). Compare the licensing of the null word by the passive agent in (36b), and the ungrammaticality of such licensing by the distributive genitive in (37b):

(36) a. demonstrant byl zaderžan milici-ej
demonstrator was detained militia-INSTR
'The demonstrator was detained by the militia.'
b. demonstrant byl zaderžan $\emptyset_{\exists x}$
demonstrator was detained
'The demonstrator was detained (by someone).'
(37) a. smotri, na jabloki na-lete-l-o ptic-ø
look on apples DISTR-fly-PAST-NEUTER bird-GEN.PL
'Look, birds flew over to the apples.'
b. *na jabloki na-lete-l-o $\emptyset_{\exists x}$
on apples DISTR-fly-PAST-NEUTER

As in Kinyarwanda, the ban on the non-specific null word in the distributive construction indicates that the distributive genitive has the complement, not adjunct, status.

3) RELATIVIZATION. In Russian, both terms and non-terms can relativize on a relative clause introduced by *kotor-* 'which, who'. For example, the passive agent 'by militia' in (36a) can relativize as in (38):

(38) milicija kotor-oj byl zaderžan demonstrant
militia REL-INSTR.FEM was detained demonstrator
'the militia by whom the demonstrator was detained'

Example (39) illustrates the relativization of the locative phrase *v zal*, occurring in (37a); this phrase is a default non-term:

(39) zal v kotor-yj nabilos' zritelej
hall in REL-ACC.MASC packed spectators
'the hall which was filled by spectators'

Next, a number of genitive nominals can relativize, for example, possessor genitive (as in (40a)). In standard Russian, it relativizes with the relativizer *čej* 'whose', as in (40b); in spoken Russian, it also relativizes with the relativizer *kotoryj*, as in (40c):

(40) a. sobaka moego prijatelja ubežala
     dog my.GEN friend.GEN ran away
     'My friend's dog ran away.'
   b. moj prijatel' č'ja sobaka ubežala
     my friend whose dog ran away
     'my friend whose dog ran away'
   c. moj prijatel' sobaka kotor-ogo ubežala
     my friend dog REL-GEN.MASC ran away
     'my friend whose dog ran away'

Unlike terms and other non-terms, the distributive genitive does not control relativization. Thus, (41b) is ill-formed:

(41) a. zritel-ej na-beža-l-o v zal
     spectator-GEN.PL DISTR-run-PAST-NEUTER in hall
     'Spectators packed the hall.'
   b. *zriteli, kotor-yx
     spectators.NOM.PL REL-GEN.PL
     na-beža-l-o v zal
     DISTR-run-PAST-NEUTER in hall
     'spectators who packed the hall'

4) WH-WORD. In Russian, non-terms can license Wh-word, either moved or in situ, as illustrated by (42a, b) for the passive agent (the corresponding passive sentence is given in (36a) above):

(42) a. kem byl zaderžan demonstrant?
     whom.INSTR was detained demonstrator
   b. demonstrant byl zaderžan kem?
     demonstrator was detained whom.INSTR
     'By whom was the demonstrator detained?'

Unlike other non-terms, though, the distributive genitive cannot license a Wh-word; thus, examples (43a, b), which correspond to the declarative sentence in (41a), are ungrammatical regardless of the position of the question word.

(43) a. *kogo na-beža-l-o v zal?
     who.GEN DISTR-run-PAST-NEUTER in hall
   b. *v zal na-beža-l-o kogo?
     in hall DISTR-run-PAST-NEUTER who.GEN
     'Who packed the hall?'

5) MODIFICATION BY A RELATIVE CLAUSE.[19] The distributive genitive, unlike terms and other non-terms, cannot be modified by the descriptive relative clause introduced by *takoj ... čto* 'such that'. Compare the grammatical (44a) with the distributive nominative and (44b), which is either ill-formed or marginal (for some speakers):

(44) a. v sad   na-lete-l-a   takaja   saranč-a,
         in garden DISTR-fly-PAST-FEM such.NOM locusts-NOM.SG
         čto daže naša sobaka ispugalas'
         that even our dog   got scared
         'Such locusts filled the orchard that even our dog got scared.'
   b. */?v sad   na-lete-l-o   takoj
         in garden DISTR-fly-PAST-NEUTER such.GEN
         saranč-i   čto daže naša sobaka ispugalas'
         locusts-GEN that even our dog   got scared
         'There were such locusts in the orchard that even our dog got scared.'

For some speakers, the distributive clause with the genitive can take the verbal modifier clause introduced by *tak ... čto* 'so that'. Example (45) shows the *tak ... čto* clause modifying a VP that consists of a single verb; in (46), the same type of clause modifies the verb and the distributive genitive:

(45)   on tak govorit čto ničego neponjatno
       he so speaks that nothing ununderstandable
       'He speaks in such a way (so) that it is impossible to understand.'
(46)   %v sad   tak naletelo saranči, čto daže naša sobaka ispugalas'
       in orchard so flew in locusts that even our dog   got scared
       'The orchard got so filled with locusts that even our dog got scared.'

Thus, the distributive genitive differs from other non-terms and requires a special analysis.

The results obtained for the inverted nominal in Kinyarwanda and for the distributive genitive in Russian are quite similar: in both languages, the respective nominal corresponds to a subject in another construction, has neither subject properties nor any term properties, and differs from other non-terms in several syntactic effects. Unlike other non-terms, it cannot license the non-specific null word, which is indicative of the fact that this nominal is an obligatory complement of the verb and not an adjunct.

---

[19]This dissimilarity between the distributive genitive and other non-terms is weaker than the others because it is attested only in some idiolects of Russian.

3. Subject Inversion in Kinyarwanda and Distributive Genitive in Russian: Toward a unified analysis

This section will present a unified analysis of the two clause types discussed in this paper. I begin with several constraints on the predicates in the SI clause in Kinyarwanda and in the distributive clause in Russian (section 3.1). Section 3.2 argues for the VP-internal status of the inverted and distributive nominals, and section 3.3 presents evidence in favor of an Incorporation analysis of these nominals.

3.1. Predicate restrictions

There are several important restrictions on the type of predicate that can occur in the SI and distributive clauses discussed here. Despite the differences between the two constructions, these restrictions are similar in Kinyarwanda and Russian.

1) TRANSITIVITY RESTRICTION. First, the verb in the SI construction has to be genuinely intransitive or detransitivized by passivization or antipassivization. Evidence for this restriction in Kinyarwanda and Kirundi is presented in (Polinsky 1993a); see also (Bresnan and Kanerva 1989) for Chichewa). Similarly, in Russian, the subjective genitive can occur only in an intransitive or passive clause. The construction does not allow transitive or middle verbs, even with the unexpressed object, as shown by (47a, b) (see also Polinsky to appear).[20]

(47) a. *detej po+na-kupi-l-o morožénoe
children-GEN.PL DISTR-buy-PAST-NEUTER ice cream
'Lots of children bought ice cream.'
b. *na rynke na-torg+uet žulik-ov
on market DISTR-trade+FUT.3SG cheater-GEN.PL
'There will be a lot of cheaters trading at the market.'

Thus, the Subject Inversion and the subjective distributive construction are possible only with intransitive or detransitivized verbs.

2) STAGE-LEVEL RESTRICTION. Carlson's (1977) distinction between individual- and stage-level predicates was introduced as a primarily semantic contrast between more or less permanent and temporary/transitory activities and states. From the semantic standpoint, Russian distributive verbs are undoubtedly stage-level: their telic/perfective characteristic implies a temporal limit to the respective activity and rules out the permanent (individual-level) interpretation.

---

[20]If the distributive verb is transitive, only the object can be coded by the distributive genitive, see (23b) above.

In Kinyarwanda, the impossibility of individual-level predicates in SI can also be illustrated by the following example:

(48) *ha-ø-komer-a aba-antu muri iyi inzu
CL16-PRES-be strong-IMPF CL2-person in this house
'There are people strong in this house.'

In addition to semantics, the stage- and individual-level contrast has been shown to have syntactic corollaries (Kratzer 1989; Diesing 1992: Ch. 2). Specifically, it has been suggested that stage- and individual-level predicates have a different argument structure: stage-level predicates have a SPATIO-TEMPORAL (EVENT) argument, while individual-level predicates lack such an argument. Locative modifiers represent a particular case of the event argument. As was shown above, the locative modifier is obligatorily expressed or is contextually recoverable in the Subject Inversion and distributive construction, which proves that the predicate in these constructions has the stage-level interpretation.

3) UNACCUSATIVITY. The relationship between Locative (Subject) Inversion and unaccusativity has been subject of much debate: on the one hand, the inversion construction often has the unaccusative character, on the other, certain unergative verbs (verbs of motion, verbs of light and sound emission) can also appear under Inversion (Hoekstra and Mulder 1990; Levin and Hovav 1994). It seems that the discussion is further complicated by the existence of two opposite approaches to unaccusativity itself, either as a syntactic phenomenon (Perlmutter 1978; Rosen 1984; Levin and Hovav 1994) or as a semantic phenomenon, also described as "split intransitivity" (VanValin 1990). In this paper, I assume that unaccusativity is tied to a specific syntactic configuration but may also have regular semantic corollaries. Thus, the syntactic criterion is given precedence, but semantics can also reflect the same distinction.

Both languages discussed here have syntactic correlates of the unaccusative/unergative distinctions. In Kinyarwanda, unaccusatives form the morphological causative with the help of the suffix -*y*-, while unergatives and transitive verbs form the causative with the suffix -*íish*- (Kimenyi 1980: 77; Overdulve 1975: 209-210; Polinsky in preparation).

The relevant question is whether unergatives can appear in the SI construction. The causative of intransitive is transitive, therefore, this causative cannot occur in the SI construction (see above on transitivity restrictions). However, if this causative is passivized, it meets the necessary condition on the types of predicates allowed under Subject Inversion.

Example (49a) shows that the verb *kuríriimba* 'sing' is indeed unergative, as it causativizes on -*íish*-. Example (49b) illustrates the passive of the causative appearing in (49a).

(49) a. umugore ya-ø-ríriimb-íish-ije abashyítsi
woman CL1-PAST-sing-CAUS-PF guests
'The woman made the guests sing.'
b. aba-shyítsi ba-ø-ríriimb-íish-ijw-e (n'umugore)
CL2-guest CL2-PROGR-sing-CAUS-PASS-PF by woman
'The guests were made to sing (by the woman).'

The passive causative in (49b) can undergo Subject Inversion, as shown by (50):

(50) mu gisagâra ha-ø-ríriimb-íish-ijw-e abashyítsi
in village CL16-PAST-sing-CAUS-PASS-PF guests
'In the village, guest were made to sing.'

Importantly, the verb in (50) can only form its causative as an unergative and cannot causativize on the -y- suffix, as an unaccusative; thus, (51) is ungrammatical:

(51) *ha-ø-riríimb-yi+jw-e abashyítsi
CL16-PAST-sing-CAUS.UNACCUSATIVE+PASS-PF guests
'Guests were made to sing.' (lit.: There were made to sing guests)

If, indeed, it were possible to form two different causatives from the verb 'sing', namely, *kuriríimb-íish-a* and **kuririimbya*, we could posit two homonymous verbs 'sing', one unergative and the other unaccusative. This solution is ruled out by the ungrammaticality of the second causative.

In Russian, unaccusativity interacts with negation: only direct objects and subjects of unaccusatives can be coded by the genitive of negation (Pesetsky 1982: 40-90; Perlmutter 1990: 28-31); compare the well-formed (52b) and the ungrammatical (53b):

(52) a. grib-y zdes' ne rastut
mushroom-NOM.PL here NEG grow
'Mushrooms don't grow here.'
b. grib-ov zdes' ne rastët
mushroom-GEN.PL here NEG grows
'Mushrooms don't grow here.'
(53) a. det-i zdes' ne igrajut
children-NOM.PL here NEG play
b. *det-ej zdes' ne igraet
children-GEN.PL here NEG plays
'Children don't play here.'

Non-distributive verbs of motion are unergative and do not take the genitive of negation; this is illustrated, in (54a), by the impossibility of the genitive of negation with *priexat'* 'arrive'. The corresponding distributive verb does not allow the genitive of negation either, as shown by (54b):[21]

(54) a. *det-ej   ne   priexalo
      children-GEN.PL NEG arrived
      'Children didn't come.'
   b. *det-ej   ne   po+na-exalo
      children-GEN.PL NEG DISTR-arrived
      'Children didn't come.'

In the debate about Locative Inversion, two approaches to the unaccusativity problem have been proposed: the construction should be interpreted as an invalid unaccusative diagnostic or as a construction where an otherwise unergative verb appears as an unaccusative (see Levin and Hovav 1994: chapter 6, for an extensive review and discussion of the problem). The Kinyarwanda data rules out the second interpretation, and the Russian material provides evidence in favor of the first solution: the unaccusative test does not apply to the distributive construction, which otherwise resembles the Inversion construction.

4) AGENTIVITY RESTRICTION. So far, I have been concerned with the syntactic characteristics of verbs occurring in the SI and distributive constructions. In this section, I will look at a semantic characteristic of these constructions, namely, the co-occurrence with agentive adverbials.

Though some verbs that appear in the SI and in the distributive constructions have the agentive interpretation (for example, 'sing', 'dance', verbs of motion), the constructions do not allow agentive adverbials such as 'purposely', 'vigorously', 'willingly', etc.. Thus, Kinyarwanda (55b) and Russian (56b) are ungrammatical. Meanwhile, as it is shown by (55a) and (56a), the same verbs can co-occur with agentive adverbials in a regular intransitive construction without subject demotion:

---

[21]In general, distributive constructions are hard to negate. This difficulty in negation is due to the propositional structure of the construction, which is a subtype of the existential predication. In the distributive clause, the verb and the genitive constitute a single assertion (the propositional structure, in its turn, can be derived from the syntactic structure discussed in 3.3). Keeping the genitive nominal outside the scope of negation destroys this propositional structure (Polinsky to appear). The best way of negating a distributive clause is by embedding it under the matrix negation; then, the verb and the genitive nominal are in the scope of negation. Thus:

(i) nepravda, čto ponaexalo detej
     wrong   that arrived   children
     'It is not true that there arrived a lot of children.'

Similar results are observed for SI in Kinyarwanda: the only way to negate an SI clause is by embedding it under the matrix negative verb.

(55) Kinyarwanda
a. abashyitsi barariríimba nkána   (mu gisagâra)
    guests   are singing purposely iñ village
    'The guests are singing (in the village) on purpose.'
b. *mu gisagâra harariríimba   abashyitsi nkána
    in village there is singing guests   purposely
    'In the village, guests are purposely singing.'

(56) Russian
a. deti   naročno   priexali v samoe neudobnoe vremja
    children purposely arrived in most inconvenient time
    'The children purposely came at the most inconvenient time.'
b. *det-ej   naročno   po+na-exa-l-o
    children-GEN.PL purposely DISTR-arrive-PAST-NEUTER
    v samoe neudobnoe   vremja[22]
    in most inconvenient time

The non-occurrence with agentive adverbials is a common semantic correlate of syntactic unaccusativity;[23] however, it was just shown that unergatives can occur in SI in Kinyarwanda, and that the unaccusative diagnostic does not apply to the distributive construction in Russian. Thus, this type of correspondence of syntactic and semantic features is irrelevant here.

Alternatively, the non-occurrence of agentive adverbials in SI and in the distributive construction may be explained in the following way. Agentive adverbials characterize the action performed by the referent of the demoted subject, which presumably may have thematic role agent; the demotion of this argument leads to the suppression of its agentive characteristics, which prevents the occurrence of the respective adverbials (for a similar semantic analysis, see Kirsner 1979: 95). Note that adverbials characterizing the entire situation, not just the action performed by the argument of the verb, occur freely in both languages:

(57) Kinyarwanda
    mu gisagâra ha-rariríimba abashyitsi byiíza
    in village is singing   guests   pleasantly
    'There is pleasant singing by the guests in the village.'

(58) Russian
    neožidanno v komnatu naletelo   ptic
    suddenly   in room   flew.DISTR birds.GEN.PL
    'Suddenly the room filled with birds.'

---

[22]The construction with the distributive nominative does not allow the agentive adverbial either; see Polinsky (to appear).

[23]Being a semantic correspondence of unaccusativity, this feature alone does not constitute an unaccusative diagnostic (Polinsky 1990: 354-355).

3.2. The inverted and distributive nominal as VP-internal arguments

As was shown in the preceding section, the predicate of the SI and distributive construction has stage-level characteristics only. Stage-level predicates can, in theory, have either external arguments (in GB terms, adjoined to [Spec, IP]) or internal arguments (adjoined to [Spec, VP]). If the argument of the stage-level predicate is external, it can have its own modifier; if the argument is internal to the VP, only predicate modification is possible (see also Kratzer 1989). The contrast is illustrated by the following English examples, where in (59a), the nominal is external and in (59b), internal to the VP; the parentheses indicate the scope of modification:

(59) a. all the (students in this class) got sick
     b. all the students (got sick in this class)

Kinyarwanda example (6b) above illustrated the impossibility of 'only' modifying the nominal 'guests': in this example, 'only' modifies the predicate, thus:

(6) b. muri iyi inzu harasiinziira abashyitsi gusa
        'The only thing happening in this house is that guests are sleeping.'
        *'There are only guests (and nobody else) sleeping in this house.'

The VP-internal status of the inverted nominal and the distributive genitive allows us to explain a number of facts discussed above, namely: the restriction on transitive verbs, whose agent has to be VP-external (3.1.1); the ban on agentive adverbials, which normally modify the external agent but cannot reach this nominal if it is internal to the VP (3.1.4);[24] for Russian, the possibility of the predicate modifier clause introduced by *tak ... cto* and the ill-formedness of the clause that modifies the distributive genitive alone (2.3).

Thus, the following condition can be formulated on the Subject Inversion and distributive construction: these constructions are allowed only with the VP-internal argument. As to the thematic role of this internal argument, it remains possible that this argument is an agent, with agentivity suppressed, probably due to the VP-internal status.

Being internal to the verbal phrase does not exhaustively describe the relationship between the verbal phrase and this argument. In the next section, I will discuss the possible analyses of this relationship.

---

[24]This also explains, trivially, why the adverbials modifying the proposition and not just the agent are allowed in the SI and in the distributive constructions: they modify the head verb with its internal elements (57), (58).

3.3. Incorporation Analysis

A possible argument about the relationship between the verb and the internal argument would be the interpretation of this argument as the VP-internal subject, along the lines of the VP-internal subject hypothesis, developed within the GB framework (Kuroda 1988; Chomsky 1991).

Some recent publications have discussed differences between VP-external and VP-internal subjects in several languages. Thus, for German, it has been argued that VP-internal subjects are accessible to certain extraction processes and to topicalization (Diesing 1992: 32-37). For several Austronesian languages, it has been argued that extraction and quantifier float characterize external subjects, while reflexivization and control, as theta-sensitive properties, characterize VP-internal subjects (Guilfoyle et al. 1992). Even if we ignore the disagreement between individual languages (which may be tentatively explained by the distinction between right- and left-branching languages), it is obvious that the VP-internal subject has at least some properties indicative of syntactic activity.

As for the nominals examined above, it was shown that they are syntactically even more inactive than some other non-terms. In particular, they do cannot serve as antecedents of reflexives (8b), (32); have no control properties (7b), (28c); do not extract (39c), or relativize (10), (43). Thus, it would be implausible to identify these nominals as VP-internal subjects because this would require a separate set of rules determining suppression of subject properties. On the other hand, these nominals consistently differ from other non-terms in the two languages.

The status of the inverted nominal and of the distributive genitive can be adequately explained under the Incorporation analysis. A detailed discussion of Incorporation within the GB framework is given in Baker (1988); see also Marantz (1984). Analyses based on other syntactic approaches are given in Mithun (1984) and Sadock (1986); a comprehensive review of different approaches can be found in (Spencer 1991: 262-296).

Under the Incorporation analysis, the verb and the nominal form a SINGLE CONSTITUENT, which in this case is a compound predicate. Structurally, the compound has the same syntactic function as the head element, while the incorporated element loses the syntactic function that the free element has in the corresponding construction.[25]

The Incorporation analysis is compatible with the non-term status of the inverted nominal in Kinyarwanda and the distributive genitive in

---

[25]The incorporated nominal does maintain a certain projection into clausal syntax: it can have certain, semantically restricted, free modifiers in the clause structure (Polinsky 1993c, on Kinyarwanda; Polinsky to appear, on Russian). As I demonstrate in the cited papers, the syntactic analysis of the relationship between the incorporated head and its free modifiers can be maintained in terms of discontinuous constituency (see also Dahlstrom 1986).

Russian. It also accounts for the inability of these nominals to license the null word (18), (37b). The null word can be licensed either by the head element (in this case, the verb, thus, the result would be verbal gapping) or by the whole compound, but not the non-head constituent alone. Next, the Incorporation analysis explains why only predicate modification is allowed in these constructions (6b), (44b), (46), (57), (58) and why agentive adverbials cannot occur even with presumably agentive verbs (55b), (56b).

The superficial problem that this analysis may face is that Incorporation in Kinyarwanda and Russian does not have a clear morphological realization. This problem is resolved differently for the two languages discussed here.

In Kinyarwanda, there is indeed evidence of the morphological fusion of the verb and the inverted nominal. The arguments in favor of such fusion come from phrasal phonology (see example (12) above) and from the ban on lexical material intervening between the verb and the postposed nominal (16a, b). Thus, the Incorporation does find morphological realization, though the degree of fusion between the verb and the incorporated element is less than in such incorporating languages as Chukchee (Polinsky 1990), Eskimo (Sadock 1986), or Southern Tiwa (Allen et al. 1990). In these languages, the incorporated element is positioned between the inflectional morphemes; in Kinyarwanda, all the verbal suffixes precede the incorporated nominal.

In Russian, the fusion between the verb and the distributive genitive is much less obvious; the verb and the genitive remain separate words, the genitive can be fronted and or separated from the verb by light lexical material. However, unlike other non-terms, it cannot extract into the matrix clause and cannot cross over heavy parentheticals (Polinsky to appear). This type of complex predicate formation, which is not accompanied by overt fusion, can be accounted for as Abstract Incorporation or Reanalysis (Baker 1988). Under Abstract Incorporation, the nominal still forms a single constituent with the verb, but this constituent can be realized as a discontinuous one.

This analysis means that both the Kinyarwanda and the Russian constructions discussed here have the same basic structure. In this basic structure, the verb and the nominal form a single clause constituent, a compound predicate. This structural analysis then explains the communicative features of the construction: the compound predicate forms a single focus, and the locative, temporal, or possessive argument is easily topicalized. The fusion of the verb and the predicate also explains why they form a single assertion rather than different elements of the proposition (see fn. 21).

The construction with the incorporated nominal corresponds to a non-incorporation construction, where the respective nominal is an intransitive subject (see example (4a) for Kinyarwanda, (22a) for Russian). If a stratal representation is assumed, for example, in Relational Grammar terms, the representation of the SI and distributive construction will be:[26]

(60) P   1
    P   chô

This links the SI construction and the distributive genitive construction to the constructions with incorporated intransitive subject found in Southern Tiwa (Allen et al. 1990: 330-333, 336-338) and in Chukchee (Polinsky 1990). The only difference, again, is in the degree of fusion between the verb and the incorporated nominal. It is possible then to establish a cross-linguistic continuum of Noun Incorporation, with languages like Chukchee, Eskimo, and Southern Tiwa representing the highest degree of verb-nominal fusion, and languages like Russian at the other extreme, representing Abstract Incorporation.

References

Allen, Barbara, Donald Frantz, Donna Gardiner, and David Perlmutter. 1990. Verb Agreement, Possessor Ascension, and Multistratal Representation in Southern Tiwa. *Studies in Relational Grammar 3*, ed. by Paul M. Postal and Brian D. Joseph, 321-384. Chicago: The University of Chicago Press.

Babby, Leonard. 1980a. *Existential Sentences and Negation in Russian*. Ann Arbor: Karoma.

Babby, Leonard. 1980b. The Syntax of Surface Case Marking. *Cornell Working Papers in Linguistics* 1: 1-32.

Baker, Mark. 1988. *Incorporation: A Theory of Grammatical Function Changing*. Chicago: The University of Chicago Press.

Bresnan, Joan and Jonni Kanerva. 1989. Locative Inversion in Chichewa: A Case Study of Factorization in Grammar. *Linguistic Inquiry* 20: 1-50.

Carlson, Greg. 1977. *Reference to Kinds in English*. Ph. D. Dissertation, University of Massachussets, Amherst.

Chomsky, Noam. 1991. Some Notes on Economy of Derivation and Representation. *Principles and Parameters in Comparative Grammar*, ed. by Robert Freidin, 417-454. Cambridge: MIT Press.

Chvany, Catherine. 1975. *On the Syntax of Be-sentences in Russian*. Cambridge: Slavica.

Dahlstrom, Amy. 1987. Discontinuous Constituents in Fox. *Native American Languages and Grammatical Typology*, ed. by Paul Kroeber and Robert Moore, 53-73. IULC.

---

[26]Because the unaccusative diagnostic may not apply to the constructions discussed here, I leave open the question whether the first stratum in (60) has to be preceded by the unaccusative stratum (P 2).

Diesing, Molly. 1992. *Indefinites.* (*Linguistic Inquiry Monographs,* 20.). Cambridge: MIT Press.
Dressler, Wolfgang. 1968. *Studien zur verbalen Pluralität. Iterativum, Distributivum, Durativum, Intensivum in der allgemeinen Grammatik, im Lateinsichen und Hethitischen.* Wien: Carl Winter.
Franks, Steven. to appear. Parametric Properties of Numeral Phrases in Slavic. *Natural Language and Linguistic Theory.*
Freeze, Ray. 1992. Existentials and Other Locatives. *Language* 68: 553-595.
Gerdts, Donna B. and Lindsay Whaley. 1991. Locatives vs. Instrumentals in Kinyarwanda. *Proceedings of the Seventeenth Annual Meeting of the Berkeley Linguistics Society: Special Session on African Language Structures,* ed. by K. Hubbard, 87-97. Berkeley: The University of California Press.
Gerdts, Donna B. and Lindsay Whaley. 1992a. Kinyarwanda Multiple Applicatives and the 2-AEX. *Papers from the 28th Regional Meeting of the Chicago Linguistic Society,* 186-205.
Gerdts, Donna B. and Lindsay Whaley. 1992b. Two Types of Oblique Applicatives in Kinyarwanda. *Proceedings of the Western Conference on Linguistics* 1991, ed. by K. Hunt et al., 138-151. Fresno: The California State University Press.
Guilfoyle, Eithne, Henrietta Hung, and Lisa Travis. 1992. Spec of IP and Spec of VP: Two Subjects in Austronesian Languages. *Natural Langage and Linguistic Theory* 10: 375-414.
Hetzron, Robert. 1971. Presentative Function and Presentative Movement. *Studies in African Linguistics, Supplement* 2: 79-105.
Hetzron, Robert. 1975. The Presentative Movement, or Why the Ideal Word Order Is VSOP. *Word Order and Word Order Change,* ed. by Charles N. Li, 345-388. Austin: University of Texas Press.
Hoekstra, Teun and René Mulder. 1990. Unergatives as Copular Verbs; Locational and Existential predication. *The Linguistic Review* 7: 1-79.
Kimenyi, Alexandre. 1979. *Studies in Kinyarwanda and Bantu Phonology.* Carbondale-Edmonton: Linguistic Research.
Kimenyi, Alexandre. 1980. *A Relational Grammar of Kinyarwanda.* (*UCLA Publications in Linguistics,* 91.). Berkeley-Los Angeles: The University of California Press.
Kirsner, Robert. 1979. *The Problem of Presentative Sentences in Modern Dutch.* Amsterdam: North Holland.
Knjazev, Jurij P. 1989. Vyražrenie povtorjaemosti dejstvija v russkom i drugix slavjanskix jazykax. *Tipologija iterativnyx konstrukcij,* ed. by Victor S. Xrakovsky, 132-145. Leningrad: Nauka.
Kozinsky, Isaac. 1983. *O kategorii "podležaščee" v russkom jazyke.* (*Int-t russkogo jazyka. PGÈPL. Preprint,* 156.) Moscow.
Kratzer, Angelika. 1989. Stage and Individual Level Predicates. *Papers on Quantification.* University of Massachussets, Amherst.

Kuroda, S.-Yuki. 1988. Whether We Agree or Not: A Comparative Syntax of English and Japanese. *Linguisticae Investigationes* 12: 1-47.
Levin, Beth, and Malka Rappaport Hovav. 1994. *Unaccusativity: At the Syntax-Semantics Interface.* Cambridge: MIT Press.
Marantz, Alec. 1984. *On the Nature of Grammatical Relations.* Cambridge: MIT Press.
Mithun, Marianne. 1984. The Evolution of Noun Incorporation. *Language* 60: 847-895.
Neidle, Carol. 1988. *The Role of Case in Russian Syntax.* Dordrecht: Kluwer.
Overdulve, C. M. 1975. *Apprendre la langue rwanda.* The Hague-Paris: Mouton.
Padučeva, Elena V. 1985. *Vyskazyvanie i ego sootnesennost' s dejstvitel'nost'ju.* Moscow: Nauka.
Perlmutter, David. 1978. Impersonal Passives and the Unaccusative Hypothesis. *Berkeley Linguistic Society. Annual Meeting* 4: 157-189.
Perlmutter, David. 1990. *Demotions to Object, the Successor Demotion Ban, and the Class of Careers.* MS, UCSD.
Pesetsky, David. 1982. *Paths and Categories.* Ph. D. Dissertation, MIT.
Polinsky, Maria. 1990. Subject Incorporation: Evidence form Chukchee. *Grammatical Relations. A Cross-theoretical Perspective*, ed. by Katarzyna Dziwirek, Patrick Farrel, and Errapel Mejías-Bikandi, 349-364. Stanford: CSLI.
Polinsky, Maria. 1993a. Locative Inversion and Related Constructions. *Proceedings of the Western Conference on Linguistics 1992*, ed. by Vida Samiian. Fresno: California State University Press.
Polinsky, Maria. 1993b. *Oblique Objects as Terms: Evidence from Kinyarwanda and Kirundi.* Paper presented at the LSA Annual Meeting, Los Angeles.
Polinsky, Maria. 1993c. Subject Inversion and Intransitive Subject Incorporation. *Papers from the 29th Regional Meeting of the Chicago Linguistic Society.*
Polinsky, Maria. 1995. Double Objects in Causatives: Towards a Study of Coding Conflict. *Studies in Language* 25.
Polinsky, Maria. to appear. *Ponaexalo tut vas*: Russian Distributive Clauses with the Bare Genitive. *Proceedings of the Second Workshop on Formal Approaches to Slavic Linguistics*, ed. by Steven Franks.
Polinsky, Maria, in preparation. *Unaccusativity in Kinyarwanda.*
Polinsky, Maria, and Isaac Kozinsky 1992. Ditransitive Constructions in Kinyarwanda: Coding Conflict or Syntactic Doubling? *Papers from the 28th Regional Meeting of the Chicago Linguistic Society*, 426-442.
Rappaport, Gilbert. 1984. *Grammatical Function and Syntactic Structure: The Adverbial Participle of Russian.* Columbus: Slavica.
Rosen, Carol. 1984. The Interface between Semantic Roles and Initial Grammatical Relations. *Studies in Relational Grammar 2*, ed. by

David Perlmutter and Carol Rosen, 38-77. Chicago: The University of Chicago Press.
Sadock, Jerrold. 1986. Some Notes on Noun Incorporation. *Language* 62: 19-31.
Spencer, Andrew. 1991. *Morphological theory. An Introduction to Word Structure in Generative Grammar.* Oxford: Blackwell.
Timberlake A. 1979. Reflexivization and the Cycle in Russian. *Linguistic Inquiry* 10: 109-141.
Timberlake A. 1980. Oblique Control of Russian Reflexivization. *Morphosyntax in Slavic*, ed. by Catherine Chvany and Richard Brecht, 88-110. Columbus: Slavica.
Van Valin, Robert D. 1990. Semantic Parameters of Split Intransitivity. *Language* 66: 221-240.

A Glance at French Pseudopassives

PAUL M. POSTAL

New York University

The ostensible defining characteristic of English pseudopassives like (1), is that the superficial subject of an otherwise straightforward passive clause corresponds to the head of a headless prepositional phrase (PP), yielding a 'stranded' preposition.

(1) a. Anthony was voted against by most of the population.
     b. Such subjects should not be talked about in public.
     c. Civilians should not be fired at.

So in the nonpassive correspondents of (1) in (2), the analogs of the subjects head the relevant PPs.

(2) a. Most of the population voted against Anthony.
     b. One should not talk about such subjects in public.
     c. One should not fire at civilians.

It is commonly assumed that pseudopassives involve 'reanalysis', with preposition incorporation into the verbal complex somehow rendering a PP object equivalent to a direct object (Chomsky (1975: 242 n 43;1981: 123, 292–300), Riemsdijk (1978: 215ff), Hornstein and Weinberg (1981), Williams (1980: 204), Bresnan (1982), Kayne (1984: XII, 45, 65, 82, 114–116, 123), Riemsdijk and Williams (1986: 203), Lasnik and Saito (1992: 206). Were this the proper treatment of English pseudopassives, I would not be discussing them. But in Postal (1986: Ch. 6) I presented never answered arguments that 'reanalysis' does not exist and sketched an alternative treatment in the Arc Pair Grammar framework of Johnson and Postal (1980), now Metagraph Grammar. Unfortunately, the present discussion involves appeal to technical aspects of the framework, which it is unreasonable to assume are known but which space precludes explicating.

In the Metagraph analysis of pseudopassives in Postal (1986), nominals bearing diverse grammatical relations advance to direct object, leaving associated invisible copy pronouns that are the heads of the PPs. Subsequent theoretical refinement of that analysis gives example (3a) Metagraph structure (3b).

(3)   a. Peter was talked to by the guard.
      b. = revision of <6.28> of Postal (1986)

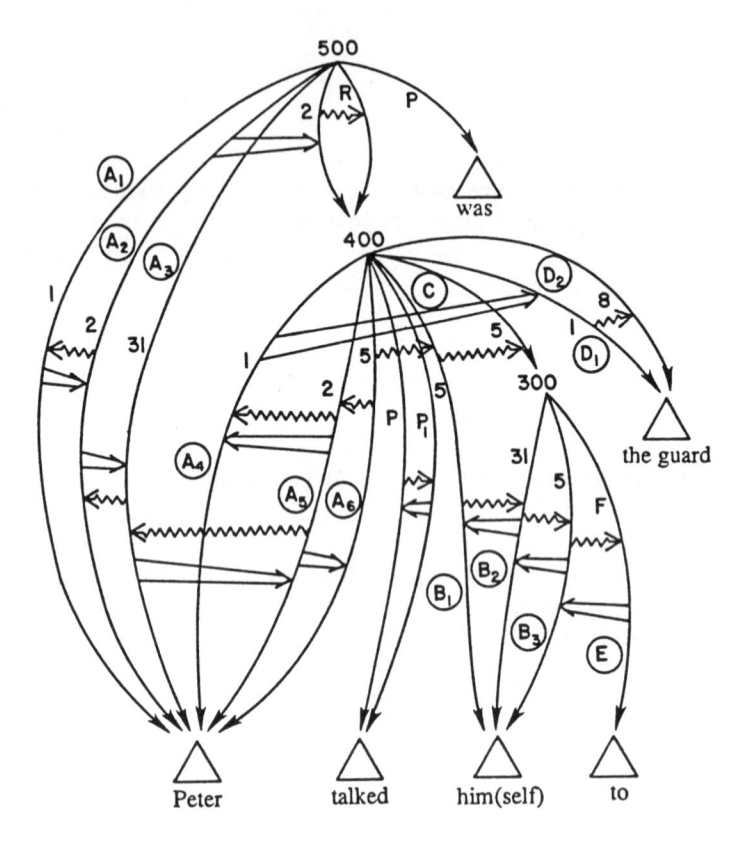

My goal is not to justify (3b) but only to clarify the kind of object it is. Diagram (3b) consists first of nonterminal NODES represented as arbitrary numbers, 500, etc. linked by curved oriented EDGES labelled with circled capital letters. The labels are simply a convenience. The orientation is represented by the arrowheads. These edges represent primitive LINES, each associated with some RELATIONAL SIGN (R-sign). The interpretation is that the HEAD node, occurring at the arrowhead, bears the primitive grammatical relation named by the associated R-sign to the TAIL node. (4) lists relevant R-signs and named relations.

(4)   **Relation**   **R-sign**

    a. Nominal

        subject   1
        direct object   2
        indirect object   3
        subobject   4
        semiobject   5
        quasiobject   6
        chomeur   8

    b. Predicational

        predicate   P
        primary subpredicate P_1
        union$_1$ U_1

    c. Other

        escape   31
        flag   F
        pronominal clitic   ¢

So in (3b), the arrow labelled A$_6$ indicates that *Peter* bears the semiobject relation to node 400. Arrows A$_5$ and A$_4$ specify that this nominal bears other relations to that node. A quadruple consisting of an edge, its R-sign, and its head and tail nodes is called an ARC.

In addition to arcs, (3b) manifests broken and double arrows. Where the smooth single arrows link nodes, these connect arcs and represent the two primitive metagrammatical relations posited in Metagraph grammar, SPONSOR and ERASE. In the current formulation, not all arcs are sponsored, that is, lie at the heads of broken sponsor arrows. Unsponsored arcs like A$_6$ are called INITIAL. That A sponsors B means A's existence is a necessary condition for B's. The interpretation of Erase is that it picks out from the collection of all arcs a subgraph called the SURFACE GRAPH, roughly all and only the unerased arcs. In (3b), although the nominal *Peter* heads six arcs, all are erased except A$_1$, which gives the surface status of that phrase: main clause subject.

Structure (3b) meets the assumed proper definition of passive clause in (6), formulated on the basis of the definitions in (5).

(5) **Definitions**

   a. Arc A is a SUCCESSOR of B (reciprocally, B a PREDECESSOR of A) if and only if B sponsors A and A and B OVERLAP (have the same head node).

   b. A relation between arcs (like Successor) is respectively LOCAL/FOREIGN depending on whether the arcs involved are NEIGHBORS (have the same tail node) or not.

(6) **Definitions**

   a. Substructure Universally Defining a Passive Constituent

   B = prepassive arc; A = arc-passive arc

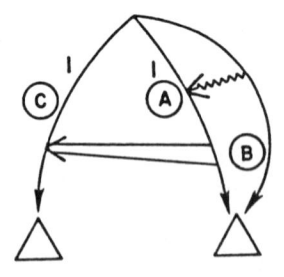

   b. B is a PREPASSIVE arc and A an ARC-PASSIVE arc if and only if A is a 1-arc local successor of B which locally erases a 1-arc.

   I assume condition (7)

(7) **English Prepassive Arc Condition**

   If A is a prepassive arc, A is a 2-arc (or a 3-arc).

This is not met in (3) by the initial arc, A_6, headed by the passivized nominal, *Peter*. A_6 is a 5-arc, which in English determine PPs for their heads. But, a prepassive arc satisfying (7) exists as a result of advancement, since A_6 has a 2-arc local successor, A_5. Given this, pseudopassivization reduces to standard structures and actually represents not a kind of passivization, but a special sort of advancement to object having three key features. First, it is associated with a copy pronoun, represented in (3b) by the COPY ARC B$_1$. The head of this is embedded in a PP structure defined by arcs C, B$_2$, B$_3$ and E. Second, resumptive pronoun heads of such phrases must be invisible, indicated in (3b) by the erasure of B$_3$ (by E), yielding a PP without a surface NP. The preposition, which instantiates the flagging of a copy pronoun, really results from copy advancement to direct object. Without the invisibility requirement, a pseudopassive like (3a) would have form (8).

(8)   Peter was talked to him(self) by the guard.

Third, English grammar demands that the advanced nominals passivize, blocking 'pseudoactives' like (9):

(9)   a. *The guard talked Peter to.
       b. *One should not talk such subjects about in public.

Although justifying the invisible resumptive pronouns of pseudopassives was a burden for my 1986 analysis, recognition of such is the key link with the French cases referenced in the title. Talk of French pseudopassives seems initially bizarre since French participial prepositional passives are sharply ungrammatical (Blinkenberg (1960: 92),[1] Kayne and Pollock (1978: 609 fn17), Pollock (1979), Zribi-Hertz (1982: 3, 28), Kayne (1984: 103, 196), Postal(1986: 204–205)), Riemsdijk and Williams (1986: 146–147) and Baker (1988: 259–260), as in (10), which translate the sentences in (1).

(10)   a. *Antoine a été voté contre par la plupart de la population.
       b. *De tels sujets ne devaient pas être discutés de en public.
       c. *Les civils ne devaient pas être tirés sur/dessus.

Moreover, French also has reflexive passives, and prepositional analogs of these fail as well.

(11)   a. Un compromis pareil, ça se rejette.
       "A compromise like that is rejected
       b. *Un pont pareil, ça ne vole pas (des)sous.
       "A bridge like that is not flown under"

---

[1] So Blinkenberg (1960: 92) states, typically, (my translation, PMP), "If for example English admits correspondences like 'they laughed at him—he was laughed at' nothing similar can exist in French".

Speaking of French pseudopassives is nonetheless sensible because of sentences like (12), hereafter, referred to as RESUMPTIVES, a term based on the view that the highlighted pronominal forms are resumptive.

(12) a. Daniel se fera moquer de *lui* (par Jean).
"Daniel will get made fun of (by Jean)"
b. Daniel se fera moquer de *ses* oreilles (par Jean).
"Daniel will get made fun of his ears (by Jean)"

Although complex morphosyntactic issues arise in their analysis, Resumptives do reveal clear passive-like properties; one is that the superficial subject is understood as the (prepositional) object of (12a) and as the possessor of the prepositional object of (12b). Another is the presence of a nominal in a *par* phrase understood as the logical subject, both features of French participial passives. Resumptives like (12a) have puzzled and disturbed grammarians concerned with French for more than a century,[2] traditional grammarians sometimes remarking that Resumptives are 'barbarous', 'illogical', etc., which amounts to declaring them incomprehensible. Since there seem to be no modern analyses of Resumptives in any terms, I conclude they remain as perplexing and unanalyzed in 1994 as they were in 1886.

The present remarks are fragments of an unfinished project from 1986-1991. Its descriptive goal was to uncover the proper grammatical analysis

---

[2]Tobler (1905: 239fn) [orginally written in 1886] claimed that (my translation: PMP): "nothing excuses" a sentence like (i) and that such a fashion of speaking is a "pure barbarism".

(i) Celui qui...agiterait gravement de telles questions se ferait justement moquer de lui.
"One who would get seriously excited about such matters would justifiably get made fun of"

Grevisse (1969: 563) speaks of a "curious" construction *se faire moquer de soi* in which *moquer* has simultaneously the status of a direct transitive, as in *se faire blâmer*, and the status of an intransitive, as in *faire rire de soi*. He claims that in the latter case, *soi* is "inexplicable logically", while in the former *se* is "inexplicable logically".

Sandfeld (1965: 180–181) says of the same sentence type that the ordinary construction with this verb (hereafter: V) is *se moquer de quelqu'un* and that "one has added *de soi* in an entirely mechanical way without realizing that the regime of the verb was already expressed" (i.e. by *se*: PMP).

for Resumptives, thereby to also further support the nonstandard analysis of English pseudopassives sketched above, and to advance and support the Metagraph framework.

Although Resumptives fall into neither of the two best known French clausal classes reasonably categorized as passives, its participial and reflexive passive structures, a key to understanding them is a third structure type rarely considered in the anglophonic literature, clauses such as (13).

(13)   a. Marcel s'est fait pincer par un flic vicieux.
        b. L'institutrice s'est fait dire par Marcel de sortir.

These look like *faire par* subvariants of the causative construction. And, on one reading, glossed in (14), they certainly are.

(14)   a. Marcel had himself grabbed by a vicious cop.
        b. The school teacher had herself told to leave by Marcel.

On that reading, (13a,b) are active sentences whose main clause logical subjects are identical to complement logical objects, making (13a) a reflexive variant of the wider paradigm which includes the nonreflexive element of (15).

(15)   Marcel l'a fait pincer par un flic vicieux.
        "Marcel had him (≠Marcel) arrested by a vicious cop."

But in addition and, in these cases, more naturally, (13a,b) are interpreted like English *get* passives and are respectively equivalent to (16a,b).

(16)   a. Marcel got (himself) grabbed by a vicious cop.
        b. The school teacher got told to leave by Marcel.

As remarked in the French literature,[3] on this second reading, no agentivity

---

[3]Danell (1979), Dubois (1967: 123–4), Stimm (1957) Dubois (1967: 123–4), Spang Hanssen (1967), Chocheyras (1968), Gaatone (1970), Shyldkrot (1981), Roggero (1984), Postal (1985, 1992b), De Groof (1983), Van Oevelen (1985), Tasmowski-De Ryck and van Oevelen (1987). Martinon (1927: 456) states (my translation: PMP):

"In the same way pronominal constructions such as *se laisser fléchir, s'entendre insulter, se voir dépasser,* and even *se sentir toucher* can be considered as equivalents of passives [such as] *être fléchi, insulté, dépassé, touché.*"

Spang-Hanssen (1967: 141) indicated (my translation: PMP): "Even if one or causativeness is associated with (13a,b), whose main clauses are understood to have no logical subject.

At this point a terminological categorization like (17) is useful.

(17) **French Passive Types**

    a. PARTICIPIAL PASSIVE

        Jacques a été arrêté par un flic vicieux.
        "Jacques was arrested by a vicious cop"

    b. REFLEXIVE PASSIVE

        Un criminel pareil (ça) s'arrête.
        "A criminal like that gets/should be arrested"

    c. UNION PASSIVE

        Jacques s'est fait pincer par un flic vicieux.
        "Jacques got nabbed by a vicious cop"

And, since Union passives involve passivization of either direct or indirect objects, I call the former type UNION-2 PASSIVES, the latter UNION-3-PASSIVES.

The Participial and Union passive sentence types are, I believe, both

---

requires in order to speak of a passive the possibility of a simple transformation not yielding any change in the semantic content, *se faire* + infinitive can, justly, be considered as a passive construction. In the following phrases, faire doesn't add any causative idea and the temporal equivalence with the corresponding active sentence is perfect." He then gave the following:

(i)   M. Pisani se fait suivre par une dame.
        "M. Pisani gets followed by a lady"

Moreover, as Spang-Hanssen notes in (ii), this construction has the unique (internal to French) property of permitting the passivization of an indirect object.

(ii)   "*Se faire*+ infinitive also serves...for the transformation of the indirect object of the active sentence into subject of a passive sentence. For these constructions the term passive is perhaps not universally adopted, but the phenomenon is fundamentally the same: a simple transposition permits going back to an active without changing anything of the content".

biclausal. The characterization 'passive' is technically only relevant to their subordinate clauses. In most contexts though, no confusion arises from using these terms for the overall constructions. (18b) represents my account of the typical French Participial passive (18a).

(18) a. La voiture sera laveé par les étudiants.
"The car will be washed by the students"
b.

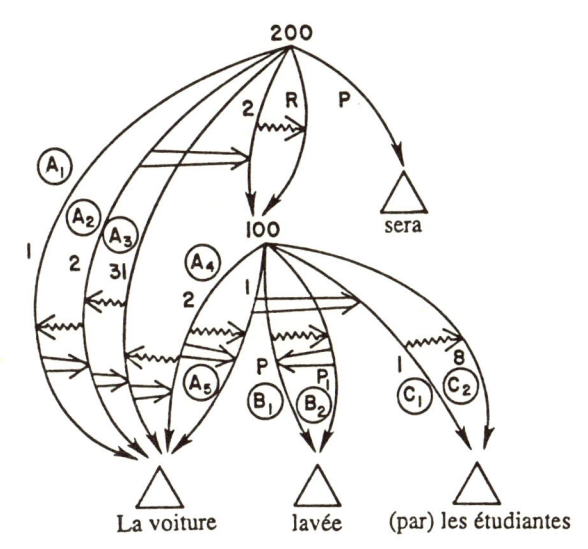

Although both clauses 100 and 200 there contain 1-arc local successors, namely A₁ and A₅, only clause 100 satisfies the passive structure definition, since A₁ erases no other 1-arc. In (18b), local successor A₅, is erased by its predecessor. Such successors are referred to as TYPE II successors; TYPE I succcessors erase their predecessors, these being mutually exclusive. See (19).

(19) **Definitions**

Assume A is a successor of B. Then A is a type I successor of B if and only if A erases B and a type II successor if and only if B erases A. In any other case, A is a type III successor of B.

A key consequence is that passive clauses like 100 in (18b) have no final subjects, critical in explaining certain participial passive properties.

I turn to the Metagraph grammar notion of CLAUSE UNION

construction since, as the name in (17c) suggests, I take Union passives to instantiate this. (20) is a typical French clause union example.

(20)   a. Marie leur fera répondre à Georges.
       "Marie will have them reply to Georges"

       b.

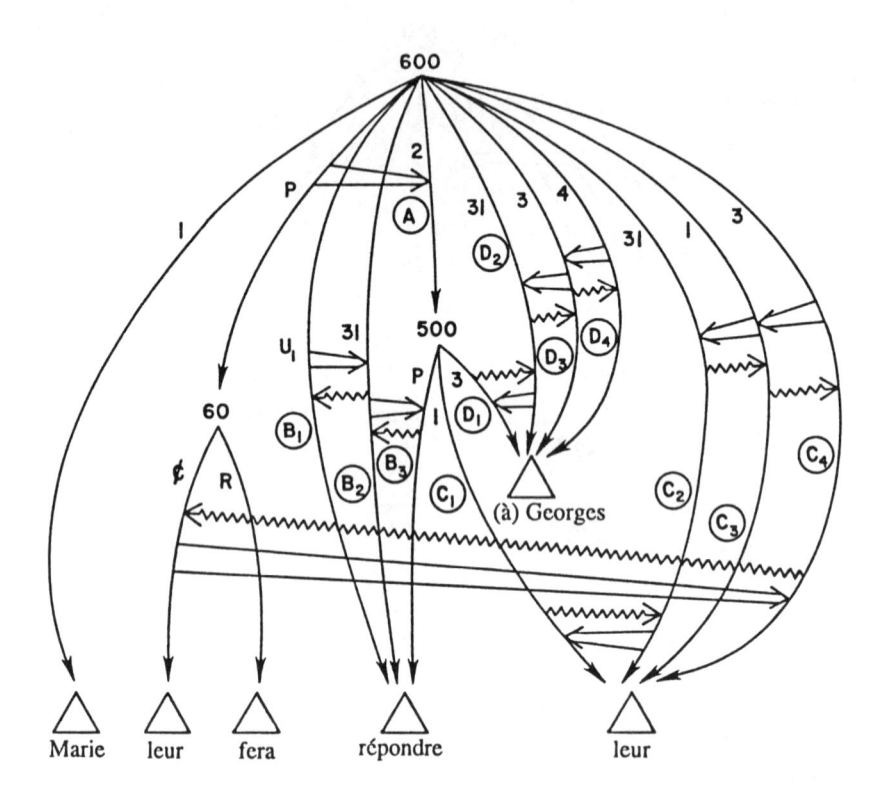

For me, the characteristic features of such constructions are that a complement-defining arc, here the 2-arc A, is erased by its neighboring P-arc, and that the P-arc branch of that erased arc, here B3, has a foreign successor in the main clause. I assume now, inessentially, that there is only one foreign successor relation in natural language, whose R-sign is 31. That foreign successor, B2, then has a U1-arc local successor defining the final status of the complement V in the main clause. These features force all the otherwise unerased neighbors of the complement P-arc, called

LAUNCHERS, to themselves have type I foreign successors in the main clause. So C_1 and D_1 are launchers. Those foreign successors must have type I local successors equivalent in R-sign to the launchers. So C_3 has the same R-sign as C_1, D_3 as D_1, etc. Those local successors in turn must themselves sometimes have local successors. For instance, since the complement subject in (20a) ends up as an indirect object, the complement indirect object, which otherwise would be the final main clause indirect object, ends up bearing a relation I call subobject. The analysis determines that every arc defining the complement clause is erased and thus not a surface arc; so that the complement is not a surface constituent.

Union passive sentences like (13a) are structurally ambiguous. On each reading, the complement clause is the same kind of passive. The sentence where the main V manifests semantic content, is a special case of the transitive *faire* construction, a clause union structure in the sense just specified. On this analysis, (13a) parallels the English (21), except that the latter lacks the clause union-defining features.

(21)   Marcel had himself arrested by a vicious cop.

Although the Union passive analysis involves the same morphological main V and complement type, there are two distinctions. First, the Union passive main V is semantically empty, like a Participial passive auxiliary. Indeed, the Union passive main V's role significantly parallels that of the Participial passive auxiliary, modulo that, as argued in Postal (1985) contra Fauconnier (1983), only the Union passive structure instantiates clause union. Second, a Union passive main clause involves no initial 1-arc.

I suggest that the structure of Union passive (22a) is (22b), whose complement clause satisfies the passive clause definition and is of the type II variety.

(22)   a. Michel se fera répondre par Louise.
       "Michel will get replied to by Louise"

b.

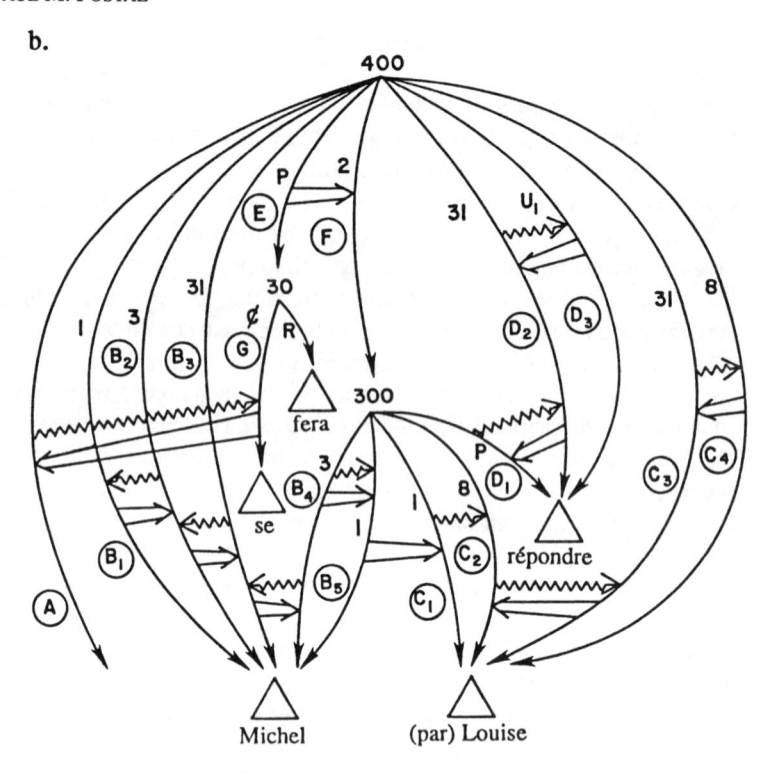

Here the prepassive arc B_4 is a final arc and launcher. That B_4 is a 3-arc is irrelevant to satisfaction of definition (6), which does not limit the prepassive arc R-sign. The main clause local successor B_2 satisfies the condition requiring launcher foreign successors to have equivalent local successors. That B_2 itself has a 1-arc local successor is due to factors parallel to those leading to advancement to subject in unaccusative clauses.

The complements of (22b) and the participial structure (18b) are essentially parallel, differing significantly only in the erasure of their P-arcs. In (18b), the P-arc has an erasing local successor and the clause is not a clause union complement. In (22b), the P-arc has, due to the clause union structure, a type I foreign successor. However, each complement P-arc is erased, and thus there is no instance of what I call a PERSISTENT CLAUSE corresponding to the complement; see (71). Only persistent clauses are subject to the law requiring a final 1-arc. Note that it is the type II character of the arc-passive arc in (22b) which makes B_4 a launcher.

Against this background, Resumptives resemble pseudopassives in being 'excess' passive clauses. Pseudopassives seem to be 'excess' in that the ordinary 'formula' for forming an English (Participial) passive would not yield them, just as parallel 'formulae' in other languages correctly do not. Such a 'formula' might say a passive can be formed only by making the direct object of a transitive V, V_x, into the subject of a form of the auxiliary (*be*), embedding the past participle form of V_x below it and optionally representing the original subject as head of a *by* phrase. Since pseudopassive superficial subjects do not correspond to direct objects, the problem of pseudopassive description becomes in part that of providing a mechanism which allows (only certain) non-direct objects to feed the passive 'formula'. The difference between English and languages having passives but not pseudopassives, e.g. German, is the absence of that addditional mechanism in the latter. The mechanism proposed in Postal (1986) and illustrated in (3b) is copy advancement to direct object with the requirement that the resulting 2-arc local successor be prepassive.

Resumptives link to the overall class of Union passives essentially as pseudopassives link to the overall class of English Participial passives. Like standard Union passives, Resumptives are bipartite, with a main clause based on a reflexive form of known clause union triggering Vs, and an infinitival complement. In both, a *par* phrase can correspond to the complement logical subject. But like pseudopassives, Resumptives are 'excess' sentences given the usual 'formula' for Union passives. The latter might say that a Union passive can be formed by making either a direct or indirect object the subject of a reflexive form of *faire* (or *voir*) and embedding the infinitival form of the original V below it, optionally representing the original subject as the head of a *par* phrase.

Resumptives deviate from the Union passive 'formula' first in having main clause subjects corresponding not to direct or indirect objects but to certain *de* phrase heads, in general not possible sources of Union passive subjects. (23b) shows the standard result of forming a Union passive on such a phrase.

(23)   a. Jacques a rêvé de Marie.
"Jacques dreamed about Marie"

b. *Marie s'est fait rêver par Jacques.
"Marie got dreamed of by Jacques"

Nonetheless, the correspondence between a Resumptive subject and a *de* phrase is clear. The subject is understood in the same way as the propositional object of the active sentence and the pronoun occurring in the *de* phrase of a Resumptive must agree with the subject. So, in (24a), the subject plays the same semantic role as the object of *de* in (24b). (24c,d) show ungrammaticality where agreement fails.

(24)   a. Marie s'est fait moquer d'elle par Michel.
       "Marie got made fun of by Michel"

       b. Michel s'est moqué de Marie.
       "Michel made fun of Marie"

       c. *Marcel s'est fait moquer de Louise/ta mère.

       d. *Marcel s'est fait moquer de vous/elle/eux.

A second reason why Resumptives are peculiar Union passives is that, like English pseudopassives, they contain a surface residue of the ultimate subject source; in English, the stranded preposition, in French, *de* followed by an agreeing pronominal form. The explicit resumptive pronoun in Resumptives plays a role quite parallel to the only inexplicit pronoun posited in my analysis of pseudopassives.

Resumptives are puzzling Union passives in a third way based on one class of Vs which permit them. This includes those like *moquer*, which are, Resumptives excluded, only inherently reflexive, requiring a reflexive clitic not corresponding to a logical element (Haggis (1971: 7) states (my translation: PMP): "We add here *se moquer* and *se souvenir*, *souvenir* and *moquer* not being used in the language of today".) So, sentences of the form (25) are ungrammatical with *moquer* although grammatical with a transitive V like *louer* 'to praise'.

(25)   a. On a loué/*moqué Marcel.
       "One praised/mocked Marcel"
       b. Marcel a été loué/*moqué par les étudiants.
       "Marcel was praised/mocked by the students"
       c. On a laissé louer/*moquer Marcel par les étudiants.
       "One let Marcel be praised/mocked by the students"
       d. Marcel s'est fait louer/*moquer par les étudiants.
       "Marcel got (himself) praised/mocked by the students"

Resumptives excluded, *moquer* occurs only in sentences like (26).

(26)   a. Marianne s'est moquée de Marcel.
       "Marianne made fun of Marcel"

b. J'ai laissé se moquer Marianne de Marcel.
"I let Marianne make fun of Marcel"

Thus many Resumptives manifest otherwise obligatory inherently reflexive verbs nevertheless occurring without inherent reflexives, where the latter contrast with 'true' reflexive markers like that in (27) which represent 'coreference'.

(27)   Marcel se critique tout le temps.
       "Marcel criticizes himself all the time"

An account of the absence of inherent reflexives in Resumptives formed on inherently reflexive Vs is informally given below.

Incidentally, one must not confuse, as did Sandfeld in footnote 2, the main V reflexive clitic of Resumptives with the inherent reflexive required on Vs like *moquer*. One argument that these are independent depends on the broader class of Vs permitting Resumptives, so far exemplified only with *moquer*. Resumptives are also formable on the Vs of (28); see also (29).

(28) **Some Verbs Occurring in Resumptives**

   a. Class A

      se charger 'to attend to, take charge of'
      se défier 'to distrust, mistrust'
      se désintéresser 'to lose interest in'
      se ficher 'to make fun of'
      se foutre 'to make fun of'
      se gausser 'to ridicule'
      se jouer 'to make sport of, deride'
      se marrer 'to laugh strongly at'
      s'occuper 'to take care of'
      se plaindre 'to complain about'
      se rappeler 'to remember'
      se rire 'to laugh at'
      se separer 'to separate from'
      se servir 'to make use of'

b. Class B

abuser 'to wrongly take advantage of, seduce, dishonor'
causer 'to chat about'
douter 'to have doubts about, mis/distrust'
jaser 'to chatter about'
parler 'to talk about'

(29) a. (i) Nicole se charge de Georges.
             "Nicole takes charge of Georges"
       (ii) Georges s'est fait charger de lui part Nicole.
             "George got taken charge of by Nicole"
     b. (i) Nicole s'est plaint de Georges.
             "Nicole complained about Georges"
       (ii) Georges s'est fait plaindre de lui par Nicole.
             "Georges got complained about by Nicole"
     c. (i) Nicole se sépara de Georges.
             "Nicole will separate fronm Georges"
       (ii) Georges se fera séparer de lui par Nicole.
             "Georges will get separted from by Nicole"

That reflexive clitics also occur in Resumptives based on the nonreflexive Class B Vs shows that the Union passive main clause reflexive clitic is independent of inherent reflexives.

Both Class A and Class B Resumptive-forming Vs permit, as (30) illustrates, *de* phrases which alternate with the clitic *en*, indicating that Resumptive superficial subjects correspond to a natural class of phrases in nonResumptives.

(30) a. Nicole s'en charge/plaint (, de Georges).
         "Nicole takes charge of/complains about Georges"
     b. Georges en abuse/parle (, de Nicole).
         "Georges takes advantage of/talks about Nicole"

Strikingly though, despite the possibility of *en* in non-resumptives like (30b) corresponding to Resumptives, no Resumptive can contain *en* instead of a pronominal *de* phrase; see (31).

(31) a. Georges se moque d'elle.
         "Georges makes fun of her"

b. Georges s'en moque, de Louise.
"Georges makes fun of Louise"
c. Louise, Georges s'en moque.
"Georges makes fun of Louise"
d. Louise s'est fait moquer d'elle par Georges.
"Louise got made fun of by Georges"
e. *Louise s'en est fait moquer par Georges.
"Louise got made fun of by Georges"

An explanation of restriction (31e) is sketched below.

Not just any V taking *en*-determining *de*-phrases permits Resumptives, which is only possible for intransitives; see (32).

(32) **Transitive Structures with *en*-inducing *de*-Phrases**

    a. (i)   On a extorqué 100,000 dollars de Claude.
             "One extorted one hundred thousand dollars from Claude"
      (ii)   *Claude s'est fait extorquer 100,000 dollars de lui.
             "Claude got extorted 100,000 from him"
    b. (i)   Edwin a hérité cette maison de Louise.
             "Edwin inherited that house from Louise"
      (ii)   *Louise s'est fait hériter cette maison d'elle par Edwin.
             "Louise got inherited that house from her by Edwin"
    c. (i)   Maurice obtiendra des drogues de Tony.
             "Maurice will obtain drugs from Tony"
      (ii)   *Tony se fera obtenir des drogues de lui par Maurice"
             "Tony will get obtrained drugs from him by Maurice"
    d. (i)   Mon chef a exigé cela de moi.
             "My boss required that of me"
      (ii)   *Je me suis fait exiger cela de moi par mon chef.
             "I got required that of me by my boss"

Further, (33) lists unergative intransitives which (34) show appear not to permit it.

(33) **Some Intransitive Verbs Occurring with *en*-inducing *de* Phrases Which Do Not Permit Resumptives**

    a. Class A

    s'approcher 'to approach'
    se débarrasser 'to get rid of'

se défaire 'to get rid of'
se désengager 'to disengage from'
se désespérer 'to lose hope in'
se déshabituer 'to become unhabituated with'
s'enticher 'to become infatuated with',
s'éprendre 'to become enamoured of'
s'inquieter 'to worry about'
se lasser 'to tire of'
se soucier 'to worry about'
se souvenir 'to remember'
se raffoler 'to be wild about'

b. Class B

bavarder 'to talk, chat about'
débattre 'to debate about'
discourir 'to discourse on'
douter 'to have doubts about'
hériter 'to inherit from'
rêver 'to dream of'
saisir 'to seize hold of'
triompher 'to triumph over'
vouloir 'to want'

(34)   a.   (i) Marcel s'est approché de l'institutrice.
"Marcel approached the female teacher"
(ii) *L'institutrice s'est fait approcher d'elle par Marcel.
"The female teacher got approached by Marcel"
b.   (i) Candice s'est désespérée du swami.
"Candice lost hope in the swami"
(ii) *Le swami s'est fait désespérer de lui par Candice.
"The swami got lost hope in by Candice"
c.   (i) Le capitaine s'est entiché de cette serveuse.
"The captain became infatuated with that waitress"
(ii) *Cette serveuse s'est fait enticher d'elle par le capitaine"
"That waitress got fallen infatuated with by the captain"
d.   (i) Les dactylos ont bavardé de Michel.
"The secretaries chatted about Michel"
(ii) *Michel s'est fait bavarder de lui par les dactylos.
"Michel got chatted about by the secretaries"

The distinction between the intransitive Vs of (33) and those of (32) apparently requires brute listing.

I have not argued beyond generalities that Union passives are passives. For justification, one should show that Union passives share properties with uncontroversial passive structures. Given the uncontroversial passive status of Participial passives, one should consider ways in which Union passive behavior parallels that of Participial passives. I simply list a few such parallels, space precluding going into detail.

First, they show the same alternations in marking of what, under a passive analysis, would be passive chômeurs or their variants, *par* with most Vs, *de* with a very restricted subclass; see (35).

(35) a. Claudine sera aidée par/*de sa mère.
      "Claudine will be aided by her mother"
      b. Claudine sera détestée *par/de sa mère.
      "Claudine will be detested by her mother"
      c. Claudine se fera aider par/*de sa mère.
      "Claudine will get aided by her mother"
      d. Claudine se fera détester *par/de sa mère.
      "Claudine will get detested by her mother"

Second, like Participial passives, Union passives obey the 1 Advancement Exclusiveness Law. This determines the impossibility of passives with unaccusative, inversion and any other Vs whose clauses contain a 1-arc local successor independent of that connected to a passive structure. See (36) and (37).

(36) a. (i)   Louise lui a succombé, à Hervé.
                 "Louise succumbed to Herve"
          (ii)   *Il a été succombé à Hervé par Louise.
                 "It was succumbed to Herve by Louise"
          (iii) *Hervé s'est fait succomber par Louise.
                 "Herve got succumbed to by Louise"
      b. (i)   Un spectre lui a apparu, à Hervé.
                 "A ghost appeared to Herve"
          (ii)   *Il a été apparu a Hervé par un spectre.
                 "It was appeared to Herve by a ghost"
          (iii) *Hervé s'est fait apparaître par un spectre.
                 "Herve got appeared to by a ghost"
      c. (i)   Une lettre lui parviendra, à Hervé.
                 "A letter will reach Herve"
          (ii)   *Il sera parvenu à Hervé par une lettre.
                 "It will be reached to Herve by a letter"

　　　　　(iii)　　*Hervé se fera parvenir par une lettre.
　　　　　　　　　"Herve will be reached by a letter"
　　d.　(i)　　　Cette femme lui a déplu, à Hervé.
　　　　　　　　　"That woman displeased Herve"
　　　　　(ii)　　*Il a été déplu à Hervé par cette femme.
　　　　　　　　　"It was displeased to Herve by that woman"
　　　　　(iii)　　*Hervé s'est fait déplaire par cette femme.
　　　　　　　　　"Herve got displeased by that woman"

(37)　a.　(i)　　　Louise lui a téléphoné, à Hervé.
　　　　　　　　　"Louise telephoned Herve"
　　　　　(ii)　　Il a été téléphoné à Hervé par Louise.
　　　　　　　　　"It was telephoned to Herve by Louise"
　　　　　(iii)　　Hervé s'est fait téléphoner par Louise.
　　　　　　　　　"Herve got telephoned by Louise"
　　b.　(i)　　　Louise lui a cédé, à Hervé.
　　　　　　　　　"Louise gave in to Herve"
　　　　　(ii)　　Il a été cédé à Hervé par Louise.
　　　　　　　　　"It was given in to Herve by Louise"
　　　　　(iii)　　Hervé s'est fait céder par Louise.
　　　　　　　　　"Herve got given in to by Louise"
　　c.　(i)　　　Ses enfants lui ont survecu, à Hervé.
　　　　　　　　　"His children survived Herve"
　　　　　(ii)　　Il a été survecu à Hervé par ses enfants.
　　　　　　　　　"It was survived to Herve by his children"
　　　　　(iii)　　Hervé s'est fait survivre par ses enfants.
　　　　　　　　　"Herve got survived by his children"
　　d.　(i)　　　On lui a craché dessus, à Hervé.
　　　　　　　　　"One spit at Herve"
　　　　　(ii)　　Il lui a été craché dessus, à Hervé.
　　　　　　　　　"It was spit at Herve"
　　　　　(iii)　　Hervé s'est fait cracher dessus par Lucille.
　　　　　　　　　"Herve got spit at by Lucille"
　　e.　(i)　　　On lui a tiré dans le pied, à Hervé.
　　　　　　　　　"One shot Herve in the foot"
　　　　　(ii)　　Il lui a été tiré dans le pied, à Hervé.
　　　　　　　　　"It was shot in Herve's foot"
　　　　　(iii)　　Hervé s'est fait tirer dans le pied par Lucille.
　　　　　　　　　"Herve got shot in the foot by Lucille"

A further argument appeals to the unique properties of controlled infinitival complements with the main V *menacer*. As Gross (1975: 86-7) noticed, both main and complement clauses with *menacer* can be either active or Participial passive, but the only grammatical forms are those in which both clauses are active or both are Participial passive; see (38).

(38)　a. Jacques a menacé Marie de la virer.
　　　　"Jacques threatened Marie to fire her"
　　　　b. Marie a été menacée (par Jacques) d'être virée (par Luc).
　　　　"Marie was threatened (by Jacques) to be fired (by Luc)"
　　　　c. *Jacques a menacé Marie d'être virée (par Luc).
　　　　"Jacques threatened Mary to be fired (by Luc)"
　　　　d. ?*Marie a été menacée (par Jacques) de la virer.
　　　　"Marie was threatened (by Jacques) to fire her"

Significantly, the same pattern is found with Union passives, as (39) illustrates:

(39)　a. = (38a)
　　　　b. Marie s'est fait menacer (par Jacques) de se faire virer (par Luc).
　　　　"Marie got threatened (by Jacques) to get fired (by Luc)"
　　　　c. *Jacques a menacé Marie de se faire virer (par Luc).
　　　　"Jacques threatened Marie to get fired (by Luc)"
　　　　d. ?*Marie s'est fait menacer (par Jacques) de la virer.
　　　　"Marie got threatened (by Jacques) to fire her"

Generalization (40) can only apply to e.g. (39) if Union passives are in fact passives.

(40) Schematic Clause Compatibility Condition for *menacer*

A main clause whose predicate is *menacer* and whose complement C is infinitival is in Voice N if and only if C is also in N, where N = <Active, Passive>

Principle (40) allows either the main or subordinate clause to be either a Participial or a Union passive, which is correct:

(41)　a. Marie s'est fait menacer (par Jacques) d'être virée (par Luc).
　　　　"Marie got threatened (by Jacques) to be fired (by Luc)"
　　　　b. Marie a été menacée (par Jacques) de se faire virer (par Luc).
　　　　"Marie was threatened (by Jacques) to get fired (by Luc)"

(42) a. Marie s'est fait menacer (par Jacques) de se faire refuser l'entrée.
"Marie got threatened (by Jacques) to get refused entrance"
b. Marie s'est fait menacer (par Jacques) de se faire tirer dessus.
"Marie got threatened (by Jacques) to get shot at"
c. Marie a été menacée (par Jacques) de se faire refuser l'entrée.
"Marie was threatened (by Jacques) to get refused entrance"
d. Marie a été menacée (par Jacques) de se faire tirer dessus.
"Marie was threatened (by Jacques) to get shot at"

A final ground for the passive status of Union passives is that various apparently lexical constraints on Participial passives are mirrored in Union passives; see (43)–(46).

(43) a. Jacques aura ma voiture demain.
"Jacques will have my car tomorrow"
b. *Ma voiture sera eue par Jacques demain.
"My car will be had by Jacques tommorrow"
c. Marie n'a aucune résidence connue.
"Marie has no known residence"
d. *Aucune résidence connue n'est eue par Marie.
"No known residence is had by Marie"

(44) a. Jacques a eu des servants loyaux.
"Jacques had loyal servants"
b. *Des servants loyaux se sont fait avoir par/de Jacques.
"Loyal servants got had by Jacques"

(45) a. La plupart des seigneurs ont eu des esclaves.
"Most of the lords had slaves"
b. *Des esclaves se sont fait avoir par/de la plupart des seigneurs.
"Slaves got had by most of the lords"

(46) a. Mon pére veut cette Rolls-Royce.
"My father wants that Rolls-Royce"
b. *Cette Rolls-Royce est voulue par mon pére.
"That Rolls-Royce is wanted by my father"
c. Mon pére veut cette esclave.
"My father wants that slave"
d. *Cette esclave s'est fait vouloir par mon pére.
"That slave got wanted by my father"

The arguments just skimmed provide basic support for the passive character of Union passives, meaning that both Participial and Union passives must be instances of similar abstract structures, a desideratum met by the structures proposed in (18b) and (22b).

There are two alternative ways to analyze Resumptives as Union passives. The most straightforward denies that only direct and indirect objects form Union passives. Rather, these would also be fed by the kind of *de* phrases found in Resumptives, taken here to represent the relation Quasiobject. French quasiobjects are the forms which require the marking of nominals with *de*, determine the pronominal clitic *en* and yield the relative form *dont*. Proposal one is that Union passives are directly fed by direct and indirect objects and by quasiobjects. Alternatively, only direct and indirect objects would provide the requisite prepassive arcs and Resumptives would represent advancement of a quasiobject to direct or indirect object just as the necessary prepassive arc in my analysis of pseudopassives results from advancement. The latter more indirect proposal has immediate advantages linked to the invariant presence of the resumptive structure. For, under the second proposal, Resumptives involve at least two distinct complement phenomena: advancement of a quasiobject to object and the standard link between an object-arc and a 1-arc, found in all Union passives. Resumptives aside, the latter never yields any resumptive structure. Generality can thus be maintained if the type II 1-arc local successor of an object arc characteristic of Union passives uniformly does not determine a resumptive and the pronominal element in any Resumptive is associated with quasiobject to object advancement, which feeds the linkages to subject characteristic of Union passives. Like English pseudopassives, French Resumptives then involve not a special type of passivization but advancement to object necessarily linked to passivization.

A second reason for not viewing Resumptives as involving direct quasiobject passivization is based on cases like (12b) where the underlying quasiobject surfaces not as a subject but as a quasiobject containing a possessive resumptive pronoun. No subsumption of (12b) under the same principles as (12a) can appeal to direct passivization of quasiobjects. (47), a partial structure of (12b), brings this out.

(47)

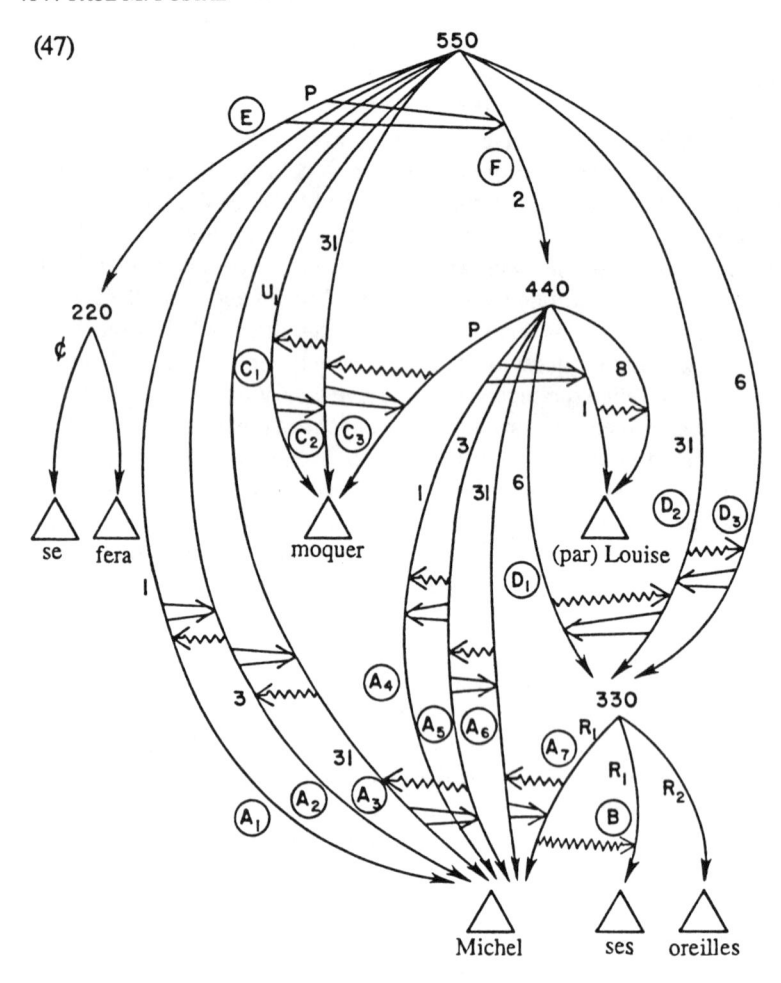

Since, independently of Resumptives, Union passives are based on either direct or indirect objects, there exist the plausible proposals in (48) as to the nature of the characteristic advancement to object.

(48) **This advancement is:**

    a. exclusively 6 to 2 advancement; i.e. Resumptives are Union-2-passives.
    b. exclusively 6 to 3 advancement; i.e. Resumptives are Union-3-passives.
    c. indifferently either 6 to 2 or 6 to 3 advancement; i.e.

Resumptives are ambiguously Union-2-passives or Union-3-passives.

Surprisingly perhaps, considerable evidence supports (48b); that is, Resumptives are based solely on quasiobject to indirect object advancement. Asssuming that, Resumptive (49a) has a structure like (49b), paralleling (22b).

(49)   a. Michel se fera moquer de lui par Louise.
       "Michel will get made fun of by Louise"
       b.

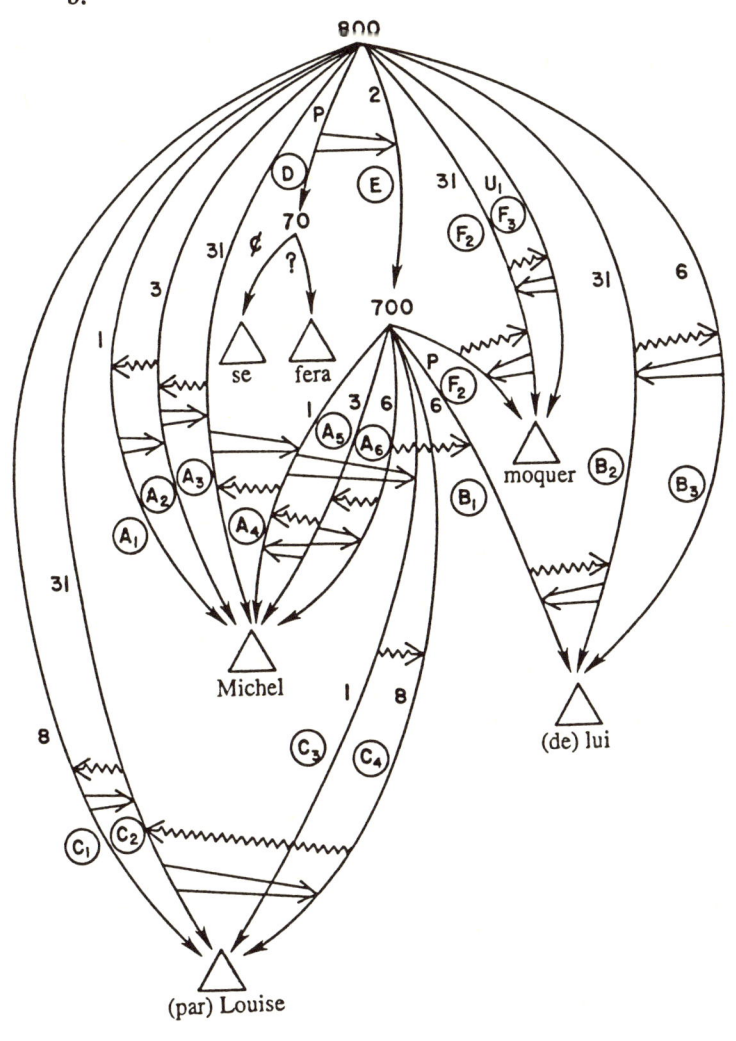

The conditions governing 3-arc local successors of 6-arcs have three principal features. First, only those intransitive Vs in (28) permit it. Second, such is only possible in passive clauses, in Resumptives or those clause union cases surface-identical to Resumptives. Were it not so limited, 6 to 3 advancement with e.g. *moquer* would yield grammatical active structures like (50), which are invariably ill-formed, parallel to English pseudoactives like (9).

(50) a. *Louise se moquera à Marcel de lui.
"Louise will make fun of Marcel"
b. *On s'est moqué à moi de moi.
"One made fun of me"

Third, 6 to 3 advancement evidently requires the presence of a resumptive pronoun as (the head of) a surface quasiobject. Otherwise, (51b) would be well-formed as well as (51a).

(51) a. Marcel s'est fait moquer de lui par son chef.
"Marcel got made fun of by his boss"
b. *Marcel s'est fait moquer par son chef.
"Marcel got made fun of by his boss"

Despite certain differences, these conditions on Resumptives parallel my account of pseudopassives, in which only certain intransitive Vs permit the phenomenon, the advanced nominal must passivize and a copy element is obligatory although invisible, resulting in the stranded preposition.

Given the Metagraph framework and previous assumptions, restrictions allowing e.g. (51a) but blocking (50) and (51b) can be simply formulated as in (53), appealing to definition (52).

(52) **Definition**

Arc A copies arc C if and only if there exists a B which is a successor of C and A replaces C.

(53) **French Quasiobject Advancement Rule (First Version)**

If A is a local successor of a 6-arc, B, then A is a prepassive 3-arc, some arc copies B, B has no 2-arc neighbor and B's P-arc neighbor is headed by *moquer*,...

The first consequent conjunct of (53) eliminates any instances of 6 to 2 or 6 to 1 advancement and also blocks examples like *(50a,b), where there are no erased 1-arcs but initial 1-arcs which are also surface 1-arcs. The second consequent conjunct blocks (51b), which lacks a resumptive structure. The third expresses the constraint which blocks Resumptives of transitive structures like (32dii) and the fourth is the intransitive listing.

When combined with the standard relational view of impersonal passives, rule (53) also predicts that there is no French 6 to 3 advancement in impersonal passives; see (54).

(54)   a. Le comité a discuté de Pierre.
       "The comittee discussed Pierre"
       b. Le comité en a discuté, de Pierre.
       "The comittee discussed Pierre"
       c. Pierre s'est fait discuter de lui par le comité.
       "Pierre got discussed by the comittee"
       d. Il a été discuté de Pierre par le comité.
       "There was discussion of Pierre by the committee"
       e. *Il a été discuté à Pierre de lui par le comité.
       f. *Il lui a été discuté de lui par le comité.

Space precludes discussion.

Features of rule (53) support the view in (48b) that Resumptives represent exclusively 6 to 3 advancement. Although (53) says nothing explicit about Union passives or the differences between them and either Participial or Reflexive passives, (53) suffices to block either Participial or Reflexive passive analogs of Resumptives, which do not exist; see (55).

(55)   a. Quelqu'un s'est moqué de Michel.
       "Someone made fun of Michel"
       b. Michel s'est fait moquer de lui par quelqu'un.
       "Michel got made fun of by someone"
       c. *Michel a été moqué de lui par quelqu'un.
       d. *Un type pareil (,ça) se moquerait de lui.
       <<OK only on irrelevant active reading>>

Rule (53) blocks (55c,d) as follows. Independently of Resumptives, French grammar must entail that both Participial and Reflexive prepassive arcs are exclusively 2-arcs, to block, for example, the (ii) and (iii) forms of (56).

(56)   a.   (i)   Jacques mentira á Louise.
                  "Jacques will lie to Louise"

(ii) *Louise sera mentie par Jacques.
"Louise will be lied to by Jacques"
(iii) *Une femme pareille, ça se ment.
"A woman like that is lied to"
<<OK only on irrelevant nonpassive (reflexive) meaning>>
b. (i) Arthur enverra ce livre à Thomas.
"Arthur will send that book to Thomas"
(ii) *Thomas sera envoyé ce livre par Arthur.
"Thomas will be sent that book by Arthur"
(iii) *Un type pareil, ça ne s'envoie pas de livre.
"A fellow like that isn't sent books"
<<OK only on irrelevant nonpassive (reflexive) meaning>>

Since direct objects passivize in all three passive types, but indirect objects only in Union passives, a rule like (57) is motivated independently of Resumptives; (58) is evidence that obliques do not passivize in any type.

(57) **French Prepassive Arc Restrictions (First Version)**

If A is a prepassive arc, A is a 2-arc or a 3-arc;
and if A is a 3-arc, then A is a launcher.

(58) a. Marie-Claire travaille contre les communistes.
"Marie-Claire works against the comunists"
b. *Les communistes sont travaillées par Marie-Claire.
"The communists are worked against by Marie-Claire"
c. Ce garçon habite avec Louise.
"That boy lives with Louise"
d. *Louise est habitée par ce garcon.
"Louise is lived with by that boy"
e. On tomberait sur des rochers.
"One would fall on the rocks"
f. *Des rochers, ça ne se tomberait pas.
"Rocks should not be fallen on"
g. On réfléchit à ça.
"One thinks about that"
l.. *Ça ne se réfléchit pas.
"That isn't thought about"

The key in (57) is the specification that a prepassive 3-arc has to be a launcher. Since launchers occur by definition only in clause union complements, the consequent's second conjunct limits French prepassive 3-

arcs to Union passives; for among French passives, only these have a clause union structure. This is obvious enough for Reflexive passives, and argued at length in Postal (1985) for Participial passives.

Consider an arbitrary 3-arc local successor, A, of a 6-arc. According to rule (53), A must be prepassive; but given rule (57), neither Participial nor Reflexive passives can allow prepassive 3-arcs, blocking e.g. (56aii,iii). Moreover, our assumptions do not allow a grammatical case where a 3-arc local successor, A, of a 6-arc would have a prepassive 2-arc local successor. For (53) requires that A itself be prepassive.

Rule (53)'s ability to block the ill-formed versions of (56) without explicitly referencing particular properties of Participial or Reflexive passives is a good initial argument for assumption (48b). Considerable other evidence takes the form of data showing that Resumptives manifest constraints otherwise holding for non-Resumptive Union-3-passives, but not for Union-2-passives.

First, the Stylistic Inversion construction involves postverbal positioning of the subject of an uninverted clause. Stylistic Inversion occurs in subjunctive complements, where it is as available for Union-2-passives as for Participial ones; see (59).

(59) a. Elle veut que se fasse arrêter Claude (par la police secrète).
b. Elle veut que soit arrêté Claude (par la police secrète).
"She wants that Claude get/be arrested by the secret police"

But subjunctive complement Stylistic Inversion is impossible with Union-3-passives, as (60) shows.

(60) a. Elle veut que Claude se fasse téléphoner/sourire/tirer dessus (par quelqu'un).
b. *Elle veut que se fasse téléphoner/sourire/tirer dessus Claude (par quelqu'un).
"She wants that Claude get called/smiled at/shot at (by someone)"

Under present assumptions, the constraint in (60b) linked to indirect objects correctly predicts the incompatibility of Resumptives and stylistic inversion in subjunctive complements illustrated in (61).

(61) a. Elle veut que Claude se fasse moquer de lui par l'assistance.
b. *Elle veut que se fasse moquer de lui Claude par l'assistance.
c. *Elle veut que se fasse moquer Claude de lui par l'assistance.
"She wants that Claude get made fun of by the audience"

If, contrary to (48b), Resumptives represented advancement to direct object, the reduction of *(61b,c) to *(60) would collapse, given the well-formedness of (59a).

A second ground for the claim that Resumptives are Union-3-passives hinges on the impossibility of embedding Union-3-passives under an additional clause union V, although this is possible for Union-2-passives, as shown by (62) and (63).

(62)   a. J'ai vu se faire arrêter Claude par la police.
"I saw Claude get arrested by the police"
b. J'ai laisse se faire critiquer Claude par mes étudiants.
"I let Claude get criticized by my students"

(63)   *J'ai vu se faire téléphoner/mentir/tirer dessus/refuser l'accès à Claude par quelqu'un.
"I saw Claude get called/lied to/shot at/refused access by someone."

The constraint in (63) combines with hypothesis (48b) to predict that Resumptives are incompatible with such multiple embedding, which (64) shows is correct.

(64)   a. *J'ai vu se faire moquer de lui Claude par quelqu'un.
b. *J'ai vu se faire moquer Claude de lui par quelqu'un.
"I saw Claude get made fun of by someone"

A third support for the Union-3-passive character of Resumptives derives from contrasts such as (65), an instance of the *faire par* construction. See Kayne (1975), Postal (1992a), Legendre (1990) and references therein for further discussion.

(65)   a. Marcel a fait arrêter/virer/interroger Lucille par Valerie.
"Marcel had Lucille arrested/fired/interrogated by Valerie"
b. *Marcel a fait mentir/répondre/tirer dessus/envoyer des paquets Lucille par Valerie.
"Marcel had Lucille lied to/answered/shot at/sent packages by Valerie"

In all of (65a), the complement postverbal nominal corresponds to a direct object. In the bad (65b), it is an earlier indirect object. And there is also no correspondent of (65a) based on a Resumptive-like structure, as (66) shows.

(66)   a. *Marcel a fait moquer Lucille d'elle par Valerie.
       "Marcel had Lucille made fun of by Valerie"
       b. *Marcel vous fera moquer de vous par Valerie.
       "Marcel will have you made fun of by Valerie"

This follows from the view that Resumptive copy advancement is exclusively to indirect object, which permits subsumption of (66) under the principles independently needed to block (65b). If, on the contrary, French permitted copy advancement to direct object, nothing would preclude (66) from being part of the well-formed pattern in (65a).
   To clarify and strengthen the argument, consider contrast (67).

(67)   a. Marcel a fait répondre à Lucille par Valerie.
       "Marcel had Lucille answered by Valerie"
       b *Marcel a fait moquer à Lucille d'elle par Valerie.
       "Marcel had Lucille made fun of by Valerie"

(67a) differs from (65b) in that the downstairs object of a *faire par* construction appears as a an indirect not a direct object. Since this is possible for undisputed indirect objects like that in (67a), why is it impossible for those taken here to result from advancement to indirect object, leaving (67b) ungrammatical? An answer is required to ground my earlier claim that not only is 6 to 3 advancement limited to passives, but specifically to Resumptives and their look-alikes. For, although controversial, there is a case that the complements of examples like (67a) are passives. If so, it remains obscure why (67b) is bad, for its ungrammaticality follows from neither of rules (53) or (57).
   Fortunately, no ad hoc rule linked exclusively to Resumptives is required; the relevant constraint can be taken to be that needed for restrictions like (63), whose contrast with (62) illustrated contexts where clause union complements involving indirect objects were more restricted than those involving direct objects. Just such a pattern is, of course, found in (65).
   Further perspective on the problems just introduced focusses on examples parallel to (67) and adds transitive ones to yield (68).

(68)   Le père a fait écrire (une lettre) à Jacques par le comité.
       "The father had Jacques written (a letter) to by the committee"

Two distinct analyses are possible for the complement of the long form of (68), even under my controversial assumption that it, like all *faire par* complements, is a passive clause. It could involve a prepassive 2-arc headed by *une lettre*, or a prepassive 3-arc, headed by *(à) Jacques*. Both would, without ad hoc statements, yield the longer form, since in each case the prepassive arc would be a launcher, given the type II analysis of the relevant passives. However, I suggest that the long case of (68) is structurally unambiguous, manifesting only a prepassive 2-arc. This claim, for which there is no direct factual evidence, can be implemented by stating that a French prepassive 3-arc is not only, as in (64), required to be a launcher, but is further possible only in Union passives or their active look-alikes. The latter proposal directly determines that the short version of (76), whose complement is intransitive, also does not involve a prepassive 3-arc. This leaves its structure obscure, since it might appear that it contains no prepassive 2-arc.

But earlier work of mine argues that the short version of (68) does involve a prepassive 2-arc of the type occurring in impersonal passives. This asssigns the short form of (68) a complement structure paralleling the nonauxiliary clause complement of (69a), rather than the complement of (69b).

(69) a. Il a été écrit à Marie par le comité.
      "It was written to Marie by the committee"
      b. Marie s'est fait écrire par le comité.
      "Marie got written to by the committee"

The latter involves a prepassive 3-arc of its *écrire* clause; the former a prepassive dummy 2-arc in its *écrit* clause. The contrast in (67) then follows since, for reasons beyond this discussion, inherently reflexive verbs forming Resumptives never permit impersonal participial passives. So my proposal reduces the difference in (67) to that between (69a) and *(70).

(70) *Il a été moqué de Marie par le comité.
      "It was made fun of Marie by the committee"

That a French prepassive 3-arc must not only be a launcher but of the sort occurring in a Union passive can be formalized by a minor extension of rule (57). Where the latter does not block a prepassive 3-arc analysis for either version of (68), the refined version requires the 3-arc launcher referenced in (57) to bear a certain relation to a 1-arc, as in (72), given the definition in (71).

(71) **Definition**

Arc A is Persistent if and only if A has a P-arc neighbor B, and B is not erased.

(72) **French Prepassive Arc Restrictions (Final Version)**

If A is a prepassive arc, A is a 2-arc or 3-arc and a prepassive 3-arc is a launcher that is remote erased by a final persistent 1-arc.

Note that REMOTE ERASE is just the logical ancestral of Erase. Rule (72) explicates the otherwise puzzling contrast between Union-2-passives and Union-3-passives when embedded as clause union complements, as in (62) and (63). Such embedding determines that the final 1-arc of the Union passive main clause, which remote erases the complement 3-arc, is not the final 1-arc of a persistent clause. Hence that 1-arc remote successor of the prepassive 3-arc does not help satisfy (72) and there is no other 1-arc which does. Thus rule (72) is unsatisfiable by prepassive 3-arcs in clauses embedded below an additional clause union complement, but not so for prepassive 2-arcs.

Rule (72) predicts the contrast seen in (65), and, given hypothesis (48b), the ill-formedness of structures like (66), related to Resumptive structures, follows. Similarly, (72) combines with the view that (67a) involves impersonal passive complements (hence prepassive 2-arcs) and the fact that those inherently reflexive Vs permitting Resumptives preclude impersonal passives (see (70)), to yield the contrast between (67a,b). So various apparently anomalous restrictions on clause union cases with Vs like *moquer* follow from the independently needed rule (72), which does not mention such Vs or Resumptives. These facts support assumption (48b), and rules (53) and (72), which claim that all Resumptives are Union-3-passives.

There are three unsettled points. First, why must inherently reflexive Vs like *moquer* occur in Resumptives without the inherent reflexive? A rather simple answer follows from the type II 1-arc local successor analysis of Resumptives and Union passives in general, which determines that the passive constituent of a Resumptive has no final 1-arc. Therefore, if the inherent reflexive rule is, informally, like (73), the facts are explained.

(73) **Inherent Reflexive Rule (Highly Informal Version)**

A 1-arc A of a clause K is linked to an inherent reflexive in K if and only if A is final and K's main verb is *moquer*, or ....

A second question is why a Union passive main V requires a reflexive clitic, making Union passives superficially identical with 'coreferential' reflexive causative structures. The answer is that semantically empty reflexives are required not only in certain lexical contexts but also in certain syntactic ones. Since, under my analysis, Union passive main Vs take clause union complements but have no initial 1-arcs, I propose condition (74).

(74) **Initially Subjectless Clause Union Rule (Informal Version)**

A 1-arc A of a clause union main clause K is linked to an empty reflexive in K if A is final and K has no initial 1-arc.

This not only predicts the necessarily reflexive clitics of Union passives, but also specifies those of (75):

(75)   a. Ce vin se laisse boire.
"This wine lets itself drink = is drinkable"
b. si le besoin s'en fait sentir
"if the need for it is felt"

A third issue is why, as (31) documents, the *de* + pronoun of Resumptives cannot alternate with the clitic *en*. I derive this from the property that the pronoun in question is abstractly reflexive, combined again with the type II 1-arc local successor analysis of Union passives as these factors interact with a principle limiting pronominal cliticization of reflexives. This says, roughly, that a reflexive arc Q can sponsor a $\cent$-arc only if Q is anaphorically paired to a final 1-arc. Under a type II analysis, this assumption can explain the well-known fact that a so-called 'corefrerential' reflexive clitic is impossible in Participial passives; see (76aiii).

(76)   a. (i)   J'ai décrit Jacques à lui-même.
"I described Jacques to himself"
(ii)   Jacques a été décrit à lui-même.
"Jacques was described to himself"
(iii)   *Jacques s'a/s'est été écrit (à lui-même).
"Jacques was described to himself"
b. Jacques s'est décrit cela (à lui-même).
"Jacques described that to himself"

Essentially, (76aiii) is then bad because although a reflexive 3-arc exists in the complement of the passive auxiliary and that 3-arc is linked to a 1-arc, namely, the type II arc-passive arc, that 1-arc is not final.

An exactly parallel account holds for Resumptives, except that the reflexive arc is a copy 6-arc, and not a result of the replacement of overlapping initial 3-arcs arcs as in the so-called 'coreference' cases.

To conclude, (77) summarizes the main points about Resumptives I have made in these remarks.

(77) **Basic Elements of the Analysis of Resumptives**

    a. Resumptives are Union passives.
    b. Union passives are biclausal.
    c. Union passives are clause union structures.
    d. The main clause in a Union passive contains no initial 1-arc and its main V is meaningless (like the participial passive auxiliary).
    e. The complement of a Union passive contains a type II arc-passive arc.
    f. Any French prepassive arc is a 2-arc or a 3-arc.
    g. The prepassive arc in a Resumptive is a 3-arc.
    h. Although the (unergative) Vs which permit Resumptives take no initial 3-arcs, (77g) can hold (for type (12a)) because French allows 3-arc local successors of 6-arcs, provided that at least (77i) is true:
    i. the 3-arc is (I) prepassive, (II) a launcher and (III) has a remote successor which is a persistent final 1-arc; and (IV) the 6-arc is copied.
    j. The main clause of a Union passive requires a reflexive clitic because this is requisite for all French clause union main clauses not having initial 1-arcs.
    k. The subordinate clause of a Resumptive based on an inherently reflexive V must lack an inherent reflexive because it has no final 1-arc.
    l. The *de* + pronoun of a Resumptive cannot alternate with the pronominal clitic *en* because of the interaction of a law linking reflexive pronominal cliticization to arcs anaphorically paired with final 1-arcs, not found in Resumptive complements under a type II analysis.

References

Baker, Mark C. 1988. *Incorporation*. Chicago: The University of Chicago Press.
Blinkenberg, Andreas. 1960. *Le problème de la transitivité en français moderne*. Copenhagen: Munksgaard.
Bresnan, Joan. 1982. The Passive In Lexical Theory. *The Mental Representation of Grammatical Relations*, ed. by Joan Bresnan, 3–86. Cambridge, Massachusetts: The MIT Press.
Chocheyras, J. 1968. Un nouvel outil grammatical en français moderne: le verbe voir. *Le Français Moderne* 36.219–225.
Chomsky, Noam. 1975. *Reflections on Language*. New York: Pantheon Books.
Chomsky, Noam. 1981. *Lectures on Government and Binding*. Dordrecht, Holland: Foris Publications.
Danell, Karl J. 1979. *Remarques sur la construction dite causative* Stockholm: Almqvist and Wiksell International.
De Groof, Christine. 1983. *Remarques sur la construction causative* Antwerp, Belgium: Dissertation, Universitaire Instelling Antwerpen.
Dubois, Jean. 1967. *Grammaire structurale du français: le verbe*. Paris: Librairie Larousse.
Fauconnier, Gilles. 1983. Generalized Union. *Communication and Cognition* 16.3–37.
Grevisse, Maurice. 1969. *Le bon usage*. Gembloux, Belgium: Editions J. Duculot.
Gross, Maurice. 1975. *Méthodes en syntaxe*. Paris: Herman.
Haggis, B. M. 1971. Verbes réfléchis ou verbes pronominaux. *Le français dans le Monde* 79.6–13.
Hornstein, Norbert and Amy Weinberg. 1981. Case Theory and Preposition Stranding. *Linguistic Inquiry* 12.55–91.
Johnson, David E. and Paul M. Postal. 1980. *Arc Pair Grammar*. Princeton, New Jersey: Princeton University Press.
Kayne, Richard. 1975. *French Syntax*. Cambridge, Massachusetts: The MIT Press.
Kayne, Richard. 1984. *Connectedness and Binary Branching*. Dordrecht, Holland: Foris Publications.
Kayne, Richard S. and Jean-Yves Pollock. 1978. Stylistic Inversion, Successive Cyclicity, and Move NP in French. *Linguistic Inquiry* 9. 595–621.
Lasnik, Howard and Mamoru Saito. 1992. *Move α*. Cambridge, Massachusetts: The MIT Press.

Legendre, Géraldine. 1990. French Causatives: Another Look at *faire par*. *Grammatical Relations: A Cross-Theoretical Perspective*, ed. by Katarzyna Dziwirek, Patrick Farrell and Errapel Mejías-Bikandi, 247–262. Stanford, California: CSLI.
Martinon, Phillipe. 1927. *Comment on parle en français*. Paris: Librairie Larousse.
Pollock, Jean-Yves 1979. Réanalyse et constructions impersonelles. *Recherches Linguistiques* 8.72–130.
Postal, Paul M. 1983. On Characterizing French Grammatical Structure *Linguistic Analysis* 11.361–417.
Postal, Paul M. 1984. French Indirect Object Cliticization and SSC/BT. *Linguistic Analysis* 14.111–172.
Postal, Paul M. 1985. La dégradation de prédicat et un genre négligé de montée. *Recherches linguistiques* 13.33–68.
Postal, Paul M. 1986. *Studies of Passive Clauses*. Albany, New York: State University of New York Press.
Postal, Paul M. 1989. *Masked Inversion in French*. Chicago: The University of Chicago Press.
Postal, Paul M. 1990. French Indirect Object Demotion. *Studies in Relational Grammar 3*, ed. by Paul M. Postal and Brian D. Joseph, 104–200. Chicago: The University of Chicago Press.
Postal, Paul M. 1992a. Phantom Successors and the French *faire par Construction*. The Joy of Grammar: A Festschrift for James D. McCawley, ed. by Diane Brentari, Gary Larson and Lynn MacLeod, 289–321. Chicago: The University of Chicago Press.
Postal, Paul M. 1992b. Un passif sans morphologie spécifique. *Hommages à Nicolas Ruwet,* ed.by Liliane Tasmowski and Anne Zribi-Hertz, 475–484. Ghent, Belgium: Communication and Cogniton.
Riemsdijk, Henk van. 1978. *A Case Study in Syntactic Markedness*. Dordrecht, Holland: Foris Publications.
Riemsdijk, Henk van and Edwin Williams. 1986. *Introduction to the Theory of Grammar*. Cambridge, Massachusetts: The MIT Press.
Roggero, Jacques. 1984. Le passif, le causatif et quelques autres formes assez étranges. *Travaux cercle linguistique d'Aix en Provence* 2.25-39.
Sandfeld, Karl. 1965. Syntaxe du français contemporain: l'infinitif. Genève: Librairie Droz.
Shyldkrot, H. 1981. A propos de la forme passive "se voir+V_{inf}". *Folia Linguistica* 15.387–407.
Spang-Hanssen, Ebbe. 1967. Quelques périphrases passives du français moderne. *Actes du 4ème congrés des romanistes scandinaves dédiés à Holger Sten.* Copenhagen: Akademisk Forlag. (= Revue romane, numéro spécial 1. 139–147.)

Stimm, H. 1957. Eine Ausdrucksform passivischer Idee im Neufranzösischen. *Syntactica und Stilistica, Festschrift E. Gamillscheg*, 581–610. Tübingen: Niemeyer.

Tasmowski-De Ryck, L. and H. van Oevelen. 1987. Le causatif pronominal. *Revue Romane* 22.40–58.

Tobler, Adolph. 1905. *Mélanges de grammaire française*. Paris: Alphonse Picard and Fils.

Van Oevelen, Hildegard. 1985. *Se Faire Infinitif- Se Laisser Infinitif: Restrictions d'emploi*. Antwerp, Belgium: Doctoral Dissertation, Universitaire Instelling Antwerpen.

Williams, Edwin. 1980. Predication. *Linguistic Inquiry* 11.203–238.

Zribi-Hertz, Annie. 1981. *Towards a Transformationally Expressed Explanation of Passive Verbal Morphology in French and English*. Bloomington, Indiana: Indiana University Linguistics Club.

Underspecifying grammatical relations in a constraint-based morphology

KEVIN RUSSELL
University of Manitoba

In this paper, I would like to consider how best to treat cases where morphological agreement markers seem to need to refer to sets of grammatical relations rather than single grammatical relations, for example, an agreement marker that appears if either the subject or the direct object is second person singular. Such morphology is common in languages of the Algonquian family of North America. The examples in this paper will be drawn from two of these: Cheyenne and Potawatomi.

The framework of this paper will involve the emerging ideas of constraint-based morphology. Starting out from work in Declarative Phonology (e.g., Bird 1990, 1992, Scobbie 1991), a constraint-based approach to morphology centres on the idea that morphemes are not pieces of phonological representation that need to be stuck together, nor are they rules or operations that build these representations piece by piece. Rather, morphemes are constraints on what pieces of phonological structure and what pieces of syntactic (and semantic) structure can co-occur.

Unlike rules or operations, these constraints cannot be ordered, either extrinsically or intrinsically. They all apply at once, and they all must be satisfied.[1] In the most extreme versions of the approach, constraints apply to only a single level of syntactic representation and a single level of phonological representation. Despite these limitations, such an approach is fully capable of handling the intricacies of an Algonquian morphological system.

This claim is in marked contrast to those claims that Algonquian person agreement requires some kind of inversion operation that applies in the course of a derivation in virtual time to reverse (syntactically or morphologically) the positions of the subject and the object. This is not to say that there may not be good *syntactic* reasons for such an

---

[*] This paper has benefitted from discussions with Jean-Roger Vergnaud, David Pentland, and the participants at the Grammatical Relations conference. Part of this work has been supported by a fellowship from the Social Sciences and Humanities Research Council of Canada.

[1] In this respect, the approach is unlike the Optimality Theory of Prince and Smolensky (1993) or McCarthy and Prince (1993).

inversion operation, for example, those proposed by Perlmutter and Rhodes (in preparation) for Ojibwe. But if these syntactic reasons are absent, as they seem to be in many Algonquian languages, there are no morphological reasons to insist on inversion.[2]

In order for a constraint-based analysis to work in a principled fashion, it is necessary to accept an idea that has already been argued for by some syntacticians, namely that grammatical relations (GRs) can fall into natural classes and that grammatical principles (in this case, morphemic constraints) can refer to these natural classes. Put another way, morphemes can be underspecified for the GRs of the arguments whose features they are interested in. I shall show that even analyses that use an inversion operation will still need to make use of some sort of GR underspecification. I shall also try to show that explicitly referring to natural classes of GRs is superior to approaches that try to accomplish the same work as a side-effect of the general formal principles for referring to arguments (e.g., Anderson 1992, Steele 1992).

1. The general problem

The sort of inflectional marking we shall be dealing with is well illustrated in the following set of Potawatomi verb-forms:[3]

(1) nwapma 'I see her/him'
n-wapUm-a
1-see   DIRECT

(2) kwapma 'you (sg.) see her/him'
k-wapUm-a
2-see   DIRECT

(3) nwapmək 'she/he sees me'
n-wapUm-Uk   '3sg sees me'
1-see   INVERSE

---

[2] Potawatomi also seems to lack syntactic grounds for assuming an inversion operation, as Anderson (1992) admits. Cf. Wolfart (1973) and Dahlstrom (1986) on Plains Cree.

[3] Data are from Hockett (1949). (See also Hockett 1939.) The /U/ that appears in the morpheme-by-morpheme glosses is the archiphoneme proposed by Hockett for a schwa that alternates with zero.

(4)   kwapmək 'she/he sees you (sg.)'
      k-wapUm-Uk   '3sg sees you(sg.)'
      2-see   INVERSE

In (1) and (2), a 1sg and 2sg subject respectively is acting on a 3sg direct object. The prefix before the verb stem wapəm marks first person (n-) and second person (k-). In the next two words, (3) and (4), the situation is reversed: a 3sg subject is acting on a 1sg or 2sg direct object. Yet the prefixes continue to mark first and second person in exactly the same way they did in (1) and (2). The only way to determine which argument the first and second person prefixes are agreeing with is the suffix that has come to be known in the Algonquianist literature as the direction marker. If the direction marker is in the "direct" form, the first or second person is the subject, if in the "inverse" form, the object.[4]

The entire paradigm for the main-clause form of the verb wapUm- 'see', where one argument is a third person and the other is a first or second, is as follows:[5]

(5)

Subject:	Object: 3sg	3obv	3pl
1sg	nwapma	nwapman	nwapmak
2sg	kwapma	kwapman	kwapmak
3sg		wapman	
1pl.i	kwapmamən		
1pl.e	nwapmamən		
2pl	kwapmawa	kwapmawan	kwapmawak
3pl		wapmawan	

---

[4] While I shall often refer loosely to "objects", it should be noted that these are somewhat different in Algonquian languages than in many more familiar languages. In ditransitive sentences, it is the indirect object that patterns with the direct object of transitive sentences. Following Rhodes' (1990) discussion of object GRs in Ojibwe, I shall refer to transitive direct objects and ditransitive indirect object as "primary objects", and to ditransitive direct objects as "secondary objects".

[5] "3obv" stands for the third person obviative. In Algonquian languages, only one third person referent in any stretch of discourse can appear in the unmarked (or "proximate") third person form. All other third person referents must appear in the marked or "obviative" form. Obviative expressions are neutralized for number. Because an obviative third person is necessarily disjoint in reference from a proximate third person, obviatives have sometimes been called "fourth persons".

(6)

Object:	Subject: 3sg	3obv	3pl
1sg	nwapmək		nwapməkok
2sg	kwapmək		kwapməkok
3sg		wapməkon	
1pl.i	kwapməknan		kwapməknanək
1pl.e	nwapməknan		nwapməknanək
2pl	kwapməkwa		kwapməkwak
3pl		wapməkwan	

In all these forms, we can see the basic generalization that if a first or second person serves as either the subject or direct object of the verb, it will be marked by a prefix. The same general principle extends to verbs with both first and second person arguments. In cases like this, it is the second person prefix that appears, as in (30) and (31) below.

We can informally state the generalizations for prefix selection as:

(7) a. if subject or primary object is 2nd person, the prefix is k–; otherwise
 b. if subject or primary object is 1st person, the prefix is n–; otherwise
 c. if subject or primary object is 3rd person, the prefix is ?–

In his study of Cheyenne morphology, D. Russell (1987) lists the three approaches to dealing with this generalization more theoretically that have played a role in the Algonquianist literature:

a. "highest-person" approach: prefix marks the highest person on the animacy hierarchy

b. "surface subject" approach: inverse forms have undergone obligatory passivization; prefix marks the surface subject

c. "Bloomfieldian" approach[6]

The "highest-person" approach depends on the assumption that grammatical persons can be ranked in a hierarchy that determines which one

---

[6] Although Bloomfield is often believed to have argued for the highest-person approach, D. Russell shows that his actual analysis was somewhat different.

is given preference in selecting the prefix. The section of the hierarchy that most Algonquianists agree on is:[7]

(8) Animacy hierarchy:
     2 > 1 > 3 > 3 obv

The operation of the animacy hierarchy applies to the verb prefixes we have been discussing so far. Verb suffixes are determined by more complicated principles that often refer to the person/number values of more than one argument. But, as with the prefixes, it is typically the case that these suffixes will not be concerned so much with the exact GR of the argument bearing a certain person/number value, but simply with whether or not that person/number value is present somewhere in the argument structure of the verb. Two typical suffixes of Cheyenne, with their uses as described by D. Russell, are:[8]

(9) Cheyenne $-m\acute{e}_1$ (D. Russell 1987: 59):
     Of the two sets {1pl, 2pl} and {1sg, 2sg, 1pl, 2pl, indef}, the Subject is a member of one and the Direct Object is a member of the other.

(10) Cheyenne $-n\acute{o}_1$:
     Of the two sets {1pl} and {2sg, 2pl}, the Subject is a member of one, and the Direct Object is a member of the other.

It is this ability (or necessity) for the principles determining suffix selection to look for person/number values in more than one argument of the verb that will be the focus of this paper. In particular, we shall be concerned with whether this ability is a side effect of some other grammatical rule (such as an inversion transformation), or a side effect of the conventions for interpreting rule formalism, or whether it is the

---

[7] D. Russell argues that the "direction" markers are really person markers and that the animacy hierarchy is in fact a collection of GPSG Linear Precedence Rules. For example, given two sisters, the left-hand one cannot bear a first person feature while the right-hand one bears a second person feature. In what follows, I shall assume that the effects of the animacy hierarchy can be obtained by an analysis along these lines.

[8] The same person/number values are often present in both sets of the morpheme characterizations given by Russell. This is because Russell analyzes reflexives as morphologically transitive verbs. This does not seem to be a necessary part of the analysis, and it may be that reflexives in Cheyenne will, like those of other Algonquian languages, turn out to be formed by detransitivizing derivational morphology.

result of morphemes referring to a natural class of GRs, that is, whether morphemes can underspecify information about GRs.

2. A constraint-based morphology

It is one of the basic assumptions of what have been called the "unification-based" approaches to grammar that linguistic signs are complexes of various kinds of information, e.g., syntactic structure, semantic structure, phonological structure. Using the traditional matrix notation of these frameworks, the highest level of a linguistic sign might look something like:

(11) $\begin{bmatrix} \text{PHON} & [\,...\,] \\ \text{SYN} & [\,...\,] \\ \text{SEM} & [\,...\,] \end{bmatrix}$

Work in various frameworks of unification-based syntax has explored what the syntactic and semantic parts of this structure might look like. Work in Declarative Phonology (e.g., Bird 1990, 1992, Scobbie 1991, K. Russell 1993) has explored what the phonological part of this sign structure might look like. One of the common threads of the entire research program is the hypothesis that morphemes (or, often, "lexical entries") are licences that allow the pairing of a certain syntactic structure and a certain phonological structure within one sign.

Morphemes are often diagrammed using the same matrix notation that is used for actual linguistic representations, such as the following diagram of the Potawatomi morpheme for the stem 'see':

(12) $\begin{bmatrix} \text{SYN:} & V^0 \\ \text{SEM:} & see' \\ \text{PHON:} & /\text{wapUm}/ \end{bmatrix}$

But, since the clear distinction between representations and *descriptions* of representations (or constraints on representations) was argued for by Johnson (e.g., 1988, 1991), it has been recognized that matrix diagrams like (12) are really only convenient abbreviations for a constraint or a description of a legal structure. The "morpheme" in (12) is thus merely an abbreviation for a logical description that might look like the following:[9]

---

[9] This "description" is itself highly abbreviated. For some proposals on what descriptions of phonological structures would have to look like, see Bird (1990) or K. Russell (1993).

(13)   for all X
       if $X = V^0$ and $Sem(X) = $ see' then $Ph(X) = $ /wapUm/

Such a constraint essentially says: "If there's a V^0 node in the syntactic structure that's associated to a semantics of *see'*, then there had better be a corresponding section of the phonological structure that has a *w* followed by an *a* followed by...or *m*, or else the entire structure will not be a legal sign of the language."

Additional constraints will determine where the stretch of phonology corresponding to a syntactic node X must lie with respect to the stretch of phonology corresponding to its sister Y. The scope of these alignment constraints may be narrow (e.g., a single morpheme) or quite wide (e.g., all heads precede all non-heads).[10] A typical alignment constraint might look like the following, which demands that the stretch of phonology corresponding to V^0 precede that corresponding to Agr:

(14)   for all X,Y
       if X and Y are sisters and $X = V^0$ and $Y = $ Agr then
       $Ph(X) \prec Ph(Y)$

2.1. Application to Algonquian morphology

Treating the morphemes for Algonquian verbal prefixes and suffixes as constraints, we immediately run into a difficulty. The second person prefix *k–*, for example, would seem to need two constraints:[11]

(15)   for all X
       if $X \approx [Person_a, independent]$ and $X \approx [agr: [subj: [pers: 2]]]$
       then $Ph(X) = $ /k/

---

[10] With wide scope, they act like the Linear Precedence rules of GPSG's Immediate Dominance/Linear Precedence distinction.

[11] For concreteness, I am treating argument structures as attribute value matrices with the attribute AGR and GRs as the attributes of subordinate attribute value pairs. This is similar in many ways to their treatment in LFG, but is not a crucial aspect of the main argument being made in this paper. With a small amount of complication in the formulation of morphemic constraints, GRs could be treated more as they are in HPSG. Of course, the arguments presented here would not be compatible with a claim that each argument of each verb has a unique and primitive GR. No matter what else may be in the internal structure of a GR, it is crucial that there be some features in common between the arguments of different verbs.

(16) for all X
if X ≈ [Person$_a$,independent] and X ≈ [agr: [p.obj: [pers: 2]]]
then Ph(X) = /k/

(15) is needed in order to require the presence of a k– when there is a second person subject, and (16) for when there is a second person primary object. But this exact duplication would be needed over and over again in Algonquian morphological systems. The Cheyenne suffix –mé$_1$ of (9) would require two constraints, like:

(17)
a. $\left[\text{agr:} \begin{array}{l} \text{subj:} \quad [\text{1sg} \lor \text{2sg} \lor \text{1pl} \lor \text{2pl} \lor \text{indef}] \\ \text{p.obj:} \quad [\text{1pl} \lor \text{2pl}] \end{array} \right]$

b. $\left[\text{agr:} \begin{array}{l} \text{subj:} \quad [\text{1pl} \lor \text{2pl}] \\ \text{p.obj:} \quad [\text{1sg} \lor \text{2sg} \lor \text{1pl} \lor \text{2pl} \lor \text{indef}] \end{array} \right]$

The suffix –nó$_1$ of (10) would also require two constraints. Most prefixes and suffixes would require two constraints, with a regularity that should lead us to worry that we are missing a generalization.

One possible way of doing this would be to refrain from spelling out exactly which GR the constraint is looking for, using instead a variable for it and restricting the range of values that that variable may have.

(18) for all X
if there exists a U such that
X ≈ [Person$_a$,independent] and X ≈ [agr: [U: [pers: 2]]] and
U=subj or U=p.obj
then Ph(X) = /k/

This allows us to collapse two constraints into one, but it is not entirely satisfactory. Variables restricted to just these two GRs would appear in morpheme after morpheme in Cheyenne and Potawatomi. There is no reason we should expect variables to be restricted to *subj* and *p.obj* any more frequently than to *subj* and *s.obj*, to *p.obj* and *loc*, or to any other pair of GRs. If we find one particular pair of GRs showing up over and over in variable restrictions, we should again suspect that we are missing a generalization.

One possibility that I shall be exploring in this paper is this: the pair of GRs *subj* and *p.obj* occur together so often in morphemic constraints because they form a natural class that the grammar of a language is able to refer to. The existence of this natural class is already widely recognized and used under various names. For example, Relational Grammar refers to the GRs 1 and 2 together as "nuclear" terms. It is generally assumed that a principle or law that refers to nuclear terms is more natural and less "costly" than one that refers to a random collocation of GRs.

Following the Jakobsonian principle that natural classes are defined by shared features, it can be proposed that within linguistic representations, GRs have some sort of internal structure and that some feature (or features) of this internal structure is shared by the members of the natural class consisting of *subj* and *p.obj*. Referring to the shared feature(s) as F, we can collapse the two schematic diagrams of the second person prefix morpheme in (19) into the single statement of (20).

(19) [agr : [subj : [pers: 2]]]
      [agr : [p.obj : [pers: 2]]]

(20) [agr : [[...F...] : [pers: 2]]]

Some research into the possible natural classes of GRs has already been conducted by syntacticians. In the LFG framework, for example, Bresnan and Zaenan (1990) propose the following classification and featural representation for the four GRs, subject, primary object, secondary object (O_θ), and oblique (cf. Levin 1986):

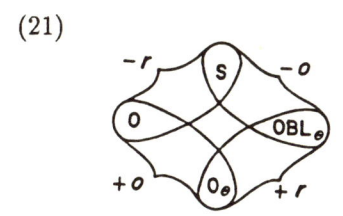

(21)

(22) [+r] *restricted* (as to thematic role)
      [+o] *objective*

The natural class we have found at work in Algonquian morphology, *subj* and *p.obj*, is the class defined by the shared feature [−r], that is, those GRs that are unrestricted as to what thematic roles they may be associated with.[12]

---

[12] Recall that in Algonquian languages, it is the secondary object (the direct object of a ditransitive verb) that is restricted in the thematic roles it may be associated with, while the primary object (transitive direct objects and ditransitive indirect objects) is relatively free.

Using the feature [±r], we can rewrite the schematic representation of the morpheme in (20) as:

(23) [agr : [[–r] : [pers: 2]]]

Underspecifying GRs in this way allows us a simple and natural characterization of the kinds of morphemes needed for Algonquian agreement affixes. For example, the Cheyenne suffix $-mé_1$, already seen in (9) and (17), can be characterized as:

(24) Cheyenne $-mé_1$:
$$\left[\text{agr:} \left[\begin{array}{l} [-r]_i : [1pl \lor 2pl] \\ [-r]_j : [1sg \lor 2sg \lor 1pl \lor 2pl \lor indef] \\ \quad i \neq j \end{array} \right] \right]$$

Notice that the morpheme is making demands of two different arguments, one argument of unrestricted GR, i, that is either first or second person plural, and a second argument of unrestricted GR, j, whose feature/number value must come from the set {1sg, 2sg, 1pl, 2pl, indef}. The morpheme further demands that the two arguments i and j be distinct, with the result that one must be the subject and the other the primary object.

This requirement of disjointness is by no means a necessary fact of Algonquian morphology. It is quite possible for a morpheme to impose two demands on the argument structure and not care whether it is the same argument that satisfied both demands. For example, Cheyenne has a suffix $-no_3$ that we may characterize with the following diagram, without any proviso that $i \neq j$:

(25) Cheyenne $-no_3$:
$$\left[\text{agr:} \left[\begin{array}{l} [-r]_i : [-\text{animate}] \\ [-r]_j : [+\text{plural}] \end{array} \right] \right]$$

$-no_3$ occurs if either the subject is plural and the object is inanimate, or the object is plural and the subject is inanimate, or the subject is both plural and inanimate, or the object is both plural and inanimate.

Finally, it should be noted that it is not necessary for a morpheme to restrict its attention to any particular subset of GRs. It may look for a certain feature in any argument. We can symbolize this with an empty matrix in place of the GR attribute, that is, the morpheme makes no demands at all on the internal structure of the GR of the argument bearing the relevant feature:[13]

---

[13] Jean-Pierre Koenig points out that the classification of GRs in (21) by

(26)   Cheyenne $-o_1$:
appears if either the Subject or the Direct Object or the
Indirect Object is plural
[agr: [[ ] : [+plural]]]

3. Other approaches

There are other recent attempts to analyze Potawatomi that should be compared to the approach argued for here. These include Anderson (1992) and Steele (1992). Both are framed within processual models of morphology that make use of operations applying in virtual time.

The significant aspect of these analyses is that they both make use of mechanisms that are suspiciously similar to GR underspecification, but in both cases this underspecification is made to seem a side-effect of the formalism rather than something that the grammar is explicitly doing.

3.1. Anderson (1992)

Anderson's (1992) theory of morphology uses the full power of the transformational machinery of the 1960s and 1970s, complete with curly braces. His treatment of person agreement in Potawatomi is essentially the obligatory passivization analysis of LeSourd (1976) or the inversion analysis of Perlmutter and Rhodes (in preparation), the only difference being that he believes that this operation applies in the morphological component rather than in the syntax.

Anderson's Morpho-Syntactic Representations (MSRs) encode the agreement features of the various arguments of the verb using a layering technique:

---

the features [±r] and [±o] is unable to treat exactly the set {subj, p.obj, s.obj} as a natural class opposed to various oblique GRs. This may pose a problem for a treatment like that of (26), where the three arguments are accessed by completely underspecifying the GR, if it turns out that Cheyenne does need to have oblique arguments (e.g., the "relative root complements" mentioned by Rhodes (1991)) present in the list of arguments visible to agreement principles. Donald Frantz has argued that this is the case for Blackfoot, cf. Frantz (1991). In any event, there is a strong likelihood that the two features [±r] and [±o] will not be enough to define all the natural classes of GRs used in the world's languages and that some additions or changes will need to be made to the featural characterization of GRs in (21).

(27)
$$\begin{bmatrix} - & \text{me} \\ + & \text{you} \\ + & \text{Pl} \\ + & \text{Anim} \end{bmatrix} \begin{bmatrix} - & \text{me} \\ - & \text{you} \\ - & \text{Pl} \\ - & \text{Anim} \end{bmatrix}$$

Each layer of an MSR contains the agreement features for one argument. Agreement features are supposedly inserted into these layers by special agreement operations that apply in the syntax. Thus the MSR is completely specified before the morphology begins its work on it.

Anderson accomplishes the inversion operation he assumes with the following rule:

(28)   Inversion rule:

$$\begin{bmatrix} +\text{Verb} & \begin{Bmatrix} +\text{Obv} & \begin{bmatrix} +\text{Obv} \\ +\text{Anim} \end{bmatrix} \\ \begin{matrix} -\text{me} \\ -\text{you} \end{matrix} & \begin{bmatrix} \begin{Bmatrix} +\text{me} \\ +\text{you} \end{Bmatrix} \end{bmatrix} \end{Bmatrix} \end{bmatrix}$$

[+Verb 1 [2]] → [+Noun 2 [1]]
/X/ → /Xuko/

This rule exchanges wholesale two layers of an MSR, the outer level representing the subject and the first embedded layer the object. Besides some other changes to the MSR (e.g., changing the verb into a morphological noun), the rule has the side-effect of adding some phonology — /uko/ — to the stem.

Once this inversion rule has applied, other rules can apply to the revised MSR, secure in the knowledge that the agreement features they are looking for will be found in the appropriate layer, if they are to be found at all. For example, the rule

(29)   First person plural in inverse forms:
$$\begin{bmatrix} + & \text{Noun} & \\ + & \text{me} & (\text{X}) \\ + & \text{Pl} & \end{bmatrix}$$
/X/ → /Xnan/

applies to mark the presence of a 1pl.e in the outermost layer, relying on the fact that even if those person/number features did not start out life in the outermost layer, the inversion rule will have put them there.

Interestingly, rule (28), despite the vast power of the formalism it relies on, is not enough to do all the work required. It cannot reliably place all the agreement features that a particular affix is interested in into just one layer. One example of this inability is the first person plural suffix $-mUn$, which appears in the following two verb-forms:[14]

(30) kwapməymən 'you see us' (you ambiguous for number)
      k-wapUm-yU- mUn
      2-see-   EXT-1pl.e

(31) kwapmənmən 'we see you' (you ambiguous)
      k-wapUm-Un-   mUn
      2-see-   INVERSE-1pl.e

In (30), 1pl.e is born in the second layer; in (31), it is put there by the inversion rule because the 2pl outranks it. For these two verb-forms, the rule inserting the suffix $-mUn$ can rely on finding the 1pl.e features in the second layer. But this is not always the case. In the forms in paradigm (5), 1pl is born in the outermost layer and because it outranks the third person objects, it stays there. So the rule inserting $-mUn$ cannot rely on finding the 1pl features in a single layer of the MSR and must look for the features in both the first and second layers.

Anderson forces this wider search by leaving the brackets off of the 1pl features in the rule responsible for inserting $-mUn$:

(32) +me
      +Pl
      /X/ → /Xmʊn/

By the final convention of (33), this omission will cause the rule to look for the features in every layer of the MSR possible.

(33) Ways of referring to features (Anderson 1992: 99):
      Specific reference: e.g., [+F [-F]] (applies only if [+F] in outer layer and [-F] in inner layer).
      Outermost layer reference: [+F (X)] (applies when outermost layer contains [+F], regardless of what — if anything — is contained in subordinate layers).
      Innermost layer reference: [+F] (by convention, analyzes only the most deeply embedded level of list structure for the value [+F]).
      Anywhere reference: +F (when no bracketing is specified, analyzes any representation containing the value +F at any level).

---

[14] I have glossed as EXT or "extension" the yU that co-occurs with mUn in this environment. In forms where the other unrestricted argument is second person, $-mUn$ is first person exclusive plural, abbreviated 1pl.e.

Once morphological operations are given this ability to look at more than one layer at a time, however, the entire justification for a morphological inversion rule like (28) disappears. All the rules that Anderson formulates to look at the outermost layer after inversion can be reformulated to look at either layer. D. Russell (1987) and Steele (1992) are two examples of analyses that check more than one argument for agreement features and thereby avoid the need for an inversion operation. This is not a trade-off situation: the choice is between an analysis that needs to check more than one argument and an analysis that needs to check more than one argument and does inversion too.

3.2. Steele (1992)

While still operating within a processual model of morphology, Steele (1992), unlike Anderson, tries to deal with the concerns about restricting the power of formalism that have been the focus of so much research in both syntax and phonology during the past two decades.

The framework Steele argues for, Articulated Morphology, uses attribute-value matrices like those of constraint-based approaches (e.g., HPSG, LFG), but these are not handled in the passive constraint-checking manner familiar from these frameworks and argued for here, rather they are are actively built piece by piece by a derivation. A central tenet of Steele's Articulated Morphology is that every operation must *add* information.[15]

Steele also has a way of simulating the effects of GR underspecification. Following Anderson's notational practice of leaving off the brackets of features that are looked for in more than one layer, Steele proposes rules that look like:

(34)   X   XmUn
        [   ] → [   ]
        P:X   P: P:X   P:+speaker
                          N:unspec N:pl

Condition on Domain: First member ≠ [P: −speaker, −hearer]

---

[15] This poses quite a challenge, since in Steele's theory there can be no such thing as a completely redundant morpheme, while in Algonquian languages there are things that come fairly close. Steele has to come up with at least one piece of information that each affix adds to a verb and, harder yet, each affix in a particular slot has to add more or less the same kind of information. Because of this, Steele's proposes operations are more complicated than I believe they have to be. Still, her paper contains many insights into Algonquian morphology that may not have been possible to achieve if she had allowed herself to use a less restrictive framework.

Steele explains the effect of this notational difference:

> [T]hese operations do not specify individually the argument which the additional feature set enriches; rather this feature set 'floats' in the co-domain. ... the appropriate unification target for the additional 'floating' feature set is determined by a general strategy. (Steele 1992: 37)

To a stem that has a single person specified, rule (34) adds a second specification for a 1pl.e argument and closes off the number value of the existing argument. The features +me and −you can be be added to any argument in the list, subject to the following "general strategy":[16]

(35) **Avoid P:3**
For Suffix$_{2a}$ operations, compatible information may be unified with any member of an attribute/value structure, unless this member bears the feature/value pair [P:−speaker, −hearer].

Again, as with Anderson's analysis, this "floating" of feature values is in many ways a side-effect of the formalism. It is not an attempt to refer to a natural class of grammatical relations.

4. Underspecifying grammatical relations?

We can summarize the two competing claims as follows: for me, that certain morphemes refer to the natural class of grammatical relations comprising the subject and the primary object; for Anderson and Steele, that certain morphemes can refer to *any* argument in the argument structure. Since Potawatomi has no agreement with secondary objects (at least as far as Hockett has revealed), these two characterizations are extensionally the same for this language. The two approaches cannot be empirically distinguished in Potawatomi.

In order to decide between the two approaches, we would need a case where the verb agrees with properties of *three* arguments, where some rule or affix treats two of the arguments as being in some sense the same, while not giving the same treatment to the third argument. Fortunately Cheyenne, which shows verb agreement with some properties of the secondary object, offers a testing ground to see which approach's predictions are borne out.

---

[16] In Steele's analysis, Suffix$_{2a}$ operations are those that take a Stem (specified for two person values and no number values) and create an Extended Stem (specified for two person values and one number value).

Cheyenne has several suffixes that allow us to decide between the two approaches. One is −vo, whose context D. Russell (1987: 66) describes as:

(36) Cheyenne ditransitive −vo:
Either a. Of the two sets {3pl} and {1sg, 2sg, 3obv, 2pl, 3pl, indef}, the Subject is a member of one, and the Indirect Object is a member of the other, and the Direct Object is animate
Or b. Of the two sets {2pl} and {3sg, 3obv}, the Subject is a member of one, and the Indirect Object is a member of the other, and the Direct Object is animate

Some examples of its use are:[17]

(37) námêtaenovo 'they gave it (obv.) to me'
ná− mét −ae   −n   −o −vo
1− give −3pl.subj−DITRANS−PL

(38) némêtonovo 'you gave it (obv.) to him'
né− mét −ó   −n   −o −vo
2− give −3sg.IO−DITRANS−PL

Here, we do find the subject and primary (indirect) object being treated alike to the exclusion of the secondary (direct) object, yet the [+animate] requirement makes it clear that the secondary object must be present in the list of arguments visible to the affix. Under the first option (36a), the affix must check for the 3pl features (among others) in both the subject and primary object, but does not check for them in the secondary object. A verb with a 2pl subject, a 3pl secondary (direct) object, and a 3obv primary (indirect) object would not take the affix −vo.

But this is exactly what should happen if the rule for −vo had the ability to search for the agreement features of 3pl in *all* argument positions, as predicted by the "Anywhere Reference" or "floating feature" conventions used by Anderson and Steele. It is clear that −vo only has the ability to look for 3pl in the subject and primary object. What characterizes just this set of arguments is membership in a natural class, specifically in the natural class we have been designating [−r].

---

[17] Although the direct object in these examples is glossed in English as 'it', it can only be used of a referent whose noun is of the animate gender-class. Several lifeless objects have grammatically animate nouns.

Note that inversion will not allow us to avoid referring to a proper subset of arguments. We cannot bring in a rule to invert the subject and primary object and rely on it to consistently put 3pl in any particular layer of the MSR. There is another set of person/number values that the morpheme is also looking for in the other [-r] argument — {1sg, 2sg, 3obv, 2pl, indef}. 3pl is in the middle of this list in terms of the animacy hierarchy: 1sg, 2sg and 2pl outrank it; it outranks 3obv and, in many versions of the animacy hierarchy, indef. So, sometimes an inversion operation would put 3pl into the outer layer, sometimes it would put it into the second layer. The morphology would still need the ability to look for 3pl only in the first and second layers, while ignoring the third, innermost layer.

The bracketless feature convention made the prediction that a morpheme should be able to check for features either in a particular argument or in all arguments. Cheyenne -vo is a counterexample to this prediction: referring to any single argument is not enough, referring to all arguments is too much. The morpheme must be able to look for features in all and only those arguments whose GRs belong to a natural class. This is the situation we are led to expect by the analysis using GR underspecifiction.[18]

Using the ability to underspecify grammatical relations, an analysis in a constraint-based morphology can formulate a morpheme that looks for the 3pl features among those arguments whose grammatical relations belong to the natural class we have been calling [-restricted]:

(39) Cheyenne -vo:

a. $\left[\text{agr:} \left[\begin{array}{ll} [-r]_i : & [3pl] \\ [-r]_j : & \left[\begin{array}{l} 1sg \lor 2sg \lor 3obv \lor 2pl \\ \lor\ 3pl \lor indef \end{array} \right] \\ [+r, +o] : & [+\text{animate}] \\ i \neq j & \end{array} \right] \right]$

b. $\left[\text{agr:} \left[\begin{array}{ll} [-r]_i : & [2pl] \\ [-r]_j : & [3sg \lor 3obv] \\ [+r, +o] : & [+\text{animate}] \\ i \neq j & \end{array} \right] \right]$

5. Conclusion

In this paper, I have tried to add morphological arguments to the already existing syntactic arguments for the claim that the representa-

---

[18] This is not to say that searching for features in all GRs is impossible, as can be seen in example (26).

tion of grammatical relations in linguistic signs must have some kind of internal structure and that features of this internal structure can be used to define natural classes of GRs. I have also argued that morphemes can underspecify GRs by referring to the features that define their natural classes, in the same way that they can refer to natural classes of properties like person by using features like [–me].

I have illustrated the widespread use of one of these natural classes in Algonquian morphology, the natural class consisting of *subj* and *p.obj*, defined by the feature [–restricted] of Bresnan and Zaenen (1990). I have tried to show that none of the other analyses that have often been applied to Algonquian morphology will allow one to completely avoid referring to this natural class. Inversion operations cannot be relied on to place features that morphemes are interested in into any single argument of the argument structure—so analyses will still need a way to look for features in more than one argument. On the other hand, a convention that allows a morpheme to look for features in any argument at all is too strong. The Cheyenne morpheme for *–vo*, for example, can look for the 3pl features in two and only two arguments, and any analysis must find a way of restricting the morpheme's attention to just this proper subset of the argument structure. An account that allows morphemes to underspecify grammatical relations can accomplish this in a simple and natural manner.

References

Anderson, Stephen R. 1992. *A-Morphous Morphology*. Cambridge: Cambridge University Press.
Bird, Steven. 1990. *Constraint-Based Phonology*. Doctoral dissertation, University of Edinburgh.
Bird, Steven, editor. 1992. *Declarative Perspectives on Phonology*. Edinburgh: Centre for Cognitive Science, University of Edinburgh.
Bresnan, Joan, and Annie Zaenen. 1990. Deep Unaccusativity in LFG. *Grammatical Relations: A Cross-Theoretical Perspective*, ed. by K. Dziwirek, P. Farrell, and E. Mejías-Bikandi, 45–57. Chicago: University of Chicago Press.
Dahlstrom, Amy. 1986. *Plains Cree Morphosyntax*. Doctoral dissertation, Berkeley.
Frantz, Donald. 1991. *Blackfoot Grammar*. Toronto: University of Toronto Press.
Hockett, Charles. 1939. Potawatomi syntax. *Language* 15, 235–248.
Hockett, Charles. 1949. Potawatomi. *IJAL* 14, 1–10, 63–73, 139–149, 213–225.

Johnson, Mark. 1988. *Attribute Value Logic and the Theory of Grammar*. CSLI Lecture Notes, Number 16. Chicago: University of Chicago Press.

LeSourd, Philip. 1976. Verb Agreement in Fox. *Harvard Studies in Syntax and Semantics, Volume 2.* ed. by J. Hankamer and J. Aissen, 445–528.

Levin, Lori. 1986. *Operations on Lexical Forms: Unaccusative Rules in Germanic Languages*. Doctoral dissertation, MIT.

McCarthy, John, and Alan Prince. 1993. *Prosodic Morphology I: Constraint Interaction and Satisfaction*. Ms, University of Massachusetts, Amherst, and Rutgers University.

Prince, Alan, and Paul Smolensky. 1993. *Optimality Theory: Constraint Interaction in Generative Grammar*. Technical Report 2, Rutgers Center for Cognitive Science.

Rhodes, Richard A. 1990. Ojibwe Secondary Objects. *Grammatical Relations: A Cross-Theoretical Perspective*, ed. by K. Dziwirek, P. Farrell, and E. Mejías-Bikandi, 401-414. Chicago: University of Chicago Press.

Russell, Dale W. 1987. *Cheyenne Verb Agreement in GPSG*. Doctoral dissertation, University of Illinois at Urbana-Champaign.

Russell, Kevin. 1993. *A constraint-based approach to phonology and morphology*. Doctoral dissertation, University of Southern California.

Scobbie, James. 1991. *Attribute-Value Phonology*. Doctoral dissertation, University of Edinburgh.

Steele, Susan. 1992. Towards a Theory of Morphological Information. Ms, University of Arizona.

Wolfart, H. Christoph. 1973. *Plains Cree: A Grammatical Sketch*. Transactions of the American Philosophical Society, new series, v. 63, part 5.

Binding and Conference in Jakaltek

FRANK R. TRECHSEL
Ball State University

0. Introduction

Facts regarding the possibilities of coreference and non-coreference between various types of NP in a sentence have long been used to motivate hypotheses regarding the hierarchical constituent structure of clauses. In recent years, these facts have assumed even greater relevance and importance in the context of theories which posit universal structural (i.e. configurational) constraints on coreference. Within the framework of GB, for example, it is often possible to deduce certain significant aspects of clause structure from information regarding the distribution and interpretation of the various types of overt and covert NP. Thus, a linguist (or child) equipped with knowledge of Condition C of the binding theory can conclude immediately from examples like those in (1) and (2) that subjects c-command direct objects in English, but objects do not c-command subjects:

(1) *He$_i$ saw Peter$_i$'s father.

(2) Peter$_i$'s father saw him$_i$.

Given the enormous practical significance of this sort of deduction (as well as its widespread use and acceptance within GB), it is important to understand the nature and extent of its limitations. In this paper, I propose to demonstrate that there are, indeed, limits to what can be deduced about clause structure from the binding and coreference facts in at least one language. In Jakaltek, a Q'anjob'alan (Mayan) language spoken in Guatemala, the facts regarding the various possibilities of coreference and non-coreference of NP are clear and unequivocal.[1] Nevertheless, they are not sufficient to motivate any specific hypotheses regarding the structural (hierarchical) relationship of constituents because the various constraints and conditions which determine these possibilities do not refer at all to configurational notions like c-command. I intend to show that the strategy of deduction illustrated above fails in this language precisely because the crucial appeal to the binding conditions is unwarranted.

The structure of this paper is as follows: In section 1, I present some minimal background information on the two distinct sets of elements in Jakaltek which can, under certain conditions, be interpreted as coreferential with another NP in a sentence. One of these is the set consisting of the twenty-four 'noun classifiers' in the language; the other is the singleton set consisting of the empty category, pro.[2] In section 2, I offer a critique of one recent attempt to deduce the hierarchical structure of clauses in Jakaltek from facts regarding the distribution and interpretation of the elements in these two sets. This is the attempt of Woolford (1991), who argues for the validity of the so-called 'Internal Subject Hypothesis' in this language on the basis of data presented in Craig (1977, 1986). Specifically, Woolford argues that transitive sentences with normal VSO word order in Jakaltek have the 'flat' S-structure represented in (3):

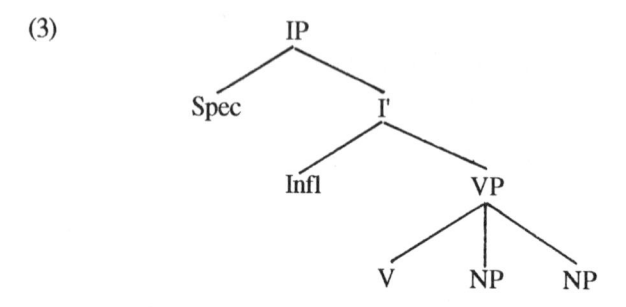

(3)
```
            IP
           / \
        Spec  I'
             / \
          Infl  VP
               /|\
              V NP NP
```

In this structure, both the subject and the direct object occur as immediate daughters of VP. They therefore appear in a relationship of mutual, not asymmetric, c-command. After summarizing the evidence which Woolford advances in support of this flat structure, I point out that her argument fails with respect to at least one type of VSO sentence in Jakaltek. In sentences of this type, elements which normally function as 'classifiers' of overt head nouns in definite and/or specific NPs function, instead, as (the translational equivalents of) pronouns. I argue that in order to account for the fact that these elements may not be interpreted as coreferential with another NP in sentences of this type, it is necessary to assume that they are not, in fact, pronominal (i.e. [-a, +p]) in Jakaltek, as Woolford claims. Rather, they are R-expressions (i.e. [-a, -p]). Given this assumption, the failure of coreference falls out, immediately, as a consequence of Condition C under Woolford's proposal. Thus, for a certain limited range of Jakaltek sentence types, her argument for the flat structure in (3) goes through.

In section 3, I consider a slightly broader range of sentence types involving the use of classifiers and show that no matter what structure is assumed for VSO sentences in this language, the binding conditions of GB are not sufficient to account for all of the relevant facts. Indeed, the examples presented in this section suggest that no condition (or, set of conditions) stated exclusively in terms of configurational notions like c-command will suffice. I argue that in order to account for the possibilities of coreference and non-coreference in these examples, it is necessary to posit at least one additional condition on the interpretation of classifiers. Since this condition is, by itself, sufficient to account for most of data which

Woolford presents, it effectively undermines her argument for the flat structure. The argument cannot be considered valid, I claim, if the crucial appeal to the binding conditions is unnecessary.

In section 4, I discuss the distribution and interpretation of pro in Jakaltek. I demonstrate, first, that the binding conditions cannot, in principle, account for the most salient and significant fact about this element - i.e. that it is always interpreted as coreferential with at least one overt NP in a sentence. I then show that the binding conditions cannot account for the distribution of this element even in cases where it is so interpreted. In order to account for the full range of facts, it is necessary to posit another language-specific condition. This condition too serves to undermine Woolford's argument since, independently of the binding conditions, it induces the correct distribution and interpretation of pro in all sentence types except one. In order to account for the failure of coreference in this one remaining type (corresponding to (2) above with pro in object position), it is necessary to assume that objects do, in fact, c-command subjects in Jakaltek, as Woolford claims. However, it is not necessary to assume that subjects c-command objects. Since this latter assumption (i.e. that subjects c-command objects) cannot be motivated on the basis of any of the facts regarding the use of classifiers or pro in Jakaltek, I conclude that Woolford's argument for the flat structure is, ultimately, invalid.

In section 5, I propose an alternative account of the binding and coreference facts. This account does not rely exclusively on the binding conditions to regulate the distribution and interpretation of classifiers and pro in Jakaltek. Instead, it relies on a combination of these conditions and a neo-Gricean conversational principle of the sort proposed by Reinhart (1983a,1983b), Dowty (1980), and others. According to this principle, the function of pro in this language is simply to disambiguate sentences in which a classifier may be interpreted, ambiguously, as either coreferential or non-coreferential with a preceding NP in S'. The binding conditions establish when a classifier may be so interpreted; the conversational principle insures that in all and only such cases, a classifier is used to unambiguously indicate non-coreference and pro is used, instead of a classifier, to unambiguously indicate coreference. I motivate this pragmatic account on the basis of sentences in which the conversational principle is, apparently, violated. I then show that it is not possible under this account to claim that subjects c-command objects in VSO sentences in Jakaltek. The flat structure is, thus, not only unmotivated by the facts. It is also, I claim, incompatible with them.

In section 6, I offer a brief summary of the paper and a conclusion regarding the efficacy and legitimacy of the strategy which Woolford and others have employed to deduce clause structure in some language from facts analogous to those in (1) and (2) above.

1. Background

Jakaltek is unusual among Mayan languages in that it exhibits two distinct sets of elements which may, under certain circumstances, be interpreted as coreferential with another NP. One of these is the set of 'noun classifiers' in the language, which has been extensively described by both Day (1973) and Craig (1977, 1986, 1990). This set consists of twenty-four distinct lexical items, which are derived, for the most part, from corresponding common nouns. Each of these items is a free morpheme which may function either as a modifier of an overt head noun in a definite and/or specific NP or as a modifier of a covert (i.e. null) head noun in an anaphoric or 'pronominalized' NP. Sentence (4) below illustrates the use of the classifier *no'* 'animal' in both of these two functions:[3]

(4) xinloq'   hune'   no' txitam b'aq'ich tu'   yinh q'inh   (= C: 142)
     I bought   one   cl   pig   fat   that   for   fiesta

     yaj   xkam   no'   ewi.
     but   died   cl/it   yesterday

'I had bought that fat pig for the fiesta but it died yesterday'

In its first occurrence, *no'* functions as a modifier of the overt common noun *txitam* 'pig'. Together with the other modifiers (i.e. the numeral *hune'* 'one' and the demonstrative *tu'* 'that'), it establishes that this noun has a definite and specific discourse referent. In its second occurrence, *no'* functions as a modifier of a covert or null head noun. In context, the NP consisting of *no'* and the null head is obligatorily interpreted as coreferential with the preceding NP, 'that fat pig'.

It should be noted that not all common nouns in Jakaltek occur with an overt classifier. That is, there are some 'unclassified' nouns in the language. Typically, these refer to abstract or 'undifferentiated' objects such as air, wind, smoke, stars, coca-cola, beer, garbage, and all items made of plastic. I follow Craig (1977, 1986) in positing a zero-classifier, ∅, for these nouns. Like its overt counterparts, this zero-classifier may function as a modifier of either an overt or covert head of NP:

(5) ilk'anab'   hun-q'ahan   ∅   tx'umel   tu'   la'   (= C: 142)
     look   one-few   cl   star   that   prt

     chawila   ∅
     you see   cl/them

'Look at those stars! Do you see them?'

It is the distribution of the classifiers in their role as modifiers of covert or 'pronominalized' heads that is most relevant to the determination of clause structure in Jakaltek. As Craig (1977, 1986) demonstrates, this distribution is heavily dependent on such surface syntactic variables as the relative linear order of the classifiers and their antecedents and the presence or absence of certain types of intervening clause boundaries. Some of these factors will be discussed and illustrated below.

The other set of anaphoric elements in Jakaltek consists of the empty category, pro. This is the normal pronoun for most other Mayan languages, which typically lack independent pronouns in the third person and delete or drop such pronouns in the first and second persons. Unlike the pro in these other languages however, Jakaltek pro may not be interpreted from extra-linguistic context but must, instead, always be interpreted as coreferential with an overt (i.e. linguistically expressed) antecedent. Although it acts, in this respect, very much like an anaphor in the GB sense, it cannot be analyzed as a pure anaphor (i.e. [+a, -p]) in this language. This is shown by numerous examples in which this category is not c-commanded (and hence bound) by its antecedent. In the following sentences, for example, pro is obligatorily interpreted as coreferential with a preceding classifier:

(6) xkolwa   [y-unin ix_i]   [yinh   s-mi' pro_i]   (= C: 161)
     helped   E3-child cl/her   in   E3-mother
     'her_i child helped her_i mother'
     (*'her_i child helped her_j mother')

(7) xkan   [y-uxhtaj naj_i]   [sk'atanh pro_i]   (= C: 162)
     stayed E3-brother cl/his   with
     'his_i brother stayed with him_i'
     (*'his_i brother stayed with him_j')

(8) xa'   [s-mam naj_i]   ch'en   melyu   [tet pro_i]   (= C: 162)
     gave   E3-father cl/his   cl   money   to
     'his_i father gave the money to him_i'
     (*'his_i father gave the money to him_j')

Since the coindexed classifiers (*ix* 'female, non-kin' and *naj* 'male, non-kin') function as possessors of head nouns in these sentences, they do not c-command (hence, bind) the empty category. I conclude, therefore, that this category cannot be regarded as an anaphor in the GB sense since this would entail a violation of Condition A in these sentences. Instead, it must be regarded as a pure pronominal (i.e. [-a, +p]). I will continue to refer to this empty category, in the text and in the examples, as 'pro'.[4]

The presence of these two types of elements in Jakaltek entails a certain amount of redundancy in the presentation. Although a given point can be established, in many cases, with reference to only one of these types, it is important to consider them both in order to insure full and complete generality. Part of what is at issue here is whether and to what extent the distribution and interpretation of both of these types of elements can be accounted for in terms of the binding theory. For this reason, the majority of the examples in the sections below come in pairs.

2. Critique of Woolford (1991)

Woolford's (1991) argument for the flat structure in (3) is based, primarily, on the fact that none of the Jakaltek sentences corresponding to (1) and (2) above permit a reading on which the pronoun (subject in (1); object in (2)) is interpreted as coreferential with the proper name. Thus, both of the sentences in (9) and (10) below are ungrammatical on their coreferential readings. Sentence (9), with an overt classifier, *naj*, as subject, only has the disjoint or non-coreferential reading. Sentence (10), with the empty category, pro, as subject, has no grammatical reading at all.

(9) xil naj$_i$ [s-mam naj pel$_j$]
    saw cl/he E3-father cl Peter
    'he$_i$ saw Peter$_j$'s father' (*i = j)

(10) *xil pro$_i$ [s-mam naj pel$_{i/j}$]
     saw E3-father cl Peter
     ('he$_i$ saw Peter$_{i/j}$'s father)

Given the flat structure, the failure of coreference in both of these sentences can be immediately accounted for in terms of Condition C of the binding theory. Since the possessor of the object, *naj pel* 'Peter', is an R-expression, it cannot be coindexed with any NP, either overt or covert, which c-commands it. Thus, the failure of coreference in these sentences provides prima facie support for at least one of the assumptions of the flat structure - i.e. the assumption that subjects c-command objects in Jakaltek. If this assumption were not made, there would be no way to account for this failure via appeal to the binding conditions. Of course, the failure of non-coreference in (10) does not receive an explanation under this account. No matter what structure is assumed, this failure cannot be attributed to the binding conditions. Sentence (10) then, on its non-coreferential reading, provides no argument either for or against the flat structure.

In order to motivate the additional assumption that objects c-command subjects in this language, it is necessary to consider the Jakaltek analogues of the English sentence in (2). The following sentences, (11) and (12), are exactly like those in (9) and (10) above except that the order (and hence thematic interpretation) of the two NPs is reversed:

(11) xil   [s-mam   naj   pel$_i$]   naj$_j$ (= W: 506)
      saw   E3-father cl   Peter   cl/him
      'Peter$_i$'s father saw him$_j$' (*i = j)

(12) *xil   [s-mam   naj   pel$_i$]   pro$_{i/j}$ (= W: 507)
      saw   E3-father cl   Peter
      ('Peter$_i$'s father saw him$_{i/j}$')

As indicated, neither of these two sentences expresses the proposition 'Peter's father saw him (i.e. Peter)'. Sentence (11), with an overt classifier in object position, only has the disjoint or non-coreferential reading 'Peter's father saw him (i.e. some other male human, not Peter)'. Sentence (12), with the empty category, pro, in object position, has no grammatical reading at all.[5] Given Woolford's proposed flat structure, the failure of coreference in these two sentences also follows from Condition C. Since the possessor, *naj pel*, is an R-expression, it cannot be coindexed with a c-commanding object. The flat structure is thus motivated, once again, by the fact that it affords a simple and straightforward account of the failure of coreference in these sentences. The failure of non-coreference in (12), however, remains unexplained.

Although Woolford's argument for the flat structure goes through with respect to at least the ungrammatical coreferential readings of the sentences in (9) through (12) above, problems emerge in connection with sentences in which the proper name *naj pel* 'Peter' in these examples is replaced by the overt classifier *naj* 'male, non-kin'. The following sentences, (13) and (14), correspond to the two sentences in (11) and (12) above:

(13) xil   [s-mam   naj$_i$]   naj$_j$ (= C: 177)
      saw   E3-father cl/his   cl/him
      'his$_i$ father saw him$_j$' (*i = j)

(14) *xil   [s-mam   naj$_i$]   pro$_{i/j}$ (= C: 177)
      saw   E3-father cl/his
      ('his$_i$ father saw him$_{i/j}$')

Like (11) and (12), these sentences are ungrammatical on the coreferential readings.[6] That is, they do not admit readings on which the possessor, *naj*, is interpreted as coreferential with the object. The failure of coreference in these cases, however, cannot be explained in terms of the binding theory if the possessor, *naj*, is analyzed as a pronominal (i.e. [-a, +p]). Condition B of the theory only requires that a pronominal element be free in its governing category and this condition is satisfied in these examples if the governing category of a possessor is taken to be the possessed NP. Even though the possessors are c-commanded by a coindexed object in the flat structure, they are still free in the subject NP. Coindexing (and hence coreference) of the possessors and the objects should, therefore, be allowed.

In order to account for the failure of coreference in sentences (13) and (14) under Woolford's proposal, it is necessary to assume either that the governing category of a possessor is not the possessed NP or that classifiers like *naj* are not, themselves, pronominals. In fact, it is fairly easy to show that the first assumption (that the governing category of a pronominal possessor is not the possessed NP) is false for Jakaltek. Consider, for example, sentence (15) in which the empty category, pro, functions as possessor of the object:

(15) xil naj$_i$ [s-mam pro$_i$]   (= C: 159)
 saw cl/he E3-father

'he$_i$ saw his$_i$ father' (*'he$_i$ saw his$_j$ father')

In this sentence, coreference between the subject and the possessor is not only allowed, but obligatory. The sentence means 'He saw his (own) father'; it cannot mean 'He saw his (someone else's) father'. Given the flat structure, the only way to permit the coreferential reading is to assume that the governing category of the possessor is the possessed object NP. If this assumption is not made (i.e. if the governing category is taken to be, say, the matrix S), then coindexing of the possessor and the c-commanding subject results in a violation of Condition B and coreference is, accordingly, precluded. On the other hand, if this assumption is made (i.e. if the governing category of the possessor is taken to be the possessed NP), then coindexing of the possessor and the subject is permitted by the binding theory since the possessor is free in the object NP. I conclude that since coreference between the subject and the possessor is possible (in fact, necessary) in this example, the governing category of the possessor must be regarded as the object NP. More generally, the governing category of a pronominal possessor in Jakaltek must be regarded as the (minimal) NP which dominates both it and the possessed noun. It is, therefore, not possible to account for the failure of coreference in sentences (13) and (14) above under Woolford's proposal if the classifiers functioning as possessors of the subjects are analyzed, like pro, as pronominals.[7]

The second assumption mentioned above - i.e. the assumption that classifiers like *naj* are not, in fact, pronominals in Jakaltek - holds considerably more promise as an account of the non-coreference facts in (13) and (14). Under this assumption, *naj*, like the proper name *naj pel* 'Peter', is an R-expression (i.e. [-a, -p]) and, therefore, cannot be coindexed with the object or any other c-commanding NP in the flat structure. The coreferential readings of these sentences then are ruled out for the same reason that the coreferential readings of sentences (11) and (12) are. In all of these cases, an R-expression (*naj pel* in (11)-(12) and *naj* in (13)-(14)) is coindexed with a c-commanding NP. This, of course, constitutes a violation of Condition C.

The assumption that classifiers like *naj* are R-expressions in Jakaltek is, perhaps, surprising in view of the fact that Woolford, like Craig before her, consistently refers to these elements as 'pronouns' in instances in which they occur in NP as modifiers of covert (i.e. null) heads. Nevertheless, it is the only assumption that appears to be warranted by the facts. As noted above, this assumption immediately yields a successful account of the disjoint reference facts in (13) and (14) under Woolford's proposal. It also yields an account of the facts illustrated in (16) and (17) below:

(16) xil   naj$_i$ [s-mam   naj$_j$]   (= C: 159)
      saw   cl/he   E3-father cl/his
      'he$_i$ saw his$_j$ father (*i = j)

(17) *xil   pro$_i$ [s-mam   naj$_{i/j}$]
      saw   E3-father cl/his
      ('he$_i$ saw his$_{i/j}$ father)

These sentences are identical to those in (9) and (10) above except that the possessor, *naj pel*, has been replaced by *naj*. Like (9) and (10), these sentences are ungrammatical on the coreferential readings. That is, they do not admit readings on which the possessor, *naj*, is interpreted as coreferential with the subject. This failure of coreference cannot be accounted for under the assumption that *naj* is a pronominal. As shown above, the governing category of a pronominal possessor in Jakaltek is the possessed NP (i.e. the object in these examples) and *naj*, qua pronominal, is free in this category. Coindexing (and hence coreference) of *naj* and the subjects should, therefore, be allowed. In contrast, if *naj* is analyzed as an R-expression, then the failure of coreference in these examples falls out immediately as a consequence of Condition C under Woolford's proposal. *Naj*, qua R-expression, cannot be co-indexed with a c-commanding NP. Coreference is therefore blocked in these sentences ((16) and (17)) for the same reason that it is blocked in the original sentences (9) and (10).

3. The Interpretation of Classifiers

Given the assumption that classifiers like *naj* are R-expressions, all of the facts regarding the interpretation of these elements in the sentences above can be accounted for, straightforwardly, in terms of the flat structure and Condition C. However, as I will now show, there is at least one other fact about classifiers in Jakaltek which cannot be accounted for in these terms. In order to account for this fact, it is necessary to posit a separate, language-specific constraint on the distribution and interpretation of these elements. Since this additional constraint is, by itself, sufficient to rule out the ungrammatical coreferential readings of many of the sentences above, it effectively undermines the argument which Woolford advances in support of the flat structure. This argument cannot be considered valid if the crucial appeal to the binding theory (specifically, Condition C) can be shown to be unnecessary.

Consider the sentences in (18) through (20) below:

(18) xkolwa   [y-unin ix_i]   [yinh   s-mi' ix_j]   (= C: 161)
      helped   E3-child   cl/her   in   E3-mother cl/her
      'her$_i$ child helped her$_j$ mother' (*i = j)

(19) xkan   [y-uxhtaj naj_i]   [sk'atanh naj_j]   (= C: 162)
      stayed   E3-brother cl/his   with   cl/him
      'his$_i$ brother stayed with him$_j$' (*i = j)

(20) xa'   [s-mam naj_i]   ch'en   melyu [tet naj_j] (= C: 162)
      gave   E3-father cl/his   cl   money to   cl/him
      'his$_i$ father gave the money to him$_j$' (*i = j)

These sentences are identical to those in (6) through (8) above except that the empty category, pro, in the latter has been systematically replaced by a classifier (*ix* in (18); *naj* in (19) and (20)). As indicated, all of the sentences are ungrammatical on the readings where the classifiers are interpreted as coreferential. Regardless of whether these elements are analyzed as pronominal or non-pronominal, this fact cannot be attributed to the binding conditions. Since the classifiers function, in every case, as either possessor of a noun or object of a preposition, they do not stand in a relation of either mutual or asymmetric c-command. Coindexing (hence, coreference) of these elements should, therefore, be allowed.

In order to rule out the ungrammatical coreferential readings of the sentences in (18) through (20) above, it is necessary to posit at least one other condition on the interpretation of classifiers in Jakaltek - i.e. a condition independent of those imposed by the binding theory. Woolford (1991:506) mentions one possibility in passing. This is formulated as the Disjoint Reference Condition in (21) below:

(21) Disjoint Reference Condition (adapted from Craig (1977))
      A classifier must be interpreted as disjoint in reference from
      any NP which precedes it in the same (minimal) S' (= CP).

This condition, a reformulation of one originally advanced by Craig (1977), prohibits coreference between a classifier and any NP which precedes it in the same S' (= CP).[8] It therefore accounts immediately for the failure of coreference in sentences (18) through (20). However, as Woolford acknowledges, it also accounts for the failure of coreference in sentences (11), (13), and (16). These sentences ((11), (13), and (16)) then cannot be used to motivate the flat structure since their ungrammatical readings are ruled out, independently of the binding conditions, by means of the DRC in (21).

The DRC in (21) may profitably be considered to be part of a much more general constraint in Jakaltek that prohibits coreference between a classifier and any R-expression that occurs, anywhere, in the same (minimal) S'. In her grammar, Craig (1977:150) notes that 'a pronoun form [i.e. a classifier] never precedes its controller NP'. She captures this fact by requiring that the rule of 'Pronominalization' in the language (i.e. the transformational rule that she claims is responsible for the distribution of coreferential classifiers) must always proceed from left-to-right. Given the fact, then, that there are no cases of 'backwards' pronominalization (in her terms) in Jakaltek, the DRC in (21) can be reformulated as in (22):

(22) Disjoint Reference Condition (revised)
A classifier must be interpreted as disjoint in reference from any other R-expression in the same (minimal) S' (= CP).

This constraint prohibits coreference between a classifier and any R-expression which either precedes or follows it in S'. It is, therefore, a stronger and more general constraint than that formulated in (21). Like that constraint, it rules out the ungrammatical coreferential readings of all of the sentences in (18) through (20), as well as those of the sentences in (11), (13), and (16). Unlike that constraint, however, it also rules out the ungrammatical coreferential reading of the sentence in (9). Since this is the only sentence involving classifiers that remains from section 2, I conclude that there is no argument for the flat structure based on the distribution and interpretation of these elements. Although the ungrammatical coreferential readings of all of the sentences in (9), (11), (13), and (16) can be ruled out via appeal to Condition C under Woolford's proposal, they can also be ruled out via appeal to the independently motivated condition in (22). Woolford's argument for the flat structure is invalid because it is not necessary to appeal, specifically, to the binding conditions in order to account for the disjoint or non-coreferential interpretation of classifiers.

4. The Interpretation of 'pro'

Having established, then, that the flat structure cannot be motivated on the basis of the sentences (9), (11), (13), and (16) involving the use of classifiers, I now propose to demonstrate that this structure can also not be motivated on the basis of the sentences (10), (12), (14), and (17) involving the use of the empty category, pro. I will establish, first, that this element, like the classifiers, is subject to an independently motivated constraint in Jakaltek. I will then show that this constraint is, by itself, sufficient to account for the failure of coreference in sentences (10) and (17) and, therefore, these sentences too are irrelevant to Woolford's argument. Since these are the only sentences left from section 2 which motivate the claim that subjects c-command objects in Jakaltek, I conclude that this particular aspect of the flat structure cannot be established on the basis of any of the facts regarding the distribution and interpretation of either the classifiers or pro in Jakaltek. Although the facts are explicable in terms of a structure in which subjects c-command objects, they are also explicable in terms of a structure in which they do not. Woolford's argument for the flat structure fails, in this case, because there are other, more articulated structures available which are equally consistent with the data.

As mentioned earlier, the sentences in (10), (12), (14), and (17) present two distinct problems for a theory of anaphora in Jakaltek. On the one hand, these sentences do not admit readings on which the empty category, pro, is interpreted as coreferential with another NP. On the other hand, they also do not admit readings in which this category is interpreted as non-coreferential with another NP. Given the flat structure (and the assumption that classifiers like *naj* are R-expressions in Jakaltek), the first problem at least is easily overcome by a straightforward appeal to the binding conditions. Condition C prohibits the coindexation of pro and any proper name or classifier which it c-commands. The second problem, however, is not so easily overcome. Condition B requires that pro be contra-indexed with all NPs that c-command it in its governing category, but nothing requires that it be contra-indexed with other NPs (i.e. NPs that either do not c-command it at all or that c-command it outside its governing category). Since the proper names and classifiers in sentences (10), (12), (14), and (17) function, syntactically, as possessors, they do not c-command pro in any category. Therefore, contra-indexation of pro and the possessors in these sentences is allowed by the binding theory. The sentences are predicted, incorrectly, to be grammatical on their disjoint or non-coreferential readings.

In order to account for the ungrammaticality of the non-coreferential readings of the sentences in (10), (12), (14), and (17), it is necessary, I believe, to posit an independent, language-specific condition on the interpretation of pro in Jakaltek. This condition, formulated in (23) below, requires this element to be interpreted as coreferential with at least one other NP in the same minimal S' (= CP).[9] In addition, it requires that the antecedent of pro be overt (i.e. linguistically expressed). This latter requirement is necessary in order to rule out cases in which pro is interpreted as coreferential with another, distinct instance of itself and nothing else:

(23) The 'pro' Condition (first approximation)
'pro' must be interpreted as coreferential with at least one overt NP in the same (minimal) S' (= CP).

This condition can obviously not be satisfied in sentences (10), (12), (14), and (17) above without inducing a violation of Condition C. Therefore, these sentences are correctly predicted to be ungrammatical on both their coreferential and non-coreferential readings.

Although the 'pro' Condition and Condition C together yield a successful account of the ungrammatical readings of the sentences in (10), (12), (14), and (17), they do not yield a successful account of the ungrammatical readings of the following (= (14) with the order of pro and the classifier reversed):

(24) *xil   [s-mam   pro$_i$]   naj$_{i/j}$
       saw   E3-father   cl/him
       ('his$_i$ father saw him$_{i/j}$')

The 'pro' Condition, by itself, rules out the ungrammatical non-coreferential reading of this sentence. However, nothing rules out the ungrammatical coreferential reading. There is no violation of Condition C since the classifier, *naj*, is not c-commanded (hence, bound) by pro. There is also no violation of Condition B since pro is not c-commanded (hence, bound) by the classifier in the governing category of the possessed subject NP. In order to account for the ungrammatical coreferential reading of this sentence then, it is necessary to revise the 'pro' Condition in (23) above and make it refer, specifically, to the relative linear order of pro and its antecedent. The following formulation requires pro to be interpreted as coreferential with at one least one overt NP that precedes it in the same (minimal) S':

(25) The 'pro' Condition (revised)
      'pro' must be interpreted as coreferential with at least one
      overt NP that precedes it in the same (minimal) S' (= CP).

This condition suffices to rule out the ungrammatical coreferential reading of (24) since the classifier in this sentence does not precede pro, but rather follows it. I submit that this is the only way to account of the failure of coreference in this sentence. As demonstrated, no appeal to the binding conditions can suffice.

It is worth mentioning that the revised 'pro' Condition in (25) follows, in a straightforward way, from Craig's (1977) transformational analysis of the distribution and interpretation of pro in Jakaltek. According to her analysis, pro is derived through the operation of an obligatory rule of Noun Classifier Deletion. This rule applies, within the domain of a single S', to delete classifiers which are interpreted as coreferential with another NP. Since the coreferential classifiers are, themselves, derived by means of the rule of Pronominalization, which, as noted above, only applies from left-to-right, they never precede their antecedents. Therefore, the rule of Noun Classifier Deletion, which also applies from left-to-right, never results in an empty category (i.e. pro) which precedes its antecedent. This, of course, is exactly the distribution which is entailed by means of the revised 'pro' Condition in (25) above.

Having motivated the 'pro' Condition in (25), I now proceed to the comparatively easy task of showing that this condition undermines Woolford's argument for the flat structure. Notice, first, that the revised 'pro' Condition accounts not only for the failure of non-coreference in (10), (12), (14), and (17) above but also for the failure of coreference in (10) and (17). In these sentences ((10) and (17)), pro precedes the proper names and classifiers. Coreference is therefore blocked, correctly, by means of the revised 'pro' Condition in (25). Since it is not necessary to appeal to the binding conditions in these cases and since the 'pro' Condition does not, itself, refer to the structural (hierarchical) organization of clauses, it is not possible to motivate the flat structure on the basis of either of the sentences in (10) and (17).

This leaves the sentences in (12) and (14). Unlike the sentences in (10) and (17), these sentences apparently do require an appeal to the binding conditions. As noted earlier, they are ungrammatical on both their coreferential and non-coreferential readings. The latter (non-coreferential) reading is ruled out by means of the 'pro' Condition. The former (coreferential) reading, however, is not (since pro follows the coindexed NPs and thus satisfies the 'pro' Condition). In order to account for the ungrammaticality of the coreferential readings of these sentences then, it is necessary to assume 1) that objects c-command subjects in Jakaltek and 2) that classifiers like *naj* are R-expressions. Given these two assumptions, the failure of coreference in both of the sentences in (12) and (14) falls out immediately as a consequence of Condition C.

Notice, however, that the appeal to Condition C in these two cases (i.e. sentences (12) and (14) on their coreferential readings) only provides an argument for one of Woolford's claims - i.e. that objects c-command subjects in VSO sentences in Jakaltek. It does not provide an argument for the other claim - i.e. that subjects c-command objects. In fact, given the independently motivated conditions in (22) and (25) above, there is no argument for this latter claim based on any of the sentences in (9) through (17) above. Although the facts regarding the distribution and interpretation of the classifiers and pro in these sentences are consistent with this claim, they are also consistent with the alternative claim that subjects do not c-command objects in VSO sentences in Jakaltek. I conclude, therefore, that Woolford's argument for the flat structure is invalid. The crucial claim that subjects c-command objects in this language cannot be established on the basis of the binding and coreference facts alone.

5. A Pragmatic Account

In the preceding sections, I have argued that the flat structure cannot be established on the basis of the evidence regarding the distribution and interpretation of either the classifiers or pro in Jakaltek. In this section, I would like to argue, further, that this structure is, in fact, incompatible with this evidence. That is, I would like to demonstrate that the flat structure is not only unmotivated for VSO sentences in this language, but also wrong. I propose to do this by presenting, first, an alternative account of the binding and coreference facts. I will then show that this account yields a fairly conclusive argument against the flat structure. Specifically, it yields an argument against the claim that subjects c-command objects in VSO sentences in this language.

Perhaps the most salient and significant fact about the distribution and interpretation of classifiers and pro in Jakaltek is that the latter occurs in all and only positions in which the former are obligatorily interpreted as non-coreferential with some preceding NP within the same S'. This fact is explicitly captured in Craig's transformational analysis (Craig, 1977). As noted earlier, her obligatory rule of Noun Classifier Deletion is specifically designed to delete classifiers (i.e. replace them by an empty category) in all and only instances in which in they are interpreted as coreferential with another NP. It therefore induces a kind of complementary distribution of these two types of elements within the domain of S'. Classifiers occur in this domain in all and only positions in which they are interpreted as non-coreferential with other NP; the empty category (analyzed here as pro) occurs in all and only positions in which it is interpreted as coreferential with at least one of them.

I have already demonstrated that the distribution and interpretation of the classifiers and pro cannot be accounted for, in all cases, by means of the binding conditions. Condition C requires that the classifiers, which I have argued are R-expressions in this language, must be contra-indexed with all c-commanding NPs in a sentence, but this is not sufficient to induce contra-indexing in all of the relevant cases. Condition B requires that the empty category, pro, must be contra-indexed with all c-commanding NPs in its governing category, but this in no way guarantees that this element will always be coindexed with an element outside this domain. Clearly, in order to construct an adequate theory of anaphora in Jakaltek, it is necessary to look beyond the binding conditions. I take it that a minimal requirement for such a theory is that it account, directly, for the complementary distribution of the classifiers and pro within the domain of S'. That is, it must account for the fact, noted above, that pro occurs in all and only those positions in which a classifier is obligatorily interpreted as non-coreferential with some preceding NP in the same (minimal) S'.

The account which I propose is essentially a pragmatic one based on the fact that classifiers (analyzed here as R-expressions) are free to receive any index at all in a sentence except in instances in which they are required, by Condition C, to be contra-indexed with another NP. Thus, the classifiers which appear in sentences (18) through (20) above, for example, may be either coindexed or contra-indexed with one another by virtue of the fact that they do not appear in a relation of either mutual or asymmetric c-command. As far as the binding theory is concerned, these sentences are ambiguous with respect to the interpretation of the classifiers. On one reading, the classifiers are interpreted as non-coreferential. On the other reading, of course, they are not. The point is that both readings are available in principle. Neither can be ruled out by appeal to Condition C or any other condition currently recognized in GB.

In order to avoid the ambiguity which is, I claim, inherent in sentences like (18) through (20), speakers have adopted a strategy whereby classifiers which are interpreted as coreferential with another NP in a sentence are obligatorily replaced by pro. By convention, this element (pro) must be interpreted as coreferential with at least one preceding NP in a sentence. Thus, the sentences in (6) through (8) above are completely unambiguous and only have the readings on which the classifiers and pro are interpreted as coreferential. This leaves the sentences in (18) through (20), with overt classifiers, to express the other, non-coreferential, reading. In effect, speakers use and interpret sentences with classifiers and pro according to the neo-Gricean conversational principle stated in (26). This principle has many precedents in the literature (cf: Reinhart (1983a, 1983b), and references cited there). The formulation here is based on one presented in Dowty (1980:32):

(26) Given two sentences, A and B, such that A is ambiguous
      between meanings X and Y and B has only meaning X,
      cooperative speakers will choose the ambiguous sentence,
      A, to communicate meaning Y and reserve the unambiguous
      sentence, B, to communicate meaning X.

My claim is that sentences containing a classifier are always ambiguous between the coreferential and non-coreferential readings unless the classifier appears in a position in which it is required, by Condition C, to be interpreted as non-coreferential. In contrast, sentences containing pro are always unambiguous (i.e. have a coreferential reading only) since this element, by convention, must be interpreted as coreferential with at least one preceding NP. Sentences with classifiers, then, correspond to the ambiguous sentences of type A in the conversational principle above, and sentences with pro correspond to the unambiguous sentences of type B. Speakers of Jakaltek conform to this principle by employing sentences with classifiers in instances in which they intend to communicate a non-coreferential reading and by employing pro in instances in which they intend to communicate the opposite, coreferential reading.

Interesting support for this pragmatic account may be derived from sentences in which a classifer can be interpreted as either coreferential or non-coreferential with a preceding NP in violation of both the DRC in (22) and the conversational principle above. As Craig (1977:181) notes, sentences like that in (27) below are structurally ambiguous in Jakaltek:

(27) [b'oj   s-mam   ix]   xil   naj   (= C: 181)
     with   E3-father   cl/her saw   cl/he/him
     'it is with her$_i$ father that he saw her$_i$/it'
     'it is with her$_i$ father that she$_i$ saw him'

It is not possible to tell, on the basis of the surface form, where the empty category (i.e. pro) is located. Hence, it is not possible to tell whether this category functions as a coreferential subject or a coreferential object. In this particular case, where neither the subject nor object is c-commanded by a co-indexed NP, speakers may resolve the ambiguity by introducing the overt classifier *ix* 'female, non-kin' in place of the empty category. This yields one of the two sentences in (28) and (29) below in which the position (hence, grammatical relation) of the classifier is apparent:

(28) [b'oj   s-mam   ix]   xil   naj   ix   (= C: 182)
     with   E3-father   cl/her saw   cl/he   cl/her
     'it is with her$_i$ father that he saw her$_{i/j}$'

(29) [b'oj   s-mam   ix]   xil   ix   naj   (= C: 182)
     with   E3-father   cl/her saw   cl/she cl/him
     'it is with her$_i$ father that she$_{i/j}$ saw him'

These sentences, of course, are ambiguous with respect to the coreferential vs. non-coreferential interpretations of the classifiers, but they are not ambiguous with respect to the position (hence, grammatical relation) of these elements. The fact that overt classifiers may be interpreted as coreferential with another NP in sentences like (28) and (29) shows that the interpretation of these elements is not determined by a syntactic constraint of the sort represented by the DRC in (22). Rather, it is determined by a pragmatic constraint of the sort represented in (26). Because this constraint is motivated solely by the exigencies of successful communication, it can be (and frequently is) violated in instances in which the use of the empty category, pro, would result in a significant loss of information. Such principled violations are difficult, if not impossible, to explain under an approach in which the interpretation of classifiers is induced by means a syntactic constraint like the DRC in (22).

Given the conversational principle in (26), it is not necessary to assume either the Disjoint Reference Condition in (22) or the 'pro' Condition in (25). Recall that both of these conditions were introduced in order to account for facts that could not, in principle, be accounted for in terms of the binding conditions. The DRC was introduced in order to account for the fact, illustrated in (18) through (20), that a classifier cannot be interpreted as coreferential with another R-expression within the same S' even in cases where these elements do not appear in a relation of either mutual or asymmetric c-command. However, precisely because the failure of coreference in these cases cannot be accounted for in terms of the binding conditions, it can be accounted for in terms of the conversational principle in (26). Since the classifier is not required, by Condition C, to be contra-indexed with the other NP, it can, in principle, be interpreted as either coreferential or non-coreferential with that NP. Given the availability of pro however, the conversational principle in (26) requires that the classifier be interpreted as non-coreferential. There is, therefore, no need to appeal to the DRC to rule out the possibility of a coreferential interpretation of the classifiers in these cases. The DRC in (22) is entirely redundant (hence dispensable) given the binding conditions and the conversational principle in (26).

The 'pro' Condition in (25) is likewise dispensable. I have already stated that the interpretation of pro in Jakaltek is a matter of convention among speakers. Although it is possible to assume that this convention has been 'grammaticized' in the form of a special syntactic and semantic condition like that in (25), it is also possible to assume that it has not been. That is, it is not necessary to assume that the 'pro' Condition, or something like it, has been specifically incorporated into the grammar in order to account for the fact that pro is obligatorily interpreted as coreferential with at least one overt NP in the same S'. This interpretation can be viewed, I believe, as a simple matter of convention.

Of course, it is still necessary to account for the fact that pro may not precede its antecedent. Earlier, I proposed the 'pro' Condition to account for this fact. If this condition is dispensable, as I claim, then, obviously, this precedence requirement must follow from something else. I suggest that it follows from the conversational principle above together with the condition, motivated in Craig (1977:150), that prohibits coreference between a classifier and any NP that follows it. If, as I claim, pro occurs only as a substitute for a classifier which may, in principle, be interpreted as either coreferential or non-coreferential with another NP, then it cannot occur as substitute for a classifier which is required, by this independently motivated condition, to be interpreted, unambiguously, as non-coreferential. Thus, it is not necessary to posit the 'pro' Condition or any other special condition in order to induce the requirement that pro follow its antecedent. This requirement follows, automatically, from the conversational principle above plus the condition that a classifier may not be interpreted as coreferential with any NP that follows it.

Consider now what this pragmatic account entails about the flat structure. As demonstrated in section 2, the binding conditions make very strong predictions about the distribution and interpretation of classifiers in this structure. In particular, Condition C predicts that a subject classifier may not be interpreted as coreferential with a classifier (or, other R-expression) functioning as possessor of an object. It also predicts that an object classifier may not be interpreted as coreferential with a classifier (or, other R-expression) functioning as possessor of a subject. Thus, the classifiers which occur in the two sentences in (30) and (31) below can only be interpreted as non-coreferential. Given the flat structure, they all appear in a relation of (asymmetric) c-command. Coindexing (and hence coreference) of the classifiers is therefore precluded by Condition C:

(30) xil   naj   [s-mam   naj]   (= (16))

(31) xil   [s-mam   naj]   naj   (= (13))

Since none of the classifiers in these sentences is ambiguous in reference, the conversational principle in (26) predicts that none of them can be replaced by pro. This prediction is correct for the two classifiers in (31) (cf: the sentences in (24) and (14) above). It is also correct for the first classifier, functioning as subject, in (30) (cf: the sentence in (17) above). It is not correct, however, for the second classifier, functioning as possessor of the object. As demonstrated in sentence (15), this classifier can (indeed, must) be replaced by pro if the coreferential reading is intended. Given the flat structure, of course, this replacement constitutes a violation of the principle that pro may only occur in positions in which a classifier may be interpreted, ambiguously, as either coreferential or non-coreferential with some other NP.

In order to permit the replacement of the second (possessor) classifier in (30) by pro under the pragmatic account, it is necessary, I believe, to give up the flat structure and assume, contrary to Woolford, that subjects do not, in fact, c-command objects in VSO sentences in Jakaltek. Given this assumption, the facts in (30) fall out. The empty category, pro, is allowed in possessor position because the classifier which it replaces is not required, by Condition C, to be unambiguously interpreted as non-coreferential. Rather, it (the classifier) may be interpreted, ambiguously, as either coreferential or non-coreferential with the subject by virtue of the fact that it is not c-commanded (hence bound) by this NP.

Giving up the flat structure has at least one undesirable consequence, however. If subjects do not c-command objects, as I claim, then it is not possible to appeal to the binding conditions to account for the fact that the classifier in subject position in (30) may not be replaced by pro. This classifier is obviously not c-commanded by the possessor of the object. Therefore, it is not required, by Condition C, to be unambiguously interpreted as non-coreferential with this NP. Since, according to the binding conditions, the subject classifier in (30) may be interpreted as either coreferential or non-coreferential with the possessor, the conversational principle predicts that it should be possible to replace this classifier by pro. However, as demonstrated in sentence (17) above, this prediction is false.

Fortunately, the difficulty just mentioned can be easily overcome by appealing to the condition, cited above, which requires a classifier to be interpreted as non-coreferential with any (non-pronominal) NP which follows it. Since the subject classifier in (30) precedes the possessor, it cannot be interpreted as coreferential with it. Therefore, it is not ambiguous in reference and, in accordance with the conversational priniciple in (26), cannot be replaced by pro. The facts in (30) are thus consistent with the claim that subjects do not c-command objects in Jakaltek given the conversational principle and the independently motivated constraint against coreference between a classifier and a following (non-pronominal) NP. The first (subject) classifier in this sentence cannot be replaced by pro simply because it cannot be interpreted, ambiguously, as either coreferential or non-coreferential with the second classifier functioning as possessor.

Notice, however, that the facts in (30) are not consistent with Woolford's alternative claim that subjects do c-command objects in this language. As noted earlier, the flat structure predicts, incorrectly, that the second (possessor) classifier in this sentence cannot be replaced by pro because, by virtue of Condition C, it can only be interpreted as non-coreferential with the subject. Since it is not ambiguous in reference, it cannot be 'disambiguated' through obligatory replacement by pro. I conclude, therefore, that the flat structure is incompatible with the facts regarding the distribution of pro in (30). This structure cannot be maintained in any analysis which attempts to account for this distribution in terms of the binding conditions and the conversational principle in (26).

6. Conclusion

I began this paper by asserting that it is not possible to motivate any specific hypothesis regarding the structural (hierarchical) organization of VSO sentences in Jakaltek solely on the basis of facts regarding the distribution and interpretation of the various types of overt and covert NP. Given the conclusions of section 5 however, it now appears that this initial assertion was too strong. In fact, it is possible to motivate one hypothesis —i.e. that objects c-command subjects, but subjects do not c-command objects. This hypothesis follows under the approach, advocated in section 5, in which the binding conditions serve only to establish the range of positions in which a classifier may be ambiguously interpreted as either coreferential or non-coreferential with another NP in S'. The obligatory non-coreferential interpretation of these elements and the obligatory coreferential interpretation of pro are both determined by means of the conversational principle in (26).

Although my point concerning the impossibility of deducing the structure of VSO sentences in Jakaltek from the binding and coreference facts is, apparently, invalid, my other point concerning the risks and limitations of the strategy of deduction is not. In fact, it is not possible to deduce the structure of clauses in a particular language from sentences analogous to those in (1) and (2) above without first determining the precise role and relevance of the binding conditions. Although these conditions do, indeed, play a role in the anaphoric system in Jakaltek, for example, they are not sufficient, by themselves, to determine all of the relevant facts. It is therefore unwise, methodologically, to try to construct an argument for or against a given structure in this language based solely on an appeal to the binding conditions. Woolford's argument for the flat structure fails, I claim, precisely because it is based exclusively on such an appeal. As demonstrated in this paper, the binding conditions are not solely, or even primarily, responsible for regulating the distribution and interpretation of either the classifiers or pro in Jakaltek.

Notes

[*] I am grateful to Judith Aissen and Ellen Woolford for their comments and suggestions regarding an earlier version of this paper. Woolford, in particular, prompted me to produce what I hope is a more coherent and explicit version. Neither she nor Aissen should be held accountable for any errors or infelicities that remain.

[1] This is the language which Woolford (1991) and Craig (1977, 1986) refer to as 'Jacaltec'. I have changed the spelling of the name in order to conform to the orthographic conventions of the Academia de las lenguas mayas de Guatemala (1988).

[2] It should be noted that I use the word 'classifier' in this paper in two different senses. In some cases, it refers to some particular member of the set of 'classifiers'; in others, it refers to an NP containing one of these expressions as a modifier of a covert (i.e. null) head noun. I trust that it will be clear from context which of these senses I intend. In contexts in which I refer, specifically, to the interpretation of a classifier, I mean, of course, the interpretation of the NP in which it appears. Since classifiers are modifiers of nouns, they never head phrases with NP-type denotations. Therefore, they cannot, technically, be interpreted as either coreferential or non-coreferential with another NP. Nevertheless, it is easier for purposes of exposition to write as though they can. I trust that this expository convenience will not engender too much confusion or misunderstanding.

[3] All of the examples in this paper are taken from either Woolford (1991) or Craig (1977). Sources are identified by author's initial (W or C) and by page number. I have changed the orthography of the examples in order to conform to that which has been proposed and recommended for Jakaltek by the Academia de las lenguas mayas de Guatemala (1988). In this new orthography, the following correspondences hold: b' = implosive

bilabial stop; k = voiceless velar stop; q = voiceless postvelar stop; tz = voiceless alveolar affricate; ch = voiceless palatal affricate (not retroflex); tx = voiceless palatal affricate (retroflex); s = voiceless alveolar fricative; xh = voiceless palatal fricative (not retroflex); x = voiceless palatal fricative (retroflex); j = voiceless postvelar fricative; h = voiceless glottal fricative; nh = velar nasal; ' = glottal stop; and C' = the glottalized counterpart of some stop or affricate consonant C. All other values are customary. Abbreviations used in the glosses are: cl = nominal classifier and E3 = third person ergative agreement marker. Morphologically complex words are generally not analyzed.

[4] Woolford (1991) also reaches this conclusion regarding the status of this empty category in Jakaltek. See her footnote 5, page 506, for further evidence and discussion.

[5] As Craig (1977:177) notes, the sentence in (12) does have a grammatical reading 'Peter's father saw it' where 'it' refers to the denotation of one of the many unclassified nouns in the language. On this reading, the element which occurs in object position is not pro, but rather the zero classifier ∅:

xil [smam naj pel] ∅

I ignore this reading in what follows.

[6] Again, sentence (14) does have a grammatical reading 'his father saw it' where 'it' refers to the denotation of one of the unclassified nouns in the language. On this reading, the element which occurs in object position is not pro, but the zero classifier ∅. I ignore this reading here.

[7] I have been reminded by both John Moore and Ellen Woolford that this argument does not, necessarily, go through in versions of the binding theory in which the governing category of a pronominal possessor may vary according to the status of that NP as overt or covert. That is, although the argument establishes that the governing category of a covert possessor (i.e. pro) in Jakaltek is the possessed NP, it does not necessarily establish that this is also the governing category of an overt possessor (i.e. a classifier). The argument fails in the context of a theory in which the governing category of one of these types of elements may, potentially, be different from that of the other. Here, of course, I assume the more traditional version of the binding theory in which the governing category of a pronominal possessor may not vary according to the overt vs. covert status of that NP. Given this version of the binding theory, the argument in the text is valid.

[8] It is necessary to refer, specifically, to S' (= CP) in this condition since a classifier appearing in a relative clause must also be interpreted as

non-coreferential with all NPs in the matrix. As Craig (1977:192) notes, relative clauses in Jakaltek are never introduced by a complementizer or definite article. They therefore arguably belong to the category S (= IP), not S' (=CP). S' here corresponds to what Craig calls an 'opaque boundary'; S corresponds to one of her 'transparent boundaries'.

[9]Again, it is necessary to refer to S' (= CP) in the statement of this condition since a pro occurring in a relative clause (analyzed here as an expression of category S (= IP) in Jakaltek) may find its antecedent outside the relative clause. See Craig (1977:165-167) for examples.

References

Academia de las lenguas mayas de Guatemala. 1988. *Documento de referencia para la pronunciación de los nuevos alfabetos oficiales*. Guatemala City: Instituto Indigenista Nacional.
Craig, Colette. 1977. *The Structure of Jacaltec*. Austin: University of Texas Press.
Craig, Colette. 1986. Jacaltec Noun Classifiers: A Study in Grammaticalization. *Lingua* 70: 241-284.
Craig, Colette. 1990. Clasificadores nominales: una innovación Q'anjob'al. *Lecturas sobre la lingüística maya*, ed. by Nora C. England and Stephen R. Elliot, 253-268. Antiqua, Guatemala: Centro de Investigaciones Regionales de Mesoamérica.
Day, Christopher. 1973. *The Jacaltec Language*. (Language science monographs, 12.) Bloomington: Indiana University Press.
Dowty, David. 1980. Comments on the Paper by Bach and Partee. *Papers from the Parasession on Pronouns and Anaphora*, ed. by K. J. Kreiman and A. Ojeda, 29-40. Chicago: Chicago Linguistic Society.
Reinhart, Tanya. 1983a. Coreference and Bound Anaphora: A Restatement of the Anaphora Questions. *Linguistics and Philosophy* 6: 47-88.
Reinhart, Tanya. 1983b. *Anaphora and Semantic Interpretation*. Chicago: University of Chicago Press.
Woolford, Ellen. 1991. VP-Internal Subjects in VSO and Nonconfigurational Languages. *Linguistic Inquiry* 22: 503-540.

P201 .G679 1995